Scene in the marketplace at Dubno, eastern Poland, October 1919. Public domain. Source: Library of Congress Prints and Photographs Division, Washington, DC. Photographer: Capt. Marshall, American Red Cross. Not in the original book.

Background: During the First World War, Dubno often changed hands between the two conflicting sides, and its economy plummeted. Epidemics of smallpox and typhoid struck, and there were repeated pogroms. In July 1919, Soviet authorities had ordered liquidation of the kahal, the Jewish communal umbrella organization.

Sources: Virtual Shtetl (sztetl.org), *Encyclopaedia Judaica*

Dubno

Memorial Book
(Dubno, Ukraine)

Translation of
Dubna: Sefer Zikaron

Original Book Edited by: Y. Adini

Published in Tel Aviv 1966

A Publication of JewishGen, INC
Edmond J. Safra Plaza, 36 Battery Place, New York, NY 10280
646.494.5972 | info@JewishGen.org | www.jewishgen.org

Dubno Memorial Book (Dubno, Ukraine)
Translation of *Dubna: Sefer Zikaron*

First Printing: July 2022, Tamuz 5782
Second Printing: August 2022, Av 5782

Editor of Original Yizkor Book: Y. Adini
Project Coordinator: Anna Grinzweig Jacobsson
Editors of Translation: Anna Grinzweig Jacobsson and Shirley Ginzburg
Name Indexing: Jonathan Wind
Reproduction of Photographs: Allen Ginzburg
Cover Design: Nina Schwartz

Printed in the United States of America by Lightning Source, Inc.

Library of Congress Control Number (LCCN): 2021933471

ISBN: 978-1-954176-06-5 (hard cover: 692 pages, alk. paper)

About JewishGen.org

JewishGen, an affiliate of the Museum of Jewish Heritage - A Living Memorial to the Holocaust, serves as the global home for Jewish genealogy.

Featuring unparalleled access to 30+ million records, it offers unique search tools, along with opportunities for researchers to connect with others who share similar interests. Award winning resources such as the Family Finder, Discussion Groups, and ViewMate, are relied upon by thousands each day.

In addition, JewishGen's extensive informational, educational and historical offerings, such as the Jewish Communities Database, Yizkor Book translations, InfoFiles, Family Tree of the Jewish People, and KehilaLinks, provide critical insights, first-hand accounts, and context about Jewish communal and familial life throughout the world.

Offered as a free resource, JewishGen.org has facilitated thousands of family connections and success stories, and is currently engaged in an intensive expansion effort that will bring many more records, tools, and resources to its collections.

Please visit https://www.jewishgen.org/ to learn more.

Executive Director: Avraham Groll

About the JewishGen Yizkor Book Project

Yizkor Books (Memorial Books) were traditionally written to memorialize the names of departed family and martyrs during holiday services in the synagogue (a practice that still exists in many synagogues today).

Over the centuries, as a result of countless persecutions and horrific atrocities committed against the Jews, Yizkor Books (Sefer Zikaron in Hebrew) were expanded to include more historical information, such as biographical sketches of famous personalities and descriptions of daily town life.

Following the Holocaust, the idea of remembrance and learning took on an urgent and crucial importance. Survivors of the Holocaust sought out other surviving residents of their former towns to memorialize and document the names and way of life of those who were ruthlessly murdered by the Nazis. These remembrances were documented in Yizkor Books, hundreds of which were published in the first decades after the Holocaust.

Most of these books were published privately, or through landsmanshaftn (social organizations comprised of members originating from the same European town or region) that still existed, and were often distributed free of charge. Sadly, the languages used to document these crucial histories and links to our past, Yiddish and Hebrew, are no longer commonly understood by a significant percentage of Jews today. As a result, JewishGen has undertaken the sacred responsibility of translating these books into English so that the culture and way of life of these communities will be preserved and transmitted to future generations.

In 1986, a group of farsighted JewishGenners started a project to pool their efforts together in groups based upon their ancestors from each town and donate money to get the Yizkor books of their ancestral towns translated into English. As the translated material became available, it was made accessible for free at www.JewishGen.org/Yizkor. Hardcover copies can be purchased by visiting https://www.jewishgen.org/Yizkor/ybip.html (see below).

It is our hope that the translation of these books into English (and other languages) will assist the countless Jewish family researchers who are so desperately seeking to forge a connection with their heritage.

Director of JewishGen Yizkor Book Project: Lance Ackerfeld

About JewishGen Press

JewishGen Press (formerly the Yizkor Books-in-Print Project) is the publishing division of JewishGen.org, and provides a venue for the publication of non-fiction books pertaining to Jewish genealogy, history, culture, and heritage.

In addition to the Yizkor Book category, publications in the Other Non-Fiction category include Shoah memoirs and research, genealogical research, collections of genealogical and historical materials, biographies, diaries and letters, studies of Jewish experience and cultural life in the past, academic theses, and other books of interest to the Jewish community.

Please visit https://www.jewishgen.org/Yizkor/ybip.html to learn more.

Director of JewishGen Press: Joel Alpert
Managing Editor - Jessica Feinstein
Publications Manager - Susan Rosin

Notes to the Reader

The original book can be seen online at the Yiddish Book Center web site:

https://www.yiddishbookcenter.org/collections/yizkor-books/yzk-nybc314184/adini-yaakov-dubno-sefer-zikaron

OR
 At the New York Public Library Digital Collection:

https://digitalcollections.nypl.org/items/31976d00-6c7d-0133-037f-00505686a51c#/?uuid=321ccf20-6c7d-0133-4e70-00505686a51c

To obtain a list of Shoah victims from Dubno the reader should access the Yad Vashem web site listed below; one can also search for specific family names using family name option. These lists are continually updated by Yad Vashem, so it is worthwhile to periodically search these lists.

There is more valuable information (including the Pages of Testimony, etc.) available on this website: https://yvng.yadvashem.org/

A list of all books available from JewishGen Press along with prices is available at: https://www.jewishgen.org/Yizkor/ybip.html

The cost of this translation was defrayed by a subsidy from the following organizations, gratefully acknowledged:

The City of Göteborg, Levande historia, Sweden

The Swedish Arts Council

The Heckscher Foundation, Sweden

The Yiddish Culture Society in Göteborg, Sweden

The Swedish Jewish Genealogy Society

Acknowledgements and Information to the Reader

The project of translating the Dubno Yizkor book to English started in 2017. During the course of five years we have seen the book emerge, chapter by chapter, a sensation that must be similar to that of an archeologist excavating an hidden ancient city. The work has also connected us with devoted and skillful people and created many strong bonds. Our warm thanks to all translators who have tirelessly contributed to the project; Selwyn Rose, Pamela Russ, Aryeh Sklar, Jerrold Landau, Sara Mages, Yocheved Klausner and Ilana Goldstein. Many thanks also to the Yizkor book project manager Lance Ackerfeld for continuous and professional support.

The original book was written mainly in Hebrew, with a smaller Yiddish section comprising about a quarter of the book. Most of the Yiddish chapters were duplicated in the Hebrew section, but not all. In this English version we have tried to keep the Hebrew chapter structure and inserted the unique Yiddish chapters where we found it appropriate. In a few cases we have moved Hebrew chapters to improve the chronology.

The fact that the original book is a mix of two languages affects the English spelling of certain words. The reader will find a difference between chapters translated from Hebrew (e.g. *Heder, Hanukah*) and from Yiddish (e.g. *Cheder, Chanukah*). Please also note that there are two kinds of brackets in the text; (original) and [translator].

We have tried to spell city names and other geographical names according to the historical time period. As an example, we use *Lemberg* during the Habsburg era, *Lwow* during the Polish inter-war era, and *Lvov* after the annexation by the Soviet Union in 1939. For well-known city names such as Warsaw and Moscow we use the established English names. Valuable support regarding correct geographical spelling has been kindly provided by Staffan Böös.

The images constitute a very important part of the book. We are most grateful to Allen Ginzburg who has put in a great labor, scanning the images from the original book and postprocessing them for improved quality.

The translation project has been funded by multiple sources. It is not possible to mention all private donors here, but we wish to express a special thanks to George Ow, Junior, whose generous contribution in 2017 made the project launch possible.

Anna Grinzweig Jacobsson, Göteborg, Sweden
Shirley Ginzburg, Santa Cruz, California, USA
July 2022

Credits and Captions for Book Cover

Front Cover:

The marketplace, 1929. Courtesy of Oren Perlson and Yona Malar.

Back cover:

Down From Top:

The great synagogue and old Jewish neighborhood, 2008. Source: Photo Archive of Yurii Pshenychnyi.

Ethel and Azriel Ross with their uncle, Shamai Ross, c.1907. Courtesy of Meir Razy.

Zvi Malar (back row on ladder), and Lazar Genirberg (back row at far right) clown around with friends from Hashomer Hatzair, c.1934. Courtesy of Oren Perlson and Yona Malar.

Golda Peysikh Goldvoug, née Shtreyman, Dubno, c.1890. Courtesy of Marigold Fine, James Stanford, Carolyn Rosevelt, and Deborah Naples.

Geopolitical Information

Dubno, Ukraine is located at 50°25' N 25°45' E and 210 miles W of Kiev

	Town	District	Province	Country
Before WWI (c. 1900):	Dubno	Dubno	Volhynia	Russian Empire
Between the wars (c. 1930):	Dubno	Dubno	Wołyń	Poland
After WWII (c. 1950):	Dubno			Soviet Union
Today (c. 2000):	Dubno			Ukraine

Alternate Names for the Town:

Dubno [Rus, Pol], Dubna [Yid]

Nearby Jewish Communities:

Mlyniv 9 miles NW
Muravytsi 10 miles NW
Varkovychi 10 miles ENE
Verba 11 miles SSW
Ozeryany 13 miles ENE
Kozin 16 miles SW
Mizoch 18 miles E
Torhovytsia 18 miles WNW
Demydivka 18 miles W
Krasne 19 miles WNW
Ostrozhets 19 miles NNW
Olyka 21 miles N
Kremenets 22 miles S
Velikiye Berezhtsy 23 miles SSW

Zdolbunov 23 miles ENE
Baremel 24 miles W
Rakhmanov 25 miles SE
Klevan 25 miles NNE
Podlesnoye 25 miles S
Rivne 26 miles ENE
Shums'k 26 miles SE
Berestechko 28 miles W
Mochulki 29 miles NNE
Katerynivka 29 miles SSE
Lutsk 29 miles NW
Radyvyliv 30 miles SW
Kuniv 30 miles ESE
Pochayev 30 miles SSW

Jewish Population: 7,108 (in 1900)

MAP OF UKRAINE IN 2014

Map of Ukraine with **Dubno** indicated

TABLE OF CONTENTS

Foreword

Translated from Hebrew by Selwyn Rose

About ten years ago we, "ex-patriots" from our community of Dubno, among the remnants of our people now in Israel, met together to create a fitting memorial to those upon whom had fallen the great Holocaust that had struck the whole House of Israel. We took upon ourselves the Holy task of eternalizing for future generations a portrait of Jewish Dubno throughout its history, its institutions, its intelligentsia, its Rabbis, its parties, and movements – a true portrait of its happiness and its somberness. As remnants of the generation that had lived through that fateful era, we saw it as our obligation to leave no stone unturned in hunting down memories and to record for posterity the period of riots and disturbances in the life of the town's Jewish population and to shed light on the public, cultural, religious, economic, and national experience before they all become swallowed up and lost in the depths of oblivion.

We did not delude ourselves; we knew the way would be long and hard until we achieved our goal of bringing the idea to fruition in a book. We knew that it was not to established writers we would be turning to record their memories but to those from the town – simple every-day folk, preserving in their hearts many important details of the life of our community and our town and by their own hand, join in recreating their past in all its splendor and brilliance. But we hoped that those who had taken upon themselves the burden would wonder the past of our town and investigate its sources and origins throughout the generations; to uncover documents and records, advertisements and historical material and collect together it all together on the threshing-floor and select everything that will illustrate the history of the Jewish life of Dubno in all its aspects and be privileged and blessed to see the fruits of their labors as a finished product. Alas it was not so – taken from the world leaving behind them only raw material virtually untouched barely enough for one or two articles.

Right at the beginning of the task of preparing the material for publication our active member on the committee Dr. Meyer Zohar (Lichtenstein), was taken from us, the man who with his broad intellectual ability and wide authority knew well to consider everything that came before him, bringing wise practical advice. Hardly had we recovered from the great loss when our colleague and friend Eliezer Czerner, the "lion" of our group took to his sick-bed and rose from it no more.

Our spirits fell. We asked ourselves: "Can we - will our strength be sufficient to continue with this project and bring it to a conclusion? Or must we accelerate the work, decrease the use of material already accumulated and rush ahead as fast as possible to bring the book to publication?"

While we were still considering our options and our way ahead the editor and architect of the book, Yacov Netaneli Roitman was uprooted from among us and left us groaning.

We became utterly depressed; the pain was great but greater still was the responsibility we felt towards the future generations and our martyrs – and ourselves, together with all the survivors from our town who answered us with their material for the book already hoping for years for its appearance. We gathered our remaining strength of purpose and continued. We continued – and failed. Whether from lack of experience and expertise or simply from neglect that dragged on because we relied on those who had left us. Thus, the years passed, and our townsfolk were pressing…

Eventually our efforts were crowned with success; we began to advance the work and published the book that now appears before us.

Thus were the labor-pains of this book and its contents.

The material brought before you here are presented chronologically: the town and its sources, Jewish settlement in the town, life in the town throughout the generations as represented in documents, certificates and newspapers and the traditions of the residents who live with us yet today – until the destruction at the hands of the Nazis. We have written as best we could, related what we have remembered and perpetuated for posterity in these pages what is holy and dear to us. The entire town is concealed within these pages, the town and its streets, its houses, its throngs of Jews, Study-Houses, and gardens – a clear picture of what was and is no more. We do not ignore that there are defects and faults and certainly the book will elicit comments from several quarters, and we know there is no way of being perfect in all eyes. We have done the best we can knowing the holy obligation we have taken upon ourselves and our dedication to this holy work will in the coming years stand firm before those who will come and criticize what we have done and what we have left undone.

We have produced a section in Yiddish in which appear condensed versions of the most important items for those of our town who are not over-familiar with Hebrew.

It is a pleasant obligation to acknowledge our grateful thanks to all those who cooperated and took part in the preparation of this book, either with advice or in more practical ways: to the people of Dubno in Israel and in other parts of the world wherever they may be, to the members of the editorial board, the editor Mr. Yacov Adini, Mr. D. Sztokfish who translated the monographs into Yiddish, to the organizing committee of the Dubno society in Israel, to Mr. Eliezer Steinman for his cooperation with his monographs, to the National Library of Israel for permission to use material from the *Pinkas HaKehilot*[1] and copies of the microfilms, to the *Sifriat Hapoalim* for permission to use the material of Mr. Raphael Mahler – all of them are worthy of blessings.

The Editorial Board

Translator's Footnote

1. Pinkas HaKehilot is an extensive series of journals recording the histories of hundreds of Jewish communities throughout Europe devastated and mostly lost during the Holocaust

7

The Editorial Board
Sitting (from right to left): Shmaryahu Roitman, Yisroel Pfeffer, Moshe Cohen, Nisan
Drori
Standing (from right to left): Zelig Freiman, Benjamin Bardiga, Asher Reichman

A Jewish Metropolis

A. Avtichi-Hadari

Translated from Hebrew by Sara Mages

Dubno, one of the most famous ancient cities in the province of Volhynian Russia (Wołyń in Polish) since the beginning of the second millennium AD, is tied with many strings to the history of the Ukrainian Jewry. Jewish refugees from the German principalities, who sought refuge in the nearby countries including Volhynia and its ancient cities Ostrow (Ostrów, Ostrog, Ostroh), Dubno, Lutsk (Łuck) and others, settled there in the 10th century.

The name Dubno, or Greater Dubno as the Jews called it in the distant past, evokes many memories, good and gloomy, about the living conditions in the diaspora for more than nine hundred years. During this period, the Jews of Dubno saw a lot of darkness and little light and went through great sufferings and little peace. They suffered from persecutions, oppressions and annihilations in time of wars and libels; exchange of occupiers, rulers and leaders; the decrees of 5408 and 5409 [1648/49]; the oppression of the Russian Tsarist authorities; the hostility of the Polish government; and last – Hitler's terrible Holocaust which brought the destruction and the annihilation of all the European Jewry including more than ten thousand Jewish residents of Dubno, and with them many thousands of Jews, men, women and children, from the surroundings that were brought to the Dubno ghetto by the Nazis and found their death there.

It can be said, without exaggeration, that the Jews had a large and important part in the building and the development of Dubno. The Jews have shaped its public and economic image, despite the difficulties and the limitations from which they suffered at different times. The adaptability of Dubno's Jewish residents and their talents helped them at all times. They were able to initiate, create and perform many enterprises that benefited the city's residents, including the Jews.

Since Dubno was close to the Austrian border it developed commercial ties across the border and served as a window to the west for Russia and Poland. At the end of the

18th century, its geographical situation and developed trade attracted major "fairs" and the well known "contracts" that took place there for nearly a century. "*Vaad Arba Aratzot*" [The Council of the Four Lands] discovered that Dubno was a worthy place for its meetings and conventions in which they revised regulations, set instructions, and made decisions for all the Jews. The city grew and flourished, and its name was known in faraway places. Many flocked to Dubno from near and far, and it became a center for the towns and cities across Volhynia.

Already in the earlier days, the community of Dubno was organized like all the other Jewish communities in Volhynia, and had Torah, charity, and benevolence institutions which were common in Jewish communities. Throughout the generations the community of Dubno appointed community leaders, public activists, Torah sages, scholars and leaders. The community was rich with synagogues and Beit-Midrash. Many genius Rabbis and famous scholars sat there and never stopped studying the Torah.

Dubno is the city of "*Shelah ha-Kadosh*" [the holy *Shelah* - Rabbi Yasaiah Horowitz], the Dubner Maggid and Avrom Ber Gotlober. Dubno is the city of the first Jewish press in Poland-Russia. Dubno is the city where loyal Zionist activists excelled during the last generations, starting with R' Zalman Ashkenazi who carried the nation's vision since his youth and infected many like Mordechai Blat, David Horowitz, the Perl brothers and others. Thousands of teenagers, who were educated in the spirit of the Hebrew language in the city's Hebrew School, were members of pioneer youth movements - *Gordonia*, *Hashomer Hatzair*, *Hechalutz* and others, and many of them immigrated to Israel and were among its builders and defenders.

Dubno's name, a metropolis with a rich and glorious past in the Volhynia diaspora, will remain forever in the history of the Jewish communities.

The City and its History

Yakov Netaneli Roitman

A. The Outline of the City

Translated from Hebrew by Sara Mages

Dubno, the province city, sits on the left bank of the Ikwa River, which draws its water away from the city to a distance of 5.6 kilometers until it spills into the Styr River near the town of Targowica [Torgovitsa]. Dubno is close to the central rail station of the Zdolbuniv-Radyvyliv railway, on the junction of the main line Brisk-Kiev. This central station is located in the village of Straklov, a distance of 12.7 kilometers (6 Russian versts) from the city, between Ozeryany and Rodnia stations.

Dubno is built on the edge of the Galician-Volhynia ridge, which turns its shoulder here to the east. It is surrounded on three sides by the waters of the Ikwa River, which block the access to the castle and to the city and serve as a natural barrier against attackers. In addition, the right bank of the Ikwa River is lower than the left bank, and the riverbed is swampy. Extensive swamps and deep-water lakes, which extend over large areas, prevent the access to the riverbed, and therefore Dubno was well protected from enemies in ancient times.

At the edge of the ridge, above the left bank, where the Ikwa is flowing in a semicircle, rising a red-brick castle whose enormous walls stand vertically above the river and serve as a shield against attackers, while two tall towers fill that role from the south and the west. On the western side, a wide deep moat separates the castle from the city; at time of emergency the moat was flooded with water from the river, so the castle was completely cut off from the city and stood like a fortress in the heart of the river. In ancient times, a portable bridge linked the castle to the city, and when necessary, it was raised with chains to the castle. In recent generations it was replaced by a permanent wooden bridge.

The Market

West of the castle stretches a spacious square plaza; it is the main market. In the middle stands the Council House (Rathaus), a large square building with a central courtyard that four arched open gates lead to it from the market. Muzzles of old cannons protruded from both sides of the gates, and their barrels were embedded vertically in the pavement by the doorposts. Many shops surrounded the Council House on all sides, and also the square around the Council House.

Straight streets opened from the market to all sides of the city. They were divided at right angles by side streets: Aleksandrowicz Street, formally called Grodski, a main promenade which wasn't very long; Machenskyi Street, named after the conqueror of the city during the Polish invasion; Castle Street (Zamkova); Szeroka Street, that led to the suburb of Zabramie, two additional streets branched off it: Parna Street and Panienska Street.

In the center of town, north of Aleksandrowicz Street, the Catholic Church, named after John Nepomucena, closed the passage with a wide white façade and a Latin inscription in large letters was fixed on it: "Gloria Tibi Domine" ("Glory to Thee, O Lord"). The priests of the Catholic religion, which ruled many towns in the environment, settled here. Behind the church there is a spacious garden surrounded by a white wall. Inside it is a green lawn and many barren trees: linden, chestnut, and white poplar.

Aleksandrowicz Street ended in the crossing corner of Machinski Street. From here it sloped to the Ikwa River and to the ancient Jewish Street. The Great Synagogue, which was built between the years 5543–5554 (1782-1794), stood close to the river.

Aleksandrowicz Street

It is told about the synagogue[1]:

"The synagogue in the city of Dubno is a very beautiful stone building, its height is about thirty cubits (21 meters), and its dome rests on sixteen pillars that were built in four rows. Its construction lasted approximately twelve years, from 5543 to 5554, when – as is written in the community ledger - they started to pray there. Its builders worked hard to find the large sums of money they needed to spend on it, and without the aid of Prince Michael Lubomirski, the city's leaders couldn't carry out their good ideas and all their hard work were in vain if this good master hadn't come to their aid. He sent his peasants' servants to work in this building for very small wages, and for the stones,

[Columns 27–28]

bricks, sand, raw material and the lime that they bought from him for this building, he only took half of the asking price. He helped them every day with everything that he could and directed them with his advice. Twenty-five years have passed since a reliable man, an old man of about seventy years, told me that he had heard in his youth from his father, who was eighty years old at that time that he was there when the cornerstone was laid for the synagogue's building. He saw with his own eyes how the townspeople, their chiefs and notable persons sat around the tables, which were made of wooden planks that were placed on top of empty wine and brandy barrels, and glass of brandy and honey cakes before them, and in their company was also this prince, a great respected minister of the Polish Kingdom and one of the military leaders, who drank a glass with them after he told them a few things and after he blessed them: 'That they'll finish successfully what they have started to build, and they'll pray in this synagogue to God who created the heavens and the earth, and all living things upon the earth".

"And in memory of the good thing that this nobleman has done, the masters of the city, together with our brothers, placed a gilded iron plate over the entrance to the synagogue, and on it the coat of arms of this respected noble family and the initials of the name of the prince, Michael Lubomirski, and under the sign – the verse: 'To the house of God we will go in the lightning, thunder, rain and snow' – 5554."

"*Aron HaKodesh* [the Holy Ark] in this synagogue is a work of art and very beautiful, on it, on its doors and on the pillars on its sides, there are gilded wood carvings, buds and flowers, seraphs, cherubs and grape vines, which attract the eyes of those who look at them. But over the years, this Holy Ark started to break down, and a few toys [ornaments] that were on it fell and decreased, and its gold fell and darkened, until the former Gabai of this synagogue, the chief philanthropist, our teacher and rabbi Shmuel Horowitz May God protect and preserve him, didn't rest until they fixed it and regilded it and now it is more decorated than before, this repair cost more than two thousand rubles. Also, the thick oak floor, that the builders of the synagogue made, rotted over the years and it was difficult and dangerous to walk on it, HaRav S. Horowitz removed it and replaced it with a solid limestone tile floor, beautiful and comfortable for those who walk on it."

"About sixty Torah scrolls, big and small, stand in *Aron HaKodesh,* and most of them are proper to read. Sacred vessels of silver, crowns, *Etzi Hayim*[2], fringes, *Yadim* [3], lamps, bowls and jugs that the Cohanim will use to wash their hands with next to the pulpit, also *Parochot*[4] and*Kaporot*[5], and a lot of expensive covers, the work of artists, are to be found in the synagogue."

"The Hanukah Menorah, that they also light candles in every Friday night and on holidays, is of pure silver, big and heavy, and was gloriously made with a double headed silver eagle on top. Two small silver plaques are attached to the menorah and these things are written on one of them: 'This menorah was refurbished by the Barkeepers Society who added a lot of silver to it 5576 (1816)', and written on the second: 'In everlasting memory of the Barkeepers' treasurer and the members of the Society, in the year 5597 (1827) the pure menorah, that they donated to the synagogue, was stolen and found missing, and with their kindness they repaired it again, beautiful and pure, it was ready on *Hoshana Rabbah* 5598 (1838) and it will exist for eternity until the arrival of the Messiah'."

"It is told: this menorah was stolen by Herel who put out the candles on Friday nights, after he broke it, he put its shafts and its parts in a sack and brought it to one of his associates to sell, and there was one man there who saw it, and from him it became known to the people of the community, the thief was sent to prison and the menorah was returned to the synagogue."

"As we said, there are many *Parochot and Kaporot* and covers in the synagogue, and they are always replaced on the Sabbath, festivals, and the Days of Awe. On Friday night the Ark is covered with a light blue *Kaporet* and *Parochet*. Stitched the *Kaporet* in silver letters: 'Donated by our teacher Yosef son of our teacher Avraham May God protect and preserve him, in the year 5500 (1740) by the abbreviated era'. The entire Sabbath *Kiddush* is stitched on the *Parochet* and above it says: 'Donated by our teacher and rabbi R' Tzvi Hirsh son of our teacher and rabbi R' Eliyahu May God protect and preserve him and his wife Mrs. Gitel'. And above: The year 5527 (1767) by the abbreviated era'."

"On *Sabbath Mevarchim*[4] they'll put on the Ark a *Parochet* and a *Kaporet* with the blessings of the month in silver letters, and at the bottom of the *Parochet* 5510 by the abbreviated era (1750). On a Friday, when there is *Brit Milah* in the city, and also on a weekday and on the Sabbath, they'll cover the Ark with a *Parochet* and a *Kaporet* with the blessings that are recited during the circumcision. On *Leil Yom Tov* [Friday night] they'll cover the Ark with an expensive red *Parochet* on which all the entire *Yom Tov Kiddush* is stitched in silver letters and the inscription: Donated by the modest noble woman Mrs. Hinda Chaya daughter of the late preacher our teacher Yermiyah HaLevi of blessed memory'. There is also a silver bowl from her with the inscription: 'Donated by the modest Mrs. Hinda daughter of our rabbi our teacher and rabbi R' Yermiyah Segal'. Written on another *Yom Tov Kaporet*: 'I have set the Lord always before me', donated by our teacher Eliezer son of our teacher Yosef for his son the boy Eliyahu, May God raise him to the Torah and to good deeds Amen *Selha*'. And written on another *Kaporet*: 'Donated by the chief, our teacher David son of our teacher R' Nisan of blessed memory in the year 5537 (1777) by the abbreviated era'. Written on a beautiful expensive Turkish, *Parochet*: 'Donated by the important noble woman Mrs. Ester May she live, daughter of the prominent scholar our teacher and rabbi Yoel, May the memory of the righteous be of a blessing'. But on most of the *Kaporot* and the *Parochot* there aren't any inscriptions and dedications. During the *Musaf* on the seventh day of Passover, and on *Shemini Atzeret*, they'll hang on the Ark an ornate expensive *Parochet*, the work of artists,

[Columns 29–30]

and embroidered on it with threads of silver and gold, large pillars and grape vines in various beautiful colors, and in the middle, there is a pattern of a horned bull standing next to a water well, and on this *Parochet* it is written: 'The year 5487 (1727) by the abbreviated era. By the worker who deals with the work of holy garments Yakev (Yakov) son of HaRav R' Yehudah Leib of blessed memory, and by the worker who deals with the work of holy garments Tzvi Hersh son of HaRav R' Yehudah Leib of blessed memory'."

"All the vessels and holy garments are stored in the cellar under a door and iron bars that were made by the Gabai of that time, the late R' Meir Shumski of blessed memory, whose heart and soul always benefited the House of God, and so was his late son, R' Chaim Hirtz of blessed memory, who was the synagogue's Gabai after him. All these valuable objects were donated by people who lived in recent centuries."

"There are four women's galleries in the synagogue that span to north and to the south, two of them upstairs and two of them downstairs. At the entrance to the synagogue, on both sides, there are four small houses of prayer, two downstairs and two upstairs. Most of the population and the tradesmen prayed there except for the High Holidays when everyone prayed in the synagogue."

"Besides the synagogue and the four houses of prayer at the entrance to this building, there are additional seventeen houses of prayer and Midrashim in the city, because in the city of Dubno, like in all the cities in Lita, Poland and Rusyn [Ruthenia], each association, each Hassidic sect, and all the tradesmen had a special house of prayer that carried the name of its founder, the name of the association, the Hassidic sect or the tradesmen who prayed there."

*

Close to the Great Synagogue stood in all of its gloom the ancient Bathhouse, not far from it the *"Hekdesh"* – a shelter and hostel for poor passers-by, and also the home of the president of the rabbinical court, and the Chief Rabbi.

Near the Great Synagogue was also the end of Zydowska Street – a long meager shapeless street, which started somewhere in the suburb of Zabramie on the bank of the murky Ikwa River, that reeds, thorns and weeds grew in its neglected yards.

Before the First World War the city of Dubno was paved and clean. Policemen and inspectors were strict about cleanliness, and homeowners

[Columns 31–32]

were given fines or even thrown in jail if the street near their houses was dirty. Therefore, you would have found each morning, when you passed through the streets, many important homeowners holding a twigs' broom with a long stick, cleaning the sidewalk near their house and half of the adjacent road, while the neighbor across the street was cleaning the second half of the road. The roads were paved with red bricks and not with stone slabs. The curbs were high and upright, and puddles ran along the sidewalk because the city didn't have a sewage system.

Many of the large buildings were not plastered and whitewashed because they were only built with red bricks, and for that reason they were the pride of their owners. There were many homeowners in the city because it was considered to be demeaning to live as a "neighbor" with someone. There were few apartment buildings; most of the buildings were of one storey with an attic; two-storey buildings were only in the market.

The Post Office

The city's homes were lit by kerosene lamps, but the lighting in the streets was poor and meager. Kerosene lamps hung on special posts and city employees, the "Lampers", lit them every evening. In the years 1910–1912, the kerosene lamps were replaced by "Lucas" lamps on the main streets. They were raised to the top of the posts with steel cables, and since the "Lucas" lamps were the height of progress in Dubno, masses of idle youth gathered every evening to watch how the "Lamper" lights the "Lucas" lamp, and shout "Hurray!" when a blinding white light penetrated from the modern lamp.

In Dubno they drank water from the Ikwa River. Every morning the water-drawers went down in horse drawn barrel-carts to the shallow places on the shore of the Ikwa, drew murky water with a long-handled ladle, and poured it into the barrels through a wide funnel. They transported the water from the river to the houses and sold it with a measuring cup.

One day, "Kazapim"[4], who knew how to drill, were brought to Dubno. An artesian well was dug in the heart of the market, and its pristine water flowed in abundance from open taps. The municipal council built a shelter over the taps to protect them from damage and from freezing in the winter. Indeed, even then the water didn't flow through pipes to the houses, but the water-drawers no longer treated the homeowners with muddy water full of filth but provided them with clear drinking water.

The suburb of Surmicze

In the description of the city, we can't forget the suburbs: Zabramie – to the west, by the Russian Orthodox Church; Surmicze to the east, with three bridges over the Ikwa's tributaries and the mighty dam; and Pantalia – to the north. Semi-rural life flowed in these

[Columns 33–34]

suburbs: Jewish blacksmiths flattened iron, Jewish carpenters planed beams, Jewish chimney sweepers walked blackened and jolly from house to house, and gentile farmers harvested the produce of their fields.

There were many boulevards, which were planted with ornamental trees, in the city like: Panienska Boulevard, which is planted with shady linden trees, and Pantalia Boulevard that passes over the Ikwa River, with a vast marshy prairie on both sides, to the modest pleasant Pantalia grove. Also, the slope of Gorbachina Street, west of the city, served as a place for a stroll. On one side of the street stood the walls of the church and the state prison, and on the other side was a wide green plateau, which was lost in the vast horizon.

Panienska Boulevard

A few kilometers out of the city, on the Zabramie's side, there was an elegant wide green park, Palastini. Inside stood the monument of Tsar Alexander III, which commemorated his visit to the city in 1890, during his tour of the southwest region of his kingdom that bordered with Austria.

There were hardly any antiquities in Dubno – there weren't any special buildings, there weren't any monuments or ancient water wells like those that are found in western cities; only the Russian Orthodox Church and the monasteries with the "onion domes" that gave the city an Eastern Slavic color, and the Baroque Polish Catholic Church of "Saint John".

Most of the city's 19th century buildings were wooden structures, but due to the frequent fires in the city and the primitive fire fighting conditions (they were forced to bring water from the river), the city council forced homeowners to build stone houses in the main streets and cover their roofs with tin or tiles.

One and only was the Polish castle, which was called by the Jews "Der Schloss" (the castle), it stood in the heart of the city and reminded the horror of the past. During the Russian rule military barracks were built in the castle's courtyards.

Original Footnotes and Translator's Comments

1. According to the book "*Dubno Rabati*" [Dubno the Great] by Rabbi Hayim Zev Margaliyot, Warsaw 5670 (1910), with small variations.
2. Etz Hayim (pl. Etzi Hayim) - tree of life - one of two wooden handles of a Torah scroll.
3. Yad (pl.Yadim) – hand - a ritual pointer, used to point to the text during the Torah reading.
4. Parochet (pl. Parochot) – ornamental curtain covering the front of the Holy Ark.
5. Kaporet (pl. Kaporot) – covering of the Holy Ark.
6. Sabbath Mevarchim - "Sabbath of Blessing" - the Sabbath on which the forthcoming new month is blessed.
7. "Kazapim" - Ukrainian derogatory name for the Russians.

B. The Jews of Dubno

Translated from Hebrew by Selwyn Rose

A

The earliest reliable information we have concerning Dubno is dated from the late 14th Century, in the period of the founding of the Principality of Lithuania under the rule of Witold[1], the Grand Duke of Lithuania and a blood–relative of Jogaila the son of Algirdas the King of Poland. At that time the Principality of Volhynia (Wołyń) constituted a part of the Principality of Greater Lithuania and three cities in Volhynia formed the southern defensive line – Lutsk, Ostrow and Kremenets (Krzemieniec); Dubno was considered a second line of defense.

Within a few years, at the beginning of the 14th Century, there were Jewish communities in the towns of Lithuania and Volhynia, in spite of the fact that Jews were not mentioned as residents of Dubno until 1530. The communities were connected with the towns of Brzesc[2] Grodno, Troki and Lutsk. On 28th June 1388 the Jewish people of Lithuania in the town of Lutsk were given a notarized documentary "Bill of Rights" recognizing their existence. The document was known as "The Certificate of Troki" and it promised the Jews the following rights: unrestricted movement throughout the State; identical taxation for Jews and Christians alike; the identical rights of citizenship as the Christians (regarding the present "…lack of assistance extended to Jews in distress at night" the Christian to be punished as a thief; for breaking and entering a Jewish home or plundering, the Christian will be charged as if stealing from the Kingdom's coffers; when a Jew casts a suspicion of murder on a Christian the Duke will designate a police officer to undertake a full investigation; for murder and rape of Jews by Christians the offender will be prosecuted to the full extent of the law, and so on), defense of Study–Houses and Jewish cemeteries (for violating a Study–House fines will be imposed and violating a Jewish cemetery, property will be confiscated). A Jew can only be tried on the evidence of two witnesses – one Christian and one Jew "known to be faithful to his religion". In the same "Bill of Rights" the basics of Jewish communal autonomy were laid down that confirmed the authority of the Jewish *Beit–Din* over the community and its members.

The few sources from which we can draw details of Jewish life in Lithuania and Volhynia in the 14th and 15th Centuries are the Jew Kalman of Breslau, Germany who visited Kamianets–Podilskyi (which belonged to Lithuania), in 1390, and found Jews there, and also the Dutch tourist Guillebert de Lannoy[3] who writes concerning his visit to Troki in 1415: "There are living here Ashkenazis (Germans), Lithuanians and a large number of Jews, all of them speaking in their respective mother tongue". It is also known that the Jewish people in those areas spoke "Yiddish, Byelorussian and the Tatar language."

Suddenly in the year 1492 – the same year as the expulsion of Jews from Spain and Portugal – The Duke of Lithuania, Alexander Jogaila, expelled all the Jews and confiscated all their possessions. Although, ten years later in 1503 Alexander Jogaila rescinded the edict and the Jews began to return to Lithuania and re-establish themselves. On 21st March 1514 a "Bill of Rights" was given by the Duke, in Vilna (Wilno), to the Jews of Troki, Grodno, Brzesc, Lutsk, Pinsk and Kovrin in which he re-affirms the promise of his brother King Alexander: "…to exempt them from the obligation of supplying the army with a thousand horses and taxes paid by them will be identical to those paid by all the other citizens and they can practice arts and craftsmanship without restriction or interference."

Additional evidence concerning the favorable situation of the Lithuanian Jews of the period can be found in the report of the Catholic Bishop Comedani who was the Pope's representative at the court of Zygmunt II August, the King of Poland at the end of the 16th Century[4]: "They are found there (Volhynia and Podolia) in considerable numbers and they do not provoke contempt as they do in other places. Generally speaking, they do not make a living from despised businesses, like loans at interest and involvement in trading suspect goods, although there are among them some who are attracted to such dealings. The Jews are land-owners, traders, and dedicate themselves to study, literature, medicine and astrology. Some of the Jews are very prosperous and belong to the dignified and respected class of society. The Jews are not required to wear a yellow patch on their clothing in order to distinguish themselves from the Christians. They are permitted to carry a sword and arms and they enjoy the identical rights and privileges as the rest of the citizens."

B

Jews, as residents of Dubno are mentioned for the first time in a document from 1552[5] which, among other things, discusses Jewish dealers in beef who bought bulls in Wallachia: "Michal of Vinnitsa – 2080 bulls; Issatchko of Ostrow 1500 bulls; the Jew Laschiak of Dubno bought 309 bulls. He and Michel of Ostrow have 120 bulls."

[Columns 37–38]

Clear proof of the existence of a Jewish community in Dubno is the oldest gravestone in the old Jewish cemetery from the year 1581[6] a fact indicating that the Jewish community was so firmly established that it was able to acquire a plot of land to use as an independent cemetery. Another ancient gravestone dated 1604 is mentioned in the book by Rabbi Margalit "Greater Dubno": "Here is interred the old woman Mrs. Khinka, daughter of Yitzhak. Passed away 5th Elul in the year 5634 (1604). May her soul be bound up in the bond of eternal life."

Evidence supporting the advancement of the Jewish community in Dubno can be found in the book "The Gate of the Letters"[7] by *Hash'lah Ha–Kadosh*[8]: "When I was in Volhynia, I asked those same traders if they had stocks of non–Kosher brandy in casks that they were selling to the Holy Land (to a non-Jew), before Passover: how can they do it? They said that they have been doing so for generations." Rabbi Pinchas Pesses[9] explains: "*Hash'lah* the Righteous was the Rabbi in Dubno in 1600 and in Ostrow in 1603 and it appears that many years ago the expression "for generations" meant at least 100–150 years ago before the question arose – about 1450–1500, so we can assume that at that time there was a Jewish community worthy of that designation, in our town."

Thus, Rabbi Pinchas Pesses relies upon the evidence of Mr. Balhass, the archivist of the Princess of Aratinska, the royal lady of Dubno at the end of the 19th Century who discovered a Latin inscription in the archive's repository referring to "…the small town of Dubno close to the County capital of Ptycha," confirming the accepted tradition of the local Jews and that the settlement of Jews in Dubno and the surrounding area commenced in the years 1450–500. He, too, relies on information from 1552, "…that Jews from Dubno bought 309 bulls in Wallachia", as proof of a Jewish community in Dubno in the middle of the 16th Century.

C

The rights of the minority Jewish community in Volhynia during the 16th and 17th Centuries were based on the Lutsk "Bill of Rights", Brzesc and other towns, and the Jewish population did not suffer from discrimination by the princes of Lithuania, with which Volhynia was amalgamated from the middle of the 14th Century. Thanks to that lack of discrimination the Jewish communities of Lithuania and Volhynia expanded in most of the towns and cities and their economic situation was stable, although in Professor Sergei Bershadski's opinion there was much significant poverty among many Jews, as he states: "Large proprietors and exporters from among the Jews were a mere handful and for most of them the returns on their businesses and trading enterprises were small. The 'fortune' that most of the Jews had was a mere handful of rubles (at the 1882 exchange rate); more than that – the interest to the Tatars, farmers and the townspeople of loans was so small that the Jewish holder of a so-called 'fortune' was himself forced to mortgage his household goods with the priesthood, government officials and 'nobles' in order to obtain some cash."

The annexation of Volhynia to the Polish kingdom by King Sigismund – in August 1569 – brought with it many changes in the social and economic structure and had a decisive influence on the whole of Jewish Poland.

At that time the "Council of the Four Lands" was founded in which heads of the Jewish community of Greater Poland (Poznań), Lesser Poland (Krakow), Russia (Podolia, eastern Galicia – Lwow (Lwów, Lemberg, Lvov, Lviv)) and Volhynia (after the annexation to Poland). The functions of the Council were: "…to determine and mark the borders of community authority, lest one authority encroaches upon a neighboring one, to clarify and pass judgment on disputes between one community and another and between a community with an individual, to levy taxes, to arbitrate in negotiations between communities in religious, educational and economic matters, to offer counseling in lobbying nobles where necessary[10]."

Among the towns of Volhynia, the fourth of the "Council of the Four Lands" that became prominent after a while was Dubno, mentioned once in the 18th Century, while Kremenets and Ostrow were mentioned in the 17th Century. Dubno was the most important of the Jewish towns in Volhynia and was known as "Greater Dubno" in several books and in the Journal of the "Council of the Four Lands".

Already in 1634 in the foreword to the book "*Torat Hayim*" by the *Gaon*, Abraham Hayim ben Naphtali Hirsch Schor, Father of the Rabbinical Court of the Holy Community of Stanow, printed in Krakow that same year, the following signature occurs: "A short declaration by Tzvi, known as Hirsch (son of my lord and father) the wise Rabbi Ozer (may he be remembered in the world to come), I place my standard, for the time being, here in the Holy Community of Greater Dubno, 1634."

In 1663, the name "The young Nahman, son of our Rabbi and teacher Meir, Righteous Cohen Rappoport[11], may he be remembered in the world to come, who has settled in the Holy Community of "Greater Dubno", appeared among the signatories of the Council of the Four Lands decision not to print "The *Shulhan Aruch*[12] since it had not been sufficiently edited". And on the gravestone of the Rabbi, bar Josef of Dubno who died and was buried in Lwow in 1664 is the inscription: "And Moses went up unto G–d on the 9th day of the month Sivan 5425 (1664) being the Great Gaon and Rabbi of our Rabbi and Teacher Rabbi Josef, Father of the Rabbinical Court of Greater Dubno. He taught Torah humbly and modestly, nourishing the minds of his generation. May his rest be honorable until the dead are revived."

[Columns 39–40]

The Castle, which was called "Der Schloss" by the Jews

"Greater Dubno", as such, is mentioned for the first time in 1709 in an "approval" of the book "*P'nei Ari Zuta*[13]": "Thus said Shmuel Avraham our Father, Teacher and Rabbi, who has supplanted the Priest from Krakow and settled himself in the Holy Community of Greater Dubno, on the 5th day of Tammuz 1709." While in 1724 one of the Dubno Rabbis together with a Rabbi from Lwow, Lublin, Opatow, Zamosc and Krakow signed an approval on a book entitled "*Yeffe Mareh*" "The diminutive Yehoshua Herschel" our Rabbi and Teacher, the noted Rabbi Eliezer the incumbent of the Holy Community of Greater Dubno on the fourth day of Elul 1724... when the Rabbis of the Four Lands were officially registered in the office of the wise men of Jaroslaw" while in the official minutes of Dubno on page 51 column 1 the year 1742 the following signature appears: "41 – Yitzhak Moshe Kahana resident in the Holy Community of Greater Dubno (May it be established on High, Amen), 1742.

We find in the statistical report of 1765 much evidence confirming the large number of Jewish citizens in Dubno, compared to other towns in Volhynia: Dubno– 2492; Lutsk– 1845; Konstantin (new and old)– 1801; Lublin (the town)– 1634; Kowal– 1516; Rowno (Równe, Rivne) – 1422; Lubivne (Liuboml)– 1226; Kremenets– 1029. That same year there were 6877 Jews in Brody and 6378 in Lwow.

Regarding the social standing and equal rights situation of Dubno's Jewish population, we learn from an order published in the name of King Wladyslaw IV in the middle of the 17th Century: "The Jews in the town of Dubno will retain the use of their synagogue and use it according to their practices, they may trade and manage their businesses and trading as they were permitted to do before times. In addition they will pay taxes equally with other citizens since they are in business together with them and derive the same benefits..."[14]

D

At the end of the 16th Century many Jews migrated eastwards from Poland to Ukraine and settled there, but their settlements were razed during the Khmelnytsky uprising that reached as far as Poland and tens of thousands of the Jews were killed during the pogroms. In the years 1648–1649 the Khmelnytsky Cossacks destroyed many towns in Podolia and Volhynia among them Brzesc, Pinsk and Kobrin, Brody, Dubno, Kremenets and Ostrow and their Jewish residents were put to the sword.

Regarding the destruction of Jewish Dubno, Nathan ben Moses Hannover tells us in his book "*Yeven Mezulah*"[15]: "…And the evil oppressor [Khmelnytsky] (May his name be forever blotted out and erased), marched with his army on the Holy Community of Konstantin and from there to the Holy Community of Ostrow the capital. These communities were already destroyed by the soldiers…and from there they marched on the Holy Community of Greater Dubno. There, too, was a strong fortress unlike any in the whole state of Poland … and behold – when the Duke and Nobles fled from the war and remained in Dubno several hundred Jews who were there sought to find refuge in the fortress…and when the ruffians came close to town one prince came in to town with eighty heroic soldiers…and they closed the fortress gates and bolted them and held the fortress and refused entry to the Jews…and one thousand one hundred Jewish souls were slain in front of the fortress…"

In that year according to the archives of 1650 there were 47 Jewish homes in Dubno and 141 Christian homes[16]. All the houses became fuel for fires. Additional evidence on the destruction of the Dubno community that same year can be found in the archives of the Principality of Aratinska where it is written: "…the slaughter of the Jews was carried out on the heights by the fortress and on that hill of mourning the people of the G–d of Abraham fell victim to the envy of a cruel people. And the burial place of these martyrs can be found outside the city wall in the grounds of the Great Synagogue and the people of the town went there on the ninth of Av. In a house next to the synagogue was the home of Rabbi Tovia, (Z"L) the ritual slaughterer and inspector, there stands a pillar surrounded by a wooden fence about 2 feet high and it is believed here are buried a bride and groom from among the martyrs of 1649.

A tradition accepted by the Jews of Dubno relates that in that same year of 1649 the daughter, Esther, of Rabbi Meir, the son of Rabbi Moshe Katz Ashkenazi, head of the Religious Court of the Holy Community of Dannhausen, who arrived in Dubno from Mogilev and died in 1643, sister of Rabbi Shabtei Cohen, died as a martyr[17]. The noted Rabbi of that generation, Rabbi Avraham bar Shmuel Ashkenazi delivered a eulogy[18] as follows:

We searched our way and examined it:

In the Holy Community of Dubno the Capital,

As an illuminating crystal,

Replete with soul, counsel and heroism…

On the fifteenth of Tishrei, the Rejoicing of the Law,

The Children of Israel walked to the elegant synagogue

And opened their mouths in song and chant,

And in an aura to thank and praise G–d.

And they finished praying elegantly, with joy and respect

Intending to fulfill the commandment and erect their Succoth rapidly,

A threat and horrifying defilement came,

And murdered hero and heroine

With their children – their crowning glory

And not a trace of them remains…

And four thousand great and small,

Our Rabbi and Teacher, Yehuda, Master of Kabbalah and tradition,

Careful and quick in memory and preserving,

They bound him up as with a grape–vine…

They killed him by stoning, fire and strangulation

Who can imagine…

And put to the sword some of our Holiest expositors

And a scandal was perpetrated…

E

Twenty–three years after the destruction of Dubno's Jewish community by Khmelnytsky's Cossacks, in December 1671, a French diplomat, Ulrich von Werdum wrote about Dubno in the journal he kept of his travels[12]:

[Columns 45–46]

"Dubno is a medium sized town. Its houses are long, but narrow, wooden and overpopulated. The streets of the town are straight and long and also the alleys cross them but the whole town is paved. On the edge of Dubno stands an elegant Bernadine monastery with its wide entry. Apart from the monastery there also exists a Catholic church and four Russian houses of worship and also a synagogue for the Jews, all brick buildings. Outside the town, on the shores of the lake, rises the monastery of the Russian monks. A brick building and on the other side of the lake opposite the monastery is a wooden convent that houses the Russian nuns."

"The town and the castle stand close to the lake on a long ridge on one side of which is the lake and on the other side flows the river Ikwa. The Castle is located on the highest edge of the ridge, near the exit to the town. On the widest section of the ridge, approaching the town, two trenches were dug and strong solidly built batteries although at the extremes the construction was not so strong. Between the embankments is the elegant gateway built of stone, to the town."

"The castle is surrounded with a broad trench on the side facing the town and projections of the walls are faced with stone. The castle has a high wall with several turrets rising up above the walls. From an architectural point of view the roof is flat as is the style in Italy."

"To the left of the castle is a building in the Italian style, a stoa of columns of dwelling places. To the right is a single-storeyed building of stone also containing living quarters. At the edge of this building are a wall and a trench that give entry to the old castle where all the structures are of wood partially surrounded by a wall and towers and partially by an earthen embankment. The old castle is mainly just a pile of rubble. Neither of the castles has been maintained."

"From the castle one passes over a long moat-like depression between a marsh and the lakes to the village of Rachyn that is situated on the banks of the lake. A long wooden bridge leads from the town to the moat."

"About twentythree or twentyfour years ago the Cossacks laid siege on that castle and rained bombshells on it but failed to subdue and conquer it. Nevertheless, those same Cossacks stormed the town, conquered it and laid waste to it. There is now no bastion to defend it other than the lake…"

"We lived with a Jewish man who lighted a candle for his mother–in–law who had died the previous year on this day. Once a year he is obliged to light a memorial candle to her memory. On Friday evening, with sundown, they lit four candles because there were two women and on the Sabbath eve the Jews are commanded to light two candles for each woman living in the house…"

Hand—drawn map with numbered locations made by Ulrich von Werdum (columns 43–44). 1. The village of Raczyn. 2. River Ikwa. 3. Convent. 4. The New Castle. 5. The Old Castle. 6. The City Hall. 7. Synagogue. 8. Jewish Quarter. 9. Christian Quarter. 10. Italian Stoa. 11. Apostolic Church. 12. Russian Orthodox Church. 13. Russian Orthodox Church. 14. Gateway to the suburb of Zabramie. 15. Bernadyn Monastery. 16. Russian Orthodox Church. To the left of 13 the steep Gorbaczyno slope. (The map was copied by hand by Abba Fenichel Pinx in 1959.)

F

Sixtyfive years after the destruction, in the year 1713 the Jewish population of Dubno was greater than that of the Christians as we learn from the assertion of the noble, Prince Alexander Dominick Lubomirski who granted the city council the right to levy taxes on the Jewish residents amounting to two thirds of the total while the Christians would pay only the remaining one third while the other obligatory civic works falling upon the citizens – like road repairs, bridge maintenance – were shared equally among them, Jewish and Christian alike and "a fine of one thousand Grivna will be the punishment with imprisonment for all defaulters".

The same Prince Lubomirski issued an order in 1727 in Dubno to the council concerning the Jews specifically[20]:

"Clause 2. Disputes between the Jews and other residents will be adjudicated by the city's chief inspector and claims before the court without the intervention of the chief inspector. The guilty party will be sentenced to seven days' imprisonment under guard."

"Clause 4. The citizens will themselves elect the officers of the city and there will be one Jewish representative from the Community."

"Clause 13. Citizens will not go to the public bathhouse together with the Jews but segregated and for that purpose days of the week will be designated for the separate faiths as follows: Tuesdays and Saturdays for the Christians, Thursday and Friday for the Jews. The enforcement of this arrangement will be controlled by the municipal inspectors and offenders will spend four days in the prison. The law will be written into the statute book of Dubno."

During the reign of the Princes of Lubomirski over Dubno, the extent of Jewish settlement in the town increased and in the 17th Century the Jewish Street extended in a straight line from the Zabrama Gate along the Ikwa River as far as the Great Synagogue. In the year 1742 Prince Stanislaw Lubomirski sold to "…the Jew of Dubno, Yehuda Libowitz, a plot of land to build a house"[21] in a street close to the Catholic church. His grandson, Berish Roitman built his well-known hostel in 1813. On the same street, close to the same period, the houses of other families: Yoshie "the farmer" and the family home of Joel Mandelkern.

G

In spite of the equal rights enjoyed by the Jews of Dubno during the reign of the Princes of Lubomirski, there were, for all that, pressures from the Christian residents as is seen from the record of a trial that was held by the City Council in Dubno in 1716[22]:

[Columns 47–48]

"And this is the verdict brought in by the Magistrates of the City of Dubno, after the required investigation that was undertaken according to the City prosecutor in the matter of two women suspected of the heresy of accepting the religion of Israel, on 5th March 1716."

According to Dubno town's attorney the townswoman of Vitebsk, the widow Marina Davidovna Surawicza and the townswoman, the maiden Maryna Wojciechówna were taken for questioning for accepting the Hebrew religion. During the investigation the first woman stated that she was the daughter of a Pravoslav Priest of Vitebsk and was married to the Christian David Surawicz and remained with him for ten years. After his death she accepted the Hebrew faith of her own free will and without the intervention of any third party because she heard from her father the Priest what seemed like a suggestion that the Hebrew faith was superior to the Christian one. No one knew that she had converted and during the whole journey from Vitebsk to Dubno she had ridden on horses given to her by the Jews because she had told them she was Jewish and in Dubno she had slept only one night and the following day she had been arrested and brought before the court.

"On being asked: would you consider reconverting to Christianity? She replied she would not and that she would suffer agonies and die as a Jewess as a martyr in the name of the living G-d."

"When she was asked under severe tortures and one hundred and eighty lashes, she repeated the words she had spoken at first…"

Maryna Wojciechówna was caught under the wedding canopy during a marriage ceremony to a Jew. She stated that in her hometown, Milica, she worked as a housemaid in a Jewish home and after a time moved to another small settlement where the Jewish man, Pasternak and several other Jewish people moved her intensely to the extent that she accepted the religion.

"When asked three times under severe torture and had received sixty-six lashes she said the following and then only after receiving an additional forty-four strokes:

'Now in my heart I hate the Jewish faith and as before I am a Christian and am prepared to suffer agonies and die for it..."'

Five other Jews were brought to the prison from under the wedding canopy: Ephraim Jacobowitz, the bridegroom of Maryna Wojciechówna; Leib Abramowitz, an inspector of the hospital in whose home the wedding was taking place, Ya'acov Barchowicz, organizer of the ceremony; Leib Mofsowitz, who traveled several days with Marina Woczkowa and Ya'acov Yuspowicz, who wrote the ceremonial document.

This last said that he was ill and was not completely aware of what he was writing. When asked under torture and beaten with a strap, each one of them three times, all of them, unanimously claimed that they did not know she was Christian.

"On the basis of Common Law and the laws of "Speculum Saxonum"[23], anyone who leaves the Christian faith shall be burned with fire, the judges condemn the widow Marina Davidovna Surawicza to have her flesh torn off with pincers and to afterwards be burnt at the stake while her soul yet lives within her; and the maiden Maryna Wojciechówna they sentenced to be decapitated and her remains cremated..."

The Jews, except for the sick Ya'acov Yuspowicz, and those from another place, were sentenced to suffer one hundred lashes at the stake and to be banished from the town.

"The citizenry of Dubno, because of their frivolousness either deliberately or unknowingly, in allowing the apostates a place among them for a week and permitting them to carry out the religious ceremony – will pay a fine in wax and wax candles for the benefit of every house of Christian prayer in the town of Dubno and to the State treasury, the Prince, the castle and the city council and to return to the Christian citizens of Dubno all the expenses of this trial."

"In addition, it is forbidden to the Jews to employ workers and house servants of the Christian faith from now on and to confine a Christian who works for them to a prison, under a penalty of one hundred Grivna."

H

The Jewish community of Dubno is again mentioned in 1755 at the time of the big dispute concerning the false Messiah Shabtei Tzvi in connection with the ostracism of Rabbi Jonathan Eybeschtz by Rabbi Ya'acov Emdan concerning certain supposedly heretical amulets written by the former "…in the of name of the Lord G–d and his faithful Anointed one, Shabtei Tzvi"[24]:

"With G–d's help, today Tuesday 1754, may we be increased for good, here in Dubno. Ya'acov, our teacher and Rabbi, Rabbi Ya'acov, (may his lamp illuminate us), and I stand on guard in this Holy Community of Konstantin, and afterwards I will make my way to the country of Russia."

Dubno was also mentioned in the text of the extensive boycott and excommunication against Shabtei Tzvi and his disciples: "Whosoever, within the Holy Community of Lwow and the Holy Community of Lutsk and the Holy Community of Brody and the Holy Community of Dubno and all the associated districts… any man or woman connected with the evil ones mentioned above, doing business with them or bargaining with them or eating of their food will be excommunicated as are they…"

[Columns 49–50]

And again the community of Dubno is mentioned when the representatives of the "Council of the Four Lands" congregated near Krakow on the 7th of the month of Av, 12th December 1760, to discuss the situation of the Jews at that time, after the Shabtei Tzvi affair, Nathan Ha'azti and Jacob Frank[25] who did great damage to the Jewish world, and the Chairmanship of Rabbi Meir ben Joel of Dubno and "…the public image of the 'Four Lands'."

This same Rabbi Meir ben Joel was a man of great prominence, generosity and public activity and in 1754, together with other elders of Dubno was a signatory to a decision "…in the matter of engaging 'ten community members to be available at all times for prayers and the reading of Psalms'" at public expense and a year later his signature appeared on the acceptance of a rabbi for Dubno.

In 1761 Rabbi Meir ben Joel of Dubno wrote several articles repudiating the blood libels against the Jews of Poland and paid 2400 Florins out of his own pocket for their publication. He also made sure that copies of other important documents of the official library were made, thus turning them into official instruments requiring state and priesthood authentication.

Three years previously in 1758 a special delegate, Rabbi Ya'acov Eliachim ben Asher Selig from Yampil (Yampola) representing the "Council of the Four Lands" went to Rome and met Pope Benedict XIV to protest the blood libels being carried out against the Jews of Poland[26] and to seek a Bull of protection.

His mission entailed high expenses, and, on his return, the presidential committee sat to debate how to compensate him. The receipts, totaling 3,046 Adumin were presented to the committee's Elder, Rabbi Meir of Dubno. The "Council of the Four Lands" had no such sum and decided to levy a one–time tax on every Jewish family. Only the destitute and scholars were exempt, and the decision was confirmed in writing on 2nd on Nisan (6th April 1761) by the treasurer of Poland Theodore Wessel.

The following summer the presidential committee of the "Council of the Four Lands" again convened in Piltza near Krakow from 8th to the 18th of Av, – July 1762 – chaired by the Committee's elder, Rabbi Meir of Dubno. Present at that meeting was the county minister as representative of the Minister of Finance Theodore Wessel.

At the center of the debate was the question of the large lingering debts owed by the Committee and the Provinces and the Committee decided to reject the claim of the interest and place upon the County committees to cover the fund in four annual payments. The decision was recorded in Polish in order that the authorities will recognize the document.

At that same presidential convention of the "Council of the Four Lands" a special tax for the Royal Household was also debated and "…in the presence of the noble gentleman, the Finance Minister and with his agreement…" it was decided to collect that tax and a suitable sum was apportioned to each of the Counties. Four representatives of "Greater Poland" and four representatives of "Lesser Poland" took part and one from the county of Chelm, one from Zamosc and the Holy Community of Rzeszow (Reisha)…"

The expenses of the convention – rental of the hall in which the meetings took place, in the amount of 100 Florins and a "tip" for the representative of the treasurer to the amount of 370 Florins – were paid for by the Elder Rabbi Meir ben Joel of Dubno.

And yet again, a year later from 21st – 28th Elul (September 1763), another convention of the "Council of the Four Lands" took place in Piltza and again the chairman was Rabbi Meir ben Joel of Dubno. His deputy was Rabbi aim Aaron Rappoport, Rabbi and Father of the *Beit Din* of the Holy Community of Lwow.

The meetings confirmed the previous year's decision of paying a special tax to the Royal Household and also confirmed "…the agreement with the Holy Community of Przemysl (Pshemishl) to return excess if the taxes levied upon them exceeded 1300 Florins. "In addition, 1000 Florins were budgeted for the refurbishment of the synagogue in Piltza with the assent of the Minister of Finance who indicated that "…the 'Council of the Four Lands' in earlier times would donate funds for the construction of new synagogues." Therefore "…it is also given to the 'Council of the Four Lands' to cover the expenses of Rabbi Meir of Dubno with a payment of 6010 Florins".

That same meeting of the 'Council of the Four Lands' was the last one at which Rabbi Meir ben Joel acted as Chairman and Elder.

Less than a year later on 6th June 1764 on its 24th sitting the Sejm decided to dissolve the "Council of the Four Lands" and the Councils of the various counties and took a census of all the Jews of Poland and imposed on every Jew an annual poll–tax of two Guilders. The State Treasurer formed a "Liquidation committee" that made a demographic and financial survey of the "Council of the Four Lands" and the councils of the counties at the time of their "demise".

In 1765 Rabbi Meir of Dubno claimed 2,400 Florins from the "Liquidation Committee" owing to him as payment for the publication of his letters four years previously protesting the blood libels and 1,390 Florins for various other expenditures of the Council of the Four Lands but the committee rejected the claim and even fined him 500 Florins for the crime of "forging and searching through public documents."[27]

I

During the sixth decade of the 18th Century the sad fate of Ukrainian Jewry came to pass – the days of the terror Khmelnytsky riots that spread to the Jewish towns and villages of Poland. The Hetman Maksym Zalizniak and his Haidamak brigades raided cities and villages in Poland and carried out slaughters of Jews and Poles alike.

[Columns 51–52]

The reaction of Dubno's Jews was the declaration of a year of mourning in 1761 which was stated thus:

"Our disbelieving ears have heard, and our souls languish in sadness and our eyes are dimmed from the tragedies and libelous lies…we have been sent like lambs to the slaughter, debased, dishonored, shamed…therefore we place upon our souls a whole year of lamentation from today in order to mourn appropriately this great devastation. We will inflict upon our souls for a whole year the wearing of our ordinary clothes on the Sabbath, men and women, and on feast days no festive wear will be seen for this year, only Sabbath and weekday clothing. Nor will we wear silver and gold ornaments or even a bracelet, and silver– and goldplated will be forbidden for six years.[28] Only a headscarf will be worn by women on Sabbath, gold and silver will be plain and simple and not beaten even on festivals. All this in our community alone but traveling we shall allow our citizens to wear the normal dress, especially for weddings. It is also forbidden to send honey in silver containers or to wear fine silk. We will not go to celebrations and even for a Mitzvah and certainly for any other gathering and we will not send friends wine or such."

"All of the above is being enacted with the agreement of the distinguished leaders of the community on this day 19th day of Tammuz) 5521 (21st July, 1761) together with Rabbi the Gaon, lover of justice, head of the *Bet–Din* and *Yeshiva*. His honor the Rabbi and his household are not included in the prohibitions. Signed Arieh Leib and David ben Nisan and the Reverend Yehoshua Heschel and Reverend Kalonimus–Kalman…"

J

The liquidation of the Polish Kingdom by command of the ethnographic unit of the state following the division of the country among three of its neighbors – Russia, Austria and Prussia in the space of three years, 1772, 1793 and 1795 led to fundamental changes in the lives of the Jewish population and ruptured the thread of the unified and fixed lifestyle – habits, traditions and its deep–rooted, many–branched autonomic structure. Volhynia and with it Dubno became part of the expanding Russian empire.

For almost onehundred and fifty years, from the days of the Khmelnytsky riots of 1648 and 1649 until the final dissolution of the Kingdom of Poland in 1795, the Jewish community of Dubno prospered and expanded and its number increased from 235 souls (47 families), in 1650 to 2525 souls (331 families), in 1788 in the town of Dubno and together with is suburbs and satellite villages 3022 souls. The economic standing of Dubno's Jews during those years can best be illustrated by the following numbers:

In the year 1765 Dubno was owed 18,000 Polish Guilder by the Volhynia–Kiev State Council as repayment for excess taxes that had been paid to the Council.

In 1778 the Dubno community collected "a large amount of silver" as ransom to redeem "many souls" imprisoned in a private prison of Pan Wieliczka, the owner of the village Kopalnia.

In 1792, just before the second division of the Kingdom, the community of Dubno went bankrupt.

K

After the annexation of Volhynia by Russia, Dubno became the most important commercial center in the western area of the Russian Empire. Especially prominent was the trade in agricultural products although there was significant trade in furs, hides and livestock at the "Dubno Fairs". Jewish traders came from all parts of "old" Poland to these fairs. Dubno was also a center for the export and import trade dealing with the various Principalities of Germany and with Hungary, from where they imported wines in wholesale quantities.

Indeed, even before the annexation there were big traders in Dubno who attended famous fairs in Leipzig, Saxony and in 1728 the businessman Herschel Isaac from Dubno, accompanied by his bailiff Michael Samuel and also from Dubno the businessman Laybl Lipmann; Raphael Moshe also a trader from Dubno visited Leipzig in 1755.

In 1774, two years after the annexation of Eastern Galicia and Lwow to the Kingdom of Austria the Contractors' Fair transferred from Lwow - now Lemberg - to Dubno "in consequence of which a powerful industry developed."[29] The fair took place annually in Dubno until the annexation of Volhynia by Russia in 1794 and then transferred to Kiev and what had been called in Dubno "The Contractors' Fair" until after the First World War was nothing more than a congregation of horse dealers from Podolia as far as north Volhynia, who would meet there in July each year.

[Columns 53–54]

A map of "The Four Lands"

41

That same year 1794 the first Hebrew printing house in Dubno was established by Yohanan ben Ya'acov from Wilamowice in Silesia[30] where he had been a proof-reader for the Krügera publishing house in Nowy Dwor and later an agent for a commercial house in Warsaw dealing in books. The printing house was established with the assistance of the Master–Printer Michal Piotrowski and together they were "partners and involved in the art".[31]

The town's administrator, Prince Michael Lubomirski, granted them permission to open the printing house and as a mark of recognition, they printed on the opening page of their books the noble Family escutcheon of his House crowned in which were intertwined the initials of the Prince M.L.

The typesetters were Nathan Fajtel (Z"L) the brother of Yohanan, who had been a type–setter at the Krieger printing house in Nowy Dwor – "the type–setter who sets type so elegantly in new type – to pass on his lore to posterity"; Benjamin ben Tzvi Hirsch (Z"L) of the Holy Community of Wishnowitz (Wishnewitz, Wisnewitz, Wisniowiec). The press operator was Josef the son of Shlomo from the Holy Community of Ostrow.

The process of proof–reading and editing was carried out by Yohanan the printer, himself because it was his favorite task and the "apple of his eye" and he would rid the books of *errata* and his first printed book "*Shibolei Haleket*"[32] he prefaced with the following:

"May the creator be blessed and eternally praised with wonderful prayers, since all beginnings are difficult especially printing with new types, therefore I will make a comment lest I be accused of evil intent and my stature…it ails me that the reader of this book should find an occasional error possibly even the most minor one, therefore do not place me on the scales of demerit, for I have already expressed my apologies…may the Almighty judge us and console us with Zion and Jerusalem and bring upon us goodness without end…"

About twenty years after the annexation, 1816–1819, after Napoleon's failed attack on Russia, Dubno traders supplied textiles to the reorganizing armies of Tsar Alexander the First. From 1852–1883 in the reign of Tsar Nikolai the First, the tradesmen of Dubno were among the most important clients of the Berdichev (Berdyczów) Fair during the period when the Fair was the most important and publicized one in Russia and took a leading place together with Jewish traders from Vilna, Brest–Litovsk, Shklow (Szkłów) and Ostrow as Russian exporters to Prussia and Austria.
It was during this period that the industry of fur hat–making also developed in Dubno and the products sent all over Russia. The raw material – untreated sheepskins – were brought from Poltava, in Ukraine.
The economic situation of Jewish Dubno at that time was good although the financial situation of the community as a whole was not always so. On occasion when the

Community Council was short of money the Council would borrow money from the Church at low interest. It was quite regular throughout Poland at that time because Christianity did not permit the lending of money to Christians for interest according to the Papal directive, therefore the Church loaned its money to the Jews and they used it either for their own needs or they re–loaned it to Christians…

L

The lives of the Jewish community in Dubno were well organized almost from the first days of their settlement in the town and from 1715 a "Community Journal" was kept for more than a hundred years. "The Journal" opened "with the light of day 19th Iyar 1715 as has been shown and closed "Sunday 12th Av 1823."

The organization of the Community is described in the "Journal" on page 34 1747 as follows:

The Community Council was composed of four "Elders", three other residents of High standing and six from the general ranks of the citizens. Adjunct to the Council were the following treasurers: a committee of six senior treasurers, a committee of Charities and a treasury committee of the two synagogues in town each one numbering three members. In addition, there were three rabbinical courts in town each one staffed by three "Dayanim" (Rabbinical judges).

Jewish artisans were organized in their own unions operating according to their internal constitutions. There were Unions for tailors, furriers, weavers, butchers, bakers and a "Company of Bartenders".

The Community Council carried out assessments of the taxes due to the "Council of the Four Lands" and the regional councils and the community leaders had the right to execute a "Right of Exemption" to Rabbis, and wealthy benefactors of the community from these taxes and occasionally from among themselves also – a procedure that was acceptable to the ruling houses of Poland concerning "special privileges".

One of the severest ordinances that the Community Council corrected was the "Prohibition by Boycott" that effectively stopped Jews from purchasing houses or "foreign Territory" from Christians and even to rent from them apartments and shops. It was an "ancient

Frontispiece of the book "Shibolei Haleket" (Sheaves of Gleaning).
Printed in Dubno in the year 1798 in which appears the "Coat of Arms" of Prince Michael
Lubormirski

ordinance". Exceptions were those who were able to donate to the community large sums and undertook to pay all the Council's taxes. The explanations for the ordinance were to prevent the Jews from intermingling with the Christians in order not to be liquidated in times of woe and in order to prevent Jews from evading the general levy of taxes on the Community and to preserve the purity of the Jewish family in danger of being assimilated if they lived among the Christians.

The Council preserved the fairness of trade in the market and shops and in accordance with an ordinance from the year 1717 it was forbidden for middle–men to purchase goods themselves "in order to inflate a higher price". They were also forbidden for them to go to the shops with a Christian or his master". In 1775 an additional ordinance was passed that forbade "market regulars" who dealt in fruit and haberdashery to return as merchants.

The Community Council also regulated public institutions – the bathhouse, the ritual bath, the treasury and the cemetery; on charity – a collection box was used every day of the year for approved necessities and especially on the eve of the Day of Atonement; on the dress of men and the adornments of women, the arrangements for parties and festivals; on the Talmud Torah, study house for children, aid for the needy and the dowry for the bride.

There were plenty of frictions as well and in the middle of the 18th Century the Community leaders "shut down" the unions of the artisans because of their "anti–establishment" opposition. The artisans took an openly aggressive stand against the authoritarian stand of the Council's heads although they, because of their connections with the Government and especially the "lord of the town" Prince Józef Aleksander Jabłonowski, succeeded in 1765 in acquiring a dissolution order to liquidate the unions of the weavers, the butchers and bakers and forbade them to reorganize, with the claim that "the artisans suppress the needy of the community".

Nevertheless, a year later, in 1776, the Community heads were compelled to recant because the new ordinances of the Council determined that in a special meeting three "prefects" will be elected and in their hands will be the authority to inspect the expenses and incomes of the Community heads. It was also ordained that the town elders would also be "denied the right to grant themselves a monthly salary or demand a fee for their signatures for official documents of the Community".

In continuation of the struggle between the artisans and the Community heads, in 1781 and again in 1793, a correction was made to the system of payment of the special taxes for Kosher meat and the system of payment by the community "in order to prevent more shouts of despair from the poor and to lighten the load of the people". In 1793 an ordinance was enacted obliging the residents to pay a slaughtering fee and the special tax "even if they are not coming to town during the High Holidays".

M

In conclusion, it is interesting to present a few details on the growth of the Jewish population in Dubno during two periods: The Polish authority during the years 1650–1788 and that of Russia from 1796–1897.

According to the Polish census the Jewish population of Dubno numbered as follows:

1650	47 Jewish homes and 470 souls[33]	144 Christian homes 1440 souls
1765	178 Jewish homes and 1795 souls	391 Christian homes
1788	321 Jewish homes and 2525 souls	106 Christian homes.

In 1796 the Russian authorities declared Dubno to be the County capital and the Jewish urban population numbered as follows:

1797	Urban Jews – 2780 souls
1799	2799 souls
1803	2784 souls
1847	6339 souls
	Urban Christians – 7149 souls
1897	Urban Jews 7108 souls

The number of Dubno Jews after the First World War in 1921 was 5315 souls.

Original Footnotes and Translator's Comments

1. Vytautus (Lithuanian)– 1350–1430
2. Brest, Brest–Litovsk, Brisk–de–Lita {Brisk (of) Lithuania – Yiddish}.
3. See: https://en.wikipedia.org/wiki/Guillebert_de_Lannoy
4. From the book "A Study of the History of the Jews and the Karaite sect" by Thaddeus Chaczyk, this appeared in 1807 and quoted Bishop Comedani's book of 1614, published in Paris.
5. Prof. Sergei Aleksandrovich Bershadski "The Jewish–Russian Archive" Petersburg, 1882, Vol. A', pp184–185.
6. Mentioned in the book "The Town of Dubno and her Sons" by Rabbi Pinchas bar Yesheyahu Pesses of Dubno, Krakow 1902
7. Translator's comment: A thorough search of many relevant sources on the internet both Hebrew and English failed to discover any book of that name, especially not one ascribed to this renowned and holy author or his equally illustrious family. However, the Rabbi is known to be the author of a book entitled "The Gates of Heaven" that he wrote as a testament and willed to his children which is still today a much acclaimed spiritual guide and it is possible that our present writer made an error when writing the title – _unless_ itself is a chapter in "The Gates of Heaven".
8. An acronym derived of the words *Shtei Luchot Ha–Brit* which means "Two Tablets of the Covenant" the nickname of the author himself Rabbi Isaiah bar Avraham Ha–Levi Horowitz known for his book:"The Tablets of the Covenant"
9. In his book "The Glory of the Levites" Warsaw 1902.
10. Prof. Tzvi Hirsh Graetz: "Chronicles of Israel" Vol. 7: pp351–352.
11. See: https://en.wikipedia.org/wiki/Rappaport
12. See: https://en.wikipedia.org/wiki/Shulchan_Aruch
13. Printed in Wilmersdorf, Germany, in 1680
14. Matthias Barzon "Diplomacy"
15. "The Abyss of Despair" Published by the United Kibbutz Movement, 1944. See also: https://en.wikipedia.org/wiki/Nathan_ben_Moses_Hannover
16. South–West Russian Archives Year 'B', vol. 42.
17. Shabtei Cohen (1621–1662), Rabbi and expounder of the Talmud, one of the greatest such of his generation. He was a noted Dayan (Judge), in Vilna and later a Rabbi in Dreznitz and later Holeov. He described the riots and pogroms of 1648–9 in his book *"Megillah Afah"*. There are those who believe that his sister Esther was the basis for Shaul Tchernichovsky's heroine in the ballad "The Rabbi's daughter" during the riots that opens "Let the youth of Dubno be praised…"
18. The eulogy can be found in the book "Treasures of Literature" by Isaac Shaltiel Graber, Krakow (1888) and also in Haim Yona Gorland's book: "History of the (Khmelnytsky pogroms) Edicts".
19. Translated in its entirety to Polish and appearing in the book "Foreigners in Poland" by Ksawery Liske, Lemberg 1876. The [Hebrew] translation presented here is from that work pp167–168.
20. From the book "Greater Dubno" by H.Z. Margoliot, p. 11.
21. According to an original document, written on parchment signed and sealed with heavy wax seal "Guardian of the Great Seal; Military Commander of His Highness the Prince Stanislaw Lubomirski".
22. Op. Cit., H.Z. Margoliot.
23. See: https://en.wikipedia.org/wiki/Sachsenspiegel and also: https://www.wdl.org/en/item/11620/ et. al.

24. Rabbi Ya'acov Emden "Edut be–Ya'acov" p. 55; col. A. See also: https://en.wikipedia.org/wiki/Jacob_Emden et. al.

25. See: https://en.wikipedia.org/wiki/Jacob_Frank and http://jewishencyclopedia.com/articles/6279–frank–jacob–and–the–frankists

26. See: https://www.studylight.org/encyclopedias/tje/e/eliakim–ben–asher–selig.html

27. Most of the material cited in this section was extracted from "Journals of the 'Council of the Four Lands'" pps 416–440.

28. Author's own footnote suggests that the statement was intended to read "six months."

29. "Greater Dubno" by Rabbi Chaim Mordecai Margoliot.

30. Many years previously he had also been a resident of Dubno and from 1768–1782 was a distinguished "Elder".

31. See the excerpts in columns 111–112 in the "Journal of Greater Dubno"

32. Rabbi Zedkiyahu ben Avraham Harofeh (13th Century)

33. From the national census carried out on the number of houses, estimating an average of ten souls per dwelling.

C. The Scholars of Dubno

Translated by Selwyn Rose (Hebrew) and Pamela Russ (Yiddish)

A significant part of this Hebrew chapter (C) and the following ones (D, E, F and G), i.e., columns 61–98, is also found in the Yiddish section on columns 583–603. This text is a combined work by two translators, translated partly from Hebrew and partly from Yiddish, and merged into one seamless piece.

There were three major spiritual streams flowing throughout Jewish Europe at the end of the 18th Century: the *Hassidut*, the *Haskalah* (the Jewish "Enlightenment") and the *Mitnagdut* (opposition to *Hassidut*). The *Hassidut* brought a lifting of the spirits for the *hoi polloi* by giving a new content to their lives in driving away the sense of rejection and inferiority that had enveloped them in the face of the "Scholars". The *Haskalah* constituted the basis for a revival of Hebrew language literature and formed the cornerstone of a modern investigation of Judaism and was the foundation-stone of the struggle for equality throughout Jewish Europe, while the *Mitnagdut* was used as a foundation for the normalization of the Jew as a man and a guardian of the purity of the Torah against the spread of both the *Haskalah* and *Hassidut*.

Of the heroic personalities who left their mark on European Jewry of that era, the names of two, who brought the city of Dubno to world fame, must be underlined: the meticulous and sharp commentator Rabbi Shlomo Dubno. Born in Dubno, he was one of the first who laid the foundation of the *Haskalah*, along with the Jewish philosopher Rabbi Shlomo Mendelssohn; Rabbi Ya'acov Krantz, known by the title of the Dubno *Maggid* (preacher), editor and author of parables (fables), a guest in the house of the Vilna *Gaon* genius) Rabbi Eliyahu. His scholarly thoughts on *Mitnagdut* were brought closer to the hearts of the people.

Rabbi Shlomo bar Yoel of Dubno ("Rashad")

Born in the year 1738 in Dubno, as a youth he was a student and served under the well-known *Gaon* the Ra'avad (Rabbi Avraham ben David), religious leader of the city, and Naphtali Hertz. In the year 1767, as a 19-year-old young man, he left for Amsterdam, Holland, where, for over five years he worked on researching the grammar and traditions and history of the Land of Israel. He also tried to write "Occasional Poetry"[1] as was the custom of that time.

In the year 1772, Rabbi Shlomo continued to travel to places of *Torah*, and from Amsterdam arrived in Berlin, and there met with the scholar Moshe Mendelssohn. In Berlin, Rabbi Shlomo supported himself by giving lectures on grammar. One of his students was also Mendelssohn's son Yosef, as was expressed in the letter to his friend the scholar Avigdor Levi of Glogow: "And behold, one dear to the Lord has brought the wise grammarian, teacher and Rabbi, Shlomo, may his light shine, to instruct my son Yosef in the laws of grammar for an hour each day."

Rabbi Shlomo Dubno left a deep impression on Mendelssohn with his overall knowledge, and right away Mendelssohn gave him permission to publish his German translation and commentary of the Torah, as this becomes clear later on in the above-mentioned letter to Avigdor Levi:

"…and when the above-mentioned Rabbi saw the translation in my hand, he was most pleased with it and asked permission to print it for the benefit of all Jewish children and Jews generally, who had need of a "commentary of the Holy Writings" other than the incorrect ones generally available, and he nodded his head in agreement…"

With the giving of his agreement, Mendelssohn made a stipulation that he would compare the translation and commentary with those of the five greatest Jewish expositors of the Middle Ages: Rashi, Rambam, Ra'aba (Rabbi Abraham ibn Ezra), Ramban, and Rabbi David Kimchi – and from this he relied on his knowledge and ability.

שלמה מדובנא

Rabbi Shlomo was excited by the idea of printing the German *Torah* with its translation and new commentary, and in 1778 published a pamphlet entitled '*Alim le-Terufah*,' "Information with extracts from the publication of the Five Books of Moses with German translation by Mr. Moses Mendelssohn, with commentary and revision by Rabbi Shlomo Dubno, Amsterdam, (1778)," with an additional elegy "'Ask not the way to Zion'" (Jeremiah 50:5) by Rabbi Yehuda Levi, translated into German from the *Ramban*.

[Columns 63–64]

That year, Rabbi Shlomo began to prepare his commentary on corrections of the traditional scribes, to the Book of *Bereshit* (Genesis) and the introduction to the Book of *Shemot* (Exodus) that he dedicated to "*Tikunei Sefarim*"[2] and on which he toiled for ten months.

It seems that the introduction to the Book of *Shemot* brought about a disagreement between Rabbi Shlomo and Mr. Moses Mendelssohn, according to a letter the latter wrote to his friend the above-mentioned Avigdor Levi of Glogow: "It seems I have indeed come to a disagreement with our esteemed Rabbi and Teacher Rabbi Shlomo Dubno, may his light shine, and G-d Almighty Himself knows that I am not the guilty party in this….Only time will tell if we can get together again…"

51

No one knows exactly what the reason was for the argument between Rabbi Shlomo Dubno and Mr. Moses Mendelssohn, and many have been of the opinions as to the cause. It is possible that it was because of a criticism of Mendelssohn by Rabbi Shlomo's Rabbi, the kabbalist Rabbi Naphtali Hertz, as Rabbi Shlomo wrote in 1789 from Amsterdam to his friend the grammarian Rabbi Benjamin Ze'ev Heidenheim: "In 1778, while I was toiling over the introduction to *Shemot*, Naphtali Hertz of Dubno passed through Berlin and confronted the author of the work on his commentary – a man, who in the opinion of the great ones of his generation, the author of "*Nodah Biyehudoh*" Rabbi Yehezkiel Landau, Father of the Prague Rabbinical Court and Rabbi Raphael HaCohen, that 'their intention was to uproot at its source the traditional texts of the Holy *Chumash*...' and Rabbi Naphtali Hertz called to the attention of Rabbi Shlomo the verse "Because thou hast joined thyself with AHaziah the Lord hath broken thy works." (Chronicles 2:20; 37), intimating that the material situation of Rabbi Shlomo will be 'broken down' that same year.[3]

Clearly, between Rabbi Shlomo Dubno and Mr. Moses Mendelssohn, there were differences in interpretations that brought about the separation between them. Rabbi Shlomo left Berlin. He stayed for some time in Frankfurt-am-Main, "...in order to encourage subscribers to fund the publishing of his books and commentaries" ... and from there he returned to Amsterdam.

During the years that he was in Amsterdam, Rabbi Shlomo managed to collect a significant number of original writings and books, and he even compiled an inventory of his own library. But in his final years, he was forgotten and lived in loneliness. He died in the year 1813. He was 75 years old.

Rabbi H. Z. Margalit writes, concerning Rabbi Shlomo Dubno's library, in his book "Greater Dubno":

"Most of his books remain in manuscript form and were preserved by the linguist Rabbi Sh. Y. Fein, whence they came to the Aziali (Asiatic) Museum in the royal city of Petersburg, according to the observation of the bibliographer Rabbi Shmuel Wiener, the controller of the Hebrew section of the above-mentioned museum."

The Dubno Maggid [4]

The *Maggid* Rabbi Ya'acov Krantz was born in Zhetl (Zietil), in the district of Vilna, in the year 1741, in his father's house, Rabbi Ze'ev, and his mother, the righteous Hinda, daughter of the *Gaon* and the Kobriner Rabbi.

As a young man of 18, he left to Mezrycz (Międzyrzecz), near Brisk, to study Torah there and without any remuneration he would lecture the congregants of the *Beit Midrash* (Study House). While in Mezrycz, he married and for some time had room and board in the home of his wealthy father-in-law, and even helped him manage his businesses. But it didn't last long, his father-in-law became impoverished, and the son-in-law Rabbi Ya'acov, had to earn his own living through his preaching and oratory.

Rabbi Ya'acov lived in Mezrycz for two years and from there, he was taken on with great honor as the preacher in Zolkiew (Żółkiew, east Galicia). From Zolkiew he began to wander from city to city and from country to country and became increasingly famous as a *Tzadik* (righteous man) and excellent orator. During those years, he also came to Berlin and encountered Moshe Mendelssohn, who became enlivened through the *Maggid's* fables and nicknamed him the 'Jewish Æsop', 'the wise man of fables.'

At the age of 32, Rabbi Ya'acov Krantz was invited by the Dubno community leader to become a lecturer and orator there. He remained there for 28 years. His income consisted of six Polish zlotys weekly and a secured home in one of the community's houses. A record was found in the community's records concerning Rabbi Ya'acov Krantz, that had been kept in the safe-keeping of the synagogue's manager, Mr. Meir Chomsky (d. 1886): "…and in a meeting it was agreed by the community leaders to add to the salary of the *Maggid* Rabbi Ya'acov two zlotys a week and at the town's expense to repair the stove in his apartment."

The years when Rabbi Ya'acov lived in Dubno were years of mutual influence: He spread his many creations and beautiful fables across the city and made them world famous, and similarly, the city gave him its name and his timeless preservation among the nations: "The Dubno *Maggid.*"

Rabbi Ya'acov merited a separate connection with the Vilna *Gaon* Rabbi Eliyahu, who was renowned for his secluded meditations and loss of even the minutest amount of time from his *Torah* studies. In the year 1791, Rabbi Ya'acov was invited to his home, through a letter filled with love and praise:[5]

B"H

Monday 2nd *Parshat Va-Yeshev* 5551

Much peace, to my soul's beloved, who is none other than the wondrous and famous Rabbi of the *Torah*, praise and honored is our Teacher and our Rabbi, the Teller of Fables of the Holy Community of Dubno. After these greetings of peace, I ask that my soul's beloved will visit me and it is a wonder in my eyes that he has not come to me these thirteen years.

I come to awaken him as a loved and faithful soul, praying for his peace and welfare.

Eliyahu Shlomo Zalman, may his Righteousness be remembered in the world to come.

From this letter it is clear that the first visit of Rabbi Ya'acov to the Vilna *Gaon* and Rabbi took place in 1778, five years after he arrived in Dubno, and his second visit was the year of the *Gaon*'s letter which was the last year he dwelt in Dubno (1791).

After he left Dubno, Rabbi Ya'acov dwelt in Chelm for two years and then moved to the community in Zamosc where he stayed for more than twelve years and where he died on 17 *Tevet* 5565 (1805).

On the tombstone of the *Maggid* of Dubno were engraved the following lines:

May peace come upon him - Psalm 141

The great and famous expositor,

[Columns 65–66]

"His fame went out throughout all the provinces" (*Megillat* Esther 9:4).

"Before him there was not and after him…there will not be a man to whom G-d spoke."

Our Teacher and our Rabbi Ya'acov the just and honest *Maggid* and expositor.

The son of Rabbi Ze'ev (Z"L)

Rabbi Ya'acov officiated in the Holy Dubno as *Maggid* in the days of the kabbalist *Gaon* Rabbi Naphtali Hertz and the *Gaon* Rabbi Ze'ev Wolf. His son, Rabbi Yitzchak, also occupied himself with the telling of fables to various communities in the surrounding area, and his daughters married in Dubno and continued living there.

The books of the Dubno *Maggid* were printed after his death, by his son Rabbi Yitzchak and his disciple Rabbi Avrom Berish Flamm. These books were:

"*Ohel Ya'acov* [The Tent of Ya'acov] – exegeses on the *Torah*

"*Kol Ya'acov*" [The Voice of Ya'acov] – exegeses on the five *Megillot* [Scrolls]

"*Kochav M'Ya'acov*" [Star of Ya'acov] – exegeses on the *Haftorot* [selections from the Prophets read on Sabbath, after the *Torah* portions of the week]

"*Emet Le'Ya'acov*" [The Truth for Ya'acov] – An explanation of the *Hagaddah* for Passover

"*Sefer Hamiddot*" [A Book of Behavior] - Eight lessons, commentaries and remarks about correct behavior.

D. The Hassidut of the Baal Shem Tov

The *Hassidut* of the Baal Shem Tov never really had a dominant role in Dubno – not in its beginnings, nor in its later years, even after the *Hassidut* spread and took over in all the provinces in Poland, Ukraine, Russia, and Lithuania. There were *Hassidim* in Dubno – and some were Baal Shem Tov followers: absorbed in *devekut* (meditative closeness to G-d), people who loved to be friendly and be joyous. But there were also *Hassidim* of Rabbi Yehuda Ha-Hassid, and his followers: self-punishers and strictly observant.

The majority of Jews in Dubno were opponents to *Hassidut* and its influences. Even when the Baal Shem Tov was still alive, before *Hassidut* became fortified in the Jewish communities of Eastern Europe, in the year 1752, one of the great Dubno scholars, Rabbi Moshe Osterer, along with the *Gaon* and head of the Jewish court Rabbi Yehezkiel Landau (the "*Nodah Bi-Yehuda*") declared a ban on the amulets of Rabbi Yonatan Eybeschütz. Rabbi Moshe Osterer had a standing of importance in Dubno not only on his own account but also because he was a descendant of great Rabbis – the son of the *Gaon* Rabbi Hillel, Father of the Rabbinical Court of Zamosc and the grandson of Rabbi Ya'acov Tammerlisch of Worms, nicknamed "Man of G-d," a kabbalist, and renowned as a mystic who officiated as preacher in the Holy Community of Brody and was the Rabbi of the famous Rabbi Mordecai 'the Righteous' Margalit.

After Yisrael Baal Shem Tov was taken to the "*Heavenly Yeshiva*" on the eve of *Shavuot* 1760, he was followed by his disciple the *Maggid* Rabbi Dov Ber of Mezrycz and Rabbi Nahman of Horodenka, Rabbi Ya'acov Yosef HaCohen of Polonne, Rabbi Levi Yitzhak who later settled in Berdichev and Rabbi Elimelech of Lizhensk who spread his teachings. At the head of and leading the *Hassidut* of the *BESHT* (Baal Shem Tov) stood Rabbi Dov Ber.

Rabbi Dov Ber was born in 1704 in the village of Lokachi (Lokatsh) in his father's house. His father, Rabbi Abraham, was a poor scholar. In his youth he [Dov Ber] "poured water on the hands"[a] of Rabbi Yehoshua, Rabbi and Father of the Rabbinical Court in Lwow and author of "*Penne Yehoshua*." He later moved to the village of Torczyn where he served for a time as teacher and even married the daughter of the Rabbi Shalom Schachne. From Torczyn he was called to serve as preacher in Korets

(Korzec), and later as preacher in Dubno. From Dubno he moved to Mezrycz where he stayed many years and later came to be known as the "*Maggid* of Mezrycz."

For the twelve years during which Rabbi Dov Ber officiated as the spiritual heir of the *BESHT* the *Hassidut* spread throughout Eastern Europe, and congregations of *Hassidim* were created in virtually every town and village.

[Columns 67–68]

The spread of the *Hassidut* awakened resistance among the Rabbis and the "*Mitnagdim*" who instituted a crusade of harassment and boycott of the "cult" – as they called it. Ruthless propaganda in the form of speeches, sermons, pamphlets and proclamations of such venom that one of them "*Igeret Kanna'ut*" – "Zealot's Letter" – written by "a prominent and respected man" in which "details of the crimes of the *Hassidim*" in the Vilna community are exposed, was delivered to the leaders of the community in Brody early in 1772. The writer of the "*Igeret*" based himself upon his reading of the boycott against the *Hassidim* by the "true genius, the kabbalist Eliyahu Ha-Hassid," who ordered the merciless harassment of the cult." The "*Igeret Hakann'ut*" was copied in Brody by the writer Rabbi Yehuda Arieh Leib bar Mordecai and published on 9 *Iyar* 1772 (12ᵗʰ May). The "call to war" against the *Hassidim* aroused hordes of the public and in some communities the rioters carried out punitive measures against them, as happened in Vilna where "terrible and harmful deeds were performed" against Rabbi Chaim the preacher and Rabbi Isser who were originally close to the *Gaon* of Vilna and later joined the *Hassidut* movement; or in Pinsk where the mob broke into the house of Rabbi Levi Yitzchak (one of the *BESHT*'s and Dov Ber of Mezrycz students) and "vandalized the home."

By chance, during those same days the leaders of the *Hassidut*, *Ha-Maggid* Rabbi Dov Ber of Mezrycz and his close friends were convening in Dubno to take counsel with each other on how to counter the harassment. But when Rabbi Levi Yitzchak read the letter he had received from Pinsk on the damage that had been done to his house, Rabbi Dov Ber remained silent.

The persecution of the *Hassidut* movement continued for many years and the last inflammatory "*Igeret*" was published in 1796, a year after the Third Partition of Poland. During the entire time of the spread of *Hassidut* and the war opposing it, it was as if Dubno was standing on the sidelines and was careful with its *Mitnagdist* conservatism. There is much of interest in the memoirs of the ADMOR⸢ Rabbi Shmuel Halevi Yozpov, grandson of Rabbi Pinchas of Korets, who settled in Dubno in the middle of the 19th century, who relates, concerning the period:

"As we know, in the years 1815-1825, Rabbi, the *Gaon*, Haim Mordecai Margalit, author of "Gates of Repentance," brother of Rabbi the *Gaon* Ephraim Zalman Margalit of Brody, officiated as Father of the Rabbinical Court and like his older

58

brother was involved in trade and commerce and declined to use his knowledge of the *Torah* as a basis for his living, even when he was actually the Rabbi of Dubno. Because of that, many of the citizens of the town who were *Hassidim* of the famous Rabbi in Volhynia, the Righteous and Holy Rabbi Moshe Ephraim of Sudylkiv (Sidilkev, Sudilkov), the grandson of the *BESHT*, approached their Rabbi with a complaint against the Rabbi of Dubno that in the conduct of his business he neglected his study of the *Torah* and that he wasn't a *Hassid* and not connected with their Rabbi and they demanded that the Rabbi install another Rabbi who will be a *Hassid* and more learned in the *Torah*."

"The Rabbi from Sudylkiv answered them saying he knows the Dubno Rabbi very well and that even when he was busy with his commercial interests he was deep in *Torah* as well and the *Mishnah* said of him: "Torah is good together with the way of the world,"[8] meaning that for those who can cope well with both – so be it. And concerning that he was not of the *Hassidut* – he *was* a *Hassid* and was becoming more so... and warned them that they would not have another Rabbi in Dubno and they should respect the one they have for being the great Rabbi and *Gaon* that he is."

"And from then on strong bonds of love and friendship existed between the Rabbi from Dubno and the Rabbi from Sudilkov, author of "*Degel Machaneh Ephraim*," as there was love and friendship between his brother the *Gaon* from Brody with the Rabbi and righteous *Gaon* from Opatow (Apt), author of "Love Israel," in spite of the fact that they had differing opinions concerning each other's work."

60

E. The Haskalah Era and Its Personalities

The circle of *Maskilim* that existed at the beginning of the 19th century was exceptional for its attributes of brotherliness and friendliness, characteristics for each ideologue who was striving to great and lofty heights. But at the center of this was a group of believers in the light of knowledge and good fortune of progress that primarily believed in the eternity of the People of Israel and that removed themselves from assimilation in all forms – dress, traditions, and copying the non-Jewish people.

Characteristic of the mood that reigned among the Dubno *Maskilim* is the letter of thanks that they received in the year 1848 from Rabbi Shneur Zaks of Berlin: Rabbi Shneur Zaks was a historian and researcher of antiquity and critic of the Holy Writings, who, on his travels and because of a false accusation was captured and imprisoned in Dubno, and thanks to the efforts of the *Maskilim* in town and from the surrounding areas, he was freed, and then remained in Dubno for a year, in the warmth of his friends and fellow *Maskilim,* whose names he mentions with love and emotion in writing "*Kanfei Yona*" ("The Wings of a Dove").

He begins the long letter with general words of greetings and then he turns to each of his friends individually about personal issues, disguised and implied, out of fear of the police and censors.

Among the personalities in the Enlightenment era in Dubno, we will mention some of them individually, those who were exceptional in their own and later generations:

[Columns 69–70]

"To my loved ones of Dubno – friends of my soul and the best of sages and Holy writers of scriptures and pure-hearted scholars ––-

"Rabbi Tzvi Hirsch Ashkenazi – from sturdy and wise roots my father Tzvi Zalman Ashkenazi –

"Rabbi L. Glasberg – Please me, brother, with thy wonderful eloquent speech and my regards to your dynamic brother ---

"Rabbi D. Weisberg and his dear brother Rabbi Yehuda ---

"Rabbi H. Elias, please me by seeing your name at the end of a book of *Mehilta*[21] of your son-in-law the Rabbi -- please me also, my dear, with your eloquent speeches --

"To Rabbi N. Margalit – How are you, delight of my eyes? And how is every one of yours? Please know that forever you are implanted in my heart ---

"Please offer my greetings to your dear father and dear brothers in Kremenets --- and where is our dear friend Yona Margalit? --- Thy mother? ---

"To Z. Marszalkowicz ---

"To R. Y. Kalischer and his dear brother Dr. Reuven Kalisch --- How are you today my dearest, with your wonderful abilities? Please write to me! --- and all that accompany you and your friends in G-d's Camp.

"To Hemlitz Lerner. Where is our industrious clever man Rabbi Z.W. Addas today? ---

"To dear Rabbi Shimshon Bar'az ---

"And to all my beloved scholars there, much love and affection. Peace. A thousand thanks for the past!"

In a letter of thanks from Dr. Yitzhak Arthur of Brody to Rabbi Leibush Glasberg of Dubno for the help given by the scholars of Dubno to Rabbi Shneur Zaks that was published in Berlin in 1857 among other remarks was written:

"How numerous are my thanks to you dear man! And the other generous donors, the wise and scholarly Rabbis of your town who girded themselves like soldierly heroes to extricate a dear soul from distress, to loosen her fetters, in order that she can complete her skills and qualities and be in the coming days an honor and splendor to us!"

"How thankful I am to the famous leader Rabbi Hirsch Ashkenazi – may his light shine forth, who added my friend to his household and entertained him with meals at his table!"

"The names of these honored people are engraved on my heart and will never be erased from my memory!"

"It is a blessing dear man! My soul's happy desire is your friendship ---."

*

Among the scholars of Dubno of the period a few are indicated here, their legacies especially conspicuous either during their own generation or later.

Rabbi Nahman Tzvi Hirsh, son of Rabbi Yeshaya Linder, born in Dubno in the year 1791. He belonged to the circle of scholars and writers at the beginning of the 19th century. In his youth, he studied under Rabbi Eliezer of Kolczyn, author of the book of questions and responsa *"Turei Even"* ("Rows of Stone"). For many years, Rabbi Nahman Linder was a teacher in the Jewish government school in Zhvil (Nowogrod-Volhynski). He died in the year 1851. He was famous as a mathematician and for his three books of research in mathematics, written in Hebrew, which were published after his death.

"The Table of Logarithms" on the natural numbers in *"Masechet Trumot"*[110] and the manner of their usage in calculations, Königsberg 1854 .8⁰ 5+49+3 pages.

"The Ingenuity of Numbers" (algebra and arithmetic) the study of mathematics and its application, Warsaw, 1856. 8⁰ 144 pages.

"Euclid" – on the ingenuity of calculation, the translation of books 11-12, Part A. Six articles with addenda and diagrams, Zhitomir (Żytomierz) 1875. 199 pages.

The scholar Ze'ev Wolf Adelson was born in the year 1798 in Lithuania, and in his younger years he was a student under the renowned *Gaon* Rabbi Menashe ben Porat from Ilya (1767-1831), author of the books *"Alfei Menashe"*[111] and *"Shekel Hakadosh"* ["The Holy Shekel"]. He belonged to those who strove to bring improvements to the lives of the younger generation, both in the acquisition of a general education and also through economic reconstruction. As a young man, Rabbi Ze'ev Wolf was a teacher in Brest-Litovsk and then went to Ukraine. In the year 1833, he arrived in Dubno.

He was the type of *Maskil* who loved knowledge and he alone realized the efforts needed for becoming a perfect person. When he arrived in Dubno, where there were many who strove to learn and to be educated, he taught anyone who was interested, without any compensation. He nourished himself with a piece of bread, the edge of a herring, and a little bit of water, and used to sleep on the floor. Among his best pupils and attendees of the lectures, were the grammarian Haim Tzvi Lerner and Tzvi Hirsh Greenberg of Katerynivka (Katerburg, Katrynburg) near Kremenets, who later converted to Christianity.

Even though he had many friends and followers who would call him "the Jewish Diogenes," Rabbi Ze'ev Wolf evoked anger and jealousy from the *Hassidim* and fanatics because of his teachings and critical speech. They made his life miserable with every means possible. He left for Mezrycz where he supported himself by giving classes to the children of the wealthy businessman and *Maskil* Rabbi Yehuda Khori. From Mezrycz he went to Odessa and died there in great poverty in the year 1866.

He was buried seven days later when the neighbors discovered his body.

Only a few of the writings of Rabbi Zev Wolf Adelson have been preserved in the hands of Rabbi Joel Ber Flakowicz and L. Chary and among them *"Megillot-Esther."* It is assumed that the many manuscripts that he left behind were consumed by the fire during the fumigation of the room in which he died.

Rabbi Haim Tzvi Lerner (*Hatzal*) was born in Dubno on the eve of Passover of 1815. The likelihood that his origins were in poverty is evident because during his childhood years he studied in the *Talmud Torah* of Dubno. In his youth he went to Odessa and studied there and worked in researching the Hebrew language and also taught himself Russian, German, Italian, and French. In 1838, he returned to his hometown of Dubno and lived there for three years, sustaining himself by giving classes to wealthy students.

At that time, the city of Radziwill (Radziwiłłów) developed near Brody, and many wealthier families settled there. Rabbi Haim Tzvi lived there for eight years (1841–1849) as a teacher of wealthy students.

Rabbi Haim Tzvi was renowned for his love of, and deep connection to the Hebrew language and for his expertise with its grammar and literature. When the government Rabbinic seminary opened in Zhitomir, Rabbi Haim Tzvi was invited there as a teacher of Hebrew language and literature. He taught in the seminary until its closing in the year 1873.

Rabbi Haim Tzvi Lerner was a prolific writer and creator, writing the majority of his books about Hebrew and Aramaic grammar, compilations about the history of grammar, and also about the grammar of the *Talmud*, and so on. His book *"Moreh Halashon"* ("Teacher of Language") had many editions, and his children received 2,000 rubles for the rights of reprinting – a huge sum for those days.

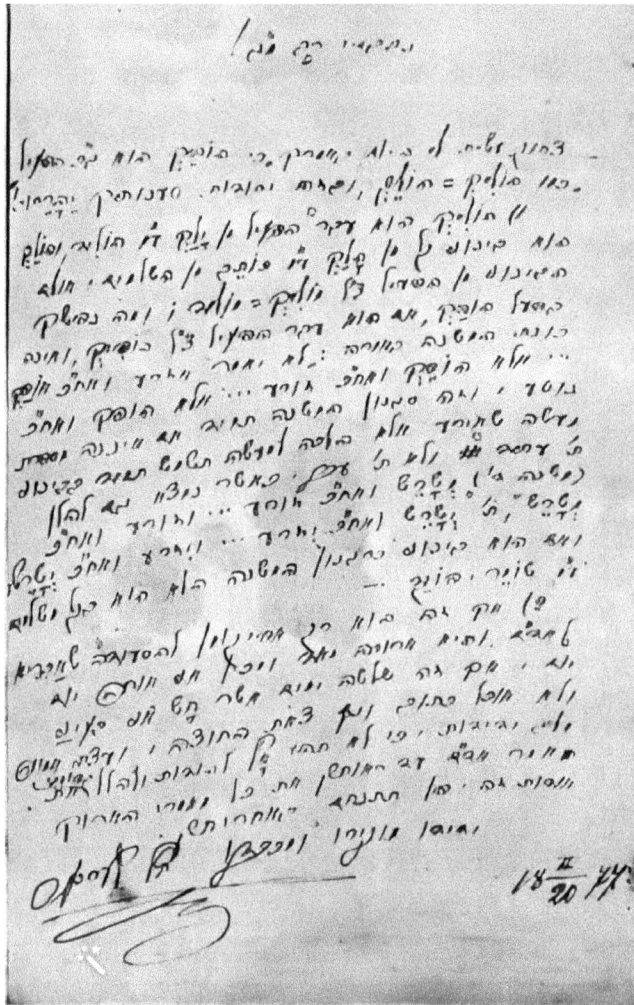

Indeed, a heart full of national feeling beat within the heart of Rabbi Haim Tzvi Lerner and many years before the creation of the "Lovers of Zion" movement he published in "*Ha-Maggid*" a poem to *Hanukah* in which he expressed his concerns for the future of his people:

The Sexton

Verse 1

The light of this noble candle

Stands before his brothers

He is thought a slave; there is none to honor him!

His goodness a traitor betrayed him...

Verse 2

He also threw light of the Land's people

With the light of his faith – an inheritance from heaven,

But they breached it - breach after breach.

Scorned and ridiculed, Ha! Drinking like water…etc.

Rabbi Haim Tzvi Lerner died in Zhitomir in 1889, after he established a generation of people knowledgeable in the Hebrew language and its grammar.

Tzvi Hirsh Greenberg – the convert Vladimir Fyodorov – was born in the year 1815 in the town of Katerburg, Kremenets region. He was a poor child. When he came to Dubno, he studied in the *Talmud Torah* and had "days" (daily assigned meals in designated homes). He was drawn to education, and under Rabbi Ze'ev Wolf Adelson, he became close to the youthful Avraham Ber Gotlober, and to the elderly Rabbi Yitzhak Ber Levinson of Kremenets.

As was the tradition among those who studied *Torah* at that time, Tzvi Hirsh married young to a butcher's daughter from Dubno – and in about one year's time, they had a baby girl.

Sometime later, Tzvi Hirsh left his wife and child and went to Kamenets-Podolsk, where he was accepted as a student in the government gymnasium. When he completed the gymnasium, he asked to be taken on as teacher in one of the Jewish schools which were opened in specific locations by Dr. Lilienthal. For an unknown reason, he was not given the position. Then he left the faith of his parents, converted to Christianity, and changed his name to Vladimir Vasilevitch Fyodorov.

As for any Christian, the gates of the universities in Kiev opened to him, and after completing his studies there, he was hired as a high official in the Kiev General Government, with the task of censoring Jewish books.

Here he found a broad field for his task, and he began to spread education among the Jews. In the newspapers, he published many articles and essays about the Jewish schools in the country, and even in the name of the General Government, he opened a platform for Jewish writers so that they could express themselves and openly discuss the problem of spreading education among their nation.

The convert Vladimir Fyodorov did not neglect his family. He divorced his wife, and when his daughter's time to be married had arrived, he came to Dubno and gave her a respectable dowry. The daughter married a cousin, the government-appointed Rabbi Weinryb from Artemivs'k (Bachmut).

During the final years of his life, the convert Vladimir Fyodorov was hired as the censor of all Jewish books in Warsaw, and there befriended the editor of *Ha-Tzefira* ("the Siren"; Hebrew language newspaper in Poland) – Haz's (Haim Ze'ev

Slonimski) and Na's (Nahum Sokolov) and even got involved with translating the *Talmud* and with translating German. He died in Warsaw at the end of the year 1870.

[Columns 73–74]

Dr. Reuven ben Moshe Kulisher – a writer, doctor, and all-round community activist, was born in Dubno in the year 1828. At the age of 20, he managed to become a regular student in the University of Petersburg. He was the second Jewish student there. After eight years of studying, in 1856, he completed his medical-surgical studies, and in the years 1869–1876 he specialized in hygiene and military medicine financed by the Russian government.

Dr. Reuven Kulisher published many science studies, originals and translations. One of these concerned skin diseases, according to the Jewish sources (appearing in "East and West" Issue No. 3) and the well-known Professor Munack based his research of leprosy on a paper by Dr. Kulisher. In 1862, he also published a series of articles explaining the theories of natural forces as understood by Helmholtz, and in 1868, a paper on the physiology of "Hunger and Thirst."

Dr. Kulisher was a community activist and active Jewish writer. In his youth, he was among the admirers and friends of writer Isaac Baer Levinsohn of Kremenets and their correspondence was published in the year 1896 in a publication of Y. Weinberg. He put a lot of energy into spreading general education among the Jews. As a student, in the year 1849 he wrote a poem in Russian "A Response to the Dictionary," which was distributed in his own handwriting because of the prohibitions of the censor (in a few years, it was published in print in a journal). He wrote in *Ha-Melitz* and *Ha-Tzefira* (Hebrew newspapers), and other Jewish periodicals. He also published a critique of Mandelkern's Russian translation of the *Chumash* (Five Books of Moses). In the year 1861, his famous song "The Fugitive Jew to His Fugitive Brothers" was published, which was very interesting both from its thematic perspective and from its style.

In distress and joy, in gaiety and in mourning,

I am with thee, with thee in the universe,

If I forget thee, O Jerusalem, may my right hand lose its cunning!

My People I will not abandon you!

In the terror of the tempest and the raging of the storm,

In the pellets of hailstones and the loud voice of rebuke,

In fire and brimstone, in the midst of a flood,

With the death of all creatures and the passing of life,

With beasts and Seraphim, and the Heavenly angels,

In distress and joy, in gaiety and in mourning,

I am with thee, with thee in the universe,

If I forget thee, O Jerusalem, may my right hand lose its cunning!

My People I will not abandon you!

..................................etc.

At the end of the poem the poet observes: "I wrote this poem in 1850 when I was at St. Petersburg University studying medicine," and the editor of "*Ha-Melitz*" added: "He wrote this cherished poem in Hebrew and Russian in his memoirs that was presented to the Tsar on his coronation day in the name of the Jewish people."

Dr. Reuven Kulisher's memoirs, "generally of hope and of the outlooks of the Jews in Russia over a period of 50 years – 1838–1888," were published in "*Wuskhad*" in the years 1891-1894.

Dr. Reuven Kulisher died in Kiev in the year 1896.

Lithograph of Avraham-Ber Gotlober

Avraham-Ber ben Rabbi Haim HaCohen Gotlober, known for his literary pseudonyms "*Mehalelel*" and "AB'G," is considered one of the most prolific writers of the *Haskalah* period. Although he was not born in Dubno, he is considered one of its greatest residents because his fame evolved at the time when he lived in that city.

Avraham-Ber Gotlober was born on December 10, 1810, in Old-Konstantin, Volhynia. His father was the city's *Hazan* (cantor). As a five-year-old boy, he began to study in a *Heder* and at the age of nine, he was already reading the "*Shirei Tiferes*" ("Songs of Glory") of Rabbi Hertz Wiesel. His father, the *Hazan,* did not oppose the young boy studying *Tanah* (The Old Testament) with the commentaries of Mendelssohn. The young boy, Avraham-Ber, read *Hassidic* stories, philosophy, and *Haskalah* books. At eleven and a half years old, he was matched up with a ten-and-a-half-year-old girl. He was married as a bar mitzvah boy. At the age of fifteen, he tried his hand at poetry and composed an elegy over the death of Tsar Alexander I and a love song for Nikolai I.

In the year 1828, he and his father stole across the Austrian border and they entered Galicia. They did this in order to avoid his conscription as a *Cantonist* in the Tsarist army. Avraham-Ber was in Galicia for some time, in Ternopol, and there met Yosef Perl. Later, when he lived in Brody, he became friendly with the young *Maskilim* in town. These meetings sealed his fate of adherence to the *Maskilim* for all time.

69

From Galicia, Avraham-Ber and his father left to go to Moldova, but his father died there. At that time, Avraham-Ber returned to his wife and the three-year-old child that had been born to him when he was 17. They lived with his father-in-law in Czernikhov, near Zhitomir. Someone told the father-in-law that his son-in-law belonged to the *Maskilim*. With the decree issued by his Rabbi, Avraham Dov of Obrocz, Avraham-Ber was forced to separate from his wife. The divorce, which he gave his wife whom he loved, leaving her and the child, ended in tragedy; as a *Cohen*, he was forbidden to court and marry her a second time.

Avraham-Ber later married for a second time. He left Czernikhov and settled in a small village in Podolia. After a short time, he left this wife too, and in the year 1830, he left for Odessa, which was the center of the Jewish *Maskilim*. He befriended some of them, such as: Bezalel Stern, first director of the Jewish government school; and Rabbi Simha Pinsker, a teacher in the school. There, he read Yitzhak-Baer Levinson's (Ryv'al) book *"Teudah b'Yisrael,"* and became a great follower of his. In Odessa, Gotlober was a private tutor in a rich Jewish home.

He did not remain in Odessa for long, and he soon began his wanderings. In 1831, a cholera epidemic broke out in the city. He left Odessa and went to Dubãsari (Dubasar), in the Kherson province. Here he also did not remain long, and at the beginning of 1832 he arrived in Dubno for the first time.

 Here he found friends and fellow *Maskilim* and scholars, *Haskalah* books, and religious books in Hebrew and in German and most important – an atmosphere of tolerance and understanding. His song collection, *"Nitzanim"* (buds), was published in Vilna in the year 1851, in which he recalled his time in Dubno with great longing.

In autumn 1834, he left Dubno and went to Mezrycz-Volhynia, and in Lutsk he visited the Karaites,[12] in whom he became interested when he was in Odessa. Later, he was married for a third time, to a woman from Kremenets and he went to live in the house of Ryv'al. In 1836, he went to Warsaw, and one year later, in 1837 his first book of songs *"Pirah Aviv"* ("Flowers of Spring") was published in Jozefow (Jozifiv). He collected funds for this book; and it was for that reason that he had wandered across the difficult roads of Poland, Volhynia, and Lithuania.

[Columns 77–78]

Once again, Avraham-Ber Gotlober took to wandering. He came to Mogilev-Podolsk and stayed there until the year 1844. That year, he heard about the establishment of government schools for Jewish children, directed by Dr. Menahem Lilienthal under the auspices of the Russian education minister Uvarov. He approached Dr. Lilienthal with a prepared list of recommendations by Jewish *Maskilim* and their addresses. For this reason, he left Mogilev-Podolsk and once again came to Berdichev.

From time to time, he would visit his family, wife, and three children, who were in Kremenets. Since he did not have a steady job, in the year 1849 he went to the convert Vladimir Fyodorov (Tzvi Hirsh Greenberg) and approached Dr. Leon Mandelstam to take him on as a teacher in the government Rabbinical seminary in Zhitomir. But he was not hired. He then decided to take the exams in the gymnasium in Zhitomir, in order to acquire certification as a teacher. He was successful in Jewish and general studies.

Until he took the position as teacher in Kamenets-Podolsk in the year 1851, he published his second book of songs – "*Nitzanim*," that was also subsidized thanks to "funding from before" by 800 subscribers. Because of that, he once again had to continue wandering across Warsaw, Brisk, Brody, Tarnopol, and Odessa.

In Kamenets-Podolsk he was a teacher for three years and there he met Mendele "*Moher Seforim*," "The Book Seller" (Yiddish writer) and even helped him send his first works to *Ha-Maggid* (Hebrew language weekly). Also, the educated daughter of A.B. Gotlober helped Mendele prepare himself for the government exams, where he was successful in acquiring a teacher's attestation.

Avraham-Ber Gotlober once again had to take his staff in hand, and in the year 1854, out of his own desire, he went to his place of birth, Old-Konstantin, where he was a teacher for eleven years. Among his students in the town was also Avraham Goldfaden, the father of Yiddish theater. While he was there he succeeded in obtaining a holiday and went on a visit to Vienna where he translated Ludwig August Frankel's book of his travels (1860). And in his last year in that town, in 1864, he published two books: one with financial help of the Russian Ministry of Education, "A History of the Karaite Sect," and the second regarding Hebrew poems: "A balanced evaluation of the Hebrew Poem in Germany and Slavic countries."

In 1865, AB'G received a post as teacher of the Talmud at the government *Beit Hamidrash* (Study House) for Rabbis in Zhitomir after being recommended by an official at the Russian Ministry of Education, and he maintained that position for eight years until the school was closed in the summer of 1873. While he was resident in Zhitomir his literary output increased and in 1866 he published "A Psalm of Thanksgiving" for Tsar Alexander II's escape from an assassination attempt on his life by the Nihilist Karakozov on April 4, 1866, for which he was thanked by the Tsar; he translated "Jerusalem" by Moses Mendelssohn and published the first part of "The History of Kabbalah and *Hassidut*." He argued passionately with the owner of "*Ha-Melitz*" Alexander Zederbaum and the critic Avraham Uri Kowner.

With the closure of the "*Beit Hamidrash*" for Rabbis in Zhitomir, AB'G requested a paid holiday from the Russian Ministry of Education because "...from my extensive work my eyes have now dimmed," but he was rewarded with a one-time benefit and an allowance for one year only and he was forced to return to his daughter, who was married to the government appointed Rabbi Bornstein in Dubno. Dubno was no longer the town of great Hebrew scholars of forty years previous, but a town where the young scholars were mostly interested in following the cultures of Russia and Europe. In great sadness he left Dubno and moved to Galicia to sell his translation of Lessing's "Nathan the Wise" and then went to Brody, Lemberg, Krakow, Jaroslaw, and Tarnow. He was in Vienna and Prussia and again Vienna, but without success.

In Vienna he met the founder and editor of "The Dawn," Peretz Smolenskin, who helped him significantly, but their paths separated in 1875 when Smolenskin took an antagonistic stand in "The Dawn" against Moses Mendelssohn and the "Berlin *Haskala*" while AB'G was an admirer of Mendelssohn and defended him and even founded "The Morning Light," a monthly journal a year later with an entirely different approach to Jewish issues from "The Dawn." Smolenskin's "The Dawn" was a flag signalling the national rebirth of Israel while Gotlober emphasized in his journal's name with Mendelssohn and the *Haskala*. The light already illuminated the morning after the darkness of the Middle-Ages and the spread of the *Hassidut*.

When AB'G founded the "*Haboker Or*" ("Morning Light"), he was already an older man, and the work was not easy for him. At the time, he lived in Dubno (Russian Volhynia), while the newspaper was published in Lemberg (Austrian Galicia), because under the Tsar Alexander II Jews were not permitted to publish newspapers and journals. Within ten years – 1876–1886, only seven issues of "*Haboker Or*" were printed: In the years 1876-1878 it was published in Lemberg; from April 1879-June 1881 it was published in Warsaw; it stopped appearing from summer 1881 to the beginning of 1885, from 1885-until January 1886 it was again printed in Warsaw and then stopped completely. AB'G was not available to edit it because he was burdened with financial problems and the practical issues of editing were performed by others. In Lemberg the coordinator was the writer Reuben Asher Braudes while in Warsaw at the beginning it was Eliezer Yitzhak Shapira and then Avraham Zuckerman.

[Columns 79–80]

Despite its brief life, the "*Haboker Or*" of Avraham-Ber Gotlober served as the primary place for young working men, many of whom later held a respected position in Jewish literature and culture. Here were the first songs and ballads of "*Kiddush Ha-Shem*" ("Sanctification of G-d's Name") of Y.L. Peretz. Konstantin Abba Shapira published his first poems of "*Al Meshorerei Bat Ami*". And the first compilations of David Frishman saw their real light in "*Haboker Or*" – and the poems – "There is Hope," "On my Birthday" and "Behold – Today I am Fifteen," the story "On the Day of Atonement" and the pamphlets "Pen-sketches."

Among the participants in the Journal were the grammarian Haim Tzvi Lerner, the researcher Ya'acov Reifman, the author of a treatise on the prophets David Kahane, the historian Ze'ev Yavetz and the publicist S.Y. Horowitz. Mendele "The Book Seller" also contributed "A General Overview of Fish" that was a part of his series on "The History of Nature," N. Rochel excerpts from "*Pinkas Dubno*" and the writer Zalman Epstein his essay on F.N. Dostoevsky, "In Memory of a Great Man." In 1879, AB'G received a license to publish "Morning Light" in Warsaw and in April of that year came to settle there - and there, in the shabby, editorial offices he was visited by the young, spiritual Ahad Ha'am (Asher Ginzburg) who was then aged 22.

In 1881, AG'B was to celebrate his seventieth year and the Hebrew press of the day, *"Ha-Melitz," "Ha-Maggid"* and *"Ha-Tzefira"* lauded the activities of the celebrant and called upon the public to support him lest he be forced once again to wander the world seeking subscribers for his journal "Morning Light." But it seems that the cry for help went unheeded and the celebration held in St. Petersburg on October 8, 1880, was not a financial success.

In the years 1881–1885, when *"Haboker Or"* was no longer published, he left Warsaw and returned to Dubno to his married daughter. Because of the pogroms in southern Russia in 1881, and because of his disappointment with the *Haskalah* in terms of its wages, he joined the *Hovevey Tzion* ["Lovers of Zion"] and began to write a series of Zionist songs: *"Yisrael Mekunan,"* "The Eternal Wandering Jew," "A Voice from the Window Sings" and *"Le-Menatze'ah al Mechalat bat ami b'Romania"* (meaning Russia), in which he summons his brothers to return to the Land of the Fathers.

"Who is there among you of all his People? The Lord his G-d be with him and let him go up."[13]

In Dubno, he also wrote his famous songs *Die Stürmedike Schiff* ("The Stormy Ship") December 1883 and *Yehuda and Ephraim* (Tevet - January 1884) – against assimilation, changing one's name, the language and dress of the *Maskilim,* and against the lessening of faith in nationalism.

The Stormy Ship[14]

Amid the wild noisy sea

A ship tosses and turns,

Swinging around and around

Atop the crest a moment then falling.

etc.

Yehuda and Ephraim[15]

Go, Germany and gaze in earnest

If they will be borne there by force,

They have turned their backs on their peoples,

Erased all Memory of Zion and Jerusalem

From their hearts and their prayers –

And still the scorn and curses...

[Columns 81–82]

The last year of "Morning Light," during which only five editions appeared, was 1886. It was also the year of AB'G's seventy-fifth birthday and the completion of fifty years of his literary output. Sages and authors from all over Russia and abroad showed him great respect. Among those who respected him was Mendele "The Book Seller" who recalled the kindness shown to him in his youth and sent a heartfelt and sensitive letter under the name "S.Y. to the teacher" (a clue to his real name: Shalom Ya'acov Abramowitch).

After the final appearance of "Morning Light," AB'G changed his place of residence together with his daughter and son-in-law from Dubno to Rowno and later to Bialystok, where he became blind. In Bialystok, he was visited by the young writer Joseph Klausner who was impressed by his dignified mien telling of respect and his outpouring of sayings displaying his wisdom and intellect, humor, and scholarship.

In the last three years of his life, AB'G did not leave his house because of his blindness and found himself in complete solitude. On June 12, 1899, he died at the age of 88.

Dr. Shlomo ben Simha-Dov Mandelkern, the man from Greater Dubno, as he used to call himself during his youth, was born on the second day of Passover, 1846, in Mlynow (Młynów), a town near Dubno.

During his childhood years, he studied a lot of *Torah* with Rabbi Pinhas in the town of Torhovytsia (Trovits, Targovitza), in the Dubno district, when his father died in the year 1862. When Shlomo was 16 years old, he left for Dubno and studied *Torah* there with Rabbi Tzvi Rappoport HaCohen and with Rabbi Yitzhak Eliyahu Landau. When he was studying in Dubno, the young Shlomo Mandelkern dedicated himself to Kabbalah, went to the Kotsker Rabbi Menahem Mendel of Kotsk (Kock), befriended his son Rabbi David'l, and together with him studied Kabbalah and *Hassidut*.

When he returned to Dubno from Kotsk, he became busy with *Tanah* research, with the literature of the Middle Ages, and grammar of the Hebrew language, and he also began to write for the weekly *Ha-Maggid* ("The Preacher") 1856, the first Hebrew language weekly newspaper in Lutsk, Poland] (1865) and in the periodical "*Ha-Melitz*" ("The Advocate"); the first Hebrew language newspaper published a few months after "*Ha-Carmel*)", and "*Ha-Carmel*" (1860, first Hebrew weekly then monthly in Russia), which were published in Odessa and Vilna. In 1864, he married in Dubno, and about a year later, they had a son. But he left his wife and child to study in the Zhitomir Rabbinical seminary, and from there – in the Rabbinical seminary in Vilna. There he met AD'M HaCohen,[16] who befriended him warmly.

In 1868, Mandelkern completed his studies in the Vilna Rabbinical seminary, and he was awarded with ordination as the government-appointed Rabbi. He returned to Dubno, divorced his wife, and left for Petersburg. He was accepted into the university and there studied Oriental languages. After five years at the university (1868–1873), he completed his studies with excellence and received a gold medal for his concordance of the *Tanah,* the Septuagint and the Vulgate and his paleographic study of certain biblical locations. He was given the position of representative of the Rabbis in Odessa, and during the eight years of living in the city (1873–1880), he completed his judicial studies in the University of Odessa and was given the title of "Candidate for Judicial Science." During the holidays he studied in the university in Jena (Germany) and there he was granted the title of Doctor of Philosophy for his dissertation about the differences between the Book of Prophets and *Divrei Hayamim* (Book of Chronicles).

In the year 1880, he stepped down from the Rabbinic position in Odessa and went to Leipzig (Germany), and then worked for 16 years preparing his concordance of the *Heichal Hakodesh* (Hebrew and Aramaic concordance of the *Tanah*), a monumental and all-encompassing work that serves as a basis until today, for all studies of *Tanah* research. He also planned for a large concordance of the Talmud, but his energy had been spent on the enormous previous task and he did not have enough funding for this endeavor.

Dr. Shlomo Mandelkern published many articles in Hebrew, Yiddish, Russian, German, and English, and also wrote songs and ballads. He was a delegate at the First Zionist Congress in Basel. On March 24, 1902, he died of a mental illness in a Vienna hospital and was brought for burial to Leipzig.

F. Hovevey Tzion and the Beginnings of Zionism

In the '80s of the 19th century, the *Haskalah* light began to fade among Eastern European Jewry. The ideals of the *Haskalah* movement, struggle against superstition, and the low level of religious life, the mockery of *Hassidut* and rabbis, the efforts to be an "individual in the street but a Jew at home" – did not survive the test of the times. The pogroms in southern Russia in the year 1881 that were marked with the allegorical name of "Storms in the Negev" broke the belief of many intellectual personalities of that period. The problem of emigration from all the Russian provinces which, in the last few years had become stronger and became a mass fleeing to Germany, England, America, and Argentina – increased the pace of the development of the *Hovevey Tzion* movement and the colonization work in the Land of Israel.

Among the Dubno Jews, there was a young scholar from a prestigious family – Rabbi Zalman Ashkenazi, who was active in the *Hovevey Tzion* and Zionist activities.

He was born in Dubno in 1848, at the beginning of the *Haskalah* movement. His father, Rabbi Tzvi Hirsh, was well known as a scholar and *Maskil*. At that time, there was a youth group in Dubno, to which Rabbi Tzvi Hirsh belonged, which strove for knowledge and education.

In his father's house, Zalman had the accepted *Torah* upbringing, and as a youth he was sent to Lemberg to receive a general education. When he returned to Dubno with a lot of *Torah* and knowledge, and since he was already well known, he began working with pharmaceuticals, got married, and set up a rich, Jewish home. He had only one son, and he soon began his community activities.

Rabbi Zalman Ashkenazi's first steps to speak on behalf of *Hovevey Tzion* was after the visit of the renowned lecturer Tzvi Hirsch Masliansky in Dubno (1893), who, in the *"Resursa Obywatelska"* (Citizens' Club), called a meeting of "worldly" Jews, who came in large numbers, and he earned significant approval from them.

In order to bring the people closer to the *Hovevey Tzion* movement, Rabbi Zalman organized Maccabi celebrations (Maccabi-fest) each year, for which he arranged renowned speakers and activists, and most illuminating was the article of one Pinhas Pesis in *"Ha-Melitz"*[17] in 1894 concerning a *Hanukah* celebration of the *Hovevey Zion* that same year in Dubno:

"On Saturday night, as the Holy Sabbath ended – the first night of *Hanukah* – there gathered together by invitation the *Hovevey Zion* group in the home of the respected Mr. Reuven Stahl (with authorization from the County Governor). Many dear women, members and other guests, delegates from neighboring towns were also there…the number of participants exceeded three hundred persons. They gathered in four large rooms, pleasantly illuminated, and in the main hall the men and women sat apart from each other. In one of the rooms tables were set up laden with produce from the Holy Land, the results of the labors of our brethren working with the sweat of their brow on the mountains of Israel: wine and cognac from Rishon Le-Zion; citrus from the Holy Land; and other various sweetmeats, most of which had been prepared by our sister members."

"The opening ceremony was conducted by our representative Mr. Z. Ashkenazi who blessed the first *Hanukah* light using olive oil brought from the Holy Land, and a choir afterwards sang 'A Song of Praise and Dedication' and '*Hanerot Halallu.*' After the lighting of the candle, Mr. Z. Ashkenazi delivered a sermon on the verse: "Then shall thy light break forth as the morning…"[18] and "And behold, the glory of the G-d of Israel came from the way of the east…"[19] After him, the honored delegate Mr. Tzvi Prelutzky of Kremenets spoke for about an hour on the topic of the 'Return to Zion' from the period of Zerubabbel until the time of the Hasmoneans…the lecture made a deep impression on the entire gathering, even to the extent of some of them shedding tears, and a deathly silence fell over the audience. At the end, he received great acclaim and shouts of appreciation. After that the chorus sang the song "*Maduah*" (Why), by the poet M.M. Horwitz, and then Mr. Ashkenazi raised his glass and proposed a toast blessing several notable participants and their respective organizations both at home and abroad, especially mentioned were Paris, Kremenets, Rowno. Mr. Prelutzky toasted Dubno and the Holy Land ---------- It was five in the morning when the gathering finally dispersed, satisfied, and went home."

"The prepared tables yielded a net income of one-hundred-and-twenty silver rubles for the benefit of settlements in the Holy land."

Rabbi Zalman also wrote songs, all of which were dedicated to Israel. Apparently, two typical verses of a poem that appeared in the same year in "*Ha-Melitz*":[20]

A poem in Honor of *Hanukah* by Zalman Ashkenazi on lighting the *Hanukah* Candle (1895).

These lights…

The clouds disperse, the heavens clear,

The starlight shines around with noble light.

No longer will the face of Jacob pale with shame,

These lights we which we ignite…"

All creation is in shadow – brothers and friends,

A plethora of blessings and joyfulness are poured forth…

These lights which we ignite…

When the *Hanukah* celebrations were being organized, Dr. Tuviah Hindes and Tzvi Hirsh Prelutzky of Kremenets helped Rabbi Zalman, because his activities were not only in Dubno, but he would travel on the difficult roads to the distant Volhynia towns in order to "snatch up souls."

For the entire time of the activities of the Odessa committee of *Hovevey Tzion*, Rabbi Zalman was its authorized director in Dubno. He was the "living spirit" in organizing the distribution of money on the eve of *Yom Kippur*, distributing it to the right destinations, empowering others to become active as well.

In the year 1897, he was selected as a delegate for the First Zionist Congress and took upon himself the responsibility to tell his electors about the Congress and his problems in *Ha-Melitz*, dated 5 Shevat 5659[21] [January 1899]:

"From Dubno comes the announcement that on Tuesday, the 6th day of *Hanukah*, the Zionists celebrated the "Festival of the Maccabees" in great elegance in the home of Mr. Zalman Ashkenazi. The Zionists congregated in the hall at 10 in the evening. Mr. Ashkenazi opened the evening with burning issues of the day…and after a short break began to relate – as the Zionist delegate of Volhynia - the events that took place in Basel in all its details, and significantly engaged the hearts of his audience reporting almost word for word the speech of Max Nordau concerning the diplomatic work of Dr. Herzl… and the hearts of his listeners were filled with hope and love for the Ancestral Home and its People…"

Rabbi Zalman Ashkenazi did not make light of any smaller jobs, no matter how trivial, provided they were related to Hebrew or the Land of Israel. Wherever he went, he spread the Hebrew books from the publications of *Ahi Yosef* and *Toshia* that were being printed at that time. It was understood *a priori*, that products of the Land of Israel – the wines of *Carmel Mizrahi* and olive oil, almonds and raisins – were always to be found on his table, even the Land of Israel's *etrog*[22], which was far from profitable and close to proving a loss, failed to dissuade him, and it too found its way to Dubno.

When the Jews in Russia, during the first election of the *Duma* (1904), believed that in the Russian Empire it was now also a time of "spring for the people," Rabbi Zalman was of the first to assess the importance of the Jews' participation in the elections, and thanks to his caution and activities, all the Jewish electors came to the ballot box. No one failed to vote – something that did not happen anywhere else.

Rabbi Zalman Ashkenazi was an exceptionally good-looking person, and his manner of dress was fine as well, and he was religious. Every Sabbath, he prayed in the *Beit Midrash* of BR'T (Rabbi Ya'acov ben Meir). He was a good speaker, he wrote articles, songs, and pamphlets that were often published in *Ha-Melitz* and in the *Luah Ahi Yosef*. A friendly and kind person, he found time to play chess with his friends, where he made an exceptional impression.

On Sabbath, 21 Tammuz, July 10, 1909, he died at the age of 71. His death left a tragic mark on all the Jews of Dubno. Thousands of his followers and friends of the city and the surrounding areas came to pay their final respects. His funeral was a powerful demonstration of Zionism and showed how deeply he had planted roots in the people.

From various sources and the descriptions of David Lander, the friend of Mr. Zalman Ashkenazi, from the "Volhynia Journal" 1 Nisan, 1940

G. Dubno Rabbis

Until the end of the 17th century, the names of the Rabbis of Dubno were not recorded, not by their study groups, not in the contracts, and not on the tombstones. But beginning in the year 1600, the names of the rabbinic leaders and heads of the Rabbinical courts of the city were known – until the murder of the Jewish community by the Nazis.

The first of the Dubno Rabbis at the end of the 16th century was the *Gaon* Our Rabbi Yeshaya Halevi Ish Horowitz, called the *Shelah Hakadosh* (the Holy Shelah) named after his book *Shnei Luhot Habrit* ("Two Tablets of the Covenant"). His progeny, generation after generation, until Rabbi Shmuel Halevi Ish Horowitz, and his son Rabbi David Halevi, may his blood be avenged, were Rabbis in Dubno. They died in the first days of the German invasion of the city, in the year 1941.

Rabbi Yeshaya Halevi Ish Horowitz, the son of Rabbi Avraham Bar Shabtai Sheftel Bar Yeshaya Halevi, leader of the Jewish community in the city of Hovice, in Bohemia, was born in Prague in the year 1575. In his childhood years, he and his father left Bohemia and went to Krakow, Poland. He was closely associated with his teacher the *Gaon*, Rabbi and Teacher Yehuda Leib, Father of the Rabbinical Court in Polonne.

In the year 1600, his name was mentioned for the first time with Dubno and its circle, because, it seems, of the answer of the *Maharam* (Meyer Ben Gedaliah) of Lublin, on Monday, 13 Adar 5360 (28th February 1600), regarding nullifying a divorce because of a change of name:[23] "Shalom, to you - Shalom my beloved and exalted friend, whose name is known in heaven, Head of the County and town Rabbi, our Teacher and Rabbi. Concerning the *Get* (divorce document) granted there near the border, and the woman in the domain of the Rabbinical court of his honor and Torah in the Holy Community of Dubno, etc., etc…"

In the years 1603–1606, he was Rabbi and Father of the Rabbinical court in the Holy Community of Ostrow and the region and possibly also Poznań, and later was installed in Frankfurt-am-Main where his salary was "…400 guilder a year, and he was obliged to purchase for his son and son-in-law citizenship of the town." He remained in Frankfurt until 1614 when he and the Jews of Frankfurt were exiled, and moved to Prague where he officiated as Rabbi and Father of the Rabbinical court together with the *Gaon* Rabbi Ephraim Luntschitz, of Łęczyca (Lintshits), author of *"Olelot Ephraim."*[24]

On the death of his wife the *Rabbanit* Mrs. Haya in 1620, he decided to go to the Holy Land – his secret dream, passing through Germany via Frankfurt-am-Main and Venice in Italy, whence he sailed to the Holy Land, arriving in 1622 at his longed-for destination - Jerusalem. There he completed his major work "The Two Tablets of the Covenant" in 1624. The following year he was imprisoned by the Turkish Pasha together with another 15 Rabbis on false charges. That same year he escaped from Jerusalem to Safed, where he died in 1630, and was laid to rest there.

After the *Shelah Hakadosh,* the successor to the Rabbinical Chair in Dubno was the *Gaon,* Rabbinical scholar and leader Shmuel Aharon Halevi Ish Horowitz – from 1625 until about 1630. Then he was established as the head of the Rabbinic court in the city of Lubovna (Lubomel) and that is where he died.

For a short time (1632–1634), the Rabbinical office in Dubno took on Rabbi *Ha-Gaon* the Rabbinic leader Tzvi Hirsh son of the Rabbi Our Teacher Ozer, son-in-law and disciple of the *Gaon* Avraham Haim Naphtali Hirsh Shorr, Rabbi in Satanova, (Satanów). Rabbi Tzvi Hirsh wrote the foreword to the book *"Torat Hayyim,"* authored by his son-in-law, printed in Krakow in 1634 and inscribed by him with a formal elegant dedication.

It is generally considered that in the years 1642–1643, the rabbinic seat in Dubno was occupied by the *Gaon,* Our Teacher Meyer Katz, son of *Gaon* Moshe Katz Ashkenazi. This opinion is supported by the script on the tombstone in the Dubno cemetery.

> A righteous and holy man, a revealer of wisdom and *Halacha,*
> Our Rabbi and Teacher Meir the son of Maharam Katz,
> He passed away on Tuesday, 3 Kislev.
> *May his soul be bound up in the bond of everlasting life.*

Maharam (Our Teacher and our Rabbi, Rabbi Meir) Katz was at first the Rabbi in Amstibovo and afterwards in Mogilev, on the Dnieper (Molev) until 1642. Later he moved to Dubno and died there. Relying on the clause "…an illuminator of wisdom and *Halacha,*" one may assume he was the head of a college and a righteous teacher in Dubno until the day of his death.

[Columns 89–90]

The *Gaon* and kabbalist Rabbi Yehuda, may his blood be avenged, mentioned among the fallen martyrs of the year 1649 in the book *Tza'ar Bat Rabim,*[25] was almost certainly the head of the Jewish court and was murdered by Khmelnytsky's thugs, along with the Dubno Jews, and did not have a Jewish burial.

For about nine years, 1649–1658, there was no Jewish community in Dubno. In those years, Dubno was given a "charter" by Prince George Sebastian Lubomirski. Then the *Gaon* Avraham Halpern, Our Teacher and Rabbi, the son-in-law of the *Gaon* Mordecai Yeffe author of "*Halevushim,*" was elected as the Rav, where he held his position from 1660-1662 when he became the honored Rabbi of the Holy Community of Kowel, where he was laid to rest.

For eleven years (1663–1674), the Rabbinical seat in Dubno was held by the great, renowned *Gaon* of his generation, Our Rabbi Nahman HaCohen Liptzis, who was the Rabbi of Lwow (Lwów, Lemberg, Lvov, Lviv), Kremenets, Chelm, and Belz (Bełz). He was the grandchild of the *Gaon* Our Teacher and Rabbi Gershon HaCohen Rappoport, a scion of the family of Rabbi Moshe of Speyer, known as Liptzis after his mother the wealthy Mrs. Liptzis, the grand-daughter of the *Gaon* Rabbi Yitzhak Shrentzel, Father of the Rabbinical Court of Lwow. He was installed as Father of the Rabbinical Court of the Holy Community of Dubno in 1663, as proved by the signed "agreement" in his name: "…and it was agreed in 1633 to print '*Shulhan Aruh*' with clarifications by the Maharal (Judah Loew ben Bezalel), '*Be'er Hagolah*' in its first printing in Amsterdam, together with the Rabbis of the Council of Four Lands at a conference held at a fair in Yaroslav together with the author of "Columns of Gold" ('*Turei-Zahav*' also his nickname), Rabbi David Ha-Levi Segal, on Monday, 15 Elul, 5423 (17ᵗʰ September 1663), from Nahman in an anthology of sayings gathered by Meir Katz Rappoport who had settled in the Holy Community of Greater Dubno."
In 1675, he had already approved of the work '*Nahamot Tzion*' as the Rabbi of the Holy Community of Belz and died there that same year.

Following him – the great *Gaon* Moshe Bar Yosef, but we do not know about his position in Dubno, other than the writing on his tombstone in the cemetery in Lwow:

> And Moshe went to G-d, 16th of Sivan, 1684.
> The great Gaon Our Teacher the Rabbi Yosef –
> Father of the Rabbinical Court of the Holy Community of Greater Dubno.
> Preacher of the Torah in his generation to the needy and poor and
> population of G-d.
> May he rest in honor and peace until the dead arise.

After Rabbi Moshe Bar Yosef, head of the *Beit-Din* in Dubno was the renowned *Gaon* of his generation, *Gaon* Yisrael son of the notable Rabbi Avraham Yoleh's (after his mother's name Yoleh) of Krakow. He was the son-in-law of the community leader of his generation the Rabbi Berish son of the *Gaon* Rabbi Hershel of Krakow.

Rabbi Yisrael who was also known as Rabbi Swinocher, held the position in Dubno for one year (1684–1685) and then with the highest honor, he was given the Rabbinical seat in Lutsk, where he died. His daughter was the wife of the *Gaon* Our Teacher and Rabbi Simha Katz Rappoport the son of Rabbi Nahman Katz who officiated after him as Father of the Rabbinical court in Dubno.

From the year 1685, the Rav of Dubno was the *Gaon*, the great leader Simha and the *Gaon* Rabbi Nahman Katz Liptzis Rappoport. He was born in Lwow where his father was the *Dayan* [judge] and the head of the *Beit-Din*. In 1685, he married the daughter of Rabbi Yisrael Swinocher and came to Dubno along with his father and when his father took his seat in Lutsk, he filled his father's place in Dubno.

It is not clear how long Rabbi Simha occupied the Rabbinical seat in Dubno, but in 1694 he approved the book *Zafnat Pa'aneah Hadasha* [26] (Frankfurt-am-Main). "Pleasure beyond words for our Teacher the great *Gaon* Our Teacher and Rabbi Nahman Katz Rappoport (His Righteousness will be Remembered in the Next World), of the holy community of Dubno and now in the holy community of Grodno." He died in 1717 in Szczebrzeszyn (Shebreshin).

From the years 1691 until 1698, there was no Rabbi in Dubno. In that year, 1691, the *Gaon* Rabbi Simha moved to Grodno. In 1698, the Dubno community invited the Rabbi Yosef Yazki, son of the Lublin Rabbinical leader and kabbalist Yehuda Yodel who had been Rabbi and Father of the Rabbinical court in Lwow, in Minsk, and then Kowel.

Rabbi Yosef approved of the book "The Satisfaction of Naphtali" [27] and wrote: Yosef – the famous Rabbi, our Teacher Rabbi Yodel (Z"L), residing in Minsk from where his influence was spread wide in the Holy Community of Greater Dubno. He was the Rabbi of the kabbalist Our Teacher and Rabbi Tzvi Kaidanower, author of the book *"Kav Ha-Yashar"* (*The Just Measure*) to which he added elements of wisdom and morals. He also authored *"In Honor of the Holy Sabbath"*. [28] Rabbi Yosef died in 1706 in Dubno on the evening preceding the month of Iyar (approximately January/February), and the congregation would recite the *El Maleh Rahamim* prayer for the dead on the anniversary of his passing.

Following the *Gaon* Rabbi Yosef Yazki, of blessed memory, the Rabbinical seat was held by the *Gaon* and wealthy man, the leader Shmuel *"Hagvir Haparness"* Rabbi Shlomo Shahne Katz of Krakow. Before this, he was the Rabbi in Neustadt and afterwards the Father of the *Beit Din* [30] in Dubno; we have an approval by him of the book *"P'nei Arieh Zota"* (Wilmersdorf 1720), "Signed, Shmuel son of my beloved father

Our Teacher the Rabbi Shahne of Krakow, dwelling in the community of Greater Dubno."

[Columns 91–92]

He officiated as the Rabbi of Dubno for six years, from 1706–1712. He died in Brody in 1729 and on his tombstone was inscribed:

> Here lies buried the great Gaon Rabbi
> Rabbi of the Community of Dubno
> Our Teacher and Rabbi Shmuel Shalom Shahne Katz
> 21st Sivan 5489 (20th May 1729)

In the years 1712–1715, the rabbinic seat in Dubno was held by the leader Yitzhak Isaac the son of the *Gaon* Rabbi Sha'ul Ginzberg. He was the father of the *Gaon* Meir Ginzberg, Father of the Community of Wieczyn and brother-in-law of the Teacher and *Gaon* Tzvi Ashkenazi. He was the son-in-law of Meshulam Zalman Mierlisch (Mirels), Chief Rabbi of the Community of Hamburg. Then, in 1715, he was invited with great esteem to come to Mogilev on the River Dnieper.

In the years of 1715–1719, before the Holy *Gaon* and leading community personality Eliezer Beharav came to Dubno, the son of Our Teacher and exalted Rabbi, the *Gaon* Rabbi Issachar-Berish ("Rabbi of all exiles"), he was Rabbi in Ruzinoy (Różana). He left Dubno for the position as Rabbi in Brody, and he died there.

He was the grandfather of the *Gaon* Rabbi Yehezkiel Landau, the author of "*Nodah Biyhudah*" (Known in Judah), who was the son of his daughter Mrs. Haya and Rabbi Ya'acov'ke the son of Our Rabbi and Teacher the exalted Rabbi Yehezkiel Landau who refers to him in the preface of his book "*Nodah Biyhudah*" as a "…righteous element of the world."

In the year 1719, the *Gaon* Rabbi Yehoshua Heschel, son of our leader Eliezer Beharav, also called the 'Little' Rabbi Heschel, was Rabbi and Father of the Rabbinical court in Dubno, and when his father left for Brody in 1719, he officiated there for ten years. On 27 Nisan (approximately April/May), 1720, he was one of the signatories in the community journal to a document pertaining to medical and nursing protocols in the town, and in 1724 he approved of a book "His Hand against All"[29] (Frankfurt-an-der Oder, 1727) and signed: "Yehoshua Heschel son of Our Teacher the *Gaon* Eliezer, the 'Light of Israel,' resident in Dubno.

He died in Dubno in the year 1729 and left behind an inheritance of 400 gold zlotys for charity. Two-and-a-half percent of that sum – 10 zlotys per annum – was designated to support those who studied Torah.

The *Gaon* Our Rabbi Ephraim son of Sha'ul, Rabbi in Ludmir, held the Rabbinical position in Dubno for only one year (1730) and left the city for an unknown reason. For the next five years, Dubno was without a Rabbi. During these years, the *Beit Din* judged the people.

In 1735, the community notable Rabbi, Our Teacher and Rabbi Avraham the son of the *Gaon* Shmuel Kahana, came to Dubno and was installed as the Rabbi after having had many adventures.

Rabbi Avraham, who was the son of the *Gaon* Rabbi Shmuel Kahana – the nephew of Rabbi Shalom Shahne Katz of Krakow – was previously Rabbi and Father of the Rabbinical court in Brody and was invited by the community of Ostrow to accept the chair of the Rabbanut there, after its Rabbi, Rabbi Naphtali Katz, immigrated to the Holy Land. He arrived in Ostrow, but "...his wife was remarkably beautiful and the town's head authority was captivated by her; the *Gaon* our Teacher and his wife escaped by night from Ostrow, and on their way to Brody passed through Dubno." He died in Dubno in about 1741.

After he died, his eldest son, Rabbi Yitzhak Moshe Kahana took the rabbinic seat. His signature appears on many regulations in the town's constitution in the years 1741–1742. He left behind a *parohet* (curtain covering the Holy Ark) in the Great Synagogue, beautifully woven with the two large symbolic hands of the priesthood, as well as a Torah scroll.

He did not live long, dying in 1745.

Rabbi Yitzhak Moshe Kahana's inheritor in 1745 was his brother-in-law, the renowned *Gaon* Rabbi Sha'ul, son of Rabbi Arieh Leib. Rabbi Sha'ul, son of Rabbi Arieh Leib, the grandson of the *Gaon*, Our Teacher Sha'ul, Father of the Rabbinical court of Lokachi (Lokatsh), Krakow, and Amsterdam, the father-in-law of the "Great Eagle" the wise Tzvi Ashkenazi.

Rabbi Sha'ul the son of Arieh-Leib was born in 1717 in Rajcza (Reitcha), and in 1734 he married the daughter of the Dubno Rav-Rabbi, Rabbi Avraham Kahane. When he was about twenty, he was accepted as the Rabbi of Lokachi, his aged father's community, and in 1745 after the death of brother-in-law Rabbi Yitzhak Moshe Kahane he was invited to accept the Rabbanut of Dubno and officiated there until 1757.

In 1749, he "endorsed" the book "Blessed Be the Children of Asher"[134] (published in Zolkiew) and "*Shash Katan*" (published in Amsterdam) and wrote: "The Holy Sha'ul, *Gaon* and Our Teacher Rabbi Arieh Leib (Z"L) resident in the Holy Community of Dubno and the Holy Community of Amsterdam." And indeed, after the death of his father the Rav-Rabbi of the Holy Community of

Amsterdam, he was elected in his place as the Rabbi of the German community when he was only 32 years old. He served there for 35 years and died there in 1790.

[Columns 93–94]

Rabbi Arieh Leib wrote songs and also wrote a book *"Binyan Ariel"* ("The Building of Ariel") that was printed in two volumes in Amsterdam in the year 1778. The son of Rabbi Sha'ul, Rabbi Arieh Leib, took as a wife the daughter of the uncle of the Gaon Ya'av'etz (Rabbi Ya'acov Emdan, the son of Tzvi Ashkenazi, also known as "Tzvi the Wise").

After the departure in 1757 of Rabbi Sha'ul the son of Arieh Leib, to officiate as the Rabbi in Amsterdam, the kabbalist and *Gaon*, Our Teacher and Rav-Rabbi Naphtali Hertz, the second son of the *Gaon* Rabbi Tzvi Hirsh Father of the *Beit Din* Halberstadt, was called upon to occupy the seat of the Rabbinate of Dubno. (Rabbi Tzvi Hirsh was the son of Rav-Rabbi Naphtali Ashkenazi, Father of the *Beit Din* in Kowel and Lwow and the son-in-law of Rabbi Moshe Pinhas known as the *"Harif"* – sharp-minded.

Rabbi Naphtali Hertz studied Torah in Brody, together with his brother-in-law Rabbi Yitzhak Halevi Ish Horowitz, Rabbi of the three towns: Altona, Hamburg, and Wandsbeck, and with the *Gaon* Rabbi Yehezkiel Landau author of "Known in Judah" ("Nodah Biyhudah"). He was the son-in-law of the Lwow notable and Father of the Rabbinical court Rabbi Yankel'e, and while still young became the Father of the Rabbinical court in Kowel where, in 1755, he was a signatory to "the Excommunication Edict against the Frankists and Sabbateans concerning Market Days in the Holy Community of Brody in 1755,"[132] together with his uncle the *Gaon* Rabbi Haim Cohen Rappoport, Father of the Lwow Rabbinical court, his brother Rabbi Simha Father of The Rabbinical court of Dessau and brother-in-law of Rabbi Yitzhak Halevi Ish Horowitz Father of the Three Towns: "Signed, Naphtali Hertz."

He was the Rabbi of the sage Rabbi Shlomo bar Yoel of Dubno and it is thought reasonable that he was a contributor to the argument between Rabbi Shlomo and Mr. Mendelssohn, causing their mutual separation.

Rabbi Naphtali Hertz died and was laid to rest in Dubno on 10 Iyar, in the year 1777.

The inheritor was his son the *Gaon*, Rabbi Ze'ev Wolf, who was born in 1745 in Brody, and who, as a young man, received his Rabbinical ordination in the city of Radziwill. In 1792, his wife Mrs. Yuta, the *Rebbetzen,* died; she was the daughter of the *Gaon* Our Teacher and Exalted Rabbi Nahman Halperin Father of the Rabbinical court in Kalisz and Brisk in Lithuania.

When he was thirty-two years of age and with the death of his father in 1777, he occupied the Chair of the Rabbinate of Dubno. His signature is found in the Journal of the Dubno community from 28th (month illegible) 1778, where he gave his approval to the book *"Margoliot Ha-Torah"* ("Pearls of the Torah") on 22 Elul, (14th September 1787), and on the book *"Bat-Oni,"* Dubno 1788, and on *"T'shuat Khen,"* Dubno 1797.

Rabbi Ze'ev Wolf was a prosperous man all his life, and in 1792, with the death of his wife Mrs. Yuta, he "spent 1,000 Polish zlotys for charitable needs setting aside 10% for a memorial prayer for his wife on the anniversary of her death." He also donated money to the synagogue for an expensive curtain for the Holy Ark, embellished with the *Kiddush* prayer for each of the three pilgrimage festivals, costing in Danzig 500 silver rubles.

In 1800, he died at the age of 55 leaving his son Rabbi Haim Ya'acov then about 25 years old. One of his descendants, Our Teacher and Exalted Rabbi the *Gaon* Menahem Mendel Auerbah, erected a new tombstone in 1884, on which was inscribed:

> Here lies buried Rabbi Ze'ev Wolf
> Father of the Rabbinical court of our community,
> Son of the Great Rabbi the revered *Gaon* of his generation,
> of blessed name,
> Rabbi Naphtali Hertz (Z"L),
> Father of the Rabbinical court Our Rabbi and Teacher.
> He left orders which were obeyed,
> not to eulogize him or praise him beyond measure.
> *May his soul be bound up in the bond of everlasting life.*
> In the year 5560 from the creation of the world

In 1800, the Rabbinical seat of Dubno was taken by the brother-in-law of Rabbi Ze'ev Wolf, the leader Rabbi Natan Halevi Ish Horowitz, the son of the *Gaon* Rabbi Yitzhak Halevi Ish Horowitz, Rabbi of "The Three Towns." His signature is found in the Community Journal from the 26th of Sivan, 5560 (19th June 1799): "Natan Halevi Ish Horowitz, Biala Cerkiew (Biala Tserkva, Vais Feld)." He died in Dubno in 1815, leaving no children.

During the days of *Harat Olam* (the *Rosh Hashanah* and Day of Atonement period, when this prayer is recited), when the Russian Empire made life difficult for religious Jews, three rabbis took over the Rabbinical positions in Dubno: Rabbi Natan Halevi Ish Horowitz – for about fifteen years during the time of the Napoleonic Wars. He was also Rabbi in Biala Cerkiew. We don't know if he presided over both cities, Dubno and Biala Cerkiew, at one and the same time.

After his death in 1815, Rav Haim Mordecai Margoliot became the head of the *Beit Din* in Dubno, the former Rabbi of Berestechko (Beresteczko), brother of the renowned *Gaon* Ephraim Zalman Margoliot of Brody. In his approval of the book "Half a Shekel" (published in Pavlivka, Poryck, Poritsk, 1819), on Wednesday, 15th Shevat 1816, he wrote: "Haim Mordecai Margoliot, abiding in the Holy Community of Greater Dubno and the Holy Community of Berestechko." He also gave his approval to "The Two Tablets of the Covenant" by Yesheyahu (the Holy *Sheloh*) Halevi Horowitz (Pavlivka 1817), and on "My Prayer Book" Part B of 11 Elul, 1819.

It was he who stated: "Let no cook come to the house of inspection when the slaughterer examines his beast, and if he passes by, or looks at the house through the windows, he is again forbidden to be a cook..." and ordered it to be inscribed in the community's journal.

[Columns 95–96]

Rabbi Haim Mordecai Margoliot was one of the three-man Rabbinical delegation who had to present themselves to Tsar Alexander I in Petersburg. In 1818, he started a printing company in Dubno, and there he printed his book "*Sha'arei Teshuva*" ("The Gates of Repentance"), "*Shulhan Aruh* – Way of Life" and an expository work on "*Yad Ephraim*" by his brother. He also published his brother's book "Ephraim's Gate." Rabbi Haim Mordecai also positioned himself as a trader on behalf of his brother Ephraim Zalman in order not to find sustenance from his learning as a scholar of Torah, although eventually the business failed because of associates who went bankrupt, and finally he had to leave Dubno in 1829 when a fire destroyed his printing company and his books.

The third one who occupied the chair was the *Gaon* Rabbi Haim Ya'acov, the son of the *Gaon* Rabbi Ze'ev Wolf Halberstadt, who had earlier been Father of the Rabbinical court in Rowno. He held the Rabbinical position for the years 1829–1850 and died at the age of 76.

Rabbi Haim Ya'acov was the disciple of Rabbi Nisan, the Dayan, *Gaon* and Righteous Teacher in Dubno, author of the book "*Etzei Lavuna ve-Ma'yan Ganim.*"[133] Rabbi Haim Ya'acov, who was the son-in-law of Rabbi David Pranz, who officiated as Rabbi in Dubno from 1829 until 1850, when he died aged 76.

In 1850, in place of his father-in-law Rabbi Haim Ya'acov Halberstadt the great *Gaon* and Rav, David Tzvi bar Haim Auerbah-Rosenfeld was Rabbi in Dubno for thirty years, until the year 1881, when he died and was buried in Dubno.

From 1882–1884, the Rav Moshe Natan Rubenstein, author of the book "*Elef Hamagen*"[134] ("A Thousand Shields") and *Klilas Hamenorah* ("Light of the Menorah"), and after that he became Rav in Vinnytsia (Podolia).

From the year 1884, *Ha-Rav Ha-Gaon* Menahem Mendel Bar David-Tzvi Auerbah-Rozenfeld held the Rabbinical seat in Dubno, having previously been Father of the *Beit Din* in Berdichev, and with him as teacher his brother, the righteous, modest Rabbi Ze'ev Wolf.

Rabbi Menahem Mendel and he held this high position with pride for fifty years and did not fear the attacks of the population. He took care of the community's needs and of everyone who approached him – they knew they would be welcomed and attended to. He was not interested in money and everyone knew that he had "clean" hands.

Rabbi Menahem Mendel was short, resolved in his own views, and called everyone "you" (informal address), was always cleanly dressed, with black polished boots and a walking stick with the silver knob in his hand. They say that because of his speed and motion, the *shamash* (sexton) had difficulty keeping up with him.

In his youth, Rabbi Mendel traveled to the Righteous One of Skvyra (Scowar), left the school of *Hassidut* after a few years, and adhered to the *Mitnagdim* for the rest of his life. His favorite remark was: "I ask only one thing from the Holy One after a hundred and twenty (years): that I may be permitted to see how the Rabbis are facing the real world…" and not for nothing did he object to the appointment of the scholarly *Hassidim* of the town of Kotsk headed by Rabbi Berish, although he bore them no grudge after his appointment was confirmed. Politically, he was Conservative and loyal to the Crown.

Rabbi Menahem Mendel married the daughter of Yitzhak Weisberg of Berdichev and they had one son, Rabbi Hershel of Zhitomir, and one daughter, Mrs. Shifra, who married Rabbi Nisan of Radziwill.

During the First World War, he went to live in Zhitomir to avoid mobilization, but in 1916, the survivors of Dubno Jewry asked him to return to Dubno.

From that time on, he never left the city, not even during the Ukrainian pogroms nor when the city was twice assaulted by the Bolsheviks.

He died in his old age, in the year 1933.

The Chair of the *Rabbanut* was inherited by his son, Rabbi Hershel of Zhitomir, who acted as his father's advisor during the latter's final years.

This might be a good place to say something of the Rabbinical family of Auerbah-Rosenfeld. This family name was Auerbah while Rosenfeld was an addition tacked on to avoid military service. And from where comes the name Auerbah? They say that the patriarch of the family Rabbi Leibush Stanislaw, from the generation of the BESHT the name (the acronym of the Ba'al Shem Tov), had a line of descent from Rashi about whom they say that when his mother was pregnant with him, she passed through the town of Troyes[35] and was walking along a narrow lane when two horsemen suddenly came galloping down the lane endangering her life. She pressed herself against the wall which miraculously created an alcove-like depression deep enough for her to step back out of the way, providing what would seem to be an air-cushion for her protection (evolved into "*Auer-buh*" in Germano-Yiddish). The dynastic record was held by *Rabbanit* Esther-Etta, the wife of Rabbi Simha HaCohen Rappoport of Zhitomir until the First World War.

Rabbi David Tzvi the son of Haim Auerbah-Rosenfeld, who occupied the Chair as Dubno's Rabbi for thirty years, had four sons and each was a scholar of the Torah: Rabbi Menahem Mendel, Father of the Rabbinical court; Rabbi Yitzhak Weisberg of Berdichev; Rabbi Ze'ev-Wolf, Teacher and Expositor in Dubno, and married to a woman from Tetiyiv (Tetiev) in the district of Kiev. They said of him that "Walls melted when he would shake the world with his Day of Atonement prayer of '*Al Het...*'"; Rabbi Leibush, Rabbi ---- Shteibel of Uman, who knew word-for-word by heart 500 pages of the *Gemara* and lived in Chishinau (Kishinev) and Rabbi Tzadok, *Gaon* and with a penetrating mind, Rabbi Elisha Halperin of Uman were also residents in Kishinev.

The Dynasty of the *Gaon*, Rabbi Menahem Mendel Auerbah-Rosenfeld (His Righteousness will Protect us), Father of the Rabbinical court of Dubno.

The dynastic Patriarch was Rabbi Leibush Stanislaw of the generation of the BESHT and he, a male child, Rabbi David Tzvi the Great was born through the legendary intervention of the BESHT himself.

The son of Rabbi David Tzvi the Great was Rabbi Naphtali Hertz, Father of the Rabbinical Court of Halberstadt.

His son was Rabbi Ze'ev Wolf who officiated as the Father of the Rabbinical court of Dubno.

His son was Rabbi Haim Ya'acov who also officiated as father of the Rabbinical court of Dubno. The son-in-law of Rabbi Ze'ev Wolf was Our Teacher and Rabbi David Tzvi Auerbah-Rosenfeld the husband of Sarah Feyga (Z"L).

The son of Rabbi David Tzvi was Rabbi Menahem Mendel Auerbah-Rosenfeld, Father of the Rabbinical court of Dubno for fifty years.

The son of Rabbi Menahem Mendel was Rabbi Heschel of Zhitomir who inherited the Rabbi's position and remained there until the Shoah when he perished together with most of his community.

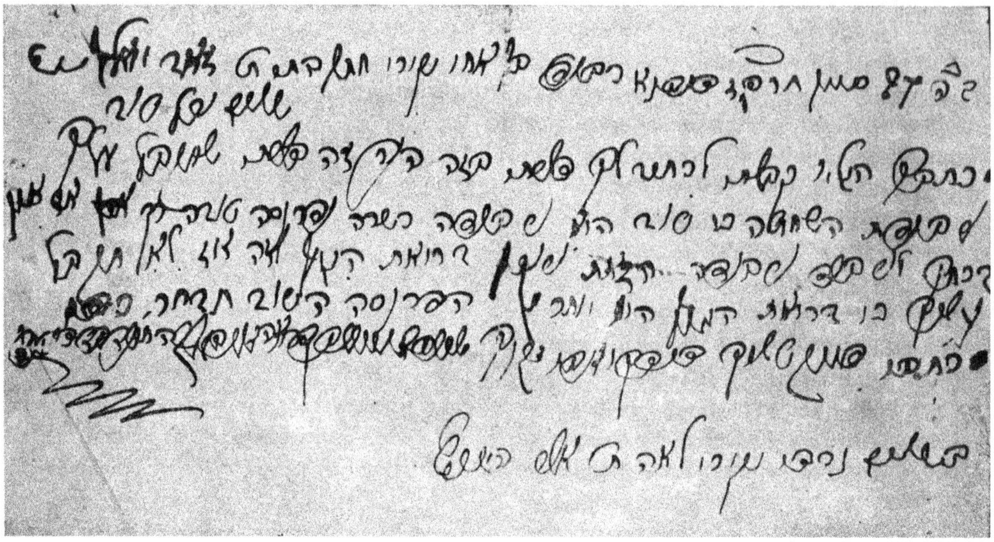

Original Footnotes and Translator's Comments

1. See: https://en.wikipedia.org/wiki/Occasional_poetry.
2. *"Tikunei Sefarim"* is an expression used for scholarly workers who correct perceived biblical errors from creeping into the Holy script, therefore diminishing its authority – see https://en.wikipedia.org/wiki/Tiqqun_soferim
3. You may consider reading this excellent, somewhat esoteric – and subjective – article that gives much more background to this topic and contains much of interest - Trans.: http://www.chareidi.org/archives5760/metzora/features.htm
4. See also the works of Eliezer Steinman about the Dubno Maggid.
5. See the section "The Dubno *Maggid*"
6. An expression denoting apprenticeship, a disciple, devotion to, aiding or otherwise serving a recognized superior, and taken from Kings 2: 3:11 – the Prophet Elisha's "public debut".
7. ADoneinu, MOreinu Rabbeinu" Our Lord, our Teacher, Our Rabbi.
8. According to Hassid Rabbi Gamliel, the son of Rabbi Yehuda Ha-Nasi said: "An excellent thing is the study of the Torah combined with some worldly occupation, for the labor demanded for them both causes sin to be forgotten. All study of the Torah without work must in the end be futile and become the cause of sin." (Ethics of the Fathers 2:2); All those who work with the public will work with them for the sake of Heaven, us and Hassidim, by Dr. S. A. Horodatzki, Part A. Published by Dvir, Tel-Aviv, 1952.
9. See: https://en.wikipedia.org/wiki/Mekhilta.
10. See: https://en.wikipedia.org/wiki/Trumot.
11. "The Thousands of Menashe" a direct reference to Deuteronomy 33:17 q.v.
12. A sect of the Jewish people who do not accept the oral law. see: https://en.wikipedia.org/wiki/Karaite_Judaism.
13. A reference to Chronicles 2:36: 23
14. From all the poems of the Mehalel
15. One of the last three verses. (The previous ones are not shown in the original text, so the full context cannot be illustrated – Trans.).
16. Avraham Dov Levinsohn HaCohen
17. Volume 281, 19/31 December 1894.
18. Isaiah 58:8
19. Ezekiel 43:2
20. Vol. 276, 13/25 November 1894
21. Vol. 273, Petersburg 1898.
22. A member of the Citrus-fruit family, used in ritual during the festival of Succoth
23. "Questions and responsa" Maharam of Lublin.
24. "Gleaning of the Grapes of Ephraim" - a reference to Judges 8:2.
25. Loosely translated as "The Grief over the Daughters of Many," a Eulogy on the Jews, victims in the 1649 massacres in Poland, by Avraham ben Shmuel Ashkenazi, published in 1848.
26. "A New Decryption Decoder" the name of a large number of books published throughout the ages by different scholars designed to assist scholars in understanding all the difficult references in early scholarly works by such luminaries as Maimonides, e.g.
27. Deuteronomy 33:23 (Amsterdam 1698).
28. A shortened title of the original – (a comprehensive book giving clarification of the preparations and rituals for the Sabbath – Trans.).
29. A literal translation of the title but taken basically from Genesis 16:12.
30. Rabbinical Court
31. Taken from Deuteronomy 33:24.
32. See: https://en.wikipedia.org/wiki/Sabbateans.

33. An apparent but slightly paraphrased reference to "Song of Solomon" 4:15.
34. The Song of Solomon 4:4.
35. By all accounts, Rashi was indeed born in Troyes, but this reference to Troyes for the incident is clearly an error on the part of the writer since the legend is well-established as referring to Worms where the "depression" in the wall can still be clearly seen in the sidewall of the Rashi Synagogue and is pointed out by guides. The "horsemen" similarly is a carriage in most accounts – Trans.

H. The Government-Appointed Rabbis of Dubno

Translated from Hebrew by Selwyn Rose

Due to the lack of sources, it is not possible to prepare a complete and definitive list of the official, government-appointed Rabbis who officiated in Dubno. The registry given here was scoured from the Hebrew press beginning from the '60's of the 19ᵗʰ Century.

1862	The first appointed Rabbi in Dubno Mr. Shpetlezahn (Adar 'A' 1862).
1870–1874	A. Bornstein, the son-in-law of Avraham bar Gotlober.
1875–1878	Rabbi Meir Pesis the grandfather of Rabbi Pinhas Pesis. Author of the book "The Town of Dubno and her Rabbis".
1878–1882	Rabbi H. Z. Margoliot, Author of "Greater Dubno".
1882–1893	Rabbi Shalom Meierzahn.
1894–1902	Rabbi Pinhas bar Yeshaya bar Meir Pesis.
1902–1911	Rabbi H. Z. Margoliot.
1911–1914	Rabbi Sacher.
1914–1920	"Interregnum" – First World War – No Rabbi was installed.
1920–1942	Rabbi Tzvi Hirsch, may G-d avenge his blood, the son of the Rabbi and Father of the rabbinical court, Rabbi Mendele Rosenfeld, May his Righteousness be remembered for a Blessing.

I. Dubno Mirrored in the Press

Translated from Hebrew by Selwyn Rose

The many changes that began to take place in Europe half-way through the 19ᵗʰ Century, found echoes in the demographics of Jewish society and they may be readily seen reflected in the Jewish press of the time. To our regret, we are unable to present here examples of the newspapers since they are not available here in the country.

We are forced therefore to be satisfied with Hebrew journals and magazines that began to appear in the second half of the century in Eastern Europe and we will try to extract from them typical material on Dubno and its Jewish community:

a. *"Ha-Magid* "which began to appear in Ełk (Lyk), East Prussia, in 1857, edited by Eliezer Lipman Zilberman.

b. *"Ha-Melitz"* which began to appear in Odessa in 1861 edited by Eliezer Zederbaum-Erez.

c. *"Ha-Tsfira* "which began to appear in Warsaw in 1862, edited by Haim Zelig Slonimski (Hazas).

Before we bring the items from the Hebrew periodicals, we will introduce two pieces of information that appeared in the Polish press at the end of the 18ᵗʰ Century that touch on Dubno:

The "Warsaw Gazette" issue 56 from 1782 reports that when two young princes of the Lubomirski family entered Dubno, they were greeted at the gates of the town by Jewish youths dressed in their finest, who showered them with flowers.

In the "Craiova (Krajowa) Foreign Correspondent" that was published in Warsaw from the 13ᵗʰ April 1793 it was reported that the Dubno community had gone bankrupt because of non-payment of dues to the Polish government.

*

Ha-Melitz No. 10 and 12 (second year) (3/17 October 1861)

Excerpts from an article on Dubno signed with the name "Shohad Tuvtam" (Tzvi Greenberg, a.k.a. Vladimir Feodorov).

And so, I see that our town Dubno, although a town that in age and wisdom can compete with the other large and respected towns in our country, has thus far had nothing befitting written about her ------- two, are her highly honored qualities, one is graciousness and forgiveness, the second is *Torah* and wisdom. And in righteous pride, Greater Dubno can boast in the presence of all the cities of Volhynia that she is the "grandmother" of wisdom; she is the town that has entwined within her *Torah* and charitable graciousness, productivity.

Already some decades ago, at a time when heavy clouds rested upon Volhynia, a bright star shone over the town of Dubno and her skies were filled with the glowing light of knowledge --- out of which shone the wise and divine grammarian Rabbi Shlomo who was like a brother with our Master, Moshe ben Menahem Mendelsohn and close to the great expositor and legendary teller of fables, who was nicknamed "the Jewish Æsop" (Rabbi Ya'acov Krantz), and apart from these wise men there were many more --- knowledgeable in grammar and logic and among them especially the rest of the academic subjects: algebra, engineering and mathematics, like the fiery *Gaon*, Rabbi Eliezer (Z"L), from Kałuszyn (Kalushin) and from among his students, the wise Rabbi Nahman Tzvi Linder. They all stood like a fortified wall against the scourge now sweeping throughout Volhynia, namely the *Hassidic* Movement that had engulfed all the regions of that county --- until it reached the town of Dubno in the mouths of ne'er-do-wells, the *Hassidic* Rabbis, saying as a taunt: "Dubno the rejected and sinful town" ---

Our town was the first town in the county to establish a school for Jewish girls, standing as a fortress for three years, programmed and built by someone born in our town, the wise magnificent Berman.

Who will speak of the donors, the greatest and richest of our town ever since it *was* a town! Until today the poor of our town eat the fruit of their charity, all of them left behind them blessings: stone-built homes, shops, canopies, leaving them permanently for charity to be for the needy of our town.

Study houses, thirteen in number, apart from the Great Synagogue from the point of view of its income, was plenty ---
Who would not wonder at charitable deeds performed with wisdom and knowledge --- by the town notable Our Teacher and Rabbi Zadok Marshalkowycz (Z"L) ---

For he gave much money to the lords of the town during the days of the respected Prince Michael Lubomirski who undertook and promised that he would donate several hundred trees from his estate's trees every winter, to the needy poor of the town ---

The hospital stands on an ugly and dirty street. The students of the *Talmud Torah*[1] usually playing boisterously, poorly clothed and bare-foot on the streets. And why don't they unite the Talmud Torah with the exalted government school? Why are house owners ashamed to send their sons to the school? Why do they send their daughters to the school and their sons to the dark *Haderim*[2] to be educated? –

[Columns 101–102]

*

Ha-Melitz No. 23 (8/20 March 1862)

A poem about Dubno in the dispute surrounding Hassidut and the Haskala by S.M.R. Mandelkern

Verse A	O, beautiful daughter of Dubno: In flight at night Limb and courage displayed And performing valor…
Verse C	Palace of the gods A house made with planning There where the waves Are struck into drops
Verse D	Many were they as perfect To hold fast to the way they saw Consumed in the blazing fires Defiled, defiled they cried.
Verse I	And beautiful daughter of Dubno After she stood at birth She shone and gathered together She cried and fell:
Verse M	Ha! O, honored wisdom Wonders came down The wretched senselessness Arose ever upwards…

Ha-Melitz (1/13 14th Iyar 1865)

--- The residents of Dubno bought an imposing, elegant house in a clean street and dedicated it for use as a hospital, adorned with a surrounding garden for the inmates to enjoy to their heart's content. ---

Ha-Magid issue No. 18, 14th Iyar (18.5.1865)

That town that from the beginning was known for its many wise men, writers, knowledgeable in *Torah* --- in recent times --- became much impoverished. Also today the remainders of earlier generations have been lost to her with the passing of the surviving member of the magnificent Berets family who was conveyed to his grave, the righteous modest *Gaon*, famous for his respected writings our Teacher and Rabbi Tzvi Hirsch Rappoport --- who added clarifications to the book of Leviticus called "Guide for the Priests" --- Our town Dubno lost in him a force for righteousness, a warm-hearted, modest, loving man, a searcher for peace who left no one comparable to follow on.

Ha-Tsfira (6th September 1875)

On September 11th last year, in the periodical "*Ha-Tsfira*" the teacher H. Shansis called to the attention of readers in Dubno to consider with some seriousness the intention to erect a school in which their children will learn language, literature, *Torah* and good manners - all in order to become good citizens. It was a "voice crying in the wilderness."

A few months later the scholar Gotlober, who lived at the time in Dubno, awoke to the idea and requested a license from the authorities to open a school with two classes for the Jewish youth and when he received the license, he posted announcements on the synagogue walls hoping that the parents will send their children to the school. But the "unenlightened" zealots tore down the announcements from the walls of the synagogue and poured from their full bitter cup of wine their punishment, erasing his dreams; the school was not opened ---

The writer concludes:

If you recite the weekly passage of the *Torah* and the daily page of the *Gemara,* shouldn't H. Gotlober and the teacher also have a part to play in this? --- wake up dear brothers, lest you wait too long.

A Guest invited to Stay[3]

100

*

Ha-Magid (8.9.1875) in a letter by A.B. Gotlober:

I said the residents of my town will be pleased --- that I have the authority to open a school to bring success to the children of their parents with the *Torah* of G-d and the tradition from the hand of G-d for the good I will yet do, for I will teach them the language of the Land of Israel --- and not one of the residents of the town have come to me and asked that his son be taken into my school and have me spread my wings over him ---

Is this really the town Dubno that more than forty years ago, when I came in the days of my youth, the youngsters of our people came running to me from every direction and asked to learn *Torah* from me? And in those days, there was the honored sage, Rabbi Ze'ev Adelson (Z"L) who taught many students...

*

Ha-Tsfira No. 47 (6ᵗʰ September 1876/77)

--- Last night 250 wounded soldiers were brought here to Dubno from the battlefield.

All the officers and clerks, the local police commissioner and the general, rushed to the

[Columns 103–104]

railyard to greet them sympathetically. The whole route was illuminated with oil lamps and whatever else could be used as torches...

The Senior Officer in charge honored each and every one of them with a glass of wine and tea, cake and a cigarette. All the townspeople welcomed them as well --- the respected resident Mr. Itche Halbirt presented five hundred cigarettes. The excellent scholar, Rabbi Lazar Shreier of Viliya donated sugar. The scholar Rabbi Yisrael Leib Gilberg donated two kilograms of tea and 3 rubles.

Chaim Asher Bernstein Born in Dubno.

*

Ha-Tsfira No. 16-18 (18/30 April 1878)

--- The mists and fogs of woefulness placed upon Greater Dubno a deep feeling of mourning --- on the second day of Passover the Lord poured out his anger on our town and early in the morning, a fire broke out. Within two hours over two hundred shops were devoured in their entirety by the flames down to their foundations together with the contents thereof and also many homes were fuel for the hungry flames with no one to save them --- how extensive and widespread was the confusion that occurred as the fire broke out and swallowed everything in its path --- people ran naked from their home leaving behind them everything they possessed, without food to sustain their souls --- the value of the damage was estimated at 500,000 rubles. ---- Blessings upon the heads of our brethren and the charitable organizations in the neighboring towns like Rowno, Lutsk, Rodvil (Radyvyliv), and others --- who sent matzot and potatoes and piled up money for the desperate and destitute burnt out of their homes and possessions. The notable and known scholar Rabbi Meir Chomsky will be remembered for his good deeds for he advised the towns immediately by telegraph to arouse themselves and support their brethren ---

Written in a spirit of sadness ---–

Zeinvyl Safian

*

Ha-Melitz (1878)

We are informed from Dubno, Kobryn (Kobrin) and other towns that our brethren will welcome with bread and salt and much happiness the battalions as heroes returning from their war with Bulgaria and the Balkans ---

*

Ha-Tsfira No. 33 (Elul 1881)

Wednesday 17th Av. The minister who had always been known as a fervent humanist and lover of mankind in general and the "Children of Israel" in particular was gathered unto his people. When storms gathered over the heads of our brethren in Russia, the General was there to cover us and secure our safety preventing anyone from harming us. We who dwelt in the town of Dubno owed him our respect and were not ungrateful to him and we eulogized him together with our Christian brethren.

We did the noble gentleman much honor and the whole town accompanied him to the railroad station, from where he was taken to be buried with his fathers in Moscow. His name will never be erased from our hearts. May he rest in peace.

Akiva Cohen Rappoport

*

Ha-Melitz **(1882) 1st Nisan (9/21. 3.1882)**

Dubno 12 Adar. ---- In our town we were called upon to pray to G-d on the Fast of Esther and plead with Him to soften the government's heart; the Government Rabbi Shalom Meirzahn prayed with the congregation in his services in the Baratz synagogue and all the people cried in sorrow for their brethren (the pogroms of 1881).

--- During those few days the scholar Haim Ashkenazi took the initiative and organized a collection of money to clothe and feed the people of our town and to train them for work---and until today, five youngsters are trained at a school for artisans. The Lord acts and does good for his people. ---

*

***Ha-Melitz*,** **6th Tishrei (7/19.9.1882)**

--- Our town – considered a tower of scholarship was also struck in the last two weeks by a plague --- it was a case of the "Four prime causes of injury"[4]

    A. The holy Rabbi Shlomo Malek
    B. Hanka
    C. Son of the Rabbi of Rodvil (the son of Rabbi Mordecai)
    D. The last but not least - an anonymous boy from Galicia.

The first gained from his disciples more than 1000 silver rubles---

After him, Hanka and the son of Rabbi from Rodvil who extracted no less than 500 silver rubles. The fate of the Galician boy was very bad --- for him they waited another day---

Didn't the people of the town do well --- to repair the destroyed hospital and build a hostel for the poor? ---

Halevi

*

Ha-Tsfira **issue 28 (1883)**

A "voice crying in the wilderness" for the esteemed liturgist A.B. Gotlober whose condition was desperate after losing his source of sustenance.

[Columns 105–106]

----------Have we no generous hearted donors? Every donation will be sent towards forwarding the publication of "Hymns of Praise", the least considered as great as the greatest.

The donors' money will be forwarded to his dwelling place in Dubno to the hands of the esteemed poet in Dubno, Rabbi Meir Chomsky.

P.S. I have added here Dubno and the publication of "Hymns of Praise" more than fifty silver rubles placed in the hands of the above esteemed notable.

H. Margolit.

*

Ha-Tsfira (4/16.1.1883)

On the day of the coronation of his Imperial Majesty, the Mayor and his advisors and H. Kahana collected 225 rubles to provide lunches for two battalions garrisoned here.

H. Zukerman

*

Ha-Melitz No. 83 15ᵗʰ Heshvan (16.10.1884)

Yesterday, 8ᵗʰ MarHeshvan here in Dubno we celebrated with the greatest possible "pomp and circumstance" the one-hundredth birthday of the lover of Israel and great philanthropist, Sir Moses Montefiore.

  After a congratulatory telegram was sent, a large crowd gathered in the synagogue in celebration. The distinguished *Torah* and G-d-fearing scholar, the respected Rabbi and notable Rav-Rabbi Shalom Meirzahn preached a sermon before the congregation on the events of the day and after presenting his sermon, the government appointed Rabbi, the learned scholar Rav-Rabbi H. Z Margolit spoke. The synagogue Cantor Rav-Rabbi Ya'acov-Ya'akel son of the well-known Cantor, Rav-Rabbi Yeruham of Berdichev blessed the righteous Knight and wished him a long life and the congregation all answered, "Amen!"

A.B. Gotlober

*

Ha-Melitz No. 3, 6th Shevat (11/23.1.1885)

From Dubno comes an announcement that on Saturday night a fire broke out in the Baratz Study House. The fire consumed it and two other houses. A Scroll of the Law was also lost to the flames. The Christians and army officers together made strenuous efforts to contain and quench the fire.

*

Ha-Melitz Wednesday 22ⁿᵈ Elul, (10/21.9.1886)

---------------It is not heroic that a few Jewish families are travelling from here to the New World (America) and a few other families are also preparing to sail across the ocean in the coming days.

Ya'acov

105

Ha-Melitz 21ˢᵗ **Kislev, (1890)**

---The idea of resettlement of our Holy Land, that of itself had smoothed pathways into many towns in Israel did not find its way into our town. The collection-bowls placed in every synagogue --- with my own eyes, I saw that the wealthy and respected tycoons were not in a hurry to donate the five kopeks. Also, in the matter of the revival of our sacred language found little support among our few intelligentsia ----

Dubno resident.

*

Ha-Melitz **issue 94 (1894)**

Dubno 25ᵗʰ Nisan. The seventieth birthday of our *Gaon* the first of the "Lovers of Zion" ADMOR Rabbi Shmuel Mogilever, the "Light of Israel", Father of the *Beit Din* Bialystok, was, for us, the "*Hovevey Zion*" of Dubno a festival in every sense of the word. As evening arrived, we all gathered in the great Baratz *Beit Ha-Midrash* and the sagacious and esteemed advisor, chief delegate "*Hovev*" in our town Zalman Ashkenazi, preached a deeply moving and soul-stirring appreciation of the spirit of the times clarifying the immensity of the "Man of the Hour" for the good of the settlement of the Land of Israel from the first moment of the birth of the idea up until the present day.

, How ennobled and pleasant were his words and their content! And what testimony from Jewish history, for every idea was beautiful and correct and in true and honest perspective; he found and presented the great among our people and our sages from each generation – even from within the lands of the strangers, he toiled and suffered to implant them in the Garden of our Faith. So many times, he spoke of the concept of "Lovers of Zion" and the purity of his faith for the whole House of Israel.

We send today, on his seventieth birthday this congratulatory epistle of blessings and tribute to the celebrant, signed by all the notables of our town together with a "Poem of Gold" composed by the sagacious poet H. Ashkenazi. There was also a sum of money provided… to plant an "etrog[5] garden" in the Holy Land as an eternal memorial to his name.

Michal Burstein

*

Ha-Melitz (1894)

(Dubno) With much pomp and splendor, the *Hovevey Zion* in our town today, the 12th Tammuz celebrated the seventieth birthday of the venerable elderly gentleman, the gracious philanthropist, Kalman Ze'ev Wyzotsky. The event took place in the evening in the home of the wise and excellent author, H. Zalman Ashkenazi --- and presented just one of the thousand noble contributions – that of the school in Jaffa.

The Cantor Rabbi Meir Teitelman delighted his audience with his renderings.

[Columns 107–108]

*

Ha-Melitz issue 210, Elul, 1894

A crate of etrogs arrived in Dubno for Rabbi Menahem Mendel Oyrbah, Father of the *Beit Din* of our town and they are wonderful. Z. Ashkenazi sent to Odessa for some Palestinian wine. It is hoped that the collection-bowls will reflect everyone's appreciation…

Pinhas Pesis

*

Ha-Melitz issue 237, Heshvan, 1894

(Dubno). The collection-bowls that were placed everywhere on the evening of *Yom Kippur* were successful. Libelous pamphlets and the failing, unsuccessful "*Ha-Havazelet*" paper were sent in their hundreds, if not thousands, to all the Jewish settlements of the Children of Israel yet not one arrived in our town because there was no place in our town for the irreverent writings of the "poorly clothed just for the sake of appearances"[a] because of Rabbi and Father of the *Beit Din* Rabbi Menahem Mendel Oyrbah and the Righteous Teacher Rabbi Moshe Halevi Rubinstein (author of the book "*Elef Hamagen*" – "A Thousand Defend" – and "*Klilat HaMenorah*" – a study book on the *Talmud*), among the *Hovevey Zion*. That year many new members joined the support committee in Odessa. *Hovevey Zion* here wait every day for olive oil to arrive from the Holy Land that has been despatched directly from Jaffa and the delegate Rabbi Zalman Ashkenazi will send to it the towns of Kremenets and Rowno for lighting the *Hanukah candles*---

*

Ha-Melitz issue 261, 1894

(Dubno). The *Hovevey Zion* is continuing to grow and spread in our town and has had great success and made an impressive reputation comparing itself favorably with all the bigger towns. The love of our holy language is growing from day-to-day to the extent that even the girls are beginning to like it and its literature – sadly because only two competent teachers of the language exist here ---

*

Ha-Melitz issue 267, 1896

(Dubno). Yesterday, the fifth day of *Hanukah*, *Hovevey Zion*, under license from the town authorities, celebrated in magnificent style the success of the Maccabean Revolt. Members of the *Hovevey Zion* from other towns came to celebrate together with us: Zhitomir – Mrs. Fleicher, from Kremenets, Doctor Litvak and Mr. Tzvi Prelutsky, from Rowno, Mr. Rubinstein and Mr. Hershtein - and others. At 9 o'clock in the evening all the invitees gathered together - about 200 people in the large hall belonging to H. Berger and the celebration began. The synagogue Cantor and his choir sang "God Save the King" in honor of the Tsar and the Hebrew song "These Candles…". After that, Mr. Z Ashkenazi spoke of the rise of the Movement's ideology and its history - in raising the spirits of the people. After a recess, Mr. Prelutsky spoke of the four rebirths of Israel – the first after Babylonian exile that was completed during the period of the Hasmoneans. After that Doctor Litvak and H. Rubinstein spoke --- wine-glasses were raised to praise Mr. Ashkenazi, the organizer of the festival and to the above speakers and all the leaders of the *Hovevey Zion* and the pioneers of the resettlement of the Land. Mrs. Fleicher raised a glass honoring the girls of Zion who were learning their holy language. After, all began singing zionist songs with delight until dawn.

*

Ha-Melitz, 28th Nisan 1897

(Dubno). On the Festival of Passover, the notables of our town celebrated the event to the full measure of the commandment "Holidays, festivals and seasons are for rejoicing!" according to the Jewish culture. Virtually every member of the Jewish "supporters of the workers of the Holy Land" came to the home of the community representative H. Ashkenazi where they were welcomed with a celebratory glass of wine from the vineyards of our Holy Land "Rehovot and Hermon", taking much spiritual pleasure to hear from his earlier words, spoken with emotion, as an enlivening and at one and the same time, eloquently poetical speech on the documentation of the festivals of Israel and awoke in the hearts and ears of his gathered audience a love of Zion and all the holy ones of the nation.

---In his honor, those gathered collected for the benefit of the toilers on the land the sum of 22 silver rubles --- and may it be pleasing to the organizer and those gathered and may the work of their hands be strengthened and blessed. Selah.

Joel Friedman

*

Ha-Melitz, 17ᵗʰ Sivan 1897

(Dubno). On the first day of the Festival of Shavuot, Mr. Z Ashkenazi spoke on a theme taken from chapter three of "Ethics of the Fathers" penetrating deep into the soul of all who were gathered there. After which the members of the *Hovevey Zion* who were present offered up a toast in tribute to Baron Rothschild, the committee in Odessa and the farmers in Palestine. Here I express gratitude to our honorable delegate, Mr. Z. Ashkenazi for his toil and his dedication both materially and spiritually to the ideology of resettlement.

P. Pesis

*

Ha-Tsfira, issue 201 1901

From Dubno comes the announcement via H.A. Bernstein that the residents recently celebrated the ritual sanctification of a new Holy Ark for the synagogue. It is the handiwork of the artistic master-craftsman Wolf Sirkis who devoted an entire year to its creation. Beautiful to behold it is indeed a work of art demonstrating only too clearly the creative and professional competence of its maker.

Those taking part in the consecration ceremony were the congregation and donors together with senior official citizens of the town, President of the town, his deputy and senior clerks.

A List of Journalists of Dubno Writers in Newspapers and periodicals

Newspaper	Year	Journalist
Ha-Melitz	1861	Ze'ev Woolf Neimark; Tzvi Greenberg.
	1862	Sh. Mandelkern.
Ha-Magid	1865	Leibush Steinberg.
Ha-Tsfira	1875	Arieh Leib Scheintziz.
	1877	Haim Asher Bernstein.
	1878	Zeinvil Sapien.
Ha-Melitz	1878	Yoel Albert.
Ha-Tsfira	1879	Yoel Albert; H Margoliot.
	1881	Akiva Cohen Rappoport.
Ha-Melitz	1882	Halevi.
Ha-Tsfira	1883	S. Zukerman; Eliezer Lippa Rokach.
	1884	Yachaz (?)
Ha-Melitz	1884	Shimon Bernstein; Eliezer Lippa Rokach
	1886	Ya'acov Heilman
	1887	Marnanan (?)
	1890	Dubna
	1894	Michael Burstein; Pinhas Pesis
	1896	Ben-Amram; Yabaz (?); David Lewittan.
	1897	Yoel Friedman; P. Pesis.
Ha-Tsfira	1901	A. Gaski; H.A. Bernstein

An announcement from the "Wolhiner Leben" 1924–1925

Dubno. A town resident Mr. Sh. Horwitz donated a building that contained a cinema and hall for various performances as a present in the founding of a professional school for deprived and needy children. Although Mr. Horwitz is known in our town for his generosity, many were surprised by this pleasant act and he is promised wide-spread acknowledgement of his generous donation.

7th December, 1924

Thanks to Mr. Levinsohn, our delegate to the Sejm, the orphanage that had been administratively closed on order by the hospital three years ago, has now been returned to the hands of the Department of Nursing. As of now, major refurbishment operations are being undertaken to prepare it for use in its original function for the local orphans.

Y.L.
18th November 1924.

*

Dubno. 9th December. A celebration took place at the premises of the Artisans' Bank marking two years since its foundation. Attorney Pinhosowitz, Chairman of the management, briefly explained to the people gathered there, the importance of the event: "This institution that was established two years ago with a capital of 70,000 marks developed in the desired direction and today the value is 4,000 gulden as share value and several hundreds of gulden as investments. The first loans earned 500 marks and today we have out on loan about 11,816 gulden. The Bank, which suffered in 1923 from a loss, has now achieved a clear profit of 1,227 gulden. The speech ended with an expression of the opinion that a bright future awaited the Bank and that the Bank will continue to offer help to small traders and artisans. Those gathered greeted his words enthusiastically.

Mr. Hamish proposed that the Society of Artisans acknowledge and express gratitude, while the treasurer, Mr. Zimmerman spoke widely on various activities of the Bank.

Additional compliments were added by Mr. Zaiger, a manager, and the gentlemen Streiger, Tauwster, Gitleman, Korin, Barkowsky, Leizman, Plauder and others. The meeting ended in high spirits.

Ya'acov Semigran
19th December 1924.

Translator's Comments

1. Religious Hebrew primary school for the younger pupils, usually until about the age of 13.
2. *Hader* (-im pl.) – a class-room in a typical *Talmud Torah*
3. This was the title of a book written by S.Y. Agnon and published in the 1930's
4. Taken from the Mishnah Bava Kamma -1 Sefaria "There are four primary causes of injury and damages…"
5. An etrog is a member of the citrus family, similar to a lemon and is traditionally used during the autumn "Festival of Booths", (Succoth) as one of "The Four Species".
6. A free translated interpretation of the original Hebrew text taken from Zachariah 13:4 – (see also the preceding verse3)

J. From the Pinkas [Record Book] of the Dubno community

Translated from Hebrew by Jerrold Landau

Parts of this chapter can also be found in the Yiddish section (columns 577–582).

We find written in the *Zohar*, "Everything depends on luck, even the *Torah* scroll in the sanctuary." – and luck indeed was on our side. For the Jews of Dubno decided to transfer a precious remnant of the past to Jerusalem even before the Nazi Holocaust – the list and memories of things of more than 250 years ago, when the community of Dubno was connected to the greater Polish Jewry – the Community Journal of Dubno.

In his book "Greater Dubno" Rabbi H. Z. Margolis, the government appointed Rabbi of Dubno, writes that he had access to the Communal Journal from the days of the Preacher (*Maggid*) Rabbi Ya'acov Krantz, already during the 1890s. In it was written about a decision to raise the salary of the *Maggid* to two zloty per week. This Journal, "with all the other ledgers and communal manuscripts" went up in flames during the great fire, in which a third of the houses of the city were burnt on 18 *Iyar* 5655 (1895).

However, it was not only the great fire of 5655 that destroyed the "ledgers and communal manuscripts." The ledgers of the *Chevra Kadisha* (burial society), which were maintained in the city until the middle of the 19th century, and included "the enactments and customs of the society, and the procedures for the feasts that were conducted at specific times[1], as well as the memorial list of events that took place in the city" was confiscated by the government in the wake of the bitter battle that broke out within the *Chevra Kadisha* in the year 5610 (1850). The ledger was not returned to the *Chevra Kadisha*, and H. Z. Margolis testified, "When I met the court prosecutor at the beginning of the 40s of their counting[2] (the 1890s, about 40 years after the outbreak of the dispute) I asked him, "Why have you not returned the ledgers of the society to us, and where are they now?" He responded, "The ledger was condemned to be burnt as a piece of evidence of no value."

However, one volume from the ancient Jewish archives, *Pinkas Dubno*, which was transferred to the National Library in Jerusalem in the year 5697 (1937), contains

113

original authentic material. This volume has 177 large–size pages (text footnote: consisting of 354 folios), and is bound with old leather. Its reference number in the National Library is Heb. 40 – 349 M.S. 382.

The ordering of entries in the *Pinkas Hakehillot Dubno* is not chronological through the page numbering, indicating that the "compilers" or article writers in the ledger did not write the entries in accordance with a straightforward historical style, but rather incidentally as the events took place, or in the best–case scenario in accordance with the year alone. This led to no small amount of confusion amongst the researchers and scholars who quote citations from the ledger.

[Column 112]

In any case, the Ledger of the Community of Dubno is a fruitful treasury of historical–sociological material. We will include typical sections of the life of the community from it, as written, but organized in chronological order with modern script and punctuation.

*

The ledger opens in the year 5475 (1716) with an unsigned article stating that the heads of the community who "sit in the ranks" have reached a decision "to enact enactments on which the world will stand," however "for unknown reasons there was not enough time to complete the task." For it is now impossible, since we have been completely surrounded, as if with swarm bees[3]..." This was because in that year (5475 or 5476) a court case took place in Dubno concerning two women from Vitebsk and Malecz who had converted to Judaism and were sentenced to death by burning. The verdict was carried out[4].

The scribe of the city of Dubno writes on page 49, folio a.:
"Since every institution, building, and situation in the community is dependent on the foundation of the charter of each and every community, it is very clear, and as the sages have said, "If there is no vineyard, there is no boundary." – the opposite is also true: "if there is no boundary, etc.; and since everything is dependent on the lions of the society who sit in the ranks, with proper and complete agreement, to enact enactments upon which the world, our community, may it continue, shall stand, and for unknown reasons there was no time to complete the work, and it is now impossible to wait due to the tribulations that have surrounded us like a swarm of bees… And in places where it has been said we should shorten, we have no right to elongate: they agreed around the pure table to be patient, and to wait until next *Cheshvan*, may it come upon us for the good, to make the enactments. Until the time comes to make the enactments, the original ones will remain in force as appropriate, without even one

point falling away. They will remain in place, with no one disputing them. To further strengthen the matters, we have come to sign: today is the 17th (day), since the good light has been put in place, 19th *Iyar*[5]."

The instructions to maintain modesty during religious festive meals, found on page 57, folio b, were copied there by the scribe in the year 5479 (1719) from the Ledgers of the Council of the Four Lands, and rendered appropriate for the needs of the community of Dubno:

"The Council of the Four Lands opens with curses and castigations from the leaders of the Four Lands, may they continue to exist well, regarding festive meals in which literally more than a fifth goes to waste. We have already shouted out about this on several occasions, so we now come to make an enactment that is not to be changed.

[Column 113]

One whose assessment is a large coin[4] has the permission to invite two *minyanim* [i.e. 20 people] over and above the Rabbi and head of the rabbinical court, mediator, monthly administrator, cantor, and one beadle based on lottery. The celebrant has the right to register whomever he wants, even several *minyanim*, and the beadle will determine by lot the two *minyanim*, and not one person more. Someone whose assessment is greater than a large coin has the rights to invite three *minyanim* [i.e. 30 people] in accordance with the above procedure, over and above the Rabbi and head of the rabbinical court, mediator, monthly administrator, and one beadle in accordance with the aforementioned lottery. Someone whose assessment is greater than two large coins has the right to invite even four *minyanim*, aside from the aforementioned obligations, but no more. This is even the case for someone whose assessment is ten Polish large coins. For every large coin, the celebrant has the right to invite two respectable poor people. The regulation is the same for a circumcision, a wedding, or any other religious festive celebration.

All the above has been issued by us with the participation of the honorable Rabbi, the great luminary, the head of the rabbinical court, and head of the *Yeshiva*. It should not be changed by even one small iota, and should be maintained with full force, as is registered in this ledger on *Nisan* 1, 5479 of our calendar.

We have not come to block or to explain that which is written on the other page, with several points, as is explained in the older enactments – that is the enactments explained in this ledger that were enacted on *Rosh Chodesh Sivan* 5477 (1717) – that someone who has had one honor is not entitled to another honor that same week, even if there are other feasts that week.

Thus, is spoken by the aforementioned Yehoshua Heshel, who lives here in the community of Greater Dubno.

Signed: Mordecai the son of Rabbi Shimon (Z"L).[7]

Signed: Tzvi Hirsch the son of Rabbi Yisrael Katz, the memory of the holy ones should be a blessing.

Signed: Shmuel the son of Rabbi Shimon the Levite."

Regarding the enactments to organize education in the community and designating who is fitting to teach, the number of students that each teacher is permitted to teach, the amount of tuition, and the penalties for anyone violating these enactments, the scribe writes as follows in the year 5501 (1741) on page 68, folio a:

"Since the work of G–d is being cheated, regarding cases where teachers of children have not learned properly[8], who do everything in the name of money, who aggrandize and adorn themselves to increase their salary and to take on too many students, a large number of students for increasing their own honor,

[Column 114]

who puff themselves up by enlarging the number of students to increase their income – we have come to make the following restrictions, among which are:

Those teachers should follow the explanation of *Tosafot*[9] that one should not take on more than ten students, and that their salary should be 15 *adomim* (a type of gold coin) for a term, and no more. Those who teach only *Gemara* [i.e. higher–level teachers] may take on fifteen students, and their salary shall be 200 zloty and no more. The primary teachers may take on 25 students, and their salary may be 150 zloty and no more. It is completely forbidden for the teachers to take on too many students, or to have a salary larger than the aforementioned amounts. Every teacher is obligated to bring a roster of his students in writing to the chief and monthly administrator two weeks after the start of the term. If a teacher is found to violate the enactments and falsify his roster, he will be punished with harsh punishments for violating our decree. The fathers of the students must pay tuition on a monthly basis. If the tuition is not paid for one month, the teacher has the right to expel the son from his *Heder*. It is forbidden for any teacher to violate any of the aforementioned in his *Heder*. This has been determined and set by the group of leaders and chiefs of the community, with the participation of the honorable Rabbi, luminary, head of the rabbinical court and *Yeshiva*, may his lights shine.

Signed: Yitzhak Moshe Kahana of Greater Dubno.

Signed: Yitzhak Dovber the Levite.

Signed: Avraham the son of Rabbi Yosef, may the memory of the holy be blessed.

Signed: Yosef the son of Rabbi Ezriel, may the memory of the holy be blessed.

Signed: Menahem Minis the son of the leader Rabbi Avigdor of blessed memory."

Special enactments regarding modesty in dress and jewelry were enacted in 5507 (1747) during the reign of King August III. The evaluation that was done at that time for tax purposes indicated that there were 170 Jewish "houses" in Dubno, and 1,923 individuals. These enactments were written by the scribe on page 93, folio a. The preface indicates that it is "A time of tribulation for Jacob [i.e., for the Jews"[10].

"It is a time of tribulation for Jacob, trouble for his stormy sister[11], groping like a blind person in the dark, and we continue to be diminished like sheep brought to slaughter. He placed me as the main wanderer amongst the nations, the hand of fate is upon us like a wanton person in the desert, and it would be appropriate for us to remove our decorations, wear sackcloth, and place ashes upon our heads, upon the nation holy to G–d that has fallen to the sword. We have opened our eyes to this, and have become diligent regarding the enactments of our townsfolk that we not be a source of jealousy among the nations in which we live during this bitter exile.

This is what has come from us, the chosen ones from amongst the people, the leaders and chiefs of the community, both new and old, in cooperation with the exceptional individuals, everyone agreed unanimously, without one absent,

[Column 115]

all have accepted it upon themselves and upon their children, to fulfil all that has emanated from us, without omitting a single thing.[12]

a. The daughters of our city are forbidden to wear on weekdays any silk clothing, with the exception of vests, bodices, and short jackets which may be made of silk, as well as of old *partur*[13], as long as they have no covering of silver or gold. Of course, the rest of the weekday clothing must have no covering of silver or gold – whether the jacket, dress, or kerchief. However, *pasiman*[13] vests, which have few silver or gold threads, are permitted on weekdays, and it is permitted to encircle the weekday dress with the aforementioned *pasiman* one time.

b. They should not wear any *shlamin*[13] clothing, fox furs, or other furs from foxes. However, it is permitted to put these at the bottom of their Sabbath clothing. One can have such furs on their weekday clothing, but from now on it is not permitted to make new fox furs unless they are worth less than four gold coins – that means that the entire garment, from top to bottom, with that fur, must all not be worth more than approximately four gold coins.

c. Newly made Sabbath and holiday clothing is permitted to be made simply, without gold or silver ornaments; but it is forbidden to make new *dreit*,[13] damask, *partur*[13] satin, or velvet. A person who already has clothing of *dreit* or damask is permitted to wear such on Sabbath and holidays, but they should not be decorated with any gold or silver. And satin, silk, and *partur*, even old, are forbidden on Sabbath and festivals. Also, vests and jackets and bodices are permitted, even decorated ones. On Sabbath and festivals, at a festive meal of a circumcision or wedding on a weekday, it is permitted to wear Sabbath and holiday clothing, as mentioned earlier.

d.   It is not permitted to wear any type of jewelry, gold and pearls and precious stones, including the headscarf, into which decorations have been placed, even fake ones, and it should not be worth more than five gold coins. An earring with a ruby is permitted, without anything dangling. It is forbidden to hang even one pearl. Corals are permitted, but there should not be any jewelry or decorative hanging, even fake ones.

e.   Unmarried girls are permitted to wear anything, and the abovementioned decrees do not apply to them until after they get married. This is what the jewelry of the unmarried girl should be: a chain with a value of not more than five gold coins, a *binda*[13] with pearls with decorations, and a *konik*[13], and nothing more. Also, earrings with decorations are permitted, and those who do not have a chain should wear four pearls with five strings, and no more. And all this is for Sabbath, festivals, and also for a wedding. On weekdays, their regulations for jewelry are the same as for other women.

[Column 116]

f.   On weekdays, men may not wear any satin clothing, and it is also forbidden to make new clothing of *schlek*[13] velvet for weekdays. Someone who already owns such is permitted. Only for a festive meal of a circumcision or wedding, or in honor of a guest can one wear new clothing of *schlek* velvet. The regulations for men are the same as the aforementioned regulations for women. They are permitted to men even on weekdays, as on the Sabbath and festivals; and with the above conditions, it is permitted to make the clothing of *schlek* velvet even for weekdays.

g.   Sabbath and festival clothing can only be from *gredtor*[13]. However, one who already has satin or *dreit*[13] clothing can wear the headdress on a festival, but not on the Sabbath. Gabardine is completely forbidden.

h.   One cannot send any wine at all from the community to any citizen or Rabbi. The community is also not permitted under any circumstance to drink wine from communal funds, even at a party.

118

i.   No householder is permitted to send *shalach manos* [gifts/foods for *Purim*] to anyone in the world in a silver dish, and also not to bring the *etrog* [citron for *Succoth*] to the synagogue in a silver holder.

j.   All these regulations apply to all the residents of our city, excluding our esteemed Rabbi, his wife, and their children.

k.   It is forbidden to give out more than eight honors at a circumcision, aside from the *mohel* [circumcisor], *kvater* (person who carries in the baby before the ceremony), the *sandek* [person who holds the baby during the circumcision], the person who holds the baby during the blessing, and the one who brings him to that person.

l.   For a woman in childbirth, one cannot send any potion, except to the Rabbi's wife and the midwife.

m.   A householder is prohibited from housing any teaching assistant in his house who shaves his beard, and even more so does this apply to the teacher. A householder also cannot keep a servant who shaves his beard. No teaching assistant or child worker may wear a satin yarmulke, or a *spodek* [Hassidic fur hat] covered with satin or other type of silk.

n.   Anyone making a wedding for his daughter outside the city is not allowed to invite residents of the city via the *Shamash* (beadle) or his emissary, with the exception of first–degree relatives[14]. He is also obligated to give payment to the Rabbi, cantor, and *Shamash* who conduct the wedding ceremony in any place that is not subordinate to our community, just as he would if he were making the wedding here in our community.

These matters apply to residents of our city, young and old.

May these matters be good and pleasing to G–d, who should put an end to our tribulations, and lead us speedily and upright to our Land through the harbinger of peace [the Messiah], who will announce peace in our precincts.

All the aforementioned is enacted from today and onward for a period of three consecutive years and applies to all residents of our city. Anyone who leaves here to go to another place may do so and will not be obligated by the stringencies of the place that he left. [Enacted by] the 24 elected honorable leaders of the community, new and old, along with the aforementioned special individuals, with the agreement of the honorable, renowned Rabbi, the head of the rabbinical court of Chodorow (Chodorów) – today, *Elul* 22, 5507.

> Signed: Aryeh Leib the son of Rabbi Shmuel, may the memory of the righteous be blessed.
> Signed: Yosef the son of Rabbi Ezriel, may the memory of the righteous be blessed.
> Signed: Meir the son of Rabbi Yoel of blessed memory.
> Signed: Yitzhak Izik the son of Rabbi Asher Anshel of blessed memory."

An acknowledgment and thanks for the help for several communities of Volhynia to the community in Dubno during the days of the "burning fire" when there was a pogrom against the Jews run by the Ukrainian Haidamaks (comprised mostly of local free Cossacks, peasants, and rebels), who rose up against the Polish aristocracy – is written by the scribe in the year 5512 (1752) on pages 59, folio b:

"Their righteousness should stand for ever, as we will note those communities who committed to help out of the goodness of their hearts, and sent (provisions) to our community, after the "burning fire" that took place here on *Elul* 12, 5512, to be distributed to the poor of our community

The community of Konstantin – 400 zloty to the administrator of providing sustenance to the poor.

The community of Olyka – six gold coins (*czerwony*) in cash to dispense among the poor immediately; they also sent wagons filled with corn, bread, meat, and dishes.

The community of Kremenets– five gold coins (*czerwony*) to distribute among the poor immediately.

The community of Ostrow sent a wagon of bread and foods.

The community of Brody – sent thirty–five gold coins (*czerwony*) to distribute among the poor …

After this, we, the leaders of the community, send ten gold coins to the emissaries of the community of Konstantin to discharge some mix–up in that city, may G–d save us. After the great fire that took place in our community, may G–d save us, we gave them 300 groszy via the emissaries of our community. We also gave them two gold coins through their emissaries to help in the completion of the building of the synagogue."

The three entries next included here clarify the battle of the community against corruption – holding of stolen property, misappropriation of trust, drunkenness, etc.

[Column 118]

At the end of page 62, folio b, the following is written, without a date, but apparently from the year 5500 (1740).

"Rabbi Meir Haim the son of Rabbi Mordecai did evil by supporting sinners and becoming an adjunct to them. Stolen goods have been noticed in his possession on a repeated basis, as this is now the second time that such has been found with him. It is appropriate to deal with the matter and conduct a serious trial for such wrongdoers, but we must be wary lest things get too harsh[15] by matters becoming too stringent through their (i.e. the secular) law. Our master the general gubernator has decreed that his iniquity be inscribed and sealed in the ledger, so that it not be repeated; and if stolen property is found in his possession again, his decision is firm that the verdict be carried out on his soul[16] in accordance with the ordinance of our master the gubernator, so that (it) be removed, and no one dare to perpetrate such an evil again."

On page 59, folio b, the scribe writes about an incident that took place in the year 5518 (1758): where the cantor was removed from his post due to drunkenness, and was restored to his position after expressions of regret and taking an oath to not repeat the abomination:

"A representative who did wrong, the representative of our community[17], (is he not) (his name and the name of his father are erased) and after we saw that his behaviour was inappropriate, for he placed his eyes on the cup and did not act with propriety. Therefore, we have convened as a group, with a full table, and decided to dismiss him. He is now dismissed from his position, and Heaven forbid that we return him to his job without the unanimous agreement of the community, which can stop the judgment. (Agreed to) by all the heads and chiefs of the community, new and old together, today, Thursday 12 *Nisan* 5518 (1758), with the participation of the Rabbi, the renowned head of the rabbinical court and *Yeshiva* head of the community of Chodorow.

> Signed: Aryeh Leib the son of Rabbi Shmuel, may the memory of the holy be blessed.
> Signed: Yirmia the Levite.
> Signed: Avraham the son of Mordecai, may G–d protect him.
> Signed: Yehoshua Heshel the son of Rabbi Tz. H. may his light shine.
> Signed: Tzvi Hirsch the son of Eliahu Katz.
> Signed: David the son of Nisan of holy blessed memory."

[The following is written] further on, at the time that the cantor expressed remorse, and was obligated to take an oath to not repeat his travesty:

"I, the person who signed below, have come with regret for my earlier behavior, and hereby request from the leaders and chiefs of the community to accept me for the holy service of serving as the communal representative (prayer leader) of the community. I have done wrong, perpetrated a travesty, and have (now) accepted upon myself through a stringent oath

[Column 119]

through taking hold of a (holy) object in the presence of two representatives of the rabbinic court and the communal intercessor to adjure myself to keep away from wine and any other intoxicating drink, liquor or liqueurs. Heaven forbid that I even taste such forbidden material. I take this upon myself through an oath that applies on weekdays, Sabbaths, festivals, and even for festive religious celebrations – it is forbidden upon myself for the entire year."

On page 27, folio b, there appears the text of a declaration through an oath regarding the evaluation of property for taxes. The declaration is written in a mixture of Hebrew and Yiddish. It is not dated, but it is surmised to be from the year 5522 (1762).

"I hereby swear with the approval of the Omnipresent and the communal trustee, and take the oath without any subterfuge or deceit, that this notice that I am giving to the communal trustees is true and correct. I claim nothing more than what is stated in this notice, and I am hiding nothing that is not in this note. I also include in my oath that I have no knowledge that my wife has money or any deposit. In my estimation, she has nothing. And I am not hiding any cash, cash equivalents, gold, or jewelry – whether beads, pearls, ovals [evidently a type of jewelry item], gold or silver chains – or merchandise or debts that I have, and which I owe to other people. I am also not hiding that which is due to me in accordance with the ordinances of the community. I have not given over, lent or deposited anything to be hidden until after the oath and then returned to me. I have also not deposited sums of cash or jewelry with our sons or daughters, and not deposited toward any inheritance or marriage contract, even for a dowry for our sons and daughters – anything that can be spoken by the mouth or thought of in the heart. Our property is no more than what is stated in the notice that I have given over to the trustees. If my oath is, Heaven forbid, not true, then may G–d not desire to forgive me and may all the curses and maledictions written in this book fall upon me[18]; and may He who exacted punishment from the generation of the flood and the generation of the dispersion exact punishment from anyone who acts with guile regarding his oath[19], and may all of Israel be free from this iniquity. If my oath is true, may G–d continue to grant me success in my endeavors, and may my curses turn to blessings, Amen."

On page 56, folio a and b, there is a list of donations received from the heirs of "the late, scholarly, wonderful wealthy man, Rabbi Kalonymus Kalman the son of the late Rabbi and wealthy man Moshe of blessed memory," in which he allocates bequests in his will for synagogues, various institutions, poor people, redemption of captives, etc. From this list, the date of which is 5538 (1778), we

[Column 120]

can deduce the religious and communal activities of the Jewish community of Dubno at the end of the 18th century.

"Money has no value to a person on the day he passes from the world. The late wonderful, scholarly, wealthy man, Rabbi Kalonymus Kalman the son of the late Rabbi and preacher Rabbi Moshe of blessed memory commanded his children to distribute from his fortune on behalf of his soul. The following list is what their father commanded them and let their sons do as their father has commanded.

To the Small *Kloiz*, 1,000 zloty.
Regarding the above, the leaders of the community received from the trustees as was written with the signature of the leaders who gave the aforementioned sum to the Small *Kloiz*.
To the *Chevra Kadisha* (burial society), for *Mishnayot* in the aforementioned Small *Kloiz*, 100 zloty.
To the *Chevra Kadisha*, an eternal light in the Great Synagogue 200 zloty.
To the Large *Kloiz*, 400 zloty.
To the *Chevra Kadisha*, a prayer candle for the aforementioned *Kloiz*, 100 zloty.
To the *sandek* Society[20], 100 zloty.
Total of the above shall be given over the head, Mr. Izik the son of Reb Anshel. For the needs of the public, 200 zloty. The aforementioned sum is given as a loan by the aforementioned Izik the son of Reb Anshel, with the will of the group, to Reb Meir the son of Reb Haim Farber, through an act of acquisition[21].

For sustaining the poor, 400 zloty, discharged through a receipt.

To the Society for the Visiting of the Sick, 200 zloty, discharged by a receipt.

For the redemption of captives, 139 good and large zloty, discharged by a receipt. The sum of 60 good and large zloty still remains to be discharged in accordance with the will of the aforementioned deceased man.

To the synagogue, through a receipt from the trustees of the city, 400 zloty.

The total of what is due from the heirs of the aforementioned deceased man in accordance with the aforementioned list comes to 3,300 zloty and was discharged as above. Still owing is the aforementioned payment of 600 zloty.

Tuesday, 11 *Tammuz*, 5538 (1778), as we count here in Dubno.

So that this document can be preserved, I have written it with an iron and lead pen.

Aharon the son of the great, renowned Rabbi, Rabbi Yisrael of holy blessed memory."

On page 109, folio b, there appears a directive from the year 5542 (1782) forbidding the imposition of new taxes for the building of the Great Synagogue of the city. From this we must surmise that sufficiently heavy taxes had already been imposed on the community in its time.

"With the help of G–d, since our spirit was awakened, and we set our hearts on building a great house with walls, splendid and glorious, to exalt the house of our G–d with a miniature sanctuary[22], the holy synagogue of our community may it be protected.

[Column 121]

Given that we now are concerned lest some leaders of the community renew some obligations on the members of the community in accordance with the tax evaluation, we state that they have no permission at all to do this. Any one of the card holders is allowed to stop things so that no obligation based on tax evaluation be imposed for the purpose of the building of the synagogue.

> Signed: Ze'ev Wolf the son of our Rabbi and *Gaon* N. H., may the memory of the holy be blessed.
> Signed: Yitzhak Izik Margolis.
> Signed: David the son of Nisan, may the memory of the holy be blessed.
> Signed: Shalom the son of Rabbi Sh. Zalman, may he be protected.
> Signed: Meir the son of Mr. Moshe of blessed memory.

(And nine more signatures)

Today, Tuesday, 15 *Sivan* 5552 (1792) in Greater Dubno, with the participation of the local Rabbi and head of the rabbinical court."

Regarding the participation of the Jews of Dubno in donations for the benefit of Ashkenazic poor of the Land of Israel during the 18th century, we can see from an entry that appears in the ledgers from the year 5543 (1783) on page 107, folio a. This is a copy of the certificate received from the rabbinical emissary from the Land of Israel:

"Today, *Tevet* 3, 5543 (1822), I received a holy emissary of the Four Lands of the Land of Israel[23], may it be rebuilt speedily in our days, Amen, from the heirs of the late renowned Menahem Manes of blessed memory a sum of 400 gold coins for the poor of the Ashkenazim of the Holy Land, may it be speedily rebuilt. From the aforementioned sum, I am obligated to give the sum of 42 Polish zloty to the widow of the late famous *Hassid*, Mrs. Freidel of blessed memory[24], who is a relative of the deceased of blessed memory – over and above the distribution of money for the Land of Israel that is due to her from the distribution of the Ashkenazic sages of the Holy Land, may it be speedily rebuilt, Amen.

As a proof, I am signing, today, on the aforementioned date, Eliezer Zisman the son of Rabbi Yitzhak, may he be remembered for life in the World to Come, the head of the rabbinical court of the two communities of Safed and Tiberias, may they be speedily rebuilt, Amen."

The entry on page 113, folio b is especially interesting. It is also from the year 5543 (1783), and deals with changes in the collection of taxes, "to reduce and not to add in accordance with the needs of the times." These changes include reductions in tax owing granted to merchants, shopkeepers, and tradesmen, as detailed here:

"The owners of rented shops and stores, not "ones they own"; the shopkeepers who receive their merchandise on credit, and the merchants who maintain property – houses, shops, stores, and stalls –

[Column 122]

whether "by contract" or "by rent"; small–scale tradesmen ("household servants will give nothing"), sellers of salt in wagons and blocks; importers of wine from Hungary to sell wholesale; makers of "malts" to put in beer, as well as anyone who "wishes to tell their choice" in the *Kloiz* or the *shtibel*. Only [three types of payment listed here][25] must be given by everybody" …

The entry concludes as follows:

"All the aforementioned has been agreed by all of us, the enactors of enactments who were chosen by the community, the merchants, tavern keepers, and estate owners, with the authorisation of the great master, the Commissar, may his glory be raised. It has been enacted and concluded for the benefit of the community on Tuesday, 17 *Iyar* 5543 (1783).

> Ze'ev Wolf who lives here in Greater Dubno.
> Signed: David the son of Nisan of blessed memory.
> Signed: Chaim the son of Rabbi Tzvi Hirsch of blessed memory."

An enactment related to leasing the meat taxes for a group of Jews, including two people not from Dubno, enacted in *Elul* 5553 (January 1793)[26], during the time of the Second Partition of Poland, which was a time of tribulations and lack of political and economic stability. It was decided from the outset that a change in the situation of the butchers who leased the tax, resulting from the economic situation, will be dealt with by the heads of the community regarding paying of the lease fees, as is related on page 139, folio a and b:

"We, the communal leaders who signed below, convened and leased the tax of ritual slaughter to the wealthy people Tz. H. Charta'z, Fishel Bara'n, Itzin of Zloczow, and Y. Tzvi Hirsch the son of Fishel of Kremenets for the duration of an entire year, that is from the 25th of *Elul* 5553 until the 25th of *Elul* 5554, for the sum of 350,000 zloty as explained on the next page. The communal leaders are obliged to receive it when the aforementioned discharge their obligation. If, Heaven forbid, some sort of scandal or any other issue arises regarding the aforementioned taxes, everything is the responsibility of the leaders of the community. Similarly, if the scarab[27] affects the cattle, this too will be the responsibility of the communal leaders.

As a proof, the leaders who own the aforementioned tax themselves sign below on Tuesday, 25 *Elul* 5553, here in Greater Dubno."

In the year 5564 (1804), after the Russian conquest, the residents of Dubno were ordered to provide residence ("quarters") for the occupation soldiers. The task of

[Column 123]

allocating the soldiers to the houses of the Jewish residents fell upon a *Shamash* [communal worker] named Ya'acov. He apparently favored the wealthy, and, in exchange for gifts and bribes, did not house the soldiers with them. After the facts were brought before the heads of the community, the *Shamash* Ya'acov was dismissed from his position forever, and it was decided to not give him any communal work or position. This is described on page 173, folio b.

"Behold, we have seen the great obstacle that stemmed from Mr. Ya'acov the *Shamash* regarding the allocation of lodging for soldiers in our community. He had been responsible for the determination of lodging. The aforementioned Mr. Ya'acov acted deceitfully, favored the wealthy, received gifts from them, and placed the soldiers only with the middle–class and poor of the city. The house of anyone who gave him a bribe was free from soldiers. He did not do good amongst his people, for he stole from the masses. Who can close their ears from hearing the cries of the poor people who shouted out that the aforementioned Mr. Ya'acov demanded from them and from all their neighbors every month, "give, give, lodging money?" After an investigation and inquiry, it became clear to us that he was guilty of theft from the public, that he continued to sin, and acted brazenly with brazen forehead in front of a table full of the communal leaders.

Regarding this, the leaders and heads of the community have agreed that, from this day forward, the aforementioned Mr. Ya'acov will be permanently dismissed, and he will have no position or tasks from the communal leadership under any circumstance. This will be enacted with strength and force.

These are the words of the honorable leaders and heads of the community, today, Thursday 8 *Adar*, 5564 (1804)." (No signatures)

It seems that eleven years later, in the year 5575 (1815)[128], two *Shamashim* (communal workers) from Dubno, who were in charge of housing Russian soldiers in the homes of the residence, once again corrupted their duties. When the matter was brought before the communal leaders, the leaders found it appropriate to dismiss them from their positions and to forbid their future employment in communal affairs "with a strong ban, for all the generations of the world." However, due to a command of the Russian police chief in the city, apparently issued in writing, the heads of the community lifted the ban on one of the *Shamashim* after two months and returned him to his position. This is noted on page 171, folio a:

"The people of the community, may it be established, came to us with a great complaint regarding the *Shamashim* of the housing commission of this community, Reb Avraham Jaszikisz and Mr. Yosef the son of Gershon, and stated how those *Shamashim* assign housing to soldiers in an unjust manner in accordance with their will. This has caused a dispute, resulting in the dismissal of the aforementioned *Shamashim*. Therefore, we have accepted their words and issued a stringent decree that from today and onward, for all the generations of the world, the two aforementioned *Shamashim* were sentenced to

[Column 124]

permanent dismissal. They will never be permitted again to serve, and no permit will ever be of benefit to them, and nobody can prevent this. Other *Shamashim*, who will be acceptable to everyone, shall be immediately appointed in their place. If it happens that those new *Shamashim* also act improperly, they will also be sentenced to dismissal. As proof, we, the honorable leaders and chiefs of this community have signed, together with the deputy of the commission as well as with honorable Rabbis of renown, the righteous rabbinical judges of this community. We have signed on Monday, 4 *Tammuz* 5575 (1815).

Signed by Ari Leib son of Rabbi Hillel of blessed memory; Signed by Yosef the son of Y. Gabmo of blessed memory; Signed by Ya'acov Mordecai Halperin;

Signed by Shimon the son of Reb A. deputy;

Signed by Yisrael the head of all the organizations.

There is a permission that comes from the ban. Since, on account of disputes and strife, we have installed new *Shamashim* to the housing committee, and since we have seen that the new *Shamashim* are not able to act appropriately in providing housing, and furthermore, we have received a command from the police chief that we specifically employ the original *Shamashim*, we have lifted the aforementioned ban with a complete permit, and have accepted Reb Avraham Szajikisz as a *Shamash* in the housing committee as previously, for the majority of the residents of our city have requested this from us.

This shall be established with power and authority, today, Sunday 19 *Elul* 5575 (1815).

Signed: Aryeh Leib son of Reb Sh. Of blessed memory."

From what is stated on page 132 it seems that the community of Dubno was diligent in the support of the Jews of the Land of Israel, for we find details regarding the donation that was given in the year 5583 (1823) to the "emissary from Hebron in the Holy Land":

"Today, the emissary from the holy city of Hebron came here, with a roster of donors from several cities who agreed to send donations every year. It is clear from that roster that 200 zloty have been pledged annually. After we have seen that the emissary has the permission from the people of Hebron to act on their behalf, we have compromised with the aforementioned emissary and have discharged our obligation from the past to the present, in a manner than from this day forward, the leaders of our community are free from the aforementioned donation forever. The aforementioned emissary has signed this compromise with his own signature in the aforementioned roster today, Sunday, 12 Av 5583 (1823)."

The Jews of Dubno did not use family names until the beginning of the 19th century. They sufficed themselves with their first names, their descriptions, and the names of their fathers. Very few family names appear in the Ledgers of the Community of Dubno until the year 5591 (1831), even though an edict of the Russian authority obligated them in this already from the year 5573 (1813).

[Column 125–126]

128

On page 171, folio a of the ledger, the first lengthy list appears of signatories with surnames appears, in an entry regarding the giving of vessels of silver and gold to the scholarly young man Mr. Shimon the son of Reb Yeshaya of blessed memory. The protocol was written on Wednesday, 14 *Iyar* 5591 (1831) here in Greater Dubno.

"Signed by Jarasz Baskis,
 Ziskin Optyk,
Avraham the son of Reb M. P. Chawkin,
Yisrael Hirsch Baskis,
Shmuel Ajzenhart,
Zalman Parnas,
Rafael the son of Reb M. Rafalowicz,
Berish Feuersztajn,
Kalonymus Kalman the son of Reb D. Mraszolkewicz,
Yisrael the son of Reb Z. Parnas,
Yosef Manilsohn."

Hand–written page from Dubno p. 349–4. The Israel National Library and Hebrew University.

Original Footnotes and Translator's Comments:

1. It is the general custom of *Chevra Kadisha*s [burial societies] to observe a fast day on a certain date, which varies between communities, to be followed by a major gala feast.

2. I am unsure as to what this date reference means. The 1890s would correspond to the 5650s in the Jewish calendar. From the context, it seems to refer to some court counting from the beginning of the case.

3. Based on Psalms 117:11–12, recited as part of the *Hallel* service, referencing a person being surrounded by enemies, like trapped bees.

4. Original footnote: see Tur 48.

5. The next three words are a partial quote of a Biblical phrase (with the first word slightly misspelled). This type of phraseology is used as a mnemonic code for a specific year.

6. Original footnote: "Large" refers to a coin of specific value (Groszy); Assessment – his evaluation, according to which the taxes that he must pay to the community is determined – based on his economic situation.

7. The term Rabbi used in the signatures may not be literal. The term "our teacher the rabbi" is often used as an honorific for an honorable, respectable person. That appears to be the style in the signatures in this ledger.

8. Original footnote: Regarding those teachers of children who had not learned themselves and are not appropriately exacting.

9. *Tosafot* is a set of commentaries on the Talmud.

10. Based on Jeremiah 30:7.

11. Jacob here refers to the Jewish people, and the sister refers to Jewish women.

12. I based the translation of many of these protocols from the analogous article from Hebrew column 577. The Hebrew version had more detail, so I modified and added to the translation as necessary.

13. I could not find the meaning of these textiles or garments.

14. Relatives whom one is forbidden to marry by Torah law (parents, children, grandparents, grandchildren, aunts, uncles, in–laws, etc.).

15. Original footnote as follows: We must be wary that things do not become more severe than they should be. (Translator's note: a secular court would deal with this more harshly than a Jewish court, and the community evidently felt that there is reason to avoid such.)

16. I believe, but am not 100% certain, that this is a reference to the death penalty.

17. *Shliach Tzibur* – communal representative – is a term referring to a prayer leader or cantor who represents the community in prayer.

18. Some of this is paraphrased from Deuteronomy 29.

19. A paraphrase of the *Mi Shepara* curse imposed upon those who do not fulfil their words (Mishna *Baba Metzia* 4:2).

20. Seemingly a society for the provision of funds for circumcision ceremonies for the poor.

21. Literally: *Kinyan Sudar*, a transaction enacted by picking up an object of some small value, usually a piece of cloth.

22. A term for a synagogue, as opposed to the Holy Temple (which would be the Great Sanctuary).

23. There is a footnote in the text here: the four lands of the Land of Israel are Jerusalem, Hebron, Safed, and Tiberias.

24. The "of blessed memory" seems out of place here, and likely applies to the late husband. There seems to be a misordering of clauses, which is not uncommon in such documents.

25. '*Kumin gelt*' – possibly arrival money; '*paglon*' – unsure of the meaning; '*shnit gelt*' – probably money for tailoring.

26. Seemingly an error here, as *Elul* is August / September, and not January.
27. I am unsure what this means in this context, but likely refers to some cattle disease (the transliteration is *skarb*).
28. The text indicates 1875, but either the Hebrew or, more likely the secular date provided is in error.

The Dubner Maggid

134

The Sage and His Town

by Eliezer Steinman

Translated from Hebrew by Selwyn Rose

Rabbi Ya'acov Krantz was born in *Zhetl*, Wilna region and died in Zamosc, Poland. He functioned as a teller of fables and preacher in Międzyrzec (Mezerits de Lita) and Zolkiew, in Galicia and for only eighteen of the 64 years of his life did he actually live in Dubno and even then, much of his time was spent on the road travelling from town to town, country to country, delivering his sermons – but his name is forever linked to the town of Dubno.

Apparently, the town was especially privileged in that his revered name should be so closely connected to it and it was an added privilege that the reputation of Ya'acov Krantz throughout the world should be transmitted not by his personal name nor by his famed book "Ya'acov's Tent" but simply as "The *Maggid* of Dubno".

We find many instances o f our sages being recognized by their writings like: Rambam, Rashi, the *Maharsha* [an acronym for Rabbi Shmuel Eidels – **M**oreinu **Ha–R**abbi **Sh**muel **E**idels]. *Ha–Taz* [Rabbi David Ha–Levi Segal after his renowned book "*Turei Zahav*" – "Pillars of Gold"]. *Ha–ShaH* [Rabbi **Sha**bbtai ben Meir Ha**C**ohen "*Siftei Cohen*" – "Lips of the Priest"] – nicknamed "Known in Yehuda" – among many other élites who were named for their towns such as: *Ha–Maharal* of Prague, The *Gaon* of Vilna, Rabbi Yisrael of Medzhybizh (Medzhibozh, Mezbizh), The Preacher of Mezerits (Międzyrzecz), Rabbi Levi–Yitzhak of Berdichev. The *Maggid* of Dubno dwells among an élite society indeed.

So, what is the difference between them? The amazing thing is that all these sages mentioned here, except the *Gaon* of Vilna, spent very little of their lives in the towns they are named for. *Ha–Maharal*, although he spent some time there during his lifetime, actually moved there shortly before his death as the town's Rabbi. The *Ba'al Shem Tov* of Medzhybizh; Rabbi Nahman was neither born nor died in Breslev; Rabbi Levi–Yitzhak became Rabbi of Berdichev and later the Rabbi of several other towns; thus, it was with the *Maggid* of Dubno. So, what's the point of it all?
I think there is.

These sages of the towns are mostly men drawing the core of their wisdom from the wellspring of the people, not only *Hoi Polloi* but from the élite, worthy, riffraff and peacemakers as well. They were more than teachers, they were informers, and beyond making demands they bestowed and shed a new light on the lives of the people in general and the individual in particular. It was as if they lifted a heavy burden from the souls of the populace and increased the vitality of their being.

All these special qualities we find in Rabbi Ya'acov Krantz. He is a man of the *Torah* but especially a man of wisdom: he preached ethics but more than that, he preached sympathy and concern. He seemingly stood on the high dais of the homiletic interpreter but was humiliated to see the woes of the Jewish people and the sufferings of all of Israel. From within his people, he sits and his soul speaks. He wears no clothes of honor; he is not installed as a rabbi nor was he considered as the local rabbi, nor was he a community's leading figure or a guide. He was a simple Jew wandering from place to place without claiming to inform "*Ya'acov* and *Israel*" of their sins but only to confirm with his pleasant words. For indeed "*Ya'acov*" will arise, although he is small and his haters many and large in number. But his faith is stronger and shields him with the upper hand on his fate and will not allow "*Ya'acov*" to fail; it is his strengthening girdle. But in parallel with the division within the faith, flowing within his sermons, there is found that tiny rivulet of common-sense demanding recompense for the good and revenge upon the evil. Support ("tana d'ma'asay")[1], for common sense is at the heart of the merciful claimant for justice.

The *Maggid* of Dubno is wise-hearted. Mercy is the basis of a wise heart. Because Rabbi Ya'acov Krantz is not an ordained rabbi or *Dayan*[2], he refrains from embellishments and passing judgments. His heart overflows with compassion. The power of a merciful one is his complete modesty and unpretentiousness. With what shall he boast of with his fellowman? What advantage has he – greater wealth, power or wisdom or any other pleasant attribute. But the possessor of a great heart doesn't keep its goodness to himself because the advantage he has is to be shared and not kept to himself. If he is a distinguished scholar, he shows graciousness to those who are not so endowed with *Torah* as is he, and if he is wise and just, he feels sorry for all those who are untouched by the light of wisdom and righteousness. More than that: the merciful one is forever engulfed within the emotions of the heart and has no time to recognize his attributes; the *Maggid* of Dubno had no idea that he was the *Maggid* of Dubno, that his name was carried far and wide by many diverse routes; he knew not of his noble spirit. It is quite likely that it never occurred to him that he was unique to his generation if not to many generations. He had no time to be self-appraising; his soul was flooded with the wonder of the Holy One blessed be He, of the people of Israel, of the legends and the countless homiletic interpretations that were retained in his memory as if in a safe. He was *the* safe of Israel's homiletic interpretations and by his countless proverbs and pleasant stories from life

[Column 135]

136

itself. He laid the cornerstone of Modern Hebrew literature, illustrating reality but he didn't know that. There are geniuses that are aware of their strengths and there are geniuses blithely unaware of the fact; he was entirely unaware. Wisely innocent or innocently wise – herein lay the pith of his course. His excessive modesty was fed and nurtured by his naïveté. In his conversations with the *Gaon* of Vilna, who takes upon himself the persona of the poor whom in the congregation of the respected, will not be honored, will not be greeted with cries of "welcome" and not be granted a place at the table; but he stands at the entrance or somewhere in the corner; he is not offered a portion of food, nor a spoon or fork and on his own volition he stretches forth his hand and selects items from what is on offer, in no order of preference, a piece of roast or a slice of salted fish, eating the last scraps. Therefore, he is unable to compose an organized book of *Torah* interpretations but snatches every morsel presented to him from the heavens, whether an exposition on Balak or Isaiah. He lives on what fortune provides. He sees himself as a bypasser, boarding any wagon that chances by and simply goes wherever it takes him.

All the fables of the *Maggid* of Dubno unite seamlessly with moral lessons but the lesson of his own poverty is unsuccessful. His is rich in spirit and has exceptional

[Column 136]

organizing ability. He never speaks spontaneously but ponders carefully beforehand. The poverty is found in his lessons because his heart is with the poor and all his spiritual life is with the pauper. He is close to the simple people. He is one of *Hoi Polloi*. I feel sure that the *Maggid* of Dubno never rebuked or censured or thundered from the pulpit, only ever spoke in tranquility. The meek dare not be seen as rowdy. No, he was no "loud speaker" but the "people speaker" – the people spoke through his voice. His spirit was recognized on the pulpit, not in the disguise of a *Gaon* but from the awe of glory and fear from the people. He not only speaks to the people he is also within the body of the public. Every public delegate is, in truth, in fear of the people because the people delegated him, and his fear is that he does not fulfill their wishes.

The *Maggid's* heart was full of fear, but the congregation was warmhearted toward him when listening to his sermons. The congregation heard the voice of their fathers, and forefathers dispersed throughout the Diaspora, the voice of future generations hoping for salvation and redemption. The voice of Rabbi Ya'acov Krantz spoke for the people: "The voice of the bride and the voice of the prayers and the voice of the dances of *Simchat Torah*[3] and the voice of joy and the voice of happiness and the voice of gladness."

The *Maggid* of Dubno is significant as the *Maggid* of the people. Dubno won the right that the *Maggid* of the people dwelt within their midst, therefore Greater Dubno was a town AND the people of Israel.

Translator's Comments

1. Aramaic expression of support
2. A recognized rabbinical judge
3. The Festival of the Giving of the *Torah*

The Fables and Parables of the Maggid of Dubno

by Eliezer Steinman

Translated from Hebrew by Selwyn Rose

Rabbi Ya'acov Krantz, known to the entire, dispersed House of Israel by the nickname The *Maggid* of Dubno, acquired an excellent reputation and the love of the people through his many pleasing parables that were understood by everyone and were acceptable in everyone's opinion and were integrated into his sermons on portions of the *Torah* and the five scrolls: The Song of Solomon, Ruth, Lamentations, Esther and Ecclesiastes.

The *Maggid* of Dubno had not intended at the outset to record his fables, as did many of the sages in Israel and the other peoples of the world had done. He was a preacher and interpreter of homiletic texts in the "*Musar*"[1] tradition. What was important to him was the moral lesson. The proverb he introduced as if by chance, to penetrate the ears of his listeners. Nevertheless, every fable of his has a life of its own and speaks for itself; it even speaks to our heart as if it is the main reader in every event and chapter. And he is not a lesson only for himself for he comes to teach us something – the laws of the *Torah*, or the legends of the *Midrash*[2] or simple good manners and courtesy and life's experiences. He has triple charms – his natural inborn charm, that of the benefit of retrospect and that of innocence, that all come by chance.

But more than that: every fable of the *Maggid* of Dubno is much more than just a fable. It is a short story, a description of a human being, a living picture of the way of life in those days. We call that "Chapters from Life". Even though the way of life seems to be relevant and exclusive only to its period and in the following era it changes shape, the changes are minor and maybe major but the core detail always remains intact. In the same way, Man's face does not change from generation to generation except in small ways. Thus, the face of life in its basic form remains the same; the Earth is unchanging. The nature of humanity can be compared to the sea whose waves are constantly changing but it still remains the sea.

As a result, take a look around and see how many it seems are the changes that are being generated in our way of life, the way of negotiations among people, the appearance of the towns, and their size, the style of houses and especially the family table. In the days of the *Maggid* of Dubno, for example, we would travel by horse and wagon and not by railroad or car. There were no coffee houses, but wine shops, bars and public houses were found everywhere. Therefore

[Column 137]

the "scene of momentous events" of most of the *Maggid's* stories and activities is a wine shop, a public house, the front or rear seat of the wagon jouncing and bouncing along the road. It is there that most of the souls in his fables are found, inn, or hostel keepers, wagon masters, the trader travelling to or from a market town fair, the rich, the beggar or the philanthropist. But what about the way that the implements serving a person were lost to him and others came in their place to be used? Implements come and go but the main hallmarks of one's temperament and character are recognizable in all generations. The qualities remain standing. There are those with good qualities and those with bad qualities, creative and constructive people and destructive ones. We find active people and indolent ones, voluble ones and silent ones, hurrying people and moderate ones, easy to anger and be angered and those able to conquer their anger. There are wise men who examine the sources and attributes to be found in human nature, even if he discusses matters of the moment, and describes them in the context of the present, his words are relevant to our lives and are integrated with what happens in the present and on into the future.

Rabbi Ya'acov Krantz, the *Maggid* of Dubno was a sage of the type who debated in the present and creates and sees the newborn, and above all, he sees the continuity that is present in human nature, the permanence of its weaknesses, its transgressions and its failures. But even the temporary is raised to the permanent by him. He always grasps the general rule and the specific. Because of this, his influence spread far and wide in time from his era. His fables and his conversations talk to us today as if they had just been spoken.

Rabbi Ya'acov was not only a preacher, advocate and censurer. He was, first and foremost an expositor. He was a great expositor of the *Torah* and great also was his strength as an expositor of the Jewish heart – and that one heart is in all the generations. In the same way, he asserts the *Torah* and the commandments of the Almighty, blessed be He, so he addresses the people of Israel. And to all he speaks of the generations of the people, describing their deeds as a sort of theatrical play with their various incarnations and evolutions. The sorcery of his language created living souls. He was the actor playing the lead role presenting the sorrows and grief and he is also the vision of consolation and salvation of great futures and exalted hopes between Israel and their G–d.

140

Rabbi Ya'acov Krantz speaks with sublime grace. He wants to know the Jewish soul and its path in the end of days in the lands of Poland and Russia, Ukraine and Lithuania, and will not cease reading the book of Chronicles. Do not tell me you have read enough. Never ever enough. The depths of Israel's soul is frequently reflected in homiletic literature. The wisdom displayed there is very spiritual. There it is simple clear and straightforward *Torah* and prayer.

Among the community of preachers and tellers of fables, the *Maggid* of Dubno has carved uniqueness for himself. He is the most diligent and studious among them, the most straightforward and simplest with his explanations, the wisest, the poet and most imaginative. He is full and overflowing with *Torah* and his contribution to research is great but, in his conversation, it is just simply one man talking to another.

[Column 138]

If we were to extract all the souls that the *Maggid* of Dubno created in his books and stories there would appear before our eyes an entire community of humanity's creation – Jewish almost the entire House of Israel with its divisions: the poor, the rich, the customs official, the trader, the rabbi, the sexton, the treasurer, the cantor; the matchmaker, the resolute, the community head, the scholar, the barman, the wise son, the silk trader, the simple son, the evil one, the only son, the hostel keeper, a man just as he is, or special with his group, students of the *Yeshiva*, house owners, itinerant beggars and traders going about their business. The wagon master, his horse and his whip, he is one of the leading actors for the Jew was always travelling. Most of the things Mendele and his mare saw on the Jewish wagon in his clear mirror preceded the *Maggid* of Dubno. He saw everything, as in a blurred cloud of smoke rising from the flame of his feelings.

I would be amazed if there is, among the fabulists and preachers in Israel one to match the *Maggid* of Dubno in all his attributes. Rabbi Ya'acov Krantz is clear in his knowledge and expressiveness. He is sharply intelligent with good taste. He is simplistic with his explanations and very close to his hearers, intelligent and educated, well informed in worldly matters. He is desolate because of the schism in his people outraged at the woes and sufferings that fall upon the House of Israel, vigorous in his pleadings before the Lord of the Universe with courage and earnestness. In his opinion, the Creator, may He be blessed, brought very little of his promises to pass for our forefathers: He brought them to the Promised Land but exiled them from it; He brought them out of their exile in Egypt but tortured them with other exiles; He built for them two Temples and then destroyed them; He gave us the *Torah* – the *Torah* of life – but life he failed to give us, that we could expand and perform the commandments of that *Torah*. We never experienced a complete redemption. Only in the place where you find rebellion do you find his hopes and commiserations. On every teardrop there are many dewdrops; on every cup of agony and suffering he pours out four cups full of salvation and consolation.

A man is good if his conversation is good – that is the perfect fitting description of Rabbi Ya'acov Krantz. A man remembered for his good qualities. A man always remembered only for good things and his compassion. In his writings, there are no curses or expletives or anger. Hades is not a common word in his books. Rabbi Ya'acov is never aided by admonishments and punishments. He teaches only with a gentle heart and there is no strap in his hand and no reprimand on his lips. He never suffers from impatience.

Because the man is inherently good, how is it possible to pour upon him anger and disdain? Even the evil in the world will not find words spilling anger from his lips; on the contrary – he shows pity for the unhappy individuals, we who are not showered with those lusts. "Eyes they have but see not, ears they have but hear not"[3] common sense they have but no understanding because their souls are forfeit here in this world and not in the world to come.

[Column 139]

Because he is good hearted, he is forever soaked in sadness when he sees the House of Israel insulted.

He had unlimited pity on Israel and the holy ones. Have they anything in this world? They have no fields and no heritage, no assets and no authority. For all the peoples of the world all is well and for Israel – calamities and divine punishment.

Rabbi Ya'acov sees in earlier generations that they had no pleasure in this world. Go and look what befell this people: From its earliest days, it had no satisfaction. No promise given to it by the Holy One, blessed be He, was kept and fulfilled by Him. The Creator promised the Holy Land to our forefathers and even that promise was not kept except for a few hundred years and immediately they were banished from the land and the Temple destroyed. But what are a few hundred years in the life of a nation? The House of Israel has many complaints against the Lord of the Universe, and he, Rabbi Ya'acov, is their defense attorney. For Israel, Rabbi Ya'acov is a great light, and against the Holy One, blessed be He, he is most severe, painstakingly and punctiliously calling Him to account on every woe and disturbance. His complaints to the Creator are made loudly and forcefully saying: We are entitled to the Holy Land, we are entitled to our fields and our inheritance; they are signposts of our people and by rights must speedily come into our hands. He is sitting, watching and expecting the return to Zion. The Land of Israel is on his lips and in his heart. Certainly, the Messiah will come and redeem us but we, too, must voice our rights. The Owner of the land isn't claiming it is His. The *Maggid* of Dubno makes unceasing claims.

The fables of the *Maggid* of Dubno are full of various themes – poetry, emotions, the investigations of humanity [*Sifrei Hakira* – Trans.], and opinions on life. Rabbi Ya'acov read and changed a lot, he lived a lot, gazed upon the way of the world, and had experienced many events. In addition to being worldwise, he was a great student, highly perceptive and a specialist in all aspects of the *Torah*; in the *Tanah*[4], legends and *Midrashim* [see footnote 4], in Investigative Books and books on *Mussar*. His expertise in all the literature of *Ha–Rishonim* and the *Aharonim*[5] is astounding. More than that, we are amazed by the expansive knowledge and understanding that he brings up in confirmation from the very verse. There are in these proverbs basic lines of world views, general rules of life.

These are briefly some of the headings:

Pleasant is the man created in G–d's image that is to say, that he has a measure of intelligence and strength of will and choice. Indeed, all of creation worships G–d and performs his will but they always act according to the natural human nature given to them. In the way that fire burns and water douses, cold cools without knowledge and intent. So, man and animals fulfill their roles in life. Man himself is gifted not only with the strength to desire, but also with the ability to choose.

[Column 140]

Because of this, he rules over creation, but he is only custodian and responsible for it and he is a delegate for every living thing, to bless, to thank, to praise, to exalt the Creator for all His benevolence on his creation. Man is not simply superior to all of creation but also to his own small world that includes all of nature and its qualities, its many attributes, both good and bad, of animals confined within it. Man knows the soul of the living beast and of every living creature there is a spark in Man's soul.

The might of Rabbi Ya'acov's belief is, at best, a source of blessing and an honor for the triumph to come that is waiting in his mouth, strength greater than the calamity. Evil passes, Evil has no legs, it has no truth and no reality. But its good deed is its immediate foundation whose fruit is preserved into the future. Light shines over the righteous, and only the honest are happy and joyous. The evil have no joy, no peace of mind, no tranquility. They appear as succeeding and the immediate present seems to favor them. But their sinful manipulations gain them nothing if the joy of life eludes them, if their hearts are never at peace? And so, Rabbi Ya'acov Krantz was wont to say: "Sufficient unto the day is the evil thereof"; crying never lasts forever but genuine happiness is enduring and long lasting. Generation after generation of the righteous, communicate the joy of fulfilling the commandments and performing good deeds. Wonders and miracles, salvation and comfort that in early times encouraged and pleased our hearts do so today. That is the way of the Lord of the Universe, to provide a healing for every woe. The Creator created evil and created the *Torah* as a healing herb against the woe. And so, the Devil is ill-conceived and is rejected. Man has to take the test, and it is good that he does so. The tests strengthen and heal him.

The *Maggid* of Dubno considers that all the woes will eventually evolve into salvation and comfort. The troubles are a combination of exposed sicknesses and hidden cures. A good ending is a condition of every beginning. The bad is bitter before it is healed. All medicines are bitter.

The *Maggid* of Dubno debates a lot on medical matters. The topic is very close to him. Most of his fables in some way involve doctors and medicines. According to him in the beginning, there was the medicine. Just as all herbs are encoded in medicine, so all the actions of the Creator are cures for disease, between the ills of the bodies and the diseases of the soul. He never seeks to equate the functions of the body with the needs of the soul. The lynchpin of his interest and the one that mostly occupied his mind, was the wisdom of the mind as the doctrine of education. He poses a serious question: Why was evil (Satan) created? Why did the Creator embed within our nature the attribute of evil? Why do we have within us pride, anger, cruelty, hatred, envy? The excuse is that the negative attributes are measures against the evil. Not only that, but they are also used as motivation to perform good deeds, such as by which they fight exploitation and diverse forms of greed and plunder, stand to the right of the persecuted and the despised, they hate the evil, and give

[Column 141]

them the tools to educate the mind to proper leadership. The youth flooded with lust for gambling and pleasure is made more alert than his companions, and will become as light as an eagle courageous as a lion and a scholar of the *Torah* performing good deeds.

All matters of exile and redemption, the destruction of the Temple and the return to Zion, and the calamities that have fallen upon Israel in their northern lands and good destinies for the future to come, all the reproach to them by our Prophets and all their Northern influence in the future, are made intelligible in his clear mind. Israel and its advancing country were not as the Gentile resident in his homeland, we were at home. There is no comparison, says Rabbi Ya'acov Krantz, between a home and clothing. A house moves from hand to hand. Clothing doesn't transfer from body to body, except if one cuts it and restitches it to fit the new body. And that is the point: every Gentile resides in his country as an individual in his house and he can exchange house for house. But the Land of Israel is as if a garment measured and made according to the measurements of Israel. Israel cannot remove the garment except it be ripped from his body and his land will not fit any other nation. Except if it is cut into shreds and resewn into a different pattern. According to this Israel went out of its land — in dignified exile and sits as a widow, desolate and abandoned. This is evidence that Israel is not simply a purchasable piece of merchandise that can be exchanged between proprietors like a passing shadow. The Land of Israel may be called a purchase of truth by Israel, given to us for eternity. All people are sinners, no land in together with its people. Every nation that sinneth, its land sinneth not with it; Israel's sins impose a defect on the Holy Land, tearing its finest purple[a], again the torn garment does not fit our nation and we go out to exile. You learned that exile is not simply a physical blow to the body, but a fault of the soul, a blemish on the image of

G–d. The curse of exile – he says that our people are no longer fed by the blessings of his land, but by the residual wealth of the nations of the world.

It is a *mitzvah*[1] to gather together all of the *Maggid* of Dubno's proverbs, just for their own inimitable value, so they will be in all minds. Not only preachers and expositors took them and used them for their own talks, but many authors of practical stories also dug into the gold mine of his works and raised nuggets for their stories. Jews are distracted by the legend or fabled world experience that they have integrated into their own from the scribe, and it is the fate of the most illustrious figures who have had their works made famous, and their famous names repeated so often that the teller no longer mentions the names of the authors. The *Maggid* of Dubno was in opposition to the *Hassidut* movement but their most prominent and learned scholar also "dipped" into his fables to "spice" their own points of view. Thus, many quoted or paraphrased him without mentioning his name. Anyone who calls anything by name, saying so brings the redemption closer, and he that does not do so, delays the redemption.

[Column 142]

Many are they who delay the redemption because of Rabbi Ya'acov Krantz. His fables are for the trader, the rabbi, the hoe-holder, the preacher and many, many more. His words dissolve into the conversation of the Jews as easily as salt dissolves in water.

It is therefore only just to at least bring redemption to Rabbi Ya'acov Krantz and present him with his portion and name the fables in his name.

We love the *Maggid* of Dubno whose fables are not just fables but pleasant stories and his wisdom is not just pungent wisdom but also cleverness that warms the heart. He encircled his fables of the Five Books of Moses, the Prophets and the Writings, *Midrashim* and legends – and the Jewish heart, with a golden girdle.

For examples, we bring three of his fables together with their lessons:

We have in our hands but a moment

A poor man came to a rich man and asked him of a loan of a 100 zloty and to repay him every week one zloty, part of it for a charity and a few zloty as interest. The rich man refused to loan the poor man money.

The poor man asked him: "Why not? You'll get your money back and also a small profit."

The rich man replied: "In my opinion it's a false accounting. What do I get in return? For 100 zloty, he gives me only one zloty, every time just one zloty. But one zloty every time does not add up to 100 zloty. From my side it is more like giving a 100 zloty and getting back only one zloty, for he will be paying me back only bit by bit. The one zloty he gives me will be gone before he gives me the next payment; it's not worth making a deal."

The lesson behind the parable:

Thus, it is with a person's lifetime. If we would tell a person in advance that he will live to the age of 80, he would really feel that he is getting 80 years. But this is not how it works. Rather, a person receives life only one moment at a time. As each moment comes, it seems as if his lifetime consists only of the moment he is living right then, for the previous moment has already gone, and he does not know whether he will get the next moment. Thus, King David declares (Psalms 39:6): "Behold, You have made my days like handbreadths, and before You my time in this world is like nothing. " Elsewhere David states that man's days are "like a passing shadow" (ibid. 144:4). This is what the *Midrash* is saying. Our days are not like the shadow of a wall or a tree that remains in place for an extended time. Rather, they are like the shadow of a bird while it is flying. At each moment a new shadow appears, while the previous shadow is uprooted and vanishes.

Our Spiritual Endowments Are the Tools of Our Craft

The *Maggid* presents a parable. A skilled craftsman fell into bankruptcy and was threatened with jail by his debtors. He escaped and ran away from his hometown leaving behind all his possessions specially his beloved tools. He wandered from place to place, town to town, suffering many privations. He was so burdened with his situation that all he could think of was his physical sufferings. Occasionally he bemoaned the loss of his beloved tools because with them he made wonderful things and he had no idea where they were or what was happening to them. Then one day heaven smiled on him again and he returned home. But things were never the same again and the replacement tools he found were never good enough for him and he found fault with all of them. He bewailed his loss.

The lesson behind the parable:

The Holy One blessed be He, planted within the Jewish heart precious attributes with which all the Holy work could be accomplished – the *Torah* and the Commandments. And the Lord instilled in our hearts the love of the Lord saying to us: "Love thy neighbor as thyself." And commanded us "Honor thy father and thy mother," instructing us how to live a life of holiness and all these measures became hidden within us in good measure. But with the constant exile and wanderings the baser instincts gradually grew from day to day and the Children of Israel did not notice the steady erosion and the loss of the finer qualities. It was only when Ezra[8] came to help them and opened up the *Torah* before them reading the laws and Commandments to them explicitly they understood what had happened to them, for there was not in their hearts the love for the Creator nor the fear of Heaven.

One Must Love the Land of Israel for its Name's Sake Alone

Two childless neighbors went together to a great righteous man, a miracle worker, to plead for a miracle for them and a promise that G–d will bless them and that each shall have a male child. The righteous man gave them his blessing and instructed them to take rigorous care of the boys for a year, commanding them to bring the children to him when they reached their third year of life so that he could congratulate them, and so they did.

At the appointed time, when the children reached the age, the righteous man had designated, and the fathers brought the two boys to him. The righteous man looked at each of them carefully and said: "That little one will be a great scholar – a fitting, happy, heaven-fearing Jew. But his companion will be shameful, a fool, involved in fights and as far as the *Torah* is concerned, uninterested. You will do well as a parent to keep a sharp eye on this wild child and teach him how to behave."

The father of the good child was happy while the father of the bad child was sad and disheartened at what had befallen him. The days and weeks passed into years and the children became youths but not as the righteous man had predicted. The youth he foresaw would have a blessed and honorable future because he was a good child, was insensitive and hardheaded and unmindful of education; while the other child, for whom had been predicted a wasteful and inattentive life, turned out to be attentive and quiet in his ways, learning *Torah* and running eagerly each day to study with his rabbi. When the father saw that all the predictions of the righteous man had reversed, he went to the miracle worker, telling him of his woes and unhappiness saying: "Oh, woe is me, woe is me! It is not enough that I hoped to raise a good child, a great scholar, a Jewish man, as you have promised me. Your Honor, there is a great trouble for me in my home and I have a bad son of shame, a sorcerer and teacher [of sorcery], a hater of *Torah* and morality."

The righteous man began to console the stricken father speaking to his heart, because in the end the boy would change his ways, his actions and in his desires for his studies and be a credit to himself. But the man cried bitterly and said: "Why are you consoling me your Excellency, while my soul is inconsolable? Do not my eyes see what evil and bitterness has befallen me? Two children are before me, my neighbor's and mine: mine – only bad things I see, he is not studying neither is he behaving well and courteously, he is nothing but a wild man. In fact, one of the teachers came to take him to the classroom and he refused to go. I thought to run to him at noon and took a handful of nuts for him and he threw them in my face; he did the same thing with some apples that I took for him. In contrast to that, the neighbor's son goes willingly to school and accepts easily the tempting nuts and apples; the lad walks happily because his soul is steeped in *Torah*. And after all, you have witnessed the difference between the stubborn, dumb son and neighboring son who is a benevolent son, blessed seed, a comfort to his parents, and happy for all to see."

The righteous man answered him:

Nevertheless, my judgment is sound; everything that I have predicted concerning the two boys will come to pass, not one element will fail. Do not judge on what you see now, as

[Column 145–146]

the lads are yet young and have little sense in their hearts. And from where will the lad have the taste to be a scholar of the *Torah*? It is natural that there is little taste for study. But what? The neighbor's son sees as his rewards from the *Torah* nuts and apples and all kinds of sweet things, so he tries very hard in his studies to earn these "rewards". Here we have the evidence that he is naturally lustful. His heart doesn't yearn after the *Torah* but its rewards, apples and nuts and so on. When he grows up, he will also follow his lusts and stray from the straight path, and he will no longer have the guidance of his parents to give him rewards for good deeds. But your son from his childhood has known not to allow his desire to govern him. It is impossible to tempt him to study – not with nuts, apples or anything else. When he grows, he will be the master of his creativity and not the slave. His eyes will be opened, and he will see how goodly is the *Torah* and how pleasant its ways. My promise for your son stands and I trust in your son's good future; he will provoke the evildoers and be a great, heaven-fearing Jewish scholar.

The lesson behind the parable:

Even if the love for the Land of Israel in the beginning was closer to the hearts of the people, who were attracted by the imagined attributes like the good fruit, the fresh air and the rest of the other impressive qualities of human enjoyment – and this is what the *Midrash* has been saying: In this world, everything was desirable in the Land

148

of Israel because of its earthly and pleasant virtues, and this in itself caused them to become sinful until they found out. But in the future, God will uproot the evil out of our hearts and slowly our sin and iniquity will be on us and our desire for the land will be on the purity of holiness and our sons "will be planted on their land and will no longer be crushed."[9]

Translator's Comments

Note of thanks: For the three sequential parables and their interpretations commencing on column 142, I am indebted to David Zucker, who's immensely rich and scholarly website is dedicated to The *Maggid* of Dubno. http://jlm–dubno–maggid.org/blog/

1. See: https://en.wikipedia.org/wiki/*Musar*_movement
2. Broadly speaking the interpretation of Holy texts, it can also apply to the methodical ways of interpreting them.
3. Psalm 135
4. The complete Old Testament comprising the Five Books of Moses – **_Torah_**, the Prophets – **N**evi'im and **K**etuvim ('Writings')
5. See: https://www.jewishvirtuallibrary.org/a–H–aronim
6. A reference to the "Royal purple" – i.e. the "finest of the finest"; "to be born into the purple."
7. A blessed commandment – more generally any good deed.
8. Ezra the Scribe is credited with instituting *Torah* readings in the reconstructed Temple after the return from Babylon and basically introducing public prayer into the life of the Jewish people resulting in what has become the basis of our synagogue service today.
9. Amos 9:15

Some Fables of the Dubner Maggid[a]

By Eliezer Steinman

Translated from Yiddish by Pamela Russ

The Parable with Diamonds and Herring

In a town, there once lived a successful merchant, who was a scholar and a very smart man. He noticed that there were wealthy people living in the town, really rich people. He opened a diamond store for them, and he had many customers. But sometime later, he settled in a small town and many poor people lived there, paupers really poor people, sadly, poor devils, so sad. So, the smart merchant went and opened a store for them. Not an ordinary store, but a store of herring, of salt, of kerosene, of other basic material. And the hands that used to hold diamonds, these same hands now held herring and some kerosene. And just as the merchant was satisfied with the other store, he was now happy with this poor store. No, he was even happier. He bore everything with joy.

That's how it went, until a friend of his from the larger town approached him and said to him: "I don't understand. How is this fitting for you, for a diamond and jewel merchant to deal with herring and salt and with other simple things?"

The good and smart merchant replied:

"It's not good that you don't understand. Listen as I explain what this is: In the large city, there were people with lots of money, with their own diamonds, and they were very knowledgeable about expensive jewelry. But here live poor people, simple workers who sadly work and struggle very hard. They don't need diamonds and they don't understand anything about that. What they do need – is a small piece of herring, some salt, and a small piece of bread."

This allegory, the Dubner Maggid sharply imprinted on the mind of the arrogant scholar who was preparing himself for the ordinary people with this scholarship.

151

The Blind Man and the Seeing Man

It is told: The Dubner Maggid was asked why a rich man would give a contribution more readily to a blind, poor man, or a lame man, or a limping man, before giving a contribution to a poor man who is a scholar. The Dubner answered briefly and sharply:

[Column 610]

That is because the rich man himself is not certain that he himself could one day become blind or lame. But one thing he is certain: He will never be a Torah scholar.

A Fool Does Not Know What He Is Missing

The Dubner was asked: Why is the Maggid seen going to wealthy people, but you never see the wealthy person going to the Maggid? It's simple. The Maggid knows well that he has no money, so that's why he goes to rich men. But the rich man does not know that he is missing Torah, so he never comes to the Maggid.

A Court Case with a Horse

Once, a modern person said to the Dubner: "So, let's test each other, and we'll see who is right."

The Dubner looked at the rude person and said, in his usual manner: "Young man, I'll tell you a parable about this:"

"Once, a Rav was riding with a wagon driver to Vilna, and the horse had to pull the wagon across a very hilly road. The driver went down off the wagon so that it should move more easily for the horse. Immediately, the Rav also went down off the wagon. And the driver said to the Rav:" "'You can stay in the wagon. You are a passenger and you paid for the ride.'"

"The Rav answered: 'But the horse can have a complaint against me, that it is a huge hill, and he can summon me to Jewish court. I might win, but I do not want to go to Jewish court with a horse.'"

They Are All Right

The Dubner once said: "It's a strange thing with the *chassidim*. If I am speaking to a *chassid* from Kotsk, he wants to offend the Rebbe from

[Column 611]

Monastrycz. If I am speaking with a *chassid* from Medzhybizh, then he wants to defame the Rebbe from Rydzyina. One does not believe the other. I, however, believe all. They are all right…"

The Wise Man and the Evil Man from the *Haggadah* [Passover]

They once asked the Dubner this question: "What is the difference between the question that the Wise Man asks in the Passover *Haggadah* and the question that the Evil Man asks? It's almost the same thing. If that's the case, why should they call the Evil Man *Rasha*, and why should they push him away and almost curse him? What does the Wise Man say? He says: 'What are the witnesses, and the laws, and the behaviors that our God has instructed you?' 'And what does the second Son who is called the *Rasha*, say?' He says: 'What is the worship that you are doing, what does it mean?' There is really very little difference in their words."

The Maggid replied: "I will present you with a parable for this. Once, the Sultan dreamed that he lost his teeth. He asked his wise men to interpret this dream. One wise man said to him: 'The dream means that your wife, your children, and all your good friends will die within your lifetime.' The Sultan became very angry with these words and he demanded that this man be put into prison. After that, the Sultan asked another wise man, and that wise man replied: 'The dream shows that you will live a long life and that you will outlive your wife and children, and all your court friends.' These words pleased the Sultan greatly. Only later did these wise men realize that the only difference between the two messages was the tone and manner of speech. The first wise man delivered the message in a negative way, but the second wise man expressed the same idea in a positive manner."

[Column 612]

"From that," concluded the Dubner, "you see the difference between the first two sons of the *Haggadah*."

From this parable and moral ending, you can see the Dubner's manner of *Mussar* [admonishment], and his manner of speaking to the people. Always better to take a positive outlook rather than, from the outset, complaining in a negative manner.

A Peasant in a Handsome Coat

Once, a peasant came to town to buy a few things. It was a cold, winter day. The peasant was wearing a warm, old fur coat, and under the coat he was wearing old, shabby clothing, and on top of that, he was wrapped in rags, all to keep warm. He sees a store with beautiful, warm clothing. He looks and says to himself: "If I would put on that beautiful coat, I would look like a dandy, no worse than Prince Enescu."

The peasant goes into the store and asks for a nice, black coat, just as the important people wear. The smart storekeeper soon sees what size the peasant needs and so he gives him a coat and takes him into a separate room to try on the coat. The storekeeper waits a minute, then another minute, and the peasant does not come out of the room. He goes into the room and sees how the peasant is struggling to get into the coat – but he is not succeeding. The peasant begins to shout: "What kind of coat did you give me? It is not my size. Are you making fun of me?"

The storekeeper replies: "I am not making fun of you, but you are making fun of yourself. The coat is exactly for you. But before you put on such a coat, first you have to toss off your own fur coat and all the rags that you are wearing."

[Column 613]

This is the parable; this is the story. And what is the moral of the story? The moral can be a simple one, like this: If a person does not toss off the coarseness from himself, then he can never become a respectable person…

But the Dubner made the moral a deeper one. He placed the moral onto the People of Israel, and with his warm melody, he began to say: "And here is the moral of the story, which is telling us this:

[Column 614]

The Holy Torah and its commandments which God, may He be blessed, gave to us, was appropriately created for our use, according to our nature and our needs. But we place all kinds of rags onto ourselves, all kinds of bad habits and bad sins. Then we complain that the Torah does not work for us, and that it is difficult to keep all the commandments. Rabbis! Leaders! First, let us throw down the rags and only then will we be able to see that the Torah is perfect for us…"

Original Footnote

1. From the book: B.Y. Bialostotzky – "The Fables of the Dubner Maggid and Other Essays." Tsika Publisher, New York. 1962, p. 374.

The Maggid of Dubno and His Fables

by Y. P. Ben–Haya

Translated from Hebrew by Selwyn Rose

The *Hassidut* Movement existed in Dubno over fifty years ago as it did in the rest of the towns in Ukraine and was showing sign of decline although it still had some influence in a few sections of the community that were mainly concentrated in the various Study Houses and *Kloizim* of the *Hassidim*. There, it was possible to find groups of young and old between the afternoon and evening prayers – the hour during which the daily page of the *Gemara* would be studied, or engaged in some kind of *Shaklah ve–Taryd*[1] on some rabbinic point or other of the "*Shulhan Aruh*" – and discuss the doings of the fathers of the *Hassidut*, the *Ba'al Shem Tov* and his students, preparing themselves for the *Rebbe's* planned visit to the town.

If you were to enter the Study House on Sabbath, or the festival of Shavuot in the afternoon, or the evening of the Festival of the Giving of the Law, before the traditional parading of the scrolls, you would find the place humming with the groups of *Hassidim*, passionately singing the festival hymns and melodies creating a special atmosphere such that even if you were not to take part in their joy, the atmosphere would enwrap you completely. He who would be a part of this, or a similar group, would incline the ear, and drink thirstily of the stories and deeds, the "wonders" of the first of the *Rebbes*; you could hear also about the "misdeeds" of those opposed to the movement – the "*Mitnagdim*" in their attempts to prove the worthlessness of *Hassidut*.

In these Study Houses and *Kloizim*, you could also hear the Fables of the *Maggid* of Dubno that were well known and repeated by students and scholars of those institutions carried down from mouth to mouth throughout the generations.

*

Rabbi Ya'acov Krantz was young at the time – he was born in the town of Zdzięcioł (*Zhetl*), near Vilna, the county of the "Litvaks" – when he was invited to the town of

Mezrycz in Volhynia to function as a preacher. In those days, the end of the 18th Century, Mezrycz was an important center of the *Hassidut* Movement. The influential Rabbi Dov Ber officiated there and was accepted as the chosen heir of the *Ba'al Shem Tov* himself, to succeed him after his death. In *Hassidut* circles, there was a feeling of comfort and satisfaction that the *Maggid*, Rabbi Ya'acov had been invited to Mezrycz by the *Mitnagdim* there as a counterbalance to the highly influential Rebbe since it was known that the *Maggid* was a strong supporter of the *Gaon* of Vilna and a fierce proponent of the *Mitnagdim*.

Rabbi Ya'acov Krantz remained in Mezrycz for only a few years. He moved to the village of Zolkiev in Galicia and from there to Dubno but even from there he moved on and became an itinerant preacher in many towns and villages but was always known a the "*Maggid* of Dubno".

*

They say that the *Maggid* was once asked: "How is it that you can weave a fable spontaneously, on the spot?" The *Maggid* replied instantly with this:

"An estate owner once sent his son to the army barracks in town to learn how to shoot accurately. The son remained there many years in the barracks learning and eventually specializing how to shoot until he became an expert. In time, he left the barracks to return to his father's estate. On the way

[Column 147]

he passed through a village and noticed that on one of the houses, the wall was entirely peppered with bullet holes and each and every one was right in the center of a white chalk target. The young man was stunned at the accuracy of the unknown shooter and asked to see him. The villagers brought before him nothing more than a simple young village boy. The estate owner's son turned to the village boy and asked him how he could possibly shoot with such unerring accuracy. "Please tell me how you can shoot so accurately that every shot hits the target?" The young village boy answered him saying: "What is so wonderful about it? First I shoot all the bullets into the wall and then I take a piece of chalk and draw a small white circle round the bullet hole."

The *Maggid* wandered all over Ukraine, Lithuania and Poland visiting many villages and towns appearing as a teller of fables and preaching morals, calling for good deeds and influencing the people to walk the straight path. He pleaded for help for the needy and to give charity to the poor and especially to donate for the release of prisoners and made collections to accumulate money for that purpose and made sure to visit the homes of the important and wealthy.

They tell, that once one of the stately personages asked him: "Rabbi Ya'acov, we see you visiting the homes of the wealthy. Why don't we see them visit you?" He immediately replied: "The Holy One, blessed be He, blessed me and gave me knowledge; therefore, I can understand that I lack money. The Lord gave them money, but they do not understand that they lack knowledge, so they do not come to me ..."

The *Maggid* was once asked: "Why do you receive payments for your sermons, while your whole intention is to set an example to the people?" He replied: "Even the Holy One, blessed be He, does not afflict His people, Israel, for free..."

They also asked the *Maggid*: "What is the point in a notable tending to give donations to the poor, blind or crippled and not donate to the poor scholar?" The *Maggid* replied: "It's quite simple: the notable has no idea what fate has in store for him and one day he also may find himself handicapped; but about one thing the notable can be sure – he will never be a scholar..."

There were many *Hassidim* who never missed an opportunity to listen to him but there were also those who opposed him, who even hated him, among whom were many heretics, agnostics and secularists.

It is related that one such said to the *Maggid*: "Rabbi, they say about you that by the force of your arguments you inspire the spirit of regret and repentance in the heart of a man and that your power is so great as to convert a strict epicurean to become a repentant. Show me, now, this power and cause me, too, to repent."

The *Maggid* replied: "I'll tell you a story. It concerns a Jewish man

[Column 148]

who had lived all his life in a village and one day came to the town and saw a blacksmith using his bellows on his fire. He liked the idea of the bellows and thought to buy a present for his wife to use on her kitchen stove. On his return home, he gave the bellows to his wife and said to her happily: 'Now it will always be easy for you to get our stove burning well'. The following day, his wife came to him complaining bitterly: 'What kind of bellows have you brought me? I pump and pump and pump and nothing happens!' The man approached the stove and saw that it was full of coal but there wasn't a single spark of fire there. He laughed at his wife and said to her: A fire you can ignite if there is at least one single spark; although the stove is full of coal there isn't a single spark there to start the fire.' Thus, it is with you." The *Maggid* added to the epicurean: "When there is in a Jewish heart, a single spark of Jewishness, it is possible to light the fire of repentance in his heart and cause the fire to burn fiercely and the man to become a repentant. Not so with you – your heart is empty and there isn't a single park of Jewishness, so what will it help all the hard work of my bellows?"

157

*

Although the *Maggid* of Dubno was an expert in his knowledge of the *Torah*, he preached to his congregations in simple language that was understood by everyone and when he heard a rabbi giving an explanation on the *Torah* in language that no one understood, he told him a parable:

"This is about a smart businessman who arrived in a large city. When he learned that there were many rich people in the town, he opened up a shop dealing in diamonds and other precious gems and he had many customers. In time, the businessman left the town and went to live in a small village where he opened a small shop selling food and provisions. One day he was visited by one of his old friends from the big city who, finding him in his small shop said to him:

"Is this indeed so pleasant for you – a successful trader in diamonds and precious jewels, to trade in such items as food and trifles?" The businessman answered him thus: "In the big city there were many rich people, and they understood the value of jewels while here, in this small village most of the people are simple villagers who don't understand jewels and don't need them either. What they need is food and other domestic trifles."

"Thus, it is with the scholarly rabbi, preaching to a congregation of poor, simple folk who never learned. What will they understand from these sayings of the scholar?"

*

Many were the parables of the *Maggid* of Dubno and they spread all over the Jewish world and when you mention the town of Dubno – the immediate response is: The town of the *Maggid* of Dubno."

Only for eighteen years did Rabbi Ya'acov Krantz reside in Dubno, but his name is forever known as "The *Maggid* of Dubno" and the honor bestowed upon him reflected upon all her sons.

Translator's Comment:

1.   An Aramaic expression literally meaning "Clean and Fresh" but usually interpreted as "discussion", "debate" or "negotiation"

The Dubner Maggid – the Expert in Parables and Messenger of Realism

by Rafael Mahler

Translated from Hebrew by Jerrold Landau

Just as the Gaon of Vilna attempted to breathe the breath of life into the dry bones of halacha through an innovation in the style of learning, so did one of those close to him, the Maggid of Dubno, like a final manifestation of creative energy in the arena of traditional preaching after it withered with old age. The Maggid of Dubno, Rabbi Yaakov Kranz (1740–1804), a native of Zhetl [currently Dzyatlava] in the area of Vilna, aside from speaking as the "speaker of righteousness and preacher of uprightness" in Międzyrzec, Zolkiew, Chelm and Zamosc, where he died – traveled around, delivering his sermons through many communities in Poland and Lithuania. He even reached Germany in his travels. He was known by the people simply as the Maggid of Dubno, after the city in which he had lived for 18 years. This name remained with him forever, in love and honor in the midst of his nation. The special skills of this expert preacher, who was loved by the people more than all the preachers that preceded him or followed him, were natural, both in the form and ideas of his sermons.

A populist, heartwarming charm enveloped all the sermons of this preacher and expositor, the spiritual heir of the best of the masters of lore and Midrash based on the Mishnaic and Talmudic sages, on Rashi and Rabbi Yehuda Ha-Hassid[1]. Unlike the preachers of his generation, whose ideas were immersed in a pile of didactics and sharpness, the Maggid of Dubno was wonderfully straightforward in his preaching and explanations. Even though he was an expert scholar, who swam in the sea of Talmud and Midrash, as well as delving deep into the philosophy of Duties of the Heart[2], Guide for the Perplexed[3], *HaIkrarim*[4], *Akeidat Yitzchak*[5], and the other books of investigation and morality of the Middle Ages, he would explain his teachings in popular language, and in words that emanate from the heart and penetrate the hearts. He was graced with the ethos of a poet, and with deep talent in observing the happenings of life. He used parables, in the pattern of the master of lore of yore. However, despite the fundamentally allegorical parables in the lore of the Talmud and Midrash, therefore restricted in words solely to the essence, they required an

159

explanation of the referent of the parable; the parables of the Maggid were expressed calmly, broadly, in the manner of a populist storyteller who brings enjoyment to his audience – and incidentally to himself as well. They were told with full detail of the narrative, in a way that captured the imagination of the audience and won over their hearts. Even though the Maggid was preceded in this regard by the Hassidic parable tellers, some of whom were greater than him with their creative imagination that enthuses the eye with its treasury of colors, such as the Baal Shem Tov and his great-grandson Rabbi Nahman of Breslov – the parables of the populist preacher had a special character, for most were taken from the realities of the world, from the abundant, vibrant, day-to-day life. The repertoire of the Maggid was also full of common parables, in which the characters of the king, the son of the king, ministers, and villagers appeared frequently. However, these allegories

[Column 150]

were only one in sixty[a] for him in relation to parables taken from the flowing reality and experience. On account of this, the sermons of the Maggid peered upon Jewish life in Poland and Lithuania at the end of the 18th century as if through a lens[b].

The weltanschauung of the Maggid of Dubno was a definitive outlook of fear of Heaven, still embedded in the roots of the dualism doctrine of the Middle Ages: the purpose of man is to observe the commandments and study the Torah, and to make the good inclination overcome the evil inclination in order to merit life in the World To Come. The true pleasure is the spiritual pleasure and the perfection of man through the perfection of the soul, and purity in the service of the Creator with the heart and with love. However, the most wonderful part of his sermons was specifically the sprouts of ideas of the relationship of obligation and reality of the world of action – expressed and emanating as heralds of renewal from the realm of the ancient doctrines of man. The Maggid, of the generation of the founders of the Hassidic movement, also yearned for a spirit of optimism. Like them, he too trusted with his full heart in the mercy of the Creator who wishes good upon His creations. Unlike the masters of morality who preceded him, he did not threaten his listeners with the torments of hell, nor did he frighten them with punishment from Heaven, but rather encouraged them through words and strengthened their trust and hope. Like the Hassidim, the Maggid was far from the spirit of self–flagellation prevalent in the Middle Ages. Like them, he made the first breaches in the wall of duplicity that completely nullifies [the value of] this world. The Hassidim attempted to overcome the duplicity by sanctifying physicality and raising it to the level of spirituality, whereas the theory of the Maggid of Dubno was based on compromises with things required for "the ways of the world" for the proper running of the world – without which the worship of the Creator would be impossible. Regarding the verse "And you shall be completely happy" (Deuteronomy 16:15), he expounds, "Indeed, a person cannot rejoice unless his heart is sated with meat and wine, therefore there is a commandment to enjoy G–d through

160

pleasures of good foods, as well as to sacrifice voluntary offerings, but the main joy is to rejoice by being drawn close to: my beloved is mine, and I am his[8] – – – ...." The Maggid continues and explains why "we do not recite a blessing on any good thing that is given, that He gave me bread – – – that He gave us clothing, only on the Holy Torah that He gave us, the Torah of truth – – – for behold, everything that our eyes see in this world that is given to our hands – – – despite all this, it is accepted by us that a person should only use and take from them what is necessary

[Column 151]

to complete one's holy work that he must study, teach, observe, perform, and fulfill. Anyone who benefits from this word without a need deducts from his account – – – therefore, we do not recite a blessing on anything that He gave other than the Torah." (*Ohel Yaakov*, Portion of *Re'eh*, page 77).

The difference between the Misnagdic Maggid and Hassidism relating to the duality of the reality of this world on the one side, and the service of the Creator on the other side, stands out in particular in his theory regarding the trait of trust. Hassidism, in the wake of the idealistic humanism of its outlook, stresses the trait of trust through all the deeds of man, when he lies down or is awake. This trait shows its value particularly in matters of livelihood. The Maggid placed the trait of trust as a fundamental in his doctrine of Fear of Heaven. However, in his tendency toward realism, he restricted its actual role to areas not related to livelihood. His teaching in this matter is based on a psychological-social outlook and elaborates on the outlook of the Talmud and Maimonides regarding the deeds of man that are "necessary for human society." In the opinion of the Maggid, "Trust is not natural in the ways of the soul, but man can plant it into the channels of the heart by choosing good. Thus, it is the wisdom of the Creator to create man in a world that is not based on trust, for it is the desire of the Blessed One to complete it [the world] through human beings who work with their hands, for this is the culmination of the deeds of influence." Even though "the vessels of deeds and the means of influence are many, are much better than the deeds of man, and are stronger than them – as the heavens give the early and late rains, and the land therefore gives of its fat after the cattle plow, and the like, for these are the things necessary for the influence of life. Nevertheless, the main part and the culmination of the work is from man, for without his efforts and work, the land would remain desolate." The work of man creates civilization, or "human society" in the language of the Talmud, which is the culmination of the work of creation. The inclination to work is, however, nothing other than the evil inclination, the work of "folly," demonstrating a lack of trust in the Creator of the World. However, this inclination is compared to Mephistopheles in Goethe's Faust[2], whose inclination is toward evil, but nevertheless expresses good. For "if trust was naturally fruitful within the soul, man would loathe his work, and would not make the effort. He only makes a strong effort when he understands the weak ability to obtain his food without the agreement of the Supreme Benefactor, may He be blessed." – – – On the contrary, to the extent that the "folly," "nonsense," and "foolishness" of man increase in his pursuit of pleasures and excesses of the "vanities of this world"; so does his role in building civilization increase. From here also arises the social class differentiation in levels in accordance with the level of creativity in obtaining their desires in this world "For you will see their efforts in the achievements of this world, for the thoughts and customs of the villager are not far from the truth, for he only desires that which he can obtain to feed his family and till his soil

[Column 152]

so he can be sated with bread. Above him is the bourgeoisie, and further above are the large-scale businessmen, whose folly is very great in terms of amassing a fortune to conduct business afar." Relying on a statement of Maimonides (in his introduction to the Order of *Zeraim*) "Were it not for the crazy ones, the rest of the world would be destroyed," the Maggid explains his psychological theory, according to which "The greater something's supervision and guarding, the greater is its charm in the eyes of people regarding things that exist" – such as "pearls and precious stones." Thus he explains that people are prepared (in accordance with the words of Maimonides, ibid.) "to move to far off countries, to go on a ship, to traverse the paths of the seas – – – to put themselves in danger, to fetch and find precious stones with which they can conduct business" … It is desires for excess "for unnecessary things" planted in the hearts of man at the will of the Creator "for the Holy One Blessed Be He did not create anything for naught and desires the existence of all part of reality for the special benefit of all who are here in the world." This desire is also the primary factor in the development of economy, since it provides work for many workers: "and all this is for the needs of human society, that the masses will sustain themselves through their work in helping them conduct their work, and furthermore, the builders build up the ruins as well as halls of pleasure. They also work in gardens and orchards, without which numerous people would be unable to obtain their sustenance and bounty[10]. – – – It shows that the large–scale merchants, who were part of the realities of the Maggid to the extent that they served as the most precious topic of his parables, instilled their spirit and world outlook upon him – the commercial world of capitalism.

Just as the desires implanted in man lead to the constant advancement of economy and civilization, so too was man created with the insatiable desire to delve into the secrets of wisdom, and through the force of this desire "The righteous ones will continually march forward to the perfection desired of him by the Blessed One, without ever ceasing" … However, the force of desire is the same, whether in the souls of the righteous or in the souls of the "evil ones who divert this force to the vanities of the world, there is no end to their desires, for this force will maintain its nature… and this is the principle… for the soul is never sated." This is how the Maggid expounds the verse in Kohelet [Ecclesiastes 10:1] "a little folly outweighs wisdom and

162

honor." Regarding this, he made a crisp parable: "G–d gave a bit of foolishness to people, and on account of this, his soul desires day and night to stand for what he is lacking. Through this, he searches through all the rooms of Torah, so that perhaps he might find something that his heart desires. Through his delving and searching, he succeeds in finding many things, which are wisdom – – –" (*Kol Yaakov*, page 126–127). Therefore, the Maggid does not negate secular wisdom out of principle. He is certain and relies on "everyone who occupies himself with Torah for its own sake – – – honor will eventually come, for the secrets of Torah and all external wisdom are revealed to him." On the other hand, he derives from the verse "external wisdom

[Column 153]

sings out" about "One who is empty of Torah wisdom and occupies himself with external wisdom" (*Ohel Yaakov*, Portion of *Shemini*, page 22).[111]

The sparks of realism that exemplify the weltanschauung of the Maggid of Dubno are also evident in his grasp of the idea of redemption and the return to Zion. This idea is woven as a scarlet thread in all the sermons of the Maggid. He does not leave any opportunity, such as the Torah portions of the Exodus from Egypt, the sacrifices, the tabernacle, the priestly gifts, and most certainly the reproof and promises of redemption in the Torah – to explain in a comprehensive, fundamental manner the concept of exile and the return to Zion. There is no doubt that, similar to the majority of the leaders of the generation, both in the Misnagdic camp and the Hassidic camp, the populist preacher was overtaken by longings for redemption with greater strength in the wake of the disturbances of the stormy era. Several of his sermons were written in the latter years of his life[112], when new hopes for a speedy redemption were aroused in the hearts of the nation in the wake of the victory of the revolution in the west, and especially after the news spread about the Bonaparte plan to restore the Jewish state in its land. It is superfluous to state that the Maggid regarded the redemption as a salvation from Heaven that is not dependent solely on repentance. He was also effusive in his praise of the redemption as a spiritual redemption, as at the End of Days, when "the Holy One Blessed Be He will renew his supernatural actions" (*Ohel Yaakov, Bamidbar*, page 17), and the Jewish person will arrive at "spiritual completeness of the soul) (ibid. conclusion of the book, page 124); "In the future, G–d will bring joy to us when He gives us a clear spirit, wholesome knowledge, and true wisdom…" (ibid., *Balak*, page 100). Nevertheless, through the expression of these traditional ideas of faith, he always exposed his heart as a leader of the nation, pained by all the tangible tribulations of the exile, which lifted his soul toward the economic and political rectification of his nation in its homeland.

The Maggid, who delved deeply to understand the economy of human society built upon labor, could not avert his eyes from the shaky structure of the livelihood of the Jews in the lands of the Diaspora. A deep aspiration to agricultural work, such as plowing, planting, and harvesting, could be heard from his longings for the return to

Zion. He never tired of comparing the life of the nation "from the earlier times when we dwelled in the lands of living in the Holy Land, each person under his vine, etc." (*Ohel Yaakov, Vayeira*, page 97) with the inferior livelihood in the exile. The situation would be rectified when "every person would earn their livelihood from their own labor. The body would be sustained through the work of the land with one's body – – – but all this was when we were on our land – – – not so now, for we do not have a known occupation for sustaining the household, neither from the storehouse or from the vineyard, not from the dew of the heaven, nor from the fat of the land. We only have the plowing of the heart from morning

[Column 154]

until evening. His heart does not rest even at night, for he only thinks about business affairs, how can he fetch his livelihood from afar – – –" (ibid. *Vayeilech*, page 120). In the Diaspora, the joy of the festival is also not complete, "for we do not now have a field or vineyard with which to rejoice with the gathering of our produce from the field" (ibid. *Pinchas*, page 11). The Maggid repeats over and over the bitter truth that in the Diaspora, the Nation of Israel is only sustained by the leftovers of the nations, "for the dew of the heavens and the fat of the earth are not ours, but rather theirs, for the land is theirs – – – they have the inheritance of the field and vineyard." And that which the nations themselves "snatch and pillage one from the other, what can we hope from them anymore" – – – and this is "You turn us away from our adversaries, for our enemies pillage us" (Psalms 44), and it is apparently appropriate to state that they pillage us, but the matter is such that it is mitigated by a parable of a proper poor person who goes to the party of a certain wealthy householder. Immediately upon his arrival at the door of the house, as he looks at the gathering of invitees and their activities, he turns back and returns to his house. The householder runs after him and asks him, what did you see that you do not want to sit at the table – – – is it because you did not have a place to sit at the head of invitees? The poor person responds, on the contrary, I am already used to sitting with the poor and lowly – – – but here I saw that the high ones themselves grab and trample one another, so what more can I hope for. Without doubt, nothing will remain for me..." (*Kol Yaakov, Megillat Eicha*, page 99).

In the Diaspora, even wealth is not secure with its owners, for "our lives are hanging in the balance, and we are not sure of it for even one hour, and how much more so our money and property" – – – This is compared to a person who built "a splendid house – – – in the location of a large river covered with heavy ice during the winter, and thought that this was the ground of the world – – – and the sun warmed up, melted the ice and the frost, and the entire building sunk..." (ibid. page 75). However, the livelihoods of the Diaspora, aside from not being built firmly, are "spoiled bread... the sin of usury and trespassing, and the like. All the toil of man in accordance with his mouth and soul will lead to mourning, for his business and affairs are all thorns in your eyes and sticks in your side – – – and this is what the prophet said (Hosea 4) – – – that there is no truth, etc. rather lies, etc. – – – like most of them, they sin to me, all according to the size of their wealth will their sins increase" (*Ohel Yaakov*, *Vayeira*, page 97). Regarding this bread "that is repugnant by trespassing and by theft, false oaths and dishonest weights" Ezekiel prophesied (4:17) "thus shall the Children of Israel eat their impure bread among the nations" (ibid. 338, page 74).

According to the statement of the Talmud (*Brachot* 13) "the latter tribulations make the earlier ones be forgotten" the Maggid explains the reason with his deep psychological understanding, that the Children of Israel in the Diaspora long for the redemption primarily because of the tribulations in the lands of the dispersion; "For every person according to his status and his habit thinks about what he lacks. One who is constantly used to meat and wine, if you feed him bread

[Column 155]

and water, he will think of this as torture in comparison to what he was formerly accustomed to. Not so someone who is sustained all his life with bread and water – he will not consider this as torture, only if he is hungry and thirsty – – – " Thus also "The order of the exile from the light to the heavy, from oppression to oppression, for at first they will consider it as a land that is not theirs with sufficient disgrace and wrath, but after they get used to it and they do not consider this painful, they will 'enslave them' – – – and after they get used to that as well without being sad over it, then they will 'torture them' – – – ." However, in truth, the essence of the exile is "that we left our dwelling and settled on foreign soil" … (*Kol Yaakov*, *Megillat Eicha*, page 76). The pain of the exile is that G–d "separated between the joined parts, that is between Israel and the pleasant land, of which there had never been such an honorable match of two things from the day G–d created the land and the heavens". According to a statement in the *Yalkut* and in the spirit of the opinion of Rabbi Yehuda Halevi, the Maggid expounded the verse "He stood and measured the land" (Habakkuk 3:6) thus, "for the Holy One Blessed Be He measured all the lands and measured all the nations, and gave a dwelling place to every nation and tongue, each one according to the desires of their heart and according to their temperament, for every country is unique in its traits and attributes – – – and G–d weighed the traits, temperament and essence of the Israelite nation, for it only succeeds in honor in accordance with the pure statements of G–d. The proper place for this honorable matter is only above the head, in the chief area of Jerusalem and all its precincts, in the place fitting for prophecy and for attaining the holy spirit and the secrets of the Torah – – –" (*Ohel Yaakov*, *Bechukotai*, pages 159–160). The Land of Israel "Is the place of our life, the life of the soul like water is the place of life for all found therein – – – And, when we left it, there is no punishment greater than that, for we are like fish caught in a trap – – – and this is the greatest of all the troubles that have been sent to us in the exile, that which we live on impure land – – – and this is – – – if I do not place Jerusalem as my chief joy demonstrates that even if we have all good and are sated with joy, in any case we should not harden our hearts from remembering Jerusalem, for in truth, what is more dear to us than the preciousness of Jerusalem, and what can be compared to it." (*Kol Yaakov, Megillat Eicha*, page 83). Israel was also the object of another parable of the Maggid: "It is literally like a garment made to measure for a person, which does not fit anyone else unless you dismantle it and changes its measure, both in length and width[113] – – – This is what the author of Lamentations states: Look and see our disgrace, for our inheritance has been turned over to strangers. That is to say, that they ruined it from its former splendor – – –" (ibid. page 97). The Maggid similarly explains the longing of the nation for the return to Zion in a popular parable that touches the heart: "It is the image of someone who lost a chicken and went to search for it. Perhaps

[Column 156]

he would find it at one of the neighbors. He went to one neighbor and saw the chicken, with its leg tied to one of the legs of the bed. He said to him, "this chicken is mine." The man argued with him, "It is mine. I bought it from so and so." Then the one who recognized it said, "Here is the sign that it is mine. Loosen its bonds from its legs, open the door, and your eyes will see that it will immediately fly to my house and to my land." This is literally the argument of Israel with the Holy One Blessed Be He: – – – For our hands our bound in the places of our dispersion, and this is the sign for us that when the Blessed One will loosen the ropes of the displaced one, we will immediately run after him in joy and gladness of the heart to the place where our G–d was at first. This is "Who are these who fly as a cloud, like doves to their dovecote?" (Isaiah 60:8) – – –" (*Ohel Yaakov, Tavo*, page 100).

"With the completion of the benefit of the public, the benefit of the individual will also be completed" (*Ohel Yaakov, Vayeilech*, page 117). Each Israelite person will only be saved through the solidarity of the entire nation. "And this is literally like a brand of fire that fell in a house between other houses. If every homeowner leaves his own house and they assist together in putting out the fire, they will succeed, because the fire will be easily extinguished... It will not be so if everyone works on their own to empty their house of belongings – – –." Therefore, "We have been compared to a worm – 'do not fear, oh worm of Jacob' (Isaiah 41:14) – for... if a worm is alone, it is nothing" ... "If, heaven forbid, everyone's goal is for themselves, this will be the reason for the prolonging of the exile." (*Kol Yaakov, Megillat Eicha*, page 84). Rather than every person of Israel praying for their own soul, for their own livelihood, they should rather request the redemption of the nation "for the city that is destroyed and desolate, for the Holy of Holies, for the ingathering of the exile, for the rule of the House of David[114]. The nation in exile is compared to a sick person, and "The most severe sign of the sick person, testifying to the danger and the severe blemish, is when the sick person does not sense his pain." (*Ohel Yaakov, Vayeilech*, page 117). Regarding the efforts of the nation to arrive from the Diaspora to the resting place, the Maggid states the following parable: "Orphans had a great inheritance with many rooms, lower story, second story, and third story, and someone was living in the house, whereas they were living in the house of a stranger. Eventually a fire broke out in the city. They began to make efforts to save the house in which they lived. One wise person said to them: "Why are you toiling so much over the inheritance of a strange person. How do you abandon your honor? How have you forgotten that you are supposed to toil to save the house of your fathers, for it is an eternal bequest to you." (*Ohel Yaakov, Shlach*, page 74). In contrast with the small mindedness of those "Who love the dispersion, saying that only at their (the nation's) hands will they obtain

[Column 157]

their livelihood, and the livelihood of their house – – – So what connection do they still have with the inheritance of G–d in the Holy Land, what connection do they still have to Zion and Jerusalem?" (*Ohel Yaakov, Shlach*, page 71). The Maggid arouses the nation to national pride with a parable that penetrates the heart: "It is compared to a king who was angry with his son and sent him away from his house and his city. The lad went and wandered about for bread until he was forced to knock on the door of a lowly person, for perhaps he will at least have a place for him to sleep. The person rose to his voice and brought him into his house – – – to serve him and perform his work. Several years passed until he forgot his nation and his father's house, and he performed the village work as if he had done so[15] since birth. Eventually, the villager died, and he served his son. However, his son was a wicked, evil man, who worked him with mortar, bricks, and all sorts of hard labor, and also did not give him an appropriate portion of bread. It was very bitter for him, and he wished to die. In those days, the king became saddened over his son, for he had not heard from him for a number of years – – – he took council, and went to travel through the land – – – He went on his way along with one of his friends… Every place he went, he commanded that a declaration should be made in the marketplaces and the streets saying: anyone who has a request from the king, to ask for a judgment between friends, or for a servant to his master, all shall come before the king – – – and he will take up their argument – – – The king's son also came – – – to curse his master – – – and he did not recognize his father – – – And it was, when the king saw his beloved son – – – He fell on his neck, kissed him, wept bitterly and said to him: "My son, my son, how did you forget your glory and pride, how did you forget that the kingdom was waiting for you, and when you were in my house, several ministers and deputies would bow to your majesty and glory. And how, how have you fallen so low, forgotten all this, and only asked that you find favor in the eyes of a villager to lighten your work, and to add a bit of bread to your allotment." (*Ohel Yaakov, Emor*, page 115; with a bit of change of text – ibid. page 74).

Indeed, the psychological, social realism stood for the Maggid of Dubno, who saw with open eyes the negative factors that prevent the nation from remembering its homeland and pining for redemption in Zion. He expounded the verse in the book of Lamentations [Eicha]: "Judea was exiled from poverty – – – She dwelt among the nations and did not find rest – – – " in accordance with the Midrash "Had it found a resting place, it would not return – – – the Holy One Blessed Be He – – – exiled us from our Land, and we became accustomed to this as well and found a resting place among the nations, then the Holy One Blessed Be He added to our troubles, with afflictions and poverty. All of this was to arouse our hearts – – –" (*Kol Yaakov*, *Megillat Eicha*, page 92). When he explains the promise of the Torah "When you are in the straits, and all these things overtake you in the latter days, and you return to the Lord your G–d"

[Column 158]

(Portion of *Vaetchanan*, Deuteronomy 4:30), the Maggid gives a sign to recognize the purpose of the afflictions of the nation of Israel: "If the Holy One Blessed Be He afflicts us with one punishment – – – the intention is – – – to purge our sins – – – and to thereby save us from the judgment of Gehinnom [Hell]". It is not so with the many troubles that surround us – – – All have gathered around together, and this is a sign and portent that the Holy One Blessed Be He has come to arouse our hearts to ask for mercy and return us to Jerusalem – – – to ingather our exiles from the four corners of the earth. This is literally like someone who is chasing after his slave who escaped from him. If he comes to him and wishes to catch him and blocks his route so that he will come back to his house, there is a field before him to the right and the left. This is not the case if you come and surround him from three sides so that there is no way to turn to the right or left. Then, he must return to his place. Thus, the Holy One Blessed Be He forces us to return to our place by sending us many bad tribulations that surround us from all sides and all corners – – – Then, they are forced to ask about Zion, behold the path is before them" (Jeremiah 50:5). One of the Maggid's parables is about the force leading the nation to longing for a return to Zion: "A great minister whose son transgresses – – – and, perforce, his father exiles him to a far–off land. Since the mercy of the father toward the son is very great, the father sends him anonymous gifts in overt and covert ways, so that he will not die of hunger – – – As the time moves on, and the minister goes about with a distraught face because he is sad about his son, and it is not honorable to write to him to come to his house. Given the disgraceful things that the son did, how can the father go to appease him? He goes about with a bitter heart, and half his flesh is consumed. One of the ministers sitting before him approaches him and says, My master – – – I will advise you and he will come by himself – For my soul knows very well that the livelihood of your son during these times is certainly only from your hand – – – for, from what does he live. Therefore – – – return your hand to your bosom, and, from today, do not send him

168

any livelihood. When he does not find anything, perforce his uncircumcised heart will be subdued, and he will come to you, and appease you, so that he can return to your table." (*Ohel Yaakov, Vaetchanan*, page 22).

Appropriate to the best of the tradition of the nation that evolved from the visions of the prophets on the matters of the future period, the Maggid of Dubno also sees the redemption during the time of the Messiah as a complete redemption – both national and social. "This entire way" (that is, the division of the world into rich and poor) "is only in this world as long as the leaders (the trait of justice and the trait of mercy) set the scales one against the other. However, regarding the future, it is stated "And the redeemed of G–d shall return and come to Zion with song, with eternal joy over their heads. They will attain joy and gladness, and agony and sighing will disappear" (Isaiah 35:10, 51:11). That is to say, the trait of justice will not rule, to set bad against good. There will only be peace, truth, joy, and gladness from all sides. Agony and sighing will disappear, and one will no longer be against the other." (*Ohel*

[Column 159]

Yaakov, Re'eh page 66). He continues to explain matters through a comparison: "And when we delve into the section of land which we are upon, it is not level, but rather has ascents and descents, mountains and valleys, ravines and hills. The intellect indicates that something missing here is extra in another place. About the future it is said (Isaiah 40): Every valley will be raised, and every mountain and hill will be lowered, so the land will be level" (ibid. page 67). Indeed, complete social equality is only possible in the future. The world will run in accordance to its custom until the time of the Messiah, and there will be a social division between the rich and the poor, in accordance with the simple explanation of the verse, "For there will not cease to be poor in the midst of the land."[116] The social problem, the problem of the reason for the reality of poverty in the world and the obligations of society toward the poor, is one of the themes upon which the sermons of the Maggid were based. He explains in accordance with the same theories that are known from his sermons on the redemption of the nation in Zion. The two pillars with which the Maggid delves into ways of life, and which serve as the primary theme for his parables, the large–scale merchants on one side, and the poor on the other side, are also the two poles of the outlook of society. However, at the same time as the Maggid, with his general outlook, displays a positive side of the spirit of capitalistic effort and bourgeoisie individualism, especially regarding the class of large-scale merchants; when he approaches the question of poverty, he remains almost completely immersed in the organic–feudal concept of society, and in the traditional religious concept of charity. Even in his doctrines of the ways of the world, in which G–d "provides the livelihood of the poor through the wealthy," as well as his claim of that generosity in charity is an obligation and not a kindness, the Maggid of Dubno meets up with the best of the Hassidic preachers of his generation; however, the fundamentals of the populist preacher are exposed here too in the craft of wonderful explanation unique to him, in a manner, through parables that are direct and heartwarming, the secret of which only he knows.

About the Way of the Maggid of Dubno in Parable and His Social Teaching

1. Through Parable

The Maggid was especially involved with the realities of the two classes standing at the two edges of the nations – the merchants on one side and the kilns of the poor and beggars on the other side. These merchants and poor people are most prevalent as the heroes of his parables.

Some of the merchants travel to Leipzig alone or in a caravan, and others import merchandise through their emissaries; a merchant "who owns many factories, with many people standing to do the work," and one "all of whose merchandise had been obtained from a craftsman and worker"; a merchant who purchases merchandise with cash, and a merchant who purchases on credit; "a large scale merchant who travels with twenty wagons laden with merchandise for distribution"; a merchant who travels to the fair and to the market day, a merchant of new clothing, and a merchant "whose merchandise

[Column 160]

is worn out, used clothing"; a merchant of silk, embroidered products, and a merchant of precious stones; merchants who are "trustworthy, whose intention and will is to pay," and merchants whose "intention is to no longer travel to Leipzig, to no longer appear before the merchant"; a merchant in accordance with the law and custom, and a merchant "about whom rumors are spread that he deals with forbidden products"; "a shopkeeper who sells merchandise in a store to a few people," and a traveling peddler who is "a representative" for a large scale merchant who "travels with the merchandise to sell in the towns"; the servant of a merchant and "the scribe in the shop of the merchant, who received a set annual salary." By nature, the gallery of poor people is not as variegated as that of the merchants, but they too have healthy beggars and blind beggars; a beggar who goes door to door in his city, and "a poor person whose livelihood comes from a known wealthy person"; "a beggar who goes from city to city to collect donations," and "poor people who go in a group, and carry a bit of merchandise with them in the manner that poor people carry, such as tzitzit, and mezuzas." If the doctor is mainly an allegorical type, tradesmen appear in the parables in their true essence. These include "tradesmen of precious material" such as diamond cutters and the like; a butcher, a baker and a tailor "who comes with the measuring stick" "measuring and doing business" with the groom before the wedding; a tradesman who is independent, and a tradesman "who works for the business of a merchant, who received half the payment"; bartenders, middlemen; teachers, the head of the stall, the matchmaker, and the cantor; wagon drivers, and tavern keepers. To fill out the picture, the preacher presents for us, with precious humor in several of his parables, the thieves with their caprices and tricks, as well as characters such "as someone who earned his livelihood from news, that is, when he heard good news about someone, he would hurry to tell the subject"; or, such as the idlers in the *Beis Midrash* who were jealous of the servants and representatives of the merchant who went to Leipzig and Danzig, and who received a raise in salary after the strike "and they also acted with caprice, gathered all together, went to the wealthy person and advised him with an excuse that he should add to their weekly salary"…

Here is one of the examples of the penetrating gaze of Maggid of Dubno into the economic–social life of his time, which served for him as a complete source of his doctrine. Regarding the verse in the Torah "You should not harden your heart, and you should not close your hand from your impoverished brother" (Deuteronomy 15:7), he makes the following parable in his introduction to the statement in *Pirkei Avot* "Let your house be opened wide and let there be poor people among your household"נחל: "A poor person sells fruit in the market and thereby earns his livelihood, but there are no customers where his house is, for he lives in a grove on the slope of the city at the edge of the population. What does he do? He builds a hut among the stores of the wealthy people, next to the house of a wealthy person who sells food and drink. Many people are found there, and there he too can sell the bit of fruit in his hands. In this way, the wealthy person does not give this poor person anything of his own, other than allowing him to set up a place near his house, thereby giving him his livelihood. On the contrary, when he impedes him [i.e., the poor person], even though he does not

[Column 161]

take anything from the poor person, he cuts into his livelihood. The referent: the source of livelihood and fortune of the poor person is very difficult and withheld from him. However, the wealthy person has good fortune from heaven to receive a bounty in a generous fashion. If the wealthy person volunteers to give bread to the poor person every week, the wealthy person does not give anything of his own, for the Holy One Blessed Be He bestows upon him the portion of the poor person as well. This is nothing other than the livelihood of the poor person passing through his hand via his house – and this is the meaning of the statement, "Let your home be opened wide," for what does it matter to you if a poor person is included in your household. This is the meaning of "And let poor people be among your household," and you will not be lacking anything due to them. This is "And you shall not harden your heart, and you shall not close your hand." It is only that the livelihood of the poor flows through the purity of your heart. Through opening your hand, by including him as well in accounting for the needs of your household, you will be bestowed in a greater fashion,

171

so that there will be enough for him as well, as it says (Proverbs 18), "The gift of a person broadens him."

The Maggid, the craftsman of parable, also knew how to dive into the secrets of Jewish folklore and to weave popular stories, full of wisdom, wit, and satire, embroidered as one in his sermons on morality. A parable of this nature also exemplifies his characteristic talent: "It is compared to a poor man who had a prominent, wealthy relative, and the wealthy person had to make a wedding for his son. – – – This poor person said in his heart, I too will be invited to the table of my uncle, and therefore I will prepare for this by not eating anything in my house. – He fasted for two days so he would be hungry and would then be able to enjoy himself in the meadow of sweet delicacies. Toward the evening of the second day, he felt very faint. He looked out the window to see if the servants had begun to go to the wealthy people to summon them to the feast. He saw that the servants were all passing by the door of his house, neglecting him. He was very bitter and told his poor wife to give him something to eat from what was in the house. She gave him lots of bread, onions, radishes, and other such bitter and sour foods. Since he was hungry, nothing was left over. After he ate all this, his uncle's servant came to him to tell him that his master had requested his presence on the day of the wedding and joy. He went with a bitter soul. When he sat at the table, they first brought fish, and he did not find any taste in the fish, as he was already full. Then they brought roasted meat in gravy. When he took a spoonful of the gravy to his mouth as it was still hot, his stomach exuded the bitter taste of onions and radishes, and this honorable food tasted bitter and sour. He sat there the entire meal and did not eat one morsel of all these tasty foods.[18] – – – The referent: for in truth, the Holy One Blessed Be He invited us to Torah and the commandments, all of which are beloved, pleasant

[Column 162]

and sweeter than honey and honeycombs. Someone who approaches them with a pure soul and a proper spirit will sense their sweetness. Not so with us, who have already sated our souls with the lowliness of the vanities of the evil drives… And this is what was said: woe to those who call evil good, and good evil, etc. They exchange bitter for sweet, and the sweetness is bitter. Our rabbis of blessed memory have already advised in a Midrash (brought in *Tosafot, Ketubot* 104a, starting with *Lo*), the Holy One Blessed Be He said: As long as you pray that the words of Torah enter your innards, also request that the words of vanity literally exit your innards, as is written (*Ohel Yaakov*, Book of Exodus, Portion of *Pikudei*, Warsaw edition, 1873, pp. 151–152).

2. "The Philosophy of Poverty" in the Teaching of the Maggid

In the opinion of the Maggid, based on Talmud and Midrash, there are two reasons for the existence of "poor people" in the world, why G–d did not make it "that everyone will be wealthy"; One is that poor people are trustworthy to worship the L–rd with a full heart (according to *Midrash Rabba, Mishpatim*, 31, in the commentary of Psalms 61, 8: "Had I made My world equal, mercy and truth would not be preserved!") The second is to grant merit to the wealthy through the commandment of charity (according to *Bava Batra* 10a: "So that we will be thereby saved from the judgment of Gehinnom", *Ohel Yaakov, Bahar*, page 142). However, also according to this theory, according to which G–d "provides livelihood to the poor through the wealthy" the Maggid expounds a fundamental theory: G–d sustains the poor through the wealthy "both in ways that they know, and in ways that they do not know" in various ways, and not only through charity: "For He prepares pretexts to change things for the wealthy, or the wealthy person will be forced to invite the poor person to his house to help him with some work or task, or the wealthy person will lose something and the poor person will find it, and many other situations of this nature where the bounty of the wealthy transfers to the poor" (*Ohel Yaakov, Re'eh*, page 66). This strange doctrine of philanthropy only serves for the Maggid as a support for the commandment of charity: The poor "in any case, only get their sustenance from the hand" of the wealthy, for "the poor will never cease in your land"[119]. The explanation of "I will not abandon him – – – to be cast off and abandoned to death by hunger," for if he is not sustained through acts of charity, he will be sustained "through causes and reasons," in that a bit of the wealth will roll over to the hand of the poor person. Therefore, the Torah adjures, "You shall surely open up your hand to him – – – surely give"[120]; the explanation is: "Give to him out of the free choice of your good heart, and through your hand – – – for if he gets his livelihood from you without your knowledge, and without your choice, nobody will lose other than you, for it will not be considered for you as charity – – –" (ibid).

Furthermore, the statement in the Midrash (*Midrash Rabba, Mishpatim*, ibid.) regarding the punishment of poverty awaiting the wealthy person who does not support the poor, is explained by the Maggid in accordance with his theory of the two reasons for the existence of poverty in the world.

Regarding the verse "A poor and rich person meet, G–d made them all" (Proverbs 22:2)[21], the Midrash expounds: "If a poor person extends his hand, and the householder does not want to give to him, G–d made them both. He Who made this person rich will eventually make him poor, and He Who made that person poor will eventually make him rich." The Maggid explains and adds: If the rich people do not support the poor "then this reason is not relevant" to the existence of poverty, that is to give merit to the wealthy people for fulfilling commandments. Rather, the first reason applies, "That the world cannot exist without poor people." However, in this case, "This person does not have to be poor, and that one rich, for the world can exist even if it was the opposite – – –"(*Ohel Yaakov*, ibid.)

In the wake of this theory, the Maggid explains and teaches the theory of the Alshich[22], that "The wealthy person does not give anything of himself, for the Holy One Blessed Be He also bestows on him the portion of the poor, and this is nothing other than the livelihood of the poor passing through his household" (*Ohel Yaakov, Re'eh*, page 68). (Compare the aforementioned parable in which the poor person sells fruit in "a hut between the stores of the wealthy.") Even in this situation, social differences of the earth are noted, for it has mountains and valleys – – – hills and ravines," "for what is missing here is made up for in another place" – – – "Indeed, and thus we deduce that what the poor are lacking for their needs will be added to the wealthy people, for Heaven forbid should the Holy One Blessed Be He give to the wealthy person that for which he has no need, unless the wealthy person has only what the poor person lacks." It is compared to "the dream of Pharaoh, who saw that the bad cows swallowed the good ones. It can be seen that the additional bounty of the seven good years was that which was lacking from the seven bad years. Therefore, the command was issued to gather up heaps, and to leave over the excess for the years of famine." The act of charity is nothing other than justice, in the simple sense of the term, in that the wealthy person gives the poor person his portion, "and this is literally the statement that there will be no indigent among you, Heaven forbid, that the portion lacking from him will be extra for you, and therefore the wealthy person is obligated to bear the burden of the poor person and to sustain him, for he is giving him that which is his" (*Ohel Yaakov, Re'eh*, page 68). As an additional proof, the Maggid also goes beyond the straightforward meaning of the verse that is the foundation of the justification of the poor person in the world: "For the poor will not cease from the midst of the Land – that is to say, I did not withhold from the poor by not giving him his share in the land." – – – "The Holy One Blessed Be He commands the wealthy person, who continues on with the blessing for himself, to save some of his blessing to give to the poor his portion" (ibid. pp 73–74).

From this theory, according to which the "excess" portion in the hands of the wealthy is nothing other than the portion of the poor that has been given to his hand, the Maggid also derives the theory of the decisive connection between the wealth of the wealthy and the poverty of the poor. Already in the Midrash (*Shmot Rabba* ibid.) the parable is found that the world is compared from a social perspective to the "wheel in the garden, the earthenware vessel in which those who are lowly rise up

and those who are above descend empty." However, the Midrash states the parable regarding the exchange of fate between the wealthy and the poor as a wheel that turns ("Not everyone who is rich today will be rich tomorrow, and not everyone who is poor today will be poor tomorrow"), whereas the Maggid of Dubno uses that parable to prove that, to the extent that the rich person gets richer, the poor person gets poorer. "For the poor and the rich are both weighed on a scale, with scales of justice one against the other, for to the extent that the rich person attains wealth, the poverty of the poor person will be deepened. Then, is it not the law that the rich person be given enough to provide for the poor during his time of poverty, as per the following parable: Two people tied their utensils to two ends of the rope on the wheel. When one pulls the rope to raise his items from the pit, it is appropriate for his friend to help him. For as long as he is involved with raising his own, he is also involved with lowering those of the other. The referent: whomever has mercy upon the poor, bears the tribulations of his poverty and provides his needs, justice will have it that he will be wealthy, and he will be granted wealth in relation to the poverty of the other person. However, if the rich person averts his eyes from the poor, why should the poor person bear the burden of poverty on behalf of the wealthy person? Therefore, He Who made this person rich can also make him poor – and this is what it means 'if there will be a poor person among you'[23], rather than 'if there will be a poor person with you' – for the poor person is as if cut from a piece of the rich person, for the poverty of the poor will be in accordance with the weight of his wealth."

Since the division of bounty in the world is compared to scales, in the sense of "this in comparison to that," we find that someone who enjoys the excess, such as the excess of wealth, is stealing from the poor: for "as the wealthy person gets richer, grows greater, rises up, and basks in his wealth, justice forces the poverty of the poor to become heavier (ibid. *Bahar*, page 142). Even Rabbi Wolf of Zhitomir[24] thunders against the life of excess, and regards such people as stealing directly from the portion of the poor that has been placed in the hand of the rich person. Nevertheless, the reasoning of the Maggid of Dubno has a greater level of social realism, as explained and proved by the following parable: "If food is placed on a table, and the food is too meager for those seated around the table, then if one of them eats too much, perforce another will remain hungry." – "Thus, someone who amasses wealth and greatness is certainly stealing from others." – "And this is the meaning of: do not steal from the poor, for stealing from the poor, etc. and you should understand" (ibid. *Kedoshim*, page 93). With great psychological understanding, the Maggid explains the custom of the rich to invite poor people to a celebration. It is as if to assuage their guilty conscience:

"One can say that because of this, when people make a celebration for some good thing, they have the custom of making others happy as well, for the joy is a reason for causing sadness to the poor, based on the scales of placing one against the other. When one person is given more joy, pain and mourning will be added to the other. Therefore, he is obligated to make others happy." – This is literally the meaning of the dance of the poor at the wedding of the wealthy person in Anski's Dybbuk...

[Column 165]

The Maggid, who was good at observing the way of life of the wealthy people, also knew that not only did they not fulfill the commandment of charity according to its law, to grant the poor person "his portion" to give him "what is his"; but they also used every excuse, such as bad business, to restrict their donations or to withhold all support from the poor. Regarding this, the Maggid relates one of his most pointed satirical parables: "It is like a wealthy person who did his business over the great waters and went with a boat laden with a great deal of wares. He also had books with him so that he could study a lesson every day, as well as his tallis and tefillin, and other such things. Once, a windstorm broke out, and they saw that the boat was already sinking too much into the water. The captain called out to him and told him to quickly lighten the weight of the boat, without sparing his merchandise – to throw into the water whatever came to his hand, for otherwise, they would all perish and be lost. The merchant was very frightened, so he quickly took his tallis, tefillin, and all his books, and tossed them into the sea – – – The referent: The needs of people are very great, and their expenses through the months of the year amount to a great sum. How many thousands does he spend on himself, his wife, and children for food, drink, clothing, and jewelry? He also gives a minute amount to the poor; however, it is negligible in comparison to the vast sums that he spends on his household. When he sees that fortune is not good to him, it would be fitting to minimize the spending on his household, so as not to disburse money on things that are not necessary. That way, he would be able to have enough money. He does not do this, but rather "and your eye becomes mean toward your poor brother"[25], that is, he withholds everything from him.

The continuation of that verse (Deuteronomy 15:9), "And he will call out to G–d about you, and you will have a sin" is explained by the Maggid with a parable of the realities of the people of his generation: "It says, 'and he will call' and not 'and he will shout', for we know that all the prayers of the wealthy are only accepted through the poor. – – – This is the matter of a wealthy person who marries off his daughter to a prominent lad from a splendid family, and he did not sustain him properly with food on his table or fine clothing, and the lad suffered bad things from him. The lad was silent and held his peace. As time went on, he had a large judgment with the minister of the city, as the minister wanted to disrupt and destroy him. He found nobody to intercede on his behalf to beg for his life from the minister, other than the uncle or cousin of his son–in–law. He sent his son–in–law to the home of the redeemer relative to ask him to do this for him. The lad went to his relative to intercede for his father–in–law. When the lad came to the house of his uncle, his uncle saw how distraught his face was, with a dark complexion, naked, and barefoot. He asked, "Why are you so poor, my son?" Those standing around responded that this was from the miserliness of his cruel father–in–law, who treats him with the evil eye. When he heard these things, and also heard that he had sent his son–in–law to find someone to intercede for him before the minister, his wrath was kindled greatly, and he said: "Now you will see what I will do to him, for briers and thorns will be his, and

[Column 166]

I will uproot all his grain." The referent: And I will call out to G–d about you, for now you ask that he call out to G–d on your behalf. Not only will this not arouse mercy, but also "it will be a sin for you." For when the memory of the poor person comes before the Blessed One, with his poverty and bitterness, and you prevent kindness for him, the trait of justice will strengthen "[26] (ibid. pp. 69–70).

One of the pearls of Jewish folklore on the topic of social satire is the parable that the Maggid uses to explain the verse "If your brother becomes poor..." (Vayikra, *Bahar*, 25:35). The Maggid brings a verse from Proverbs (19:17) that the Midrash uses in this context: "One who has mercy upon the poor lends to G–d, and He will repay him." He prefaces this with the verse in Isaiah (58:13–14): "And you shall call the Sabbath a delight, to sanctify for the honorable G–d – – – Then you will delight in G–d – – –". He makes the parable: "It is compared to a tycoon who has two sons in far–off places, one rich and the other poor. These brothers had not seen their father for many years. Once, a letter came from the wealthy father that the son of his old age was about to get married, and he asked to celebrate with his other sons on the day of the wedding and rejoicing. He wrote a letter to the wealthy son asking him to come along with his brother to the wedding, and not to worry about the great expense for the honor of their father, for he would pay everything in fine fashion. When the wealthy son received this letter from his father, he went quickly to the store to purchase a great deal of valuable merchandise. He made splendid clothes for his wife and children and prepared to travel. Before he ascended the vehicle, he reminded himself, and said, "Summon my brother quickly, for I need him greatly." They summoned him in haste, and the poor person asked, "What do you want?" They told him, "What are you asking, come with me onto the vehicle." He came aboard and sat down, and they went. As this vehicle approached their destination city, and news reached the home of their father that his sons and daughters–in–law were approaching, the in–laws went out with the musicians to greet them in joy. The rich person descended from the vehicle dressed in splendid clothing, and the in–laws asked who he was. They said, "This is the son of the wealthy man." Then the poor person came down after him, tattered, naked, and barefoot. They asked about him, and they said that he too is a resident in the city of his brother, that they are brothers. They were silent and nodded their heads. They came to the house, the musicians played, the wedding ceremony took place, and they rejoiced greatly. After two or three weeks, the rich son said to his wealthy father, "My dear father, I have done everything that you commanded me, to come and rejoice together, and now you know that I am a businessman, and how can I leave my business for this entire month." His father said, "Do what you need to, my dear son, and who is stopping you. You can travel to your home in peace." He listened to the words of his father, and it was like

[Column 167]

air locked into his bones regarding the great expense that he expended, and that his father had promised to repay sevenfold. Now he sees his father evading this, and he is forced to return back to his home. He says to himself, "Why am I silent and holding back. I must ask with my mouth." He went before his father and presented him with the long accounting of all the great expenses that he made. Thus was the cost of the clothing that he made, thus was the clothing that he made for his wife and children, thus were the expenses of the journey. His father said, "You made clothing for yourself, use them, wear them out, and then you will get new clothes for yourself." He said to his father, "But you promised me that all the expenses will be on your account." He said to him, "Don't lie, my son, for this is a lie." He then took out the letter in his father's handwriting, and showed the letter to his father, saying, "See my father, that the truth is with me." His father then said, "Read out loud the words of the letter." He read to him, that it is written therein that all the expenses that you make in my honor I will pay you. "Now see, my son, that if you really did it in my honor, how is it that you did not remember or concern yourself with my honor, in that you took your poor brother with you, naked and barefoot, wearing worn–out, torn clothes, and you did not remember to dress him in a fashion that will be honorable to me. See, everything that you spent, and all the great expenses were for you, so what are you demanding of me?" The referent: The Holy One Blessed Be He, so to speak, also wrote a long letter to the person that He will repay all the expenses that he makes for the honor of G–d in the enjoyment of the Sabbath and festivals – – – So how can he enter in to the Sabbath day dressed splendidly and eat fine foods, while his poor brother sits as a mourner eating seeds? – – – And this is the sweetness of the adage, if you lend to G–d: who lends to G–d? One who is merciful toward the poor. He will be repaid also

[Column 168]

for the expenses that he pays for himself – – –". (*Ohel Yaakov, Bahar,* pp. 139–140).

Charity is giving to the poor what is owed to them. The Maggid warns, "It is not that one should be aroused by the pain of the poor, as is said (Proverbs 31), 'her hand is spread open to the poor', etc., one should not wait for the poor to extend his hands to request his bread – as the pious one of blessed memory writes (in *Chovot Halevavot*)[2] regarding one who is merciful to the poor to remove his own pain, to push off the pain that afflicts him by seeing the agony of the poor, thereby redeeming himself from great agony through a smaller agony. Then it is only like he is serving the desires of his own heart, as one who hits someone in his anger is serving his own anger…" (*Ohel Yaakov, Re'eh*, page 75). Similarly, the Maggid expounds the verse "If your brother becomes poor, you shall support him, and he shall live with you"[27]: The explanation is that when you see him tottering, but he has not yet fallen, you must not say, "I will wait until he has no support." – – – Rather, before he falls, you should arise and help strengthen him, so he can maintain his status. – – – This is as is written, "and you shall strengthen him." You will only have to strengthen him a bit, and he will live with you. That is, his own energy will join in partnership with your power and hold him up (ibid. page 74).

The social teaching of the Maggid of Dubno is fundamentally similar to that of the Hassidic preachers, especially of Rabbi Binyamin of Zalowice. However, there is something in the sermons of the Hassidic Maggidim, from the perspective of form and content, that does not exist in the sermons of the Misnagdic Maggid, wonderful in their parable: the explicit, sharp social protest directed toward the rabbis and communal heads who commit sacrilege in their roles. This is no surprise: In contrast to the Hassidim, the Maggid of Dubno does not speak in opposition to the communities and does not desire a change of guard. Therefore, he does not berate, but rather preaches. He does not pillory, but rather convinces with words. He does not protest, but rather explains.

Original Footnotes and Translator's Comments:

1. See https://en.wikipedia.org/wiki/Judah_ben_Samuel_of_Regensburg
2. See https://en.wikipedia.org/wiki/Chovot_HaLevavot
3. See https://en.wikipedia.org/wiki/The_Guide_for_the_Perplexed
4. See https://en.wikipedia.org/wiki/Sefer_ha–Ikkarim
5. See https://en.wikipedia.org/wiki/Isaac_ben_Moses_Arama
6. An expression of minimalism, common in traditional Jewish thought.
7. Original footnote: See the chapter "on the Methodology of the Maggid of Dubno in Parable, and his Social Teaching" columns 159–160 further on.
8. A verse from Song of Songs 2:16, considered to reflect the mutual love of G–d and the Jewish people.
9. See https://en.wikipedia.org/wiki/Mephistopheles
10. Original footnote: Brought down from *Sefer Hamidot* [Book of Traits], chapter of trust, fourth chapter, and from *Ohel Yaakov*, Portion of *Tazria*, page 64.
11. In other words, secular wisdom without Torah wisdom is problematic.
12. Original footnote: Compare *Ohel Yaakov*, portion of *Nasso*, published in 1874, page 21: "This honorable thing I heard in the name of our master, the Gaon of Vilna, the leader of the nation. The Gaon of Vilna died on the Festival of Sukkot, 5556 (1797).
13. Original footnote: This parable is based on the Midrash (*Bamidbar Rabba*, portion 23) "There is a person who is handsome, but his clothing is ugly, who is ugly; but Israel is pleasant for the Land, and the Land is pleasant for them."
14. Original footnote: In this reproof, the Maggid is definitely influenced by Rabbi Yehuda HaLevi. Compare the *Kuzari*, section II, 24: "And our speech is not about bowing to His holy mountain, bowing to His footstool, and may the Divine Presence return to Zion. On the contrary, it is like the hissing of the hounds and the like, for we do not think about what is said about this and the like…"
15. Original footnote: It seems that there was a printer error here, and it should have said "a servant forever".
16. Deuteronomy 15:11
17. *Pirkei Avot* 1:5
18. Original footnote in the text here: That parable is told in the name of the Maggid with a change in the ending, as a satire on a Maggid who stole the lesson from him. Compare A. Steinman, "From the Writings of the Maggid of Dubno" Volume I, pp 383–4 (section "Counting and with G–d" 21).
19. Deuteronomy 15:11.
20. Deuteronomy 15:8.
21. There is an error in the quote of this verse here. It should be "The wealthy person and the poor person meet, G–d made them both".
22. See https://en.wikipedia.org/wiki/Moshe_Alshich
23. Deuteronomy 15:7. A nuanced change in one small word in the verse.
24. See https://www.encyclopedia.com/religion/encyclopedias–almanacs–transcripts–and–maps/zeev–wolf–zhitomir
25. Deuteronomy 15:9.
26. I.e., you will be judged harshly.
27. Leviticus 25:35 (with some words missing).

The City and its Residents

Dubno Eighty Years Ago [1880]

by Yitzchak Ajzik Feffer

Translated from Yiddish by Pamela Russ

Introduction translated from Hebrew by Selwyn Rose

In the winter of 1956 when it was decided to publish "Greater Dubno" the memorial book for the Holocaust fallen, the editorial board approached a surviving town Elder, an old man who had accumulated much wisdom and knowledge during his long life, Mr. Yitzchak Ajzik Feffer who was at the time 94 years of age, in order to reveal to the readers of the book, a portrait of Dubno as it was clearly drawn in his memory. But before he was able to see the fruits of his labors he passed on.

Mr. Yitzchak Ajzik Feffer, the tutor of Rabbi Elisha Feffer, one of the offspring of Rabbi Leyb Sharhass a student of the Ba'al Shem Tov (May his name be preserved), was born in the village of Olik (Olyka) on the 5th of Av 1862. His mother was the granddaughter of Rabbi Yitzchak Ajzik, leader of the Rabbinical Court of Korets. He immigrated to Palestine during peacetime and settled in Petah Tikvah and was one of the strong preachers of *Torah*. He lived to see his children and grandchildren established in the Homeland and died at a good old age at 96. He was interred in Kfar Saba on *Rosh Chodesh Iyyar* 1958. *May his soul be bound in the bundle of life.*

*

183

In the year 1880, when I was eighteen years old, after my marriage to Khaya Laya Rinzberg, [sic] I left my hometown Olyk, not far from Dubno, and settled in Dubno proper.

Unlike the regular life of the youth in that period, who for years used to eat *kest* [regular meals as part of the dowry] at their father-in-law's home, and who spent regular time at the *Beis Medrash* [Study Hall] and in the *kloizen* [small Chassidic circles or courts], I went to work in trade, being certain that I would earn a living from that.

At that time, the main business for the Jews of Dubno was stores and shops. Rent for one such store was generally about six rubles a year, and the value of an average shop was between eight and ten rubles. If there was about twenty rubles worth of material in a shop, the merchant was considered to be a wholesaler. Taxes did not bother the merchants and shopkeepers. They paid government tax (*"promislovi nalog"*; "guaranteed taxes") of about 30 kopeks a year, according to the number of candles the women used to light and bless on Friday night. The taxes were not paid directly to the government, but to the collectors (*"zborschtchik"*), such as Reb Moti Waldman who would collect the leasing taxes from the government, collecting the debts with the help of other collectors, all of them our Jewish brothers.

The Russian authorities in the city were represented by few officials, the highest of which was the chief of police, along with his two helpers, inspectors, and 2…3 policemen (*"desyatnikes"*; "of ten men" sergeants), who maintained order. Among these, I remember the old policeman Kuzma.

This is how the local authorities were, and their relationship with the people was very good.

There was a prison in town called "*Dvoryanskaya Turma*" ["The Nobleman's Prison"], a large room where they detained criminal citizens by day, and then they went home at night to sleep in their own beds…

In the year 1880, the southwest train was already working, which at Radziwill cut across the Austrian border and from there went to Brody and beyond to Lemberg. During the summer, in town, people rode in *kibitka* [Russian carriages] and in the winter – in peasant sleds.

The population in Dubno a hundred years ago, as the old people would recount, was – a small Jewish settlement. They would

[Column 615–616]

describe the place as "Dubno near Murawiez" in the 80s of the former century – about 5,000 souls, and they earned a living as shoemakers, smithies, harness makers, tailoring, carpentry, and masonry. As Jewish workers, there were chimney sweeps, limestone workers, dyers, folk doctors [barber surgeon], haircutters and shavers, and those who did drawing of blood, leeching and cupping. Jews also worked as furriers, porters, transporters, and watercarriers from the river. On the other hand, the peasants ("*Poleshukes*"); [*Poleshchuki* is the name given to the people who populated the swamps of Polesia] in the area did the wood chopping, as they were "rented" by Jewish homes to chop wood for the winter. They would do this in the summertime and store the wood in the ovens by the houses.

There were no roads or sidewalks in town, so they put boards from one house to the next on rainy days. In the marketplace, in the center of town, was the City Council building, and in their yard was residents' garbage and waste. The city owned two mills. One, the watermill of Shloss (Schloss Mill), and the other of the Princess Szubalowa and her daughters. Jews earned a substantial living and comfort from both mills.

Once a year, there was a horse fair under the name of "*Kontrakten*."

There were thick forests in the area, such as the Smyg, on the road to Kremenets, and Jewish forest merchants of Dubno employed hunters, and they chopped down the pine trees, the oak trees, and the fir trees to export out of the country. At that time, Reb Aron Aronstein was well known. He employed four hunters. His sons-in-law were Reb Nissel Wajnberg and Reb Shmuel Halevi Horowyc, descendants of the *Shelah Hakadosh* [*Isaiah ben Abraham Horowitz, c. 1555[1][2] … March 24, 1630, also known as the Shelah Hakadosh, after the title of his best-known work; was a prominent rabbi and mystic*].

The family Bratz (the son of Reb Tzadok) and the family Marszalkowyc belonged to the higher class of people in Dubno, who were blessed with wealth and fine character. The Bratz family was wealthy, and they were generous spenders with an open hand. The largest textile business in town belonged to them. They built up a beautiful *kloiz* for relatives and Torah scholars.

*

In the 80s, only traces of the Berlin *Haskalah* [Enlightenment] were still evident. But *chassidus* also made roots in town, even though not everyone embraced it. In Dubno, there were *shtiebelech* [plural of *shtiebel*, small informal synagogue] of the Karliner and Ruzhiner *chassidim*, of the Ostrower, Olyker, Kotsker, Trisk-Stoliner, and Trisker, whose rabbis were descendants of Reb Motele Czernobyler [of the Czernobyler dynasty].

The Kotsker *chassidim*, loyal followers of the Rebbe [spiritual leader] Reb Mendele, were small in number. They followed their Rebbe, and studied *Gemara* [Talmud], *Peirushim* [rabbinic elucidations], and *Tosafos* [classic commentaries on the Talmud], prayed at later times, and did not travel to their Rebbe, but regularly sent monies [as a token, redemption] every year. The four main pillars of the Kozker *chassidus* in Dubno were: Reb Berish Shmarye's (Roitman) outstanding scholarship. His parents settled in Dubno at the beginning of the 18th century; Reb Beryl Yekhiel's, originally from Poland; Reb Leybish Teumim and Reb Berish Avigdor's, from the residents of Dubno.

There was no organized life in Dubno during that period. The city did not have a decent hospital, other than the "*hekdesh*" [disorderly designated area], and also did not have a place for care of the elderly. In the large synagogue, there was a small room that was called the "community room" in which two tax collectors sat, whose job was to collect money for the most urgent expenses, such as: for the baths, cemeteries, and so on. They also were busy with community issues. The Kazioner Rav was Reb Meyer Pessye's, who would write out birth and death certificates. Reb Pinkhas Pessye's, author of the book "The City of Dubno and Her Rabbis" was a grandson of Reb Meyer and earned a living as a shopkeeper. After Reb Meyer, the next Kazioner Rebbe was Reb Khaim Zalman Margolioz, and he also

[Column 617–618]

investigated the history of the city, even though he was not a native born Wolhiner, but came from Lithuania.

*

There were six *shokhtim* [ritual slaughterers] in town at that time. Among them were: Reb Meyer son of Yosef the *shokhet* and *bodek* [examiner of the meat] and a specialist at sharpening the knives; Reb Sender son of Lippe, an expert on *sircha* [any adhesions on the lungs which may render the meat non-kosher]; and Reb Yakov Shub, son of a simple harness maker, but a God-fearing man and a great Torah scholar, and of the Zinkower *chassidim*. The tax-farmer was Reb Borukh Cohen. The head of the Jewish court was Rev Dovid Tzvi Auerbakh, frail because of his old age.

Dubno had many houses of worship, *kloizen* [private study halls], and study halls. The sexton in the large synagogue was the wealthy man Reb Meyer Szumski, an influential man appreciated by the aristocracy. Businessmen prayed there along with the ordinary people. This was a house with thick, tall walls, strong walls, and domed windows, and inside were wide, strong columns. Close to the synagogue, there was a small patch of earth, walled in, marking the bride and groom who were slaughtered under their canopy by Khmelnytsky's animals in the year 1648. The Holy Ark was a work of art made by wood carvers, and years later it was completely covered with pure gold. Precious curtain covers [of the Holy Ark], woven with gold and silver and handicraft, were often found in synagogues and on *Simkhas Torah* night [last day of Succos holiday, celebrating with Torah scrolls], they put a white satin cover sewn with pearls over the Holy Ark.

Other than the large synagogue, there were *kloizen* of Trisk, Olyk, and Stolin *chassidim*, and also of the hat makers. Day and night, you could hear the voices of Reb Avrohom Mordekhai and of Reb Aron and the sons of great rabbis learning Torah and reciting prayers. There was no *yeshiva* [religious school] in Dubno, but there were many students of Talmud and small schools for young and old, with teachers for the very young. Whoever wanted to study Jewish law and *Mishna* [Talmud] – always studied in the *Beis Medrash* [Study Hall]. One warmly remembers the teachers of the young: Reb Fishel, Reb Yoel, and Reb Leizer Poliak; the teachers of *Chumash* [Five Books of Torah] and *Rashi* [primary commentary] – Reb Naftoli and Reb Leizer Berishes; the Talmud teachers: Reb Itzik Leyb, the blind one Reb Avremele, and Reb Yosi Gutman.

*

In the Dubno region there used to be many trade fairs. On the 20th of every month there was a market day in Olyk; on the 15th of every month – in Mlynow; on the 10th – in Merwycz; and on the 20th – in Berestechko.

Traveling to these types of fairs was physically and mentally challenging. All of the roads were twisted, muddy, with ditches and hills. You would leave at dawn and get back in the middle of the night – everything for a livelihood.

Another source of livelihood for many families in town, left behind from the Polish rule, were the inns and temporary ["drop in"] houses.

In the 80s, in Dubno, there were a few leftovers of the Enlightenment generation, among them – Reb Avrohom-Ber Gotlober, the publisher of the magazine *"Haboker Ohr"* ["The Morning Light"]. There were no schools in Dubno at that time, therefore, when a Jew needed to write something in the province [government], or just to compile an address in Russian, he turned to Yossi the writer, who, with a professional handwriting, put everything on paper. Also, the young Pinkhasowyc knew how to put together requests with a nice Russian handwriting. There was one more like that in town, Khaim the writer, a man of the Enlightenment, who would always [write] satirically about the mud and dirt of the Jews that would always be removed on the eve of Passover. He used to say: "Wait, dear Jews! Wait! When the Messiah will arrive, all the holidays will be nullified, and then you will sink in dirt until over your heads, and all year round...."

In town, there was a whole institution by

[Column 619–620]

the name of *"Potcht"* ["mail"] – Leyb Silsker, with his horse and buggy. When letters were amassed, he took them from the town to the train station and from there – beyond...

In the year 1882, Dubno was boiling as a kettle: Tsar Alexander III was coming to visit the town!

The homeowners took to beautifying their houses, they whitewashed the walls, cleaned up the garbage and washed the roads. The Tsar really did come to town with great pomp, and with his successor Nikolai. Near Reb Avrohom's *kloiz* the community elders gathered, rabbis, and those who worked in the religious Jewish world, with decorated Torah scrolls in hand. But the Tsar and his escorts only drove by the town and only visited the old castle. No one even glanced at the Jewish delegation...

Greater Dubno

By Yakov Netaneli-Roitman

Translated from Hebrew by Selwyn Rose

The history of Dubno? Perhaps it is not as clear as a historian would like it to be – concrete and documented. The sad fact is that it is not possible for us to write a detailed chronological history of the rich Jewish experience steeped in tradition and faith as it was in Eastern Europe. In my grandfather's house, Rabbi Issachar-Dov ben Nehemiah Gershon, there was something that created an atmosphere of the past – it was a large trunk on wheels that occupied an honored place in the dining-room and study. The trunk was fitted with iron bands and an iron lock. Iron nails, the work of a blacksmith, were hammered into the bands and inside was a mixed collection of articles from the past like a small atlas with a stiffened cloth binding, elegant dresses from the time of my grandmother's wedding, a tooled leather document-case holding different certificates, a contract from Prince Lubomirski from the year 1742 and taxation records from the Napoleonic era and promissory-notes from the Counts of the Tarnowski, Miaczynski and Ittar families; silver spoons shaped like fishing-boats and carefully scrolled parchments and heavy silver rubles…there were also the historical records of the Municipal Council and the ancient Polish castle hidden in the misty air of the bridges and the old monasteries in the autumn-like twilight; but another "history" of deeds captured and presented in the form of well-written and documented reading books starting from some "beginning" never existed in our areas.

Perhaps earlier, when there was still an active Burial Society registering deaths and grave-sites of the deceased in the cemetery but what young person today, in the present century will find interest in those graves?

Among the Polish Christians, owners and landlords of great estates in the county such records certainly existed; they had it all – large castles, thick forests, hunting rifles and antique weapons, fields of rye and wheat, hop-fields and real library collections of classical literature and philosophers in books from earlier generations and more modern works. But among the Jewish people of Dubno at the beginning of the century there were only the physical remains of the bride and groom, slaughtered by the Cossacks while under their very wedding-canopy next to the Great Synagogue and the gravestones in the cemetery of the *Torah* Luminaries of the Holy Community from four-hundred years earlier and of the Holy Ark of the synagogue, with its gilded floral decorations.

The Dubno Jews bought from the Ukrainians the produce of their fertile fields – rye, wheat, potatoes, sugar-beet, clover seed and corn; the collected produce was passed on to other Jewish traders, wholesalers, who in turn exported it to the countries of the Imperial Austro-Hungarian Empire, corresponding in documents written half in Hebrew and half in Yiddish; the agents in the Holy Community of Brody had already concerned themselves in finding different agents in all the other European countries.

The Jews of Dubno built hop-kilns for drying and raking hops that had been brought in enormous sacks looking like feather pillowcases two meters long, from the plantations of Czech and German settlements; they treated the bitter-smelling produce, sorting it by color and aroma and the year of its harvesting, drying and storing it in well-ventilated silos in order to ship to breweries in Germany, England and South Africa. Dubno's Jews harvested clover-seed, cleansed it and transferred the valuable commodity to Danzig and northern countries, areas where the plant failed to thrive or germinate, or taverns and bars serving raisin-wine and mead. People who weren't traders, saloon-owners or hostellers sat on benches and tarred laces for the Gentiles' boots, sawed logs, worked the bellows in smithies, plastered walls or worked in cement works or brick foundries. Some made iron grills or swept the soot from factory chimneys… (no one in the Austro-Hungarian Empire had ever heard or seen, nor would they believe such a thing) – that a chimneysweep with a blackened brush tied to his shoulder would, before their eyes enter a soot-filled chimney and sweep down on himself a cloud of soot; and what do you know – a Jew does it! And if a man had no trade and was a synagogue sexton, or cantor or – Heaven forbid – the town fool, isolated and living on the fringes of society and wandering around, even they never starved to death.

Most of the crafts and trades were present in Dubno and most of the artisans were Jewish and even house-servants and housemaids of the wealthy were Jewesses and served their employers with loyalty into old age, and their retirement to the old people's home. The Jews of Dubno always dressed in black wearing a '*kashket*'[1] on their heads, a remainder from and reminder of, the law introduced by different European countries in the 19th Century concerning Jews and even though broad-brimmed European hats were available the Jews continued to wear the black, knitted '*kashket*' and educated and scholarly Jews insisted on wearing such caps made of silk or velvet together with a long black frock-coat, slit at the back and buttoned all the way down to the waist-line on sunny and rainy days, with their trousers tucked into their boots. Shoes "booties" and sandals were permitted only to young children and babies. Long '*peyot*' were not common in Dubno and were forbidden by the ordinance of the authorities but most of the male householders left their *peyot* untouched. Those who shaved were considered 'outsiders' and 'Epicureans' and their numbers small - Shmulik the watch-repairer, a known 'outsider' in town, of whom it was said that even on the Day of Atonement he didn't Fast —in his old age was eventually made *'Commissar'* of the Police and carried a sword – even he – grew a beard.

During my years as a youth not many devoted themselves to *Torah*; all traces of 'Enlightenment' and its Jewish counterpart, the *'Haskalah'*[2] were forgotten and obliterated, or at best set aside and during the era of Avrom Ber Gotlober and his colleagues no attempt was made to deepen and broaden interest in it. If anyone in town asked about them, they would likely be stoned. Official communities, like those of the Austro-Hungarian Empire, with a community-head and leaders recognized by the authorities, were non-existent anywhere in Volhynia at the beginning of the century. The Municipality was in the hands of the small Christian minority one of whom was appointed and authorized to represent the Jewish community. A religious Rabbi and a "government appointed" Rabbi, a few pieces, not particularly impressive, of ritual religious articles and artifacts, a handful of public-spirited well-to-do citizens lobbying the town's Police Chief, the Governor and the provincial Governor – was all that represented the Holy Community of Greater Dubno at the end of the last century when the Jewish population numbered 14,257 souls compared to 7,108 Christians of all denominations – Catholics, Paraslavs (eastern Orthodox) and others. The town was not a center of *chassidism*. A few sharp-minded scholars were sent to Kotsk and later congregated in the *Kloiz*[3] of the *chassidim* opposite the Great Synagogue a couple of Karlinists[4], a few others - 'fanatics' - as they slangily referred to the young *chassidim* when they witnessed their exaggerated eagerness in lighting festival and memorial candles; there was in that pejorative nickname the very essence of muddied, inanity that attracted to itself all the idle and vacuous blindness of 'miracle-workers' and unthinking pedants. 'Fanatics' is exactly what they were.

[Columns 185–186]

And just who was an acceptable 'someone' in Dubno? A respected Jewish house-holder – a Jew living in the shadow of its walls, fronted by a large courtyard with a barn, a milk-cow and, from April to October, stacked-up logs of firewood drying in preparation for the winter to be easily chopped by hefty, broad-shouldered *"Polishukim*[5]*"* in the autumn; he had a place in the Study-House and his sons and grandchildren lived close-by. His livelihood brought him in a ruble or two by "permission and not prohibition"[6] of the local police-chief who received a "consideration" to "close his eyes". Such a Jewish man would appear outside his house early in the morning and take his cow to pasture, light the fire for the copper boiler with wood-charcoal, and make sure that it is burning correctly with no bluish smoke escaping from the chimney. He would then take a long-handled broom and sweep his yard hither and thither, clean of all the dust and dirt down his sloping yard from the red-bricked sidewalk towards the street. This led to an opportunity for a casual conversation and to sip a cup of tea with his neighbor from opposite and from there he would go to the *Kloiz*[7] and from there, at about eleven o'clock he allows himself to forsake the Holy One Blessed be He and turn his attention and hands to his own daily tasks and the needs of all flesh.

Of this you may be sure: The Jews of Dubno for generations had been successful businessmen. They were specialists in conducting business with landowners, barons, princes and other nobles acting as lumber and forestry agents and the erection of saw- and flour-mills; Polish- and stumbling Russian-speaking Jews, perhaps somewhat proud and arrogant, loving to joke at others' expense but serious among themselves, were careful in their dealings with the authorities and street-wise and wary when dealing with the "*Katchapim*"[8], reclusive within their community, relying solely on themselves and always aware of the eternal shadow of an invisible, undefined fear wafting above their heads.

*

The river Ikwa (the name of the river is not Slavic; perhaps Celtic) encircling Dubno in a sweeping arc, is a typical Ukrainian river overflowing the entire area, swampy, potentially dangerous in places, with wide expanses of reeds and other river-bank growth; there are deep and deadly fords seeming to be narrow enough to allow one to leap easily from one bank to the other. The river flows from south to north encompassing the town in a wide arc before turning to the north-west. To the east of the town are several small rivulets crossed by a bridge leading to the railroad station five kilometers distant from the town. At the peak of the arc, protected on three sides rises the fortified "palace" built of red bricks with its four rounded watchtowers at each corner. The sloping walls above the moat were without windows. There were arrow slits, wide on the inside, embedded all along the fortress walls, reminders of the snipers' nests from the days of the Khmelnitsky uprising. The deep moat, fed by the river in days of siege, surrounded it on all sides and cut the palace off from the town. At the foot of the precipice spread the old town of Dubno with its 170 Jewish houses with their two-thousand souls, according to the Polish census of 1765. In the days of Khmelnitsky there were perhaps more: "*Yeven Mezulah*"[9] mentions the slaughter of 4,000 souls in 1649 by Khmelnytsky's Cossacks. It is easy to identify the old town: at the town's center stood the Town Hall, a square solid building with thick walls and arched rooms. Four gates opening into the courtyard from all sides. At each gate stood an ancient un-mounted cannon. They stand upright on end with the muzzles pointing skywards and rainwater easily enters the muzzles. In town there were shops all rented by Jews. In the Guffa building there were large halls and private apartments – the Municipality had vacated the building for some reason or other – and a "Citizens' Club" instituted a gambling casino there for Jews and Christians alike. South of the

Municipality was the Jewish street – Sarnitzna Street, as it was called in Yiddish – an unmade street with no sidewalk, just mud and potholes. It is divided into two with one side leading down towards the river and the second towards the drier land opening out near the Great Synagogue and the bathhouse. The bathhouse was built under the auspices of Prince Lubomirski in 1699 for public use – Jew and non-Jew alike. Next to the bathhouse was a fenced-off area – a common grave with no tombstones. Here, Khmelnitsky (may his name be erased from memory), slaughtered the whole congregation with the sword and here, about a hundred years later, Gonta also slaughtered Jews. The externally unimpressive Guffa Synagogue was built in 1784, unlike the great synagogues of Lutsk and Luboml (Libevne); its domed roof was the highest building in Dubno and shaped like a Jewish cap from the middle-ages. The inside of the synagogue was flooded with light. Its pale walls and two sturdy columns supported the ceiling. The Holy Ark was decorated with pure gold from the ground up to the roof-beams. On festivals the Ark was draped with a *"Parochet"*[110] of silk decorated and interwoven with silver thread. On the festival of the Giving of the Law an even more decorative *Parochet* was used covered with precious and colorful stones and pearls. Two synagogue officials would stand guard, one on each side to ensure that none of the celebrants, when closing the Ark and kissing the *Parochet* in reverence, bit off some of the stones or pearls… the whole community was intensely proud of its Holy Ark.

[Columns 187–188]

Several streets radiated out from the Municipality: the broad Szeroka, to the north, Sawaronya, Aleksandrowicz and Panienska where the wealthy lived. Newer areas of the town purchased from the Prince at the beginning of the 18th Century were Surmicze to the east, Zabramie to the west and Pantalia to the north, neighborhoods occupied by both Jews and Christians. The Monasteries and churches imparted to the town a somewhat Christian aura. Aleksandrowicz, at the heart of the Jewish town was dominated by a tall Polish-Catholic church with its white plastered walls shaded by chestnut trees and a grassy lawn. Its bells were not hung in the steeple but set into special niches constructed in the walls of the church. Placed along the wall in *bas-relief* were the Latin words *Gloria Tibi Domine* (Glory be to Thee O Lord) – and Dubno was not at the time completely Polish and all its signs were in the Slavic language. Nevertheless, at the end of this rustic road in the suburb of Zabramie stands a Convent, one of its feet on the street and the other on the slopes of the cliff overlooking a pleasant valley! The Convent was Orthodox, and it was occupied by nuns. It is said that there was a tunnel burrowing into the bowels of the hill and running for a kilometer or two as far as the Palace. One day when the market square was being repaired opposite the Municipality, the surface collapsed, and the tunnels were found beneath the roadway: they led away to both the left and the right in the direction to and from the convent and the palace. Everyone came to see skeletons and broken vessels, rusted swords and suchlike. The gaping hole from the collapse was filled with earth, fenced all around, and nobody asked any questions…!

There was another Monastery in town near the Municipal Gardens – a pleasant corner where black pigs could be seen burrowing in the plowed field. The big Monastery, occupied by Orthodox monks, surrounded by a wall with many bells attached, stood overlooking the wooded areas of Pantalia and the meandering Ikwa beyond the town. When their Holy Days came, towards the end of Hanukkah and a bitter frost covered the earth and the trees were bare of their leaves at the end of autumn, the sound of the bells spread from the four corners of the town: the bass bell of the Catholic church and the contesting counterpoint of the Uniates: ding, dong, ding, dong…filling us with loathing; it was something of an anathema! Judgment be upon you, Greater Dubno! Nevertheless, everyone heard and listened.

*

Have you ever seen houses with un-plastered blood-red brick walls separated by thin layers of lime? There were many of them in Dubno. Their windows were narrow with six panes of glass with rounded cornices like in the Study-House. Every house was like a Study-House! In front of each house a tiny porch, about one yard long and one yard wide, with two stools at the side and steps leading up from the sidewalk. The sidewalks were also constructed of red bricks placed back-to-back, and in the evening, neighbors would sit outside and chat. Every house had a wide yard with a high gateway that was locked at night. There were stables in the yards for horses, a storehouse for wood, a hut for a small arbor and a stall for a cow. There were cherry-trees, tomatoes and apples. At that time no trees were planted in the street because the gardens of the private houses stretched out onto the street preventing trees from being planted. The town was kept very clean, even in the marketplace among the peddlers, carriage-drivers and phaetons, their black leather harness equipment and yokes were all clean and polished, the drivers, too in their rough and ready coarse fur coats wore broad decorated cummerbunds, there, too, among the wagon drivers – complete cleanliness. Greater Dubno was like no other town in the province. There was no sewage or other plumbing. At the beginning of the century the population still drank water from the Ikwa. The water-carriers, Jews who owned a barrel, would fill it using a funnel at the top and draw the water out through a tap at the bottom. They would go down to the river at dawn, enter the shallows with their horse and cart, moving about here and there up-stream filling buckets with the turbid waters and deliver the water to their customers in their homes charging the people according to the number of buckets delivered during the week. And wonder-of-wonders – the "*Kapatchim*"[11] came and sectioned off a central position in the market place and began busying themselves with pipes, drilling a hole in the ground, drawing from the hole and extracting from the thick milky-white mixture of gravel and water. They continued drilling and again drew out the rubble. The whole town one day came to see what was happening and behold – a powerful spout of crystal-clear water came gushing up out of the ground spraying everything around…they tasted it and the water was like a sweetened summer drink. An artesian well! How? No one in town knew. Later they built a small brick roofed structure over the installation. All the water-drawers were elated. No longer did they have to go to the river and draw the dirty, turbid water. They just joined the queue at the tap and without lifting a finger the clear water simply flowed into the barrel – it was a great relief.

What was it Gotlober once said to his son-in-law the doctor, (that my father (Z"L) heard with his own ears one day when he went to the artesian well)?: "The religious folk may live and study the Holy Books for a hundred years and will find no mention of wells!" But along come the modern educated people and without their knowledge of the Torah they brought us artesian wells and for all that – although they're not mentioned - they exist!

[Columns 189–190]

But never mind the well – what about the telegraph!? Is it nothing, to be discounted? Or the railway?

"Oy! Die Eisenbahn, was ist gemacht gewarden, sie fahrt passagieren,…"[12]

In any case – one must say that at the beginning of the present century the people of Dubno displayed a different spirit. The younger people began to exchange the traditional black frockcoat for a Christian manufactured shirt and those who wore hats on their head exchanged them for polished leather ones – just like the Christians. Even peddlers in the marketplace began to use Russian almost automatically in their conversation, Heaven forbid! The conflict between the two schools of educational methodology--the one leaning towards the Russian language and the traditional *Heder*-based system caused an exodus of the children from the *Haderim* and induced them to join the more modern system. Students appeared in town, Almighty G-d! In the summer heat with baskets of red cherries on the streets of the town, students suddenly appeared in white-as-snow uniforms, golden epaulettes and brass buttons and on the left side of their breast a small amulet – the insignia of their faculty; tall and handsome they were. The girls were captivated at the sight awakening the desire both overt and hidden to join the movement to secular study, obtain a graduation certificate, making it all a reality.

One of the first among these was Kagani, clownish and energetic. Nevertheless, he prayed with his father and owned a delicatessen, a likeable Jew, a member of the *Baratz* Study-House community. He knew how to read portions of the *Torah* accurately (he was a lawyer and Mayor during the days of the Revolution, swinging to the side of the Bolsheviks and back again. At the outbreak of war, he was in Dubno. Nothing is known of him after that).

*

My grandfather's house, may he rest in peace, stood firmly and stubbornly against the "disease" of the movement to secularism and the grandchildren didn't wear shirts! There were other similar houses, but the hops and clover traders were hard hit and sent their children to the private "Reali" Humanistic school in Kremenets that had been built for the Jewish people with their own money and was like a stronghold against the Christians, while the girls were sent to the gymnasium that had been founded for girls in Dubno.

Mr. Zalman Ashkenazi, a prominent member of the *Baratz* Study-House where he was privileged to have a seat against the eastern wall adjacent to the Holy Ark, was wont to say: "Such a thing never happened! Your merit will not derive from your Russian *Mandarin*-style shirt or your dress-coat but by Zion!" A Jew will not be a man like all the men of creation unless his eyes envision the return to Zion. A Jew needs to have the Land of Israel as a possession. Where is the Land of Israel? They say – beyond Odessa. And is that far? – Yes, very! They have already journeyed to the Land of Israel from Berestechko. Berestechko compared to Dubno is like a ram compared to a bull. But they are there – young stalwart men, like oaks. Mr. Zalman didn't usually converse with the simple folk. He ran a pharmacy – or rather a warehouse of medicines because he wasn't a pharmacist. He sat against the eastern wall of the synagogue, his round face shaven clean like a priest, wrapped in a silver-embroidered prayer shawl and *pince-nez* on his nose and no one knew how to interpret and expound on the liturgical poems as well as he did. He was unique; a delegate to the first Congresses. The whole Study-House could "warm itself from his fire". But what of the Land of Israel with our many sins, when the Russian lancers and the infantry brigade of her Imperial Majesty Maria-Feodorovna, who all man a garrison in Dubno right up against the walls of our house, decide to make war with our "comedian" warming with joy the hearts of all the grandchildren of our courtyard. And even the local artillery stands ready to relocate to somewhere in the Far East…

Gershon Hadmoni, a family member and a reserve soldier, was also mobilized to be sent there but deserted and was already in Brody over the border. David Dushansky, a tailor's cutter, and an officer in a cavalry brigade, told our grandfather (may he rest in peace) explicitly that it will be – bitter. And it began, indeed, to be bitter. The clouds that hung over the town on the summer evenings foretold…something. The Russians who had been brought from the depths of Russia, broad-featured and fair-bearded, to construct a dam across the Ikwa, expressed themselves in spirited singing rhythmically to the beat of their sledgehammers on the heavy sharpened logs used as pylons pounded into the earth and the bottom of the river: "O! The sledgehammers will beat on you…" – even they seemed to change their preferences and they had never seen Jews before in their lives! They lost the faith in the nation. Even Old Nikolai, our house-servant and Simon with his axe, who chopped wood in the courtyard throughout the days of winter...everything, seemed to be done under threat. We, the grandchildren, supervised the locking of the gates to the courtyard every evening, and that – we did.

We also completed among ourselves making and polishing iron daggers. I managed to acquire one broad enough, double-edged and about half a meter long with a good point and most evenings I spent polishing it. I fashioned a hilt as a good handhold and I had in my hand a dagger fit for a Cossack. My heart felt a little easier.

Dud'l, the eldest of us grandchildren at home, didn't take part with us "infants". He disappeared each evening into the Pantalia marshes, over the bridge with five apprentices of artisans. It was an overnight activity. The artisans began to behave with an exaggerated sense of self-importance. As an old proverb says: "Shoemakers and tailors aren't men" ...imagine! Dud'l, the son of Rabbi Shlomo Berish-Shmaryes escaping with apprentices – it's almost unbelievable! But we knew: and for sure so did he; and they have pistols! How, how?

[Columns 191–192]

Like this. Tie it to Nadziratan's nose... Dud'l brought back from his nights in the Pantalia marshes osteo-tuberculosis but nothing happened in Dubno. Later on – years later, we understood: it was too close to the Imperial Russian Empire...here nothing could happen. But in Kishinev and Odessa things were different. And once again the imbeciles in town sneered at the crude words of the song: "In Harbin it's good but in Mukden it's better...[113]"

In the Study-Houses they debated the actions of General Tojo and passed judgment on General Stoessel, spoke about the Battle of Tsushima, the Commander of Port Arthur, Rozhdestvenskii, or just sought explanations and interpretations of insults and slurs, claiming there was no way out except "*Svoboda*" – Freedom! And one day it was announced that Tsar Nicolai had given them freedom! Freedom was declared in the first Duma and no one in the town knew whether to be joyful or to cry. It was a "dish" that we had not yet tasted. The provincial governor was also confused. In any case he immediately ordered an inspection of the central prison, repairing and repainting it, transferring the prisoners to the internal courtyards so no one outside would hear all the rumbling and speculation going on inside...and a sort of calm prevailed. The sounds coming from the workers in the workshops carried beyond the walls a different type of music, Russian and Jewish, that captured the hearts with their rich sweetness and wealth of courage.

And night after night trains rumbled down the railroad from east to west, from Kiev, Poltava and White Russia to Dubno and from there to Radziwill, Brody and beyond that to the world. Only it should be far from Russia, as far as possible from "Freedom".

Beyond the border, in Brody everything was grotesque and crazy: *Streimelech*, top hats, strange Jews with too many "please" and "thank you" and adjacent to the railroad station was an old man singing a song:

Maybe you want to know if a Russian is a man?

His boots are torn, his fur-hat cocked to one side –

A Russian is a thief, a Russian is a thief.[14]

For all that he was there, beyond the border, every Russian Jew was already over the border.

Translator's Comments

1. A cap usually made of felt, worn mainly by Hasidic Jewish children as an alternative to the kippah (skullcap). It has a crown, a band and a peak. From the beginning of the 20th century until the Second World War, many Russian and Polish Jews wore this cap as part of their everyday dress.
2. For a full account of 'Haskalah' see: https://en.wikipedia.org/wiki/Haskalah.
3. A Yiddish word referring to a special study sanctuary closely associated with but usually detached from a synagogue building
4. See: https://www.encyclopedia.com/religion/encyclopedias-almanacs-transcripts-and-maps/karlin
5. A pejorative term for the people of Polessia.
6. A Talmudic concept derived from the Talmudic phrase *Mai nafka minnah*. See: https://en.wikipedia.org/wiki/Nafka_minnah for a complete explanation.
7. A small Study-House usually housed in and/or affiliated to the synagogue of a senior scholar or rabbinical luminary.
8. A somewhat derogatory, pejorative slang term for the Russians
9. A record of the Khmelnitsky Pogroms by Rabbi Nathan Hannover.
10. A highly decorated curtain covering the front of the Holy Ark containing the scrolls of the Torah, usually embroidered with gold or silver thread.
11. A pejorative slang term the Ukrainians had for the Russians.
12. "The railroad that has been invented is finished and working, carrying countless passengers hither and yon…." (a free translation of a popular song from 1870's. A free translation from the Yiddish/German and Hebrew footnote – translator).
13. This seems to be a reference to an event during the Russo-Japanese war at the beginning of the 20th Century. An intensive and exhausting search of the internet failed to provide any alternative explanation – Translator.
14. A free translation from the Yiddish via a footnoted Hebrew translation

[Columns 191–192]

Dubno on the Eve of the First World War

by Agronomist Eng. Yisrael Feffer

Translated from Hebrew by Selwyn Rose

Education

A

Until the end of the 19th Century Jewish Dubno was a quiet town and education was carried on according to the earlier traditions: toddlers learned with various teachers in the *Heder*[1], among who was Rabbi Motel Loitzky-Bronstein who was very sharp-minded and witty. Above the *Haderim* for the tots were the *Haderim* of *Torah* studies, Rashi and *Gemara* where children studied for three or four years and the outstanding among the teachers was Rabbi Lazar Pollack. There were no *Yeshivot*[2] in Dubno but there were Study Houses that bore the style of a *Yeshiva*. The *Haderim* were under the approval of the authorities and the instructors were required to hold a teaching certificate; Rabbi Lazar Pollack had a certificate on the wall of his *Heder* and when a Russian inspector would appear in town teachers who hadn't one would send the pupils home. The Study Houses would be used as a sort of unlicensed "study studio".

B

At the beginning of the present century two "unclassified" schools were founded in Dubno where school was taught in Russian. I was a pupil in one of them and I still remember two of the teachers: Mrs. Esther Spitzberg and Mr. Kromm. The unclassified schools prepared pupils for the municipal (classified) school where Russian was also the language of instruction. The municipal school was composed of three grades and two classes and the pupils wore school uniforms. It was difficult for Jewish children to be accepted into the municipal school and so their numbers were small although few of the Jewish pupils there doubted their capabilities and knowledge among the Ukrainian Christian children. The Christian children came to the municipal school from the Church school. The headmaster of the school was the inspector Doroschenko and his teachers were quite liberal. Fistfights and arguments were a regular daily occurrence between the Jewish and Christian children but many of the Christian children needed the assistance of the Jewish pupils with their lessons and assignments and I well remember the pupil Avraham Shpak, who, with his strength and courage stood up well in the conflicts against all the Christian pupils in the school.

In the three lower grades the pupils, boys and girls, learned together while in the two higher grades they studied separately. The hours of study were from eight in the morning until two in the afternoon and the boys had some pre-military training and would take part in official parades. Every morning the priest would hold prayers before lessons and the Jewish pupils were obliged to attend; late arrival for the prayers was met with severe punishment. A conspicuous aim of the school was to instill in the pupils a patriotic feeling for Russia and festivals were held to honor Russian literary personalities in which the Jewish pupils played an active role. At the close of the school year certificates were distributed and school-leavers were permitted to work in pharmacies as apprentices. They were also eligible to enter the gymnasium.

Group of graduates of the Russian Gymnasium in Dubno (1921)

C

A great advancement in the education system in Dubno occurred in 1907 with the opening of the first Russian gymnasium in town and among the founders was a Polish pharmacist named Witecka. The excitement of the parents was immense and the rush to the gymnasium was great not only from the residents of the town but also from the local villages. The registration fee for the gymnasium was one hundred rubles and a year's tuition fee 60 rubles – vast amounts for the period. Jewish pupils were accepted in the gymnasium without consideration of the *Numerus Clausus*.

But the joy of the beneficiaries was short-lived – the gymnasium didn't receive sufficient support and no privileges and closed two years later.

D

Two years later a government gymnasium was established in town for boys, where Jews were accepted after a difficult entrance exam but only according to the "norma" (*Numerus Clausus*) – 10% of the general student population. Many students studied in the government gymnasium and the young *intelligentsia* that was concentrated there and that tended even earlier towards the spirit of modernism, introduced sparkle and life into the Jewish youth circles in Dubno.

Because of the *Numerus Clausus* Jews were only accepted almost exclusively through influence, leaving it only for the wealthy families who were required to finance the studies of tens of non-Jewish students in order to obtain entrance for 1% of their children.

The zealousness of the young Jewish students, wearers of the uniform, was intense but nevertheless they were obliged to attend religious classes in the afternoon because it was unthinkable in those days that a Jewish youth would go against his parents and disengage from his Jewish roots.

Girl's gymnasium (1914)

It should be pointed out that from the beginning of the nineties of the 19th Century there had been a gymnasium for girls with six classes in Dubno but without the right to obtain a matriculation certificate. Young Jewish girls who wanted to complete the gymnasium were forced even at the end of the first decade of the present century to travel as far as Odessa where, at the gymnasium of Mrs. Jabotinsky-Kopp[3] they were able later to learn a profession, especially dentistry.

The government gymnasium for boys in Dubno existed for four years from 1910 until 1914 when, with the evacuation of all Russian institutions, it moved to the town of Vovchansk in the Kharkov district. It returned to Dubno in 1916 and from then was headed for many years by Mr. Possfischel, a teacher who taught Latin and was of Czech origins. He was a very liberal man (I can testify to that because in 1922 he gave me a letter of recommendation

[Columns 195–196]

to Mr. Krammersch, member of the Czech Parliament and among the leaders of the National-Democratic Party in Prague and editor of the "*Narodni List*" – "National Newspaper", to help me obtain entrance to the University).

In addition to the schools mentioned, in 1910 a governmental Jewish school was opened, and the teachers were graduates of courses for teachers in Grodno and Zhitomir. The teachers at the school and the pupils wore a school uniform. The standard of this school was low, somewhat similar to a municipal school with two classes, while the municipal school would grant to graduates the status of a "class-two volunteer" that decreases military service from two-and-a-half years to one-and-a-half, something the Jewish school couldn't do.

Group of Russian students of the gymnasium in Dubno (1921)

E

With the conquest of Dubno by the Bolsheviks in 1919 education was renewed in the government gymnasium that was now established with seven departments instead of eight. The pupils were given a certain freedom and they organized and created a "Student Committee" with students from other schools. I was elected, together with Ilya Makhrok, of blessed memory, to the Students' Committee.

The government gymnasium continued to function during the era of the Hetman Skoropadski and Hetman Petliura and included a solid amount of Ukrainian literature and language under the supervision of the previous management. But with the preponderance of Poles in town and the reversal of the government gymnasium to Polish – the wheel took a backward turn: the Jews were no longer accepted at the gymnasium and even those who had studied previously were met with difficulties with the examinations.

From this arose the need to establish a Polish-Jewish gymnasium and the first Head was Mr. Kammerman. The Chairman of the Parents' Committee was Mr. Avraham Karaulnik.

F

An event of special note in Dubno regarding Jewish education was the school teaching in Hebrew:

In 1917, during the Kerensky administration, a school was established in Dubno named as the "*Tarbut*"[1] comprising six classes. Its first founders and teachers were the veteran teacher Elimelech Blei, of blessed memory, Mr. Balaban, of blessed memory and Mrs. Eichenbaum, may G–d avenge her blood. The establishment of the school was financially difficult because the parents were not yet accustomed to maintaining a private school, so a public committee was formed to concern itself with the maintenance of the school; at the head of the public committee were Avraham Huberman and Shimon Bar Yitzhak-Isaac Feffer. The school reached the peak of its development during the establishment of the Central Council of the *Tarbut* system in Poland.

Public and Party Activism

A

Public activism may have started in Dubno in 1917 after the Kerensky revolt, when freedom of action was given to all residents, including the Jews. Indeed, Jewish activism on a restricted level was occurring even before the revolution but that was based principally on "lobbying" and the activists were very few in number.

For various reasons there was a small group of Jews in Dubno close to the "centers of power" for instance: The Province Governor, who, by the very nature of his function, controlled lobbying through blackmail and bribery of the members of the administration in order to prevent unfavorable decrees and to protect the Jewish residents from economic and political setbacks. It is worth noting here that when there was a change of officials in the administration the Jews would pray that the incoming clerks and officials would not be worse than their predecessors – meaning that they, too, would accept bribes...

The Jewish activists were dedicated and extended help to all the needy without thought of reward and mentioned in this context are Volodya Mandelker and Mr. Avraham Korin, a very popular figure and a warm-hearted Jew who was elected in 1917 in a free vote as Chairman of the Jewish community thanks to his generosity.

The Jewish "lobby" was also activated in special cases, like securing an entrance to the gymnasium for a Jewish student beyond the "norma" or obtaining a resident's permit in a village for Jews who were often under threat of expulsion because of a law from the eighties of the previous century that prohibited them from residing in the villages.

B

At the beginning of the revolution in February 1917 – the Kerensky revolution, the first signs of budding modern Jewish activism began: the first Jewish trade organization was established, as was the official Zionist Federation and a committee founded for election to the first municipal institute in Dubno – the Municipality – and the Jewish Community Council. A general public Jewish committee was also established in which activists from all layers of the community participated. The function of the committee was to represent the Jewish community before the authorities. The influence of the committee on the Jewish public was considerable. At its head was Ze'ev Burstein. A veteran loyal Zionist, a shop-owner, and there were two energetic activists, Avraham Huberman and Shmuel Barchash whose activism sprang from a sense of public responsibility and of a Jewish national awareness. The office of the Jewish Public Committee was located in the large central building of Mr. Greenberg and in the evenings his room hummed like a beehive with activity.

It was a period of general excitement, of liberalism and rosy hopes illuminating the skies of the Russian Empire, and with it came a wide awakening of Jewish public and political activity. The Zionist Federation broadened and strengthened itself and acquired for itself control of the "Jewish street" while all public issues were curtailed in the Committee's offices until its activities ceased after the free elections to the two important institutions – the Municipality and the official Jewish Community Council.

C

The elected Chairman of the Zionist Federation in Dubno during that same period was an excellent person, distinguished for manner and qualities, a short man, physically with an intelligent smile always on his lips: Moshe Zimmerman from Lubaczowk, near to Berestechko. He was submerged in Jewish and Hebrew culture, zealous for the Hebrew language and the possessor of superior qualities. He owned a library considered among the finest in town that contained the finest works of the end of the 19th and beginning of the present centuries. His two brothers, Chaim, of blessed memory – and spared for a long life – Shmuel, immigrated to Palestine in 1908-1910 and were among the founders of Yavne'el in Lower Galilee.

The finest of the Jewish youth of Dubno were centered in the Zionist Federation at this time and among them were a large proportion of the Jewish students of the Russian gymnasium. Most of them later became conspicuous as active founders of "Hechalutz"[5] and "Hashomer Hatzair"[6] and the Jewish sports club. Together they undertook propaganda activities in the elections for the proposed all-Russia congress and to struggle against the "Bund" and the "Social Zionists".

Nevertheless the "Bund" had many supporters but only a few of them were local from Dubno. Most were recently demobilized soldiers stationed at that time in the villages and towns near the Front. These soldiers had the right to vote in the places where they were stationed although their influence on the Jewish public was not great. It is true that a strong supporter of the "Bund" and a brilliant orator was Dr. Levinson, an educated man who succeeded in attracting many listeners until it was discovered that he had ties with the "Bund". Most of the meetings took place in the synagogue in the absence of a suitable public facility and at one of the meetings Dr. Levinson tried enthusiastically to prove that the Socialist swindle was a Jewish phenomenon from ancient days and brought as proof the deceit of our biblical Patriarch Jacob in depriving his brother Esau of his birthright by fraud as a clear case of Socialist economic preference…before he had finished speaking most of the audience rose in anger and left the synagogue and Dr. Levinson was obliged to reduce his activities with the "*Bund*". His influence among the general public soon disappeared as if it had never been.

A small party that earned for itself some attention was the Zionist Socialist Workers' Party; at its head was Dr. Borodianski who was also a doctor in the military and Mikhail Huberman, born in Dubno, talented and a dedicated public activist. The small Polish "People's Party", headed by the multi-active attorney Mr. Yosef Pinchoshovitz also claimed some importance and "wide influence on a broad mass of the population". Indeed, it was not worthwhile for any small party to engage in the political struggle…

These were great days for the Jews of Dubno. At the head of the list for the all-Russia legislative council representing the Jews of Volhynia stood Rabbi Dr. Mazeh of Moscow and for the first time in Dubno's history Jews were elected to the city Council by most of the population: Avrasha Kahana, a young lawyer well-known and liked by all the residents; Eliza Kagan, an educated young woman; the son of Rabbi Yisroel *Sofer Stam*[1] as the delegate of the Social Democrats and Jewish social revolutionary representing soldiers quartered in the town who were enfranchised. This town council was active until the Hetman Skoropadski head of the Ukrainian independence movement revolution in 1918.

D

During this same period a small group of Jewish Bolsheviks began to become conspicuous, drawing encouragement from the success of the Bolshevik revolution throughout Russia. Among the activists in this group were two students from the University of Kharkov, Aaron Kagan and Joel Kellner.

The Bolshevik group did not manage to gain for itself

[Columns 201–202]

support from the Jewish public of Dubno. In fact, the opposite is the case: its activities gradually faded during the turbulent changes in government in the fateful years 1918/1919 – from the overthrow of Hetman Skoropadski by Hetman Petliura; the weakening of Petliura's regime by the local terrorist gangs and his final removal by the conquering army of Poland, the temporary authority of the Bolsheviks on the county and then the re-conquest by Poland.

E

In conclusion, it is fitting to note that the activities of the Jewish public of Dubno in the years 1917–1919 were not a spontaneous awakening caused by events of the moment but the result of the new spirit that came about in Dubno during the years of the Russian revolution of the 1903-1905. As a matter of fact, the Jewish "proletariat" in Dubno was none other than a small weak number of artisans, a few apprentices and a passing propagandist who remained in Dubno for a short while, although the revolutionary spirit and the pogroms that it brought on their wings awakened the young people in town to the need to organize itself for self-defense.

The Jewish "Defense" was created in those years in the underground organized in "quartets" at the head of which were young Jewish social revolutionaries. One of them, David Ber Shlomo Roitman, was training his quartet in small arms in the swamps of Pantalia when he caught a severe cold that developed into tuberculosis from which he never recovered. Another young person who was active in the "Defense" organization was Moshe Rosenfeld who was tried for revolutionary activities and sentenced to two years in the infamous Shlisselburg prison; he was much publicized in those days.

Self–Defense in Dubno in 1919

The idea of self–defense for the Jews of Dubno was born in the days of the 1903-1905 Revolution and the seedlings began sprouting already in those early days although the organization as such began to exist only with the fall of the Kerensky regime in 1917 and the changes in authority that came following after: the Ukrainian Hetman rulers, Skoropadski and Petliura, the first Polish conquest, the Bolshevik rule, and the re-conquest by Poland. These were two nightmare years for the Jews.

Because of the weakening local authority and the continuing confusion in town there began a period of pillaging and looting by gangs of hooligans – beginning with members of the underworld and different elements of hooligans from Dubno itself and spreading to gangs of youths from neighboring villages like Palcza and others – who would fall upon the Jews and burst into their houses in the evening claiming they were searching for weapons. When they didn't find anything, they would simply demand "ransom" money. The Jews, fearful for their lives would pay and pay again and again to anyone that threatened them.

In view of that situation a few young people aged between 18 and 30, all of them volunteers who had obtained weapons in various ways, mainly by purchasing them from the Ukrainians, banded together and organized themselves for self-defense. The

Ukrainians themselves had many weapons, some from the armed forces who were in the county during the First World War – the Russians, the Germans and the Austrians. The price of a military rifle, the principal weapon of the "*Hagana*"[8] in Dubno was then 10 rubles, a substantial sum in those days. They also obtained a Russian machine-gun and a member, Moshe Barchash, who had served in the Russian army as a machine-gunner, knew how to operate it. The only motorized vehicle in Dubno at the time was a used Russian military truck, owned by the *Hagana*. It served them as a support vehicle in times of trouble and as a tool to transport a strike-force in an attack.

The *Hagana* commander in Dubno was Yasha (Ya'acov) Horowitz the son of Rabbi Shmuel Halevi Ish-Horowitz a descendant of Rabbi Isaiah ben Abraham Horowitz, and the command-post was situated in the building formerly used as the Jewish gymnasium. The members of *Hagana* fulfilled their duties on a voluntary basis with no consideration of day or hours and with nightfall they would all assemble in the command-post for a briefing. Because of the small number of members, it was impossible to patrol the distant suburbs of town, so continuously patrols were organized in pairs and they would walk the streets armed with rifles and ammunition and from time-to-time report to the command-post on what was happening in the town.

We will recall here one "military" action of the *Hagana* that was carried out one evening against Ukrainian farmers. It was one Sunday, market-day in town, and rumors arrived in the command-post that Ukrainian farmers, who had come to town for the weekly market, were looting a warehouse of Petliura's army. While the looting of warehouses didn't affect the Jews, the farmers were likely to become "encouraged" from their own activities and continue on to attack the Jews of town. Because of this a "platoon" of ten members of the *Hagana* was sent in order to disperse the crowd. The group fired a couple of shots in the air. The crowd didn't disperse but fired back. Then reinforcements were brought from the command-post, and an exchange of fire went on for some time. One of them was hit in the stomach – the son of Yehezkiel the glazier. Eventually they [the farmers] were dispersed by the *Hagana* and order returned.

Among the members of the *Hagana* in Dubno at the time we will mention here: Yasha (Ya'acov) Horowitz, Moshe Pinchosovich, Dossia Koren, Genia Meizlish of blessed memory, Moshe Barchash and the writer of these lines.

Jewish Life in Dubno[i]

In Dubno, like in other provincial towns there were journals like the one referred to here with writers who were not actually professional journalists but possessors of a broad education and high intelligence. They would sign their pieces not with their real names but with an acrostic. From among a wealth of articles those that give us a clear picture from the "class war" spirit of that time, such as the special enforced tax on meat and candles as was prevalent in the Tsarist period and the enforcers of the tax – those with the right to enforce the tax on the Jewish residents as a fixed payment in advance, to the authorities – made for themselves a nice business and controlled the community, community interests, education and more.

The Tax of 1884

With the approach of the elections due to take place in the County town Zhitomir, householders, who including those of the rich and established class, received authorization to represent the Jewish public before the government; and in order to avoid the bureaucratic tangle of correspondence and requests, it was decided to record those with the appropriate authorization according to their given names. It was agreed with them that all the profits will be used to maintain public institutions. But already in the first year of its administration it became clear that the public representatives were not worthy of the trust placed in them. Not only were these administrators elected to public office failing to transfer funds they received to the community throughout the year, but they also refused to lower the price of meat that was higher than the fixed price in neighboring communities such as Rowno, Lutsk and others. While they fixed the price of meat on the bone at 15 kopeks a pound the price in surrounding communities was 10 kopeks a pound for boneless meat.

The tax administrators, who had the mutually agreed authority, had no wish to have it taken from their hands; they became aggressive and imposed themselves on the public by force. Thus, in order to silence their principal opponents, they were not ashamed to inform the authorities of those people from close by who came to town and had no rights to settle there since it was situated within fifty kilometers of the border. After that they didn't hesitate to "rub salt in an open wound" to draw "*hoi polloi*" to their side and the "*hoi polloi*" acquiesced that the price of meat in the first half of the year will be 14 kopecks and in the second half 15 kopecks a pound, as it was in 1883.

The sale of 240 thousand pounds of meat in the year 1884 generated twelve thousand rubles in taxes that were supposed to enter the public coffers, but the uncompromising controllers poured the funds into their own pockets and not a kopeck to the needs of the community. In 1883 2,800 rubles from these taxes were transferred to public funds for its institutions of which 1,000 went to the hospital while in the following 1884 the government representatives exploited the public and enriched themselves at the direct expense of the community.

It is superfluous to point out that the promises of the elected officials to transfer funds for building the bridge over the river for the water-carriers drawing water from the river and also the erection of a public bathhouse for the community fell by the wayside.

When complaints were made against them saying "Is this possible?" – there were those who opposed them citing their responsibility to the public: "The Jewish people are a rebellious people of 'complainers'. Didn't the Children of Israel rebel against Moses our Teacher and failed to trust him?" And indeed, they continued to enrich themselves.

Professional education in 1886

One of the journalists writing that year wrote about the relationship that was shown by the fortunate and wealthy towards their less-fortunate brethren, struggling daily to make a living, not succeeding and with no one to assist them. There were many poor children in the town but only one person of means spared a thought for them. Four years previously he had sent four of them as apprentices to various artisans where they learnt the trade and had even paid for each of the four an annual fee, while children who were physically unable to learn a trade were sent by him to study under teachers and scholars. All these children – "his" children – were distinguished by their uniform which he also supplied for them. The children who did well in their apprenticeship had their handiwork sent to the "Artisans' Foundation" in Petersburg and the administration of the Foundation for Fair Recompense. Nevertheless, as we know "One swallow doth not a summer make"! And one man cannot for an extended period, do on his own the work required by an entire institution and the work done by this one man found no one to succeed him and it stopped.

The situation for the children learning in the "*Talmud Torah*[2]" was also difficult. The teachers were without elementary education, the hygiene and sanitary facilities were beneath even the lowest of standards and the children were dressed in what virtually amounted to rags, crammed into one narrow and airless room with inadequate illumination. "One's heart goes out to these poor unhappy children whom fate had dealt so harshly with" – the writer concluded.

The Cholera Plague of 1885

After the Great Fire that occurred in town, the overcrowding became critical to the point of endangering health and influenced directly the number of people falling sick. The residents were afraid to inform the authorities of being ill lest they were confined to the hospital where – as rumor had it – the patients were being poisoned. The panic was great; residents ran from town and carried their disease with them. The army left town and with them the military doctors and the small number of doctors in town was insufficient to cope. Help was needed from outside of town.

A wooden hut was erected where free tea and boiled water were available for all. The creation of a system of rotation was also suggested with the doctors providing emergency treatment. The provincial governor proposed collecting money from the affluent to fund the struggle against the cholera outbreak. A total of four hundred rubles was collected while to finance a wedding in the cemetery – which superstition said would halt the plague – five hundred rubles were collected!

In the meantime, the plague did not cease and the results were somber and until all the good suggestions from here and there bore fruit, the atmosphere of fear did its work. Many of the workers left town and the refurbishing of the destroyed town after the Great Fire ceased. Eventually a public committee was formed with several tens of young volunteers for sanitary work and thanks to their efforts and dedication the mortality rate from the dreadful illness gradually began to fall.

The Great Fire of 1895

We are not talking here about the occasional fire that breaks out now and again because of someone's carelessness that consumes one or two houses but a serious massive blaze that flares up and consumes entire neighborhoods and changes the lives of many people overnight. One must remember: these houses were far from fireproof, and their owners couldn't expect any compensation for their losses as happens today.

A fire such as that occurred in 1895 and the damage inflicted was immense to the extent that a public committee had to be created to assist the victims. The committee used the monthly journal *"Kronika Wostoka"* to ask for financial help for the needy to be sent to two committee members: Doctor Norawsky (a Pole) and Ch. Margoles, the government accredited Rabbi.

The Community in 1891

The Jewish residents of town were mainly traders and businessmen and artisans and compassionate. Their economic position was hard and not a few were impoverished and formed the "proletariat" and there was no public body that could offer help. A few years earlier one of the public figures in town suggested forming a charitable organization to help the needy but because of diverging opinions the idea failed to germinate. The community cannot be forgiven for failing to act after all, part of its function as a communal body would be to come to the assistance of the needy. There is no forgiveness either for the religious observation "To sit and do nothing is preferable"[10]. "Doing nothing" seems to matter to them more than their concern of "Kosher and Treif[11]" while all the other troubles in our Jewish world didn't touch them at all? Are they really exempt from keeping the specific commandment: "…and if thy brother be waxen poor…[12]"!?

The Struggle for the Rabbinate

The fight for the position of the additional Rabbi in Greater Dubno began a few years before the outbreak of the First World War. At the time, the seat of the Chief Rabbi was occupied by Rabbi Mendele Rosenfeld while his younger brother Velvel served as *Dayan*[13]. Both of them served as town Rabbis for almost a full generation. Their dwelling place was in the center of town although their "domain" stretched all over the town, its neighborhoods and even its more distant suburbs. One of the important elements under their control was that of slaughtering. There were several distinguished slaughterers in Dubno at the time among them Rabbi Maril and Rabbi Sandor Sakiler.

Regarding slaughtering matters there was a special regime in Dubno controlled rigidly by Rabbi Mendele assisted by his loyal aide Rabbi Ben-Tzion who acted as a sort of "adjutant" although he was much younger than the other slaughterers and was not more knowledgeable in matters of orthodoxy than they were. One of the reasons for his strictness towards most of the Trisk slaughterers of the town was because they were of the "*Hasidim*"[14] sect – Rabbi Maril and his son-in-law Rabbi Aharon and also Rabbi Sandor Sakiler were members of the *Hasidei*-Turiisk (Turzysk, Turiys'k) sect and some of the slaughterers were from the *Hasidei*-Olyka (Ołyka) sect – while he, Rabbi Mendele, was from the "*Mitnagdim*" sect. (See endnote #14).

Rabbi Maril married his daughter to a young man named Eliyahu Guttmann, a great scholar of the *Torah* and an ordained Rabbi and ritual slaughterer. Because Rabbi Maril was already getting old he wanted to transfer his power to his son-in-law, so he took him to the slaughter-house from time to time to instruct him in the practicalities of slaughtering, as was common in those days among the slaughterers.

[Columns 207–208]

Rabbi Mendele knew of this, but he didn't react to the "irregularity" of Rabbi Maril. When Rabbi Maril announced publicly his intention to delegate his position to his son-in-law Rabbi Eliyahu, Rabbi Mendele in his wrath began persecuting Rabbi Maril whenever and however he could.

Now all the Trisk *Hasidim* came to the support of Rabbi Maril. At their head were Rabbi Isaac Feffer and Rabbi Eliezer Goldfarb, both of them confirmed *Hasidim*. The synagogue of the Trisk *Hasidim* was in turmoil and was used as a campaign headquarters supporting Rabbi Maril's attempt to pass on the slaughter administration to his son-in-law Rabbi Eliyahu as an "inheritance". The dispute and the furor went on for several months and in the meantime the support for Rabbi Mendele in his resistance to the inheritance grew and solidified and the opposing forces were about equally balanced.

Then the supporters of Rabbi Maril tried something else and some of the important people from the suburb of Surmicze came out with the rallying call "All of us stand together" and invited Rabbi Eliyahu Guttmann, the son-in-law of Rabbi Maril to take the position of Rabbi of the suburb. Chief among the candidates for the Rabbinate of Surmicze was Rabbi Eliezer Goldfarb, a rich and respected Jew who chose to forego part of his salary as Rabbi. The salaries and funding for ritual objects, the Rabbis and slaughterers were paid for from incomes from the taxes but because Rabbi Mendele and his supporters were in control and refused to recognize Rabbi Eliyahu, he was forced to look elsewhere for a living.

When Rabbi Eliyahu Guttmann became installed as Rabbi of Surmicze and began to function with his "*Responsa*"[115] it became clear that he was a highly intelligent man and pleasant to all humanity causing many people to turn to him for solutions to all manner of problems as arbitrator and adjudicator even in disputes of a private or business matter. Nevertheless, it was hard for him to make a living although his status as the Rabbi of Surmicze was secure and steadfast. The public recognized him and referred to him as "the 'young' Rabbi while Rabbi Mendele was known as "the 'old' Rabbi". Although his residence was in Surmicze, a distant suburb, he usually came to town each Sabbath to deliver a sermon before the afternoon prayer in the "Braslaw"[116] synagogue where he also expounded on a page of the "*Gemara*"[117]. He was extremely learned, and his sermons captured the attention of a growing number of listeners. In this he exceeded Rabbi Mendele who was not accustomed to preaching.

When the First World War broke out in 1914 many of Dubno's residents left town and with them Rabbi Mendele who settled in the provincial capital Zhitomir. Rabbi Eliyahu remained the sole Rabbi in Dubno and he remained there with its Jews throughout the Austrian conquest and officiated as the sole Rabbi after the re-conquest of the town by the Russians. During these years he became extremely well-liked by the Jewish townspeople and with the return of Rabbi Mendele after a two-year absence from Dubno they both officiated as Rabbis. With the death of Rabbi Mendele at an advanced age his son, Rabbi Hershel inherited his place and after the Polish conquest officiated as the accredited and official Rabbi. He and Rabbi Eliyahu Guttmann together shared the seat of Chief Rabbi until they were taken by the Nazis to an extermination camp where they died a martyr's death.

Under Austrian Rule

After the outbreak of war, the town of Dubno, which lay about fifty kilometers from the Austrian border, became the base of the various armies that passed through. The Russian army, opened with an attack on the Austrian Emperor's forces, beat them and got as far as the Carpathian Mountains. Thousands of Austrian prisoners, many of them torn and battered passed through the town. However it was not long before the Austrian army, with the help of the German army, drove the Russians back and by the beginning of autumn 1915, the approach of *Rosh Hashanah* and the Day of Atonement the Austrians had reached the town and retaken it.

A group of us young people was standing near our homes on Szeroka Street when the Austrian cavalry came in and approached us. "Which way to the bridge?" they asked in German. We pointed out the direction of the bridge near the flour mill and scampered off. The following day the entire town was in Austrian hands while the Tsar's forces dug in out of town over the other side of the river Ikwa.

For a period of 10 months the town was cut off on one side from Russia and as a front-line town from the conquering Austrian state because of the military situation – like a sort of island. The conquering Austrians related politely and generously to the population and the Jewish sector in particular felt it after having suffered badly at the crude and cruel hands of the Tsarist Russians simply because they were Jews, especially so as Jews in a border town occupied by the Austrian enemy. Thousands of Jews in border towns had been expropriated from their homes far away into the hinterland by the order of the Grand Duke Nicolai Nikolayevich (the uncle of Tsar Nicolai II). He felt the Jews lacked loyalty to the Russian authorities. They were even thought of as spies and traitors. Nevertheless, the order, so far as Dubno was concerned, never went into effect from lack of time.

During the early period of the Austrian authority over the town, the Jewish residents felt reasonably free and at ease (most of the Russian residents fled the town with the retreating Russian forces); the shops were open, and goods were being sold to whomever wanted them – although at a higher price than normal. But soon shortages in foodstuffs began to be felt because the besieged town was cut off and supplies couldn't get through.

On *Rosh Hashanah* in the middle of *Mussaf* (additional prayer), when the synagogues were full of praying people, the Russians suddenly began shelling the town from across the river directing their fire towards the area of the synagogues as "a present for the festival". The panic that ensued was great but the bombardment ended without casualties.

It was not many days until the residents began to feel the effect of the military regime. The homes on the streets alongside the river were emptied of their residents on the orders of the military commander and the homes cordoned off with barbed wire. The residents were evacuated and moved into the houses abandoned by the Russians who had departed with the army. The situation regarding food supplies worsened, especially for the poor people for whom no one cared.

As usual the confusion of the present situation gave rise to the growth of unruly behavior. There were those who were close to the top military authorities who were able to obtain travel permits to travel deep into the country far from the front – something more difficult than "parting the Red Sea"!

A variety of supplies were brought to the besieged town that was sold at exorbitant prices. There were also some members of "the fair sex" close to power that succeeded in getting permits for some "traders" who then became rich – at the expense, of course, of most of the residents.

In the spring of 1916, the Russian army began an attack under the command of General Brusilov and repelled the conquering Austrians to distant Austrian Galicia. With the liberation of the town many of the exiled refugees began streaming back to their homes and the economic situation together with the opportunities of making a living multiplied. A period of relief and affluence began and for two years the residents lived on a rising economic tide of fruitfulness and prosperity. Then came the Bolshevik Revolution and turned everything upside down again…

Original Footnote:

i.   As described in the monthly journal *"Kronika Wostoka"* ("Chronicle of the East")

Translator's Comments

1. Literally "a room" – traditionally a classroom for studying the Hebrew language and other Jewish studies from an early age on through the years.
2. *Yeshiva* – Advanced study center for *Torah Talmudic* and epigraphic scriptural literature often leading to ordination.
3. Tereza (Tamara Yevgenyevna) Zhabotinskaya–Kopp, the sister of Ze'ev (Vladimir) Jabotinsky.
4. The *"Tarbut"* school system was a "revolutionary" system, breaking away from the traditional Yiddish–based Jewish studies only in the "Heder" and introducing secular subjects into the curriculum in Hebrew.
5. Hechalutz, (*lit*. The Pioneer) was a Jewish youth movement that trained young people for agricultural settlement in the Land of Israel. It became an umbrella organization of the pioneering Zionist youth movements. For a complete history and explanation see: https://en.wikipedia.org/wiki/Hechalutz
6. Ha-Shomer Ha-Tsa'ir, (translating as the Young Guard) is a Socialist–Zionist, secular Jewish youth movement founded in 1913 and was also the name of the group's political party. For a complete history and explanation see: https://en.wikipedia.org/wiki/Hashomer_Hatzair
7. *"Sofer Satam"* is an acrostic for a scribe of Hebrew religious works such as Torah scrolls, wedding, divorce and other ritual documents. "Sofer" is a writer or scribe, "Satam" is composed of the initial letter of the Hebrew words *S'farim, Tefillin, Mezuzot* – books, phylacteries, doorposts. An extremely interesting article on this entire topic can be found here: https://www.jewishvirtuallibrary.org/modern–hebrew–calligraphy
8. *Hagana* – literally, Defense. Not the organization founded by Jabotinsky in 1920 in Palestine.
9. A religious school for young children – the *Heder*, in fact.
10. From a commentary in the *Talmud* tractate *Berachot*
11. Ritually 'clean' and allowable food and its opposite"
12. Leviticus chap. XXV; 25
13. Dayan – a Talmudic religious judge
14. For a complete explanation see: https://www.jewishvirtuallibrary.org/hasidim–and–mitnagdim
15. Rabbinical decisions, clarifications and replies to questions posed.
16. This is printed <u>in the Hebrew</u> as 'Breslau' which is in Poland (Wroclaw), and is often confused with Braslaw which is in Ukraine. Since this monograph's location is Ukraine, I suspect the Hebrew 'Breslau' is a printing error.
17. For a full description of the *"Gemara"* see: https://en.wikipedia.org/wiki/Gemara

The Purim Pogrom 5674 [1914]

by Shaul Viderman

Translated from Hebrew by Selwyn Rose

At the end of 1917, when the Bolshevik Revolution announced "freedom" for the citizens, there followed a sequence of changes of authority. The "Whites" and the gangs of the Ukrainian "Black Hundred" were not complacent about the new regime and conspired against the government, spilling their anger first of all upon the Jewish population. But the revolution and its echoes inspired the Jewish youth to stand up against the conspirators. Members of the Jewish *Haganah* [Defense] returned blow for blow and refused to allow them to harm the Jews of the town.

In the winter of 1918, the town was dominated by Ukrainian rioters at the head of which was the infamous Uskilka. On one of the Sabbathot early in the month of *Adar* (March), groups of Ukrainian hooligans from the local villages suddenly appeared on the streets of the town and began provoking the Jewish residents. Members of the *Haganah* with the help of supporters of the Revolution within the town's population overcame the riotous thugs, beating them decisively, commandeered their weapons and forcibly expelled them from the town.

The Ukrainian thugs couldn't swallow this insult and on the festival of *Purim* that began the Sabbath following the incident, a large contingent of them, mobilized from the various villages, invaded the town. They attacked the synagogue and houses dragging out the men, young and old, taking them to the White Army barracks in Surmicze. Gangs of thugs broke into shops and houses robbing and looting whatever came to hand. The Christian residents did not participate in what was going on but didn't lift a finger to help their Jewish neighbors; more than that – they marked their doors and windows with a cross in order to identify it as a Christian house and the hooligans left them alone.

The rioters continued with their activities until the evening and the Jews trembled from fear and only when darkness came were the prisoners sent home suffering abuse and beatings on the way. Nevertheless, among those originally taken there were eighteen people missing, thirteen from Dubno and five Jewish students from out of town.

For several days the families of the missing students searched for some sign trying to discover where they were, but all their efforts directed to the authorities were in vain and none of their own searches in the area bore fruit and no one had any information. Only after ten days was the mystery solved: a worried woman villager came to a Jewish wagon-driver in Surmicze and told him that between her village and the barracks she had seen the hand of a man sticking out of the ground.

The Jewish wagon-driver immediately organized some public figures and activists in town, and they went out to the place and after digging down deeply they found the bodies of the eighteen missing men. All of them had been shot by the villains and traces of brutalization found on their corpses.

The martyrs of the pogrom were brought to town for a Jewish burial in Dubno and the entire Jewish population of the town attended. That was the last "heroic" deed of the Ukrainian hooligan group in Dubno and their name lives on in ignominy.

The Rabbi's Daughter

by Shaul Tchernichovsky

Translated from Hebrew by Jerrold Landau

Let the lads of the city of Dubno be praised

In the choruses of the walls of the eye:

"Oh, they are pretty, the textile is divided into cloaks!"

They are drunk with the return of soldiers with their loot.

Drunk from blood and wine.

"Come and get the booty, the loot.

Oh, oh, the wanton life of a Cossack!"

The Cossacks shout out as they divide the spoils:

Linen, atlas silk, and fine velvet,

With Sabbath candelabra of good silver

And many soft, sparkling pearls

And goblets for Kiddush and Havdalah.

Batko was not in their company,

Alas, alas, this young Batko!

To him, why the booty, the bountiful loot?

Which contains a great deal of atlas silk, silk for

shoulders

She has eyebrows of velvet, of the black velvet,

And the pearls of her teeth are necklaces of light.
Does the light of a candle dazzle like her eyes?
Is there yet in the world an intoxicating goblet
Like the lips of the Hebrew maiden?!

He is not here, for he went to the room of the
rabbi's daughter
"But, indeed I love you, oh beautiful one!
I was still a servant to the haughty landowner,
On account of you, I put my hand before
The revolt, to you my weary soul.
On account of you, I went there with the lads,
Alas, alas, the most beautiful daughter of the rabbi.

"If I did not love you, I would have already taken you
Like all your sisters in our camp…
Become a Christian, go to Father Vasyl;
Today, yet this evening in joy and gladness
We will celebrate our wedding.
I will command for you a velvet cloak, a veil of gold,
Two hundred groomsmen!"

The maiden is pale, but she still can speak:
"Oh, would that I had tasted the bitterness of
death!
Lad, how can I rejoice in joy,
Cover myself with a veil and wear a cloak,
For I was orphaned just yesterday…
At the head of every street, first to greet
The groomsmen – would be all my slaughtered
brethren."

Then the lad pounded on the wooden table:
"Let it be according to your words, oh maiden!
I will wait two weeks. To the city of Uman
Where the Hetman of the country is, and with
him the 'beast,'
Uhlans with braided hair.
There I will go with my lads; If I am not hit by
Polish bullets – I will return."

"Wait… please wait… pay attention and listen…
Do not be afraid of a Polish bullet!
But pay attention… swear… It is a deep secret
with me…
I know how to whisper about a bullet in any
implement,
It is a tradition from my dear mother,
Why are you laughing? You don't believe? Go
flee immediately!
Shoot me – Here I am! This minute!"

And the lad took out a valuable pistol
With silver dots. "Will you believe?"
He placed a bullet in it, and poured gunpowder
Into its barrel, very finely ground.
"I will lean on the doorpost!"
The gun thundered! And with a muffled groan
The maiden collapsed beneath it.

The lad kisses with the kisses of his mouth, he raises
The eyes of the maiden, they are shriveled…
Did the bullet strengthen the whisper of the dead?
Or did the maiden make her statement prematurely

Or did she forget her motto, did she err?

Or perhaps…? Only God has answers…

Who can know the heart of a Hebrew woman!

Sonminda 1924·

Translator's Comments

1. Atlas silk -- see https://en.wikipedia.org/wiki/Atlas_silk
2. A Hetman is a military commander.
3. The Uhlans were Polish-Lithuanian cavalry units. See
    https://en.wikipedia.org/wiki/Uhlan
4. I am unsure of the identity of Sonminda. In 1924, Tchernichovsky was in Palestine or
    Germany.
5. About Tchernichovsky – see https://www.jewishvirtuallibrary.org/shaul-
    tchernichovsky.
6. It is believed that the heroine of this poem was inspired by Esther, daughter of Rabbi
    Meir in Dubno. She was murdered during the Khmelnytsky uprising and massacres in
    Dubno 1649. See more in the chapter "The Jews of Dubno" and reference 17 therein.

Sources of Livelihood of Dubno's Jews

by Moshe Cohen

Translated from Hebrew by Selwyn Rose

The writer of this survey, who was born and grew up in Dubno, living there for fifty years and taking part in nearly every public Zionist activity in town, apologizes in advance for any errors and inaccuracies which may have been introduced here. It has been written purely from memory and there has been no possibility to refer or examine sources to compare the figures quoted.

The main sources of sustenance of Dubno's Jewish element were: Industry, inn-keeping, trading, artisanship – tailoring, carpentry, iron-working and welding, butchery, fishing, transport and porterage; free professions: medicine, education, law, clerkship and religious services.

A. Industry

In and around the vicinity there were six large, sophisticated flour-mills, the lion's share of the produce of which – after fulfilling local needs, was exported all over Poland.

Five of the above mills, "Solet", "Zamkoba", "Volhynia", "Zabramia" and "Economia" were owned by Jewish residents of town while one was owned by a non-Jew – "Wohlitzer" – that was always rented and operated by Jews. Only in 1937 was one of the large mills, "Solet" owned by Shmuel Horowitz (Z"L)[1]sold to a Polish company.

All the owners of the mills (about 25 families) were in a good economic situation and a few of them were actually rich.

Most of the workers in the flour-mills - clerks, professional- and non-professional workers – were Jewish and most of them were well situated.

In and around town there were also factories under Jewish ownership manufacturing roof-tiles and cement piping, but all the workers were non-Jewish.

These owners were also substantially wealthy. Similarly, the owners of the lime-kilns were Jewish but the workers were all non-Jewish.

There were also soap-making factories in the town owned by Jewish people. Several families made a living from them.

From 1927/8 the preparation and baking of Pesach matzoth began on an industrial scale that guaranteed employment for 40–50 families for four or five months each year.

In 1930 a Belgian company, in partnership with Polish and Jewish financial participation, opened a large factory for preserving meat and its products. One of the partners in the company was the well-known Lodz (Łódz) industrialist, Asher Cohen. The number of Jewish employees in that business was very small except for the suppliers of chickens and pluckers of the chickens.

There were twelve oast-houses or kilns, modern and well-equipped for drying hops. In these facilities the strong bitter-smelling clusters of hops were dried and raked-over before being sacked up for the beer-brewing industry.

All these installations belonged to Jews, most of them from Dubno, like the Albert brothers, David and Tzvi Perle, the Barchash brothers, the Goldstein brothers, Eliezer Fishbein, Moshe Kellerman, Yechiel Katz and Emmanuel Mazurek; there were also Pesses and Distenfeld of Lwow and Eliezer Goldfarb, a citizen of Dubno residing in Gdansk (Danzig). In 1932 Eliezer Goldfarb sold his factory to a Polish company.

During the season, that lasted from September to the end of March, about 2,000 -2,500 daily workers, most of them women from the town and surrounding villages, found work in these factories. The number of Jewesses amounted to 30–35% of the women workers. They were all daughters of poor families and their wages just about sustained them with careful planning; compared to them the salaries of the office and professional workers in the factories were satisfactory.

There were also eight grinding mills in Dubno milling buckwheat and millet into various grades and nearby oil-presses for expressing the oil, mostly for the farmers in the district who brought their crops of sunflowers. They paid partly in seeds and partly cash. Three of the mill owners mentioned here were wealthy while the rest needed to work quite hard to make it pay.

Soft drinks production, like soda-water, lemonade and other flavored drinks were manufactured in five factories. The owners worked very hard, especially during the summer months when there was a plentitude of work and were well-established. They attempted to amalgamate and form a cartel but after a couple of years, in 1936, the cartel broke up because of internal dissensions and each went his own way.

[Columns 215–216]

There were smaller enterprises operated by individual families – like in stocks and shares, the preparation of wine from fruit and raisins and the production of candies. There were also two factories manufacturing brushes, a factory for vinegar and a printing-house owned by individual families. In most of these enterprises the owners were not only workers in the factories but were engaged in selling their products, apart from the stock-market and printing-house enterprises where salaried professionals were engaged. The owners of all these enterprises did well and a few of them, the printing-house and a few of the stock-market families were rich.

Six or seven of the family-heads operated freight services via the railroad. They took care of all the documentation and formalities: invoicing, receipts and the reception and forwarding of goods. Their work was hard and carried a great responsibility, but the reward was commensurate with the effort.

B. Hoteliers

The business of hostelry and inn-keeping in Dubno began very early with its roots in the days of the Polish kingdom. There were fourteen excellent hotels relative to the period and another thirteen of a somewhat lesser standard. Most of the hotel guests were nobles or landowners from the area, owners of estates and forestry proprietors who arrived in town by horse. Nearly every hotel had stables or garage space except the "Francuski", which belonged to the Perlman family (Z"L), where travelers who came from all over Poland by railroad or even from abroad, stayed. Mostly they came for business reasons but there were also the delegates, who came from all the Zionist movements such as the Foundation Fund of Israel, WIZO, "Tarbut" and others. These guests were warmly welcomed by the owners of the hotel in spite of the fact that the meetings of these groups were often rowdy and extremely noisy, disturbing the atmosphere for other guests of the hotel. Among others who stayed there were honored guests from Palestine like Rabbi Maimon and Yisroel Ritoff, Rabbi Gold, Mrs. Pewzner the founder of WIZO in Dubno, political and social and Zionist activists and politicians, citizens of Poland like Dr. Fischer, Dr. Gottlieb, Avraham Levisohn and others.

The restaurant and beerhalls were also significantly in the hands of Jews and their owners belonged to the middle-classes of Dubno society.

227

A convention of Jewish artisans at Poland's national holiday

[Columns 217–218 - Hebrew]

C. Artisans and Laborers

Most of Dubno's Jews were artisans of different trades except for a few shoemakers, builders, bakers and smiths who were not Jewish. A number of them had their own workshops and worked alone, or were assisted by professionals, apprentices and students. But starting in 1930, in accordance with the economic policies of the anti-Semitic Polish Government, non-Jewish apprentices, children of the local farmers, began to infiltrate the exclusively Jewish professions like tailoring, hairdressing and carpentry. These students began as apprentices but in a short while began to appear as competitors to the Jewish established businesses. Foreign artisans from Poland and Galicia began to arrive in town who were additional competitors of the Jewish artisans. All the Jewish artisans were members of one of two guilds centered in the capital, Warsaw: a general one at whose head in recent times was Yitzhak Litzmann (now in Israel); the second was left-wing and under the leadership of the *"Bund"* led by the local "Bundist" politician Leib Luchnick (Z"L).

Most of the artisans – their number in total were a few hundred – barely made a living except for a few tens who were highly skilled. A few were even wealthy.

228

Butchery

There were between 20–30 families trading in this business. They bought cattle in the surrounding farms, brought the animals to town where they were slaughtered and sold to the butcher-shop owners in town. The work of these Jews was very hard, but their level of sustenance was considered secure.

Fishing

Fishing was carried out in the stream and lakes in the area by a number of Jewish families among them working as professionals who went fishing in the Ikwa. In addition, they would buy fish from non-Jewish fishermen and owners of local fish-ponds in the area and with the help of their wives sold all the fish in the local market.

D. The Free Professions

In medicine, pharmacy, dentistry and law the Jewish population of Dubno held a respectable place – about 60%-70% of the total academic professions, except engineering which was virtually entirely in the hands of the non-Jews. These professionals were respected and dignified and holders of wealth and assets. There were also a number of nurses, some of whom worked in hospitals and some privately.

Education and Instruction

Generally speaking, Jewish teachers were not accepted by the public municipal schools so their number in town was few. Most of them worked in the private Jewish schools and in private instruction. There were about 18 families of teachers and although they didn't go hungry their sustenance was insecure.

Clerical work

Jewish clerical workers were not accepted in government offices at all and until 1928 there were no Jewish clerical workers in the town's municipal offices and institutions – except Mr. Leybish Halperin Z"L, the municipal treasurer. But after the municipal council elections in 1928 a few Jewish clerical workers were taken by some of the municipal institutions but their numbers barely reached 7% or 8% of the town's clerical staff. However, in the Jewish institutions of town such as the cooperative banks and private companies the entire clerical staff was Jewish. About 40-50 families were involved and their standard of living was reasonable.

Religious services

Included in religious services were Rabbis, cantors, ritual slaughterers, synagogues and Study-house sextons and beadles, community clerical staff and sacred articles institutions – about 50 families. Of them only about seven or eight families – the ritual slaughterers – earned a reasonable living while all the rest had a less than adequate wage and a member of the family found it necessary to take on additional employment or live a life of poverty. Only the two rabbis, the two town rabbis – received a regular fixed payment but even that was miniscule.

E. Transport

Autobus service

The Jews were the first of Dubno's citizens to develop an inter-urban bus service covering an area within a radius of about 100 km – from Dubno to Lutsk, Rowno, Kremenets and Radziwill. At the start it was the initiative of a few individuals but after a short while a few companies came into existence investing much capital and effort. In time the branch was invaded by foreigners and after a period of unfair competition caused a number of the Jews to fall away. Eventually, however, they all united, fixed routes and timetables and the transport system continued to develop and function until the outbreak of war in 1939. In any case the autobus service was an economic blessing for the life of the town, its developers and workers during all the years of its existence.

Wagon-masters

From its earliest years there had always been wagon-masters and carriage drivers for the transportation of passengers within the town and its surroundings and especially to the railroad station that was about 4 km from the center of town. Apart from just two or three non-Jews all the wagoners and carriage drivers in town were Jewish and only from 1930 did a few non-Jews break into the business with their wagons, in accordance with the economic policies of the Polish

[Columns 219–220]

government. Generally speaking, about 40 families, mostly Jews of little means made their living from the transportation business with difficulty. There were also about 25-30 wagon-masters, all of them Jewish, working very hard who operated as haulers of goods and whose income was a little more secure – especially after they united in 1922 in one guild under the management of Naphtali Steinwertzel (Z"L) who through his dedication knew very well how to protect their interests and how to develop contacts with all elements connected to the transportation and haulage of goods and freight thus obtaining better deals for his members and a better living standard.

Water-carriers and porterage

Because of the non-existence of organized plumbing installation in the homes, water-carriers operated in town; they drew water from the river Ikwa and transported the water in barrels or even in buckets on yokes over their shoulders. Thus, was drinking water delivered to the homes until 1907 when an artesian well was dug in the center of town. About twenty families made a living from the transportation of water. It entailed extremely hard work especially in the cruel winter months and it didn't bring in a good livelihood. Indeed, in this occupation also there were intruders that infiltrated from the year 1930 and who, like the water-carriers, were not Jewish, and began to supply water to Polish families who, over time, had come to live and settle in town. It was somewhat paradoxical that in later years the economic situation of the water-carriers improved a lot because the job-status was considered inferior and demeaning and as such members of families of standing declined employment opportunities in the field and since the population had grown from year to year the income of the water-carriers had increased correspondingly.

The occupation of porterage was entirely in the hands of Jews until the end. About 20–25 families were occupied and the work was physical and very hard. Young people also were not attracted to this work so those who worked at porterage prospered accordingly.

F. Commerce

Commerce was the principal source of income for most of the local Jews of Dubno. And about 60%-65% of the Jewish population was involved in and secured their sustenance from it. The larger traders were organized into the 'Traders' Society' and the smaller businessmen in the 'Society of Small Traders'. The centers of both societies were in the capital, Warsaw. At the head of the 'General Traders' Society' in Dubno at the time stood A. Kahana, Shmuel Barchash and Yisroel Moshe Laschower and for the 'Small traders' Society' Ben-Zion Shtoff and Moshe Pinchosovich.

Commerce in Dubno fell into two sectors:

a. Trade in imported goods, like groceries, fuel, textiles, paper, leather for shoes, books, writing materials, haberdashery, clothing, metal-work, paints and building materials.

b. Trade in the exportation of agricultural produce like hops, clover seeds, wheat, flour, fruit, eggs, hens, furs and skins.

Wholesale trade in imports is divided into wholesalers and retailers.

Wholesale trading, found a major focus on groceries, and supplied all the needs of the retailers in town and in the surroundings for a radius of about 50 km. Until 1926 the trade was entirely in the hands of Jews. That same year a large Polish cooperative was founded in town and following it was a Ukrainian one. Both of them became the suppliers of all the non-Jewish shop-keepers in town and the surrounding villages. All other products that the shop-keepers needed were brought from Warsaw, Lodz and nearby Rowno and insignificant items, like iron- and metal-work, furs and textiles were imported from trading-posts and industries in Russia. After 1920 when the entire area was disconnected from Russia and passed to Poland most of the retailers dealt with Lwow.

Apart from two or three non-Jewish or foreign owners the retail trade was entirely in the hands of the Jewish population until 1925 when non-Jewish people streamed into town, mostly Polish, who began to enter the retail trade here and there until, in 1939 they represented about 15% and they even created a Society of their own.

In general terms about 400-500 resident families, a significant number, made a living from import and retail enterprises in town. About 60%-70% of them relied more or less on their shops and a regular circle of customers and clients. Most of these families belonged to the middle-class and about 10%-15% of them were in an even better economic position, while 20%-25% of the families less well-founded, sold their wares in kiosks or market-stalls. Their customers were passers-by or villagers from the area and in addition they needed to take their wares two or three times a week to other local village markets on their respective market days and fairs and only by those means could they hope to continue trading and survive economically but still with difficulty.

About 12–15 Jewish families were engaged in trade in building materials – with timber in all its forms, cement, plaster, porcelain etc., and lived well.

Four veteran families of long standing were in a partnership trading wholesale in the petroleum industry and its associated products: A. Kahana, Shmuel Barchash, Avraham Guberman and the Harmetz family and in recent times the Binstok brothers also entered the trade. They had large storage tanks and warehouses next to the railroad station that were used for supplying the town and surrounding areas. When the autobus and taxi service developed, they built a gas-station at the approaches to the city and at the center of town. These families were all rich and made an excellent living as did their employees – six or seven families; they received good salaries from which they could live comfortably.

Agricultural trade

There were three large trading houses for the export of eggs. They received eggs into their warehouses from the surrounding villages via small traders. Owners of these storehouses, [the longest established was the Nachtman family], specialized in the selection and packaging of eggs for export to companies abroad with whom they had made commercial connections. Only Jews – about 15–20 were working in the selection and packaging of eggs; their salaries were low and their economic situation difficult.

About 20–30 families were engaged in the chicken trade. The hens were bought either directly from farmers or from outside traders who would acquire the birds from sources at the entrance to town, markets or fairs. The lion's share of chickens was sold live at large centers, like Warsaw, Lwow and so on while the remainder, especially geese, were fattened and later slaughtered and sold to the local population. All the Jewish traders in fowl made a good living.

The trade in skins, furs and pig's bristle was also carried on by two or three traders who bought the stock from itinerant Jewish traders, from farmers or peddlers from the villages. From their store-houses in town they sorted the skins, dried and salted them, then sold them throughout Poland. These Jewish traders also did well to the benefit of their families.

As stated, the major suppliers of eggs, chickens, skins, furs and pigs' bristles, were some tens of poor families and peddlers who wandered around the markets or the suburbs of town, travelled to local fairs purchasing the above items in small quantities bringing them to town and selling to large traders. These families were mainly impoverished making their livelihood with great difficulty.

The trading in fruit was also in the hands of the Jews who bought from the orchard owners while the fruit was still on the tree and sometimes even before it blossomed. They picked the fruit at their own expense, bringing it to town, storing it in cool cellars and marketing the major portion by wagons to the large towns of Poland, while the remaining fruit was sold to shop-keepers for the local population. This sector also found employment for 30–40 families among whom the wholesalers made a good living and lived well while the other families were less fortunate, living more modestly, selling fruit via retailers to the local population.

233

There were also a few shopkeepers selling flour, grits and chick-peas. They bought their supplies from the local mills and were part of the middle-class.

G. Field produce and seeds

The entire area of Dubno, within a radius of 40-50 km., was rich agricultural land farmed mostly by Ukrainian farmers with a few Czechs, Poles, Germans and a few Jews.

Until 1861, the year that the farmers were released from what was virtually a feudal vassalage, the agricultural land, including the forests and rivers, was owned by the government, by Prince Bariatinski, the Counts of Malinov, Samorodov, Satiov and Taranowka, or to Polish lords and smaller estate owners, churches and monasteries.

With the Land Reforms of 1884 lots of about 24 hectares were given to each freed family including the small holdings they had before the Reform. The allocated lands had been taken from large estates in some cases, so small parcels of plowed fields of some of the farmers were at a distance from where they lived-- perhaps as much as 8–10 km.

Similar lots were sold at reasonable terms for the Czechs who immigrated to the Dubno and Volhynia area in 1884. Most of the Poles and Germans had no land of their own; they rented land and also forests that in time were felled, plowed and sown.

Nevertheless in 1890 there were still large tracts of agricultural land in the hands of large landowners amounting to thousands of hectares, and smaller landowners had up to one or two thousand hectares. The Volhynia farmers worked their land using the most primitive methods and without any guidance. Consequently, the produce was poor.

The produce was sold to suppliers and destined for export and for the army. It was during this period that army regiments were camped in Dubno - infantry, cavalry and artillery

[Columns 223–224]

and most of their needs were supplied by local Jewish contractors. Nevertheless, a large portion of the produce of the estates was sold to agents from Lutsk and Rowno where, apparently even by now, good connections had already been made with the wider world and only a small amount remained to be sold to the Dubno wholesalers who dealt with the export of produce, like Joel Potashnick, Meir Glazberg and Shimon Falper – all of them prosperous Jews.

In order to acquire the raw produce from the small farmers, the retail traders, who were called 'produce sellers' in Dubno, settled in all the various approaches to town and from there they 'hunted' the farmer who brought his produce for sale. Whatever remained unsold at the entrance to town and got to the market-place was snatched up by the traders there who managed to make a small profit. The retailers sold the produce to army suppliers and partly to the flour-mills, [and to feed] the draft and pack- animals owned by Jews from town. Anything left over was sold to wholesalers for export.

Particularly unusual was trade in clover-seeds. The farmers, especially the Czechs, would bring for sale small amounts of clover seeds – about 20–100 kgs., and neither the farmer nor the buyer had the least idea of the quality or the price. The retailer took a small sample of the clover, ran to the wholesaler and together they agreed upon a price, whereon he ran back to pay the farmer and immediately transferred the seeds to the wholesaler who generally treated the clover seed with special concern and stored it all in a room in the house.

The retailers of crops – 35–40 families mostly belonged to the middle-class and a few of them were in a better economic position.

In time the economic situation of the farmers deteriorated because their families grew, and the land was divided among the family members thus reducing the per person income. As a result, the amount of produce brought for sale was also reduced and the situation of the Jewish traders in Dubno worsened from year to year.

At the beginning of the present century, when rumors began to surface in Volhynia about a revolt of farmers in Russia, the estate owners, both large and small, began to offer hungry Ukrainian farmers plots of land for sale, while Poles and Germans were offered forested plots which when cleared would fetch a good price, but on condition that all the settlements that would be erected on the land would bear the name of the seller. That is why all the new settlements have names like Yanuvka (Bereslavka), Stanislavka, Vladislavka and so on. Around the same period, in 1907, the Land Reform Bill was published by the Russian Minister Stolypin according to which the authorities began to sell to Ukrainian farmers, owners of small plots of land, large plots of government land on condition that the farmer will erect his home on the land. The intention of the government was to liquidate the Ukrainian village on the one hand and to right the situation of the farmers on the other in order to neutralize the elements causing the rebellion, like what was happening in Russia. There is no doubt that the farmers benefited from the reform for it gave them the real opportunity to develop farms that would indeed give them a reasonable living standard.

The Agrarian Reform – the sale of land to the Ukrainian farmers and the leasing of land to Polish and German settlers – opened up new possibilities for the Jewish dealers in farm produce in the county. For the farmers, who were impoverished and had to pay for the land, for drilling wells on the farm, for erecting a house and farm buildings; and for the German and Polish settlers who were obliged to clear the land of trees and arrange the fields for plowing and sowing and to exist for two years until the land brought forth its produce - there was no money and they turned to the Jewish dealers and borrowed from them the required financing. In addition, the borrower was tied to conditions. The first was that he was obliged to sell his produce only to the person who loaned the money and thus the traders were guaranteed a fixed source of produce for their business. Indeed, on more than one occasion it happened that the farmer, or the settler on the land who needed the money would sell his produce at the beginning of autumn and in the height of winter would return to the purchaser and buy back produce for his household and livestock that he had sold and pay for it significantly more than he had received for its sale.

That situation continued until 1915.

In the summer of 1915, the Russian army was retreating before the Austrian army, that had gotten as far as the environs of Dubno, and the town was conquered by them [Austrians]. Many farmers fled their villages and escaped with their families to the depths of Ukraine and even to Russia. Dubno was cut-off from its surroundings because of the battles that were fought in the vicinity and that lasted for about ten months (from *Rosh Hashanah* 1915 until *Shavuot* 1916[2]), and the trade in field crops ceased in its entirety.

In 1916 with the commencement of the well-known Russian "Brusilov Offensive" a large part of Dubno was burnt and destroyed. Most of the town's citizens, who remained there after the Austrian conquest, were forced to escape westwards with the retreating Austrian army and leave behind all their possessions – some not too far away, some to Galicia and some even to Czechoslovakia.

In 1919, after the end of the war and following the disturbances and alternating authorities, the living conditions changed significantly and with them the manner in which trade and business was carried on, becoming unstable. The Jewish people continued doing business based mainly on the black market. In 1920 when Dubno and the surroundings were conquered by Poland and the peace agreement signed with Russia, according to which the border passed about 50 km south-east of Dubno, close to the town of Ostrow and about 120 km east of Dubno near the town of Korets, life slowly began to return to normal and with it, business generally and trade in produce particularly also revived.

[Columns 225–226]

In order to increase Polish settlement in the conquered territories, the Polish authorities began to transfer thousands of soldiers, released from the army to the area, apportioning land to them that had been confiscated from the estate owners especially lands that at one time had been the property of Princess Leonilla Ivanovna Bariatinskaya, later passed to Countess Shuvalova and also land from other Polish estate owners. The Government gave significant support to these soldiers, called 'settlers' and also provided agricultural guidance and training so that the new farms would operate in a modern fashion. Ukrainian farmers also benefited from the training, developing and improving their farms. The level of education in the Ukrainian villages began to rise, thanks to new schools that were built.

The economic standing of the farmers increased significantly during the years of political instability in the Province, because the price of agricultural produce remained very high owing to the depreciation of the Polish Mark. The trade was now based mainly on the increased demands of the villages that had grown from year to year. The Jewish traders also took advantage of the situation and improved their own economic standing although they decided that the time had come to stop with the black market and return to normal trading. The trade in agricultural produce was the easiest course to absorb the black-market traders since it didn't require professional knowledge and skills, had no need of a shop and it was possible to operate with modest sums of cash in order to manage a profitable business. The only necessary equipment needed was some kind of storage space in the approaches to town and a weighing machine. And indeed, within a short time span storage huts were constructed 10 or 12 kms from town because every agent wanted to be the first to greet the farmer bringing his produce to town for sale. Within quite a short period of time about 40–50 Jewish families had entered the business in addition to the 50–60 families of retailers of field produce that already existed.

The 15ᵗʰ Jubilee celebration of the members of the Cooperative bank for Artisans and small traders

During the years 1920–1924 there was a significant rise in the standard of living of the residents, both rural and urban. Thanks to the increased demand the farmers likewise increased their planting of clover and wheat and the high prices paid for the produce because of the lowered value of the currency, permitted a good profit for the traders among them the newcomers recently entering the trade. But in 1924 the situation again changed. The prices of field crops on the world markets began dropping after years of increased demand after the war and also the stability of the new Polish currency, the zloty, blocked the speculation in crops that was based on the instability of the old currency. The business of the traders in field-crops became difficult and competition between them became fierce. Several attempts by the traders at the town's approaches to organize some kind of partnership failed to materialize and those partnerships that did start broke down in a short while. The Jewish traders who began to become impoverished tried to maintain their position with many different and questionable tactics, like mixing invalid material into the bulk or mixing different products - but it didn't help.

From 1920–1924, while the Polish Mark was devaluing, a great change took place in the marketing of field crops. With the expansion of cereal crop production, a number of large, sophisticated mills were constructed in Dubno, Rowno, Radziwill, Lutsk and most of the cereal was sold to them; the Polish army boycotted the Jewish traders and the wheat not yet sold to the mills was exported to other countries. Because of the situation the wholesalers in Dubno organized themselves into two or three companies marketing field crops for export. These companies were not concerned about the future, they took no great care to ensure the quality of the produce nor were they concerned about forging good business relations with their clients. They tried their best to exploit the present complex situation to their advantage. Because of the situation the stability of the wholesalers was also undermined and a few of them also became impoverished.

In the meantime other external elements began a process of eroding the status of the Jewish traders both wholesalers and retailers; the government began increasing taxation on businesses in general and on agriculture is particular: the Polish commercial Cooperative in Dubno that, until now, had traded only in 'general necessities' now began to trade in the export business and began to apply pressure on the new Polish 'settlers' in the area, the released soldiers, to market their produce only through them. That, and more besides: the government taxes levied on the Cooperative were substantially lower than those levied on the Jewish traders. Many farmers in the area, not necessarily Poles, began marketing their produce with the Polish Cooperative and the Jewish traders had difficulty earning "a loaf of bread".

In the light of that situation, in 1927, together with my friend Sandor Schwam, I approached all the businessmen in Dubno trading in field-crops and suggested to them that we form a cooperative. After exhausting negotiations and equally long debates, with the help of A. Kahana the chairman of 'The Society of Dubno Traders', the first 'Cooperative of Dubno Traders in Cereals' - "Uniah" was formed in October 1927. The members of the Cooperative – 105 in number, were obliged by the Cooperative's constitution, to sell all their produce bought by them to the Cooperative alone, for a commission. Since all the traders paid a unified price for the produce deposited with the Cooperative and since the produce was stored in one granary it was possible to preserve the quality of the produce and thus prevent unfair competition. In addition, every member was bound to maintain a closed account in the Cooperative to the value of one percent of his turnover as savings.

In spite of the internal frictions among the members, the Cooperative succeeded in functioning well. It earned a good name in the produce Exchanges of Lwow and Gdansk and had clients of excellent standing. The Cooperative also purchased a carousel for sieving the produce and sieves for the clover seeds and was able to market grain to international standards and receive the highest prices. In Dubno itself the Cooperative had a good name and the financial institutions and the Polish Government bank in Rowno granted the Cooperative good conditions. Even private individuals, who were not traders in field crops, began to deposit their savings in the cooperative reserves, relying on a clause in its constitution permitting the transaction. In addition to all this the development of the Cooperative was aided by the overall general complexity of the field crop market at that time.

However, objectors of the Cooperative, among them members of the management who were wholesalers and had joined the Cooperative under pressure from the general corpus of the dealers, undermined the society and at the beginning of January 1929 complained in an anonymous letter to the Province's Attorney General, the police and the Treasury's department of taxes concerning 'irregularities' and 'illegal activities' in the Cooperative. On the 16th January 1929 the Police were authorized by Attorney General to conduct a search of the Cooperative's offices and store-houses. They confiscated all the books and files of documents taking them for investigation by specialists in the Department of Taxes of the Treasury.

By using secret methods and special efforts we managed, with the guidance of Dr. Rotfeld (Z"L), the well-known delegate to the Sejm, and many payments in order to get back some of the documents from the hands of the inspectors. After two or three weeks the examination failed to discover any wrong-doing and the entire documentation was returned to us and the Cooperative was permitted to continue its operations. But now the management was faced with a question: is there a way to continue operating with the present relationship between the members and the informer(s)? After much hesitation and consultations with advisors it was decided to liquidate the Cooperative. In April 1929 a General Meeting was called of all the members, in which it was decided to liquidate the Cooperative and thus, on 5th May 1929 the Cooperative ceased to exist.

[Columns 229–230]

After the liquidation, the position of the traders in Dubno worsened perceptibly and the competitiveness between the members became very harsh. The farmers became more suspicious and learned more about prices and weights, so it was harder for the traders to deceive them and the retailers. Apart from a dozen families who managed to hold out thanks to their savings from the 'good old days', many found themselves in crisis. Most of them left the trade and began several other businesses – small trading, market stalls, middle-men in the hops trade, and so on.

The situation of the wholesalers also worsened after the liquidation because the clients had become accustomed to certain high standards of produce and expected those standards to continue which required investment in storage near the railroad and the purchase of machinery for cleaning and sieving the produce. Since most of the wholesalers had no resources for that, partnerships were formed with Jewish financiers who demanded high returns for their investments.

These were the conditions in the field crop trade that lasted for about ten years until the entry of the Red Army into the area at the end of 1939.

Now is the time to note that most of the Jewish traders in field crops in Dubno, both retailers and wholesalers, failed to save money for less successful times, nor did they cultivate friendly terms with the local farmers. Apart from the two Fischer brothers and their families, now in Israel, who found security during the Holocaust with Czech friends in the nearby village of Klischykha, all the others who failed to escape to Soviet Russia before the 22nd June 1941, perished in the Holocaust.

*

From what is described above one gets the following picture of the living conditions of the Jews of Dubno:

● Until 1920 the Jewish traders, artisans and laborers among the population of Dubno were in the clear majority.

● Starting in 1920, the Polish authorities began introducing large numbers of foreign elements, first as clerks and Government employees who later transitioned into serious competitors with the Jews of town in all sectors of the economy.

● The Jews were found in all manner of employments in town and attempted to make a living from them, even with difficulty, right up until the last moment.

● The economic situation of the Jews of Dubno was generally slightly better than 'good'. There was among them a small minority who were rich relative to the concepts of the place and times and in contrast there was a large number of under- or partially-employed and even paupers.

● There were economic ups and downs for the Jews of Dubno caused by the conditions prevailing at different times but with the entry of the anti-Semitic Polish authorities the Jewish citizens entered a period of deep decline because of the entry of many foreigners into Jewish professions and trading branches and the crushing and cruel taxes that fell only upon the Jews. The pressure on the Jews became even more extreme starting in 1925 with the entry of the anti-Semitic Minister of Finance Władysław Grabski and continued unabated until the end of the Polish authority in the autumn of 1939.

It seems clear from the above why the Jewish population of Dubno became so impoverished shortly before the Holocaust and the poor and poverty-stricken comprised one of the reasons why there were so very few survivors of the Jewish community of Dubno aside from those few that for one reason or another managed to find a way to the distant reaches of Soviet Russia between autumn 1939 and 22nd June 1941.

Translator's Footnotes

1. "*Zichronoh(ah) Le-Bracha*" a Hebrew *postmortem* honorific meaning: May he (or she) be remembered for a Blessing.
2. From September until the following May – about 9 months

DUBNER LEBEN. № 1. פרייז 25 גראשען.

Opłata pocztowa uiszczona ryczałtem
ערשטער יאהרגאנג

דובנער

אנאנסען פרייזען:
פאר א כיל שורה פארן טעקסט 30 גר.
„ אין טעקסט: 40 „
„ נאכן טעקסט 20 „

לעבן

סע׳ז אינהאלט אין פארזן פון די אנאנסן איז די רעדאקציע נישט פאראנטװאָרטליך.
כאניסקריפטסן רעגען נישט צוריקגעשיקט.
פאר בריף: „Dubner Leben" Skrz. poczt. 159.
פאר געלד־זענדונגען סר. I. Rabinsztejn, Dubno.

אימפארטייאישע, געזעלשאפטליכע און עקאנאמישע צייטשריפט.

Adres Redakcji i Administracji: Dubno (Wołyń) ul. Zabranie 19   Dubno, Marzec 1929 מערץ

דובנא,

צו דער יודישער באפעלקערונג
אין דובנא און אומגעגענד !

ס׳קען זיין, אז סיוועלן זיך געפינען אזעלכע, װעלכע נישט אפשאצענדיק דעם גרויסן װערט פון אינזער ארבייט דאס ארויסגעבן א צייטשריפט. װעלן ביינוועלינ ערקלערן. אז אינזער צייטשריפט איז א װערקצייג אין דער האנד פון אוועלכע סאיין פארטיי אדער געזעלשאפטליכע אינסטיטוציע. דאריבער ערקלערן מיר זייערליך. אז די צייטשריפט טראגט דעם כאראקטער פון א אינפארטייאישען אָרגאן. װעלכער װעט שטעהן אויף דער װאך צו פארטיידיגן די אידישע אינטערעסן פין דובנא און אומגעגענד.

מיר װעלן נאסן א װארט אין אלע אנגעװעהסאאוסטע פראגן.

געבנדיק גלייכצייטיק יעדן א מעגליכקייט ארויסזאגן זיך אויף די שפאלטן פון אונזער צייטשריפט.

מיר װעלן זעהען איבערצייגס. אז דאס ערשיינען פין אונזער צייטשריפט װעט געפינען דעם געהעריגן אפקלאנג אין יערער װעלט אונז װי װייט סעגליך אינטערשטוצען סיי מאראליש סיי מאטעריעל.

רעדאקציע „דובנער לעבן"

דיבנא מערץ 1929

מיט גרויס צופרידנהייט קאנסטאטירן מיר דעם פאקס. אז אין דובנא האס אנגעהויבען צו ערשיינען א צייטשריפט א. נ. „דובנער לעבן" געװוידמעט די געזעלשאפטליכע אינז קול־טורע״ ערשיינונגען ביי אינז אין שטאס אין אומגעגענד.

דער טאג אין װערכן ס׳ערשיינט דער ערשטער נימער פון אונזער צייטשריפט זאל פארצייכענט װערן אין דער געשיכטע פון דובנא. װויל װי באװאוסט איז דאס די ערסטע יודישע צייט־שריפט װייס דער עקזיסטענץ פון אינזער שטאס.

מיר זענען נישט אוסשטאנד איבערצוגעבן אין עטליכע שורות װעלכע שטערוננגען סיר ראבן אנגעטראפן אויפין וועג. פינים ארויסגעבען אונזער צייטשריפט.

עס איז יעדן באװאוסט אז ארויסגעבן א צייטשריפט בכלל אין אין אינזער דובנא בפרט איז פארבינדן מיס גרויסע שװערי־קייסן בכדי אבער צו בעליכטען אלזװיסיג דאס לעבן פין דובנא אין אימעגעגנד אין אלע זיינע געביטן האבן מיר זיך נישט אפגעשטעלט פאר קיין סיס שטערוננגען אין אס שטעהען מיר פאר א געשעהענעם פאקט אז די צייטשריפט האס דערויפהן איהר זיין.

For the Jewish Population in Dubno and the Surroundings

Translated from Yiddish by Pamela Russ

Dubno Life No 1 [name of newspaper]
25 Groshen [price of newspaper]

Impartial, social, and financial magazine   **Sunday, March 1929 Dubno**

With great pleasure, we state the fact that in Dubno, a newspaper has begun its publication, known as "Dubno Life," dedicated to the social and cultural figures in our city and in the surrounding areas.

The day that the first issue of our publication appears should be marked in the history of Dubno because as it is known, this is the first Yiddish newspaper in the existence of our city.

We cannot explain in these few lines the obstacles we encountered en route to publishing our newspaper.

Everyone knows that publishing a newspaper in general, and in our Dubno in particular, is tied up with great challenges, but in order to permanently enlighten the life of Dubno and the surroundings and all its regions, we did not stop, no matter how hard the challenge, and so now we are standing at an auspicious point, and the newspaper has seen its publication.

It could be that there will be those who will not value the great worth of our labor of putting out a publication. They will explain, upset, that our newspaper is a product in the hands of a particular party or social institution. Therefore, we state strongly that this newspaper is an impartial publication that will be careful to share all Jewish interests of Dubno and its surrounding areas.

We will address all difficult questions, giving everyone equal opportunity to express himself in the columns of our newspaper.

We are certain that the publication of our newspaper will find its proper resonance among the broad Jewish masses and everyone will, as much as possible, support us both morally and materially.

The editor of *"Dubno Life"*   Dubno March 1929

[Column 619–620, Yiddish]

Dubno Between the World Wars

Author unknown

Translated from Yiddish by Pamela Russ

In Dubno, which had three mainland entrances and exits, there were three suburbs: Surmicze, Zabramie, and Pantalia. In these suburbs, there lived primarily Ukrainians and a few Jews, but in the city proper, the majority of residents were Jewish. In general, the city of Dubno was a Jewish one. In the surrounding villages, the population was a mixture of several peoples: a large part was Ukrainian, Czech, and a few Germans and Poles. These Ukrainians always took part in all the pogroms, most of them against the Jews. The Jewish resistance was weak. Jews would hide in their houses and the Ukrainians would, undisturbed, do their work as part of the pogrom – murder and looting.

Between one pogrom and another, the Jews sat quietly in the town, lived with their worries about a livelihood, guarded all the *mitzvos* [religious commands from the Torah], and decrees and laws of the country. The majority earned their piece of bread in an honorable manner, and there were also many social statuses: the intelligentsia (intellectuals and academics), merchants, craftsmen, laborers, wagon–drivers, and porters.

The economic life in town was divided into a few sectors: industrial, handwork, laborers, those without income, and so on. In the trade sector, there were grain merchants, who bought wheat and corn from the farmers, and sold them the milled [ground products]: hops merchants who bought this item from the Czechs in the surrounding villages, dried and sorted it, in order to be able to sell it to the beer brewers in the country. A significant part of the material was also exported to Germany, Austria, suburbs, and so on.

Another section was comprised of shops, wholesale and retail merchants of food, clothing, manufactured items, confection, haberdashery, and so on. The majority of them earned a living from the non–Jewish population that used to come into town from the surrounding villages, would sell their agriculture products, and buy whatever they needed in the Jewish stores.

245

There were also the booth owners in the city market (*toltczok*) and around the market, they used to sell manufactured items, haberdashery, and food. The peasants would also bring their fare here and would sell them through arrangements with the market, or in the market directly.

Industry in the city was small and primitive. The main work was with the hops projects. It was primarily women who worked there, but few were Jewish. Maybe ten percent. The workers there were specialists, the management, and supervisors – all Jews. The work was seasonal.

A significant portion of the Jewish population in town was employed in handwork. The vocations: tailoring, hat making, seamstresses, shoemakers, carpenters, smithies, wood turners, locksmiths. All of these

[Column 621–622]

activities employed workers, organized from the professional unions. A significant number belonged to the Communist party. The other salaried workers who were employed as trade employees, were not organized.

There was also a sector that lived from its own labor: wagon drivers, porters, [horse] cab drivers, water carriers, and water drivers. These worked hard in the summer and winter but provided for their families in a most respectable manner.

The intelligentsia lived nicely and comfortably: doctors, engineers, lawyers, teachers, nurses, and others.

There were a number of seasonal workers, such as those who were matzo bakers [for Passover]. The matzos, baked in Dubno, had a reputation because of their high quality and were sent to other cities in the country. The season of matzo export began right after Chanukah and stretched until Purim. It was only after Purim that they started baking matzos for the local residents and for the others in the area.

Among the unemployed, there were Jewish youths who also did not have an opportunity for education. It was difficult to find work. Not all of them wanted to take on any type of job. A large portion was actually embarrassed to go to work, the majority – girls, and they became a burden to their impoverished parents.

Those who were poor and those completely without any means were not a small number in the city. They did not have enough bread to eat each day. Businessmen would borrow for them, and each week they would run around to collect some products and money for the needy families so that they would not be without *challos* [braided Sabbath bread], bread, fish, and meat for Shabbos [Sabbath]; and for Passover, they should not be without matzo and other essential items. The businessmen also collected for the needy families for the other holidays. This work was conducted very discreetly, so that no one should know which were the needy ones.

246

As winter approached, a panic befell those families who did not have the means for daily life. The concerns to acquire the following were great:

a.   Heating
b.   Warm clothing and shoes for the household
c.   The necessary products for the winter

Community activists also took care of these needs. They distributed wood for heating, although not much, collected warm clothes for the needy, and so on.

All these districts lived their lives economically, each at its own level. Also, the synagogues, *Batei Midrashim* [Study Halls], *shtiebelech* [small, informal places of prayer], were divided into various categories. There were Study Halls for almost every vocation: tailors, shoemakers, hat makers, shoemakers, wagon drivers, and so on. There were also *shul*s [synagogues] and *chassidic shtiebelech*: Olik, Stolin, Breslau, and Trisk [names of various *chassidic* groups]. Here there were people of all classes and districts. Each *shtiebel* and its *chassidim* [followers of that *chassidic* group] were loyal to each other in general and in their private lives, in joys and in pain, but during a *Kiddush* on *Shabbos* [festive event following morning Sabbath prayers], during *Shalosh Seudos* [the evening meal on Sabbath day], *Melave Malka* [festive meal following the end of *Sabbath*], on the Jewish holidays, and especially on *Simchas Torah* [last celebratory day of *Sukkos* holiday], everyone celebrated as one family – young and old. Also, the children and the youth that would come every *Shabbos* to the *Beis Medrash*, became connected through games (with nuts) during the pauses while reading the Torah, and other games around the *Beis Medrash*.

There were general synagogues in town that had no connection to workers, vocations, or living quarters. From these came the large *shul* which was attended by the lovers of cantors and choirs. The beadles of the large *shul* always tried to have a famous cantor, excellent director, and first–class choir. Because of that, they would come to the large *shul* from all districts and all corners of the city, just to hear the singing.

Education and Training

In the city, there was a whole collection of learning institutions, starting from *cheder* [very young boys], to Talmud Torah [older boys], teachers in the homes, *yeshivos* [religious schools for boys], government public schools ("*powszekhne*"), the Hebrew school "*Tarbut*," the Polish–Jewish gymnasium [high school], and the Polish government gymnasium. At the beginning of 1920, there was also a Russian gymnasium and a Hebrew–Russian school.

Children aged four began their learning in the *cheder*. The children of the rabbis also went to school here until they began studying *Gemara* [Talmud], and then they went into higher level *cheder*s, where they labored with *Gemara* and *Tosefos* [commentaries]. Some of these boys later studied in the *yeshiva* of Reb Avrom Mordkhe's school, founded by *HaRav* Gutman, of blessed memory. In this *Talmud Torah*, that had its own house, children studied free of charge. It was HaRav Rozenfeld, of blessed memory, the founder of the *Talmud Torah*, who supported them.

A large number of young girls and boys did not attend the government public schools ("*powszekhne*"), because the traditionally religious parents did not want to send their children to a school that had classes on Shabbos and on religious holidays.

The wealthier Jews sent their children to the Hebrew "*Tarbut*" school. Not everyone could afford to send their children there. So, some studied in the *cheders*, in *yeshivas*, and had private classes at home with a tutor. This was less expensive.

This system also existed for the private Jewish gymnasium, where the school fee was steep. Therefore, many youths, even capable ones, could not afford any form of education.

In the Polish government gymnasium, they accepted hardly any Jews. In order to get in there, you needed exceptional skills, means, and connections. But even with all these in place, many Jewish students were refused simply because they were Jewish. The percentage of Jewish students there reached only 3%.

In spite of all these difficulties that I have described, the Jewish youth was not illiterate. A fine youth evolved, a Zionist youth, a party youth, a pioneering youth [for Israel], with ideals to achieve the Zionist dream and immigrate to the Land of Israel. Sadly, very few of them merited this, [to emigrate].

Parties and Organizations

In the city, there were many parties and organizations, from the extreme right to the extreme left: *Beitar, Gordonia, Tzeirei Mizrachi, Hechalutz, Hechalutz Hatzair, HaShomer Hatzair*, general Zionists, "Bundists" and communists.

Between World Wars

The first Olim [immigrants to Israel] from Dubno who came to Israel at the beginning of the 1920s came from *Hechalutz* [Zionist youth movement in Eastern Europe]. In their club, there were lectures on cultural and educational themes about Israel. At the same time, they created the *Hachshara*, training program for Israel life. Other than these evenings where the lectures were given, the youth gathered together at the center for friendly get–togethers, discussions, talks about the situation in the *Hachshara*, and how life looked in the Land of Israel. Also, trips were organized to the *Hachshara* points and colonies. The *Hechalutz* was a very large movement.

In the Youth *Hechalutz*, which was under the direction of the *Hechalutz*, there was education for the youth up to eighteen years old. After that, they moved up to the *Hechalutz*. Young boys from all areas were members. This was a lively, energetic youth who wanted to work, learn, and prepare for Aliyah to Israel.

Gordonia [Zionist youth movement based on Aaron David Gordon] did not have a large number of members. They would assemble in a small center. But it was not dull there. Everything bubbled with life and efforts to fulfill the dream of A.D. Gordon – to make Aliyah and build the land of Israel.

The *Shomer Hatzair* [Guardians of the Youth] was a large, strong organization to which the "better" youth belonged, the majority gymnasium students, matriculated ones. In their club, there was multi–branched political, cultural, and educational work for the *Hachshara* and Aliyah. There was also a library with fine books – Hebrew and Yiddish. The youth was drawn there to enjoy the treasury of books.

Every summer the *Shomer Hatzair* organized colonies in a cultural and beautiful fashion.

In the *Tzeirei Mizrachi*, there were only a few tens of youths, without a fixed location. With time, they joined other youth organizations in town. It was A. Blass who directed the *Tzeirei Mizrachi*.

Beitar grew into a proper organization because of their uniforms, and slogans that said to conquer with gun and sword, the entire Israel, on both sides of the Jordan. They had small groups for the *Hachshara* and few of them went on Aliyah.

Articles from "Dubno Life"
Newspaper

First article title: Real Work Is More
Important than Politics
Second article title: From Here and There
(Reflections)
Third article title: Report of the Activities
of the Dubno Magistrate for the Year
1928

Top: list of family names and some sort of
set of numbers to match
2nd from top: expenses – inventory
3rd from top – report of wood export
2nd from bottom –The Dubno Maggid,
article in the "Dubno Life" [great Rabbi
in Dubno, 1741–1804]
Bottom: "Life in Dubno" – article

געווארען אין בעסטען ארדענונג און ביי יעצטיגער צייט פערנעמט
ער א אנגעזעהן ארט צווישן די שענסטע און גרעסטע "שפּיטעלן
אין אונזער געגנד.

נאך דעם אלעמען איז פערשטענדליך וואָס דאָס אפּאָוזען־
הייט פון פערשטארבענעם סיהלט זיך שטארק.

באלד נאך דער סטירה האבען זיך פּערזאַמעלט אלע מיט־
גלידער און די האבען אויך איינגעלאדען בעלי־בתים פון שטאט ווי
עס איז אנגענומען געווארן א בשלום צו פאראייביגען דעם
נאָמען פון נסטר מיט עפּעס א וויכטיגע איינריכטונג אין שפּיטאל
היינו: מען זאל דאָס געבורטס־צימער אויסמאלען מיט אייל־פאַרב
און ברענגענד דאָס אין א בעסערען היגיעניען צושטאנד. צו דעם
צוועק האבן אלע פערזאַמעלטע געגעבן ספּעציעלע נדבות. און
דער חשובער ראש הקהלה ה' אלכסנדר טשערקעס האט גענקויפט
מיר זיין געלד א ספּעציעל געבורטס־בעט.

יעצט איז שוין אלעס פערענדיג און דאָס געבורטס־צימער
איז שוין בעצוארגט מיט אלע בעקוועמליכקייטען. אויך איז דאמאַלס
בעשלאָסען געווארן אנצוקויפן דאָס געבורטס־צימער אויף דעם
נאָמען פון נסטר און טראַק דעם אויסהענגען אין שפּיטאל קאַן
צעפּליאַריע זיין ביל'ד אין האָלצטען זיין יאָרהצייט.

עס צו דעם צוועק האבען זיך זוגמאַן ט' אייר פערזאַמעלט
אין לאָקאל פון שפּיטאל אלע מיטגלידער פון ראש און פערוואל־
טונג ווי אויך פיעל בעלי־בתים פון שטאַדט.

די סיעריגע פערזאַמלונג געעפנט האָט דער פערוואַלטונגס־מיט־
גליד ה' מענדעל קארנענסעלד מיט א וואַרימע רעדע. וועלכע איז
געוּוען געוּוידמעט דעם זכר פון ר' חיים פרעמד ז"ל און זיינע
פערדינסטען פאַר דעם יודישען שפּיטאל מיט א אפּעל צו די
אנוּוצענדע ויי זאָלן מיט אלע קרעפּטען זעהן שטיצען דעם
שפּיטאל און זאָרגען ער זאָל חלילה ניט פערשמעלערטען
זיין עקזיסטענץ צוליב דער אבוּוצונגהייט פון נסטר.

אזוי האָט מען פייערליך אבגעמאַרטינגט די אלע דריי
תפלות פון מעת־לעת און יעדעס מאָל געמאַכט א אל מלא
רחמים" דעם נסטר.

דובנער יודען!

נעמט זיך ארויס א מוסר, וואָס א מענש קאן זיך פרוווער־
בען מיט מעשים טובים.

סיי א מצוה, סיי כבוד קאן זיך א מענש שאַפען וען ער
געדענקט פאַר זיין לעבען דעם "אהבת לרעך כמוך" און יעדער
פון איך דארף זיך בעמיהען נאָכטוהן די גוטע מעשים פון
נסטר.

ל. לערנער.

א בריוו אין רעדאקציע

זעהר געעהרטער הער רעדאקטאר
פון "דובנער לעבען"

ערלויבט אונז דורך אייער חשוּבע צייטונג אויסדריקען א
דאנק דעם געשעצטען ה' לייבוש באסלין, אין ניו־יארק גאַס
בראַוועַארי נומער 314 פאַר די צוגעשיקטע דריי הונדערטס פינף
און פערציג דאַלאַר (345). וועלכע מיר האבען ערהאַלטען דורך
דעם ה' פישעל קוויס דובנא. פאַר די דריי אנשטאַלטען יודישער
שפּיטאל אין דובנא, בית־יתומים, מושב־זקנים. אלע צו 40 דאל
(פערציג דאַלאַר) רעשט פון דער סומע פאַר "דער אַרימער

בעסעלקערונג לויט דעם צונעשיקטען צעטעל. וועלכעס איז
ערהאַלטען געוואָרען פון ה' באַסלין ערשט דעם 1־סטן יוני ד.י.
אין נאַמען פון די אנגעשלאָסטען ווי אויך פון דער ארי־
מער בעסעלקערונג דאַנקען מיר דעם ה' באַסלין, און מיר בעטן,
אז אין דער צוקונפּט זאל ער פערגעסען אין זיין געבורטס
שטאָט דובנא בכלל און פון דער ארימער בעסעלקערונג בפרט.

מיט אכטונג
סערוואַלטונג פון דובנער יודישען שפּיטאל.

אל. טשערקעס. מ. פערניאַסטין. מ. קאַרנענסעלד. א. ז. בערינשטיין.
א. קעלערמאַן. ה. פישביין. פישעל קוויס. סאַמעל באַראַחאָו.
אנסיהרער: ד"ר מ. באַס
סעקרעטאָר: י. ש. ראַבינשטיין.
אנסיהרער פון מושב־זקנים: הרב ר' מענדעל ראָזענפעלד.
סערוואַלטונג פון דובנער בית־יתומים:
פרויען: ב. זעלבערטס. ר. לאַנדיס.

דובנא, דעם 3־טן יוני 1929 יאָהר.

פון דער אדמיניסטראַציע.

צוליב טעכנישע סיבות, איז אין מאַנאַס סאַי קיין נומער
ניט ערשינען, מיר האָפּען אין דער צוקונפט רעגולער אַרויסגע־
בען אונזער צייטשריפט.

פערוועלליכעס.

אונזער חשוּבער רעדאקציע־מיטגליד הער ישראל קוויס
סאַהרט ארויס די טעג קיין פּויזען אויף דער אויסשטעלונג, ווי
ער וועט פערווייילען עטליכע טעג. נאָכן צורוקקומען וועט ער בע־
שרייבען זיינע איינדרוקען אויף די שפּאַלטען פון אונזער צייט־
שריפט.

אופפאָדערונג.

די אדמיניסטראַציע פון "דובנער לעבען" פאָרערט אויף
אלע די, וועלכע זענען שולדיג דער אדמיניסטראַציע פאַר אנגאַנען
זיי זאָלן ביז דעם 20־סטן יוני רעגולירדן די חובות

רעדאקטאַר אַרויסגעבער יצחק ש. ראַבינשטיין.

די גאַנצע שטאַדט דובנא האָט זיך געוואונדערט

סאַרוואָס האָט דער דובנער רייכער בחור ר. חנונה נאַהאָב מיט
דער דובנער מיידעל ג. אהן א גראַשען נדן. נאָך א לענגערער
חקירה ודרישה האָט זיך ארויסגעוויזען, אז היינטיגע צייטען
דארף מען ניט האָבן קיין נדן, ווייל א שען מיידעל איז א גאַנצער
נדן און שיין קאָן מען זיין, ווען מען בעזוכט דעם

פּרייזער ה' איזאק אַרפּורע מאָנטשינסקיעגאַ 3

ווי ס'וערן אויסגעסיהרט די שענסטע פריזיר־ארבייטען לויט דער
נייעסטער מאָדע, ווי דאַמען שערען, עלעקטרישע מאַסאָושען א.א.וו.

בעקאַנטמאַכונג

דערמיט מאַך איך בעקאַנט די געעהרטע סוחרים אז פון דעם 1־טן
אפּריל ה. י. בין איך געוואָרן עקסטפּעדיטאָר אויף דער באַהן
איך נעם אן אלערלעי טראַנזאַקציעס צום ערלעדיגען
רעטלעס בעהאַנדלינג מעסיגע פּרייזען

מיט אכטונג "הערץ לערנער, סטאַראַ 79.

ד. קאַגאַן, דאַקטאָר דעניסיטס

דובנא, גאַס ליסטאָווסקע נומער 24

נעמט אן קעגליך פון 9 ביז 2 און פון 4 ביז 7
היילונג. פּלאַמבירטען. און אלע טעכנישע ארבייטען. פּריזיון מעסיג.

Redaktor-Wydawca i Redaktor odpowiedzialny Izaak Sz. Rabinsztejn — Drukar i Feigla i Ltw k Równe

Column 627 – continuation of article: – "Life in Dubno" author's name L. Lerner
Column 627–628 bottom article: "A Letter in the Report" editor's and publisher's signature on left, Yitzchok Sh. Rubenstein
Page 628 bottom, articles by Dawid Kagan, dentist

The general Zionists were active in the Zionist regions. Prominent businessmen of the city were connected to the Zionist movement, participated in the congresses in other countries, were active in *Keren Kayemet* and *Keren Hayesod*, and helped the poor *Olim* to fulfill their dream of immigrating to Israel.

The Polish words on the banner say "Matura" [secondary school certificate] and "Private" on one side, "Gymnasium in Dubno" on the right. The inked date at the top is 1926.

In Dubno, there was also a large, beautiful sports club that included all the areas of Jewish youth "*Hakoach*" (formerly "*Maccabi*"). The majority of those who belonged to the club were the youth of various Zionist organizations. Other than the sports activities, *Hakoach* also had a first-class wind orchestra, a good football team, and sections for other sports activities. The great hall in the center of the city attracted many adult and young lovers of sport. The events during the national holidays and the activities in the beautiful clothing, orderliness, and with the orchestra, evoked great enthusiasm from everyone.

All the organizations, even those with opposing principles, on the day of *Lag b'Omer* [33rd day of counting the *Omer* in the spring after Passover; celebratory event in memory of Rabbi Shimon bar Yochai], were all united. Each movement, under its flag and banner, was represented in the nearby village of Palestinis, in order to celebrate this holiday, in the fields and forests.

When the "White Book" of the British Mandate was published, in which it locked the gates against Jewish Aliyah, all the above-mentioned Zionist organizations protested as one – in the streets

[Columns 635–636]

in their centers – against the proclamation, or against other anti–Jewish proclamations in Poland and around the world.

*

The city of Dubno, with its Jewish streets, synagogues, learning centers, parties, organizations, and institutions, with its lively Jewish life, was erased in the years of the Second World War, all turned to dust…

Graduates of the Russian gymnasium (1920) [Column 631-632]

Elections for the 19th Congress

*"TOZ" [Towarzystwo Ochrony Zdrowia] – Society for the Protection of the Health of the Jews]
employees in Dubno*

The Jewish hospital in Dubno

Employees of Linat Hatzedek [Society for Needy] – Dubno.
Name of photographer on bottom of photo: Anshel Bitelman

255

Youth Movements

[Column 245–246]

The History of Hashomer Hatzair and Hechalutz

by Binyamin Oz and Dusia Korin

Translated from Yiddish by Pamela Russ

1917. Giant Russia awakens. The dictator regime of the Tsar is changed into a democratic system. The nation celebrates the liberation. The masses of Jews in Russia, particularly in the large centers, participate in the general euphoria. News comes from all sides that here and there the Zionist flag has been raised. Jews are presenting Israel as a salvation for their needs. Rumors of these events carry to Dubno, a typical Jewish town that did not follow the newer times. During that period in Dubno, there were no recognized Jewish organizations with independent activities. Some tens of respected Jews, who consider themselves Zionists, purchase the shekel and contribute to the national funds – but there was no real activity there.

The only light in those conditions is the Hebrew school, which thanks to the efforts of two elderly Zionists, was changed over into an important culture center. Tens of boys and girls study the Hebrew language there, also the history of the nation and its literature, and [develop a] love for the old-new Fatherland. All this continues, without stop by the devoted teachers.

But the majority of the youth was busy studying a page of the Gemara [Talmud] or with worries of earning a livelihood. The new winds had not yet reached them. Only in the hearts of individuals was unrest brewing, we have to do something for Zion, but for now they do not connect themselves to any concrete task.

In the local Russian *gymnasium*, that returned from its wartime migrations to the Kharkov region, there are some students with significant experience of Zionist activity. Slowly, a group of students in the Hebrew school befriends them. After several meetings, they decide to create a movement for Israel. A young group is set up, and takes upon itself the name *"Hechalutz"* [Pioneer]. At the beginning, the group numbered 12–15 comrades.

Their first achievement – to prepare the candidates in practicality for their voluntary *aliyah*. With the help of several old Zionists, a blacksmith's shop and a workshop for wagon repair, are created. It is from there that the settlers make their

259

preparations, training themselves for physical work. In the evenings, they meet to talk about Israel and works of the National Fund. During the holidays, they organize to do agricultural work alongside the farmers of the surrounding villages. All these tasks are not done in large numbers, since the number of comrades is small.

1920. The Polish Bolshevik war breaks out. Dubno is taken over by the Russians. Some of the comrades of the *Hechalutz* find work in the Soviet institutions and projects – and leave their organization, while the other section maintains the unity and collaborative work. With the recession of the Bolsheviks, part of the *Hechalutz* group goes along with them and remains in Kiev. Every single activity stops in the *Hechalutz*.

When the Polish-Russian agreement is signed, the comrades return from Kiev to Dubno and they renew their *Hechalutz* work. In the year 1921, anti-Jewish arrests begin in Israel, and *aliyah* goes on hold. Also, with the new Polish government there are now opportunities for work, but the *Hechalutz* falls apart because of the inactivity and the incapacity of the comrades to make *aliyah*.

For four of the devoted *Chalutz* comrades, who are devoted to the movement at all times, the idea is created of increasing the education work in the organization and to address the youth at a younger age. The question becomes: Should they organize a general youth organization Maccabi, or create a unit of *Hashomer Hatzair*, which already existed then in many cities of Poland and Galicia? Ambassadors are sent to the closest city of Lutsk, because there already

[Column 639–640]

was the *Hashomer Hatzair*. They return filled with ideas, and decide to create this organization in town.

In August 1921, the *Hashomer Hatzair* is officially established in Dubno. The four founders, thanks to their connection with the students of the Russian school, are successfully able to integrate tens of young boys and girls ages 13 to 17 into the organization. The first goal: to set up behind the town [a place for] gymnastic and scout-type skills. The friends are divided into separate groups. Each leader directs one group. On designated days, when they are free of studies, they meet outside of the city or in a friend's house. There is no defined program, but they touch on various subjects, discuss actual themes, but the Israel problem dominates. Of course, they also talk about other social problems, and they set up activities for *Keren Kayemet* [Jewish National Fund]. The younger ones receive an education in the spirit of exploration.

Meanwhile, there is no connection to any specific center, there are no instructors nor directives from Warsaw. Thanks to the expanded activities, we also gain experience, work improves, and we set roots. The activities of the *Keren Kayemet* strengthen. The Zionist shekel spreads just as does the Zionist ideology.

The first Hebrew-Yiddish library, with a large reading room, is created in Dubno. Opening festivities take place as well as other events, all with their own efforts. These groups serve as propaganda for Zionist thought and to enlighten the Jews about Israel. If at the beginning parents were worried to have their children register in these organizations, thanks to the prolific activity of the *Hashomer Hatzair,* they become loyal members of the movement and help them as well.

Efforts are now being made to receive an official government permit to make all activities legal. The issue goes on and on. The local government begins to interfere. Once, during an expedition outside of the city, the police surround the *"Shomrim"* [members of *Hashomer Hatzair*] and with the help of the Polish patrols remove all evidence and disband all the participants. The *madrichim* [counselors] become upset at the government. One of the comrades takes the entire blame upon himself and he alone is taken to court. The others are freed but the police find only this one man guilty in organizing illegal youth activities and conducting communist activities. With great trepidation the Jewish populace follows the trial and the joy is great when the youth is given a clean slate of any of the guilt. The police, however, are still following the activities of the organization. They [the *Hashomer Hatzair*] are starting to look for new foremen for work.

The meetings are held in the homes of comrades, the culture-educational work becomes more intense. Efforts are made to legalize a local *Tarbut* [secular Hebrew-language school] society. After receiving a permit, the library and the reading room are given over to the new institution. Under the banner of the *Tarbut,* many events and activities take place.

1925. The organization stands on solid ground. New, younger energy evolves, those who are fit to participate. A connection is made with the central [office], instructors and lecturers often come from Warsaw.

With this first group of comrades, their idea was that the time had come to make their long-time dream happen – to move to the Land of Israel. They start to prepare the necessary paperwork. During the years of 1925–1926, the first group of madrichim [youth or peer councelors] left for Israel, except for Eliyahu Makharok, who died prematurely. He, who gave all his strengths to the movement, did not merit fulfilling his own dream.

After them, the steady flow of young pioneers from Dubno who wanted to move to Israel does not cease. Soon after its establishment, *Hashomer Hatzair* focuses all its work on the Land of Israel, and almost all of their comrades [who became] new immigrants join the *kibbutzim* [pl. of *kibbutz*].

The activities of *Hashomer Hatzair* continue to grow. They also accept children ages 8–10. Many of the non-partisan youth are influenced by the blessed work and also join *Hashomer Hatzair* or *Hechalutz,* which had renewed its activities. *Hechalutz* profits a lot from the help of *Hashomer Hatzair* but they go their own way and mainly work with the non-partisan youth. Also, from their league, tens of youths also make *aliyah* to Israel. Unfortunately, the opportunities for moving to Israel were limited, the number of certificates - very few.

1939. The outbreak of World War Two terminates the dreams and hopes of hundreds of youths who want to build a new life in the old home. The members of *Hashomer Hatzair* and *Hechalutz* experience the tragic fate of Polish Jewry. Only a few individuals were successful in saving themselves as they fled to Russia, or by joining local groups of partisans. That year, a heroic chapter in the history of the Dubno Jewish youth was severed.

The Hakhshara

by Dusia Korin

Translated from Hebrew by Sara Mages

It was a year of historic importance for the Russian Jewry, and not only for the Russian Jewry. The revolution of February 1917 aroused hopes in the heart for tremendous changes in the public and private life in a renewed world at the end of the First World War. The air was filled with slogans about freedom and equality for all, for all - including the Jews. The parties, which emerged from the underground to the light of the world, began to influence the person on the street in order to draw him to them, and each assured him that, when it [a party] will rise to power, he would be able to see his world [i.e. expanded opportunities] in his life. However, before the revolutionary regime was able to establish itself democratically, the second revolution took place, the Bolshevik revolution, which completely changed the order of things. A working dictatorship was established, and all hopes vanished overnight. Nevertheless, many young Jews were drawn to this magic, left their parents and flocked to the great centers of Russia to build and be built there.

In all the vicissitudes of fate of that year, 1917, and the years that followed in Russia and Poland, including the border areas between these two countries, the Jewish youth, as a whole, did not lose its national face and was not caught in the spirit of cosmopolitanism which was blowing around. This youth, who had been educated on the knees of Jewish tradition, the yearning for Zion and Jewish upbringing, began to dream of immigrating to Israel and was ready to leave, in all routes, for it. In those days, organizational frameworks, in which it was possible to work towards the goal, were not yet established. However, the rumors that young Jews, from various parts of Ukraine, were concentrating in Vienna in order to immigrate to Israel, served as an incentive for the local youth to join the immigrants. In the meantime, shocking reports reached us about the pioneers who had been slaughtered on the way by rioters. The departure of those who were ready for all hardships, provided they would be able to emigrate, was delayed.

And now, the message of redemption came to us - the Balfour Declaration illuminated the dark days. Great awakening followed the declaration and the organization of the parties began. Eizenshtat, a graduate of the Russian Gymnasium, and David Feldman (Kozi), a high school student in France and a native of Dubno, formed a group of Jewish students from Dubno who returned, in difficult routes, from Kiev to their city: Eliyahu Makhrok, Yisrael Fefer, D. Korin, Binyamin Oz and M. Zekzer. Since there was no possibility of an immediate immigration to Israel, they had the idea of bringing pioneers together and teaching them manual labor until the anticipated hour of immigration would arrive. That's how the best young men in the city gathered around this group and the work began.

The founders of "Hashomer Hatzair"
Standing (right to left): Eliyahu Makhrok Z"L, Yair Zekzer
Sitting (right to left): Binyamin Oz, Dusia Korin

The large smithy on *"Breiter Gas"* was rented and the study of metalworking, wagon driving with all its accessories, and others, began. It was a big and sensational event in the life of the city. Dubno's homeowners were astonished at the sight of young men from good families who were training for physical work for an ideal that seemed so far away from them. Thirty-six people gathered in this workshop and studied the above professions.

The succession of governments, and regimes, that followed one after the other: Ukrainians, Poles, Bolsheviks, Germans with their "puppet" Scoropadsky, and, again, the Bolsheviks and Petliura with his gangs - all gave no rest to the residents in general, and tranquility to the Jews in particular and it was difficult to persevere, uninterrupted, in any kind of activity in an atmosphere saturated in pogroms, slaughters and blood. Nevertheless, and despite everything, they continued their work in the hope of better days, when rays of light from the far-near homeland will hint to them like a lighthouse revealed to a ship devoured by stormy sea waves.

"Hashomer Hatzair" - the first buds

At the beginning of 1921, the members, Eliyahu Makhrok and Binyamin Oz, traveled to Lutsk to meet with Y. Glikman, one of the first members of *"Hashomer Hatzair,"* in order to clarify the trend and methods of this movement. It became clear to them that this was a scouting movement in its foundation, and they decided to propose to the members to set up a branch of *"Hashomer Hatzair"* in Dubno. Their proposal was accepted and soon many of the youth began to come to the *"ken"* [branch of a youth movement] and to organize around it. Stratums, groups, troops and battalions were established. They were named after well-known personalities in the Zionist movement and the labor movement in Israel, such as Trumpeldor, Chizik, Drachler and others.

The command in all the activities of the "*ken*" was purely in Hebrew which, in itself, was enough to arouse great enthusiasm and yearning for a full and refined life.

In order to complete the picture of the movement's development in Dubno, it should be noted that the city, which lies geographically between Galicia and Congress Poland, was influenced by two trends: that of the Warsaw version which was based on scouting, and that of the Lwow version which excelled in its ideological influence on the circles close to it. In the course of time, Galicia's influence on our branch in Dubno grew stronger than that of Warsaw, and the members strove to deepen the idea that they professed. In the process, there was more interest in the study of the Hebrew language, manual labor, acquisition of Jewish values, socialism and general culture, apart from scouts games and military training.

*A regional conference of "Hashomer Hazair" in Kowel
with the participation of M. Yaari*

These were glamorous days for "*Hashomer Hatzair*" movement which included the best boys and girls in the city. Suddenly, in one of the summer evenings of 1922, when the groups and regiments were on their way back from Pantalia, happy and cheerful, and after a conversation on the subject "Mania Shohat and her proud war against the Turkish tyrant" (according to "Dreamers and warriors" by Yaari Polskin), the Polish police, together with activists of the Polish Scout movement, appeared before the turn to Panienska Street. The police surrounded the ranks, arrested the instructors and officially announced the dispersion of the "*ken*" of "*Hashomer Hatzair*" in Dubno.

Indeed, panic did not arise and we didn't know fear, but the mood was depressed for a while. A few days later we began to meet again in small groups in private homes, encouraged, full of faith and hope in the glorious future in the homeland. We got stronger in the hardships, learned to face the wave - and to go on.

Youth Movements in Dubno

by A. Cohen

Translated from Hebrew by Sara Mages

With the annexation of Dubno to Poland after the First World War, the city was cut off from the economic hinterland of Ukraine. The Polish government did not care at all for the development and industrialization of the region known as "Second Poland." Therefore, the city remained stagnant for years until the Polish government on the one hand, and national Ukrainian circles on the other, began to consider the development of productive and consumer cooperatives. This development harmed, deliberately or unintentionally, the traditional sources of income of the city's Jews. This, of course, hurt all the Jewish youth, who felt that the ground was gradually falling underfoot and the prospects for economic stability in the place were slowly diminishing. The new branches of labor remained largely closed to the Jews and in the municipal and governmental staff there was only one Jewish worker. The only chance for the Jewish youth was to persevere in the professions of the parents. However, this prospect did not encourage and attract the young people whose characteristics and views changed so much.

Sports team of the Maccabi Club, Dubno (written in Russian)

Our city was not distinguished by great leaders, not by excellent guides, but the intelligentsia, which had grown almost entirely on its own, especially the gymnasium graduates, who helped to shape the character of the local youth. The dissatisfaction among the youth was expressed in an extensive organization of the Zionist movement, which numbered about 700 boys and girls in the 1930s, most of them schoolchildren. However, they only constituted part of the local youth while the rest sought to find other ways: some completely distanced themselves from nationalism and Zionism and moved to the communist camp, and some began to live a perplexed life, empty of any content. The number of the latter was never large - a few dozen in all. Most were among the graduates of the Polish government gymnasium who sought to adapt to the Polish and Ukrainian-Russian environment but, of course, it ignored them and was not willing to accept them. Thus, this "golden youth," who spent its days dancing and partying without thinking about the future, remained detached from all sides.

Hakoah Orchestra in Dubno

Another part of the youth, mainly from among the workers or job seekers, was attracted, as stated, by the slogan "to repair the world in the Kingdom of the Almighty" in accordance with the promises of the Communist Party. They innocently believed that the Jewish problem would be resolved within the framework of the Ukrainian Soviet Republic that would be established, so, "down with Jewish nationalism, the entire Jewish culture and its past!" Now, here comes the time of spring for all humanity. What do we have for a Jew, what do we have for a Chinese or Turk? And the truth must be told: a great deal of work, worthy of appreciation, was done by the communists in the field of information and education - especially political propaganda, of course - among the youth. They succeeded in educating young people who were willing to sacrifice themselves on their way to realizing the goal before them. Members of this movement knew to endure years in prisons, to which they were thrown by the regime's detectives, and not to disarm their spiritual weapons until the day of their redemption. We have lost this youth, indeed it was totally lost, because when the day of their redemption arrived they soon realized that this redemption was not for them, it was only an illusion...

However, the vast majority of the Jewish youth in the city, who decided to deny the present, saw only one way of correcting the situation of the individual and the general public: pioneering and immigration to the Land of Israel. Since they decided to follow this path, they directed all their activities to self-training and preparedness for the fulfillment of their aspirations. Thus, the youth devoted a great deal of energy to two of their main institutions: the Jewish Sports Association "*Hakoah*" and "*Tarbut*" school.

"*Hakoah*" was affiliated with "*Maccabi*" in Poland and therefore officially belonged to the Zionist movement, but, in fact, it concentrated around it the youth interested in sports because there was no other sport organization. The sports association, or the "club" as it was called in the city, developed a great deal of sports activity especially football games, boxing, athletics, swimming etc. The "*Hakoah*" clubhouse, which was located at the Greenberg's house in the city center, was always full of youth and adults who were loyal to Jewish sports. "*Hakoah*" performances on the sports field gathered hundreds of members. "*Hakoah*" organized its own band which musically accompanied every national performance, and the blue and white ribbon on the hats of the members of the association publicly declared their affiliation to the Zionist movement. "*Hakoah*" was, in fact, the only organized Jewish body to participate in its blue and white flag in all the festivities and official performances in the city.

[Columns 257–258]

"Hashomer Hatzair" procession

"Hashomer Hatzair" *[Caption inside the photo - Summer colony in Brzeszcze]*

[Columns 259–260]

"Hashomer Hatzair," which gathered in its ranks the best of the city's youth, stood out among the pioneering youth movements. The *"ken"* [branch of a youth movement] was founded in the early 1920s and for almost twenty years conducted an ambitious educational program among the youth of whom hundreds fulfilled their aspirations and immigrated to Israel.

The activity of the *"ken"* was branched. As soon as it was established the foundation for a library in our two languages, Hebrew and Yiddish, was laid. Over time, the library numbered 2,500 books, half of which were in Hebrew. It was the only Hebrew library in the city. The library at "Tarbut" school, which was established later, only served the school's students. Therefore, anyone who wanted a Hebrew book had to turn to the *"ken's"* library. The library began its work in a rented room at the home of Dr. Fuks, which was located near the town hall, and relocated with the *"ken"* through many apartments in the city. With the official liquidation of the *"ken,"* at the beginning of October 1939, it was transferred to the attic of Yakov Groifen's house on Szeroka Street.

"Hashomer Hatzair" organized summer camps for the members of the movement. These summer colonies, which were organized together with other branches of the movement in the area, were usually housed between Dubno and Kremenets. The last two summer colonies, in 1938–1939, were established in the village of Mykhailivka, about twelve kilometers from the city, near Dlugopola a vacation spot for the Jews of Dubno. The last summer colony was established without a permit from the authorities.

Forty members of the younger stratum were forced to move twice from place to place in order to avoid clashes with the authorities.

Great was the part of the "*Shomerim*" from Dubno in the organization of the summer colonies near Novostav in the Volhynia region. In the last years before the Holocaust many participated in summer camps in the Carpathian Mountains. The last camp in the mountains of the members of "*Hashomer Hatzair*" from Dubno was suspended at the beginning of the mobilization for the war and the declaration of state of preparedness in Poland in late August 1939.

It is worth mentioning the activities of the "*ken*," together with other Zionist movements, during Lag Ba'Omer. They left in a procession to one of the forests around the city to celebrate and relax there, and returned singing through the city's streets. This traditional procession drew the attention of the Jewish population and became an impressive experience. In 1939, the holiday was not conducted properly since the authorities refused to grant a permit for the procession. Nevertheless, without prior notice hundreds of Jews gathered in the "Palestinian" Forest and celebrated the day with the movement.

A group of "elders" of "Hashomer Hatzair"

The educational activity of the "*Hashomer Hatzair*" movement was concentrated among the youth from the age of eleven until their departure for *Hakhshara* [training]. In fact, the "*ken*" controlled all the youth who attended the "*Tarbut*" school and was mostly organized in battalions and groups. The activity of the "*ken*" in this area was conducted in cooperation with the school's administration. Indeed, the Jewish students in the municipal elementary school (*szkola podstawowa*) were also connected to the "*ken*," and when the members of the "ken" were ordered to leave school and join the celebration of Lag BaOmer (it was in 1934 or 1935) against the principal's instructions, the Jewish students declared a strike and broke into singing and the dancing of the "*Hora*" in the classrooms. The school administration saw no other way but to make do with a mere warning and invited one of the "*ken*'s" leaders to discuss this matter. Thus, the Jewish students' right to belong to the movement was effectively recognized despite the formal prohibition that remained in effect.

[Columns 261–262]

In its educational activity the "*ken*" also used public trials to investigate several questions that arose, as well as on various books such as "I'm Hungry," "*Motke Ganev*" [Motke the Thief], "The Merchant of Venice" and more. Significant, and important, was its artistic work under the guidance of the teacher Balban: a choir was organized, plays were performed, etc.

The highlight of "*Hashomer Hatzair*" activity was *hagshama* [fulfillment]. Hundreds of young people, members of the "*ken*," passed through the movement's various *Hakhshara* points in Poland and immigrated to Israel. Many of them are found in kibbutzim belonging to *Hakibbutz Haartzi* of "*Hashomer Hatzair*" movement, from Ayalon in the north to Yad Mordechai and Negba in the south.

The "*ken*" excelled in its work for *Keren Kayemeth LeIsrael* [JNF], and for years stood in first place in this activity among the local youth.

At various times the leadership of the movement in the area was in the hands of the Dubno branch and the members worked for the movement throughout the region...

The Zionist activity in Dubno was suspended in September 1939 when the city was transferred to the Soviet authorities. The branch of "*Hashomer Hatzair*" continued its illegal activity for several months. This activity was mainly directed at organizing the resistance of the youth to the elimination of the Hebrew language and all the national principles on which they were raised and educated. In 1940, the movement's leaflet, which contained recorded information about the events in Israel, began to appear in Lvov. This leaflet was also distributed in Dubno. This was the only source of news from Israel since no one in the city dared to listen to "*Kol Yerushalayim*" [Jerusalem Calling]. In December 1939 - January 1940, activities were also organized for a departure from the city and emigration to Israel. Two groups, which together numbered eight people, tried to break through the blockade and reach Vilna - a station on their way to Israel. The preparations for their departure were kept secret and even the closest family members knew nothing of what was going on around them. Three out of the eight managed to reach Israel.

Rumors, that I wasn't able to examine, indicate that during the Nazi occupation underground groups of *"Hashomer Hatzair"* were established and a number of actions were taken, including an unsuccessful attempt to resist the Nazis. It is not inconceivable that one day we will discover details that are now unknown to us and would clarify, a little, the darkest and the most terrible period of our city, Dubno.

Hashomer Hatzair on Trial

by Nisan Doron (Mahrok)

Translated from Hebrew by Sara Mages

...the dispersion of the "*ken*"[1] had a grim continuation when the leader of the "*ken,*" the distinguished member, Dusia Korin, was imprisoned in the large prison in Dubno and brought for criminal proceedings before the District Court. In the search, which took place at the counselors' homes, they were mainly suspicious of the material found in Dusia's home. The "dangerous" material was not, heaven forbid, proclamations calling for a revolt against the Polish government, and not documents for the explosion of the "citadel" - the fortress in Warsaw, but photographs of the organized Jewish youth in Dubno.

Dusia Korin suffered in prison for three months. The "dangerous revolutionary" was not allowed to meet with anyone from the outside except for his mother. However, while Dusia suffered alone in the prison yard, and within the silent walls of his prison cell, on the other side of the tall fence all the youth of "*Hashomer Hatzair,*" and many of the city's residents, waited in great agony for the trial. The boys expressed their participation in the prisoner's suffering in whole night hikes near the prison fences, while the adults took care of preparing the defense. The trial was the talk of the days next to the vendors' stalls, in the workshops and the "*kloyzn.*" It was felt that the entire Jewish public, who wanted an independent Jewish life, was on trial.

The day of judgment arrived. The session of the District Court took place in the "*Rathaus*" hall - the municipality. Since morning, a large number of the city's active anti-Semites crowded into the courtroom expecting to see the Jews humiliated and proud Dusia receiving his punishment. However, most of the spectators were from among the dignitaries of the Jewish public, who wanted, with all their hearts, to honor the scout movement and its leader, Dusia.

The main material, for the charge of "revolt against the kingdom," was: photographs of youth from "*Hashomer Hatzair*" in different groups and ages and, as usual, on the other side of the photographs were lines of dedication in the spirit of yearning for Zion. Some were dedicated to "the leader of the "*ken* "Dusia Korin," "to the *kvutza* leader D. Korin," or "an eternal memento from *Histadrut Hashomer Hatzair.*" The judges sought to unravel the secret of the concepts: *ken*, *kvutza* and *histadrut*. For this purpose, the most loyal man to the "authorities" was called to testify on behalf of the prosecution - "*HaRav Mita'am,*"[2] R' Hesheli.

To the judges' question R' Hesheli answered that the translation, and meaning, of the word "*ken*" is "organization," the translation of the word "*kvutza*" is "organization," and the meaning of the word "*histadrut*" is also "organization."

This translation was exaggerated: is it not clear that before the judges enemy number one is hiding under different names?

[Columns 263–264]

Group of members of "Hashomer Hatzair," 5682 (1922)

To the sound of this "proficiency" in the language of the past, the Jewish audience almost lost its temper. The lawyer for the defense claimed that he did not trust the translation of the rabbi who proved complete ignorance in Hebrew. R' Hesheli, "*HaRav Mita'am,*" also did not trust his knowledge of Hebrew and agreed that another translator would be called in his place.

Within an hour, Mr. Fried, a teacher in the Jewish-Polish Gymnasium, member of "*Hashomer Hatzair*" in Vienna, an educated man in various fields of culture who knew Hebrew and Polish. He explained to the judges that the concept of "*ken*" isn't "organization" but a free meeting of friends, like the meeting of birds in a nest that is also free. "*Kvutza*" is not a concept of an organization but a voluntary definition of people getting together, just as members of a family can be photographed in a group, etc. For an entire hour they investigated these terms linguistically and the verdict was given: innocent.

Great was the joy and wide was the echo in the city and throughout Volhynia.

Translator's Comments

1. *Ken* - nest in Hebrew - a branch of a youth movement.
2. *Rav Mita'am* - a rabbi appointed by a Jewish community on behalf of the authorities. This rabbi served as a representative of the Jews to the authorities and was responsible for the management of birth and death certificates, marriage registration, tax payments, etc. The rabbis often had no religious education and many didn't know Hebrew.

Hechalutz in Dubno

by Zelig Freiman

Translated from Hebrew by Sara Mages

In the late 1920s, *"Hechalutz"* operated in a cramped little club, in a two-room apartment in the Eisenstein house on Parana Street. It was difficult to operate under these housing conditions, but regular educational activities and meetings took place there. From this club the first group of immigrants from Dubno, a few dozen young men and women, members of *"Hechalutz"* and *"Hashomer Hatzair,"* set out on their way to Israel.

That Saturday night would not be forgotten. At sunset, carriages and wagons full of pioneering youth, and hundreds of pedestrians, streamed to the train station to escort the group of immigrants. The train station was teeming with people and, in the great crowding, circles of *"Hora"* dancers joined together. And so, to the sound of singing and dancing, the emigrants left the darkening Dubno.

That day marked a turning point in the *"Hechalutz"* movement in Dubno. The influx of youth to *"Hechalutz"* grew from day to day, and further increased the overcrowding in

the club so it was necessary to leave it and move to a new spacious club on the second floor of the Gasir house in the city center. Now it was possible to develop a broad activity: a ping pong table and various other games were brought to the club; talks were held and cultural activities began. Many members of *"Hechalutz"* movement in Dubno set out for *hakhshara* [training] kibbutzim in various locations in Poland.

After a while *"Hashomer Hatzair"* and *"Hechalutz"* merged and, again, the club wandered, this time to the Sirkis house. The committee was composed of representatives of the two movements and each week a meeting was held to receive new members.

One day, in May 1930, the member Daniel Levi came from Klesow (Klesów). At the committee meeting, which was held on the occasion of his arrival, he announced that there were places available for *hakhshara* at the basalt quarry, as well as in the

279

sawmill, in Klesow. On the spot, about twenty members, including me, were approved for *hakhshara* in Klesow. We were very happy to join the kibbutz there.

The kibbutz consisted of three hundred and twenty members who worked in the quarry and in the sawmill. Most of the men worked in the quarry while the women were engaged in sawing wood. The economic conditions were very poor: the food was meager and the clothes tattered. We were almost barefoot. Our feet were wrapped in sacks with rubber soles, cut off from bus tires, tied to them. Because of the overcrowding, the sanitary conditions were also poor. We slept two in one bed, and the beds stood one above the other. Most of us suffered from skin diseases. In addition to all this, we also suffered from a severe shortage of kitchenware. We had only five spoons, five forks and five cups, and we had to wait in line to get a spoon or a cup.

The gentiles in the village were anti-Semites and their attitude towards us was bad. Every Sunday they got drunk and rioted. They came to us and attacked us with stones, knives and various tools. Then, the girls' screams rose to the heavens, but the police stood by and did not interfere. They called us "Palastinzi," and "Amerikantzi" to Kibbutz Betar which was also there.

Although our lives in Klesow were quite difficult, we slowly adapted to the hard work and also to the difficult conditions. We went out to work with a song on our lips, and returned singing. In the evenings we held meetings, danced and raised the spirit in the

"Hechalutz" activists in Dubno (1929)

[Columns 267–268]

camp, and since we knew how to ward off sadness and depression, the minister in charge of love relations came to visit us from time to time, and then, there was great joy in our home.

One day we received the news of the publication of the White Paper (Passfield White Paper) by the mandatory government. According to the paper there was no place in the country for additional Jews and, therefore, the immigration to it would cease. The black-and-white paper fell upon us like a blow and every face was gloomy. "What will happen, what will we do?" we asked each other. Is there any point in continuing to sit here, live in these unsuitable conditions and wait for immigration? When it may resume? Will it resume?

The member Daniel Levi, who was the coordinator of the kibbutz, called for a meeting in which he explained the grave state of affairs, the war waged by the movement's supreme institutions on the White Paper, and called for persistence in training until the day we would be called to immigrate. This day, he said, would come and we must be ready for it. The assembly dispersed, but the depression that descended upon us did not leave. Everyone began to do his account, account of days without a ray of light, without the hope of getting out of this circle of life-no-life and reaching the desired land in which we hoped to awaken to a new life.

The great departure began. About forty percent left the place, among them many from Dubno. The rest decided to stay, to go on, and to wait ... until the day when the closed gates of immigration would open wide before them.

At the train station in Dubno, a group of pioneers immigrating to Eretz-Yisrael (1931)

A short time later two emissaries from Israel came to us: the members Tabnkin and Levita from Kibbutz Ein-Harod. After seeing the conditions in which we lived they obtained for us all the utensils and kitchenware from "*Hechalutz*" center, so, from then on, everyone had his own utensils. This change alone was enough to elevate the mood in the camp. After that came the talks, lectures and stories about life in Israel, in *kvutzot* and kibbutzim, about the war being waged on the White Paper and about the hopes of renewed immigration. The members Tabnkin and Levita were also invited to Kibbutz *Betar* for conversations and lectures. Another spirit moved through Klesow - we were somewhat relieved although there was no change in our economic situation, which was very bad, because at that time we literally starved.

[Columns 269–270]

Suddenly, there was a turning point in the politics of the mandatory government. In April 1932, we received the news that 1,200 immigration certificates had been received and, from them, a few dozen were allocated to our members in Klesow. It is difficult to describe the great joy of the members who won these certificates.

All these changes in the state of the movement did not pass without a significant impression on the life of "*Hechalutz*" in Dubno. With the cessation of immigration many had left the movement, and with the resumption of immigration a new stream of blood began to flow into it and into all other branches of the Zionist movement in the city. At the same time, a united operation, of all the branches of the Zionist movement, was organized for *Keren HaKayemeth LeIsrael*. It was headed by the fund's authorized representative in Dubno, Mr. Dov Blatt Z"L.

Many, of those from Dubno who immigrated to Israel, continue on in the kibbutz, in the *moshav* and in the city. They are happy that they have been rewarded and redeemed in time, but their happiness is incomplete, and would never be whole again, because they always see before their eyes their family members, acquaintances, and friends who weren't able to immigrate - and perished there in the Valley of Death.

Histadrut Hanoar Hechalutz "Gordonia" in Dubno

by Zipora Ampel

Translated from Hebrew by Sara Mages

Histadrut Hanoar Hechalutz [Federation of Pioneering Youth] *"Gordonia"* was established in Dubno sometime after the establishment of the branches of this movement in the Volhynia district and was under the activity and inspiration of the regional leadership in Rowno. It was initially organized as a youth movement ideologically close to the *"Hitahdut"* movement in Poland, who advocated the values of *"Hapoel Hatzair"* in Eretz Israel. The movement took the name of Aharon David Gordon, who spread the idea of work ethics among the members of *"Hapoel Hatzair."* It was not long before the movement formed itself as an independent pioneering youth organization that aimed at training and self-realization. Immigration to Eretz Israel was compulsory for all its members.

Yosef Baratz in his visit to Dubno (1930)

283

At the time of the founding of the movement in Poland, there were already youth movements of a pioneering-educational nature such as *"Hashomer Hatzair," "Hechalutz Hatzair," "Dvir,"* and *"Hapoel HaMizrahi."* Nevertheless, great danger lay in wait for the youth from extreme left-wing parties such as the *"Bund"* and the communists, who aspired to capture the heart of the young people and put them into a political struggle, foreign to the values of Zionism and pioneering, and without Jewish-nationalist roots. Therefore, the founders of *"Gordonia"* saw before them a great task: to capture the hearts of the youth, working and studying alike, and organize them in the local branch. The members of the *"ken"* [smallest cell of a youth movement] were divided into three stratum according to age: *"Mitorerim," "Zufim,"* and *"Magshimim."* Each stratum had its educational framework with one goal before everyone - the education of people for a working Zionist fulfillment. In order to achieve this goal, each of the members had to leave for *hakhshara* [training] to prepare himself for a working life in the homeland.

In the course of their training and preparation towards the future, the members of *"Gordonia"* devoted themselves to the activities for the national funds - *Keren Kayemet* and *Keren Hayesod.* They also participated in the Lag BaOmer procession,

[Columns 271–272]

Members of "Gordonia" in hakhshara in Dubno, cutting wood

conducted pioneering cultural evenings with singing and passionate *Hora* dancing. They held in-depth debates on other youth movements, views and ideological differences, social structure, way of life in the kibbutz and the *kvotza*, and political outlook. It was a period of awakening among the youth and a great blessing was folded in it.

The training group for the members of *"Gordonia"* in Poland, which was founded in Dubno, brought in a spirit of life and aroused admiration from all. Young men and women didn't scorn the work given to them, whether cutting trees or drawing water. They saw in it the vision of all: the transformation of a non-working nation, a nation that for hundreds of years was accustomed, even against its will, to despise manual labor, to a working nation that loves manual labor, especially working the land. It was a complete revolution in the life of the Jew in the Diaspora, in his conception and his preparation for a different life, new life in the homeland. Under the influence of the training group many of the *"ken*'s" members left for *hakhshara* and, from them, quite a few managed to immigrate and integrate into the life of work and creativity in Israel.

In this way, the work, and the educational activity, continued until the day of the great and terrible Holocaust, when the evil hand was raised on the Polish Jewry and also brought destruction of the Jews of our city. In the general slaughter the lives of the youth were also uprooted and there was mourning and lamentation all around...

The Youth That is Gone

by Shimon Oz (Guz)

Translated from Hebrew by Sara Mages

Dubno has always been blessed with vigilant youth, active and vibrant. This youth constituted an abundant source for different youth movements, educational and political, and various sports organizations.

I will briefly mention some of them: the glorious "*Hashomer Hatzair*" movement, the strong *Histadrut* "*Hechalutz*," "*Hechalutz Hatzair*," "*Hanoar Hatzioni*," "*Betar*," the sports association "*Hakoah*," and the Union of Communist Youth. These organizations gathered within their ranks hundreds of members, youth, working and studying, full of joy of life and vigor.

Each of these organizations developed extensive activity in its special field, educated and trained thousands of members for immigration to Israel, members that we meet at the annual gathering of former residents of Dubno. The sports organizations reached important achievements in the physical and mental education of the youth, an education that left its mark on their proud Jewish appearance despite the anti-Semitism that raged at that time in Poland. This proud appearance created a special attitude toward the Jews by the Christian population, which was incomprehensible to those who came from central and western Poland, places where the Jews had not dared to stand tall for a long time. This is the place to mention the praised brass band of "*Hakoah*" which earned a reputation among the local population in its performances and won nationwide publicity.

With all our opposition to the communists' political line and their negative attitude toward Zionism, it is also impossible not to appreciate the courage of their youth, who operated under terrible underground conditions and suffered from the oppressive measures of the regime that prevailed at that time in Poland.

I briefly mentioned the large camp of youth, which operated in Dubno within the framework of various movements and associations, as in other cities in Volhynia. However, I will especially mention a modest organization that was established in Dubno in the last years before the outbreak of the Second World War, an organization

I was closest to as one of its founders. This organization did not demand from its members, like other youth movements, training and immediate immigration to Israel and, therefore, most of them remained in the place and the hand of the Nazi oppressor. Almost all of them were cut off from the land of the living. It was, *"Gedud Keren HaKayemet LeYsrael"* [The Jewish National Fund Battalion], an organization established in Dubno. Later, similar battalions were established in several nearby towns.

[Columns 277–278]

Initially, *"Gedud Keren HaKayemet LeYsrael,"* was a group of volunteers, who dealt with the emptying of the JNF boxes and other activities connected with donations and fundraising for the redemption of Israel. These members, who met frequently, decided to establish a framework with bylaws and regular action plans. Because of special circumstances the battalion was composed mainly of girls. These members gave up their free hours, and various cultural activities, and devoted their energy and strength to the activity that sometimes was difficult and exhausting. They walked from house to house, at times over great distances and through snowstorms and rainstorms, to empty the white-blue boxes, to collect the pennies which had accumulated from month to month to considerable sums, for the redemption of lands in the homeland.

Gedud Keren HaKayemet LeYsrael

The committee of Keren HaKayemet LeYsrael in Dubno
Sitting (right to left): D. Perl. A. Bronshtein, S. Roitman, M. Zimerman, A. Meizler
Standing (right to left): Kornfeld, H. Kagan, Z, Blat, Kolton

Keren HaKayemet LeYsrael, the committee in Dubno

289

These members, who knew that their chances of immigrating to Israel were not many, did their best to help realize the vision closest to their hearts. They gathered for a conversation, to study Hebrew together, to improve their methods of action and, indeed, they got what they wanted. The battalion was always first in the activities for the Jewish National Fund.

"*Gedud Keren HaKayemet LeYsrael*" took a special place among the Jewish youth movements in Lag Ba'Omer, when the Jewish youth in Dubno demonstrated its power and unity in a glorious procession. It was a holiday that the whole city took part in. In cohesive lines, uniformly dressed in bright white shirts, with flags fluttering overhead and bands of trumpets and drums accompanying it, the procession left for the forest outside the city and every youth movement set up its own camp. The youth spent a whole day outdoors, and returned to the city at dusk as the streets were filled with a huge crowd that welcomed them with pride and applause.

I remember a Lag BaOmer procession (in late 1930s). Anti-Semitism reached its peak, and that year the organizers hesitated to hold the procession even though a restricted permit was granted by the authorities under the personal pressure of David Pearl, chairman of the Zionist organization in Dubno. This procession was so important and precious to the city's Jews that everyone enlisted to protect it, even the bullies, the city's well-known "fist" men, came out to guard it. And, indeed, the procession passed peacefully and in perfect order, without interference and harassment of anti-Semitic elements and students, and members of the "*Endecja*" political movement, who gathered in the city from other locations.

These precious and glorious youth, which included "*Gedud Keren HaKayemet LeYsrael*," is gone. It was destroyed by the Nazi murderers during the Holocaust.

Of the many, I will mention two to whom fate was especially cruel. Liber Lerner and Lisa Leviatin Z"L, were members of a small group that joined "*Hashomer Hatzair*" movement, underwent training and managed to immigrate to Israel. Only the two of them remained - Liber, the quiet and modest, because of his dedication to his sick mother and young sister, and Lisa the brave and proud. When she was executed, she found the courage in her soul to call out to those who gathered: "Do not rest, fight for freedom until the elimination of the Nazi murderers!"

Their memory is kept in the hearts of their friends forever.

Synagogues and Batei-Midrash

Houses of Worship and Batei-Midrash in Dubno

by Moshe Kachka

Translated from Hebrew by Sara Mages

In every Jewish city there was usually one large synagogue, or two, new and old. The synagogue wasn't heated, not even in the coldest days. The rest of the places of worship were called Beit Midrash, "*shtiebel*" or "*kloyz*," and were heated from the first days of rain. In Dubno, there were sixteen houses of worship, aside from the Great Synagogue.

The Great Synagogue

Two houses of worship were located in the suburb of Surmicze, as well as Beit HaMidrash of Avraham-Mordechai, Beit Midrash Braslar, and one in the "Old Street." The house of worship of the Karlin Hassidim was located in an alley near Stary Street. The furriers' Beit Midrash had a branch on Stary Street, and the carpenters' Beit Midrash was also there. The big *kloyz* was across from the bathhouse and the synagogue. Beit HaMidrash of R' Aharon stood on Ribna Street, as well as Batei HaMidrash of the Oliker Hassidim and Trisk Hassidim. In the city, there was also a big Beit Midrash for public officials. Beit Midrash BR"Z (Ben R' Zadok Marshalkoviz) was located behind the military headquarters and Beit Midrash *"Beit-Sukkat-Shalom"* on Mayor Meczynski Street, across from the Roitman's house. R' Valvali the teacher, brother of the rabbi, *Av Beit Din* R' Mendele, prayed in the *"shtiebel"* of Beit Midrash BR"Z. On Tzarnizini Street was the shoemakers' Beit Midrash, and the rabbi's Beit Midrash was on Stary Street.

[Columns 279–280]

The prayer in Dubno was in the Volhynia style. *Strimelech,* to the heads of those walking to the houses of worship in the manner of the Galicians, were not found in the entire city, and there was no trace of that passionate devotion, the joy of a *mitzvah* in the belief that prayer connects the worshiper with God, of the Hassidim of Central Poland.

At times, a fire broke out in one of Batei HaMidrash for lack of caution, like leaving lit candles on rainy days, and the damages were enormous.

All Batei HaMidrash, places of Torah and prayer and good deeds, were destroyed during the Holocaust.

The Study Houses of the Righteous of Olik

by Z. Friedman

Translated from Hebrew by Selwyn Rose

Among the many synagogues and study houses that were in town, the one of the *Oliker Hassidim* was unique, as was its congregation. In spite of its name their number was very small since most of them were – as it happens – *Mitnagdim* [1] and at their head stood the Rabbi and head of the Rabbinical Court Pinchas Mendel Rosenfeld and his son Rabbi Heschel (may his righteousness be remembered for a blessing). When the Rabbi of Olik would visit Dubno and linger with his disciples in the study house, Rabbi Mendel and many of his congregation excused themselves from the study house and remained studying and praying in their own homes, went to the Great Synagogue or other synagogues in order to avoid coming into contact with those "bowing down to idols" – according to the perception of the "*Mitnagdim*".

Among those in the congregation with particular status was Rabbi Reuven Stahl, good–looking, wealthy G–d–fearing, good hearted, respected by the community because of his honesty and straight–forwardness, generous to all – charities and poor individuals alike. As a "*Mitnaged*" he was not welcomed by many rabbis. On the other hand Rabbi Yankel Sheines – Ya'acov Rinsberg, was a Hassid, a likeable Jew and loved by all creation.

An interesting person was Mr. Yehezkiel Schatz, nicknamed Yehezkiel the "Glazier". He was a tall Jewish man satisfied with his lot but numbered among the "*Mitnagdim*". He was among the first to organize self–defense during the days of the riots in town, and he was seriously wounded in his stomach, but recovered from his injuries. The administrative manager of the study house for many years was Mr. Ya'acov Safian and Mr. Moshe "the Deaf" acted as Beadle [shamas]. His nickname came by him simply because of his infirmity.

The Cantor Mr. Pinchas Schuchman or Mr. Pinchas Shochet, sang the prayers as Cantor for many years with his rich cantorial voice and they came from all over town to hear his melodies.

Everyone who came to the study house, whether "*Mitnagdim*" or *Hassid*, all were G–d–fearing, honest people who, though they may be separated by their diverse opinions during their lives, came together in death and perished together in sanctification of his Holy Name.

Translator's Comment

1. *Mitnagdim* means simply: opponents. This was an 18th Century rabbinic movement opposing the Hassidic philosophy. For a full explanation see: https://en.wikipedia.org/wiki/Misnagdim

The Study House of Mr. Avraham Mordecai

by Moshe Cohen

Translated from Hebrew by Selwyn Rose

During the first half of the 19th Century there lived in Dubno a Jewish man by the name of Avraham Mordecai Meierzon and his wife. Because they had no children, Mr. Avraham Mordecai dedicated his house for holy purposes on condition that the house will carry his name and that after his death his *Yahrzeit* (German–Yiddish: the annual memorial of his death) will be performed regularly. He reserved for himself living quarters in the house and a reserved seat in the study house and the place became somewhat sanctified.

After a few years, the study house in the center of town became one of the most important of the eighteen study houses that existed in town at that time apart from the Great Synagogue with its own four "*Shteibels*". As time passed, the study house was burned down twice and rebuilt. At the time of the "Great Fire" that befell the town in 1894 the third one was destroyed and a smaller house was built in its place with donations from the congregation (Mr. Avraham Mordecai was no longer alive); a building more suited to its needs. With the passage of years its administrating managers introduced many different improvements – a women's gallery was added, a "*Shteibel*", a new, beautiful Holy Ark, comfortable pews, the walls and ceiling were painted in the prevailing style and even carpets were spread. However the congregation was unable to care for the carpets and it was necessary to remove them. Nevertheless all these improvements significantly raised the profile of the study house of Mr. Avraham Mordecai.

The congregation of the study house was made up of merchants, shopkeepers, artisans, wagon–masters and porters – in short – the "*Hoi Polloi*". But there were also scholars and people of means who found their place along the Eastern wall, like Mr. Yishmael Birenboim, the brothers Yitzhak and Ya'acov Shteinshnid, Micha'el Goldberg, Haim Spunberg, Rabbi Eliyahu Guttman, the Meizler brothers and more and more. Apart from the main congregation who came regularly each morning and especially at twilight, were Jews who happened to be in town and took the opportunity to "catch" the "*Kedusha*" and "*Borachu*" prayers that are brief but integral and important parts of the daily liturgy, to hear a sermon from one of the expositors present, to study the daily page of the *Gemara* or a chapter from the *Mishnah* (each in its own right epigraphic explanatory extensions to the *Torah*), and in passing to pick up news and conversations on the political issues of the day – and sometimes just to keep a little warm next to the fire during the cold days of the winter…

[Columns 283–284]

Mr. Avraham Mordecai's study house also fulfilled a role within general public areas. Here, at the end of the nineteenth century, the charity <u>"Leinat Chessed"</u> was established offering help and succor to the sick and those in need, and especially to make all–night sick calls on the bed–ridden and homebound in order to ease the burden on the family members and to deal with any needs that arise.

There were also many Zionist meetings concerning the "*Keren Hayesod*" (The Foundation Fund) and the "*Keren Ha–Kayemet*" (The Jewish National Fund) that took place and every year a memorial service was held on 20th *Tammuz* (around June/July) commemorating the death of Herzl.

In 1939 when the Soviet authorities in town converted the synagogues to social clubs and cooperative workshops the congregation of the Avraham Mordecai Study House assembled and protested against the edict and at the same time the Beadle, Moshe Karnett and the Sexton, Joseph Zilberman met with the First Secretary of the Communist Party in town and succeeded in getting the edict annulled, so far as the Avraham Mordecai Study House was concerned.

When I chanced to visit Dubno in 1946 I found only a very few Jewish people living there although the study house still stood but instead of being a prayer house it had become – a restaurant.

Cantors of the Great Synagogue

by Moshe Katchke

Translated from Hebrew by Selwyn Rose

The Great Synagogue of Dubno on Rybne (Fish) Street stood, to the best of my knowledge, from 1782 to 1784 until its destruction in 1939 – 155 years.

On the second floor, to the north and south, were two women's galleries attached to the building and on the west side below, two prayer–rooms had been added and above them two upper prayer–rooms. Each prayer–room had a complement of about three quorums [minyans] of congregants.

The structure itself was impressive and could be seen from across town; none of the nearby towns had a comparable building in style or taste. I remember when the synagogue's sexton, Hershe'le informed the congregation that the Synagogue's archived journal identified the architect as a Russian, when the work was completed he was presented with a gift in the name of the community: a typical Russian black–lacquered peaked cap.

From 1902–1904 the permanent Cantor of the synagogue was the elderly Mr. Moshe Soroka. He was of medium height with a small white beard. He was noticeable for his clear enunciation and pronouncing the letter "r" with great emphasis. His voice was powerful with a touch of coloratura. For the High Holy Days he would form a chorus: the three Baroches brothers (two altos and a tenor) with an additional tenor Avraham Yohannis and Berl the rope–maker who had a *basso profundo*. At the end of his days, when already eighty years old, the women in the gallery began to complain that the voice of Moshe could no longer be heard by them. The management decided to place him in retirement.

Cantors from Odessa and Berdichev began to arrive for auditions in the synagogue. The candidate was required to officiate on one Sabbath service, on his own without a chorus. Mr. Seltzer, a pleasant cantorial–voiced individual from Odessa was chosen from among the candidates as the Cantor. His diction was not clear but together with the choir he was very good. His appointment came in 1909 shortly before the High Holy Days. The Beadle at the time was Solomon Fischbein, wealthy and young who was generous when it came to financing a substantial choir. Mr. Seltzer was somewhat apprehensive and demanded that Dubno invite the old conductor Ilya Izkovich Peisie. The Cantor and conductor began inviting vocalists and auditioned them. In a short while an excellent Odessa–style choir had been formed as follows:

- Conductor – Ilya Izkovich Peisie.
- First tenor: Avraham Yohannis – a somewhat weak voice but was able to read music.
- Solo tenor, strong–voiced but unable to read music: Beryl ben Breindel.
- Seamstress.
- A pleasant baritone who read music fluently.
- A bass, Berl the rope–maker, who read no music.

[Columns 285–286]

- Alto, a soloist and reader of music Peretz Markish from Konstantin (Konstanovsk). (He is that same well–known Yiddish writer murdered in Soviet Russia at the time of the Stalinist purge of Jewish writers).
- Four sopranos from among the younger generation in Dubno.
- Four altos, among them was Shikeh Spektor (who later became well–known as a Cantor in Vilna, Brody and Dubno).
- And another alto – the writer of these lines.

There were, therefore, twelve vocalists in this choir. The conditions of payment were agreed with each participant separately (I, for instance, was paid 8 rubles for the High Holy Days). The rehearsals took place until late at night, continuing until reaching a professional result. The governors were satisfied with the results.

The Cantor Mr. Raife and the Choir of the Great Synagogue. [Photo dates from 1924 or 1925.]

On the Festival of the Giving of the Law [Shavuot], the Cantor customarily paid a courtesy call with the choir to the homes of the Beadles starting with the "Deputy Beadle" Mr. Yehoshua Laschover (Z"L). We would sit with him around a large table laden with all sorts of goodies, singing one or two chosen pieces and afterwards we went to the senior Beadle Mr. Solomon Fischbein who lived next door to the hop–drying kiln. Again, we found ourselves sitting round a heavily laden table in his large lounge and Mr. Fischbein invited his wife to join us and listen to the concert. We gave forth our best and Mrs. Fischbein found much pleasure in the performance of the melodies. The delicacies and refreshments were delicious and of generous proportions and in addition Mr. Fischbein announced that he was granting 50 rubles to the choir and a sum to the Cantor.

Mr. Seltzer continued to function as cantor in Dubno until the outbreak of the First World War. As the battle–front approached and entered the town, the Great Synagogue was burned down in 1916 and only at the beginning of the 1920s was the building refurbished. Mr. Leibush Raife was appointed Cantor for two years and the same choir, to which had been added the Starr brothers: Avraham with a good tenor voice and Berl a bright baritone; and an alto Leibush Spektor the son of Avraham Yohannis. After Mr. Raife, Shikeh Spektor officiated as Cantor for a year and following him, Mr. Sherman of Kremenets who served until 1939.

Peretz Markish in Dubno

by Engineer Agronomist Yisrael Feffer

Translated from Hebrew by Selwyn Rose

When Peretz Markish first trod on Dubno's soil no one ever thought, even he, himself, ever dreamed then, that in time he would become famous as a Yiddish writer in Russia and abroad. That was in 1909 and he was still a handsome young man with no discernible literary qualities or even a spark of an author and poet. Although he sang well as an alto on stage he had no connection whatsoever with literature. He sang on the "stage" of the Great Synagogue.

The Great Synagogue

Markish came to Dubno from Zhitomir in order to sing with Cantor Seltzer from Odessa who functioned at the time as Cantor of the Great Synagogue together with the choir. The young man quickly became well–known for his solos and on the Sabbaths the congregations would leave their respective study houses and gather in the Great Synagogue to enjoy the young singer's pleasing *Mussaf* (additional) prayer and Sabbath Hymns.

Markish's family lived in the village of Polonne in Volhynia, and Markish came to Dubno to distant relations in the family of Ya'acov Rinsberg (Yankel Sannis named after his father Mr. Sanni–Nathanial who was also my grandfather from my mother's side) of the Olik the Righteous group. Most of his spare time Peretz spent in the company of members of the study house but had already begun to become known as a somewhat stormy soul, departing from the

[Columns 289–290]

accepted norms and habits in a town composed of predominantly traditionally observant Jews. Thus he would go out publicly for excursions in the company of youngsters both boys and girls and with one of the girls in particular – a young girl from an observant family to whom he paid particular attention. These excursions attracted the attention of the regular congregation who saw the free behavior of their choir's vocalist with some displeasure. Considerable pressure was put upon him by those with influence but Peretz was not an easy one to persuade and he continued to follow his own path. In the meantime something very unfortunate happened to him: his voice began to betray him; it became hoarse and began to change as happens to young men as they reach and mature. When he could no longer control his voice the interest in him among the congregation began to fade. His disappointment was great and many accused him of abandoning the G–d–given talent that had been granted him. Not long after that his fate was sealed: he was relieved of his position in the Cantor's choir, and he returned to his hometown. Almost certainly it was a blessing in disguise for him and his future as a renowned Yiddish poet and author.

Eight years later the name of Peretz Markish was linked with the group of young poets who had made a respected place for themselves in the role of Jewish writers centered in Kiev, the capital of the new Ukrainian Republic. During the years 1917–1924 Peretz Markish lived and worked in Ukraine, then Poland, Berlin and Paris. In 1924 he settled in the Soviet Union. He was among the editors of "*Ha–Emess*" (The Truth) and active in Communist institutions. In 1941 he was awarded a prize by the Soviet government for services to revolutionary literature. After the purges of Jewish culture during the Cultural Revolution in the Stalinist years of 1948–1949 all trace of him disappeared.

Rabbi Zeidel Hazan

by Yakov Netaneli–Roitman

Translated from Hebrew by Selwyn Rose

His name actually was Mr. Avraham Peres. His father was a Rabbi. Michael Peres a devoted disciple of the Admor (an acrostic for **AD**oneinu, **MO**reinu, **R**abeinu – Our lord [master], Our teacher, Our Rabbi), Rabbi Itzik'l from Radziwill. He was born in 1865 and received a traditional orthodox upbringing already recognized in his youth for his rich voice and also for his aptitude in various activities: wood–carving, musical composition, and sight–reading, knowledge of Hebrew and the *Gemara*. As a young man he moved to Dubno and there involved himself in the *Torah* afterwards moving to Bessarabia where he also immersed himself in *Torah*. At the outbreak of the First World War we find him in Dubno and after the Austrian evacuation in 1916 – as a result of the Russian bombardment of the town – the population and Rabbi Zeidel and his family moved to Czechoslovakia to the village of Bratislavci and there they remained until 1918.

Cantor Rabbi Zeidel

When the luxurious Rabbi Mogilever Synagogue was established in 1924 he was invited to officiate as the chief Cantor and he prayed together with a choir he trained and conducted. Rabbi Zeidel was something of a disciplinarian at rehearsals and complained bitterly at the late–comers among the members. It is worth mentioning an amusing incident that happened to him: Yesheyahu Spektor, a chicken trader in the market, once arrived quite late with a large cockerel tucked under his arm (it was Kol Nidrei, the eve of the Day of Atonement). Rabbi Zeidel began to erupt over the tardiness – came the sound of a cockerel calling: "Rabbi Zeidel, Rabbi Zeidel! It was the voice of Spektor – he quickly pulled out his tuning–fork and the cockerel sounded the correct note! We can start immediately…"

In addition to his function as Cantor, Rabbi Zeidel taught Hebrew and Talmud.

He established the "*Mishneh* Group" in which several of the ritual slaughterers took part: Mr. Bentzi, Mr. Tzvi, Mr. Yossel and others and every closure was accompanied with pleasure and singing.

As a Zionist Rabbi Zeidel was devoted to the concept of "liberation" and took part in the dramatic society that was founded in Dubno and coached the participants in music and singing.

Rabbi Zeidel was invited to pray in Lutsk, Kremenets and Rowno but remained with every fiber of his being devoted to the synagogue in his town and its congregation.

He died at a good old age in Dubno in 1939. It may truly be said of him "…the righteous are taken before the coming of evil." (Isaiah 57:1).

The Community's Welfare Institutions

The Jewish Hospital in Dubno

by Ze'ev Ziskind

Translated from Hebrew by Selwyn Rose

Our town did not escape the horrors of the First World War. The town was bombarded and shaken, the ancient synagogue, wherein once prayed the famed "Magid[1] of Dubno" – nicknamed "The Hebrew Aesop"[2] by Mendelssohn – prayed regularly, was damaged and many dear residents fell. The town that was known for its natural beauty, surrounded by streams and forests looked devastated, abandoned and deserted. In addition plagues began to spread like wildfire and reaped many victims with the sick crying out in pain with no one to come to their aid. The dire situation caused heartfelt sympathy among some of the intellectuals in town and in 1921–1922 they slowly began to re–establish the various charitable, nursing and aid institutions of Dubno. Since the resources available to them were very slender they turned to their brethren, the Jews of the United States to join them in the endeavor. The Jews in Dubno, for their part, gave whatever assistance they could.

The first thing the entrepreneurs did was to organize the establishment of a hospital that could extend medical help to the many pain–ridden and suffering sick. A. Czerkas, D. Horowitz, A. Bronshtein, D. Perle and the pharmacist Ashkenazi. Alongside them in that merciful and blessed work were Dr. Kahana – chairman, Dr. Hindz – general practitioner and pediatrician, Dr. Bat – General practitioner and the surgeon Dr. Roitman. Assisting them were the nurses Milova, Laschava and Spector; the House–mother was Mrs. L. Piszewska. The doctors and nurses worked dedicatedly over and above their strength in treating the people so desperate for help.

During the first years of the hospital's function there was no surgeon available and whoever needed even the lightest surgical intervention was forced to undertake the journey to Lwow. That situation changed with the arrival of Dr. Roitman and his wife who was also a surgeon, in 1925. They had the use of a large operating theater with x–ray equipment bringing a significant improvement in the treatment given to the needy.

The electricity supply was connected, as is usual, to the town grid and on more than one occasion there were outages and the hospital was plunged into darkness sometimes in the middle of an operation. Because of the obvious danger to life this created, the committee decided to acquire and operate a generator to supply electricity in the event of a blackout so that the hospital became independent from the supply from the town.

The establishment and development of the hospital and the professional standing of the doctors and nursing and general staff brought no praise or satisfaction from the Polish authorities – on the contrary, it was somewhat of a thorn in their side in spite of the fact that the Jewish hospital treated non–Jews who required help. The Government saw the Jewish hospital as a competitor and tried to wrest it from the hands of the Jews. Then Mr. Bronshtein went to Warsaw and made attempts to get the central authorities to cancel the edict. His mission succeeded and the hospital remained in Jewish hands and it continued to serve faithfully and efficiently the entire Dubno population, Jew and non–Jew alike, until the Holocaust when the Jewish community of Dubno was exterminated.

Translator's Comments

1.   Preacher or expositor
2.   Jacob ben Wolf Kranz of Dubno see: https://en.wikipedia.org/wiki/Jacob_ben_Wolf_Kranz

Welfare Institutions of the Dubno Community

by Shmaryahu Roitman

Translated from Hebrew by Selwyn Rose

Sick–bed Assistance

The society of "*Leinat Tsedek*"[1] in Dubno was founded towards the end of the 19th Century by the congregation of the Braclaw (Breslev) synagogue who became jealous of the charitable organization "*Gemilat Hassidim*"[2] that had been founded by the congregation of Rabbi Avraham Mordecai's synagogue. The object of the society is compounded in an extended description of its Hebrew name: To give aid and comfort to bedridden people – and not necessarily financially, but by visits and sleeping overnight, for the sick needing constant care and attention, the calling of doctors, the acquisition and giving of medicines, etc. The members of the society, men and women, left their homes and families and went to the homes of the sick to sleep there and care for the sick person needing constant attention, seeing in this act a great and holy mission – a "*Mitzvah*"[3] – what a man owes to his fellow man who is unable to help himself. The volunteers went out to fulfill their deed in turns and held the deed dearly and saw it as an act not to be missed.

The expenses of the institution were covered by monthly contributions from all levels of the community, those with more and those with less and the members of the public involved did so in the faithful belief that G–d will repay them for their actions. It was their faith and belief in this that persuaded them to continue to fulfill the obligation.

Their activities continued thus until the outbreak of the First World War; the various personnel at all levels changed but the acts of kindness never ceased. Even during the Austrian invasion of Dubno and the approach to the town of the Front, the institution continued its activities although in a slightly restricted format. When the war ended their activities recommenced with added determination and help from young blood that had joined them, as well as from better organizational methods. The circle of volunteers and donors widened to include not just the worshippers from the synagogues but young men and women. In spite of their more modern outlook and different thought processes, they did not keep distant from those of the older generation. They gave a hand in nursing the patients on their sick–bed. The active cooperation of the two generations did much to bring together the hearts of the two and a Miss Payele Poticha was elected Chairwoman of the institution. Her home became the central office of the organization and its operations. Among the veteran public activists at that time were: Mrs. Sarah Dovtchiss, Bracha Aronstein, Gittel–Devora Dov, Feyga Marshalkovitz, the respected Moshe Kellerman, Avraham Lichter, Lederman and others.

A few years after the end of the First World War the Nursing Society was legally registered and the elected committee headed by a chairman, a secretary and a treasurer. The nursing activities, the home visits both by doctors and volunteers were initiated in writing and the medicines from pharmacies were supplied to the patients at the expense of the Society. At the same time the number of needy people increased significantly, especially sufferers of tuberculosis and the institution did the best it could to come to their aid.

In the period between the two world wars "*Leinat Tsedek*" was the only institution in town with two generations, young and old, working together to bring to reality the Talmudic saying: "Whosoever preserves a single soul of Israel, Scripture ascribes to him as if he had preserved a complete world".[4]

The management committee of "Leinat Tsedek" of 1924

[Columns 295–296]

The operating expenses that continued to grow and multiply, forced greater and greater efforts to increase income. Indeed, when the institution became a registered Society the need to augment income was clear to the public eyes and it began to organize dances, plays, lotteries and "flag–days" in the streets of Dubno to which the public responded generously.

Old Peoples' Home

The corner of Bernardyska Street and Poczatkowa Street was one of the most carefully tended spots in the area. The houses were surrounded with gardens and orchards and among them most noticeable was the home of the short–tempered, well–known in town and the surroundings, Polish Dr. Niewierowski. On that same corner stood the house of Rabbi Isaac Bronstein. Three generations of the same family lived in the apartments there. The local children would sneak through Rabbi Isaac's yard into the garden of Dr. Niewierowski to enjoy the doctor's apples, pears and juicy plums that had provoked their appetite. Rabbi Isaac never told on them and for this he was well–liked by all the children and they were always ready to listen to his stories and jokes and even suffered his playful pinching of their cheeks.

[Plaque on the building reads "Old Peoples' Home"]

After the First World War the daughter and her family moved away, and Rabbi Isaac remained alone in his large house. One day the loneliness defeated him, and he decided

313

to convert his house to a shelter for elderly people and he himself headed it and managed it. The house was composed of two wings: the front wing was reserved for the womenfolk and the rear wing for the men where he had reserved a room for himself. Neighbors and supporters assisted in acquiring some of the beds and some of the elderly themselves brought their own beds with them. Since there was no budget for the maintenance of the home, everyone had to support themselves using the kitchen and general facilities while old, stalwart Rabbi Isaac with his own hands chopped wood for the stove for cooking, drew and carried water in buckets from the well and tried to be of service to everyone.

As time went by shortages began to appear and it was essential to find sources for food and other necessities. It was then that Rabbi Mendele Rosenfeld (Z"L), and with him my late father Gershon Roitman (Z"L), and Ya'acov Rinsberg (Z"L), took it upon themselves to worry about the institution. My father tended to services and general necessities, and Ya'acov Rinsberg to food and its distribution.

The institution was too small to provide for all who knocked on the door but nevertheless somehow managed. Help was found for most of the needy with some kind of solution for families with serious problems. Indeed, it proved itself to be an essential element, and many were the people that supported Rabbi Isaac in everything he did for them.

Translator's Comments

1. "Leinat Tsedek": Generally translated as "comprehensive home care for the sick"
2. "Gemilat Hassidim": Performing acts of kindness
3. "Mitzvah": Literally "a commandment" but used in its everyday sense as the fulfilling of a Biblical commandment or performing any good or righteous deed.
4. There is considerable scholastic and theological debate surrounding the use of the word "Israel", with the conflicting opinion using the expression "…human soul". The above version is taken from the Bavli Talmud (Tractate Sanhedrin 37a).

The Orphanage

by G. Steible

Translated from Hebrew by Selwyn Rose

The Orphanage was situated next to the Jewish hospital. The number of children resident in the facility was about 30 or more and their ages ranged from one year to sixteen. Most of them were orphaned either by one or both parents, although there were also children whose parents were still living but who found it impossible to allow them to remain in the family home for educational or social reasons.

The team of community activists that nurtured and cared for this institution executed their tasks with much devotion, caring for much more than simply their "daily bread" but created within the entire home an atmosphere of warmth trying to remove from the ambience all sense of gloom, suffering and the feeling of deprivation, and to shed light over all.

Volunteers receiving professional training for the orphanage

The house–mother, Mrs. Ita Goldseker (Z"L), dedicated her entire life to the welfare of the children who were the victims of a cruel fate, creating a warm homey atmosphere in the institution, treating the inmates as would a mother the "fruit of her womb", without any consideration of the many hours worked, without taking holidays and days off whenever she felt like it because her entire work–ethos was devoted to the institution and its inhabitants. It was not simply the house–mother alone: she was also concerned for their education and studies for those of the children who were unable to integrate into any other formal educational framework. At one and the same time, she was also a nursemaid and kindergarten nursery maid for the smaller children and toddlers. She was an extraordinary woman bringing upon the home and upon the children with her gentleness and nobility, an easing of the burden on their lives.

[Columns 299–300]

Public activists and notables of Dubno with Mr. Balkind (1921)

First row – Sitting L to R.: Z. Bornstein, Dr. Batt, M. Ashkenazi, Y. Balkind, Y Pinchasewitch, A. Blei, S. Pfeffer
Second row – Standing L. to R.: M. Zimmerman, D. Perle, A Legmann, S. Weiderman, (–), Tzvi Perle (–)
Third row – Lying R. to L.: Y Pfeffer, S Zorne

The office of secretary and treasurer was executed with extreme care and strictness by Mr. Dov Blatt who was careful to maintain a balanced budget, thus removing a great worry from the managing committee and allowing them to cope effectively with the institute's obligations towards the staff and suppliers.

The task that the Committee took upon itself deviated somewhat from its designated mandate the moment that it decided to give an opinion regarding those adolescents who were struggling to keep up with the educational program and straggling far behind, and to create for them a program of learning a practical trade and the respectability of honorable toil and hard work. For that purpose, they introduced a course of seamstress and needlework for girls residing in the institution and those outside; while for the boys, they were attached as apprentices to artisans in town. In relation to that project, I feel it incumbent upon me to mention here Mr. Yehezkiel Geierman who dedicated much time to the occupation of youth who otherwise would have wandered aimlessly around the streets with no control or direction, influencing them with his dedication.

The Committee also concerned itself in providing work for families with many children and little resources so that they were able to earn enough to somewhat ease their suffering and difficulties.

At the head of the Committee stood Mr. Hertzberg, who worried over the enterprise like a father until his illness finally conquered him and his wife, Mrs. Hertzberg then took over the continuation of the work. Together with her toiled, without thought of reward or honor, Mrs. Kagan of Zabramna, the respected Josef Pinchasewitch, Yitzhak Pinchasewitch, Yehezkiel Geierman and others.

A Passover Seder for Jewish Soldiers

by Moshe Cohen

Translated from Hebrew by Selwyn Rose

With the reinforcement of the Polish garrison in town in 1937, the number of Jewish soldiers in the force increased to about 150 men.

With the approach of Passover over the horizon the Community Council decided at one of its meetings to prepare a *Seder* for the Jewish soldiers and also to supply them with kosher food for the succeeding days of the festival.

With that decision, the heads of the Council, Dr. Goldblatt and Rabbi Herschel Rosenfeld approached the Commandant on behalf of the soldiers, requesting leave for the two nights of the festival and to permit the soldiers to enter town twice daily in order to eat the kosher meals prepared for them.

The Commandant answered the Council favorably and the military financial officials even transferred the necessary funds to the Council.

The Council immediately put the plan into operation by starting to refurbish a vacant hall in the Municipal Council–house that had been empty since the First World War, mobilizing volunteers to prepare whatever was needed for the *Seder*. The women's organizations, WIZO, and the various youth organizations all responded to the call and harnessed themselves to the mission. Only a few days later everything was ready according to the plan laid out.

On the two evenings of the *Seder* members of the Council, together with Rabbi Rosenfeld at their head accompanied by other community leaders arrived to sit around the laid tables with the soldiers and infused the atmosphere with a spirit of homeyness. The women of WIZO and the youth organizations who busied

Jewish Soldiers at the Passover Seder with the public notables

[Columns 303–304]

themselves preparing the food and serving at the tables spread a pleasant feeling of graciousness over the whole festivities.

During the meal Zionist songs were sung and when the *Seder* was over everyone began dancing the traditional *Hora*.

During the intermediate days of the festival, the soldiers came to town for a midday and evening meal, marching in military order by command of the Commandant; after the evening meal each soldier received a parcel of prepared food for his breakfast the following morning. Parcels were also distributed for those soldiers who were unable to come because of guard-duties or other military reasons.

This arrangement initiated by the Community Council was a gesture of respect for the Jewish soldiers based in a town far from their homes, replacing the need for the congregation of the synagogue to take it upon themselves individually [to host soldiers] as had been the case previously. Once instituted, the system was carried forward as an annual event in the life of the town. The next Passover *Seder* was organized by the Community Council with the help of the various institutions mentioned above and thus it continued until 1939 when the outbreak of The Second World War and the Shoah fell upon the House of Israel.

"TOZ" in Dubno

by Mania Deibog

Translated from Hebrew by Selwyn Rose

"TOZ" [Towarzystwo Ochrony Zdrowia - Society for the Protection of the Health of the Jews in Poland] was a society that concerned itself with the health and well-being of a multi-layered society of significantly limited means. It was an enterprising society and very vigilant among the local organizations in town. It had already existed many years before I came to work there as a nurse, and I was associated with it from 1930 until 1934. Apart from me there was another nurse working there named Beyla Krum.

Members of the committee and activists in support of the institute were: Dr. Ya'acov Goldblatt, Dr. Bat, Dr. Galparson, Dr. Berta Grinzweig, and the ladies Mrs.

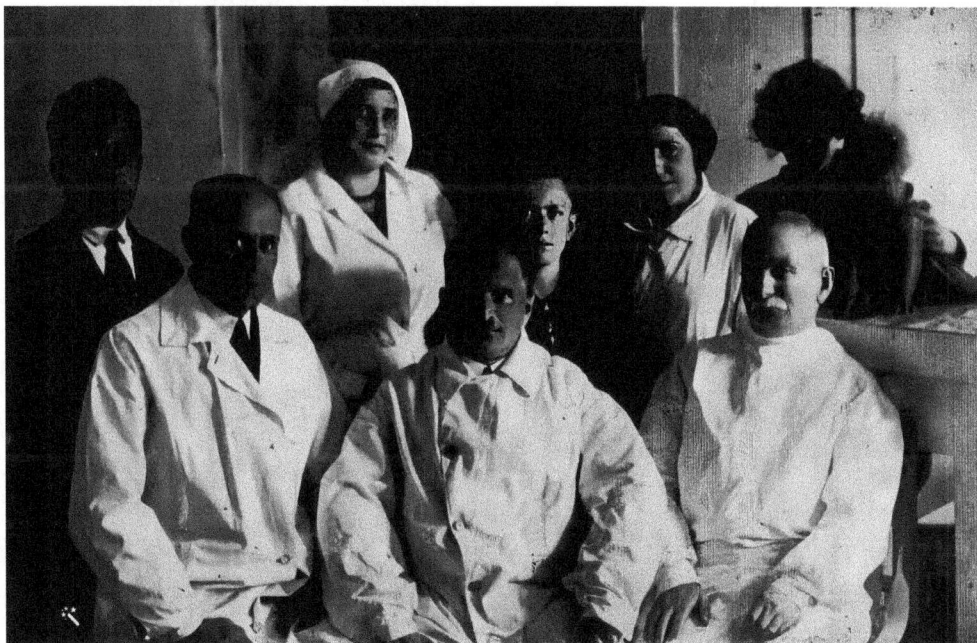

Staff of "TOZ" 1934

Greenberg, Mrs. Laszczower, Hanna Cohen, Shteinshnid and others. The secretary was Mrs. Sonia Zorne.

The budget of the institute was based on donations from its members who were themselves of modest means and on one-time projects such as performances and holidays and "flag-days". The truth must be told that the budget of the institute was never balanced and there were always deficits that were difficult to cover.

The regular activities of the society were: "Mother and child clinic" for nursing mothers and their babies, supervision and cleanliness of the poorer neighborhoods by a trained social worker, a dermatological clinic, an eye clinic, and medical examinations. The society also arranged for summer-camps for the children where they could relax and develop. The camps were a sort of "hot-houses" where the children would stay overnight, and other camps where they would stay only during the day. In these "day-camps" that took place in 1930 and 1931 in the court-yard of Mr. Goldman there were about 100 children in three cycles. The payment for their maintenance was minimal and many of the children were accepted without payment.

The children stayed in the day-camps from morning until four in the afternoon, doing gymnastics, playing all sorts of games involving physical activity and handicrafts under the control and watchful eyes of three nurse-maids under my supervision, all enjoying the fresh air and blessed warmth. The administration of the camps was in the care of the society's secretary Mrs. Sonia Zorne whose heart was dedicated to the "TOZ" project and did the utmost towards its development and prosperity.

Children in TOZ summer-camp - 1931

Culture and Way of Life

The History of the Family Name of the Historian Simon Dubonow

by Amnon Horowitz

Translated from Hebrew by Selwyn Rose

In his autobiography S. Dubonow gives a broad description of his family's origins and its history. The family had its beginnings in the middle of the 17ᵗʰ century in the time of the Polish Kingdom and in the town of Dubno in Volhynia. In the middle of the 18ᵗʰ century at the time of the partition of Poland (1772), the family moved to the town of Mscisław (Omtchislav) in White Russia which had been ceded to Greater Russia, (Mahilyow Province). When a law was promulgated in Russia requiring a family name to be registered, the patriarch of the family living in Mscisław chose the name Dubonow being the name of the town where the family had dwelt.

Our family ancestor was the kabbalist Rabbi Yosef Yoski, the son of the well-known Gaon of the time- Yehuda Yud'l from Kowel. This Rabbi Yosef Yoski occupied the Chair of the Rabbanut in Dubno during the last decades of the 17ᵗʰ century and while there authored his book "*Yesod Yosef*" but in fact the patriarch of the family was considered to be Bentzion Chatzkelovich of Mscisław.

The name Bentzion Chatzkelovich sprang from the Jewish source name Bentzion son of Yehezkiel that appeared in Russian documents – registered as Chatzkelovich and his name is found in the registers of the community among those who were elected every year beginning in 1761; the honorary title of "Head and Officer".

Bentzion Chatzkelovich was the owner of a large agricultural estate during the rule of Alexander the First and the Empress Katarina but when the law was enacted forbidding Jews to own agricultural estates, he was forced to circumvent the law by transferring title of his property to Christians at disadvantageous terms and later his descendants were to accept rent from the new owners. This situation continued for many years until a declaration of release in 1861 freed the farmers from their serfdom.

At the beginning of the 19ᵗʰ century Bentzion Chatzkelovich the "Officer" died and his place in the community was filled by his son Ze'ev-Wolf whose name was found in the Community Registry for the first time in 1823 connected with the name "Dubno"[1] – or "Dubonow" and since then the family was known by that name. Since his income and sustenance now derived as inheritance from the estate, he devoted himself to spiritual works to which he gave all his soul and strength. He attended the Study-House lessons on the *Talmud* and *Responsa*[2] and his son Avigdor busied himself with commerce, but he died young in the prime of life, circa.1840 and in his place stood the head of the Dubonow family, the eldest son, Bentzion junior (born about 1805), the grandfather and teacher of Shimon Dubonow and his brother.

Bentzion quickly realized that his living was not to be in commerce and trade since he, like his grandfather Ze'ev-Wolf leaned towards spirituality and was drawn to the *Torah* to which he indeed devoted himself and his sustenance came from the large building that he owned and rented to government offices and stores for traders, while he read and studied in the Study-House.

A story is told about him that during a fire in Dubno, he stood by calmly watching the distressing sight, the source of his income, going up in flames. His daughter stood beside him crying and wailing while he tried to calm her. She said: "Father, how are you not crying? Look! Even our neighbor, the priest is crying in front of his burning home." The old man answered: "My daughter, he has something to cry about – his god (the wooden icon), is burning up inside his home, but *our* G-d isn't burnt, and He will look after us!"

Meir-Ya'acov Dubonow, the only son of Bentzion and the father of S. Dubonow was born in 1833. When he lost his assets at the time of the fire and the family was obliged to roam from apartment to apartment, the father was forced to sustain his large family (his wife had borne him five sons and five daughters) and eventually he obtained a post with his father-in-law, his wife's father, Michael Halickman from the village of Olbrachcice, near the town of Homyel (Homl).

The father, Meir Ya'acov, was responsible for the transportation of lumber by water on boats, rafts or barges and during the summer months dwelt in Ekaterinoslav and Kherson selling the lumber to wholesalers and builders or to holders of timber warehouses only returning to Mscisław for the High Holidays and *Succoth* after the completion and settling of accounts.

[Columns 315–316]

As payment for his toil, he received a meager salary and his family rarely saw him with a happy face, a situation that caused bitterness towards the other grandfather (their mother's father) because of his meanness. The father's health was affected by his wandering far from his home and his life near the rivers – with its constant high humidity – caused him to suffer from chronic bronchitis as a result of which he passed away in 1887 at the age of 54, and that was after Mr. Michael closed his business and gave his son-in-law a distressingly small sum to build himself a house. But the father was not to enjoy even that and before the construction was completed, he passed away.

One of S. Dubonow's brothers died in childhood. The senior son, Yitzhak, died in the prime of life (1890). Two brothers of Dubonow remained alive: Ze'ev, who was two and a half years his senior and Nahman – the youngest. Both of them made their way by different paths to Palestine.

Original Footnotes and Translator's Comments

1. Original footnote: This article is from "The Past", a quarterly Journal concerning the days of Jews and Judaism in Russia, Vol. viii published in Tel-Aviv, Iyar 5721 (Spring 1960).
2. The replies and pronouncements on Talmudic legal questions. (tc)

The History of Printing in Dubno[1]

by Bernard Friedberg

Translated from Hebrew by Selwyn Rose

Rabbi Yohanan the son of Rabbi Ya'acov from Wiecki, Silesia who was a proof-reader in the Krûgera printing-house in Nowy Dwor and later the company's Hebrew agent for Hebrew books in Warsaw, founded here, in Dubno in 1754 with the help of the master "Artist" Michał Piotrowski, the "loyal working partner". The ruler of the town at the time was Prince Michał Lubomirski, and as a mark of esteem and gratitude for his permission to establish the printing-house they printed on the frontispiece of books that came off the press his monogram and his initials M.L. in large graphically decorated letters.

The following books have appeared: Zevah Shmuel, "*Hapedut ve-Hapurkan*" (Redemption and Release), "*Shibolei Ha-Leket*", "*Shulhan Arba*" (1764), "*Kerem Ein Gedi*" (The Vineyard of Ein Gedi), "*Sivuv olam*" by Petachiah Morgensperg, (two separate editions). "*Seder S'lichot*" (Prayer service for forgiveness), "*Tsad Ha-Ma'a lot*", "*Ha-Roke'ach*" The Pharmacist"(shorter edition)*(*1755), Laws governing the writing of Holy texts (1756), "*Tshu'ot-Chen*" (Shouts of Grace) (1757), "*Beit-Eini*", "*Mevasser Tsedek*" (Carrier of Justice), "*Torah*" (1758), "*Shita Mekubetzet: Nazir*", "*Tikunei Ha-Zohar*" (Additions to the Zohar) (1760), "*Machzor im Bi'ur*" (Machzor with commentary according to the Ashkenazi), (also in two editions) – (1761).

The typesetters in the printing-house were Natan Fajtl the son of Moshe Ya'acov - may he be remembered for a blessing – the brother of the printer "the typesetter of the new pleasant letters gives our *Torah* an appearance that can be handed on for generations" – Mr. Benjamin son of Tzvi Hirsch, may he be remembered for a blessing – of the Holy Community of Vishnevets (Vishnivits) "worked to honor his Creator in its production" and Mr. Yosef Haim son of Yohanan, the printer, "the faithful worker in setting the type correctly".

The maintainer of the press was Mr. Yosef the son of Shlomo from the Holy Community of Ostrow – the proof-reading was done by the printer Mr. Yohanan who followed faithfully the onus placed upon him and his love of the work – the "apple of his eye" and he removed all the errors and thorns of the text and thus his words at the frontispiece of the book: "May the Creator be eternally blessed and praised for his wonders. Since all beginnings are difficult especially with the printing of new letters, let me acknowledge at the outset, lest I be accused by all the readers of this book, and I bow down in the dust, and beg anyone who may find within it even some unproven error, that I shall not be judged badly. Many have apologized before me, but 'there is no wheat without chaff'. May the Lord judge us and grant us comfort and solace in Zion and Jerusalem and bring upon us endless good."

In 1764 a new printing-house was established here by the partners Mr. Aharon son of Yona, who was at the time the owner of a printing-house in Ostrow and his deputy, Mr. Yosef son of Yehuda Leib of Dubno who was named popularly there as printer and legislator.

At the present time, only these few books have appeared that we know of: *Letters*, *Dr. Yitzhak*, *Sayings of the Wise Men*, *The Reverence*, *The Gate of Heaven* (1764) and *Urim ve-Thummim* (completed in 1766). This book was printed by Rabbi Nathan who took upon himself the burden of the cost, helped by the financial support of Rabbi Haim Yehoshua, the son of Rabbi Yehoshua Roke'ach, Father of the Rabbinical Court of Pinsk, the son of Rabbi M. Shalom, Father of the Rabbinical Court of Tiktin (Tykocin), the son of Rabbi Eliezer the Father of the Rabbinical Court and author of the book "*Ma'aseh Roke'ach*". And in the year 1768 *Sefer Ha-Gorlot* (The Book of Fates) appeared.

The partners then separated from each other. Rabbi Aharon settled in the town of Greater Międzyrzec (Meseritch). In 1780 *"The Gates of Ephraim"* was published by the printing-house in Dubno, together with "*Shulchan Aruch*", "*A Righteous Man,*" and the book of "*Selichot Prayers for 7th Adar*"[2]. The Printer's name is not known.

Original Footnotes and Translator's Comments

1. Original footnote: From "The History of Hebrew Printing in Poland, from its beginnings in 1534, until its perfection, the chronicles of its development up until today" by Bernard (Haim Dov) Friedberg.
2. The traditional birthdate and death of Moses. (tc)

The Ikwa

by Simcha Shtibel

Translated from Hebrew by Selwyn Rose

…and there was a river in Dubno and its name was Ikwa.

This story about it is not because it belongs to the family of world famous and well–known perennial rivers – world atlases may not even record it; even the people of Dubno themselves, Jews and Christians alike, showed it little interest. Apart from a few Jewish families whose livelihood depended on fishing or the flour–mill whose wheel was driven by the river's flow – what was it to them?

Bridge over the Ikwa – the Pantalia Bridge

And the Christians, on whom Nature had bestowed an abundance of her treasures including plenty of water, had no particular need of the Ikwa.

Me? My eyes were not envious of them because of that. I felt no envy or jealousy for their "treasures" and their water, for what is the value of an abundance of water without the pleasures the water brings? For we – not they – have the prayer for "dew and rain" in our liturgy and we – not they – have the songs of our pioneers about water!

For them the Ikwa is simply – a river. They exploit it as if it were nothing. And they have no affection or feeling for it. Only occasionally, on summer days the old grandmothers will visit it, their legs spread and bared to the knees, standing like storks in its shallow waters as they wash their dirty laundry, or in the autumn when the farmers' wives come to soak their sheaves of flax in the water; or during the off season when the field laborers come to harvest the reeds, dry them and weave them into all manner of baskets for sale.

The river was not even a topic of casual conversation. Only on rare occasions was it mentioned with anger because a victim drowned in its eddies, or if the town was under siege by an enemy and they were unable to cross its waters.

[Columns 447–448]

Only we, the children of Dubno loved the river and hugged it to us; for us it was – *all year round* – an inexhaustible source of joys, pleasures and enchantments.

And on that we will talk…

And when the time comes for the fierce battles between the stubborn winter, zealously guarding its domain, and the attacking spring, slowly sending its advance platoons of salvos of rays shot from the sun's arsenal, striking and tearing at the hair of the wonderful crystal–bearded winter; and the warming gale–force winds whirling relentlessly, tearing at the thick, pure white dressing of snow and leaving behind tattered and blackened drifts to cover it's nakedness – then it is the turn of the river. There is nothing like the importance of the battlefield between the winter and the spring…

With the coming of those early spring days no "hero" could control the impulse to fly to the suburb of Surmicze to get closer and feast his eyes on the perennial struggle, and there is no *Hassid* who would not rejoice at the disappearing winter that had prevented us, the children, the many pleasures of the river. During the long months winter had ruled with unbridled authority on our river. The glorious chamomile that grew along the banks and turned them green and the noisy frolicsome waves were conquered and covered by the relentless ice.

Indeed, we were ungrateful – we the children. We did not give the winter its rightful due from the not too distant past when that same ice–covered stream provided us with hours of healthy happy entertainment on it. Now with the warm spring breezes, completely forgotten were those times on its surface from our galloping dizzy hearts, skating on the ice of the broad stream, with the wind humming pleasant tunes in our ears and the sun's rays dancing on the surrounding snow–covered fields igniting them in a blaze of color. The game was exciting and a child whose parents were unable to provide him with skates never despaired – there was always a friend who would loan him his own or give up just one of his own for the sake of a friend so both of them could hold hands and skate together as one making both as happy as can be… breathing the cold, fresh air, rejoicing and flying… the sight was unforgettably exciting.

But with the coming of spring and the thaw, an abundance of water began to flow from the fields in strong currents from all directions as if rushing happily towards the battle, trying to find a way into the swelling river. Its wall, that was trying to remain stable, succeeded in the beginning in pushing the charge of bursting waves back with disdain but slowly cracks started to appear and the charging waves, with their incessant pounding on the wall created cracks and destabilized the foundations. Then chunks of the banks were ripped away and fell into the raging waters overcoming the defenses and forces of resistance chasing after the escaping clumps of ice, tossing them aside as if they were as light as feathers, crashing them one against the other, grinding them and turning their solid state into their original state – water. Then the waters spread, swallowing everything up, piece by piece over a limitless area as far as the eye could see…and then – not the sun's happy and dancing rays and not the clear blue skies, not even the happiness of the youthful, enthralled spectators could convince any one of us that Nature was able to quieten the turbulence of the river and its stormy waves. Indeed, the river Ikwa showered upon us, the children, during those first spring days an exciting spectacle for the eyes, a breath–taking experience. Nevertheless, the joy of many of us was diminished and our hearts deeply touched at the sight of the distress caused to people living close to the river because the conquering floods didn't pass over their houses, most of them trying to save the few possessions, leaving their homes with belongings festooned on their backs…

Nevertheless, the Ikwa will not bring peace of mind to the anger and disappointment of the children. Within a very few days the river began to rein in its turbulent waters and return to its normal course; its banks became green with reeds and rushes and its waters carried along fleets of flowers, water–lilies, white and yellow with long stalks like masts, and broad leaves – and all that in order to cause the children to forget their sadness over the misfortunes of our neighbors.

Those same days – the days of Counting the Omer between Pesach and Shavuot, we, the children were forbidden to bathe in the river and only the wayward and rebellious among us disobeyed the injunction. While the majority satisfied themselves with excursions along the river as far as the bridges that bordered the town or stood and watched them and wonder at the beauty of Nature and listen…watching the sun slowly set, bestowing a rainbow of colors on the horizon, shade upon shade, listening to the frogs' and crickets' endless croaking and chirping. Thus, would we stand and listen and dream sweet dreams of summer – together…

All summer long the river had no competitor for our attention. The festival of the First Fruits (*Shavuot*), that we celebrate albeit without first fruits, awakens within us the need to pluck reeds and rushes from the riverbanks to decorate our houses and courtyards, a ritual from days gone by. The reeds are moist and give off a heady strong fragrance, perfuming all the Jewish homes. And not only that! It had an excellent characteristic: you could hold it lightly between your lips and blow it like a trumpet!

And when *Shavuot* was over, the chains were released, and we could bathe in the river freely. Then the children in their hundreds would gather and go to swim in the river. And their equipment? What child today can imagine to himself? A couple of bladders acquired from a butcher and inflated...no used tires, no inflatables – all unobtainable then, all the cars

[Columns 449–450]

that were in town you could count on the fingers of one hand...and even if a child had no inflated bladder to hang on to, nothing would stop him from the daily hours–long pleasure swimming in the river. There was rowing–boats available and rowing in them was an added pleasure for us.

We compared ourselves to – and felt like – millionaires in our loyalty and devotion to the river, we, that same group of permanently idle lads, poor, short of nearly all material items, would come every day to the banks of the river to forget their worries and problems in their noisy enjoyment and sometimes even forget their hunger...

Thus, the season would progress until the Feast of Tabernacles, coming to a close with the gathering of brushwood covering for our Sukkah (booth) and walking to the stream for the prayer of *Tashlich*[1]...

A farewell like autumn and autumn like a farewell...

Sunbeams still find their way through the gathering gray clouds covering the blue sky but their glitter gradually dims. The autumn leaves turn yellow and brown, and the colors of Fall cover the ground. The pleasant days of summer still live in our memories, but the inconveniences of winter are approaching and are noticeable in the homes where we now spend much time in the company of our parents...

Rosh Hashanah. Crowds go down to the river – for *Tashlich*, where the last three verses of the book of Micah[2] are recited and they symbolically shake out their pockets and cast their sins into the deep and the children stand next to their parents and do likewise . There were many groups of Jews, dressed formally in their dark festival clothes ...

And a choir of frogs serenades them with their croaking...

That was the river.

Thus were our lives connected to us by our festivals, the winter days as well as the summer days, with our holy days and our prayers.

Thus it has been since time immemorial.

Until that same day... the Memorial Day for our grandfather and grandmother, uncle and aunt, cousins, nephews and nieces – three thousand Jews of Dubno, men, women, babies...until that same day, when with the sunrise the river was used as a meeting place for Hitler's jackbooted blood–thirsty soldiers –

Until that same day the reeds and rushes of the river, that were always used to decorate our homes at festivals, were used as ambushes by wild beasts that fell upon our brethren and slaughtered them…and that same day as the sun began to set, the frogs of the river began their endless croaking for the children of Dubno who, for the time being at least, by a miracle have survived – Krah–krah–krah…

Evil, evil is the river Ikwa!

Evil, evil, damned and evil! …

Translator's Comments

1. A prayer recited on New Year symbolically casting one's sins into running water
2. Micah 7: 18–20

The History of the Jewish–Polish Gymnasium

by B. Bardiga

Translated from Hebrew by Selwyn Rose

Until 1919–1920 a Gymnasium existed in Dubno in which the language of instruction was Russian. After the conquest of Volhynia the Polish authorities ordered its liquidation and, in its place, a Polish Gymnasium was established that accepted Jewish pupils according to a strict percentage. After much effort the authorities gave a license to open a Jewish Gymnasium where instruction would be in Polish and that was on condition that the Polish authorities had no part in its upkeep and maintenance. The public activist, Mr. Avraham Karaulnik was installed as the "owner" of the license. Many were the pupils who graduated from the Gymnasium here and abroad and went on to complete their education in Poland and other countries.

The Jewish Gymnasium granted scholarships to families that had insufficient means to keep their children in the institution but even all those who paid the fees were unable collectively to maintain the Gymnasium without some support from the government and municipal establishments.

In 1934 the Gymnasium received grants from the government, but the financial situation was not improved, and the school stood on the brink of closure.

B. Bardiga. Graduating class of 1932

[Columns 319–320]

The entire financial burden fell upon the shoulders of Mr. Karaulnik who received no remuneration for his toil in the Gymnasium – quite the contrary: his involvement affected adversely his own sustenance. Most of the managers came from Galicia. The first was Mr. Kammerman from Lwow. After him came Mr. Scharr, Mr. Pozner and lastly Mr. Margolis. From among the teachers, we should mention Eliyahu Makhrok and Mr. Elimelech Blei, the veteran warrior for Hebrew in Dubno.

Group of pupils of the Polish–Jewish Gymnasium. Graduating class of 1932.

The Tarbut School in Dubno

by A. Cohen

Translated from Hebrew by Selwyn Rose

From the beginning of the 1920's the number of youngsters learning and understanding Hebrew began to grow. The youth groups *"Hechalutz"* and *"Hashomer Hatza'ir"* gave impetus to the trend as did the Hebrew library of the Zionist Federation that was later known as the *"Tarbut* Library" where a select choice of reading matter was provided. A number of private teachers toiled assiduously, either with individuals or in extra–curricular groups to pass on the language to the children; all that, and more with no promise of ultimate success.

In 1927 a branch of *"Tarbut"* was opened in town and the committee began to establish a school. The registration of pupils began for the year 1927/28 but the project failed to get off the ground. Only in the school–year 1928/29 was the school founded with three classes plus a preparatory class. That same year the school resided in the same building as the Polish–Jewish Gymnasium of Karaulnik and the lessons took place as an additional second–sitting period. The following year the school transferred to a building in Pilsudski Street and a few years later with its growth it took seat in Sirkis's building – a building that had been occupied by *"Hashomer Hatza'ir"* and a branch of *"Hechalutz"* who vacated the building in favor of the school.

In 1933 the first class of students of the *"Tarbut"* school graduated from their course of studies and such was the case with succeeding years.

From the moment of its inception the school became an important element in the Jewish public life of Dubno in general and the activities of Zionist circles in particular.

The pre–school experiment achieved exceptional success with the preparatory class. The gifted teacher Shlomo Balaban managed, within just a few months, to impart his young pupils with the Hebrew language so that they began to speak it between themselves and even introduced it into their parents' home.

At first it was just the Zionists who sent their children to the school although the institute slowly began to acquire standing within the town and non–Zionist parents – even those far from being Zionists – began sending their children to the school. The Jewish–Hebrew environment, the high standard and level of the instruction, the desire that their children acquire some level of basic Jewish tradition, the folk–law of the festivals – all these added impetus to the parents' sending their children to the "*Tarbut*" school.

The school's persona was clearly secular, and its spirit strongly oriented towards the Land of Israel. All the subjects were taught in Hebrew except the Polish language class that began to be taught in the second year after the children had already acquired familiarity with Hebrew. The traditional festivals and the renewed ones of Palestine were celebrated majestically within the walls of the school, but the echoes reached the homes of the parents and had some blessed influence on them. A special place of honor was reserved in the school for the Foundation Fund of Israel and its activities. There was also coordination of the activities of the youth groups and the school's program, each complementing the other.

Teachers and pupils of the second graduating class

In 1939 the number of pupils in the school reached four–hundred and fifty and the building became cramped for the number of pupils applying for entry. This was in spite of the fact that the school was "private" and received no support from the ruling authorities and the parents were forced to maintain it while the Ministry of Education paid in full for the government's school.

The school fees were not the same for everyone but were fixed individually according to the financial status of the parents but nevertheless the total revenues were not sufficient to cover the costs of paying the teachers' salary and from time to time it was necessary to run fancy–dress balls for both great and small in order to generate donations for the institute. Thus, there were big parties for *Hanukkah* and *Purim* in the municipal theater hall where the school

[Columns 323–324]

prominently displayed its achievements. It is worth mentioning here that during the first years of the school's operation no other way was found of organizing the salaries of the teaching staff in an orderly fashion, other than paying something on account each Thursday in proportion to the amount collected for that week. And when it became clear towards the end of the school–year that there were not enough funds to cover the year's deficit, the teachers saw no alternative but to agree to write–off the debt of the concluding year to allow the school to open for the succeeding one. Imbued as they were with the Zionist spirit, they could not allow themselves to be the cause of the school closing down because of the inability of the institute to pay their salaries.

The precarious situation of the school's finances made it necessary to create an organized body that would concern itself with mobilizing funds from external and peripheral sources, whether by organizing balls, flag–days or by donations from people of means or word of mouth. Thus was a circle of dedicated women created alongside the hospital with Mrs. Hanna Kagan and Mrs. Rivka Reiss Krantzov at its head who both worked tirelessly for the sake of the school's maintenance.

The secretary and pupils of the Tarbut school

The school's committee was headed by the staunchest Zionists in town, the honorable gentlemen: David Perle, A. Meizler, Mordecai Barchash, Moshe Cohen, David Horowitz, attorney Starr, representatives of youth movements, who changed from time to time, and women's representatives. Mrs. Esther Makhrok acted as secretary and contributed much to the prevailing good atmosphere of the institute.

The "*Tarbut*" school was without doubt the highlight of Zionist activity in town. The activists dreamed of moving to a new building, on the creation of a Gymnasium as a natural progression of the present one but then came the bitter reality that turned everything on its head and brought it all down…

In September 1939 the school was opened by order of the Soviet authorities as a school where the language of instruction was Yiddish and two years later, the rest of the Jews of the town, drank from the poisonous chalice…

Ha–Koah

by B. Bardiga

Translated from Hebrew by Selwyn Rose

The path of our youth between the two World Wars was by no means strewn with roses. Indeed, after the 1917 Revolution broad horizons opened up before them and carried on the "wings of freedom" many fascinating and exciting ideas and not a few of Dubno's citizens were drawn by the strong current of the Revolution. But those who remained faithful to themselves began searching for and striving towards a new organized and free Jewish life. It began with the creation of Jewish–Zionist modern, democratic social and education institutions. Thus in 1921 under the initiative the honorable and respected Z. Burshtein, Sh. Barchash, D Ganff, S. Dziura and S. Sodovitzky, the TOZ sporting club was opened and in time became the "*Maccabi*" club. The club developed and in 1924/25 was recognized officially by the authorities as the Jewish Sports club "*Ha–Koah*". The club was affiliated to the international alliance "*Maccabi*" and took its place in the general football league and many were the young people that clustered around it.

The "Maccabi" club members in 1923

There were many different sporting activities of *Ha–Koah* such as: football, handball, gymnastics, excursions, rambles and so on. In addition, the members of the club took part in all the Zionist initiatives and funds like the Foundation Fund of Israel etc., and all the public Zionist performances in town even though the fact that their ranks numbered youths with different political opinions and outlooks.

[Columns 327–327]

For special mention is the brass–band orchestra of the club. It acted as accompaniment at public performances and earned a good reputation from the entire Jewish population. Parades on "*Lag B'Omer*" in which pupils from the school and youth groups took part with the band of *Ha–Koah* at its head awakened pride among the onlookers of the parade and were welcomed with cheers and brought smiles to all faces. It was the appearance of the "new Jew", proud, upright and with a courageous heart.

Student–group of Ha–Koah during military training

Among the various classes in "*Ha–Koah*" there was also a class in self–defense; they knew how to reply to sudden attacks and to defend Jewish honor in the face of the anti–Semitism that arose with the encouragement of the hostile Polish government. More than one anti–Semitic bully felt the weight of "*Ha–Koah*'s" arm when they tried to interfere or threaten them in games or other public activity.

Thus, it was that in 1936 when the Polish scholar and Talmudic investigator Zuradky arrived in Dubno to lecture at the "*Ha–Koah*" club Polish rowdies tried to interfere with his lecture. They couldn't tolerate the idea that a Polish scholar should lecture in a Jewish club! The Defense Platoon of "*Ha–Koah*" vigorously came to his aid and the lecture took place. There was a scandal and blows and the anti–Semites made claims against them for dishonoring the Polish flag. But the matter never came to court and the incident served to reinforce the name of "*Ha–Koah*". Volunteers from among the womenfolk presented the club with a present – an artistically embroidered flag with the words: "The '*Ha–Koah*' Sport and Gymnastic Society of Dubno".

The day of presentation of the flag became a great event not only in the life of the club but throughout the entire Jewish community of the town. A special festival service took place in the Great Synagogue in the presence of the town's notables from both the club and the authorities. The jeweler, Mr. Ganff proudly decorated the flag–staff.

The Ha–Koah football team

The club was self–sustaining, without finance from external sources. The members paid membership fees and organized public sports meetings that drew large crowds, and these revenues were used to maintain the club.

[Columns 329–330]

On the eve of the war and the Holocaust many refugees arrived in the town and "*Ha–Koah*" called upon all its members to offer them all possible assistance and indeed many of them gave much help and extended a hand to their unfortunate brethren.

When the Soviet authorities took over in 1939 the "*Ha–Koah*" club became known as "*Spartak*" and the entire inventory and resources were transferred to them. But one item was not found: the wonderful flag of "*Ha–Koah*" the faithful emblem of the people to its past and its future, folded but not given to the despoilers of the people and their spirit. The hiding place of the flag was known only to Mr. Ganff; and since most of the members of "*Ha–Koah*" perished in the Holocaust it is not impossible to think that the flag was taken by them to the mass grave…

The Amateur Theater

by Moishe Katchke

Translated from Hebrew by Selwyn Rose

A

I don't know, nor will I ever know if anybody remembers the restrictions placed upon Yiddish theatrical productions by the Tsarist regime in 1907, populating different areas including Volhynia. It seems the restriction came as a collective punishment on the Jews for their participation in the 1904/05 Revolution.

I remember the group of Jewish actors' great success at their presentation at the local theater for a number of weeks, of their production in 1907. I was a young man at the time and one summer Saturday night that same year, I saw their presentation of *"Hertzel'eh Ha-Meyuhas"* before a standing-room only audience. At the end of the performance, word spread that it had been the last one and it seems as if I can still hear the rustle of surprised voices throughout the hall at the announcement of the prohibition to continue and that the ban had so suddenly come upon Dubno.

Thus, that summer brought an end to the Jewish theater until the days of the Kerensky revolution.

The Jewish population of Dubno felt a great loss with the cessation of the Yiddish production especially the working classes, since the Intelligentsia were able to patronize the Russian theater or the Ukrainian operettas like "Kamara" and "Natalka Poltavka" and only the general population remained without entertainment. There was no permanent movie theater in those years except a mobile one that would appear from time to time featuring a number of shows in the *"Rathaus"* hall.

In the meantime, at the end of 1914 a rumor was heard in Dubno that a group of amateur players in Rowno was renewing the presentation of Jewish plays; the income would be devoted to treating the war-injured and the permission for it was obtained from the Tsar's eldest daughter who administered the military hospitals in Rowno.

Following the rumor, the group of Jewish amateurs in Dubno joined together for a great struggle: it was decided to present Goldfaden's "*Bar Kochba*".

Also, when I was young, I was occasionally given a place in the chorus because of my voice. The rehearsals took place in the rooms of Tov'leh Peled (Tovel the shoemaker) in Stare Street with the following cast:

1. Wolf, the son-in-law of Brindle the seamstress, a mature baritone who could read music very well - played the role of Bar Kochba;
2. Mrs. Maria Kozier, the daughter of the old woman from Pantalia, a rich soprano and acting ability – cast as Dina the fiancée of Bar Kochba
3. Lazar Barchash, owner of a tinsmith shop opposite the city well, was cast as Eliezer, Dina's father.
4. Benzie, Tov'leh Peled's son-in-law;
5. Avraham, Yohanan Spektor's son, tenor;
6. Berl Shojcher, bass;
7. Myself, the youngest and others – the chorus.

We rehearsed for a couple of weeks. The hall was already engaged, and messengers were sent to Rowno to the government office to obtain the license for a Yiddish production for the benefit of wounded soldiers – but there was no permission and – as people say NO! With a capital 'N'! for the amateurs of Dubno and all our toil had been in vain. Again, silence rang down the curtain on the Jewish stage – until the Revolution.

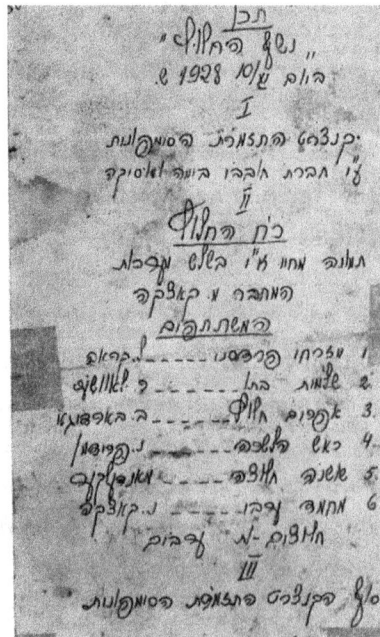

After the festival of *Shavuot* in 1918, when I returned from Czechoslovakia after a stay of three years, I discovered from an announcement that the local amateurs were going to present in the near future the musical "David's Harp" using the premises of the local dignitary, Mr. Greenberg. When that same evening I approached the booking office to buy tickets, my friends Haim Feinghort, (today in the USA) and Herschel Wilner (today in Buenos Aires), who told me that a certain actor who had been cast to play the part of Startist was unable to appear and I could be his replacement if I agreed to do so. I couldn't refuse the request of my old friends and we immediately went back-stage to the dressing-rooms so that I could make-up and dress for the role – in this particular instance – that of a woman.

As a youth I appeared in the play "David's Harp" in that same role that was also played by another young man and the fact that it was that of a female made no difference – except for the wearing of a woman's red wig with a plait hanging down the back and her little finger of her right hand held constantly between her lips all the time hanging on to her father's caftan. Occasionally the father would slap her hand and tell her to take her finger out of her mouth although Tehilah – that was the role's name – obstinately goes her own way and from time-to-time bursts into a wild neighing laugh.

The audience never discovered that I was a boy and the role of a simpleton that I played made a great impression. Eventually, at the end, when the audience expected the players to appear on stage and – as is usual without their make-up – I, too, removed my wig and before the audience stood not a girl but a young man…

Spontaneous applause broke out in the hall and from that time I belonged to the group of amateur players as an active member. The members of the group were:

Haim Feinghort, Meir Talberstein, Herschel Wilner, Shlomo Lederman, Lazar Eisenberg, Manny Kinstein, W. Poticha, Liza Rosenfeld, Bilha Kram and the writer of these lines.

B

The season didn't last long, at the most until the beginning of 1919. Then the power moved from Hetman Skoropadski to Petliura. On the eve of the *Purim* festival in 1919 the local villagers organized themselves in order to oust Petliura's men from the town and the following day the resurgent leadership based in one of the villages began moving towards town in the hundreds, Ukrainians from the suburbs of Zabramie to Surmicze and to the barracks the central

[Columns 335–336]

meeting point of the Sitsower and Galician units of Petliura forces. These regiments
were stunned at the sight of the weapon-bearing Ukrainian civilians advancing upon
them and retreated in panic as far as the railroad station intending to flee the place. At
that same time the revolutionaries were about to encircle the station approaching from
the direction of nearby villages, but the encirclement wasn't fulfilled because the
Sitsower unit began bombarding them and they retreated with heavy losses. From the
railroad station the Sitsower forces returned to town and began hunting for whoever
they could find and thus twenty-one young people, suspected of belonging to the
young Jewish activists, fell into their hands. These young people were brutally
slaughtered, and their bodies cast into an open pit near the White Barracks.

Bottom row, right to left: Diner, Nahum Katchke;
Second row: Rachel Luwshit, Lulke Kram, Sonny Freidman, M. Katchke;
Third row: Itka, Fishbein, Rivka Warech, Miriam Mendelberg, Paltenzon, Ita Frankel, Hanna Falk;
Fourth row: Poticha Michal, Gochberg Avraham, Goshkis Avraham, Gochberg, jun.;
Fifth row: Warech, Pressman Shamai (See editorial comment below)

After that black *Purim* many young people fled Dubno to the various surrounding communities and I escaped to a small hamlet on the road. There I chanced to meet Hershe'le Wilner and Eisenstadt, also from Dubno. The local Jews were as if from another continent – living quietly and undisturbed. Unemployment brought us to seek out public activity and together with the local young people we staged a musical play with the accompaniment of a local orchestra. We also staged a production of "The Estimable Hertz'la". The success brightened our lives and the income was dedicated to the local charitable organizations.

After a short time, I returned to Dubno but 1919 to 1920 were years of invasions - for a start the communists and the Poles after them, mobilization followed mobilization with no settled organization or order. Only in 1921–1922 did life return to normal when the Poles and the Russians finally came to some kind of peace agreement. Then the Jewish youth of Dubno became united with charitable Zionist organizations such as "*Leinat Ha-Tzedek*" and local hospitals. (*Leinat Ha-Tzedek* filled a most important function among the needy classes by reaching out with medical assistance and was always in need of financial assistance). Also the Jewish "Amateur Theatrical Group" renewed its activities and new young members were added: N. Kram; Chaika Feinlitt; Moshe Pinchosovich; Feyga Valder and Shmuel Toister, Feyga's husband.

The cast of "Heroes of Kastinia"

The first play we staged was *"Bubbeh Yachneh"* ("Granny Gossip"). Moshe Pinchosovich took upon himself the role of the likeable 'grandma' and it was he who brought a rousing success to the production. It was his last appearance but before every opening night he would come to rehearsals and give his professional observations and for us, the young actors, his criticisms were welcomed from all aspects.

We mostly staged dramas and operettas accompanied by the Dubno orchestra among whose players were: Moshe Streiner (violin), Mendel Katchke (clarinet), and Eliyahu Kagan (piano). In time we staged the following: "The Witch", "Chinka Pinka", "The Village Boy", "The American", "The *Yeshiva* Boy", "David's Harp", "The Estimable Hertz'le", "The Dybukk", and "The Wise Scholar". The group had its own regular prompter, Eliyahu Centner. Lazar Eizenberg was in charge of scenery and the barber, Fichanyuk was the make-up artist.

The preparation for the production was as follows:

First of all, we read the text and afterwards allocated the roles. As is usual with the *"hoi-polloi"* the allocation of roles did not go forward peacefully or without jealousy and gossip. For two weeks after, there were rehearsals, the last of which – with all the associated "business" – took place on stage. On opening night, the cast came early to make-up and attend to their costumes and with all the hurry and scurry and hesitancies the curtain went up. Obviously, there were errors, but the audience was not aware of them and the applause and acceptance were encouraging.

In 1925 the group began to disperse, this one for that reason and that one for another and the group separated. Wilner immigrated to Argentina, Haim Feinghort and Leah Rosenfeld to the United States and the writer of these lines to Mandated Palestine. With the vacuum created in the group by the loss of the veterans their places began to be filled with a group of artisans. At their head were Avraham Katchke, Ya'acov Pergamen and Meir Kubinius who were among the management. The productions were reduced to a variety of "sketches" of one type or another.

It is necessary to note that from 1922 until 1925 a number of activities gathered around the Histadrut that displayed an interest in the theater. The group took part in the academic productions and dances and created a pleasant choir conducted by the Hebrew teacher Balaban (of blessed memory).

[Columns 339–340]

At the end of 1928 when I came to Dubno from Palestine on a visit to my family, I came to know the branch of "*Hechalutz*". Its members who knew something of my history resolutely insisted that I produce something of "Zionist Pioneering" concerning which they had little or no suitable material. I prepared a sort of "audition" among the boys and girls in the branch and discovered considerable talent and from these I created a presentation in three acts of what is occurring in Palestine, together with songs and many dances - all directed to the wholesomeness of the "*Hechalutz*". The name of the show was "Strength of the Hechalutz or The Heroes of Kastinia". The committee formed from among the members Avraham Hoz, Avraham Hochberg and others confirmed the success of the production with much fanfare. As the writer and producer of the play I was very proud, and the participants were full of enthusiasm and excitement. The technical aspects and script were of a high standard. Most of the visitors were from Zionist circles and their supporters and unanimously expressed the opinion that in a short hour they felt that their spirits had been transferred to the Land of Israel. The play was also staged in surrounding towns Varkovichi, Demidovka and Berestechko. The effervescent content so excited the many national pioneering youngsters that at the beginning of the thirties many immigrated to Mandatory Palestine. With that came the end of acting and popular theatrical productions in Dubno and the county.

Translator's and Editor's Comments

1. In spite of endless attempts and searches, both in Hebrew and in English, word by word, through tens of references on the internet, professionally related to the topic, I was unable to find English language verification for several of the productions mentioned, especially (and unexpectedly) those of Avraham Goldfaden and one or two other names, etc. I beg the understanding of the reader (tc).

2. It seems, judging by the names, that the order of the third row should be read left to right. Also please note that some names are written with surname first, others with given name first (ec).

Jewish Weddings and Musicians

by Moishe Katchke

Translated from Yiddish by Pamela Russ

There was a musical band in Dubno. They played at Jewish weddings and at farmers' weddings, as well as in the courts of the aristocrats. The last of these bands were murdered by the Hitlerist demons of torture – may their names and memories be erased. Dear Jews, musicians of Dubno – God will avenge the spilling of your innocent blood...

*

Of the musicians in the band in Dubno at the beginning of the current century, I have the following individuals etched in my memory:

Reuven Tzimering, who played the clarinet, and was a genius at writing musical notes. He augmented his livelihood in that he also acted as assistant cantor in the large synagogue in Dubno. Having no choice, he was also a Torah reader in one of the *shteiblech* [informal, smaller synagogues] which was near the *shul* [synagogue] where, between the evening and night prayers [*mincha* and *maariv*] he would run in for a few minutes and also learn a chapter of *Mishnayos* [Oral Law].

Reb Eli the musician, Eli Struner, who played the second fiddle, a God–fearing man, was the sexton all his life in the shoemakers' *Beis Medrash* [Study Hall].

Reb Mendel the musician, Mendel Katchke, played exceptionally well on the cornet [trumpet], and was very skilled in writing musical notes. In Nikolai's army, he rose to the rank of sergeant. In the military band in Lutsk, he played the cornet. His religion went so far that during the four years of his service to the Tsar he never ate from the army "food." In his circle, during the High Holidays, he would lead the Musaf [afternoon] prayers for the congregation.

The other musicians in Dubno were similar to that – people with pure character and masters of the smaller arts [of music].

357

In the 90s of the previous century [1890s], there were ten men in the band. There was a *badchan* [Jewish professional jester, entertainer, rhymester; uses Torah overtones in lyrics; performs at Jewish weddings, festive events, etc.], and a first fiddle. If a good fiddler was missing, then they would hire another fiddler for "a time", that stretched from Shavuos [month of June] until the High Holidays [late September], because the summer season is a prime time for weddings. The towns around Dubno belonged to these musicians as a *chazakah* [right of ownership, after performing or enacting an event three times, this becomes a "*chazakah*"]. No other musicians from outside the town played there. At that time, when it was impossible to imagine a wedding without musicians, the monies they earned were not bad, especially since the weddings lasted almost a week. This is how they went:

For about one month before the wedding, two musicians, the most popular of the band, would visit the father of the bride to set the terms for the wedding and then also come to an agreement about the "payment." All this was – according to the status of the *mechutanim* [parents, in–laws of bride and groom] (beginning with 10 rubles, up to 50 rubles). Included with the calculations of the payment were:

"Seating the bride, meaning leading her from the place of the wedding to the wedding canopy in the large synagogue, and then back home – along with the sounds of "festivities." Often the wedding procession would wind through several streets, until the *mechutanim* were also escorted home, thus the musicians would be playing with the so–called "extended motives".

The musicians allowed themselves such a grand escort only through the streets inhabited by Jews, until reaching the wider street. So, in the streets Alexandrovka, Koscielna, Panienska, and Zamkova, these kinds of wedding processions could not take place because these areas were already mixed with non–Jews and also because the Jews there were already of a different type.

All these ceremonies were included in the "payment" but the money for the dancing was extra. Until World War One, these were the dances:

A "quadrille" performed by four couples, it cost four kopecks, and lasted about fifteen minutes. This was a respectable dance, with a slow tempo.

Then there was the "Sherele," [the "scissor dance"; see "Helen's Yiddish Dance Page" for details. One source of this dance's name is that it is originally a tailor's guild dance with the figures meant to represent a pair of shears and threading the needle.[1]]

[Column 667–668]

They took about 10 kopeks from each couple. The "Sher" was a dance that started with a slow tempo and ended with a stormy gallop.

A "*Freilachs*"[2] was a dance for only two people, a man and a woman, or two people of the same gender. In the beginning, the dancers would distance themselves four meters from each other; when the music started, one person danced toward the other, in various directions and steps, the hands positioned downwards, and the feet swinging in all sides, back and forth. They danced so long, until they fell from exhaustion. At that moment, one of the dancers would change partners by raising his hand and taking the place of the exhausted one, trying with all his strength and efforts to surpass the former dancers until both would be fired up and collapse in ecstasy, throwing their hands onto the other person's shoulders.

Then the musicians would speed up the tempo of the music and without stop, the *mechutanim* would clap their hands with appreciation and acknowledgement. The women fanned themselves with their scarves and with that, they showed their understanding of which dancer outdid his partner. This type of "*Freilachs*" cost – 20 kopeks.

There was also the "Kossak" that was the same price. These were all folk dances for adults and for the wedding families. The youth would demonstrate their capacity with waltzes, Krakowiaks [traditional Polish folk dance], and so on.

They also used to dance a Boston Waltz, and a Lezginka– Czerkes dance with a knife in hand, that was received with wild applause.

Most of the dancing took place before the *chuppah* [wedding ceremony], and a smaller portion of the dancing was after the *chuppah*, about eleven o'clock at night. After that, the tables were prepared for a festive meal. Special cooks were ordered to prepare the food. The honey cakes, fludens [fruit and nut pastry], and koumiss rolls [made from fermented brew] had an especially delicious taste.

First, they would bring the gefilte fish to the table. Then the roasted meats. Then came the lineup for the famous "golden wedding soup," with baked almond-shaped croutons made from pure wheat flour. And then, at the end, everyone enjoyed a delicious compote [poached fruit dessert].

During the entire festive meal, the musicians were not idle, and they played for the guest and for the young couple the "*Dobra Nocze*" ("A Good Night"). Before the beginning of the melody, the *badchan* [the entertainer, rhymer, singer] would call out loudly:

"In honor of the respected, important in–law…" (This was done in Hebrew.) When the melody was over, the *badchan* would once again remind everyone for whom this music was being performed.

For playing the "*Dobra Nocze*" the musicians were paid extra.

After the meal, the *badchan* recited an accounting of the dowry for the couple – all kinds of furnishings, dishes, and silverware. Then they would move the tables to the side, the musicians would play something joyous, and everyone joined in to dance the polka.

One of the *chassidim* held the corner of a scarf in his hand and the bride held the other corner – and that's how they danced the "celebration of the bride and groom." Meanwhile, it began to get lighter outside, and the musicians would escort the parents to their home.

The Tsar's police, and later the Poles' police, were not disturbed to have these wedding ceremonies. In the street, where the wedding took place, the police also came to have a look at how they were dancing. When the *mechutanim* saw the representatives of the authority, they opened the doors and invited them in, poured a double shot of whiskey and gave them a bite of food. The waltzing was "allowed" to go on, and then the couple was thanked [by the police] for having been their guests...

The *mechutanim* were proud of the police's visit and commented: "A real honor..."

If the musicians were invited by a wealthy person or by an "intellectual," they immediately went to "polish up" their instruments. They would also organize themselves, dressing in their best, and

[Column 669–670]

most beautiful [garments] that they possessed. None of the musicians was allowed to be missing from this wealthy wedding. If there was no choice, they would borrow an extra player from the Czech neighbors.

Jewish–Christian Committee for Charity Work (Doryanski Club)

In particular, the musicians would look out for a butcher's wedding, because a butcher would organize a wedding as for a king and his hand was generous for the musicians. The payment alone was high, and the "accessories" were many because the "*Freilach*" dance of the butchers was a dance with great passion. And their favorite theme [melody] was "Tzirele." During this dance, the dancers stomped rhythmically with their boots and sang along with the musicians:

"Tzirele, Mirele, hold the sack,

I will throw you a parsnip."

The musicians would leave the butcher's wedding with a profit of 60 or 70 rubles, aside from the agreed payment. They would bring along with them a closed box into which all the "accessories" had been tossed in. When they came home, in the presence of three or four players, the box was opened, the money counted, and was left with the "treasurer" to divide it all up. This dividing up took place once a month. The income was not given out just like that.

The good musician received a portion and a quarter, and many times, even two portions. Mendel the musician would get two whole portions and the bass not more than one portion. Sometimes – even less.

Generally, the "treasurer" was ignorant, but for dividing up the money, he was an expert. In Ukraine, the musicians had their own "alphabet" and numbers, and the dividing up was done according to this "alphabet," exactly to the last letter.

During the division, the members of the band would take small shots of whiskey and then each one of them hurried home, bringing his wife the "blessings" for

[Column 671–672]

which she was keenly looking out. For this "blessing," the small merchants and storekeepers were also keeping their eyes open, those who used to sell on credit, as was the melamed [children's teacher] and the landlord – one for tuition and the other for rent.

It was also accepted that the musicians would play for the *pritzim* [princes, aristocrats] in the area and for the farmers. A wedding for the farmers brought in from 20 to 30 rubles – and that was the tradition.

The groom, in the company of his escorts ("*kum*") [generally his parents], came into the city and went right to the musicians, and then negotiated the price with them. On the wedding day, a special wagon rode through the city and took the musicians into the village. The troupe was expert in wedding music of the non–Jews and played whatever the hosts wanted.

With the farmers, the tradition was that when an important guest crossed their threshold, the band welcomed him with a "march," even if because of him they had to interrupt a dance. Because of that, the guest donated money to the musicians, as much as their hearts and pockets allowed…

Often, the farmers' weddings ended with scandals and fighting. More than once, it happened that the musicians had to grab up their instruments and run home through the windows, barely alive.

If it happened that a circus came to town, the musicians quickly polished their instruments until they shone, and they played their music according to the needs of the circus. Even though the musicians were religious people, they knew when and how to play at every opportunity.

They did not leave behind any inheritance for their children and their sons did not follow in the ways of their parents, because the livelihood of the musicians was small and poor…

Translator's Comments

1. For further details, see https://www.yiddishdance.com/dance–descriptions.htm], in which there were as many dancers as they wanted.
2. Ibid

Occupations of the Simple Folk

by Asher Reichman

Translated from Yiddish by Yocheved Klausner

In general, the biblical verse in Genesis 3 "In the sweat of your face shall you eat bread" can very well refer to the majority of the Dubno Jews, who have been chasing after their livelihood - *parnasa* - and never fully reached it. Their occupations were numerous and varied: commerce on a big scale as well as small businesses, brokers, peddlers, grocers; doctors, lawyers, teachers and the like; employees and independent workers; and a significant number of people whose profession or occupation could not be exactly defined. They were the people who labored hard, doing difficult physical work - the water carriers, the carriage drivers, occupations that were practiced only by Jews.

They managed to keep proper and respectable relations, in spite of the harsh competition. A special group of people, albeit not officially organized, was able to protect the interests of the workers, just as if they belonged to official unions. Actually, there were three such unions: the carriers or porters, the carriage drivers and the cart owners. The more privileged among them were, naturally, the carriage drivers. They, too, could be divided into those who possessed beautiful, ornate and well-kept carriages and those who had the old and worn-out ones, which begged for repair and refurbishing. Their work was to drive passengers to the train station (a distance of 5 kilometers from the center of town) and back, bring the sick to the doctor, or take families to a joyous event - a wedding or a party, or just a visit. Thanks to their type of work, they were in contact with many residents of the town, and befriended many of them. They were always ready to tell a joke or some funny characteristic story about one person or another. They were the primary source of every "secret" that had ceased to be a secret, because it was told "secretly" in the ear, but it rolled from carriage to carriage and from street to street, and of course every person added a bit of information to the story…

The wagon-masters trade

Another type of people were the "*balagules*" [owners of hauling carts] whose work was to transport heavy loads or deliver merchandise that would arrive from other towns. They were simple folk, "everyday Jews," but their material situation was a better one. Their center of activity was mostly in the suburb of Surmicze, but they worked in other neighborhoods as well. Their apartments were better and more comfortable than those of other people in the same social class.

The main assembly-point of the carriers and porters was at the end of Szeroka Street, near the courthouse, always ready to go at the first call to load or unload wares, carry loads from one place to another or transfer furniture from one apartment to another. Their clothes were simple - an old and mostly torn jacket, pants tucked in their boots, which they wore summer and winter, a cap and a long rope tied around their middle: this was their working tool. Their back betrayed their occupation: it was always bent - this form given to it by the sacks of flour it had carried. In the hot summer-days they would catch a short nap in the shade of some house, in the winter they would jump and dance and pat themselves on the shoulders to get warm.

All those Jews, however, simple and humble as they were, possessed a strong Jewish-national consciousness, warm hearts and a feeling of sharing in joy and compassion in sorrow. They were hard-working Jews, who made their living with what God in Heaven had given them, friendly, ready to help each other and forgive and make peace in the case of a conflict or misunderstanding. They had their own synagogues and prayer-houses where they would feel "at home," and on the Sabbath and Holidays they felt certain that the "*Shechina*" [the Divine Spirit] was dwelling upon their houses of prayer.

But dark days have reached the town - not days of reverence, but of horror and pain. And all those strong, robust men have perished, died "*Al Kidush Hashem*" - for the sanctification of the Name of God.

Matzo-Making Machines Come to Dubno

by Moshe Cohen

Translated from Hebrew by Selwyn Rose

At the end of the nineteenth century a rumor spread around town that in the big cities, like Odessa, Kharkov, Warsaw and others they were beginning to bake matzot with machines. Only a few years later there appeared in our home a family member from Odessa Mr. Yisroel Shochet and introduced himself to my father as a specialist with matzo-making machines. He even brought with him wooden molds for producing the machine parts and proposed to my father that they create a partnership in a "modern" matzo-baking bakery. My father considered the proposition and agreed to it; he gave his partner the necessary amount of money and the man went to the factory in Mlynow to order the castings for the machines.

This was in the autumn of 1903.

In the meantime, my father looked for a suitable site for a bakery with storage space for the flour and the finished matzot, and rented a half-destroyed house of the sexton's wife, facing the synagogue. He made the necessary repairs and installed the special oven. In addition, he rented a storage space in Soroka Street for the flour and in Yankel Groipen's house in the same street a place to store the matzot.

The machine parts arrived and Mr. Yisroel Shochet erected them and prepared them for operation.

On *Tu B'Shvat* (15ᵗʰ *Shvat*), 1ˢᵗ February 1904 the oven was lighted for the first time. Everything was ready to begin the baking and the local Rabbis, conspicuous citizens and community leaders were invited to come and see the bakery in operation and grant the necessary certification for *Kashrut*. After the exacting examination the certificate was given. But with the appearance of the matzot in the market it became clear that one important fact had not been taken into account: The Jews of Dubno were accustomed to round matzot...

That same year only 40% of the baked matzot for Passover were sold while the rest were sold after the festival at half-price. The financial loss was heavy.

In the autumn 1904 my father sold the machines to Moshe Kalinowski for 150 rubles – a small proportion of what had been his total investment in the above business. Indeed after a few years bakeries were founded in Dubno for baking matzot not only for the Jews of Dubno but also for the other larger communities of Poland.

Matzo Baking in Dubno

by B. Bardiga

Translated from Hebrew by Selwyn Rose

Dubno was one of the towns in Poland to start baking matzot mechanically instead of manually. My father (of blessed memory) Mr. Yehuda initiated a foundry belonging to a Count, for the casting of machine-parts for the production of matzo in Mlynow at the beginning of the First World War. My father prepared the drawings for the casting, the result was satisfactory and Dubno began producing machine-made matzot. The factory grew with the years and created work for 400 workers especially during the winter months when there was usually considerable unemployment from January until April. The quality of the matzot created a good name for Dubno matzot and the product reached as far as Belgium.

Baking matzot

367

It is easy to speculate that the orthodox *Rabbanut*[1] tried very hard to block the production that deviated in some respects from accepted norms for baking matzot but in 1934-1936 its attitude changed for the better because the benefits to the factory and to Dubno were so conspicuous that the *Rabbanut* could no longer ignore it. By chance the pioneering youth organization "Gordonia"[2] also benefited from the factory, in that its members received employment during those same years – especially during the cold months - from the unexpected source.

For the years 1912–1914 the supply of flour came from the water-powered flour-mill rented by Mr. Yakira and his family although at the time of the Austrian invasion when there was no wheat, the town's Rabbi declared it permissible to use hulled wheat. During the hard years 1916–1917 the bakery operated as a cooperative, while in 1920 the industrialist from Lodz, Menahem Holler came to Dubno and introduced a new effervescent vitality into the industry both in the wholesale manufacture of matzot and the special packaging in cartons. The quantity of water used by Mr. Holler was very small and as a result his matzot were especially dry and crisp and the quantity he was able to export to certain locations amounted to ten thousand kilograms. Mr. Holler brought his flour from the town of Lutsk. He also succeeded in acquiring from the Rabbi Velvel'eh religious clearance for a general bakery both within and outside the town.

[Columns 349–350]

We can learn of the advances in the industrial preparation of matzot from the fact that from 1931 the whole industry became mechanized and non-Jewish employees also worked in the bakeries, under the critical supervision of the rabbinical inspectors.

From 1925 six mechanized matzo bakeries operated in Dubno: Alter Phaltz; the Great Synagogue bakery; the bakery of Hertz Tessler. The town notable, Czerkas himself supplied one-hundred and twenty thousand kilograms of matzot between 1925 and 1934 for sale outside Dubno. Before the Second World War Dubno produced to Lwow, Pashamyzl, Lodz, Warsaw, Bialystok, Katowice, Posen, Tarnow and Piotrkow. There were even enthusiastic purchasers in Antwerp for Dubno's matzot.

Translator's Footnotes

1. The Rabbinical council.
2. "Gordonia" was a Zionist youth movement. The movement's doctrines were based on the beliefs of Aaron David Gordon, i.e. the salvation of Eretz Yisrael and the Jewish People through manual labor and the revival of the Hebrew language. For a full description see: https://en.wikipedia.org/wiki/Gordonia_youth_movement

Zionism – and its Reward

by Aviezer Zaks

Translated from Hebrew by Selwyn Rose

We all know the event took place in 1906.

That same year I was living in Dubno, Volhynia County in Russia. Around the same time in partnership with three friends we opened a private school; it was a "*Heder Metukan*"[1] – we taught Hebrew in the Hebrew language and the institution earned a good reputation among the public. "*Heder Metukan*" was understandably not well-liked by the older established traditional and learned scholars who opened a concerted opposition to us, not even hesitating to tittle-tattle against us vindictively… in fact we were virtually all, professionally suited to the task and each one of us had in possession some kind of official document from the inspector of schools and educational establishments proving our fitness for the role of educator. Nevertheless, what needs to be added is an understanding of the expression "professionally suited" in the framework of the times because then – like now – much depended on "who you know" and "who knows you".

Author and poet Aviezer Zaks

It was during this period that the Zionists convened a province-wide – in effect, national – conference in the town of Rowno. In Dubno the two delegates chosen were the writer and poet Mr. Zalman Ashkenazi of blessed memory, and I. The delegates to the congress came from Dubno, Kamyanetz (Komenetz) and other places close to the Austrian border. Also taking part in the conference was the noted Zionist leader Menahem Sheinkin of blessed memory and the government-recognized Rabbi from Balta Podolia. The council conducted itself formally with elected chairmen, secretaries, veteran party members, an opposition, supporters of Herzl's ideology and those of Usushkin's – all of them pushing to make speeches, most of them saying little new. During the closing ceremonies when all the delegates were gathered together to honor Sheinkin, a delegate from one of the villages close to the border stood up and began to give voice to a serious problem: He described in touching words the fate of many refugees who had left Russia with no official passport. Their misfortune was to fall into the hands of many so-called "agents" and border smugglers. It was because of this that he had come to claim the attention and ears of the gathered Zionists, especially those from the border villages, that even though it was

[Columns 351–352]

not specifically a core Zionist issue it behooved them to form aid committees to be present when their trains arrived at railway stations to welcome them, assist them, to assist them with advice and support in safeguarding their property and belongings from would-be thieves and similar vagabonds. The Zionists must prove, he asserted, that they are the sensitive and active part of the people. After this delegate's comments the party commenced and praises and compliments were showered on the head of Sheinkin – there were those who compared him to the Maccabees while others to Bar-Kochba, and those paying the compliments returned time and time again on their flowery expressions of praise.

While the party was still in full swing a cable from Dubno was handed to me; it was from my colleague at the school, and he informed me that the police had come and closed our "*Heder Metukan*" because "it was illegal for several teachers to be giving instruction while gathered together under one roof" and only the inspector sitting in Kamyanetz had the authority to re-interpret the law and he was the only one who could give permission to reopen the "*Heder Metukan*".

Present at the party was a noted delegate from Kamyanetz named Meshullam (his family name escapes me) and when he heard of the "*Heder Metukan*" issue he promised me that he would grant me every possible assistance if I will approach him in Kamyanetz. I bid farewell to all my colleagues and hurried to the railroad station while the ceremony was still in progress, in order to arrive at Kamyanetz without delay.

Here we are aboard the train flying towards Kamyanetz and at one of the small stations a Jewish woman burst into the railcar loaded down with innumerable parcels and packages. In great agitation she told us that this is the third night she finds herself wandering around on the railways – she comes from Kyiv (Kiev) and this night she has to be in Kamyanetz and from there to a small village near the border where an "agent" will be waiting for her and together with other Jews she will be smuggled over the border. From there she will travel to her husband in America.

A warm glow swept through me and I instantly heard the echo of the delegate calling upon us to aid our brethren in distress... I sat her down on the seat and arranged all her belongings in a pile and offered her some food to revive her soul. She recovered her composure somewhat and leaning back in her seat quickly fell asleep while I sat there and looked after her belongings. At every single station ticket inspectors came aboard and woke all the sleeping passengers and checked the tickets of everyone. "Our" Jewish woman opened one eye, produced her ticket and immediately fell asleep again. Thus, the night hours passed until we arrived at Kamyanetz. Here she awoke and began to gather together all her belongings and pushed her way towards the door while I stood by and helped to make way for her. By doing this I became the last person in the car and returned to my seat to collect my suitcase and what did I see before my eyes? A woman's coat lying precisely in the place the woman had been sitting. It was clearly hers. I picked it up and hurried off the train turning this way and that to see if I could spot her along the platform – but she was nowhere to be seen so she had certainly already left the station.

I took the coat to the station-master's office and said to him: "Sir, please take this woman's coat from me, I found it left behind in the train just arrived from Rowno, in the place where she had been sitting The officer caught hold of my arm and led me into a side-room where he ordered me to shake the contents of the coat's pockets out and also to empty my own pockets all the time questioning me as to my identity, where I was from, where I was going and then asked for my passport.

I said: "Officer! What have I done that you should question me so?"

He replied: "We know plenty of "birds" like you, finding lost property left behind in the railway carriages…"

I said: "But I'm the one who brought this article to you."

He replied: "Nobody asked you to take the coat from where you found it and bring it to me"!

Everything turned dark before my eyes with the look of suspicion in the officer's face. What a nice thing that's going to be to stand before a magistrate in a Dubno court. Even if I am cleared, what will the world think, especially the teachers, about "the matter of the woman's coat"? How would you yourself feel before all of creation knowing you are innocent?

I pleaded with the officer for understanding and a measure of forgiveness, but his reply was a vehement "No!"

"We know you Yids!" he shouted at me loudly. "Who knows if you don't belong to some damned gang or other? And even if what you say is true and you don't belong to any gang – even so what you did was against the law! Who are you to me? Let the judge deal with you in your town of Dubno; let him decide who and what you are! We'll see each other; in the meantime, get out of my sight!"

My insides churned in anger but what could I do? Having no option, I went to Kamyanetz and there I found the delegate Meshullam. With released anger I told him the story of "the woman's coat and the official". Meshullam broke down in laughter, took out a note of three rubles and sent it to the inspector to appease his feelings and my passport was returned to me and not only that but the inspector also renewed my teacher's certificate for our "*Heder Metukan*".

Happy and full of satisfaction, I returned to Dubno.

Translator's Footnote

1. "*Heder Metukan*" was a late "spin-off" from the Jewish "Enlightenment" period known as "Haskala" – a response to Jewish traditional, orthodox Rabbinical Judaism. One of its more obvious and immediate "pillars" was the introduction of education for the children in Hebrew rather than only Yiddish or other National language.

Or-Torah

by B. Elimelech

Translated from Hebrew by Selwyn Rose

An ancient town indeed is Dubno in the County of Volhynia and many years ago was famous for her scholars and geniuses. There, there was an equally old *Beit Ha-Midrash* carrying the name "*Or-Torah*" and there sat the scholars of the town day and night busy with studying *Torah*. All who passed by the building, either by day or by night, heard the voice – the voice of Ya'acov - and said: "That can only be a house of G-d." Except on Friday, from noon until the hour of welcoming the Sabbath, then the voices were stilled. The sad tones penetrating the heart and soul, the sound of the *Gemara* being studied and in the building, silence reigned, a holy silence, and only the sound of the sexton's footsteps could be heard echoing throughout the building as he walked about. During these hours the scholars prepared themselves, purifying their bodies in the ritual baths readying themselves to greet the Queen –Sabbath, while the sexton cleans the candle-sticks and places in them the Sabbath candles, changes the decorated curtain of the Holy Ark with its Sabbath counterpart, fills the bowl with water for washing the hands and changes the towels for clean ones – all to honor the Sabbath.

While all this was happening, there lived a Jew in Breslau (Wrocław), Germany. The man, an illiterate peasant, knew no *Torah* as such and kept no Commandments; he had no sons. The man had heard of the Jews of the countries of Eastern Europe, knew of them being immersed in the living *Torah* and keeping the Commandments, performing acts of charity every day of their lives with their hearts and souls drawn to G-d. His heart was drawn to them more and more as each day passed; at night he was unable to sleep, and all his food lost its flavor as it passed his lips for his soul yearned after his brethren in the lands of the east. And the day came when he said to his wife: "Why are we dwelling among the Christians? The *Torah* we know not, neither do we keep the Commandments of G-d and the day of our fate will arrive. We shall be buried in the graves of the Christians and our names will be erased from the memory of Man for we have no son to remember us or to pray for our souls after our death. Come! Let us leave this place and walk to where our brethren, the Children of Israel dwell and settle ourselves with them and there we will learn from them to keep the

373

Commandments of G-d and walk in His ways and when we walk the way of all the earth we will be buried in a grave of Israel and perhaps there will even be found good people who will pray the *Kaddish* prayer after we pass away and we will rest on our eternal resting place in peace."

His wife agreed to his proposal, and they arose and departed thence. And they walked from the west to the east and came to the place that was called the "Lower (earthly) Garden of Eden"[3] which is at the "navel" of the country called Ukraine. Broad fields of arable land spread around and forests of sturdy oak trees[4] with stout branches such that the early settlers called the place "Dubno". And the man and his wife came to the place and dwelt there in Dubno. And they were happy when they saw they had come to a place of *Torah* and the fear of Heaven and they said: "If we are unversed in *Torah* and the Commandments, we will observe well what they do and we will do as they do and become like unto them and their teachers and scholars and their righteous ones will protect us with their *Torah* and their good deeds." And G-d blessed the deeds of the man and he prospered in the land and became rich. All the princes, nobles and owners of estates favored him and made of him a trader and merchant. This one sold him the produce of his fields and that the lumber of his forests; another rented him his distillery and yet another, his rivers with their fish while his brethren, dwellers of the place found their sustenance and livelihood with him because of his good heart, and all his wishes were that his brethren should live with honor and not know want.

And the man did much charity for the poor of the town. With the approach of the Passover festival, he supplied them with Passover flour from his flour mills and sent a fattened bull to the slaughter and the meat he distributed to them and fish from his rivers; and the stories spread of his good deeds both seen and unseen and multiplied endlessly. But the wise men looked not favorably upon him; they gossiped about him sitting bare-headed in the homes of nobles without even a *yarmulke*. Even tea he would drink from the cup of the nobles, shaking them by the hand on both entering and leaving their homes, even believers in paganism and astrology – and more and more terrible acts such as these.

And it came to pass, when he waxed old, he said unto his wife: "Behold I have grown old and grey and even you my wife have become so and soon the way of all the earth will come upon us... and we have no son and no daughter to remember our name. Come, let us perform some deed that there shall be some remembrance of our name in the land of the living, in the place where we have dwelt. And the man and his wife sat together and considered in their hearts what they might do that their name should be remembered. And they decided to build from anew the *Beit Ha-Midrash - Or-Torah* and call it by their name as a memorial for them. When the rumor came to the ears of the scholars, they were shocked, and their anger burned within them. "How can such a thing be," they said, "what insolence! That this peasant should build a house of study for the learned of Dubno!? By what right? No! His request shall not be granted! We shall not receive from his hand such a gift. It is better that we should crowd ourselves into our old house rather receive a gift from this peasant." The man pleaded with them to accept the gift and others also approached them in his name to persuade them – but in vain. And the man was greatly saddened and without hope.

And there came a day when the man sat in the home of one of the nobles discussing business and the noble looked upon him and saw the man's countenance was sad and asked of him: "Why is your face so fallen and sad, my friend?" And the man told him of what had befallen him. And the nobleman said unto him: "I will give you advice and if you do as I say you will succeed. Arise, purchase the land next to the *Beit Ha-Midrash* and prepare timber and all the other materials for the construction. On Friday noon, when the scholars are to be found in the bath-house, let my servants and serfs come in their numbers and in one hour they will demolish

[Columns 355–356]

the old building and erect the new one in its place. After it is done the scholars will no longer oppose it and will acquiesce and compromise in the matter of the new building." The words seemed good in the eyes of the man and he did so.

Friday noon the scholars left the *Beit Ha-Midrash* – they all went to bathe in preparation for the Sabbath. And indeed, when they came to greet the Sabbath eve – Agh! What villainy has this peasant done: has he destroyed the *Beit Ha-Midrash* of the scholars to its foundations and raised a new one in its place? The anger of the scholars burned against him and in the heat of their rage they all left and went to the synagogue in town. A scamp like that! What a nerve he has!...

And the man hid his face from the anger that sought to tear him to shreds.

Days passed; the storm passed, and the anger abated. But the new building stood silent and abashed. None crossed the thresh-hold. And the man's grief was as deep as the ocean. He went to the scholars and begged them to return to the new building, but they adamantly refused – they were firm and unequivocal. It was impossible to change their mind. No! NO!!

The day came when the man went to the Great Fair held in the town of Leipzig and he bought there three articles of value at a high price: a wonderful clock; an expensive lamp embedded with precious stones that by some hidden means extinguished itself after the prayers on the Sabbath eve when the last of the congregation left the *Beit Ha-Midrash*; and a copper bowl for hand washing that, according to all the signs was the bowl made in the days of Moses our Teacher from the copper mirrors made by the women decorating the Sanctuary in the wilderness and donated by them, their most precious possession, to make the bowl...[5]

And the man brought the three wonderful gifts to the *Beit Ha-Midrash* and enticed the scholars to accept the gifts and return to the building. And the hearts of the scholars were softened, and they were reconciled and said unto him: "We are returning to the *Beit Ha-Midrash* that you have built and accept the gifts that you have brought for it. Even more we will do unto you: the building shall be called in your name The

Breslau *Beit Ha-Midrash* in order that there shall be for you a memorial forever. But there is one condition attached to this: because you destroyed the old building without our permission and authorization and brought impure and gentile articles into this Holy Sanctuary, your seat shall be next to this basin in this *Beit Ha-Midrash* all the days of your life: not in the east, and not the west, not on the benches to the south, nor the benches of the north but only by the basin".

And the man accepted upon himself the judgment and all the scholars returned to the "*Beit Ha-Midrash*" and again the voice of the *Torah* was heard loud as in before times.

And the man sat by the basin whenever he came into the *Beit Ha-Midrash*. And indeed the building was called in his name The Breslau *Beit Ha-Midrash* until this day. But at the time of the great fire that befell Dubno the clock and the *Menorah* were consumed and only the basin remained since the fire was unable to consume it.

All who come to Dubno go to see the wondrous basin.

Translator's Comments and Footnotes

1. I draw the reader's attention to the style in which I have translated sections of this narrative; there is no doubt in my mind that the author deliberately chose to emulate a biblical-style story and I felt it proper to follow his wishes as far as I was able.
2. Or-Torah – literally translated means "'Light' of the Torah".
3. The talmudists and kabbalists agree that there are two gardens of Eden: one, the terrestrial, of abundant fertility and luxuriant vegetation; the other, celestial, the habitation of righteous, immortal souls. These two are known as the "lower" and "higher" Gan Eden. The location of the earthly Eden is traced by its boundaries as described in Genesis. See also a complete, highly esoteric discussion of the concept between the "lower" and "upper" gardens and their location(s) here: http://jewishencyclopedia.com/articles/5428-eden-garden-of
4. The word "dub" means "oak tree" in Russian and Ukrainian hence the place was called "Dubno".
5. Rashi explains that the women made mirrors from polished copper and were thus able to make themselves more attractive to their husbands and by donating them to the Tabernacle were losing their only means of beautifying themselves. Rashi goes on to explains that at first the mirrors were rejected by Moses because they were a symbol of pride, vanity and wantonness but the Holy One, blessed be He, said to him, "Accept them; these are dearer to Me than all the other contributions, because through them the women reared numerous hosts in Egypt!" (With thanks to Chabad Rabbi Mendel Adelman for this interpretation).

The Mourners of Dubno

(Illustrations from Volhyn: *Dubner Smetkes*) [1])

By Moshe Berger

Translated from Hebrew by Jerrold Landau

I am sad in your midst, Dubno, very sad.

You are surrounded by areas of rivers and lakes. You dwell in a wide area, a straight area, broad, and divided into alleyways, yards, streets. You are somnolent, calm, and monotonous. You exude silence.

Dubno has no mountains around it. There are no heights. At the time of youth, a Dubno native has a perspective of breadth: The waters of the Ikwa River move through it and nurture it. However, the tortuousness, the sidewalks and roads were constructed by the residents themselves, the work of their hands.

This city has some tall, stone houses, as a hint to what all people have. There was an electric power station and an old artesian well in the heart of the city. At the center of the city, during the nights, weak rays of flashlights flicker here and there. However, the waters of the artesian well flow slowly, as if they became congealed and rotted in the rusty pipes.

The streets are silent here, as if overtaken by the Sabbath sleep. They are silent and somnolent. The youths gather in the evening and "spend time" in a modest, discreet fashion.

There are youths who sell newspapers and offer shoeshines – two types of youths who were raised by the mother-town. There is nothing here. What is the hurry? Here

people disturb them and go down to the newspaper agents – hello, my soul! Life here has no independent form or accent. Dubno has nothing that is worthwhile for outsiders to see. There is nothing – it is as if you can grasp everything while standing on one foot. One cannot even get lost in Dubno.

Here, there is no local patriotism of people who love their native town. A Dubno native is not pampered. He takes no pleasure from his connection to his city. It is as if he does not feel an emotion or sense of warmth at all.

Dubno of the past, greater Dubno, was a city of *Misnagdim* and scholars. It was set like a sandbar in the heart of the sea of Volhynian-Podolian Hasidism. It was confined within its four ells of didactic glitter, of Talmudic disputes and differences of opinion. Here, the dry Talmudic mind pervaded even outside the walls of the study hall. In essence, the Talmudic tractate was the bounds of the world. *Admorim* (Hassidic masters) did not take their lives into their hands to cross through the entrance gates of the city. It was mortally dangerous to be trapped within the camp of scholarly buffoons. Hasidim would find no rest there.

"What is the enthusiasm and devotion for me, oh soul? What will be with Torah and scholarship? Are you an expert in the small letters?"

The renown of the scholars of the city spread afar in a praiseworthy fashion. Its rabbis were honored even far from the bounds of the city. Dubno had ambition. Its rabbis reached as far as the gates of Amsterdam. Today, the pages of the Talmud turn yellow and disintegrate on their shelves, as the *Beis Midrashes* are abandoned. Spider webs are spun at the entrance. With the suppression of the light of Torah and the silencing of the voices of the studiers, the splendor of the appointed seasons of Dubno has been removed. It is sad here.

There are no evil ones of the land, and no righteous ones of the world. There is no milk, and no meat. It is simply pareve [2]. There are no heights and no depths. A type of spirit of "that is the way it is" pervades here. There are no strong attainments or energy even in matters of This World [3]. Here, the wealthy people are mainly those who lend for interest. They are the usurers of years gone by. Their ideal is *vocher* – i.e., set weekly interest. Their bookkeeping ledger is in their apron pocket. Their list of surety is hidden in a chest. Certainty is always good...

The world war certainty affected it only because of its rivers, roadways, and railway lines. For, on the other hand, who would come to spill blood on the furnace of such a city? The ancient synagogue was also in ruins. The fine wall was burnt. The valuable, holy objects were abandoned. In their time, they were brought to the depths of Russia, and were not returned to Dubno after the war. Today, the synagogue stands as a reminder of iniquity, awaiting repair.

There are destroyed streets there, scattering into dust. Smokestacks stick out as if in shame from the ruins of the baking ovens. There are cold ovens through which gusts of wind blow.

Here, there are no builders. There is no need for such. It is as if Dubno has been frozen from below. The city marketplace is grasped by idleness. It is empty of anything and everything. There are unused benches there. The joyous shouts of babies are not heard. Childhood games, of which the mothers and caregivers are concerned about, do not exist here.

There are gloomy thoughts of Tisha B'av. Only despair pervades in the gardens. The splendid avenues along Panienjaska Street, covered with giant linden trees, the branches of which intertwine and stick to each other, are also immersed in their loneliness and longing for the youth, who were always filled with laughter, pranks, and mischief. It was as if they were pleading: come, draw near... enjoy yourselves in the shadow of our branches! Come and bask in the greenery of our canopies... Come, immerse yourselves in kisses.

There is no shortage in Dubno of the bounty of green trees, fresh air, and clear river waters. On the contrary, it is crowned with a bounty of fruitfulness, everything in generous proportion. The pollution of the outlying cities does not exist here. Dubno is not a remote town. However, in essence, nobody has a need for this cleanliness. There is no benefit to anyone from the splendid "Palestinian" market – it is far from the city, it takes excess effort to get there, and oppressive silence pervades there as well. There is nobody to listen to the songs and hymns of life. There is no exaltation of boat drivers upon the horizon of the clear rivers. Only during the summertime do the masses go out to the "Pantalia", to the bridge decorated with green, pliable willow branches. They stroll there and enjoy the pleasant aroma of cut hay. Slowly and with short steps do they stroll, and they hurry back to the city toward evening. Once again, the boredom of the summer pervades, sapping from you all desire and all internal content.

Apparently, Dubno has all the characteristics to make it vibrant and bustling: It is situated on the crossroads, it has excellent connections to Warsaw and Lwow. However, you would not stumble across it through geographical knowledge, neither from a physical or a spiritual perspective.

Scribes, artisans, and businesspeople avoid going there, almost on purpose. There is nobody on the road... It is not worth it... Even a cheap, picayune operetta would earn failure here.

It simply does not matter to Dubnoites. The only movie theater in the city is full of inferiority. The villagers of the area and people of the nearby towns do not come to the city other than for administrative affairs – for it is a district city after all. In essence, however, they obtain their provisions from other cities. Dubno has no attractive force even for the lads who have become spoiled and have turned to *Haskalah*. Here, there is no room for a Nachshon-style leap [4] ...

[Columns 359–360]

When Dubno is busy with communal affairs, activism – Heaven help us – it is centered around dispute. The actual cause of the dispute: the camp of the "elder" rabbi, and the followers of the "young" rabbi... However, do not fear! This is a dispute without fire, without cutting of *peyos*, and without slaps on the cheek, Heaven forbid. This is nothing more than ordinary talk of those who sit at the corners, the idlers of the city, Jews of the cane [5], who sit on the street all day. They even play football in Dubno without excitement, just like that, people do as they were taught...

Signs of past greatness can be found in the cemetery. There, the Torah giants, the cedars of Lebanon, a renowned amount of scholars are buried. Incidentally, there is a monograph called *The City of Dubno and its Rabbis* by Rabbi Margolis, which deals with the rich past. Throughout his life, this Last Mohawk collected an interesting and rare library regarding the city and its rabbis, which he dedicated to the studying youth. In our days it found its purpose – in a horse stable, where it is rotting, and pages are falling out...

Indeed, so it is: the rich cemetery is full of "life," and the living street is impoverished and dead. Upon this grey background I will etch some "arabesque" of a few representations of the "face" of the place. The image of Dubno will then be complete in the eyes of the reader.

The intelligentsia, with the definite article. A former student who earned great popularity. His first name, in the form of love and modesty, is known to everybody, from the water drawer up to the rabbi of the city. He was the scion of a good family. He was occupied in communal affairs, a civic advisor, a journalist, and a jurist from Petersburg. He was once chosen – when the first light breeze of freedom blew – as the president of the city. He was a dear person to the city. He promised mountains and hills. As times changed, he built a family nest. He abandoned spiritual and theoretical pursuits – as well as work for the public benefit. He abandoned his bookshelf: comic books bound together with volumes by Dubnow [6], *Sefer Ha'agada* [7] – with a catalog of wines and liquor. Suddenly, his taste dissipated, and nothing mattered to him anymore, neither the city or the community, not the communal council or the city council. It was extinguished like a Sabbath candle. Its form was removed like a beaten *Hoshana* [8]. His entire spiritual burden – a page of the daily newspaper and ruminating over old jokes...

The doctor was liked by people. He performed wonders in the heavens and on earth. He worked in the science of "medicine" and his work was honest. He was prepared to run to any call, day and night, even for the poorest of the poor – as long as he would be "honored." He was miserly, and he secured his money with real estate.

The pharmacist was an old bachelor. He was fat due to much sleep and little walking. He smiled from satiety from one end of his mustache to the other. He could prove to you two times over that it is not worthwhile to marry a woman... Every Sabbath, a group of youths would gather in his pharmacy to light a cigarette, and to smoke it while absorbing juicy jokes.

The maskil was a remnant from previous eras. He used to serve [9] A. B. Gotlober [10]. He breached the wall himself: from the *Beis Midrash* to Europe. He learned foreign languages without the help of teachers. He was full and overflowing. He lived in isolation and spent time only with his books.

He was bored with the Dubno freeze. Every new book turned into something archival in his hand. The city hall office, his writing table, and his books – this was his entire world. To hell with the rest!...

The leftist Yiddishist. Previously, he was a student in a black shirt, destined to overturn the world and what is therein. He raised a ruckus and gathered a crowd. He saw the aim in life in pedagogy. He worked in a children's home. Today he is a merchant and seller with all the badges. He is in the synagogue on Sabbaths and festivals. He is a fine young man, bringing contentment to his parents. However, it is also forbidden to overlook: He still feels faithful to his ideal – he avidly reads the *Folks-Zeitung* – as a Hassidic Jew, between *mincha* and *maariv*.

These are characters from the gallery – may G-d have mercy.

I am sad in your midst – O Dubno.

A song will not be sung about you. Your stories will not be told. It is not for naught that those near and far said about you: Dubno and its mourners…

Original and Translator's Comments

1. There is a footnote in the text here, as follows: From *Wolhiner Lebn*, issues 7-8, October 1924. The writer is a journalist who visited the city during the 1920s, after the First World War and the change of regime. He found it destroyed and desolate. This article is the fruits of his impression – the editors.
2. i.e. neutral – a euphemism here for lifelessness (tc).
3. i.e. mundane, secular affairs (tc).
4. Referring to the Midrash that at the time of the crossing of the Red Sea, the sea did not split until Nachshon the son of Aminadab jumped into the water (tc).
5. Seemingly referring to older people who are no longer employed. The Yiddish is *shtelklech-Yiden* (tc).
6. See https://en.wikipedia.org/wiki/Simon_Dubnow , as well as column 313 of this book (tc).
7. The Book of Legends by Ch. N. Bialik (tc).
8. Referring to the willow branches beaten on the ground on Hoshana Rabba (tc).
9. The phrase used for "to serve" is "to pour water on the hands of."(tc)
10. See https://en.wikipedia.org/wiki/Avrom_Ber_Gotlober (tc).

Personalities, Nicknames and Associated Names of the Townspeople

by Asher Reichman

Translated from Yiddish by Yocheved Klausner

Every town has its own ways, figures and personalities, with all sorts of names and surnames. The unique way of life in our town was expressed by the somewhat mocking nicknames given to some of the Dubno people, while for others the nickname would be an asset, making his personality lovable.

Many and varied were the types walking around in the Jewish streets of Dubno. A great number of them deserve to be remembered forever - they have earned that. These figures are standing now before my eyes, as if they demand to be revived: please tell our tale, so our nation would know about us, because everything flies by and vanishes, new people and new events come about, a new generation turns up and the old one goes away, and all is forgotten. And it is a pity, a great pity, that so many are not anymore.

It may happen that your child will ask you tomorrow: How did the Jewish town in the Diaspora look? Or, out of ignorance, the child will mock and ridicule the residents of the little towns and villages of bygone days in Russia, Poland, Lithuania, Latvia, Romania and elsewhere.

So, you must tell the child, explain and describe the life of the Jewish community, which did not have a tight budget or many paid clerks - and still the community would make sure that every hungry person would have a piece of bread and every needy would have some clothing, and the sick would be seen by a doctor and given the needed medicine. Even the dying and the lonely were not abandoned. All this, thanks to willing and warmhearted people, always ready to help others.

Days and years will pass, and our children may not be aware that in the town where their parents were born such compassionate people existed, Jews with good qualities, respected and of good spirit. They are the ones who have forged the Golden Chain of the generations, and later they pitched their tents in the Homeland that has come to life again.

So who were the Jews of Dubno?

Most of them were simple Jews, modest, without pretensions or special demands. Not many well-to-do among them; many of them were poor people. Providing for the next day was everyone's worry, and their living conditions forced them to work hard and be content with little. Together they pulled the livelihood-cart: the head of the family, the mother, the children - who were mostly undernourished. They were peddlers, day laborers, handymen and middlemen; they made a living by trading with each other and bartering with the peasants from the surrounding villages. They tried to educate their children as best they could - in the *Cheder*, in the *Talmud Torah* or in the public state-school and tried to make sure that the child knew Yiddish and a bit of "*Yiddishkeit*" and not abandon the ways of their father-and-mother and the Jewish 613 commandments.

The densely populated narrow streets created close neighbors and brought together the hearts. Everyone had a good friend, with whom he could talk heart to heart and share his joys and sorrows. This nearness caused people to assign their friends nicknames, sometimes mockingly sometimes fondly - all according to the circumstances and the feelings. Sometimes the nicknames were taken from their occupation or their origin. When a Jewish woman would say "I am going for a while to Black Bashe" or "to grandma Yente" she meant that she went to her closest friend.

The names would be inherited from generation to generation, from the great-great-grandfathers or grandmothers. From those who originated in certain places, I remember the names: Shmuel Matchever [from Matchev], Leibke Patchayever. Or by the character or a special trait of the person - Shalom God-forbid, or Don't-worry, or The-money-smells. There were nicknames by occupation or profession: Binyamin the carpenter, Welwel the cobbler and so on.

This was how the nicknames became a matter of everyday use. Through them, a special feeling of closeness and sympathy for the person was expressed.

Mattis, the water-carrier

Names and Surnames

Surname	Name	Nickname
LEHRER	Aba	
BEIDER	Avraham	
WOLITZER	Avraham	
	Avreimenyu	With the papers
BARUCH	Ide	From the eggs
	Idele	Shmaltz [chicken-fat]
TESSLER	Aizik	
IVANIER	Itzi	
COLLECTOR	Itzik	
MARKILECHES	Itzik	
	Itzik Eli	The smart
	Itzik	The bald
PERSITZ	Itzik	
KOSS	Itzikel	
	Isser	Cobbler
SIDIBITCER	Alter	
	Ester	The server
TCHOYESCH	Efraim	
	Asher	Tzimbele [cymbal]
	Bubbe [Grandma]	Yente's
	Bassie	The black
PALTIS	Buky	
	Boronio	
	Binyamin	The tall
	Binyamin	The carpenter
	Binyamin	The kid (young goat)
MARKILECHES	Bentzi	
	Bratke	
ZGATAVTCHK	Gedalyahu	
TZONDEK	David	
		The little weasel
		The cotton dealer
		The ticker
		The Turk
	Henie	Dudich's
	Henie	The buck (goat)
	Henie	From the geese
	Henietchke	
TELIGISHNIK	Hersch	
	Hersch	The pitcher
	Hersch	The rope turner

	Hersch	The *Shames* (synagogue attendant)
	Herzl	The Torah reader
	Welwele	The cobbler
		Zibele (born prematurely)
	Zisl	Grabulke
	Zalman	The yellow
	Zalman	The black
	Chantzi	The mad
	Chaia Machle	With the blue lips
BATIST	Chaim	
	Chaim	The bridge maker
	Chaim	The nouveau-riche
BENEDIK	Yankel	
SIFTSHICH	Yankel	
	Yankel	Beilitchke's
	Yankel	The tall
	Yankel	Kugel
	Yankel	*Kishke* (gut)
	Yankel	From the eggs
	Yankel	without the hand
	Yosel	Toibe's
FIDEK	Yosel	
	Yosele	*Esav* [Esau]
	Yona	The glazier
	Yehoshua	The yellow
	Yente	The Golden
	Yosel	The rag dealer
BODYONI	Israel	
	Luzer	The deaf
TOTZ	Leib	
PATCHYAVER	Leibke	
MALIER	Leib	
SCHREIBER	Leib	
PIVNIK	Leizer	
POLIAK	Leizer	
	Matye	The water carrier
	Motel	The crooked
LEWITZKER	Motel	
	Meir Moshe	Chaia Feige's
MORTCHIK	Meir	
	Meir	Knak
	Menye	The fat woman
	Mechil	The tavern keeper
	Mechil	The tall
	Meir	Tavern keeper

	Malka	The fat woman
	Motel	The red
	Moshe	"Trough"
	Moshe	The skinny
FILLER	Moshe	
FLITT	Moshe	
SHKALIK	Nachum	
	Nisel	The doctor
	Nosie	The driver
COLLECTOR	Nahman	
	Sofer	With the bass [music]
	Stisie	The fat woman
	Srulik	The world lier
	Spritiche	
KORIK	Etti	
	Pitti	The mute
	Peisie	Shikele
	Fishel	Yosi's
	Pasternak	
	Pesie	The grandma
	Kaye	The rag
		Money smell
	Kobenyu	Cobbler
	Krupnyares	
		The Ratchiner
	Shamay	The rag dealer
	Shmulik	Dog Pusher
	Shaul	Katchkes [Ducks]
SHREIBERS	Shlomo Leib	
	Shalom	Halila [God-forbid]
		Shmendritchke
OCHS	Sara'nyu	
TZAK	Shefi	
	Shtchupak	

387

Personalities and Figures

**Translated from Hebrew by Aryeh Sklar
(unless otherwise stated)**

A Portrait of the Head of the Rabbinical Court, the *Gaon*, Our Teacher and Rabbi, Rabbi Menahem Mendel

by Ya. N. A. Y.

The *Gaon* [genius] Rabbi Menahem Mendel (Reb Mendele) was born to his father, the *Gaon* Rabbi David Zvi Auerbach, the head of the rabbinical court and rabbi in Dubno, in the year 5636 [1876],[1] and he merited to preside as a rabbi in the city of his fathers for about 50 years, spreading Torah and fear of God there until his last day. When he was young, when he lived in Berdichev with his wife, Reb Mendele would attend the court of the *Admor* [an honorific meaning Our Master, Our Teacher, and Our Rabbi] of Skver. When the righteous man passed away, Reb Mendele switched to the camp of the [anti–hassidic] *Misnagdim* and remained a staunch *misnagid* until the end of his life.

Reb Mendele took on the last name "Rosenfeld" for the purposes of exemption from the Russian army, while his original family name was Auerbach, a hint to being a distant descendant of Rashi [the acronym of Rabbi Shlomo Yitzhaki, a famous 11th century rabbi]. The legend goes that when Rashi's mother was pregnant with him, she was in Troyes [France] and encountered a narrow alleyway. At that very moment, a knight passed her riding his armored steed. There was nowhere for the pregnant woman to run, placing her in grave danger. A miracle occurred, and the stones of the wall she had flattened herself against squeezed together and sunk back, like a niche, which fit her and her pregnant belly, and she emerged unharmed from that dangerous place. Therefore, her descendants were called in German "Auerbach", or "Avir–Boych", meaning "a belly filled with air."

Reb Mendele was involved in business as a young man, because he did not wish to make his Torah his livelihood [lit. "a spade with which to dig"]. After that, he was taken for the honor of being head of the rabbinical court in Rozyszcze, near Lutsk and he sat in the rabbinical seat until the year 5644 [1884]. That same year he took the seat of the rabbinate in the city of his fathers, even while opposed by the Hassidim, among whom there were many from the Kotsk sect of Hassidut.

During World War I, Reb Mendele left Dubno, which was occupied at one time by Russia, and at another time by Austria, and he went to Zhitomir, and from there to Lishinov. In the year 5676 (1916), when Dubno was occupied again by the Russians, a delegation of important individuals came out to Reb Mendele and requested of him on behalf of the residents of the city to come back to them. He accepted the request, and from then on, he continued to lead his people with integrity and justice, without favoring any man, as the commandment [Exodus 23:3] "And you shall not show deference to a poor man in his dispute." He had [Psalms 24:4] "clean hands and a pure heart," a Torah scholar, [cf. Talmud Berakhot 28a] "the same inside and out", in his appearance as well, polished and clean from head to toe, from his black boots to his knitted gloves on his hands, a fast walker and

[Column 370]

quick to perceive, he lent an attentive ear to anyone who spoke to him about their worries and troubles, granting his counsel to anyone who came to him to ask for it. His reputation preceded him beyond Dubno, to all the surrounding areas, near and far (that of Volhynia), and throughout the rabbinic circles of all of Poland.

As a *misnagid*, Reb Mendele was continuing in the position of most of the rabbis of the city, since the days of the Gra [the "Vilna *Gaon*", Rabbi Elijah of Vilna]. He would jokingly say that he hopes that after 120 years, he will merit to stand in Heaven at the time they are administering lashes to the Hassidic followers and their rabbis.

Authority was granted to Reb Mendele to its fullest extent according to his honor, even by the residents of the city who were not among the [Jewish] covenant. Before World War I, the rabbi was appointed as the rabbinical chaplain of the army, and he did much to ease the situation for the Jewish soldiers in the army. During the war, the rabbi turned to the military authorities and urged them to supply kosher meat to the Jewish soldiers encamped in the city. He [apparently] knew how to convince the heads of the military, for even during the war, the Jewish soldiers were able to observe all their religious customs. The power of his personality and his sincerity made him successful, and his influence continued to grow.

A story happened that a certain butcher had a rumor going around about him that he was feeding the people of the city meat from animals that were not kosher [*nevelot* and *terefot*]. Reb Mendele summoned him and warned him, under the principle that [Talmud Makkot 5b] "we do not punish without warning." The butcher promised to be more careful from then on, but he was careful only for a while until he went back to his old ways. The rabbi summoned him again and berated him, to which the butcher claimed that nothing happened. The rabbi sought counsel with the leaders of the community, and he decided to bring the butcher before the community to take a Torah–backed oath. This oath was arranged as per custom in the study house [*Bet Midrash*], taking place before black candles, with the specific oaths *herem* and *konam* [mentioned in the Kol Nidrei prayer of Yom Kippur]. When the butcher arose to take the oath, he had a stroke and died on the spot. From then on, the rabbi prohibited any Jew from taking such a vow.

The elders of our city tell another tale: A story once happened with Reb Alter, who lived next to the city bathhouse. One day, it was decided to install a fence around the *mikvah* [an immersion pool for purity], and they erred, and the fence encroached the property of Reb Alter. His wife burst out in a raging fury against those doing the

392

work, even trying to destroy the fence. One of the neighbors ran to the rabbi and summoned him quickly to the site. The rabbi was furious with Reb Alter's wife and reprimanded her for what happened.

[Column 371]

She declared to the rabbi, "I don't care if they are building a *mikvah*, I did not give permission for them to put a fence on our property!" The rabbi responded, "Sarah, you must desist! You will not need this land…" It was understood as a warning, and indeed, a week passed, and the woman died.

The High Holidays were memorable to the people of Dubno, when Reb Mendele would astound with his blowing the shofar, his many blasts on Rosh Hashanah, and the elongated blast [*tekia gedola*] at the conclusion of the final prayer of Yom Kippur, *Neilah*, which is meant to confuse *Satan*… His rendition of the prayer "From the Straits," would make the very doorposts quake, and fear and trembling would grip the praying congregation. It was felt that this prayer broke through the Heavens and reached the very Throne of Glory.

[Column 372]

They say about Reb Mendele that he never got sick his entire life, standing tall and strong to his last days. He would wake up around 4 a.m. to greet the morning, and he would sit and study the Talmud and the Jewish legal decisions of rabbis [*poskim*] until it was time for prayer. Whether summer or winter, even those cold wintry nights, he would travel the long distance of 5 parasangs[2] to the slaughterhouse, checking the kosher status of both small and large animals himself. He lived a long life, and died at the ripe old age of 97, in the year 5693 (1933).

During the war, when an order went out that every resident had to carry identification documents, a photographer came to Reb Mendele and took his picture [surreptitiously]. When Reb Mendele found out, he ran to the photographer, and ripped the negative to shreds. And so, the brilliant face of Reb Mendele is left etched only upon the memories of his townspeople, and his generation.

Translator's Comments

1. Based on when he died, this should say 5596 [1836]
2. An ancient Persian measurement of distance equal to about 3.5 miles. Accordingly, he would travel 17.5 miles each way

Our Master, Our Teacher, Our Rabbi [*Admor*],
R. Baruch HaLevi Yozefob

by R. Shmuel HaLevi Yozefob

My father, my master, of blessed memory, settled in Dubno in the year 5653 (1893), and was appointed *Rebbe* [Hassidic leader] by the invitation of his father's Hassidic followers, the *Admor* Rabbi Yechiel Michel of Korets, of blessed memory, who had lived there. Most of the residents of Dubno were staunch *Misnagdim*, who opposed the approach of Hassidism completely, and when my father came to Dubno, the *Misnagdim* persecuted him at first. But, in his great humility, he never said a bad word about them – just the opposite, he showed them signs of love and friendship, so much so that it wasn't long before they all became his admirers, holding him in high esteem and supporting him with generosity, so much so that he was finally able to build a house for himself and even a beautiful study house [*Bet Midrash*]. His great love of Jews did that.

My father, of blessed memory, told me a story from his holy grandfather, Reb Aharon of Chernobyl, of blessed memory, that when he first came to Dubno, great rabbis came to visit him – Rabbi Tzvi HaKohen Rappoport (the author of "Ezras Kohanim"), Rabbi Shmuel Birnbaum (the son–in–law of the great genius Rabbi Akiva Eiger), and Rabbi Yitzchak Eliyahu, a preacher of homilies who was well–known in Volhynia.) When they left his house, the righteous Reb Aharon said to his Hassidic followers that Rabbi Tzvi HaKohen Rappoport was sincere in his greetings, while the others were sarcastic, and he nevertheless loves them because of their greatness in Torah study. They deserve no guilt, however, for their opposition, for the ways of Hassidut are foreign to them.

My father, of blessed memory, told me another story that on the holy Sabbath, the righteous Reb Aharon would go pray in the Great Synagogue, and with him his Hassidic followers, as was his custom. The *mara de'asra* [lit. "master of the place," i.e., "rabbi of the synagogue"] was at that time the great Rabbi David Tzvi,

[Column 373]

author of the "Malbushei Taharah." The righteous Reb Aharon led the congregation in prayer, and when he reached the prayer of [the beginning of the evening prayer], "Borkhu," the rabbi of the synagogue sent the sexton to warn him that he should not say [the introductory prayer of] "*Kegavna*" [which, among Ashkenazim, is only said by the Hassidic sects]. The righteous man turned to the rabbi and said, "Yes, I heard from the *mara de'asra* [master of the place] not to say *Kegavna*, but what can I do, when I've heard from the *mara de'alma* [Master of the world] that I indeed should say *Kegavna*, and so the [Talmud] rule applies of "A command of the teacher and the command of the student, who does one listen to?" The rabbi accepted the righteous man's words and allowed him to continue praying according to his custom.

After that, others began to visit Dubno: both the righteous *Maggid* [preacher] of Trisk, and the righteous man from Olisk, and the Hassidic approach became accepted and spread, until three prayer–houses were established: the "*kloyz*" [small house] of the Hassidim of Trisk, the "*shtiebel*" [small prayer–house] of Stolin, and the "*kloyz*" of general Hassidim.

My father passed away in Dubno at the age of 68, on the anniversary of the death of his ancestor the holy *Admor* Rabbi Avraham Yehoshua Heschel of Apt, author of "*Ohev Yisrael*," the 5th of Nisan, 5697 [March 17, 1937]. Before his death, the rabbi of Apt commanded that they should not write any praises on his tombstone, except for the words "*Ohev Yisrael*" ["Lover of Israel"], an attribute he could boast to the Heavenly Court. So did my father, my teacher, of blessed memory, inherit from his ancestor this great attribute of love of the Jewish people and through the power of this love he could reach the opposition.

396

The Crown Rabbi[1] – Rabbi Chaim Zev Margolios

Rabbi Chaim Zev Margolios was born in Vilna ca. 5602 (1842). Most of his Torah study curriculum of Talmud with the commentaries of Rashi and Tosafot, he learned from his uncle, Yaakov Brita. At 18, he left Vilna to complete his studies abroad, traveling by foot for many days through German territories, Austria and Hungary. On his return from abroad, he entered the rabbinical seminary on behalf of the Russian government, which was in Zhitomir, finishing his requirements in the year 1870. For seven years he served as a Jewish law authority in various cities in the Volhynia region, until the government schools were closed by the authorities in 1877. The next year, in 1878, he was chosen to serve as the rabbi on behalf of the Dubno leaders and served in this role for certain intervals from 1878 until 1911.

While still a student of the study–house, he began contributing articles to the journal "HaMelitz", under the pseudonym "Chazos" ("Ch" and "Z" being the acronym of "Chaim Zev", and "os" the end of "Margolios"). In the year 1872, he published the educational book "*History of the Jewish People*" in the Russian language, which was well–received by many schools.

Of great interest is "Memories of Days Gone By" ["*Zichronot Meyamim Avru*"], which appeared in Hebrew in the year 1895, which has reliable descriptions of the lives of the hedonistic "Borsaki", who were students in the study houses of the rabbinical seminaries of Zhitomir. Another of his books, "Stories and Descriptions" ["*Sippurim ve'Tziyurim*"] (Warsaw, 1905), which appeared in Hebrew, includes many interesting facts, even if from an artistic perspective they are of poor quality. His best story appeared in "The Morning Light" ["*HaBoker Or*"] (January 1881), named "The Sinner's Sin?" ["*HaChet Cheto*"].

Rabbi Chaim Zev Margolios made a lasting memorial to Dubno, where he served, by collecting very important compositions in the notebook "Dubno Rabbati," regarding the fate of the community and its position, which was published first in the newspaper "The Morning Light" in 1876, page 313; in "*Hamelitz*" in 1893, nos. 9, 34, 51, 83, 119, 133; and in "Hatzefira" in 1902, nos. 7–11, and then in the book "Dubno Rabbati" (Warsaw 1910), which got him an award from the organization "Disseminators of the Enlightenment" ["*Mafitzei Haskala*"]. His book is used as an important source for the history of the Jews of Poland and the provinces.

– The Russian Jewish Encyclopedia[2], vol. 10, pp. 622–623
S. Stanislavsky

Translator's Comments

1. This was a position in the Russian empire given to Jewish people who acted as intermediaries between the Jewish towns and the government
2. A work published in Russia spanning 16 volumes between 1906–1913, written in Russian, on Judaism past and present. This entry was translated to Hebrew for this Yizkor book, and translated from the Hebrew to English here.

A Portrait of the Teacher Chaim–Nisan Zaks

by Naftali Toran

I was eight and a half when my mother, may she rest in tranquility, brought the "young man", Chaim–Nisan, from Oleksandria in the area of Volhynia to Klevan, my hometown, to be my teacher and educator. This is what happened:

My mother, a wise woman of good taste, traveled to Oleksandria to learn about the character of Elimelech Blei, who was suggested as a suitor for my sister, Chaya–Fayga. There she took notice of a young man dressed in tattered clothes, but with a serious look in his eyes, who was coming and going from Elimelech's house and was friendly with him. The young man piqued her interest, and she began to inquire after his situation. She was told that he was from her city, in the area of Herstadt (Volhynia), and he came to Oleksandria because of the Enlightenment. Why Oleksandria? He became enchanted by the library opened in Oleksandria by the organization in Russia called "Disseminators of the Enlightenment" ["*Mafitzei Haskalah*"], which gathered around it young men who longed for the light and enlightenment of general studies and Hebrew, and they would barely scrape by through teaching the Bible and Talmud. My mother, seeking

to find to find a proper tutor for the son of her old age, began speaking to Chaim–Nisan, and offered for him to move to Klevan with the following conditions: He should teach only four students, his wages would be 100 rubles for each semester ["*zeman*"], he would get food from the tables of his students' parents, six weeks by each one. 100 rubles was the right wage for a teacher of children, and Chaim–Nisan accepted the offer, and he moved to Klevan during the High Holidays season of 5649 (1889).

I remember when I first met with him. He would be in the synagogue for the tailors, which was next to the Great Synagogue, in the afternoon hours. No other man was there at that time. I was small and thin, and he picked me up in his arms and positioned me on the bench. I noticed how pale his face was, his cheeks smooth with no hint of beard, his posture slightly bent. He asked me questions from the Torah and the Prophets, and my answers seemed to satisfy him, for his face appeared to shine, and every so often he would say, "Good, good." I was his first student, but my mother stood by her word and worked to provide him with three more students to join me, and after the holiday of Sukkot, we began to study.

Chaim–Nisan lacked formal pedagogical training, but he was blessed with natural pedagogical abilities. We would study from 8 am until 8 pm

[Column 376]

with an hour and a half break for lunch. He would teach the Prophets with a passion, and with a melody that would penetrate the heart, explaining the words in Yiddish which was fluent in our mouths. On Sabbaths we would come to him to listen to him telling stories from history books, especially stories about the Spanish Inquisition and the Auto–da–fé in Portugal, which made a lasting impression on us. We were drawn to him, and we were treated with much affection, even though he would sometimes flog us for our misbehavior.

My heart recalls a day in winter. Between the afternoon and evening prayers, we, the children, decided to run to the river near our town and skate on the ice, not with ice skates, God forbid, like those "*shkatzim*", the uncouth teens of the village, but with our shoes on our feet. Everything was going well, we were enjoying ourselves, and no adult knew. The next day we did it again, and again everything went well; seeing this, we continued to run to the river every day and skate on the ice – that is, until Chaim–Nisan found out and punished us harshly for our mischief. Such a thing was considered a sin by parents and teachers in those days, a sin worthy of punishment, for Jewish children were not supposed to imitate the "*goyim*".

That same winter, my mother died and left me an orphan, yet my education was never interrupted. Chaim–Nisan continued to teach us a fondness for reading Hebrew literature and opening up our imagination through the written word.

Over time, youths who were fans of the Enlightenment would gather around Chaim–Nisan, and a club was organized which would meet every so often to debate various issues which were raised by articles published in "*Hamelitz*" regarding the "Love of Zion" (*Chibat Zion*) [movement]. Certain extremists would talk about the youths, especially the "young man" – i.e., Chaim–Nisan – calling him the incarnation of Jeroboam the son of Nebat, a sinner who leads the public to sin. These extremists also sought to incite simple Hassidim regarding the followers of the Enlightenment (*Maskilim*), but the inciters did so in vain. Klevan was already a progressive city, close to Rubana, a city in the province which had a mighty influence on it. But, of course, there must be fights and struggles, and from that breach [in religious isolationism], many new things followed.

During that time, we learned the Wisdom of Ben Sira in the translation of Yitzchak Frankel, and since we only had one book, we copied the chapters into our notebooks. It once happened that the sexton of the study house, while it was used by the Hassidim of Stefan (which was used by them every so often), saw what we were studying in our notebooks. He raised an alarm that we were learning heretical texts, and it aroused great agitation against the *Maskilim* in general, and Chaim–Nisan specifically. The main sexton of this study house, to whom the young *Maskilim* would sometimes gather, was a powerful Jew, and he would lobby the local authority, who greatly benefited from his lobbying efforts, and he began to move heaven and earth

[Column 377]

about this impurity that had invaded the study house. We youths knew how to wage a war in return, and we took revenge in various ways. Once on a Friday, about an hour before the start of the Sabbath, a time when the study house was completely empty of any people, I went in and wrote in ink on the wall across from the sexton's seat, "Hello thief, hello slanderer." When people came to the study house, they saw the writing, and they mocked the seat of the man whom they hated. That writing stayed where it was until Saturday night, and it perturbed the sexton that entire day. Another time, one of the children cut the corner of one of the extremists' fur coat. Such pranks, among other things we did, caused a fight of words to become a fight of fists.
It was the last day of the holiday of Sukkot [*Shemini Atzeret*], 5650 [1889]. After the party arranged for the election of the new sextons of the synagogue, when certain people of the extremists were drinking, they began to hurl invectives against

the *Maskilim*, even pouncing upon them with punches as well. The *Maskilim* and their adherents didn't hide their fists in their pockets, and they returned the punches measure for measure. After that, the struggle [between the *Maskilim* and the extremists] began to abate, until it died out completely.

The third year of Chaim–Nisan's stay in Klevan, he got married to a woman from Berezne of Volhynia, and she had several children. The first–born son was Shmerel (Shmaryahu), who lived his adult life in the United States, and he struggled mightily to make a living.

I studied under Chaim–Nisan until I turned 12 years old. I went through almost all of the Hebrew Bible, and I knew a chapter of Talmud as well.

When I became an adult, I decided I would dedicate myself to teaching Hebrew. I was 18 when I returned to Oleksandria and began giving private classes, and an idea grew in me to open a Hebrew school. I rented an apartment on the main street of the city, I ordered benches, chalkboards, and all such teaching tools, and we – my brother–in–law Elimelech Blei and I – invited my teacher of my past, Chaim–Nisan, to be the head teacher, as the principal of the school. The other two teachers would be my brother–in–law, and me. By command of the government, we had to teach the Russian language and Russian history, and as such we hired a graduate of the teacher's school in Vilna.

The school got a good reputation but could not afford 4 teachers. I therefore left and moved to Zdolbuniv and made money there with tutoring jobs, while Chaim–Nisan and my brother–in–law Elimelech continued their work in Oleksandria, until they moved after some time to Dubno, from the invitation of the Zionists there.

I know nothing regarding his life in Dubno, the years of WWI he spent in Uman, in the province of Kiev, and the end of his life in America. But, according to my brother–in–law, who would write him letters, I found out that Chaim–Nisan had a hard time scraping by in his rabbinical position in helping those who left Klevan and

[Column 378]

Dubno. Almost 8 years passed – the year 5710 [1949] – he sent money to my brother–in–law for him to publish his stories and legends that had been published in *Blossoms* [*Perachim*] by Y. H. Brenner, and in *Life and Nature* [*HaChaim veHaTeva*] by Y. H. Tevyov, and his latest stories he had published in the weekly made in Warsaw, edited by Ben–Eliezer.

Chaim–Nisan had a tremendous impact in the field of Hebrew education, influencing many students to continue his great and prolific work.

B

Chaim–Nisan, as a teacher of Scripture and of Hebrew grammar, disseminated Torah at the beginning of the 20ᵗʰ century together with the educator Elimelech Blei. He had arrived in Dubno from Klevan with his family. A young man with vigor, he tried his hand at being a business partner in a factory that made seltzer, but "he left with his hands on his head" [it was unsuccessful], and so he went back to teaching. A group of eight students was assembled by him. This was the era of the *"Heder Metukan"*, the start to a Hebrew revival for young students in schools. The main studies were Bible, grammar, the Ever language (that is what they called Hebrew, *Ivrit*, back then, which was taught in an Ashkenazi–Lithuanian accent), and a bit of Talmud. They explained the Bible in Yiddish, which was the spoken language of the children and parents, who wanted to ensure they would understand the verse in its most literal sense, without a care for the Talmudic dictum, (b. Kiddushin 49a) "One who translated a verse in its literal sense is a liar." In addition, Chaim–Nisan taught his students to write well, and paid very close attention to this [particular subject]. His influence on his students was quite great, even despite the fact that he did not spare the rod, and sometimes at a very harsh level. He demanded they learn and behave to his standards, like good Jewish children.

His teacher's wages were not minor at all, compared to the times. He demanded, and received, 24 rubles for "time"!

The great assistance to his work came from his full–bodied wife Bayla. She was in charge of two of his books: *"The Golden Book"*, and *"The Black Book."* From the outside, these books were indistinguishable; that is how they called them from the start. It once happened that Shaul'ik, a sharp–witted youth with an amazing power of recall, had heard that a fire had broken out in the city – so he stopped his studies and ran after the firefighters. Shaul'ik was all of 11 years old then. But was it possible that a youth like him would run like a barbarian [*shkutz*] in the streets of the city, bringing shame to his teacher Chaim–Nisan and his school?! After he did that, he deserved to be put in *"The Black Book"*, which Bayla took out, and in front of everyone, recorded Shaul'ik's name that he had done wrong. To no avail was his pleading and sobbing from the fear that the "*otmetka*" (Russian for "mark") meant he would certainly turn out evil – where would he go?

After a few days, Chaim–Nisan began to show an equanimity toward the lad. He would ignore his transgression if Shaul'ik would promise that he would learn the entirety of the book of Proverbs by heart.

Shaul'ik didn't recoil from such a big task, and as long as his name would be erased from his book of Hell… How great was his joy, when he began to recite Proverbs by heart in its original language before Chaim–Nisan, surely getting much satisfaction from this.

Chaim–Nisan's custom was to go out to his yard at sunset and chop wood himself for the fireplace and for the stove, and afterward sit at the table and slice a loaf of bread, dip it in oil, and enjoy it. "It's healthy", he would say.

Over the course of time, Chaim–Nisan became a well–respected individual, who took care of our fair–haired and freckled sons and daughters. He lived in an apartment that was always open, and drawn to him were the city's Zionists and anyone who loved Enlightenment and culture. One recalls the hours in the afternoon of the Sabbath and Festivals in the house of the teacher who everyone treated with love and friendship: the windows are open, its pleasant smells sweet to the outside, cups of hot drinks on the table, and Chaim–Nisan beaming with three light–shaded beards (that's how his beard grew, with three hills), sitting and going round and round with the children's stories that he had published, most of them hanging on some strange verse from the early prophets, their content filled with ethical principles, their style light yet heartening.

From the whole of the Enlightenment, Chaim–Nisan only took in a bit, and he wrestled with proper Russian grammar all his days. He didn't feel especially connected to Russian, even when teaching his students in the gymnasium. He found fulfillment his whole life in the Hebrew language, and in Zionism. His stamp was on all the literature of the day: *"Small World"* [*Olam Katan*], the books *"Rescue"* [*Toshia*], *"The Book of Legends"* [*Sefer HaAgada*] by Bialik, *"HaShiloach"*, *"The Young Worker"* [*HaPoel HaTzeir*], and more.

Chaim–Nisan created a generation of admirers of Hebrew, overflowing from his spirit and his faith to the Zionism of most of the inhabitants of the city. He left Dubno before the outbreak of the First World War and immigrated to America. He served there in the rabbinate, where he passed away at an old age.

The Lot of the Hebrew Teacher

by Nisan Machruk (Drori)

My father, of blessed memory, Rabbi David–Eliezer, was born in Lutsk in 1874. From the dawn of his childhood, he showed a great connection to his studies and to a love of books, though there was not much in the way of financial abundance in his house, and his older brothers immigrated overseas. My father left his house at a tender age, turning to Volozhin, the hub of Torah. He did not spend a full week at Volozhin, but those few days of his stay made a deep impression that carried all his days afterward. There, he "glanced and was damaged" – he glanced at the way of life of the young men of the yeshiva and was swept off by the stream of Enlightenment which was very intense in those days.

His second stay was at the Lomza yeshiva, where he studied for a number of years, though even with his deep and overall knowledge of Talmud with its commentaries of Rashi and the Tosafists, he did not wish to turn toward the rabbinate, rather putting his talents to the research of the Hebrew language and education. In 1896, he raised his family in Dubno, where he worked as a teacher for the remainder of his life.

Some years before WWI, my father founded a Jewish Enlightenment school ["*Heder Metukan*"] in his house, where his students learned Hebrew language in a Lithuanian accent. "Love of Zion" [*Ahavat Zion*] and "The Guilt of Samaria" [*Ashmat Shomron*] were the tools used for the deepening of his students' love of Zionism, and every letter in Hebrew published, every pamphlet, every newspaper, and every book that came to press in those days found its place in his library. Thus, his house turned into a meeting place of the admirers of Zion, a hub where everyone gravitated. The poet Yitzhak Lamdan, of blessed memory, also spent some time as a student of my father.

The chaos of war and the October Revolution changed many aspects of the life of the Jews of Dubno and its education.

[Column 381–382]

Community workers of KEPA (the Russian Disseminators of Enlightnment group [Mafitzei Haskala]) in Dubno with students. From right to left: Gitnacht, Goldis, Roitman, B. Cohen, Dr. Hindas, A. Wertheim, Y. Pinchasovich, and teacher D. Machruk.

In the year 1918, he founded a large school in the city according to the Zeitgeist. The studies were conducted in Yiddish, since it wasn't possible to maintain an all–Hebrew school. A war of life and death was waging between the Hebraists [on one side] and the Bund–Yevsektsiya [Jewish branch of the Bolshevik communist party] movements, who sought to completely uproot the teaching of the Hebrew language [on the other]. In this war, my father fought valiantly, even forgetting himself and the need to make a living. Many anti–Zionists and anti–Hebrew could not stand up against his ferocity, their old teacher from the past, but there were those who knew no shame, and would use any means that would help them in the war against Zionism and Hebrew. Among them was one individual, Kekhtzer was his name, a staunch Bundist, who didn't hesitate from informing on him to higher authorities, like Prusvita, the council of culture, in Kiev. My father stood strong against the waves, fighting and succeeding. He was given permission to teach 18 hours of Hebrew religion in the school, as well as in the Farber–Zabramie school. This continued to be until new winds came which were more liberal, with a change in the officers of the city and its surrounding neighborhoods.

In the '20s and '30s, my father taught hundreds of students, whom he guided and educated in the youth movement and immigration to Israel [*aliya*]. It is appropriate to note that while it is true that the students of other teachers were well–off children, educated in the Polish gymnasium, my father's students were, for the most part, from poor families. Indeed, he found a special meaning in their attachment to his group sessions specifically regarding Hebrew culture and teaching them a love for Zion.

Family tragedies crushed his spirit in the twilight of his life, and his sorrow went with his only daughter to a mass grave in the days of Nazi terror.

All his life, my father longed for the land of his forefathers, which he never merited to fulfill.

Rabbi Elimelech Blei, Teacher

by Ya. N. A. Y.

The elder of the educators of Dubno, Rabbi Elimelech Blei, was born in the year 5630 (1870) in Rowno, Volhynia. Some time afterward, his parents moved to Oleksandria, where little Elimelech spent his childhood years. He received a traditional education, and when he reached bar–mitzvah age, he went to yeshiva, molded by a rabbi outstanding in Torah knowledge and fear of heaven, Rabbi Moshe Rosenbaum. Until the age of 18, he studied Torah for the sake of Torah, without a thought of a practical purpose [*tachlis*], and without learning a trade from which to make a living. Then his parents made him a match [*shidduch*] with a woman the same age, Chaya–Fayga Zigelbaum of Klevan, who was his perfect partner until the end of his life. [As the Talmud Kiddushin 31a states:] "Can a man have a millstone on his neck [i.e., the responsibility to provide food for his family] and study Torah?" – Elimelech tried his hand at business without seeing success, and so he left it aside and turned to education. In 5658 (1898), Elimelech was invited by the head of the Jewish court, the *gaon* Rabbi Mordechai Mottel Sternberg, and the Crown Rabbi Bernstein, to teach in the "*Heder Metukan*" [school for Enlightenment–movement children] of the Oleksandria community. After 6 years, in 5664 (1904), he moved with his family to Dubno, where he founded a school on the principle of "Hebrew taught in Hebrew" [*ivrit b'ivrit*] together with the esteemed teacher Chaim–Nisan Zaks. Elimelech and Chaim–Nisan were like a single unit, working tirelessly to educate students to bear the banner of revival and love of the Hebrew language just like them. The youths of the city adapted themselves to Hebrew as a living language, and their ears held fast to the words of the Torah.

Elimelech and Chaim–Nisan did not shun the work of Zionism and [revival of] the Hebrew language; they did not rely on others to do it; they did not abandon it. They worked on the Odessa Committee,[1] disseminators of Hebrew poetry and literature, collecting members for "*HaShiloach*", distributing financial assistance in the Land of Israel, choosing representatives for the Zionist conference in Volhynia (which at the time was done in secret out of fear of the Tsarist authorities viewing it negatively), corresponding with Jewish leaders – simultaneously. Anything that had a hint of Zionism or Hebrew, Elimelech devoted himself toward it, and acted on its behalf out of the joy of doing a holy deed. I remember the letters and the postcards which Elimelech would write with holy trembling to the expert teacher Rabbi Yishai Adler in Jaffa. These letters were written in carefully beautiful handwriting, with not even a comma out of place (God–forbid). And all this activity was obviously not for him to get some reward from it; just the opposite – he worked to the core to help establish things properly.

Elimelech yearned in his soul to immigrate to the Land of Israel and to invest in it. In the year 5674 (1914), he began to take steps toward realizing this longing, turning to Dr. Joseph Klausner[2] to get his advice. In a response dated the eve of Passover, 5674 [1914], Dr. Klausner wrote to him:

> *My honored master Rabbi Elimelech Blei,*
>
> *This disease is terrible, this typhoid, which I have contracted this winter, and so I have delayed in responding to you until now, and I ask for your forgiveness. Whether there is a position in the Land of Israel of "Teacher's Assistant," and whether they would give you this position, can only be ascertained in the "place where it is practical." One must be in the Land of Israel and have proper diligence in this. From afar,*

[Column 385–386]

> *one cannot come to a conclusion about this matter at all. If you get the opportunity to travel to the Land of Israel for three months out of the year, to try this out, I will assist you in writing letters of recommendation. That is all I can do. Let me know what your daughters are writing to you.*
>
> *With blessings of peace and joy of the festival, and with the blessings of Zion,*
> *Dr. Joseph Klausner*

409

He made several preparations connected to immigrating to the Land, and then the first World War broke out. Chaim–Nisan managed to immigrate to the United States before this, while Elimelech Blei stayed. Dubno suffered many days of war and parts of it were consumed by fire. In the year 1918, the city was liberated from the Austrians, and Elimelech returned as the head of the "Tarbut" [lit. "culture"] school. In the year 1919–1920, he became the head of a school that was a mix of Yiddish and Hebrew founded through the Joint Committee. In the 1920s, with the opening of the Jewish–Polish gymnasium by Kremerman, Elimelech was invited to teach Jewish studies under the auspices of the Volhynia municipality. So it continued until 1934, the year of his immigration [to Israel].

Here, Elimelech was invited by the municipal Department of Education to teach Hebrew in night classes, as well as to take care of the office work for the classes. He continued to teach until the age of 76, and from then until the age of 80, he worked only in the office. At that point, he retired.

Elimelech also worked in publishing, mainly on children's books. His own writings were published in *"BaDerech"* in Warsaw, and in the Israeli publications *"Davar"*, *"Amar"*, and "Anthologies of Volhynia [*Yalkut Volhin*]".

Elimelech passed away at the ripe old age of 86 in Tel Aviv, 27 Iyyar [May 8th], 5716 (1956). His wife had died before him, also in Tel Aviv, in Elul [September] 5711 (1951).

Translator's Comments

1. A Russian–Jewish organization supporting immigration to the Land of Israel from 1890–1913.
2. A Jewish historian and professor of Hebrew Literature. He knew Theodore Herzl personally, and was involved in the Zionist movement, attending the first Zionist congress as well.

The Life of Hebrew Teacher Shlomo Balaban

by Asher Balaban

My father was born in Skver in the province of Kiev in the year 1889 to the family of the town's cantor [*chazan*]. He was a talented boy and excelled in his studies. He had a beautiful voice, an alto voice, and from the age of 7, he would assist his grandfather in his job as cantor for the Days of Awe. At that age of 7 he was already studying the Talmud with great diligence, and when he turned 11, his tutor sent him to the High Yeshiva ["*yeshiva gedola*"] in Kishinev, where the students were guaranteed room and board, so they wouldn't have to rely on "eating days" at local houses. [1]

To his great misfortune, he did not find a vacancy in this great house of Torah, leaving this lad of 11 years alone and penniless, without enough even for one meal, in a foreign city. He decided to turn to the study house, and who would happen to be there but one man from Skver. When he found out this boy was the son of Neta Balaban, he invited him to his house, giving him a full meal there, but could not afford to give him money for the expenses of traveling home. During their discussion, my father mentioned that he knew how to be a synagogue cantor. The man wasn't sure if the lad was telling the truth, but my father insisted, and the man took him to a certain house of study to pray the evening prayer. His voice was sweet to the congregation, and they invited him to pray on the Sabbath. The money he earned for those two Sabbaths gave him enough to get home. When he arrived home, he heard that Rowno had established a yeshiva similar to that of Kishinev, and he decided to try his luck there. He got to Rowno and was accepted as a student in the yeshiva, where he studied for 2 years.

During that same time, my grandfather emigrated to the United States, and my father was completely on his own. He began to study the Prophets and the Writings, and the Hebrew language, to read books in the [burgeoning modern] Hebrew language, and general literature. These were days of youth revolutions, of intellectual enlightenment ["*Haskalah*"], of great and lofty yearnings of the spirit to welcome new expanses and broad–minded subjects.

Indeed, my father never had a diploma or a degree, but in the field of Judaism, he excelled and transcended, and regarding secular subjects, his knowledge made my brother and me jealous, when we ourselves passed through college.

In 1910, my father was drafted to the army and was sent to Dubno. After basic training, he was accepted as a "volturno" player in the military orchestra, encamped in Farber–Zabramie. Over the course of time, by several visits to the Rubenstein family home, he met his future wife. During his service, the young soldier would delight the congregation of the "Mishartim" study house on the Days of Awe with his cantorial skills, and many, many people remembered him for this kindness for a long time.

During that same time, my father met the teacher Elimelech Blei, who had a great influence on my father, and brought him to teach Hebrew after the completion of his army service. Despite the age difference between them, they became great friends.

[Column 387–388]

But my father finished his service, and soon after the dark clouds of war began to knot the sky. That awful war broke out, and my father decided to hide rather than go to battle. He hid in secret for 3 years, and only in 1917, with the breakout of the [Russian] Revolution, he left his hiding place and began to build a life for himself. He married his fiancé, who waited for him faithfully all that time. When they had their first child – my brother – they gave him a Hebrew name: Ben–Ami [meaning, "Son of My Nation"]. This was the first child in Dubno to receive a modern Hebrew name. Even this name was only possible after a fierce argument between the two families among those who wanted to keep to tradition even in this.

My father started to work as a teacher in Dubno, first by giving private lessons, and then in the Zabramie school, where Elimelech Blei also taught. Already then, my father stood at the center of the youth cultural life of Hebrew–lovers. He organized choirs, theater presentations, managing youth movements, and teaching songs of the homeland, all this during his free time during evenings and nights. So it went until 1919, when the school closed and my father was invited to come to Zdolbuniv to teach there in the "Tarbut" school; a similar school would open in Dubno only in 1927.

In 1927, a "Tarbut" school opened in Dubno,[2] and my father was invited by Elimelech Blei to return to teach together ["in one basket"] with him. For the next 12 years, until Western Ukraine was seized by the Russians, my father put so much of his energy in this school into the education of the young generation, and the dissemination of Hebrew in Dubno.

The school salary did not provide enough for the finances of the house, and was actually lower than a teaching salary in the public schools. For this reason, many teachers sought out additional jobs by giving private lessons in the students' homes, where their parents wanted them to get some knowledge of the "Holy Language," which they would call the "Hebrew language."

Some fundamental changes began to take place within the Jewish population as a result of the annexation by the Soviet Union on September 17th, 1939. Zionism and Hebrew became ideas against the state, and anyone who was a known Zionist while the Polish were in power was recorded on a "blacklist," and many of them were sent to Siberia. All the Hebrew teachers obviously found themselves registered in this "blacklist," but one of my father's students was an important officer in the NKVD, the Soviet secret police, and he tried mightily on behalf of the teachers who had not yet been expelled from the city to let them continue teaching in the Yiddish–Soviet school. At the beginning of the 1939–1940 school year, two Jewish schools were founded, but there were many parents who did not wish that their children learn Yiddish, and they lobbied the Department of Education that they should be able to transfer their children to the schools they want – and they were successful in their lobbying efforts. After that, there was only one school left in which all instruction was in Yiddish. My father got a job there and was appreciated there. But it was hard for the Zionist Jew to adapt to the new environment, which was as yet unclear, and so the teachers had to be happy with the fact they could continue teaching in their own cities.

The invasion of the Nazis into the Soviet Union put an end to this not–so–happy situation, and also quickly put an end to the lives of the Jews in Dubno in general. My brother, Ben–Ami, was sent to prison, where they squeezed out of him any military knowledge he had from when he was stationed in Belgium in 1938, and six weeks after that, he was taken out to be killed. My father never merited to reach the land he so yearned for, where he would have been able to find hundreds of his students working its soil and shaking off its desolation. He never merited to see his grandchildren speaking a living Hebrew language as their mother tongue. He never merited, for he was forced, together with all the citizens of Dubno, into the ghetto, with all its terrible conditions, until the final round–up of the Jews, when he was a tortured and downtrodden man, taken together with my mother to be thrown into the mass graves…

Translator's Comments

1. The practice in many yeshivas in pre–war Europe was for the yeshiva to rely on the hospitality of local families to feed the students of the yeshiva in that town, on a rotation basis. The days spent at each house were called "eating days" (*le'echol yamim*), or in Yiddish, "*essen tag.*"

2. Although in the previous chapter, it states that a Tarbut school opened in Dubno in 1918, and in column 196, it says 1917. On the other hand, in the chapter on the Tarbut school starting in column 320, it says the Tarbut school opened in 1927, as we have it here. It may be, as suggested by Shirley Ginzburg, that different grade schools were opened at different times under the name "Tarbut." The earlier school of 1917 may have been ages 12–18, given that it was reported to only have 6 classes (which is usual for a Hebrew school to have less classes for older students), while the 1927 opening may have been for younger children, 7–12 years of age.

Eliyahu Machruk

by P. Y.

A politico? No, no, this is not the right word to describe Eliyahu Machruk. Yes, in his short life – quite short (1901–1927) – his positive qualities were so pronounced that he clearly stood head and shoulders above many of his peers. From a young age, his considerable talents showed in mathematics and Russian literature. Additionally, as the son of a Hebrew teacher, he knew the fundamentals of Jewish studies as well. He was greatly popular among the inhabitants of the city, and not just as a true prodigy in matters intellectual, but as one who merited to be of the first founders of the youth movements "Hechalutz ["The Pioneer"], and "Hashomer Hatzair ["The Young Guard"], at a time when most of his peers were in the dark regarding the subtleties of political movements which arose after the Revolution and the changes happening in the country. He was a well–equipped ideologue, ready for the passion necessary as a speaker and leader. He was yet a young man when he honed to excellence his sharp and brilliant oratory skills. Memorable to many was his speech given at the first year of the opening of the university in Jerusalem, a speech that turned the assembly into a beautiful rally for the Land of Israel.

His life was cut so very short – before his time! – he was only 26 years old when he died. The day before his passing, he received a notice from the Hebrew college in Lublin that he was appointed as an administrator there, after he had proved himself a gifted teacher in the Jewish college in Dubno. Many people in Israel were among his friends, his students, or his admirers, who remember him as a layer of foundation for Hebrew education in Dubno, and [part of the motivation] for their immigration to the Land of Israel.

Shlomo Reichman, Teacher

by Asher Reichman

Pinchas Pessas (son of Rabbi Yeshaya), of blessed memory, who was a friend of Shlomo Reichman, writes in *The City of Dubno and its Scholars*:

> "A community of scholars, a praised and respectable city – the Greater Dubno, a (II Samuel 20:19) 'city and a mother to Israel' from days of old. One of the ancient Jewish cities in the northern lands, it contained two yeshivas, tents of the righteous, (Isaiah 8:20) 'for Torah and for testimony'. Its rabbis, its scholars, and its teachers – the origins of the geniuses of spirit who made a name in the 'call of generations', who produced many capable students in judgement and decisions of Jewish law, many of them close to each other, of one great family, a glorious family of fathers and sons. "

It's true. If we wanted to know the spring from which they drew, those who imbued our national exile with the fierceness of their spirit and their will; if we desired to know the sources from which they nurtured their inner self and the national fortitude; we would not be able to ignore the portion and the contribution of the preacher [*darshan*], the sermonizer [*maggid*], the Zionist speaker, alongside the Hebrew teacher, who met face–to–face with his students, with the youth, guiding and explaining and lighting a fire in them for Zion and Jerusalem. They were the ones who would raise high, from pulpit to pulpit, for dozens of years, the message of national redemption, in the cities of the exile, shaping the minds of the masses in the house of Israel.

The life story of my father, my teacher, Shlomo Reichman, is a series of successful activities in education and in Zionism. The "land of his blossoming" – Dubno. As a youngster in his Zionist household (his father, my grandfather, was also a Hebrew teacher), he was raised with an abundance of love for the Land of Israel and the workers of the Land. He was fluent in Hebrew, and he used it to teach Torah – Hebrew language and the Hebrew Bible – to the children of Dubno, Rowno, and Demidovka. During the first World War, our family moved to Rowno. My father was drafted into the Russian army. When he returned from his army service, he continued to teach. The following is an account recorded by one Aryeh, son of Menahem, found in the book *The Community of Rowno*:

> "R. Shlomo Reichman, originally from Dubno, who had arrived in Rowno in the years of the first World War, taught in the school of R. Asher Lemel Kaulker, and after that in Yeshiva Eitz Chaim. But mainly, he did private tutoring in Hebrew language, and in religious studies, in the students' houses. He was a scholar and a strong advocate for Hebrew. "

After the war, my father took his family back to Dubno. My father also had a proclivity to write poetry on matters relevant to the day. He would compose them and publicize them by sticking them to the walls of the study house on the eve of the Sabbath and the Festivals. The poems were always a hit, received with great warmth by the congregation. He loved to send poems on Purim as "*Mishloach Manos*" [Purim gifts] to all his students and their parents, and so he was given the nickname, "Teacher Shlomo [*Shlomo Lehrer*]", or "Shlomo the Lion Writer [*Shlomo Leib Shreibers*]".

My father had a particular way of getting close to others and befriending them, and he thus loved entertainment and comedy. He would constantly rouse his friends, calling for them to act on behalf of the Land of Israel and the Jewish people with getting the word out.

Not for nought did they say about him, "*Reb Shlomo vet keynmal nit alt verren*– R. Shlomo will never grow old!"

The day I was set to immigrate to Israel, he presented me with one of his blessings in the form of a song and text that he would always recite called "Provisions for the Way [*Tzeda LaDerech*]":

417

Arise, my son, go up and do well!

And I after you – in the end

The people in your family with the people of our nation,

To build up and to be built upon in the land of our forefathers.

He never did [follow after me], and his death was in Rowno, where he had moved back to in order to be with his eldest daughter, in the Holocaust which ravaged the Jewish people.

R. Mott'l Loitziker

by Avraham Shritnik

R. Mott'l Loitziker was a typical teacher of young children [*melamed dardaki*], but he wasn't just a *melamed*. He worked as a matchmaker occasionally, as a real estate broker, and mediator, all with the goal of providing something for his family. R. Mott'l was a big–boned and big–hearted Jew, wise and clever, his words sharp, and very personable, yet he never gave in or stooped down for anyone.

Shortly before the first World War, he lived in Dubno, next door to the Great Synagogue Yeshiva, where about 40 young men studied. The yeshiva had been established by the Hassidic Rabbi, Rabbi Eliyahu Guttman, known as "The Young Rabbi." The butcher R. David Tzvi provided support for the institution. They also did not lack monetary support from the community. The teachers were R. Mott'l Loitziker for Talmud and Tosafist commentaries, and another teacher, Masurmitch.

I was then 16 years old. Of the 5 children in the house, it was my lot to study Torah. I can't say my heart was really into the Torah study, but I was forced to turn my ear to the Torah [lesson]. We sat from morning to evening, and we listened to the explanatory lectures – sometimes they were quite sophisticated – from R. Mott'l. And the smack of his hand upon us was not an infrequent occurrence.

"*Statskye Bosyaki*" [1] – "State Bums" – he would roar at us. And we were already older, not some children in elementary school, but adolescents past the age of bar mitzvah. But for him it was all the same – one must place fear in the students!

R. Mott'l ate the same way he taught. He would pick one of us and he would be sent to R. Mott'l's wife, "the *melamedes* – the schoolmarm," to bring him his food. And when he would eat, that was free time for us, the "state bums," a good thing for us and for him – R. Mott'l. He would sit and put a lot of salt on his food, then he would place the food slowly into his mouth and would enjoy it with every fiber of his being.

The messenger of his food was usually a boy by the name of Wolke Margolies. One time he got fed up with this responsibility and began to devise schemes to get himself out of it. What did he do? He went and bought alkaline soda, sprinkled it liberally on the food; and when R. Mott'l's fork reached his mouth, he spat three times and declared, "What happened to my holy wife today, that she burned the food?" The evil laughter of the pranksters immediately alerted R. Mott'l to the shameful deed, and the "state bums" obviously got what they deserved.

The yeshiva didn't last very long. The classes ended and the students disbanded, and R. Mott'l went back to being a *melamed*.

R. Mott'l had sons and daughters, but he got no parental pride from them – they did not follow in the religious path of their father.

Finally, he had one witty saying. One time, R. Mott'l Loitziker was standing close to the house of R. Yissochar–Barisch Roitman, and he was doing some business. A man turned to him and said, "Everyone knows that there is no difference between a *melamed* and an insane person! Yet, you are a *melamed*, and you are not insane at all – how do you explain that!" R. Mott'l responded, "Among the *melamed* teachers, I have never found an exception to that rule, me included, which would mean I count my portion among the insane… But I have one tried–and–true remedy for it. I have a drawer in my teacher's desk that opens with a key. When I end class, I take my insanity and lock it securely in the drawer… So when I am around people, I can be Mott'l and not 'the insane *melamed*!'"

Translator's Comment:

1. This is Russian which the author transliterated into Hebrew.

The Brothers David and Tzvi Perl

by Nisan

Among the most prominent public Jewish personalities in Dubno were the brothers David and Tzvi Perl, the former being the head of the Zionist movement in the city, the latter being the sitting head of Keren HaYesod. They were born in Dubno, into a family steadfast in the [Jewish] tradition. They received a traditional religious Jewish education, and they acquired their *Haskalah* [secular enlightenment] much later, through independent study. They worked in factory production and trade, with great factories producing dried and treated materials, and packaging of hops.

David Perl   *Tzvi Perl*

The period between the two World Wars was a time of explosion for the progress of the Zionist movement, as well as for Jewish nationalist life in Poland in general and Dubno in particular. And during this period the brothers David and Tzvi dedicated their best talents, their energy, and their time, to the Zionist movement, and to Jewish public life as a whole. They stood at the head of

[Column 395–396]

the fundraising campaign for Keren HaYesod and Keren HaKayemet LeYisrael; they promoted and readied immigration [to the Land of Israel], and they were among the founders of the nationalist school "Tarbut," taking part in its leadership for as long as it lasted.

Even with the dedication of their time and energy to Zionist activities and culture, the Perl brothers never disregarded the pressing needs of their own community As wealthy and high–class individuals – with connections to the authorities – they knew how to make use of their positions for the good of the Jewish community, "standing in the breach" during the time of the discriminatory laws which hung like the Sword of Damocles on the heads of the Jewish citizens. To illustrate, when the municipality declared the intent to destroy the old merchant area, which was bound to negatively affect many Jews, eliminating their ability to make a living, the members of the Jewish council, with David Perl at their head, worked their utmost capabilities to undo the worst of the decree, to allow the merchants of the area time to move to other places. They worked, and they were successful. And so they saved many Jews from peril, from losing their money and property.

In the year 1939, the Soviets seized that area of Poland. As leaders of the Jewish community and of the general area, as Zionists and wealthy businessmen, the Perl brothers did not have a smooth transition under Soviet authority. They were imprisoned in 1940, and their lot is unknown from that point on.

The Brothers Tzvi and Eliyahu Meizler

by Nisan

Originally from the city of Polonne, because of the disturbances of the war and the pogroms in Ukraine, they arrived in Dubno and set up their residence and home. They and their families soon integrated in the city scene, even becoming prominent members of the local city groups, especially as Zionists, recognizing their nation and origins.

Eliyahu Meizler   *Tzvi Meizler*

It was something of a strange fact that they appeared as if the two of them were a unified personality, and their Zionism was merged into one of them in his induction into the "*Bnei Moshe*" group of the foundation of *Echad Ha'am*. The special status of an individual as a member of the *Bnei Moshe* collective was counted from the days of R. Zalman Ashkenazi as a kind of honor, a crown on the head of a Zionist that everyone must respect, and so, even a brother can get the benefit of his brother's honor crowned in the badge of pride. Indeed, in their Zionist activities, the two brothers acted as one, their desires and thoughts completely given over to the Land of Israel.

423

David Horowitz

by Nisan

David Horowitz was born in the year 1888. The very beginning of his education, like for most others in his generation, was at the "*heder*", and he received his [secular] education at the gymnasium and then at the universities of the greater cities of Russia and abroad. Horowitz was, in his nature, a passionate soul, and he bonded well with regular folks. He was a rebel already in his youth; he rebelled against the social regime which was exploitative and discriminatory, and he also rebelled against the negative habits that clung to our nation over the course of the long exile. He was a reservoir of Jewish awareness, and he fought fiercely with this awareness.

They tell a story about him that took place during the Tsarist period. A Russian officer permitted himself to openly insult Judaism and the "kikes" [*yehudonim*] right in front of Horowitz, who responded there and then with true strikes, teaching that officer a lesson, a man of the "Black Hundreds," [1] who took what was coming to him. The reverberation of that story was great, and severe was his anticipated punishment, and so Horowitz was forced to flee the country. He was tried in absentia; the sentence waiting for him was severe, and only with the breakout of the [Russian] Revolution did he return to Dubno.

During the reign of the Ukrainian commander Symon Petliura, the terrible enemy Oskilko [Ukrainian military administrator] turned his attention to the Jewish people. Following the "Purim" pogrom, that was known to the Jewish community in its demand for heavy fines, alongside the terrible pogrom itself, they could not come up with the full amount demanded by Petliura. This attention was brought about by the campaigning and the personality of David Horowitz. Indeed, Horowitz, in his characteristically fierce passion, responded to Oskilko that the error was with him, if he thought that an independent Ukraine could be established through the blood of innocent Jews, and surely, he was not ready to lead his people day–in and day–out under the stench of spilled blood. Suffice it to say, by taking such a position, Horowitz was throwing away his life. But he knew not how to flatter, nor how to bow in submission, even before murderers. He just reacted without fear and without a care for the anticipated danger.

Horowitz was an activist who was uniquely gifted in his activism and poured himself into it. His views and opinions were related to those of the revolutionists – "Simovicim,"[2] "Bund,"[3] – but his fierce style did not allow him to connect as a follower to any particular and defined party. As a youth, his style was one of rebellion, but as he became older this turned into many constructive activities. He never became an administrator for some foundation, but he would contribute and find ways to set into motion the creation of organizations and foundations such as K.A.P.E., and A.Z.E.,[4] and he worked hard to establish and develop the Jewish hospital in the city. As an appointed official in the municipality, he did many things in the welfare bureau, concerning himself with providing professional training for the youth through the goal of founding an "ORT"[5] school, but because of the turbulence of the times, he did not succeed in doing so. During the height of the Zionist activities of the city, he was close to the "Hitachdut" ["Unity"] group, and he looked favorably at educating his children in the "Hashomer HaTzeir" ["The Young Guard"] movement.

While not many people of Dubno joined the Piłsudski–Sanation [movement],[6] Horowitz nevertheless expressed his fierce opposition to anyone who even showed a hint of willingness to join it, which he viewed as political obsequiousness, a lowering of Jewish pride and self–respect.[7]

We know only bits and pieces of the activities of the public leaders in the Ghetto, and we certainly don't know anything about the activities of David Horowitz during those terrible times in the tiny Ghetto. The few reports that have come to us by way of firebrands rescued from the literature regarding his depressed state, and his stubborn will to help others, together with the community that he had fostered and educated, he "dreamed and he fought" [chalam ve–lacham], and he found his death within the Ghetto.

Translator's Comments

1. These were gangs of antisemitic thugs who operated under the auspices of the Tsar at the beginning of the 20th century.
2. It is unclear which movement this refers to. –tc
3. The General Jewish Labour Bund was a secular Jewish socialist party in the Russian Empire, active between 1897 and 1920.
4. I do not know which foundations these are. –tc
5. ORT is a Russian acronym meaning "Association for Vocational Crafts"
6. This was a Polish political movement created between World War I and World War II. Named after the Latin word for "healing" ("sanatio"), the Sanation movement mainly comprised former military officers who were disgusted with the perceived corruption in Polish politics. Sanation was a coalition of rightists, leftists and centrists whose main focus was the elimination of corruption and the reduction of inflation. (Wikipedia)
7. A large following of the Sanation movement were those devoted to disenfranchising the Jews of Poland. After founder Pilsudski died in 1935, this part split from the group to create the "Camp of National Unity", and one part of their agenda was adopting 13 theses on the Jewish question. Modeled after the Nuremberg laws, they labelled Jews as a foreign element that should be deprived of all civil rights and ultimately expelled altogether. (Wikipedia)

Asher–Zelig Bernstein

by Nisan

Asher–Zelig Bernstein was born in the town of Berestechko, near Dubno. Yeshiva–educated and possessing a sharp mind, when Asher–Zelig moved away from home, he decided to look toward the trade business to make money. He tried to integrate into the tight–knit trade families, but he was a foreign "plant" in their midst. Only once he started to show his strength in community affairs, revitalizing it, it became clear to all, as well as to himself, that he was born to be involved in community affairs. He was a hardworking man, punctilious and meticulous, who loved order and organization, and with that always behaved with fairness toward others. With great understanding, whenever he would see a man before him, a man alone in his worries and his distresses, Asher–Zelig would work to help him however much he could. Thus, all respected him and admired him.

There is no doubt that the proximity of the town of his birthplace to Dubno was very helpful in preparing him for his involvement in public affairs and Zionism. It seemed to "overflow from its spirit" to him, granting him a strength to his communal activities before the Holocaust, as well as during the Nazi reign. Asher–Zelig invested great energy in the organization of refugees in the eve of the World War, at a time when the Nazis began the expulsion of the "Ost Yidden" [Eastern–European Jews] from Zbaszyn, a town on the Poland–Germany border.[1] These poor refugees were forced to find somewhere to live for themselves on the streets of the country. In those hard days, Asher–Zelig stood and never stopped empathizing with the utter bitterness of those strangers who lost everything and became homeless.

Translator's Comment

1. Also known as Polenaktion, it was the arrest and expulsion of about 17,000 Polish Jews living in Nazi Germany in October 1938. These deportations, ordered by SS officer and head of the Gestapo Reinhard Heydrich, displaced thousands of Polish Jews along the Germany–Poland border. (Wikipedia)

Shimon–David Feffer

by M. C.

In his youth, he was inducted into a select group of young men of study–house regulars and acquirers of general education, like many Jewish youths would at the end of the 19th century. Over the course of time, this group produced public leaders, their seals affixed upon the revival of Judaism in the city, and after Kerensky's revolution in 1917, [1] they took positions in the institutions they founded.

Shimon–David Feffer was among the founders of the Tarbut school, a member of the town committee of all the Zionist groups, and he was active in the "Keren HaYesod" institution. Out of great care and worry for the success of the Zionist movement in the city, he took an active position in the election of the local public institutions, such as the city council, the community council, etc.

He raised his children in the spirit of Zionism, and two of his children actually immigrated to the land of Israel and joined in building it up. While he himself spoke of immigrating with his wife and youngest daughter, the war broke out, killing his plans and them all together.

Translator's Comment:

1. Alexander Fyodorovich Kerensky was a Russian lawyer and revolutionary who was a key political figure in the first Russian Revolution of 1917 (Wikipedia).

A Portrait of R. Avraham–Moshe Kolton

by S. K.

A *Maskil* [1] of the previous century, Kolton's "training" was not any different than all the other *maskilim* of that era: religious studies upon the benches in the study–house of the "distinguished" Volozhin yeshiva, in the Odessa yeshiva, and the "*achsatran*" program [2] in secular studies. And in Odessa, one joined the "Hibat Zion" ["Lover's of Zion" movement] – obviously – and subsequent Zionist activities over time.

Kolton was a Zionist with every fiber of his being [lit. "with his 248 limbs" [3]], never allowing for any work or activity to not have him be a part of it. A zealot for the Hebrew language, he strove to raise his children with a Jewish education, to give to them the treasury of the nation's spirit, from which he drew and absorbed all his days. A great friend of the youth movement, he had a great influence on them in their campaigns for fundraising. He demanded from every single person in the youth movement that they practice what they preached to others and immigrate to the land of Israel. As someone who would "expound and also fulfill," [4] he sent his children before he himself would immigrate to "cherish its dirt." [5] He dreamt of immigration – but never achieved it. The Holocaust that fell upon the house of Israel also felled his longings alongside it.

Translator's Comments

1. A follower or adherent of the Haskalah movement, plural "maskilim."
2. A program of studies popular among the *maskilim* of the late 19th century, attested to in many Hebrew sources.
3. A symbolic Talmudic number of limbs, often added together to 356 muscles and sinews to equal 613 – the number of Biblical commandments
4. A phrase from the Talmud (see, for example, Hagiga 14b), meaning to practice what one preaches.
5. Cf. Psalms 102:15

Toward a Portrait of R. Yisrael–Moshe Leshchever

by Nisan

R. Yisrael–Moshe Leshchever, or, as they called him in Dubno, "Srul–Moishe Leshchever," was in the business of trees and forests, like his fathers before him. While this took a lot of his time and energy, R. Yisrael always found time for public service, which was always very helpful for the community. He never belonged to any particular faction or sect and would never push himself to the head of a line, never put on airs or put himself above anyone. His house was a meeting place, and he had a lot of authority, for he would answer anyone who would come to him seeking his counsel. He served on the city council for many years, and was appointed to deal with social work matters, and the poor and downtrodden – of which there were many in the city – would turn to him with requests for aid. R. Yisrael–Moshe, who never scorned the seemingly inconsequential, would receive them with a smile, listen to the person's request, and act to the best of his ability to help him.

He was active in TOZ [1], and he served as the sitting head of the journal "ORT," and acted in every constructive activity for the sake of the Jews of Dubno.

Translator's Comment

1. TOZ, the acronym for "Towarzystwo Ochrony Zdrowia Ludnosci Żydowskiej w Polsce," was an organization that started in 1921 that focused on the health of Polish Jewry, in the areas of hygiene, preventative medicine, and children's health, as well as providing guidance for pregnant women. Their campaigns lasted until 1938.

Chana Kagan (Cohen)

by A. C.

Chana Kagan was one of the most acclaimed public figures of Dubno in the years leading up to the Holocaust – serving her nation by dedicating her time for the good of the collective and involving herself in many causes.

Chana, the daughter of Asher–Zelig and Batya Sis, was born in Rowno in 1889. She received her elementary and high school education there, until she was displaced by the first World War and moved to Russia. In returning to Dubno, she married Mr. Moshe Kagan, and established a home that would become a meetingplace for Zionist activities for many years.

Her first public activity began in 1925, when she established a health group in the city called "TOZ." She mainly worked to establish successful children's camps and food kitchens for poor children, and camps for youth movements. She went out on behalf of TOZ to check the nutrition in these children's camps, which would get 200–300 children every year, which needed to be at a high level in the city, and she would also look at the youth camps. She was always worried about the nutrition and education of children who wandered the streets or the riverbanks during the summer.

Chana Kagan's social work activities expanded starting in 1932. That year, the municipality of Dubno decided to appoint public social workers for different areas of the city. Of these appointees, three were Jewish: David Horowitz, the pharmacist Sinegel, and Chana Kagan. Her work encompassed a sprawling area, from Tcherno Street to the First Bridge and Szeroka Street. This area was the biggest concentration of the neediest of the city, especially the poorest Jews. One of Ms. Kagan's tasks was to visit every house and report on the household's need for assistance from the municipality welfare department. She did the best she could for anybody who needed help. The needy of both Jew and non–Jew constantly appeared in droves at the door of her house to fill out registration forms for welfare. Whether in weather rainy and wet, or hot as the sun, one could find Chana Kagan on her visitation route for those who needed her help, her mouth at the ready with words of warm encouragement – she was always genuine.

She was especially concerned for the needy in the days leading up to the holidays, when complications would inevitably arise in getting food assistance to them before the holiday. She dedicated her time to provide support to them and to deliver for them, so that they could be able to afford food, and clothes for their little ones, in celebration of the holiday.

When the municipality welfare program was made defunct in 1936 with the establishment of the Economic Welfare Committee – "Ogrodki działkowe" – Chana Kagan began to work as a factory manager and served as its accountant until the outbreak of the war. She managed a campaign behind the closed doors of the Jewish population that they should join the "*Miki–mi*

[Column 403–404]

Hamashkim," [11] and she was deeply saddened by the fact that only a handful of Jewish families joined the group compared to the hundreds of Christian households.

The social work of Chana Kagan was just one aspect of her public activities. The other side was her Zionist work.

In 1937, a WIZO (Women's International Zionist Organization) branch was founded in Dubno, and Chana Kagan was chosen as its first chairwoman. Even after she relinquished her role to Ms. Starr, she remained the secretary for the branch, and she did so with a passion, especially regarding national institutions and the Tarbut school, where she would visit as a representative of WIZO.

When the decision was made to create a Tarbut school, it was clear that without wider public assistance, it would not be able to be established. Of the many activities that Chana Kagan was part of, her women's groups gave much support for the Tarbut school through monthly donations, in addition to passionately campaigning for one–time payments from others through fundraisers. Along with some of her closest friends, Dina Krantzov, Rivka Reiss, and others, she would pass house to house to collect money, sometimes for national institutions, sometimes for the school, for this was her one objective: Zionism.

With the outbreak of the second World War in September of 1939, all public Zionist activities were immediately stopped. It had seemed that an end had come to the initiative and tirelessness of Chana Kagan. But it was not so. When the Soviet soldiers entered the city, it became flooded with thousands of Jewish refugees who had no means of survival. Chana Kagan, together with Mr. Yisroel-Moshe Leshchever, decided on their own (since the organizations were no longer active) to turn toward the secretary of the Raikom (standing for "*Raionnyi komitet*" – the district committee), who also was the secretary for the Communist party, and requested that he establish a soup kitchen for the refugees. After a few days passed, they received their answer: the municipality will create the soup kitchen, on condition that Ms. Kagan manage it. And so, for a year and a half of the Soviet occupation of the city, she managed the kitchen, making tens of thousands of meals during that period for Polish refugees.

Despite her weakening and waning health, while she divided the time in her last years between her sickbed and her commitment to public service, Chana Kagan continued to act on behalf of the public, Jew and gentile alike, in Dubno. She passed away on May 21st, 1941, just a few weeks before the Germans entered the city.

Translator's Comment

1. I could not find information about this program or organization.

R. Shmuel Kaufman–Motziver

by C. Kaufman–Melamed

My father, R. Shmuel, was born in Dubno in 1878. Where did the name "Motziver" come from? From his grandfather, who came to Dubno from the town of Motziv, which is close to Kowel. This nickname stuck to the family without ceasing, though the townspeople were careful not to say it for fear of offense, while the family enjoyed it as an inside joke.

My father received a traditional education, and when he came of age, his parents said to him, "Torah goes well with work," [1] and they sent him to be an apprentice to a builder. This is what the best Torah scholars and workers did in the city. Over the course of time, after having married and started a large family, he constructed a large house for himself next to the Braslover studyhouse.

In 1912, the Zionist activists in the city decided to establish a Hebrew school. This was quite a difficult task in those days. They had to battle the conservative opinion that such schools were for the "*goyim*," the gentiles, whereas the Jews just needed a "*Talmud Torah*," religious studies schools. These "crazies" for the idea of a Hebrew school were few in number; rich in vision, but poor in material means. Among the few was my father, who was accepted in the workers' circles, and when a site for the school could not be found, for which the heads were Chaim–Nisan Zaks and Elimelech Blei, my father set aside two rooms of his house for the school, and even sent his first–born daughter to study in the first Hebrew school in the city.

It wasn't long before dark clouds spread over the European skies, with the outbreak of the first World War. Daily life in Dubno was in turmoil, for the city became split in two: on one bank of the Ikwa River was occupied by the Austrians, and on the other, the Russians, and they would alternately occupy the town for different periods of time.

And then, a revolution in Russia broke out, and then some time afterward, the Bolshevik Revolution. While the storms of revolutions were taking place in the country, the organized Polish army managed to conquer Dubno.

Slowly but surely, life began to return to normal. Committees were established for various types of aid, and the city institutions began to recover. Meanwhile,

[Column 405–406]

American aid arrived containing much needed emergency supplies, food and clothes, which was distributed to those who needed it. My father and mother took part in all of these assistance activities, and with a smile on their faces they knew how to cheer up the needy, to ease the burdens of those difficult times.

My father's activities were many–sided. He was one of the founders of the charity fund, which provided interest–free small loans, and he was also among the Jewish bank coalition and its committee. Additionally, he was appointed on behalf of the Labor ministry for candidates to receive professional building certificates. He acted to the best of his ability to help the individual and the community. That's how he became in one case a "Hassid", even though he was a "*Mitnaged*, [2]" because it allowed him to help a rabbi who was in particularly dire straits. And he was not frightened of dangerous situations, like the time he had a choice before him: to rescue a Jewish soldier who escaped captivity or turn his back on him. He surely knew that it could cost him his life, yet, despite this, he still acted to rescue the soldier.

It was his lifelong dream to immigrate to the land of Israel. When people asked him why he allowed his daughter to immigrate to Israel, he answered, "I am planting a tree in the land of Israel. When the plant matures and turns into a tree, it will bear fruits that I can enjoy." Indeed, he was fortunate to be able to immigrate; in 1935, my father left with his family to Israel, settling in Rishon LeTzion, and finding work at the Nesher beer factory, where he was quickly beloved by both his bosses and the other workers. He was happy with his lot – that is, until the second World War broke out and the crushing hand of the Nazis rose upon all the Jewish people of Poland, including the city of Dubno. His heart broke over this great national tragedy, as well as his own tragedy – his only son, who had remained there, was tragically killed in the great holocaust of the House of Israel. His depression hastened his end, and he passed on in 1947.

Translator's Comments

1. Cf. Mishna Avot 2:2
2. Literally, "opposition", this was a large portion of Orthodox Jews who opposed the Hassidic movement that began in the 18th century.

Avraham Karaulnik

by B. Bardiga

The name Avraham Karaulnik cannot be separated from its connection to an important and well–known educational institution in the city: the Jewish–Polish Gymnasium. This was the only Jewish high school that existed for over twenty years. From the day of its founding, until the destruction, it was part of Karaulnik's life. Indeed, this was even represented by his name in how he fostered the institution ("*karaul*" in Russian means a guard or someone who watches over the welfare of a thing).

In the beginning of the 1920s, when there was a change of the leadership of the city, and the city was joined to the newly–revitalized Polish nation's territory, the Russian gymnasium closed, and Jewish children were left without a high school in which to study. The Polish government's reaction was to establish a Polish state–run gymnasium in place of the Russian one that closed, but the number of spots available to Jewish students was basically zero in comparison to the demand.

In response to this new situation, several people, such as Arkhash, Zuckerman, Guberman, and Karaulnik, made efforts to create a new gymnasium for Jewish children. The municipality, viewing it as a private institution, demanded that one person be in charge of the permit for this Jewish–Polish gymnasium. Indeed, the permit provided certain benefits, but many issues too. Avraham Karaulnik overcame the issues, protected the institution from all sides, and in times of crisis, he did not rest nor remain silent, never allowing it to collapse.

Even though he was a businessman, heavily invested in his business, Karaulnik dedicated himself to the institution and took care of any problems, whether it was the building rent, purchasing inventory, or providing for the research labs and other such rooms, as well as paying the teachers their salaries – he took care of all of these things, every task, as if they were his only job. Everyone knew that if one wanted to see Karaulnik, one should look for him first in the gymnasium.

Advertisment for "The Private Gymnasium of A. Karaulnik in Dubno, with Polish as the teaching language".
The directorate informs that entry exams for all grades, except grade eight, are offered until June 27, 1932.
Registration is possible at the gymnasium office daily at 9-12.

There were many difficult decisions in trying to find a way to secure the survival of the institution. Many teachers found second jobs, and in one instance, through the initiative of Eliyahu Machruk, the teacher, they became members of a cooperative that they founded for themselves. Despite their material difficulties they encountered with the management of the institution, they still made it possible for children whose parents could not afford to pay the tuition, to be able to attend the institute. Without regard to the madness and chaos taking place in the Polish reactionary government, the institute continued to prosper and produce many graduates, who would go abroad to continue their studies. The institution proved itself capable, its pedagogy on a very high and refined level, ended up, in 1932, even then, "the evil angel is forced to say Amen," [1] and Karaulnik was granted full governmental rights. This man, who never spared any effort on behalf of the institution, merited a town full of those who appreciated him and gave him a special honor for his work.

Translator's Comment

1. See Talmud Sabbath 119b. The Talmud states that when one properly prepares for the Sabbath, a good angel blesses him that this should continue the next week, and an evil angel is forced to agree. If one does not prepare properly for the Sabbath, the reverse happens.

Leib Luchnik

by Nisan

Leib Luchnik was born in 1881 in Rowno. His father was a small businessman, and growing up, Leib only knew poverty and hard times. While still a lad, he was sent to be an apprentice for a tailor "who would make him into a man." He learned the trade – and became a man out of it.

Indeed, this apprentice developed himself alongside his skills at tailoring. He was an autodidact, and as an autodidact does, he kept becoming more and more learned, attained more understanding, and assimilated what he learned and read. During the reactionary times after 1905, he emigrated to America, but two years later returned to live close to his brother in his old hometown.

In 1912, angered over fraud perpetrated in recruitment for interning apprentices, he organized a protest. The *Ochrana* (the Russian Tsarist secret police) persecuted him because of his demands for better working conditions for workers. He was imprisoned, and his family was left hungry and impoverished. However, even his release only brought more frustration: his wife, who seemed not to understand the meaning of his activities, had burned all of his books, books he had collected and compiled through great effort, a labor of love. So, all of these events converged upon him to crush his spirit, yet he prevailed, and persecution only served to make him stronger, and he even more passionately fought for workers' rights.

He was the very definition of the "Bund" man; even though this particular political stream was not very popular in Dubno, he stood as its political leader for the small circle of followers that existed in the city, and even his ideological opponents respected him as a man of integrity.

Leib Luchnik did not know how to take a break from public activities. Three times he was elected to the city council. A man of the community, always doing the best he could to help those in need of assistance. He was there for the oppressed and the wretched, and used every means at his disposal – lobbying, persuasion, debates, raising funds, and so on – in order to lighten the weight of their bitter lots. He vowed war against the rich who also knew of this situation [and did nothing to help].

And when the Soviets came to Dubno, and the Bundists were being hunted down, this politically rebellious and public–facing man took on a decree of silence, and willingly became home–bound. He disconnected from society and put a stop to his activities, distancing himself from the public life which had been indeed his entire life, and ceased any communication with the leaders of Bund, who had been his most intimate friends beforehand.

The conclusion to this popular man's life was to be torn away from public activism in the twilight of his life, and he was brought, alongside his fellow brethren of the city, to the mass grave...

Dr. Isidore Margulies

by Nisan

Born in Brody in Galicia, Dr. Margulies received an extensive education in his childhood, drawing from Jewish traditional roots, and received a doctorate in Philosophy at the university in Vienna. At the end of the 1920s, he served as the principal of the Jewish–Polish Gymnasium in Dubno and gave his time and effort to raise this foundational institution, making it fit to be a well–regarded school in the eye of the government. In a time when educational institutions displayed open hostility towards the Jewish people, he knew how important it was to instill and strengthen the national identity within the institution, raising the feeling of self–pride in the students.

Dr. Margulies quickly integrated into public life and society in Dubno, becoming one of its leaders. In the 1930s, he was elected to serve as second–in–command to the head of the city, his prominent position like thorns in the eyes of the antisemites.

During the Holocaust, some "good" Germans tried to get him *"schayenem"*– documentation – that would give him an easier life in the ghetto, but he refused the "goodness" of his oppressors, and he remained strong–willed as ever even during times which produced in him a psychological depression. Several times he tried to take his own life, but Jewish doctors saved him. In the end, he chose to kill himself rather than by the hands of those cruel monsters, the shame of humanity.

A Portrait of Yosef Pinchasowicz

by Nisan

Yosef Pinchasowicz, or, as he was called, Yosef Borisowicz, was the very image of a public figure, outstanding at every period of his life, at all times, in every kind of situation. Though he would get involved in a public need, he would not join with the "professional" busybodies. Except for the short period in which he was involved with the "Folkists" [1] because of his friend Pryłucki, [2] he never joined a party or political movement. A man attuned to people in need, he devoted himself to the social work in the city, and any Constructivist [3] work, which he was involved with in order to help people support themselves.

A lawyer by trade, Yosef Borisowicz was unique among the people of his generation for being fortunate enough to receive an education that primed him against assimilation, and he remained a man of his people, close to the educational institutions, a member of the school's teacher council, and his passion showed. He was active in credit funds, worker's banks, as well as charity funds connected to the synagogue of Rabbi Abraham Mordechai.

According to the eye–witness testimony of one of the survivors of Dubno, she last saw Yosef Borisowicz on April 7th, 1942. She describes that day:

"That day, the day following the night of the first Passover seder, they decreed in Dubno that one of the quarters be *judenrein* – cleared out of Jews. That morning, the inhabitants of that quarter began to schlep their belongings on their backs, bringing them to the streets designated for Jews. There were no means for transportation, there

443

were no movers, and so, a person could only save what could be carried. They had limited time, just a number of hours.

One of the prominent figures with a bag on his back was Yosef Pinchasowicz, who walked with his head held high, proud, as if he were a free man. Nevertheless, alongside this pride was the knowledge of the deep, deep tragedy in his eyes of the "eternally wandering Jew". None of his good deeds, and great merits, helped him then…"

Translator's Comments

1. Also known as the "Jewish People's Party" or "Folkspartei," it was founded after the 1905 pogroms in the Russian Empire by Simon Dubnow and Israel Efrojkin. Close to the General Jewish Labour Bund for the emphasis on Yiddish and its culture, it differed from that party by its middle class, craftsmen and intellectual base, but also because of its ideological options. According to Dubnow, Jewish assimilation was not a natural phenomenon, and the Jewish political struggle should be centered on a Jewish autonomy based upon community, language and education, and not upon class struggle as advocated by Bundist theorists. It was a liberal party in economic matters, committed to political democracy and secularism. (Wikipedia)
2. Noach Pryłucki (1882–1941) was a Jewish–Polish politician from the Folkspartei. He was also a Yiddish linguist, philologist, lawyer and scholar of considerable renown. (Wikipedia)
3. This seems to be some kind of institution of a political nature, but I could not find what exactly it refers to.

Sarah'ke Dubtzis

by Nisan

No one seems to recall her from her youth. Even the oldest among us knew her as an elderly public figure. Who, then, was she, this Sarah'ke Dubtzis, among the people of Dubno?

Indeed, the image most memorable regarding this righteous woman was her short stature, her gaunt and wrinkled face, how she only ever wore one type of clothing: a black dress with a light–red shawl covering her entirely. She seemed like a typical Jewish woman – but not so! Unlike all the others, she carried a great weight on her dainty shoulders. We speak not only of the weight of a family, which on its own was almost too much, difficult and painful, but also the weight of the sum of her social welfare contributions, if we can use the modern nomenclature. Her contribution was not a pre–set amount of activity, or by supporting institutions, but toward a specific institution that concerned itself with distributing funds collected by donations to fulfill the social welfare needs of many people. She would run around to the rich people of the city, demanding – and succeeding in getting – donations from them for the social welfare needs. Her great passion convinced all to give; no person could refuse her.

Sarah'ke Dubtzis never studied psychology, nor gained expertise in social work or charity work, but she had a heart of fire, ready and willing to help all those who looked to her for help. She did that which today an institute would do to help various types of needs. Similarly, she would worry over the needs of prisoners, help the destitute sick, helping even to raise poor children, and so on.

Her warmhearted countenance, which expressed the full meaning of "Love thy fellow as thyself", added to the aura of authority and her moral power. Passing through the streets, she constantly said *"Gut morgen"* – "Good morning", to anyone she met on her way, for indeed, everyone knew her, and appreciated her for the goodness and kindness for those who needed help and compassion.

Her name became synonymous in the city for a wholesome and pure woman working to help others.

R. Avraham Lichter

by C. L.

R. Avraham Lichter was known in Dubno by the name R. Avraham Wallitzer, after the village called Wallitz where his grandfather had lived. If you asked about R. Abraham Lichter in Dubno, nobody would know who he was, or where he lived. But if you asked about R. Abraham Wallitzer – any child could show you his house.

R. Avraham Lichter was born in 5630 [1870]. Pure in his ways and sociable, R. Avraham devoted himself for many years to matters relating to charity work, out of a concern for the city's needy. As the sitting head of the charity fund, which was situated next to the religious studyhouse (he was the prayer administrator (*gabbay*) there for 20 consecutive years), he would provide interest–free loans with a collateral guarantee for anyone who needed one, which they could pay back with small payments. Obviously, the fund needed a lot of money, and so R. Avraham would visit the city elites and give rousing speeches to convince them to contribute to the fund. He instituted a custom that every year, during the week in which the Torah portion was *"Mishpatim"* ("Judgements"), [1] anyone who was called up to the Torah in any of the city's synagogues would agree to contribute to the fund, and immediately after this he would go from *gabbay* to *gabbay* collecting the money donated to the funds.

R. Avraham was also involved in other charity institutions that existed in the city, dedicating his time and energy to them. He was lucky to have such a generous and giving wife, Golda, who was forced to work very hard alone at the two stores they owned, to enable her husband to be involved in charity work.

Golda knew that she would receive merit in the next world for the charity her husband did in this world...

R. Avraham passed away on the 15th of Iyyar, 5693 [May 11th, 1933], and received much honor from the people of the city, who all came out to accompany him to his final resting place. He left behind 4 sons, 2 daughters, and 6 grandchildren. All of them, with the exception of one son who was in Israel, perished in the Holocaust.

Escorting those who were emigrating to Israel

Translator's Comment

1. The Torah is split into weekly portions to be read every Sabbath in an annual cycle. The portion referred to here is Exodus 21:1–24:18.

Yankel Sanis

by Malka Freeman

His name was Yaakov Rinsburg, but in Dubno he was called Yankel Sanis. He was a man remarkable in his ways and his refined character traits, a symbol of generosity and wholesomeness, always helping anyone who needed assistance.

His house was across the studyhouse of the Hassidic followers of Olyka, and he was the prayer administrator (*gabbay*) there for many years. His hospitality was legendary, and guests in his home were both residents of Dubno, as well as inhabitants of the nearby towns. Anyone who came to Dubno, whether for business or needed a medical specialist's opinion, whether from Mlynow, Torhovytsya, Mikovyts, or some other place – they all came to Yankel Sanis, who would welcome them with a smile, seeing himself as lucky that he could help them.

R. Yankel Sanis knew everyone in Dubno, and everyone knew him. He knew when those who struggled with making a living couldn't make ends meet, worrying over each and every one of them: This one needs food for the Sabbath, this one needs matzah for Passover, that third one needs firewood for winter... he would send them the funds – anonymously and discreetly, of course, so no one would know and he would not cause another to be embarrassed in public, God–forbid, that they needed such help. His entire life was filled with public needs: the Jewish medical clinic in the city, the old–age home, the religious school *Talmud Torah*, providing for Passover charity campaigns (*maos chitin*), and so on. He would bring starving children into his home and feed them, and then give them presents of candies and pastries.

R. Yankel had a hoarse voice, yet every so often, he would lead the prayers, for he so loved the mitzvah of being the prayer leader.

R. Yankel died at the hands of those murderers along with the rest of the community of Dubno as holy martyrs.

Ester Feffer (née Deibog)

by Y. P.

The noble image of a woman who knew, despite all the upheavals of life, how to stand strong and with pride – that was Esther Feffer. Born in Dubno to R. Chaim Deibog, a lawyer and an important person in the city, she received a higher education in music in the Academy of Music in Liége, Belgium. She began to teach music in Pryluky, and later in Dubno, and soon many parents were knocking on her door asking for her to teach their children music. She dedicated a lot of her time to the good of the community, playing concerts for the needy, for free, without any expectation of payment.

Also when in Israel, Esther Feffer donated some of her time to teach music, and though much of her time was already dedicated to pedagogical work, she knew she also needed to adapt to the agricultural work of where she lived, Kfar Saba. She became beloved and her cultured personality and her refined character traits shined through.

In her final years, she suffered a harsh sickness, and when she felt that her time was coming, she willed: "Do not oppose an autopsy after death, for perhaps they will be able to understand the disease and save others who suffer from the disease."

Eliezer Zharne

by Nisan

Born in Dubno in 1905, this stamped upon his life the mark of the Jewish sign. [1] Born to a family of businessmen, though they were constantly working on making a living, they nevertheless made sure their children received educations in secular and Hebrew studies. Good–looking, and tall like a tree, was Eliezer among his family members, and from his birth he was successful in all he did: in his studies, in sports, in leadership.

He was an outstanding student in the gymnasium, a star in the Maccabee football club, a counselor/leader in *"Shomer Hatzair"*. Like most youths in his circles in Dubno before the World War, all he desired was getting ready and leaving for the land of Israel.

His life in Israel started in 1929, in the workforce, in the kibbutz, in public activities. He had the power of persuasion, in convincing friends to get involved in public work. His words were pleasant and his sentences well–structured, precise and reasoned.

His thoughts were always on how to memorialize the community of Dubno in a book, and contributed much of his energy to organize it and realize this hope. He did not merit to see that book come to light, and, at the age of 55, disease ripped him from the land of the living.

Translator's Comment

1. This likely refers to the year of the first Russian revolution, which induced a massive wave of pogroms across the entire Pale of settlement, including Dubno.

Dr. Misha Lichtenstein–Zohar

by Nisan

Born in Dubno in 1910, he received a traditional religious Jewish education as well as a secular one. Studious from his youth, he received a doctorate already at the age of 22 for law, yet never ceased his interest in Jewish studies. He lived according to the dictum: "A Jew in the home, and a Jew in the street." [1]

His army expertise and law knowledge represented his life.

In 1939, he arrived in the Land of Israel, and as a proud Jew and army man, he immediately found his path as a leader in the Haganah. With the establishment of the State of Israel, the army integrated as a permanent fixture, and as a man of the law, he was appointed to serve in the higher military court, and in 1953, the head prosecutor in the army.

Dr. Lichtenstein–Zohar then joined the lecturer staff of Hebrew University. His analytical mind, his direct personality and his knowledge of law and order, allowed him to rise in the ranks to high positions in the international organization of military law, and he spent much time working on the adjudication of army law. Much of his work left after him is called, in lawyer–slang, "Law of Zohar."

He was a high colonel in the army, and a high champion in his talks with his friends, ears always listening to what he had to say, and he always made his point clear to others. He was rich in spirit, modest in his conduct toward others, an exemplary friend and an admirable family man. He spent much effort presenting his memories of Dubno in the book "Dubno" but did not merit in seeing the book come to light, for his tie to life was loosened in 1961.

Translator's Comment

1. A more common refrain of assimilated Jews was, "Be a man in the streets and a Jew in the home".

[Starting at column 419 Hebrew] *[Starting at column 678 Yiddish]*

Shmuelik the Watchmaker

by B. Elimelech (of blessed memory)

Shmuelik the watchmaker was the type of person about whom no one could agree: some loved him, some hated him, some praised him, some denigrated him; and so, the only thing left to do is describe him, his day–to–day life and his social life, according to the facts and real stories.

Shmuel's story begins with his service to the Dubno synagogue about 70–80 years ago. He was truly cut from the cloth of the synagogue administrator (*shamash*). Indeed, he descended from a long line of synagogue administrators (*shamashim*). It seems to be a natural law that the *shamash* must be of a hunched stature, submissive, lowly, a laughingstock, always ingratiating to the regular masses of the synagogue – just tread under every foot. But look – something different! Shmuel never inherited this "law" of lowliness from the *shamashim*. He had his own law: never meek in the face of others, never flattering others to get by, and never giving anyone a reason to belittle him. Moreover, he was bold and forward toward the synagogue–goers should anyone try to diminish his honor. "Just because I am the *shamash*," he would say, "that gives you the right to walk all over me? I am above all a human being, and all human beings demand basic respect!"

They say his outlook to life was formed already in his youth, growing up with his father and grandfather, when he saw their difficult lives and the torment of poverty that reigned over them. Shmuel did not tolerate the rich, the people who would feed themselves to the point of nausea. He was constantly criticizing them. In particular, he waged a war against Goldman, who owned a large mill in Dubno. This was a man who overworked his employees, squeezing out every drop of lifeblood they had. And when one of them would become faint from lack of strength to continue, not only would he, Goldman, ignore the person's dangerous health, but he would fire him on the spot. And there were laws and various other issues that caused the poor to be oppressed, and Shmuel fought against these as well in order to get money into the hands of the workers. He, Shmuel the *Shamash*, believed that Goldman didn't deserve, and therefore made sure Goldman would never get, a prayer lectern (a *shtender* in Yiddish) in the synagogue, not on the Sabbath, nor on the festivals, upon which he would have put his prayer book. "Such a leech! A robber, a thief, an abuser of his workers… how brazen, how shameless, for this man to come to synagogue to pray!"

During Sabbaths and festivals, the synagogue became a full and rowdy place. Shmuel would take the opportunity to heap abuse and curses upon the miller and any other rich person who deserved it. It got to such a point that they fired him from the responsibility that had been in his family for generations... [1] entirely dissolving the position.

Shmuel would not beg nor flatter. He picked himself up and found a good, honest job, though it wasn't easy for him: he became a watchmaker. He did not become another mediocre watchmaker, no. He quickly became known in the city and beyond as one of the best, a craftsman and an expert in the field. What was his specialty? If you gave him a watch to fix, he wouldn't just fix it; he would improve its function, going above and beyond the regular scope of repair, and you would know the watch would last for generations because of his care.

However, if you gave him a watch, and under his magnifying glass, he said to you, "Just throw it in the garbage," you could be sure that there was nothing that could be done – there was no "removing the evil decree" [2] – and the watch would die soon enough.

He was known to the *portzim*, the non–Jewish landlords in their mansions; they would line up at his store at opening, even though he charged three times the price, sometimes even four times the price, than what others would charge. This was an amazing thing – here was a man who always had an abundance of business, his prices high, and yet he was one of the poorest of the poor, living a life of poverty. But if you would chance a peek into his house, you would understand how this is possible – his house was always filled with people like a swarm of bees. All the wretched people, the work–weary men, the bitter women with hard lives, they would all come to his house to get his counsel and his aid. Here, a woman might express her great grief: Her husband has died, and her son is the only provider of the family. He was a worker in a grocery store, toiling like a beast of burden for the store, from early light to late night. Now they have fired him to replace him with one of their relatives. "What should we do?" she asks Shmuel, "Should we starve to death?"

In the corner sits a young man, telling his fellow: "My father, a shoemaker, is sick in the hospital. It has been such a short time, yet the administrator of the hospital tells me they want to release him before he has even recovered. What should we do? There isn't anyone at home during the day to even get him a cup of tea..."

Person after person would pour their hearts out to Shmuel, all asking him to work on their behalf. Shmuel would stop his own work, and run to and fro, from house to house. Sometimes he would plead, softening the hearts of hardened individuals, and other times he would express anger and wrath to get them to assist the poor. When he would get what he came for, his face would shine, his eyes ablaze. It was unlike anything you've ever seen before. If he was unsuccessful, he would become incensed, shouting mightily and heaping scorn upon the heads of these rich homeowners. People would often be astonished: This man lives like a dog, yet he worries after others? He was always fighting the good fight on behalf of the widowed and the orphaned. He would rescue the destitute from the hands of their oppressors; the law and justice was on his side against the powerful and rich, and he would force them to give in to his demands. Indeed, they were scared of this nudnik called Shmuel.

You might say, maybe Shmuel was influential because he was a Torah scholar. Not even close. Very little of what he learned from his rabbi in the *Talmud Torah* of his youth remained with him. Still, one thing he remembered from that time of his life: [Leviticus 19:13, 16] "You shall not oppress your fellow… Do not delay the wages of the poor… Do not stand idly by the blood of your fellow…" And he would always repeat [Leviticus 19:18] "Love your fellow as yourself", never breaking from this principle.

When Zionism appeared within the Jewish world, Shmuel became an enthusiastic Zionist. If only I could live in our land! Certainly, there our brothers only live lives of justice and morality! They all work the land and eat the bread they themselves grow. Surely there is no jealousy, no hatred, [Job 34:19] "no regard for the rich against the poor!"

Time passed, and Shmuel began chanting a new mantra; leaving aside the Land of Israel, he would instead speak of the irrelevance of country borders – human beings everywhere are all one! Love, peace, brotherhood, shall reign among peoples – Socialism! As the Bolsheviks took over, Shmuelik's dreams crystalized, and he became a Bolshevik. The Bolsheviks appreciated Shmuelik's spirit and honesty, even appointing him to Commissar! So he began wearing black clothing, letting his gray beard grow wild, always hurried, always busy, a source of astonishment for the *Chekists* [3] and the Red Guard [4] alike.

He lived a simple life at home; for food, he ate grits; for clothes, he dressed plainly; yet justice and morality were his banner. The poor exalted him, yet all luxury revolted him, and he did not flinch from taking excesses from the rich as if it were his, with the claim that wealth came from the poor, and back to the poor it should go…

His authority and rule continued until the retreat of the Bolsheviks, and he left with them on their travels. He was seen in Zhitomir wearing a Tsarist sword in his belt. He even made it to Moscow, and he regained his position there as Commissar.

With the passage of time, many things are forgotten. However, one day a letter was received from him, quite long indeed, written as a confession of a repentant man:

> *I have made a grave mistake, and great is the pain and regret. I truly thought that the rule of "And you shall love…" was known to all mankind. But to my great sorrow I must report that there are nations that never received this message. My beloved son, I ask that you seek out the educator, his name is Blei – he was always a friend to me. Ask him to teach you Hebrew language and literature, such that you will know it well. Perhaps I will merit to see you in our land, and we will be able to live according to the laws of our Torah, for only our people, who have suffered so much more than any other people, are especially capable of understanding the commandment of "And you shall love…", and only in the land of Israel can we live as a people.*

He goes on like this, full of pain and heartache about his great foolishness in his life choices. A long time passed before a new message was received: Shmuel the Watchmaker has passed away in the Diaspora. He never merited to go to the land of Israel, nor did he see his wife and son ever again...

Translator's Comments

1. Ellipses in the original, presumably for dramatic effect.
2. From the High Holidays service
3. The All–Russian Extraordinary Commission and commonly known as Cheka, first established in 1917, was the first of a succession of Soviet secret–police organizations. A member of Cheka was called a chekist. The chekists commonly dressed in black leather, including long flowing coats, reportedly after being issued such distinctive coats early in their existence. (Wikipedia)
4. Red Guards were paramilitary volunteer formations consisting mainly of factory workers, peasants, cossacks and partially of soldiers and sailors for "protection of the soviet power" between 1917–1918. (Wikipedia)

Herschel the Shamash of the Great Synagogue

by Yannai

Everyone in the city of Dubno knew Herschel, and he too knew all of them, from the youngest to the oldest. Of average height, with a black beard, he was the right–hand man of the synagogue rabbi, Reb Mendele, the righteous of blessed memory. He followed the rabbi around everywhere, the left hand of Reb Mendele holding the right hand of Herschel, and they would progress this way, hand–in–hand.

Herschel was well–known as an "Announcer and Notifier" … regarding anything having to do with the dealings of the Dubno community, and he knew of all of the city's needs. Among his responsibilities was to walk from Farber Zevromi Street to the length of the city as far as Surmicze, and make his announcements. He would do this on Sabbaths as well, during the Torah reading, in a clear and beautiful voice. As Herschel would get to the door of the building, the whispers would immediately start among the people, "Hey, hey!" Herschel would march confidently to the center of the synagogue at its raised platform, acting as if it personally belonged to him, and would begin his announcement. If he spoke at the behest of the rabbi, he would say, "As the appointee of the rabbi…" If it was a communal matter, he would say "As an appointee of the community…" And if he spoke for the Crown Rabbi, he would add, "As an appointee of the *Zhondovy Rabbin*…" – meaning the current Crown Rabbi. When he would end, the congregants would take his leave casually. Such a *"mechayeh"* – an experience – to hear how Herschel would make his announcements! Ay ay ay!

"Benedict"

by Yannai

Just saying his name conjures his image and likeness in the mind of every citizen of Dubno. A special emissary for the newly dead, he was their direct agent, making sure they went to their final resting place. It is doubtful that anyone else alive in Dubno was as famous as he, in that everyone knew him, though not everyone sang his praises. His name wasn't even Benedict.

He got his nickname from the work he did with his vehicle – to bring the dead to the cemetery. People would say, "*iz er dakh fun di royte idelekh*" (Yiddish for "he is nevertheless one of the red Jews"), or for short, "*ben adom*" – "a red person", and thus he was called "*ben adik*". [1]

A thick–bearded Jew, he was always donating to the charity fund "Charity Saves From Death". With the smile on his face, one would never know his profession was in the shadow of death.

People didn't enjoy his presence – in fact, they would keep away and keep him away from their social circles. Even worse, if one wanted to curse someone out, the worst they could say is, "Benedict will deal with you!"

A poor man his whole life, his forlorn expression proclaimed to everyone, "Riches are not forever… charity saves from death." [2]

"The greatness of charity" still did not save him from mortal danger, for he died together with everyone else in his community…

Translator's Comments

1. Unclear if this is somehow a reference to his job with the dead, and it is unclear whether he was a hearse driver, an undertaker, or gravedigger, or all of the above.
2. Proverbs 27:24, 11:4

Volodia (Frenkel)

by B. Bardiga

Solitary, a world unto himself, (Psalms 19:4) "no utterances and no words," no claims on others, generally dressing in an unkempt manner, his hair never cut – he was part of the Jewish landscape in the life of the city. With no house or place to live, he found a place for himself behind the curtains of the theater and the screens of the moviehouse. A brush and glue stick in one hand and advertisement papers in the other, ⒠ that was how he was seen every day. Only at the end of his life, on the eve of the Holocaust, he gained employment as a messenger for an organization of shop clerks and salespeople, where he could make an honorable living.

No one knew his political beliefs – he was a quiet man, never socializing with others. However, it came out afterwards that the fate and lot of his people were near and dear to his heart. He wrote a poem one year before the war broke out. Now, it does not demonstrate the work of a talented poet, but it does prove how deep his concern went for his people. This is how the poem goes:

> Lend your ear, O brothers,
> Hear me, O fellow Jews,
> Whether your flag be red
> Or your flag be the color of the skies
>
> Consider for a moment,
> Do you not see that the fire has started?
> In Romania, Poland, the Diaspora is dying,
> Judaism is wallowing in its blood,
> And in Germany, the grim reaper's blade is being whet.
>
> Ah! What will be? My God, my God!
> So, O brothers, open your eyes
> And take your fate into your own hands.
> Sharpen your weapons,
> Strengthen your unity together,
> For if not – woe to us!

About one Family

by Shmuel Kolton

The city of Dubno is surrounded by many small villages and towns; these villages and towns were where many Jewish families lived, and they would work on the surrounding farms. The Jews acted as middlemen between the farms and the city; they would purchase the supply from the farms, and market them within the city, and then they would bring merchandise from the city to sell to the farmers. They were also involved in small production companies, such as a roofing tile factory, a brick factory, a quicklime factory, a flour mill, and more. Generally speaking, the families and the farmers were on good terms with each other. The Jews, or the "*Moshko*" as they would call themselves, often would use advisers to help with their negotiations, even to clear up disputes between themselves.

In the Grodki village, a community about 12 kilometers to the east of Dubno, there lived a family among 119 Jewish families by the name "Lerner." In those days of the Tsar, the military law was that your son was only exempt from conscription if he was an only child, and so, to circumvent this, they changed their name. Thus, four sons were born to: 1) Berish Lerner, 2) Leib Perlmutter, 3) Yosef Feuerstein, 4) Neta Spektor.

The first three sons raised large and varied families, and they all lived in the surrounding area in the villages: Grodki, Nehorin, Sodowicz. The sons followed in the customs of their fathers and made a living doing business with the farmers. They fulfilled their religious duties by making do with prayer groups in one of the houses on the Sabbath and the festivals, and if they did not have a quorum of ten men, they prayed in their own houses. They sent their grown children to schools in Dubno, Kiev, or Zhitomir, and sometimes even further out than that. The young children were homeschooled, their tutors brought in from the central city areas.

Similarly, they brought in brides for their sons and grooms for their daughters from other places. Sometimes, cousins married each other, the sons from the Perlmutter and Feuerstein families marrying the daughters of the Lerner family.

This is what such families were like until the first World War.

With the change in governments because of the Russian Revolution, non–Jews began to make trouble with the Jews. Several families were burglarized, and several people were murdered, and by the time the war ended, families started to flee the villages and move to Dubno. They integrated well into the social and cultural life of the city, the children started trying out schools and gymnasiums, and the entire way of life for these families changed completely.

463

New winds were starting to blow through the Jewish communities. The Balfour Declaration was a sign for Jews, and the pioneer youth movements began organizing in Dubno as well. "*Hashomer Hatzair*" ("The Young Guard"), and "*Hechalutz*" ("The Pioneer") movements were established, and many youths from the aforementioned families began to receive Zionist and pioneering influence and education through these movements, helping them discover aspirations to immigrate to Israel, and to join its inhabitants and builders [*baneha u–boneha*]. Indeed, among the first pioneers who immigrated to Israel from Dubno, a few were from the Lerners and Perlmutters, and then others followed afterward. The Zionist and pioneer education, and the aspiration to realize their Zionism practically resulted in many of these families being saved from the decimation of the House of Israel in Poland. Many of them ran away to the forests and hid among non–Jews who agreed to hide them, and they were also saved. Some of them succeeded in getting to Russia. Nevertheless, an awful and countless number were martyred from the families Lerner, Perlmutter, and Feuerstein in the Holocaust that wiped out the Jews of Dubno.

With the establishment of the State of Israel, those members who survived the war began to make their way to Israel, and it was they who told us of these tragic details of the inhabitants of our city and this particular family tree.

Berele Gulzriker

by Nisan

In Jewish Dubno, quiet, delicate, a world unto itself, there was Berele Gulzriker, a remarkable man who excelled in the public sphere. There were different kinds of public servants – politicians, social workers, municipality workers; there were mutual aid facilities like soup kitchens, the orphanages, and so on. But one institution, the fire station, that Dubno so needed (because of all the fires that would constantly break out), was made up entirely of non–Jewish workers and managers. Berele could not accept that Dubno, which was by vast majority populated by Jews, would allow such an important institution to be run by non–Jewish people. Berele worked day and night on the firefighter's organization, until he managed to turn over this celebrated institution to the populace of the city, and he himself became its "commander". The community so appreciated him and accorded him great honor. The [Russian] word "*yeshivas*", or "firefighter", which was used mockingly by the riffraff for those who put out fires, became a term of honor and respect, as it became the mark of special and good–hearted people who stood at the guard for the belongings, and the very lives, of the citizens of the entire city.

Berele's great devotion was a symbol for altruism, and he was a role model for all. Knowing this, he would bring youngsters from all walks of life to the scenes of the fires to see the firefighters at work, so that they would appreciate the institution and its commander as well.

The Activist – Eliyahu–David (Bakraing)

by Akiva David

Eliyahu–David was born in Dubno to an ultra–Orthodox family in 1905. He received his first education at home and at the *yeshivas* and became known even then for his amazing recall and his talented mind. While yet a lad, he began to consider the paths of life, and he came to the realization that the *yeshiva* could not answer all of his issues. He directed his full passion to the idea of the return to Zion (*Shivat Zion*). As was the case back then, they placed many obstacles in his path, and they advanced vacuous arguments and, together with his father, would say, "It is forbidden to rush to end times too early!" The more pain they caused him, the farther and farther away he turned from his father's rebuke and his mother's teachings.

He was still young when he, along with a small group of friends, organized the "Pioneers" (*Hechalutz*) in Dubno. These were the days when the Bolsheviks were in power in Volhynia. With every fiber of his being, and with all of his organizational prowess, Eliyahu–David roused the community youth to wake up from their apathy.

His dedication knew no fatigue, toward any action or activism, and he took part in every Zionist event in the city. He worked during the day in the Listrin brother's shop selling metals and construction materials, and then he would sit in the late afternoon and study a page of Talmud, and at night he would dedicate his time for Zionist activities. Great was the day when the throngs came out to accompany Eliyahu–David and his friends to the train station to go to the land of Israel. "We are going to the land to build and be built by it (*lebanot u–le–hibanot ba*)" – that lyric from the poems of the pioneers who passed before the camp broke through the sky.

The situation in the land of Israel was quite difficult in those days. There were many who could not withstand it and failed, running back ashamed and embarrassed. But a man like Eliyahu–David, the pioneer and visionary, would never run away from a struggle. He put his face to the wind and was nevertheless successful in everything he did, every challenge, every job that came his way. As someone who loved nature, all living beings and all plant life, he devoted his energies to agriculture and studying the natural world. In 1927, he was an outstanding employee of the orchards of Y.L. Goldberg, and at the same time, he dedicated himself to his studies, up all night like it was daytime, until he obtained a diploma from the "Herzliya" gymnasium.

At that point, he decided to continue learning and acquiring more knowledge. He sent his diploma to the university in Nancy, France, and he was accepted as a student. With no money, and no knowledge of French, he traveled there to attend school. His diligence and industry, and his pure passion and desire, helped him overcome any hardships along the way, and he progressed further in his studies. "One clear morning" (II Samuel 23:4), we find him in Dubno, having returned from France, crowned with degrees in agronomy and chemical engineering.

Eliyahu–David would speak in the small synagogue (a "*kloyz*") of "Abraham Mordechai" before a large crowd that would hang on to his every word, listening to him speak "kindling flames" (Psalms 29:7) about Zionism and its implementation. He urged them to join the builders of the land of Israel, the implementers of the Zionist vision, by emigrating to the land.

In 1931, Eliyahu–David returned to the land of Israel, where he began a government job as Chief Inspector for "*Pri Hadar*" in Hadera, Binyamina, Zikhron Yaakov, Rehovot, and Tel Aviv. His name preceded him, and his circle of friends was always widening. He married the daughter of Dr. Mittman–Cohen, who founded the Herzliya gymnasium, and who set up a home for Eliyahu–David's family, which became a signpost of hospitality and assistance for anyone who needed help or a job. Eliyahu–David never acted high–and–mighty, and he hated the snobby, and as an activist and a pioneer, he would respond to the needy like a friend, a guide, a helper, for anyone who asked for his assistance. And Dubno natives who managed to get to the land of Israel, their first step was straight to the house of Eliyahu–David; he would counsel them, invite them to eat with him, he would concern himself with arranging jobs for them, every person according to his individual situation and abilities.

The day Eliyahu–David arrived in the land of Israel, he became an active member of the Haganah. When the situation turned dire in 1938, and the *"Kofer HaYeshuv"* called for volunteers for protection for the villages (*yishuvim*), which were failing to both work and protect themselves at the same time, Eliyahu–David immediately answered the call and enlisted. He left his house and his elderly parents, whom he had brought to the land of Israel and was their sole provider, he left the safety of Tel Aviv, his job, his educational growth, and went to Gan Shmuel, a kibbutz, to be a night guard, and to protect the corn harvests during the day. Several weeks passed at his post, when one day an enemy attacker hurled stones at him that badly injured him. He managed to return two shots that injured his attacker, but after two painful days and a fierce struggle against death, (Judges 5:27) "he lay wasted." He was just 33 years old.

Eliyahu–David was buried alongside the great heroes of Israel, and his friends and admirers expressed their grief with the following words: "You came to us a young sapling, yet you struck at deep roots." Dr. Mittman–Cohen said, "You bloomed into a great tree which bore fruit, yet you were cut short and removed from us and our land before your time." Mr. Yisrael Rokeach, the city head of Tel Aviv, said, "A new page and a shining letter was Eliyahu–David, a Tel–Avivian through and through, who died a hero's death as the first martyr of the *"Kofer HaYeshuv"* for his homeland."

His friends said, "Eliyahu–David, always in the study house, a man of culture and a thirst for knowledge, like a fine gem intertwined in the beauty of the spirit of Judaism. Always giving, a stalwart man, the first of our protectors to fall in answering the call of the *Kofer HaYeshuv*. He was a Dubno man, who gave honor and pride to our city for the sake of the homeland…"

A farewell party for those leaving to the land of Israel

The Four Who Fell

In Memory of Dubno Citizens Who Were Killed in the Land of Israel Defending their People and their Homeland

by Asher Reichman

David Meizler, the son of Eliyahu and Soibel, was born on Rosh Hashanah, 5679 [September 7th, 1918], in Polonne, Volhynia. At the age of 3, he moved with his parents to Dubno. He went to school at a "*heder*" and attended a Polish gymnasium [for high–school]. He joined the "*Hashomer Hatzair*" movement, becoming one of its counselors, and he was simultaneously an activist in the "*Hechalutz*" group, and through his activities, showed a talent for education.

David Meizler

In 1939, he immigrated to the land of Israel, continuing his education by attending a study house for teachers in Jerusalem. After he completed his course requirements, he was sent to be a teacher's assistant in Kibbutz Merhavia [1], where eventually he became a full–time member. From speaking to him and the impressions he left on others, it was known how much concern he gave to the issues of pedagogy, and how strong his desire was to improve his skills. Yet, he also longed to be a simple farmer like the rest of his friends, and every opportunity he got, he would toil [in the field] with great satisfaction. But he knew that he was meant to be an educator and to teach, and he invested the most energy into this work. Because of this, in 1945, he saw that it was necessary for him to leave his family, his wife and child, for some time, to go to Jerusalem and continue his education in the university there.

As a member of the Haganah, he fulfilled his duties during the War of Independence by guarding children. During the bombing of Merhavia on the 2nd of Sivan 5708 (June 9th, 1948), he picked his head up from the trench during an exchange of enemy fire – he was hit and died. He was laid to rest in Givat HaMoreh, in Merhavia.

He left behind a wife and son, and two sisters – all in the land of Israel. A memorial was published in the book "The Six That Fell," produced by Kibbutz Merhavia.

*

Tzvi Sternberg

Tzvi Sternberg (Tzvika), son of David and Chavah, was born in Dubno on November 13th, 1913. He attended a Polish elementary school, and stood out for his wit, as well as his good grades, especially in mathematics. At the age of 15, he joined *"Hashomer Hatzair"* and began learning Hebrew. He excelled above everyone else and was the first of his grade to become a counselor and member of the branch's local leadership. He was a counselor for 2 years, and then became secretary for the local *"Hechalutz"*. In 1933, Tzvika went for training in

Chelm and Lublin, and even there worked for them as a secretary and treasurer. He was among the hardest of workers in difficult jobs, but he became exhausted with these jobs and sought to take a break for a certain amount of time. He began to attend courses in leadership given in the Haganah, arranged by emissaries from Israel; he excelled, and became a leader of the members of his group. A short time after his wedding in 1938, he began making his way to the land of Israel with the first group of *Aliyah Bet*. [2] After about a year, his wife joined him, and they settled in a kibbutz of his party in Netanya. He worked in fruit orchards, was a leader in the Haganah, and served four years in the Jewish Police. [3]

Tzvika excelled in his work at the kibbutz as a custodian. There, he had a son. In 1943, he moved with others who were from the kibbutz to be among the first to settle the area of the Gaza Strip (first *Mitzpeh HaYam*, and then *Yad Mordechai*). After two years, he was appointed in that place to take on a Corporal uniform as part of the Jewish Police.

As the kibbutz began to plant their first vineyard, Tzvika attached himself to the plantation; with great love and devotion he cared for every sapling, as he had for the human–saplings – the children of the area. In fact, he spent time creating toys that would gladden the hearts of the children. His good–heartedness and his serenity that he had already as a youngster, shined through and had a positive effect on the youth.

In the spring of 5708 (1948), he continued to work at the plantation, to impress upon his friends, who were going through a crisis of faith, that they were not toiling for naught. A few days later, Egypt attacked. As commander at that position, he successfully stopped the advancement of the enemy troops. He was hit by a mortar shell and fell slain on May 19th, 1948. He was laid to rest in the Yad Mordechai cemetery.

*

Ozer Shehami (Ozer Perlyok), son of David and Chana, was born in Dubno on July 15th, 1915. He attended elementary school. He joined the "Gordonia" youth movement, [4] and he devoted himself to the Pioneer idea and prepared himself to immigrate to the land of Israel. He spent some time in a kibbutz training camp in Janow, and in October 1938, he immigrated to the land of Israel with the Aliyah Bet.

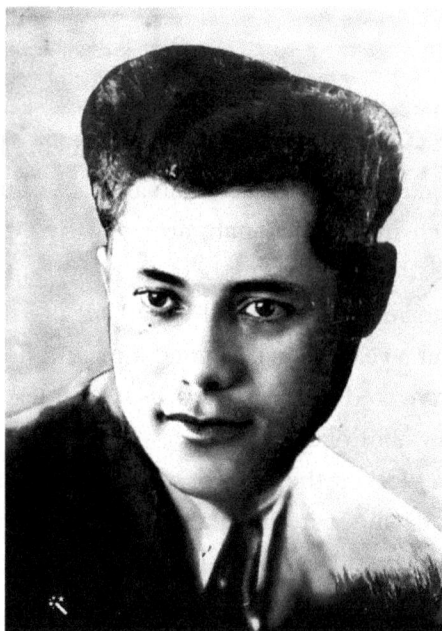

Ozer Shehami

He became a member of "Kibbutz HaSheloshah" for two years, working as a tailor. After leaving the kibbutz, he worked in a shoe shop in Tel Aviv. Diligent in his work, he made a good income for himself.

He was an active and prominent member in the "*Shura*", never missing a lecture or activity. He was also a member of "*HaPoel.*"

Ozer was a serious man, quiet, but he loved all people. He would also write poems in Yiddish. His friends and acquaintances adored him, and he would always provide assistance to anyone in need, to the best of his ability.

When the war started, some of the enlisted soldiers were sent to guard positions, and sometimes they were sent to far outposts. Ozer served in the anti–aircraft platoon. When he was positioned at an outpost near Ramla, he was struck by a sniper on November 6th, 1948. He was laid to rest at the cemetery in Nahalat Yitzhak.

He left behind a wife, two children, two brothers and sisters, and other relatives, all in Israel.

*

David Sobol, an only child born to Yisrael and Yaffa in Dubno, on December 21st, 1922. He attended elementary and high school. He entered the local "*Hashomer Hatzair*". The increase of antisemitism in Poland changed the mood of the community, including his parents, and when David asked them in 1938 to join the "Youth Aliyah" group immigrating to Israel, they did not protest. They only delayed his trip a year with the promise that when, in the following year, they would receive their grandfather's estate, they would go with him in traveling to the land of Israel. During this time, the World War broke out, and David got stuck because of the flow of refugees going to Russia. He volunteered himself to the Polish army, in the hopes that by doing this, he would reach the Middle East, and he would stay in the land of Israel. Instead, he was sent to the battalion in Germany, where he was wounded and taken captive. Disguising himself with the name "Arie", David joined the prayer sessions of the Catholic captives, sang in their choir, and he even asked for lessons in playing the organ for the services. By doing this, he survived.

[Column 435–436]

Once he was released, David dedicated himself to teaching children in the Displaced Persons camp in Austria, until he joined a kibbutz established by other displaced people. He arrived in the land of Israel with the Aliyah Bet group on June 27th, 1946. When he was accepted as a member of Kibbutz Mizra, he said with a simple joy: "This is the happiest day of my life – I now own a home." He made his home his shop and defended it in the winter of 5708 [1948]. When his friends began to be enlisted, he expressed his wish to also be enlisted in the army. His request was granted when he was enlisted according to the quota to defend the Jordan Valley against the first invasion by Syria. After his return, he said to one of his friends, "That was nothing to me. I went there because of my home that cares for me, a home that is worthy of fighting for." Standing with his class against the overwhelming strength of the Syrian military at Mishmar HaYarden, he was hit trying to get out of the line of fire with three other friends and died there on June 12th, 1948.

David was brought to be buried at Rosh Pinna the next day, but by request of the kibbutz, his bones were transferred to the Afula cemetery on December 12th, 1950.

A memorial for him was written in the publication, "*LeZikhram*" by Kibbutz Mizra.

Translator's Comments

1. Merhavia is a kibbutz in northern Israel, founded by European members of "*Hashomer Hatzair*" in 1929. It currently (2020) has a population of about 1,200 people.
2. Aliyah Bet was the codename given to illegal immigration by Jews, most of whom were refugees from Nazi Germany, and later Holocaust survivors, to Mandatory Palestine between 1934–48, in violation of the restrictions laid out in the British White Paper of 1939. (Wikipedia)
3. Called in Hebrew "*Notrut*," this was a Jewish guard brigade in the British police force during the British Mandate period (1936–1948)
4. Founded in Poland in 1925, Gordonia was a movement based on the beliefs of Aaron David Gordon, such as the redemption of Eretz Yisrael and the Jewish People through manual labor and the revival of the Hebrew language. In Gordonia the cadets learned Hebrew and the graduates organized themselves into training groups pending aliyah to the Holy Land. (Wikipedia)

Dobe Tovin-Metz

Translated from Yiddish by Pamela Russ

While still a young girl living in her parents' home, Dobe left Dubno and crossed the ocean, to the longed-for country of America. This happened about fifty years ago, when Dubno was still under the Tsarist empire. She, and several of her friends, just got up one day and left. What sort of spiritual, traditional, and domestic baggage did the young Dobe take along from her hometown to the United States?

In the course of fifty years, Dobe lived a cultured life in this big country, spoke its language, incorporating the local habits and manners. The problems of that country were as close to her as to the native-born citizens. She established a multi-branched family that planted deep roots in the free world. What tied her to her past in Dubno? During and after the last World War, Dobe knew where to find surviving members from Jewish Dubno and brought them as much help as she could. She became the

477

address to search for and find relatives from across America, and at the same time, she dedicated herself to charitable society work. She was active in women's organizations for aid and education, and thoughts of her birthplace did not leave her mind even for one minute. Despite her living in the United States for 50 years, she still sees herself as a component of the Jewish settlement in Dubno, which left its signature on her childhood years. The economic prosperity in which she lives did not make her forget the need of the flower-lined streets, and she cannot remain indifferent and cold towards the pain of others.

When she found out about the destruction that befell the European Jews and which also brought the destruction of the settlement in Dubno, she gave her contribution to perpetuate Dubno among the destroyed Jewish communities – with the publication of this Yizkor book. She also encouraged friends to collect material and financial support, and that's how she helped materialize the idea. And to her credit, it should be said that: She served – and continues to serve, after our book has already been published, as an example with her open hand – and she has a prominent share in the realizing and publishing of this book. A great thank you!

Avraham Aizik Treger

Translated from Yiddish by Pamela Russ

A man of the people
A real pauper with a
Modest soul,
He was grateful for
Having sent him two dollars from America.
This song of thanks is an original
In its style and words.

A blessing to you for your trip to America,
for Mrs. Dobe Tabachnik

1

Since your trip here
Was, thank God, a peaceful one,
Similarly, the trip back should not be difficult

2

May your trip pass
With great blessing and good fortune
And find, in good condition,
Your husband and your whole family.

3

Many good wishes and blessings
Will escort, follow you
From your family and likewise from strangers
Who have experienced your support.

4

Many sums of dollars
You have distributed here
You have helped the poor
Healing the sick people's wounds.

5

The dear God will
Repay you many times over
For one hundred there will two,
For one thousand there will be two.

6

This is a person's obligation
When he is in a situation that he has money,

To give charity and do good deeds,
During his life in this world.

7

You must and have to want
To fulfill your word
To ease up the situation here
For the Americans there.

8

And to my close friends
You should simply present
My critical situation as usual.
From me, Avraham Aizik Treger.

9

Travel in good health, and arrive in good health,
That is what I wish you now.
May your trip be like a dream
As you arrive in your country in peace.

ובערה די שוה בשם ניצי וזן לעיל- שברלין
כתי ברb אוש וברו ביים טוב ושהואוב
1
ובהרב נוצר אשרה נוצ וזהרב

אוו בשרעל בוב בפיון לווה בפלום צצוון

אווז בוה שוף בוג בלוק פיבוט ולצ

פוס בנעש ושברו בירוב רשו ונקרון
2
ובהרב נוצר צוג בלוג אבוזבר

אוו שנוט ברטה ננהה בזלבה

אש ונצון זנבואה נצוזן צון בשרו

אשוה צוג בוט ווה ער צוג בלוג ושברוה

481

The Holocaust

Two Years under Soviet Rule

by Moshe Cohen

Translated from Hebrew by Selwyn Rose

The events and details recorded here were written in April 1962, about 20 years after the actual events occurred and the writer apologizes in advance for any errors or inaccuracies that may possibly have crept in.

The writer made every attempt to recall from his memories precisely how he felt at the time of the actual events. It is possible that from the narrative itself, it will be clear and understood why there were so many Dubno Jews who were liquidated in the Holocaust compared to Jewish populations of other towns in the vicinity like Kremenets, Lutsk and Rowno that were also under the Soviet heel but so many of them succeeded in fleeing to Russia even before the arrival of the Nazi armies.

A

The middle of August 1939.

Every day the radio and newspapers brought information more and more worrying on the situation of the country. The source of the information was Hitlerite Berlin and the most worrying was the signing of the Ribbentrop–Molotov Agreement and the aggressive demands to address the status of the free city of Danzig that followed after it.

It was clear to everyone that war between Poland and Germany was virtually inevitable. On the 20th August the Polish authorities introduced mobilization of the reserves up to the age of 45. Tension and anxiety increased. The fact that so many men were mobilized and sent off to army barracks was enough to increase the worry and concern when it became clear that no one at home knew where the recruits had been taken. Fear and apprehension arose in the hearts of the families affected who were concerned about the air of anti–Semitism among the Poles and Ukrainians in town and the surrounding area.

After a few days we got to know that the men were still in the barracks because the Polish army was unable to supply them with uniforms and arms and the fact only increased the tension in town and awakened rumors of defeatism and helplessness.

In the meantime, the press and radio urged the public to store up food, clothing and boots and even advice on how to preserve and look after them. The buying mania that attacked the town caused a steep rise in prices. Everything indicated that war was getting close by the hour.

On Friday morning the 1st September the radio announced that the Germans had crossed the Polish border along its entire common frontier and were advancing eastwards into Poland. The Polish army was unable to withstand the attack and retreated eastwards towards the Polish hinterland.

The capital, Warsaw and other major Polish cities were bombed by waves of German aircraft while the Polish aircraft, far less in number and less well-trained for combat were unable to confront them. They were at a disadvantage in the air and on the ground, they were even unable to take off.

The stream of refugees began fleeing the border areas, following the retreating army in other areas as well, towards the center of the country. In trains, buses, taxis and private cars and even horse-drawn carts – all moving eastwards and by 3rd September the first refugees had reached Dubno still going eastwards towards the Polish-Romanian border.

A few days later when it became clear that the situation at the Front was worsening and there was a grave lack of arms, ammunition and fuel, the despair began to fill our hearts and hordes of people fleeing before the advancing German army filled the roads leading eastwards. Vehicles that had run out of fuel were abandoned and left at the roadside and refugees making their way on foot sought refuge at the local villages for overnight shelter.

Dubno was also filled with refugees, mostly Jews who, through lack of money and transportation were forced to stay in town. The overcrowding increased day by day and the price of food and other essential items skyrocketed. Stocks dwindled and ran out and it was impossible to bring in fresh supplies from the surroundings or from Warsaw and Lvov because of the lack of transport.

The mobilized Dubno residents that had remained in barracks mostly returned to their homes and no one even noticed; only a few remained in the army and were sent to the Front. All around town work began on digging anti-tank trenches and defense positions in preparation should the enemy reach Dubno.

Members of the Polish Parliament, the General Staff and the senior State institutions left Warsaw and they, too, made their way in the direction of the Polish-Romanian border. Many of them arrived in Dubno which sits on the highway to Romania and part of the General Staff occupied the Gymnasium. Most of the public buildings in town were commandeered for the institutions that had arrived from

Warsaw and it was rumored that even the President of the State and his retinue was to be found in the vicinity – ensconced in the Ledóchowski Palace at Smordva, about 18 kilometers from Dubno.

On the first day of *Rosh Hashanah*, 12th September, Dubno was attacked for the first time by enemy aircraft. They struck at the railway station, a factory manufacturing food-preserves and the vicinity of the mobilization center, at the entrance to town from the direction of Zabramna Street. There, many people were engaged in digging anti-tank trenches; there were several dead bodies and some injured people lying among the diggers. Close by were two damaged houses as well and buried beneath the rubble were the residents, most of them Jewish.

The anxiety of the people intensified, and panic was spreading among them. Fear of air attacks and bombing caused many to flee the town in the direction of Ostrow. Townspeople were mobilized to dig trenches, defensive positions and act as porters for the army at the railway station. The fear of being mobilized was almost as great as the fear of the enemy.

Under the pressure of the advancing German forces, the local Polish authorities left town and began moving in the direction of Brody-Lwow. The police also left, and, in their place, a civil militia was formed headed by the attorney Morovski. Nevertheless, there were quite a few of the Jewish youth in service who were armed and fulfilled their duties guarding bridges, army stores and arsenals and directing traffic in town. Even so there was much fear among the Jewish sector regarding Polish and Ukrainian anti-Semitism. The Mayor was the only Polish official who stayed in town and then he too disappeared after two months some saying he crossed the border into German occupied territory.

Two days before, the Polish army left the barracks for an unknown direction. All day and all night an endless convoy of military vehicles crossed the town in the direction of Brody-Lwow. The common belief – they were headed for the Romanian border.

[Columns 233–234]

Now only Jewish refugees arrived in town, most of them on foot and lacking everything. They left their towns literally at the last minute before being conquered by the Germans. Non-Jewish refugees were seen no more.

Sanitary conditions in town were getting worse because some of the town's doctors had been mobilized and some had left due to the bombing and the advancing enemy. In the meantime, the population grew from day to day because of the number of refugees arriving and staying, with no transport available to carry them further.

On 16th September something very puzzling happened: a convoy of army vehicles entered town from the direction of Radziwill-Brody, slowly – as if they were not certain which way to go. Here and there a soldier jumped from the trucks and hid behind a house and when the convoy passed, he turned to one of the Jewish bystanders asking

487

for civilian clothes to replace his uniform. These soldiers were Jews from the area who had decided to desert and return to their families.

At noon on 17th September the army convoy movement stopped entirely and not even one Polish soldier was to be seen in town. Apparently, the Polish authority in Dubno had been liquidated. In the meantime, the militia had been expanded. Everyone who thought it proper and correct to join the militia received a rifle and was sent to assist in keeping order in town. Nevertheless, some wild elements, mostly Christians but some few Jews as well, broke into army stores stealing things. The oast-house for drying hops belonging to a company owned by two brothers that was being used as a food-store by the army and contained much sugar, salt and other food-stuffs, was broken into and robbed within hours while the militia-men stood to one side wondering whether to intervene.

B

That same day, 17th September there was an announcement on Moscow radio that the Russian government, in view of the disintegration of the official Polish authority, had decided to liberate western Ukraine "…from the yoke of Polish over-lordship" and gave instructions to the Red Army to cross the Polish-Russian border and to enter western Ukraine in order to preserve the peace of the citizenry. The announcement added that the Red Army had already crossed the border and was close to the Rowno-Dubno-Kremenets triangle.

The announcement from Moscow radio that the Red Army was closing in on the town raised spirits and encouraged a feeling of security in the hearts of the residents, especially the Jewish sector. The militia strengthened the guard and peace reigned in the town, without disturbances, except for the robberies taking place in the army store-houses.

Towards morning of 18th September at about 4 o'clock, a crowd gathered in front of the Town Hall. Most of the crowd were Jews although all the city Council members and the president at their head were there, ready to welcome the Red Army that was already at the city gates.

At precisely 5 o'clock a convoy of Soviet tanks entered the town on Pantalia Street headed by a luxury limousine containing a uniformed Russian general. The convoy halted in front of the Town Hall and the general stepped out of his limousine and turned to the crowd that received him with cheers and applause, thanking them for their welcome and asking everyone please "to disperse and go to work." He announced that during the day additional army units would be arriving in town and that detailed information regarding the running of the town under the new authority would be published a little later. After that he entered the Town Hall and spoke with the Council, returned to his automobile and the convoy continued in the direction of

Radziwill-Brody. Throughout the day different units of the Red Army, especially tanks and artillery, drawn by tractors the like and size of which had never been seen before in Dubno, continued to drive through the town and crowds of people stood at the roadside all day watching them pass by going west, and from time to time breaking out into stormy applause.

During the day the new authority's directions were published on the streets regarding the running of the town: the residents were instructed to continue working; all the shops are to remain open; it is absolutely forbidden to raise prices or over-charge; the Polish zloty will remain as the legal tender and is equivalent to the Russian ruble; a curfew is in force between the hours of 10 at night until 6 in the morning.

Throughout the following two days units of the Red Army continued to make their way through town on their way westwards in the direction of Radziwill-Brody and a few units established themselves in different locations in town. The organization of the military authority began.

On the night of 19/20 September after the start of the curfew the sound of rifle- and machine-gun fire was suddenly heard in town. No one knew from where it came or the reason for it. Lights were turned off in all the houses and fear entered everyone's heart. In the morning there were rumors that some gangs had attacked units of the Red Army but there was no confirmation of the rumor. The victims of the shooting were one Soviet soldier killed near the post-office and the daughter of Mottel Nudler was also killed. Two Jewish women injured, apparently by stray bullets.

From that night silence reigned at night.

The gentle behavior and politeness of the Soviet soldiers, both the units that passed through and those of the standing garrison towards the population, should be mentioned here. Their manner of speech was cultured and courteous – indeed, it was a complete surprise to those who remembered the Russian soldiers from the days of the Tsar and even the soldiers of the revolutionary years of 1917–1919. The Jews of town, those who had relatives or friends in Russia and who for years had been completely cut off from contact with them, suddenly began to receive cables congratulating them, letters from their families and friends wishing them well now they have been liberated from their "Polish lords," and wishing them "a life of freedom among the

[Columns 235–236]

family of peoples of the Soviet Union." Indeed, all the cables and letters were couched in a similar unified language. At the same time, the old border between Poland and Russia remained closed for citizens of the two countries, and apart from "special cases" and visits, no one managed to go to Russia or from Russia to the "liberated" areas.

C

A few days after the entry of the Red Army the organization of day-to-day life began under the Civilian-Party authority with the blessing of the army and the N.K.V.D.

The first thing the new government did was free all the prisoners from the prisons.

The area of Dubno that in Poland's day comprised the area from Radziwill in the west to Warkowicze in the east, from Mizoch in the south-east to Malinow, Ostrow in the north, was now divided into seven districts: Radziwill, Kozin, Verba, Dubno, Mizoch, Markowitz, Malinow and Ostrow. In each sector Government institutions and independent municipalities were set up.

All the schools were reopened and even increased their absorption capability and new schools were opened. In every village an elementary school was opened, and laws of compulsory education were enacted. In Dubno an Advanced Institute of Pedagogy was opened and in Mizoch a two-year seminary for teachers.

A road-widening operation was begun that included resurfacing and the highway reached from the Russian border, though Dubno to Lvov.

An employment office was opened in order to arrange employment not only to residents who remained without the means to sustain themselves but also for the thousands of refugees who remained stuck in town. The office tried to find suitable work for everyone's capabilities. There were many varied opportunities available and it was not difficult to find the right people for the right job: clerks were required for all the administrative institutions and reorganized offices; new schools had need of teachers, administrators and inspectors; road-works were under the control of the N.K.V.D. that needed staff as office-workers, store-men and the supply of materials and food for the workers – for the "dirty" work thousands of Polish prisoners were available who were accommodated along 350 kilometers of the highway. School-leavers of middle- and high-school were designated as teachers, managers and inspectors in the gymnasium while school-leavers after seven years of the elementary schools were sent to "crash-courses" for teachers of those same elementary schools and received full salaries even during their training. "Crash-courses" were also given for practical nursing and the girls received salaries as soon as they commenced their studies.

Everyone who wanted to work, found work and everyone who wanted to study could learn at intermediate or high school and even at the university in Lvov, free of charge providing they had the appropriate certification.

The traders and shopkeepers presented a problem on their own. There were shopkeepers who didn't believe in the stability of the Russian authorities and were suspicious of confiscations. They hurried to sell their stocks at regular prices in order to liquidate their businesses and undertake "productive employment" – clerking or teaching. On the other hand, there were those, mainly the bigger dealers, wholesalers, who were doubtful of this stability and tried to "make money"; these hid most of their goods and sold them only in dribs and drabs and raised their prices as high as their patrons were willing to pay. Indeed, in time it became clear that there was a great scarcity of many basic necessities, especially clothing and footwear and the traders and manufacturers of these goods raised their prices and became wealthy.

In the meantime, the shops gradually emptied of their supplies and long queues formed. People might wait for hours upon hours and more than once returned home, as empty-handed as they had come. Soviet officers and soldiers bought whatever they could lay their hands on without bargaining and sent everything back to their homes in Russia thus increasing, on the one hand, the profits of the dealers while on the other hand hastening the end of the supplies in the town. It is true that the new regime opened a few co-operative shops later on, but the sales were restricted and the prices high and only the elite and privileged were able to buy there.

D

In the meantime, the N.K.V.D. and the militia had become organized and gave tangible signs of their authority. Jews of standing in the community and traders who owned property were arrested and accused of profiteering. Large apartments and rooms were confiscated for the use of government offices and accommodation of clerks brought in from Russia. Large houses were nationalized, and their tenants and owners compelled to pay rent to the authorities. Factories for processing and preserving meat and vegetables, breweries and flour-mills were requisitioned and transferred to the Government together with all their equipment. All the forests were also nationalized. All the schools were transferred to the authorities and the language of instruction changed from Polish to Ukrainian, except in a few cases where the parents dared to demand that another language be used – either Polish or Yiddish. The "Tarbut" school was transferred to a larger building but was forbidden to teach Hebrew, religious or Jewish subjects; the language of instruction was changed to Yiddish and Ukrainian was taught as a second language. The monastery in Panienska Street was closed and in its place a government hospital was opened. The synagogues were also closed. The first was the newest, the largest *"Mesharetei–Tzedek"* that was converted into a tailoring and shoe-making co-operative. After that, the *"Ba"ratz"* [11] synagogue was converted into a Party clubhouse. Every synagogue that was closed was allocated a new "noble function for the 'masses'".
[Columns 237–238]

All the Jewish organizations including youth organizations were forbidden to operate. The Community Council was liquidated and all the charity and help institutions that were connected with it were passed to the authorities and lost entirely all semblances of their Jewish nature and background and as a direct result thousands of helpless and destitute Jewish refugees, until now supported by those organs were affected. Only after a Jewish deputation appeared before the First Secretary of the area Communist Party, were they granted permission to open a popular "restaurant" and even granted a rationed quantity of food-stuffs. These were partly free of charge and partly at nominal prices, and free of all charge for those who were actually destitute.

With the completion of the highway widening and tarring program, work began on the streets of Dubno itself. All the shops and shacks in the center of the town that served as groceries or butchers were demolished and, in their place, a pleasant broad plaza [was built]. It changed the overall aspect of the area completely. On the expanse between Zamkova Street and the castle a new municipal park was laid out that also improved the town's appearance.

The Soviet authority was also concerned with culture. Soviet films were screened in the cinemas at prices acceptable to all levels and Soviet actors appeared in local theaters. Two "Culture-houses" were opened for the public where one could find newspapers, journals and various games but only some of the youngsters used the facilities; most of the residents of Dubno's Jews, especially the older ones, had some reservations about the new culture and were not entirely happy with it. Here, it is worth mentioning that even a few of the local Communists, who had spent years in Polish prisons and had been released only recently by the Soviets about whom they had dreamed for years, were disappointed and dissatisfied even though most of them had been given positions and provided with good apartments.

E

Life slowly returned to normal. Humanity began to adjust to the new reality and came to terms with it. Bus services that had been created with Jewish financing and entrepreneurship were nationalized and began operating again and the citizens were no longer anchored to their place and could travel again. Many of the refugees began to leave Dubno and make their way to surrounding towns and villages.

For about three months the Polish zloty remained legal tender and equal in value to the Russian ruble and all trade continued to function in that currency. The authorities even paid employees and suppliers in zloty. Suddenly, on 4th December 1939 at 9 in the morning a radio announcement informed everyone that at 12 noon that day the zloty will cease to be legal tender and the Russian ruble will replace it. The announcement fell on the town like a bolt from the blue. No one had Russian rubles; on the other had nearly everyone had sums of Polish zloty that suddenly became worthless. Intervention by the local authorities produced no results because the announcement came from Moscow. Later on, there was an announcement permitting the exchange of up to 300 zloty for rubles at the government bank providing it can be proved that the money was obtained by legal and legitimate means from government sources. All those who had kept their money in zloty managed to sell them later at 3-4 zloty for a ruble to Jews who sneaked into Nazi occupied territory where the zloty was still legal tender.

At that time the negotiations over the final borders between Russia and Nazi Germany came to an end. The border that had run along the line Lublin-Rava-Rusko-Sanok was now moved eastwards to the line Kowel-Volodymyr-Volhynsky-Lvov. Thus, the territory conquered by Germany now approached Dubno, which was only 93 kilometers distant from the border. According to Russian law foreigners were not permitted to reside closer than 100 kilometers from the border. The refugees who remained were obliged to uproot themselves and move to several small villages to the east of Dubno.

Anti-Semitism in the meantime was growing among the Poles and Ukrainians. It didn't help that many Jewish people were employed in Government and municipal institutions and part of their duties was to collect taxes, revenues and agricultural produce, operations that were not well-tolerated by the general public at the best of times.

F

And now the arrests began. On 9th April 1940 tens of people were arrested, many of them Jewish, and among them a few public activists: The Albert brothers, the Barchash brothers and the Perle brothers. No one had any idea of the why and wherefore of the arrest and anxiety hit the town. After four days, on 13thApril, all the other members of the family were arrested and exiled by the administration to Siberia and all their property confiscated.

The major impact on the Jewish population of Dubno was the arrest of the Perle brothers who were active Zionists – David Perle for many years was chairman of the local Zionist Party and his brother Tzvi was head of the Foundation Fund for Israel. Apart from their Zionism there was no palpable reason for their arrest and the Jews saw in that a clear violation of the Soviet Government's promise made when they entered the town that no one would be harmed for Zionist activities during time of Polish rule especially since such activity was at that time legal.

After a while, of those arrested at the same time, only a few were released and even they were from Soviet Russia and not Poland, among them the Albert brothers. To this day the fate of the others is unknown. The family members who had been exiled to Siberia were released in Russia after the Soviet agreement with General Sikorski on 12th August 1941 and most of them returned to Poland after the repatriation agreement of 6th July 1945.

G

In order to complete the "Sovietization" of the territory the process of exchanging legitimate Polish identification documents with Russian passports began. The majority of the town's citizens saw the action favorably until it became clear that some of them, especially the Jews, received passports that were valid for one year only instead of the usual five years. It also became clear that the holders of these passports were required to fulfill Article 11 of the Soviet Constitution. At first no one knew what Article 11 was but then discovered that according to its terms – "He who doesn't work – doesn't eat." Holders of these passports, therefore, saw themselves cast as second-class citizens and they were under certain restrictions. All attempts to nullify the decree, even in the Soviet courts with the help of Soviet lawyers from Kyiv (Kiev) who received very high fees, were unsuccessful: only a very few managed to obtain five-year passports.

The obligation to change identification documents also fell on those refugees who settled in the towns and villages and the N.K.V.D. men knew that most of the refugees were not interested in obtaining Soviet citizenship. They were offered an alternative: those who didn't want to accept Soviet citizenship were free to sign a document requesting a return to territory conquered by Germany and the Soviet authorities would return them to their previous place of residence according to the agreement that existed between Russia and Germany regarding the exchange of populations. It became clear that most of the refugees waited with great impatience for the possibility of returning to their original homes and families who had remained on the other side of the border. Although they knew that life under Nazi rule was difficult for Jews most of them preferred it to the hard life as Soviet citizens. In the meantime, those who were waiting to return to German territory began seeking opportunities to acquire Polish zloty in exchange for gold, dollars and shares they held because they knew that the Polish zloty was legal tender there and in Russian-held territory it could be bought very cheaply.

But one night it was discovered that the Russian offer was a sham and all those who had signed the request were rounded up during the night and under the guise of returning them to German-held territory were sent to distant Siberia where they were forced into hard labor. Indeed, something sweet came out of that: all those who survived the harsh conditions were released from Siberia according to the Sikorski agreement and, with the termination of the war and the establishment of the Polish Republic, about 200,000 Jewish exiles were repatriated and returned to Poland.

In the meantime, the N.K.V.D. continued with their program of incarceration, particularly of Jews, who were investigated for their political and Zionist activities both past and present. The investigations were always conducted in an atmosphere of threats and investigations of the families as well and the results were often admissions of activities that had never occurred while others, those not yet arrested, were careful not to meet even with friends and family in order not to implicate them or cast doubts upon them in the eyes of the N.K.V.D.

In the middle of 1940, all those born in 1919 were mobilized and those found fit to serve sent to basic-training camps and then transferred to units of the Red Army deep inside Russia. The fate of those mobilized is unknown to this day.

H

Not long after rumors spread in Dubno emanating from the BBC that Hitler was preparing to attack Russia and indeed, on Sunday 22nd June 1941 at 4 in the morning, we suddenly heard the thunder of artillery and explosions close to Dubno. No one knew what was happening until the announcement came at 7 in the morning from radio Moscow and Berlin that the German air-force had bombed military targets in Ukraine, in Byelorussia and Soviet Russia itself and also, an airfield being built close to Dubno was bombed. The number of people injured was small, a few killed and 20–30 injured – because it happened to be Sunday and some thousands of workers on the airfield, who had been brought from Russia, had not been at work.

Throughout the morning hours Moscow Radio continued to broadcast detailed information about the attacks of the German air-force on the military and civilian targets throughout Russia and the hearts of the Dubno residents stopped beating.

At noon we already saw convoys of Russian tanks and heavy artillery of the Red Army moving through Dubno on the way eastwards. It was clear that the Red Army was retreating before the German attackers. At the same time as the army retreated, the evacuation of the workers' families together with Soviet military personnel who came to the Ukraine also took place. The evacuation of the families took place using thousands of trucks that moved in long convoys carrying women and children, furniture and household goods in the direction of Lvov-Brody. They passed through Dubno and Rowno to the old Russian border near the town of Korets and from there onwards into Russia. The convoys of families continued without pause for twenty-four hours and then suddenly stopped entirely. It seems that all the families had been evacuated.

With the knowledge of the German attack came the immediate mobilization of all men up to the age of fifty and the gymnasium on Panienska Street was allocated as the mobilization center. Medical and management committees were set up and the examination and registration were executed rapidly. But to everyone's surprise virtually everyone who reported was sent home to await a recall. Only a few tens of them were distributed to various units of the Red Army. It seems that the decision not to activate the mobilization sprang from a certain lack of faith by the Soviet authorities in the local citizens. In September of that same year in the vicinity of Woronicze I personally met several of those mobilized and they too were removed from active duty and placed in work-units engaged in digging anti-tank trenches behind the Front.

The 23rd of June passed quietly in Dubno without any disturbance. There were no attacks by enemy aircraft and no convoys of military vehicles passed through town. In the afternoon there were no more evacuations or convoys of Soviet families. As a result, rumors spread in town that the Russians were retreating with Germany's agreement to the old Russian-Polish border from before 17th September 1939 and they stopped their attacks. On the other hand, the Russians claimed that the present quiet was due to the destruction of the German invader by the Red Army and the Communist Party Secretary in Dubno that I met in the street that same evening said: "Tell your friends that all is well. The families that were evacuated will be returning and life will resume as it used to be."

But the following morning an evacuation program was started, and the local administration institutions began leaving, travelling eastwards. Documents and files were packed, others were burnt. Rifles were distributed to the Russian workers in addition to the pistols that were already in their possession, and everyone just waited for the order to go. The request of the Jewish workers to join the evacuation was refused: "Nobody's getting ready to leave"; "Everyone is ordered to remain at his post"; "We have no transport available for you." Only a few isolated people were able to join the departing Russians at the last moment, in addition to tens of younger people, members of the Young Communists in town who had a government vehicle placed at their convenience. They were evacuated together with the Soviets who decided not to wait for the Germans to arrive and left for the Soviet Union.

There were some Jewish men in Dubno who decided not to wait for the arrival of the Germans and left of their own accord, some on foot and some on bicycles, in the direction of Mizocz and Ostrow, leaving their families and property behind them. Only a few of them succeeded in crossing the frontier to the Soviet Union; they were the ones who stayed alive.

All the rest, the entire Jewish community of Dubno decided either to remain there, to get their confiscated and nationalized property in return and try to cope with life under the approaching German army, or come to terms with the impossibility of leaving town and hoping for the best. The "Final Solution" of the Nazis was not yet known. On the evening of that same day, 24ᵗʰ June 1941 advance units of the Nazi army arrived in Dubno and the town passed to their hands. From all the Jewish people who remained no more than a handful remained alive.

I personally left Dubno on Tuesday 23ʳᵈ June towards evening on a horse-drawn cart with my son for Rowno and from there to the Russian frontier. I was one of the very few given the possibility of following the retreating Russians, thus saving my life. From all the members of my family who remained in town, I was the only one who remained alive; my father, brother and sister, and their families, I never saw again.

Translator's Comment

1. ק"בר a Hebrew acrostic for Rabbi Eliezer Zadok, a leading Rabbi of the Tannaim generation, the last of the generations of Talmudic scholars.

Layout of Dubno & the Ghetto Border

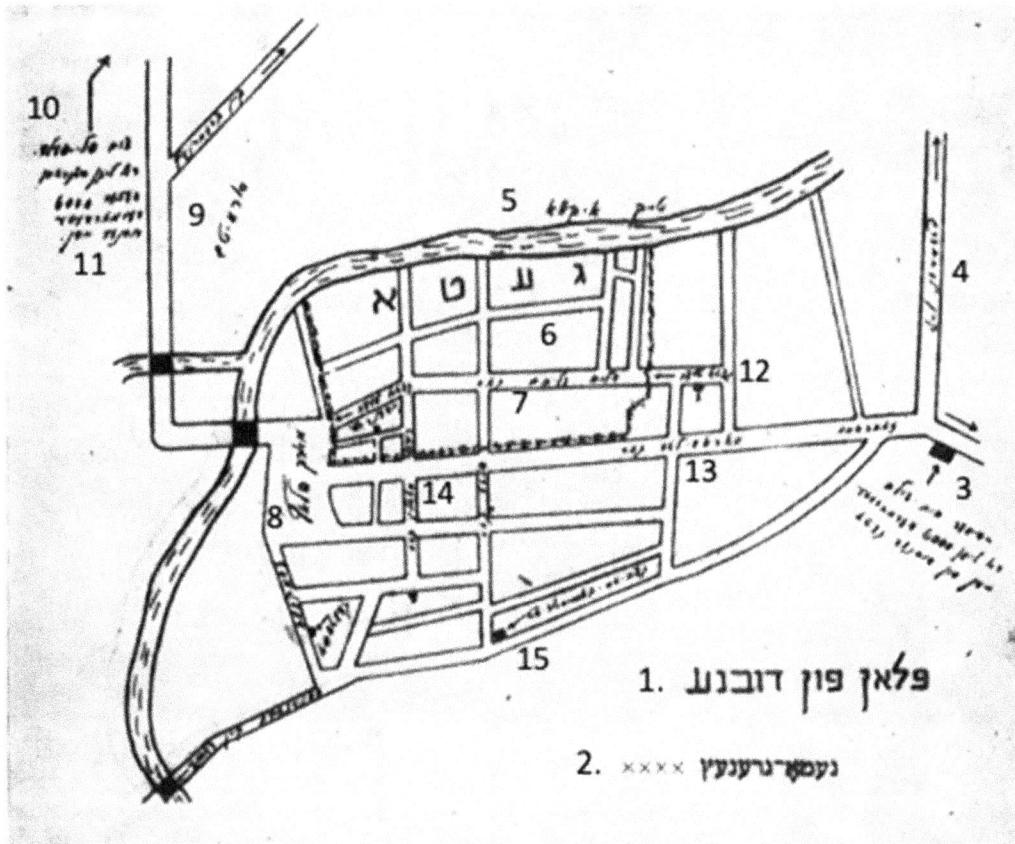

Legend (translated from Yiddish by Pamela Russ)

1. *Layout of Dubno*
2. *Ghetto border*
3. *Cemetery; here lie 6,000 dead from the Dubno ghetto*
4. *To Lemberg*
5. *Ikwa River*
6. *Ghetto*
7. *Sholem Aleichem Street*
8. *Market Place*
9. *Surmicze*
10. *To the airfield*
11. *Here lie 6,000 people killed*
12. *Ghetto gate*
13. *Wroclaw Street*
14. *Ghetto gate*
15. *Exchange Commissary Office*

The Germans Are Coming

by Moshe Weisberg

Translated from Hebrew by Selwyn Rose

Like locusts from afar they came,

Green devils borne on a wave,

With helmeted heads, astride motor–bikes –

With faces of evil, darkened with hate,

Their cheering mouths noisily laughing,

Blood and fire from their eyes flashed forth –

One fire the world entire ignited

And one bloody hangman came with.

A wild gang of hooligans rushed into town,

Galloped with flushed angry faces,

Their hands outstretched waving their guns.

They were carrying grenades and pistols;

Each weapon was loaded and drawn,

They raided the town and her streets

Robbing the Jews, dragging and beating.

An elderly man bent over with age

Was dragged; his beard was whitened and long

His body was soaking with blood.

He was kicked with their jackboots and lay trembling.

By green human–faced devils – faces of men

Against a wall with the Jew at its foot

They cut his beard: "You pig of a Jew"

The blood ran down his chest

For he was a miracle and a masterpiece.

One of them from afar appeared

Through his legs peeped the feet of a babe

The mother on her knees in his behalf pleaded

But the proud foot just trampled the tot;

A malignant curse flew from the lips of the bully

With the butt of his rifle the woman's head smiting.

He spat in her face, turned, walked away.

And while Jews were marching along,

The hail fell upon them from high.

Shovels and hoes were thrust in their hands

And while they yet lived, they were forced to prepare

Their own last resting place.

Greybeards, youngsters were all buried alive

Thus did the German foresters who invaded the town

Reign with an arrogant terror.

From the book: Mojsze Wejsberg: *Żydzi oskarżają.*
Translated from Polish by Y. Netaneli, July 1941.

The Liquidation of the Dubno Ghetto

by Yehoshua Wovek

Translated from Yiddish by Pamela Russ

On June 22, four a.m., the first German bombs fell on Dubno – and this was the beginning of the great Jewish tragedy. The Soviet families fled, and the Russian army began to recede. The municipal officials packed their suitcases, and only the Jewish residents were lost. The residents of the main streets hid in the corners and back streets.

Wednesday, 8:30 in the evening, the NKVD (Soviet Secret Police) left town. The Christian residents were in a happy mood, as they made fun of the Russians.

There were already two Jewish victims: the young man Simkha Pessy's, and the son of Dovid Poliszuk. His father did not cry. He said to me: "May his death be a redemption for all other Jews of this town…"

That same day, around two o'clock, the Germans marched into the city. Their first order was: "All Jews, from age fourteen up, must wear an armband with a blue Star of David on their sleeve.

The second command: forced labor for all Jews. He who will get out of doing this – will go to his death.

The troubles began. Ukrainian police and a city administration, composed of Ukrainians, were set up. Each day had its murders, each day had its snatching up for forced labor. At the beginning of July, 85 Jews were grabbed up – and they were never seen again.

August 21, 1941, the second *Aktzia* [round up] began. They were seizing Jews. We knew that their end would be – death. From seven in the morning, until five in the evening, they seized 900 men, except for one woman who was shot that day – the daughter of Motel Podisik. Each person died a horrible death.

The following day, an order was given to give payment to the Ukrainians for the piece of "work" that they did. They also had to give all their radio apparatus to the police. In a short time, they had seized about 80

503

residents and no one knew where they went.

The SS elder, the murderer Fafke, declared openly: "I can't close my eyes at night if they've killed only a minimum of ten Jews." SS Hammerstein said: "A Jew who does not work must be killed." And the murderer Vize remarked: "I am waiting for the day when they will kill the last Jew…"

The winter of 1941–42 arrived. Cold, frost, starvation, and grief. An order was given to give all fur coats to the Germans. For disobeying – death penalty. And a tax per head. There was also an order to bring several kilos of gold.

Yekhezkel Mendelson- as a Polish prisoner in a detention camp

The eve of Passover, another order: to set up a ghetto.

On the first day of Passover 5702 (April 2, 1942), the ghetto was created. The order demanded that by seven in the morning, all the Jews must be inside the ghetto. There was nowhere to run, but they tried to flee. They were carrying small children, they were dragging furniture, dishes, clothing; cries, wailing, and sobbing.

There was one comfort in the heart: Those who had relatives and family in Israel would be saved from this hell. But woe to those who did not live to merit this.

All were now in the ghetto.

May 15 and 16, 1942. Something was hanging in the air… They were saying that they were digging ditches. Why ditches? To hide potatoes, foodstuffs? No one knew.

May 27, 1942 (Sivan 21, 5702). At four a.m., SS men tore into the ghetto, wearing long leather coats, in one hand – a gun, in the other a rubber truncheon. "Everyone out! You are all going to your death!" The heavens and the earths all opened to the cries of the women, men, children, and elderly. The shooting did not cease until five in the evening.

The bloody toll of the day: 1,200 men, 1,500 women, 1,800 children. A total of 4,500 murdered, may their blood be avenged. On that day, I lost my wife and three-year-old dear son and 35 other souls of my family.

[Column 709]

As night fell, people began to crawl out of their hiding places: from the bushes by the river, from the closets, from the trash cans.

To those who carried out the killings, the Germans gave a day to rest: "Since they experienced so much yesterday, we'll let them rest today…"

The Strength of Liza Leviatan

Several days after the terrible slaughter, a group of Jews was sent to collect and pack up the clothing. It was horrific. Many recognized the clothing of a brother, a mother, parents, and relatives. At that time, they told the story of Liza Leviatan, the wife of Meyer Geker. Liza pleaded with the murderers to allow her to say something before her death. She was given permission – turned to the murderers and said these words to the German nation: "You Germans think that you can kill all the Jews in the world? Not true! There are Jews in Israel, and they will take revenge for the spilling of innocent blood…" After that she asked that she be shot before her son was shot. The murderers did not grant her this favor." She grabbed a piece of earth, soaked it in blood, and threw it at the Germans. After that her holy soul departed.

Itamar Klempner of Dubno, who was hiding under a pile of clothing, the clothing that had been torn off the tragic victims before they were killed, heard and saw all the horrors and heroic actions.

At that time, rumors spread that in all the surrounding towns the ghettos had been liquidated, and Dubno as well would soon become "*Judenrein*," cleansed of Jews. We began to dig hiding places for ourselves and search for escapes outside the ghetto: in the villages, the forests, fields. We prepared false Aryan documents. The person who was caught with these types of papers was killed on the spot. That is how Yakov Geker and his wife Chai'tshe Lerner were killed. They were caught in Pantalia with false papers.

In the ghetto they said: "The Germans will certainly lose – but we've already lost…"

For many years, my brother Shloime lived in the Czech village of Mirogoscz. Now he took in the family Misponis, Benny Burtnik, myself, and my sister.

Summer of 5705, we worked for a short time for the Czechs.

The Last Yom Kippur in the Dubno Ghetto

The Days of Awe of the year 5703 [1943] arrived, and I could not give up having prayers with other Jews, so I left to go to the city.

For *Kol Nidrei* [the evening ritual prayer of Yom Kippur] we assembled in the house of Sikulerin, on the shore of the Ikwa. The rooms were full. There was only one well-known cantor left in town, Reb Pinkhas Shokhet. We sat on the ground. Very often, one of the people praying would approach the *chazan* [cantor, person who leads the prayers] and say quietly to him: "Reb Pinkhas, may you merit a year of life..." Many were banging their heads in the walls, choking on their cries... so that no one would hear them outside ... After *kol nidrei*, the cantor said some other prayers. Later, all the Jews crawled back into their dark corners.

Meanwhile, more terrible rumors were heard. The threat of death was everywhere. My sister and I ran back to the Czech village. The following day, they declared in the village that all Jewish workers had to return to Dubno... My brother's family, my sister and I, hid ourselves away in a hiding place in the village, near the theater hall. We did not return to the city.

Simkhas Torah 5703 [1943]

A few days later we heard that on the day of Simchat Torah Jewish blood was running like water in Dubno. Many, with their own hands, burned their few possessions in all kinds of ways, and others took their own lives in many different ways. Not more than 25 families remained, and another 150 Jewish skilled workers.

We hid in our ditch for seventeen months. No washing, no change of clothing. It was cold all the time, and there was bad weather. This was all in our favor because

that made it easier to sneak out and find a piece of bread and some greens to keep us alive.

There were ten of us who went into the ditch, and six came out alive. Three died of hunger, thirst, filth. One, the brother-in-law of my brother, left to go find a piece of bread, and he was shot on his way to the village.

October 23, 1943, the last *Aktzia* liquidated the remaining survivors in Dubno. The city became "*Judenrein*" ["cleansed" of Jews]. The final place for this murder was the suburb of Zabramie. A small group of only 10–14 skilled specialists were left to complete all kinds of jobs for the murderers. They lived on Alexandrovska Street. In the end, they escaped. Some of them died on the roads, and some in the forests.

Once, we pushed ourselves in with Simkha Stievel and his wife Genya. They were hiding at the home of a Ukrainian. They were troubled, unfortunate, and having no means to protect themselves, they decided to return to the city and surrender themselves

[Column 712]

into the murderers' hands. We took them into our ditch, set up a corner for them for sleeping, and then they lived with us.

Finally, we merited the day of February 9, 1944, when the Soviets liberated us. It was difficult to get to Dubno, so we went there on foot. On the way, we met others from Dubno. They were dressed haphazardly, wrapped in rags and sacks, drained from hunger and illness. We could not recognize them unless someone called their names. That's how we found Khaim Segal, Abrashe Grinzweig, and the Belfer brothers.

In the town Warkowycz, we saw the first Jew. And from there, we left for Dubno after the city was freed. Our hearts were bleeding as we saw the houses, the streets, bridges, trees – were there. Only our nearest and dearest were gone, forever…

Cursed be those who did this to us! And cursed be the earth that drank in the pure innocent blood!

Der Gebietskommissar
Rückkehrerlager
Arbeitsamt Dubno

A U S W E I S

Name *Gorbatsch*
Vorname *Nikol...*
Geburtsjahr 19 1.
Nationalitaet *Peter*

ist im Rueckkehrerlager
sc...

Dubno am 1.. ... 1942

Der Gebietsk...
Rückkehrerlager
Arbeitsamt Dubn...

The Life and Destruction of the Jews in Dubno

by Moshe Weisberg

Translated from Yiddish by Pamela Russ

The regional city of Dubno lies near the river Ikwa, at the crossroad of Kiev–Rowno and Brody–Lemberg (Lwów, Lvov, Lviv), an old city that has existed for hundreds of years. Until the outbreak of the German–Soviet war, life was busy there in all areas. There were around 12,000 Jews, 60 percent of the general population. In 1941, in the beginning of the Nazi regime in Dubno, there were 13,000 Jews there.

On June 25, 1941, the Nazi thugs invaded Dubno. A terrible fear befell the Jews. The Jewish stores were looted by the Germans and the local Ukrainian residents. Looting of Jewish private properties also began, as well as the beating of Jews, coercing them into labor, and persecution in general. The bread ration for Jews was decreased to 100 grams daily. A public order was made that Jews must wear a white band 15 centimeters wide, with a blue Star of David. On October 17, 1941, the white bands were changed to yellow patches of eight centimeters in diameter, which they had to wear on the left side of the chest and on the right side of the back. The *Judenrat* [Jewish council] that was created, with magistrate Konrad Tobenfeler at the head, had to bring in all kinds of monies every day, and they also demanded contributions, such as for example, clothing, linen, furniture, dishes, instruments, and so on.

On the 22ⁿᵈ of July, a month after the Germans invaded, the first killing riot of the Jews took place. It was a Tuesday afternoon. Some trucks with SS men arrived in Dubno and mobilized the help of the Ukrainian militia, and they began the first murder–*Aktzia* [action]. The Ukrainians captured 150 men. And from the house where I was (Zabrama 5), they herded out all the men. Me and another three (Weisboim Leizer, Bortnik Mikhel, and Hersh) managed to hide. The Jews that were captured were herded together at the post office where the SS murderers were already waiting.

They threw themselves onto the Jews and beat them mercilessly. Seventy men were returned home, and eighty others were stuffed into trucks and taken to the Jewish cemetery (I lived not far from there). Ditches were already prepared there. The [Jews] were ordered to undress naked. They were beaten again, their gold teeth were ripped out, and then finally, the Jews were set out in rows by the ditches, and then shot. The following day, my Ukrainian neighbor Czerniakow brought all kinds of pictures, documents, eyeglasses, and other such things that he found in the cemetery near the ditches.

In mid–August, the Nazi military powers ordered the Dubno Jews to turn in all their gold, silver, and other valuable possessions. This order was carried out with exceptional strictness.

The second *Aktzia* took place on August 21, 1941, only for the men. It was a Thursday, and all kinds of rumors circulated, and soon, an exceptional panic as well. Jews began fleeing to their homes. Ukrainian police appeared in the streets. They were armed with pistols, steel bars, sticks, and all kinds of killing devices. The eyes and part of the faces of many of the Ukrainians were covered with black masks. The local Ukrainians tried to disguise themselves in front of the Jews who knew them well as former friends in school, in the military, from other social activities, and from other friendly situations … As wild animals, they attacked the Jewish streets, courtyards and houses, searching through cellars and attics. They dragged out elderly and young men from all kinds of hiding places. They beat and wounded and wildly chased the defenseless Jews.

That day, I was in the *Judenrat*. During that bloody day, the murderers came in about twenty times and searched for the hidden officials.

Out of 42 officials, 37 were seized. Some managed to save themselves as they locked themselves in a disguised, small house on the side, where I was as well. From that small house, we saw the marketplace where the Jews were herded together and were taken in groups to the city prison. In the yard and in the halls of the prison, Ukrainian police were set out in two rows, armed with sticks and iron bars. Each Jew had to pass through the two rows and was covered in blood after being beaten. The German murderers sat in a room where they took away all personal belongings from each of the Jews and sentenced almost each person to his death. Only a few were freed. Those sent to their deaths were driven to the Jewish cemetery, where everything else was taken from them and they were stripped naked and shot. This *Aktzia* lasted for ten hours, until seven in the evening. A thousand Jewish men died at that time.

From that day on, for about half a year, there was no greater *Aktzia* in Dubno. There were only incidents where individual Jews or smaller groups were shot, where they [the

Germans] contrived all kinds of lies. The Jews were working in various urban and military forced labor. As such, they [the Germans] diminished their morale, beat, mocked, and forced them into the most difficult labor. The greater part of the Jewish population became starved out skeletons, drained in morale, physical and psychological – to the greatest degree. The Jews comforted themselves with all kinds of made–up rumors. But confusion grew every day, primarily because of the invasion of the Nazi army on all fronts. Thousands of Soviet prisoners were brought into the city. They were tortured with beatings and starvation, no less than were the Jews. In the winter months of 1942 alone, in Rowno and Dubno 55,000 Russian war prisoners died.

The Germans also systematically destroyed the Jews. They always ordered the *Judenrat* to hand over the Jewish possessions and goods. The demands were enormous, and it was difficult to satisfy them.

[Column 696]

Confusion grew from day to day. More confusion was caused by the different news about the devastation that circulated from the surrounding, of neighboring cities and towns. From Rowno, for instance, tragic news was received, that on the 10th and 11th of November 1941, 18,000 Jews were murdered, and they were buried in nine ditches in the Sosenkas [lit: pine trees] (a small forest, five kilometers behind Rowno). Similar news also came from other Volhynian cities.

On the 5th and 23rd of March, two thorough *Aktzias* took place, for which they had to create a ghetto. For these *Aktzias*, the Germans mobilized thousands of wagons from the surrounding Ukrainian and Polish villages. Hundreds of Ukrainian policemen threw into the wagons, from all the Jewish homes, the best possessions and goods, furniture, things, and all kinds of products. All they left behind were shabby things and broken dishes. For the Ukrainian people, this was a great opportunity to rob from the Jews. The Poles, not to be left behind, also took advantage of this.

On April 2, 1942, the first day of Passover, a ghetto for the Dubno Jews was set up. By that time, there were ghettos already in most of the Volhynia cities. But it was different in the eastern Ukrainian regions. There was already no sign of any Jews there. The small, dirty Sholom Aleichem Street was designated as the ghetto in Dubno. Several other small, neighboring muddy streets that were on the shore of the Ikwa River, led to the borders of the ghetto. The place was walled in with a tall wooden wall and with barbed wire. Within one day, all the Jews of the city had to move there. For the meager eleven thousand Jews who were still living in Dubno at the time, this place was too small, and the crampedness was intolerable. All of these terrible conditions caused all kinds of epidemics.

Every morning, each day, designated groups would be marched to work,

[Column 697]

511

Return-entry pass" for workers allowed out of the ghetto for forced labor; it allowed people back into the ghetto at the end of a day's work.

and in the same order, return at night. Not one single Jew was permitted to be seen outside of the ghetto. Often, the German or Ukrainian gendarmes would conduct searches of the groups that returned to the ghetto. For discovering a few deca [small weight] of butter or other foods, the person would be murderously beaten and then arrested. This situation, for instance, happened to my friend Klara Tenenboim. She was a horticulturalist and worked as a gardener for the regional commissariat. Once, when her group returned from work, suddenly, the police commandant Mr. Popka and some Ukrainian police detained the group and conducted an investigation. They found ten deca butter on Klara. Mr. Popka beat her murderously, stomped on her with his feet, and then took her and some other girls to the police department. There he searched them again, and then when he found Tenenboim's admission certificate to the university, he ripped it up cruelly, screaming: "Jews are not permitted to have any education!" For the little bit of fat that he found, he sent the girl to be shot. Thanks to the great efforts that the regional commissioner, for whom she worked, put forth for her, she was able to save herself from death. And more so, Klara Tenenboim survived the Nazi regime and is now in Vienna.

Life in the ghetto was without hope, filled with an intense waiting for some sort of change. And a change did come, but an extremely tragic one. In mid–May 1942, six weeks after setting up the ghetto, the Germans divided the ghetto into two parts. One section was for men who were skilled laborers who received special permits, and the second section was designated for the men who were not skilled. The number of work permits that were handed out was limited. But in fact, those who received the work permits were not only those who were skilled but also those who had excellent "connections" or who paid handsomely for those papers. I myself was hired as a technical builder in the regional commission, and thanks to that I was able to provide work permits to 25 Jewish young men who were hired to work for the Ukrainian painters of the regional commission.

[Column 698]

The Jews already understood that a great tragedy was being prepared for them, and that is what happened. May 27 was a day of horrific slaughter for the Jews of Dubno, costing the lives of about 7,000 souls. The principal murderers of the Jews of Dubno in the first line were: the commandant of the gendarmerie *Pan* [Mr.] Popka; the director of the German labor office *Hauptman* Hammerstein; regional commissioner Broks; his deputy staff–director Alleter; and the inspector Wiza. *Pan* Popka was the type of criminal whose ugly, crooked, and creased face, with his whip in hand, quickly personified his character. *Hauptman*Hammerstein, who was from the Sudeten, was tall, and had a refined face and a pleasant voice. He wore glasses on his nose. Whoever spoke to him for the first time, could never imagine that this sort of person could be such a wild, slick murderer to an exceptional degree. Regional commissioner Broks was more of a quiet person. He would sign the rulings or give his consent. His bloody orders were carried out by his subordinate Germans or Ukrainians. Later, he would come with inspections to the places where there were incidents. His deputy staff director Alleter was a short man, very stern, and in reality, he directed all the work of the regional commissariat. He was the main torturer of the Dubno Jews. Inspector Wiza, as *Pan* Popka, was more of a criminal type, a sadist who would always beat each Jew who passed him, without any reason or having done any misdemeanor. He participated in every *Aktzia*.

Other than the Germans, the leaders of the Ukrainian people also had a hand in torturing the Jews. Among them, first in line, were: Mayor Burka, vice–mayor Serwas, senior official Siderovitch, and others. A certain Stashik exceeded them all. These above-mentioned Ukrainian leaders were teachers by profession, who worked with me in Soviet schools from 1939 to 1941. Then they declared themselves staunch Communists.

[Column 699]

The *Aktzia* itself happened in the following way. May 26, 1942, in the evening, the Jewish ghetto police received an order not to leave any of those non–skilled on the side of the skilled workers. At twelve o'clock at night, three shots were heard at the ghetto gate of the skilled workers, after which wild German SS men and several hundred Ukrainian police tore into the ghetto. Also, the outside of the ghetto was surrounded by armed police. They all wore helmets; and the Germans were also leading dogs. They began tearing out the Jews from their houses. Those who were ripped out of their houses were beaten mercilessly. Many women fell in a faint as they watched their young children being trampled on by murderous feet. The sick and elderly were shot on the spot. Other Jews jumped into the river (Ikwa), to encounter their death there rather than at the hands of the murderers. Many people lost their minds. One woman, Khaya Feinblit of Ribno Street, who had had no children for fourteen years after her marriage and bore her first child only after the beginning of the German occupation, when the murderers wanted to take her tiny child away during the first *Aktzia*, she threw the baby into a barrel of water, screaming: "I myself should be the one to see to the death of my long desired child!" Then she herself swallowed poison. The barbarians laughed at this, and with joy, continued on in their bloody sport. The persecuted, tragic Jews were herded together near the exit of the ghetto where there was a deathly and dark silence. From time to time, when trucks would come for the people, a last miserable scream would be heard as it cut through the surrounding silence. The victims were rammed into the trucks and driven to the place of death. Those that could not be pushed into the trucks were chased on foot. The men were herded to the Jewish cemetery; women and children – to the airfield that was behind the city near the train station in Surmicze.

One such harassed group comprised about 800 school–aged children.

[Column 700]

The best dressed children were set out in fours. They were given bouquets of lilacs in their hands. And in an irony of fate, our most beautiful children went, in the most beautiful month of the year, in May, to their own funerals – with flowers in their hands. They were chased by Ukrainians, Germans, and German women with dogs that they would incite. Many children were torn apart en route by the dogs. That's what the German women and mothers did, with their own children safely in their homes.

Groups of Jews were brought to the deep, dug out ditches. Everyone had to strip naked. They tore out everyone's gold teeth. Only very rarely, could you hear a sigh or a cry of pain. The men and women were skeletal, with pale yellow faces, more like shadows than people. They were indifferent to everything. The naked people (men, women, and children) had to kneel, with their faces lowered into the dug–out ditches and their hands placed over the back of their necks. A German sat at the edge of the ditch, holding a loaded machine gun. His feet were hanging over into the ditch and he had a cigarette in his mouth. Every few minutes, you could hear a machine gun ringing out, and twenty people fell into the ditch. That's how every few minutes a new set of twenty victims fell. Those people who were not murdered with the first shot, were murdered by the second shot. Some were suffocated under the new corpses that fell on top of them. And that's how a bloody movable mass collected in the ditches. The filled ditches were then doused in gasoline and lit. Blood oozed out into the earth in some places. Even the following day, the Ukrainians noticed how the ground in some places had shifted.

This *Aktzia* lasted until May 27ᵗʰ in the morning. On that day, the Jews from the second section of the ghetto were chased to work, as if nothing had happened. These were the remaining skilled workers for whom a small piece of white paper had delayed death for a certain amount of time.

[Column 701]

One can only imagine the psychological condition of these people who for the most part during the night had lost their families, friends, and dear ones with whom they had grown up and lived together. From time to time, cargo trucks appeared, loaded up with clothing, shoes, and various other things. These were loaded up by the Jews themselves, taken from their own brothers where they were gruesomely killed. In some places, the passing Ukrainians and Poles remained still and watched the tragic Jewish groups who were once again leaving to work. They remained still and smiled mockingly. In the best case, someone would shake his head sadly and then continue on his way. The next day, many of those sympathetic people would quietly relate how the majority of their brothers had helped the wild Germans grab out the Jews who were hiding and then delivered them to their death. A teacher who was a friend of mine and with whom I had worked, the Ukrainian Wolodka Druczenko, had himself snatched out Jewish children and delivered them to the Germans. The main role in searching out the hidden Jews was carried out by Vanka Hofman. His father was a lawyer, a Russian. As the Germans arrived, he and his family became *Volksdeutchen* [ethnic Germans, i.e., German by race, regardless of citizenship]. One of his sons became commandant of the Ukrainian police and during each *Aktzia*, he himself shot hundreds of Jews. One of the daughters also worked in the commissariat. The abovementioned Vanka played a dark role in torturing the Jews. When the work permits were being handed out, he took large sums of money for each permit and later searched out the Germans and delivered the permits to them. He even turned over his own school friend Misha Spitzman to his death (it is worth noting that Klara Tenenboim in Vienna saw Vanka Hofman there).

After the *Aktzia*, the beautiful summer days became even more difficult for the Jews. There were 3,000 people that remained alive. They were always in fear and certainty that they were being kept alive just so their last bits of capacity could be used, and their end would be – a tragic death. But there were still some naïve optimists, who

[Column 702]

comforted themselves with all kinds of contrived news from the front, from overheard talks among the Germans, or from the radio. When a German dared to say a word against Hitler or his government, that was enough for the Jews to build mountains, and then to comfort themselves for weeks… Meanwhile, the Ukrainians and Poles, for a designated time, had to learn the Jewish skills so that they would be able to replace the Jews when needed.

Sensing the approaching end for the remaining Jews, the Ukrainians and the Poles began taking the Jews' valuable possessions, promising the confused Jews that they would receive help in time of danger. The Jews gave away their best to these non–Jewish neighbors, saying: "If we survive, we may get some things back. And if not, it won't matter if things are lost." An acquaintance of mine, a Polish woman, Zophia Stepanovitchova, where I was almost every day, hid the possessions of two of her Jewish neighbors, from homeowner Bronstajn, and from the Jewish girl Adela and her mother. Besides having a cellar filled with Jewish goods, there were two closets filled with things. When the above-mentioned Adela wanted to go to her closet of things in the other woman's house, and wanted to take out a dress for herself, they taunted her and threw her out of the house. The same thing happened with the woman Bronstajn when she wanted to take some of her clothing. This is what almost all the Ukrainians and Poles did, as they became rich from our tragedy.

I myself heard such a discussion from that same Stepanovitchova. I was sitting in her room, and the Polish seamstress Kolowa came into the house. She did not know that I was sitting in the other room. Then Kolowa began speaking in a cheerful voice: "Pani [Mrs.] Zosha, can't you take a piano from a Jew for your daughter Dzidka? They are going to kill the Jews anyway. And you, *Pani*, will have a piano for your daughter. I've already taken a piano for my Helen, and thank God, they've already killed that Jew. So now I am sure that it is mine!" … And Kolowa continued: "I also must get two good

[Column 703]

fur coats for me and my husband. *Pokeh–und–lapka* coats I already have from the Jews, but I want a lambskin coat. And I'll get it … Zosha, you can't be sleepy, and you have to do whatever you can, because compared to what others have, we could choke!" The above-mentioned Dzidka, for whom she tried to prepare a piano, was one year old. Zosha, to whom her friend was speaking like that, showed with her finger at her nose that Kolowa should not say anything. Then, angry, I came out of the other room, and said in a cold and dominating voice: "Yes, you *Pani*, will play an *Oberek* [a Polish dance], Mazurka [Polish folk dance], on the piano after the Jews have been murdered. But I don't know if you'll have to play a death–march also for the murdered Poles." And that's exactly how it was. After expelling the Jews, the Ukrainians began to murder the Poles, burning and looting their possessions. These are only small incidents that characterize the relationship of the Ukrainians and the Poles towards the Jews in Ukraine. A Pole with a sincere view of the Jewish tragedy, with compassion and offering help – was a rarity. Ukrainians of this sort almost did not exist. The local Russians were also not any better. A friend of mine, the Russian Kosak, who worked with me in the regional commissariat as a draftsman, later showed his true face. When I left Dubno with Aryan papers, after some time he investigated me in order to deliver me into German hands. Only the local Czechs, in certain instances, demonstrated empathy and offered help for their Jewish friends. All the non–Jewish residents who are so busy with their fear of God and kneeling in their churches and Russian churches, were banging their heads on the floor; they who always repeated the holy words, "Love the other as you love yourself, feed the hungry, and give drink to those who are thirsty" – these, in reality, showed themselves to be gruesome and bloodthirsty murderers. And in the best case – as those who robbed the Jews' possessions and assisted the Germans in exterminating the Jews.

Meanwhile, one day followed the other in the ghetto. In the evenings

[Column 704]

each Jew lay on his cot with the feeling that this could be his last night. Many times, because of all types of rumors, people did not go to sleep at all. Many Jews prepared underground hiding places believing that there they would find protection, and in a raging time would be able to save themselves from death. The bunkers and hiding places were so cleverly disguised that they really thought it would be impossible to be discovered. But still, later these places proved themselves to be useless, thanks to the collaboration of the local non–Jewish population with the Nazis.

Slowly, life in the ghetto reached the greatest heights of poverty and depression. The bread ration was very small, and no other foods were given out. Whoever had the opportunity traded his last possessions for food in order to stay alive. For a drop of butter or little piece of meat they gave away their most beautiful suits or other valuable possessions. Very often, Jews also paid with their lives.

Regretfully, it has to be recognized that in the Dubno ghetto there was no cultural or political activity. The reason was that right after six weeks of the ghetto's existence, a large part of the Jewish residents was killed and those remaining alive continued to suffer for another four months.

From the first *Aktzia* in Dubno until the liquidation of the ghetto, the Germans used all the Jewish skilled workers. The German demands were great, and the Jews could not fill them all. The chairman of the *Judenrat*, Magistrate Konrad Toibenfeld, and the head of the Jewish work department, Rozenboim, actually lost their control, not being able to find a way to deal with demands that were impossible to meet. And on the other hand, not wanting to give the enemy a venue for imposing more problems, they did everything they could possibly do. Tragically, the largest number of Jewish skilled workers was already rotting in the earth. The head of the German labor office, Kat Hammerstein, would himself come to the ghetto and chase the Jews to work, beat them, and torture them.

[Column 705]

There were incidents when individual Jews would run from the ghetto into the forest or to familiar peasants and live there with Aryan papers.

Summer 1942, news arrived in Dubno about the liquidation of the ghettos and other Volhynian cities. Two Jews who had fled from Kremenets related about an *Aktzia* that had taken place there on July 14, 1942. About 12,000 Jews were killed in the Kremenets ghetto. They also said that until their death, the Kremenets Jews suffered a greater hell than the Dubno Jews. Between 50 to 100 Jews would die daily from starvation. Another refugee from Rowno said that on one fine July day they killed the rest of the 7,000 Jews in the Rowno ghetto. This tragic news also foretold the fate of the Dubno Jews.

In August 1942, once again 4,500 Jews were assembled in the Dubno ghetto. Included were the exiled village Jews from the surrounding areas, Jews who for generations were connected to the agricultural work with their fields and meadows. The Jews could bring hardly anything with them into the ghetto. There was an even greater hunger and lack in the ghetto. On top of the Dubno Jews' greatest level of material suffering, was the economical *Aktzia* that took place in that same August of 1942. The purpose of this *Aktzia* was to remove all food products from those Jews who were still alive. The Jews had to bring all their meager foods to a designated place.

October 5, 1942, was the day of the tragic end of the rest of the Jews in the ghetto. With Aryan papers, I was already fifteen kilometers from the city, in the village of Kurdafon. This final *Aktzia* was similar to the previous one. This was exclusively carried out by the Ukrainians, who, as envoys of the Germans, with joy and song, drove from city to city and liquidated all the ghettos, murdering those Jews who were still there from the previousious *Aktzias*. During this *Aktzia*, many Jews committed suicide by hanging themselves, ingesting poison, or jumping into the Ikwa River. My cousin Leizer Weisboim hanged himself; the dentist Kagan and Dr. Artmanova

[Column 706]

and others also poisoned themselves. Many Jews were killed right on the spot in the ghetto. Dead bodies were lying everywhere across the city streets outside of the ghetto, where they died as they tried to escape. The last holdout of Dubno Jews was also killed in the same airfield, Surmicze.

The following day, after murdering the Jews, the looting of the leftover Jewish goods began. The Germans took the better things, the rest was divided up as gifts for the local non–Jewish residents. They distributed the possessions according to official and work positions. Of the entire non–Jewish population in Dubno, there was one Pole, Popuzhinski Stefan, who was the director of the gymnasium, who had enough moral fortitude and strength to decline these gifts that were given to him from the Jewish possessions.

While looting the Jewish homes, the Ukrainians and Poles searched and found those unfortunates, and mercilessly, delivered them into the hands of the German gendarmerie. The Germans understood that there were still Jews hiding in some places. So, they posted notices ordering the Jews to come out of their hiding places. In this summons, the murderers ensured that no harm would come to these Jews because they were needed for work.

This smooth reasoning unfortunately was successful. The completely oppressed Jews began to believe that maybe, truthfully, this time good fortune would shine on them. That's how the Jews finally crept out of their hiding places. Within just several days another 150 Jews appeared in the ghetto. For a few days, they were "so called" taken to work in the workshops in order to trick even more people to come out of their hiding places. All these naïve, trusting people were shot on October 23, 1942.

That is how the Dubno Jews ceased to exist. That is how all the Jews of Volhynia stopped breathing.

In Hiding Places and in the Forests

by Yitzchak Fisher

Translated from Hebrew[1] by Ilana Goldstein and edited by Shirley Ginzburg

On June 22, 1941, the Germans invaded Russia. On that day German planes bombed our town: the first victim was a young 18-year-old man from the Polishock family. His father stood and said: "My son, may you be the last Jewish victim of our town" and he didn't shed a tear.

The panic in the town was great and the children's cries were heart wrenching, a massive flight began: The Russian Army fled without stopping. Even 12–13-year-olds were fleeing to Russia, and the Germans continued bombing…

My oldest daughter, Tzirl, and her husband Izzi Frishman, studied in an academic school in Kremenets. My wife decided to help them escape to Russia. On Monday, the 25 of June 1941, at ten o'clock (Y: in the morning) my wife rushed to the train station, but the trains had stopped running. She decided to go to Kremenets by foot, a distance of 40 kilometers from Dubno. At that time, the Germans had invaded our town and my wife could not return to us. There was tremendous panic—anyone who went out into the street was shot on the spot. People started hiding. The wheels of the Howitzer–armored vehicles and the tanks were thundering.

I fled with my two children, Rochaleh, 13 years old and Shmulik, 10 years old, to the reeds on the banks of the river Ikwa, because the Germans were bursting into the houses and beating the inhabitants with murderous force. For two days and a night we didn't eat or drink. On the third night as darkness descended, I took the children home. Oy! Our house that we found was a disaster: The glass panes of the windows were smashed, the pillows and down blankets were torn and there were feathers everywhere. Whatever was possible to steal was stolen. We found shelter for the night at one of our neighbors. On the third day there was an all–clear (signal). We went out to the street, and we found out that the Germans had rounded up 300 people and dragged them to the old castle, and there they were brutally beaten. Many died in the hands of the murderers. Eighty–five half–dead people were rescued.

521

On 2.8 (Y: 8th of February)[2], the Germans arrested the town Rabbi. He was dragged to the big jail and was never seen or heard from again.

On the 3.8 (Y: 8th of March)[3] a decree was issued to select a Jewish council – "Judenrat".

On Friday[4] toward evening the Germans made a blockade and caught 80 prominent citizens of our town. They dragged them to the old prison, beat them until they lost consciousness and took them out to the cemetery, and ordered them to dig a trench. They were agonizingly lowered in. For four days and four nights the earth was moving up and down on their grave.

On the 15.8 (Y: 8.15) villagers from outside gathered and came to town and hunted the Jewish people and killed them in various ways. A total of 1,500 people died.

There was a "Judenrat" already in Dubno, but it did not lift a finger

[Column 470]

to help save the Jews: A rumor was spread that said that it is possible to deliver packages to the already murdered for $10.00...

On 20.8 (Y: 8.20) the Jewish community decreed that everyone aged 16 to 50 must be registered to receive work permits–or else will die. There was a Jewish militia escorting the people to work and back. This continued during the whole winter of 1941–1942.

Passover eve 1942[5] a new decree: Ghetto! A Ghetto will be built!

I lived on Kantorska 39, and my relatives were with me. I built six hiding places for a hundred people. In vain. We were driven out like cattle into the Ghetto surrounded by barbed wire. The Jewish militias did not spare us and beat us, and the Ukrainians and the Germans beat us as well. But being beaten by a fellow Jewish brother hurt more...

The "Judenrat" ordered us to bring 4 kilos of gold for the Ukrainian commander or else— we will die. Each man brought his portion of gold. And again, a new decree: Furs for men and furs for women to bring to the community or else... We all obeyed this decree as well.

One day my wife surprised us—she came to the Ghetto. Our happiness was immeasurable. After a few days my sister went out to the market to buy a few onions (one hour was designated for shopping for the Jews). A "miliziant", Fada Manishevitz approached her and hit her over the head with a club. She fell fainting. I went to the head of the militia to complain about Manishevitz, but Manishevitz took out a knife and stabbed me in the rib. A man, Z.G. who stood on the sideline laughed: "No matter, a stab with a knife will not kill you..." For six weeks I lay hovering between life and death. Miraculously I survived.

And something new: the Ghetto was to be divided in two. Those destined to life and those to death. Those holding "work–cards" separately and the sheep for slaughter – separately.

One Thursday Yod Alef Sivan Tav Shin Bet—May 27, 1942, the Gestapo blockaded and slaughtered us. They murdered more than 3500 people (Y: a thousand people), among them my mother (Y: Aleyha HaShalom, may her memory be a blessing), and our neighbor with her five children.

As darkness descended, we fled toward the section of the "work–card" holders and we hid there for a few days. I found "protekzia" favoritism and we were registered amongst the living. Meanwhile the militiamen were investigating the clothes of the murdered and grabbed valuables and money.

Panic stricken, haunted by the sound of a falling leaf, we arrived at the New Year of 1942.[a] Then I heard a new rumor: Graves were being dug for the remainder of the people…

[Column 471]

We decided to run away and hide with a Polish acquaintance. We stayed with him for a month (Y: ten days.) Then came the Gentile and said: "Fisher, do you have gold— good, if not you will have to scram from here…" I returned to the town, I dug and took out a few gold coins and gave them to him, and then afterwards he chased us away from his house. "Where should we go now?"

We fled to a nearby forest. I heard voices, I listened intently – I heard Jewish voices (Y: Yiddish spoken) We approached. And there was (a group of Jews) and a bunker…

We joined them. One day we saw a man, carrying a rifle, walking, and coming near to us. It was the forester. "We must run," I told the group, and that is what we did. We transferred to another location and dug in.

It was the beginning of Autumn; it became necessary to prepare a hiding place for the Winter. We went to scout the area, when we returned, we saw a sight that made my skin crawl and my hair stand on edge: My wife and my son and with them women and children lay dead. I fell fainting to the ground. My daughter who was with me, remained alive. Eight men dug a grave and buried the dead. The day of the slaughter was ג"תש כסלו ד"כ, 3 December 1942.[a]

Barefoot, hungry, and wearing rags, we spent the nights in haystacks and during the days— in the forest. We wondered those of us who remained alive, wondered why we survived? For what purpose? Is there any hope for us? We asked ourselves.

We ran out of food. It was necessary to get some bread. I went out by myself on a dark night. Where should I turn? I went towards the Czech village, Podaheitz. I collected some food in a bag. When I went out to the villages, I armed myself with a heavy spiked club. As I left the village two loathsome youths pestered me, started to taunt me, and hit me. I feared for my life, but I did not lose my cool. I raised my club and hit one of them on the head and he fell to the ground. His friend turned to run. I kept my composure and ran after him, I caught up to him and with a heavy blow I split his head. I grabbed my bag and fled into the thickness of the forest. I sat down

to rest. In the quiet of the forest, I heard a slight whisper. I glued my ear to the ground–
– yes someone crawling on all four was searching and whispering to himself: "I will
still find him, I will find him" … I knew it was the second of the two youths. I took
my life in my hands and ran towards him. I hit him with one blow and no more.

I searched through his belongings, I found personal documents and a long knife.
I told the people what happened, and we decided to abandon the forest. A rumor
reached us that Jewish people of Dubno were hiding with a certain Polish man. We all
transferred to him. The Polish man kept me in a haystack and there I slept for two
whole days and nights. The sound of bursts of gunfire woke me.

The Ukrainians of Bandera[8], ambushed the Poles in order to kill them. The Polish
man's wife informed us of the sad rumor. For the time being the Poles were saved.

[Column 472]

Close to this place there was a forest, and there lived a Goy (Y: Christian.) We fled
there. I bought from the Goy, onions, bread, and cigarettes. The Goy would let us
know periodically what is happening in the front and where the Russians are posted.
His information cheered us up and strengthened our morale. One day we were
informed that the Banderists were surrounding us. We got up and moved to another
wooded area. It was bitterly cold, dark, and we were barefoot and naked, close to
desperation.

We lay for many hours in a ditch that we dug under the snow, and again we moved
to another forest. Suddenly we were frightened and alarmed. We heard sighs and
groans. We stared into the darkness. We saw: wild boars…

One morning we heard many marching steps: Poles fleeing…

There was an exchange of shots. We fled from there until we arrived at a fortified
Polish post: Melisharna. The occupiers of the post were young, with a lot of arms.

Christmas of 1943 was approaching. The Polish group was celebrating according
to their custom: They drank and became drunk and didn't notice that they were
surrounded by the Banderists and were taken captive, and we were amongst them…I
was horrified to see the shocking scene: the robbers were poking the Poles' eyes out
of their sockets, slicing off the women's breasts and hacking up men and women alive.
We burst into a cellar full of big barrels and we lay there for three days and nights.
After the Banderists left the killing field, we fled again to the old Goy, who entreated
us to leave, as our end will be dire. From there we moved to a cellar of an abandoned
house, but the cold and the frost were freezing us to death. At this point we were
totally desperate. My daughter wanted to go to the town no matter what. But I knew
that that would be the end. Again, I went to a Goy and bought a loaf of bread weighing
2 kg.: We dug a hideout and lay in it for two weeks until the bread was consumed. We
passed by again by the same Goy's house but as we approached, I became suspicious:
Why weren't the dogs barking? Why were the doors open? We stopped on the edge.

We heard a voice ask: "Who is there?" I answered. The Goy descended. He brought a lamp, and we could see that the house was full of Russian soldiers! ...

We remained for three days at the Goy's. Suddenly it occurred to me that we were still not in a safe place. My daughter and I went to the road, leading to Rowno. Russian soldiers loaded us onto their vehicles and brought us to Rowno. There were no Jews in the city.[9]

I went out to the road and any Jew that I met I sent to a fortified house which I chose to be in. A hundred and twenty Jews gathered. We did not reach peace.

The German bombardment was continuous day and night. After a while the bombing stopped. We headed toward Dubno to the killing field and the death train tracks. We saw the Goyim living and the Jews gone. I was fed up with the town. I took my daughter and we headed to Poland. (Y: I thought only: revenge, revenge to the Germans.)

Translator's and Editor's Comments

1. With comparison to the Yiddish (noted by Y: in the text).
2. Although the Yiddish version says February, the date was Saturday, August 2, per other eyewitnesses.
3. Sunday, August 3, was the solemn holiday of Tisha B'Av.
4. Friday was August 8, 1941.
5. Passover Eve was April 14, 1942.
6. The Jewish New Year of 1942 began September 12.
7. December 3, 1942, was Hanukkah eve.
8. Stepan Bandera, leader of the Ukrainian nationalistic organization OUN, which murdered Jews and Poles during the war.
9. In 1940, three quarters of Rowno residents were Jews, totaling some 23,000 people.

The Seven Stages of Terror[1]

By Frida Binshtok

Translated from Hebrew by Selwyn Rose

The youth leaves for the open spaces

In the year 1939, when the Germans conquered Poland, the Red Army conquered eastern Poland. Since then, those areas (Polesia, Volhynia and Podolia) were called western Ukraine. From 1939 until June 1941 Dubno was a Soviet town and we – Soviet citizens. Most of the Jews, especially the younger ones, adapted themselves to the new way of life; but there were many to whom the new way of life did not appeal, especially the wealthy. For how could they be satisfied when their property was confiscated and they themselves exiled to Siberia? But as is well known: "It's an ill wind that blows nobody good" and many of those among the dissatisfied were saved from certain death under the conquering Nazis by being in far distant Siberia and saw nothing and perhaps even heard almost nothing of the horrors of the terrible war. After the war many returned to Poland and from there scattered all over the world, some of them to the State of Israel.

The middle-classes, the wealthy, also grumbled and complained because the authorities closed their shops, requisitioned their homes, and permitted the owner of two or three properties to occupy only a single room for an entire family. If the once-Jewish owner of a large flour mill was forced to work as a clerk in that same mill, now owned by the State and his obedient employees now government workers – it is no wonder that he and his family were disappointed with the new regime, grumbling and complaining and cursing, hoping for its fall.

But the youth, at least most of them, were satisfied because they saw opening before them the gates of a new life of which they had never dreamed. For them everything was available - for example: until 1939 there had been one High School in our town that accepted about eighty pupils each year of whom only eight percent were Jews while Jews represented about sixty percent of the general population. Only the

527

wealthy were able to study in the High School as the fees were quite significant and... one also needed influence to have a pupil accepted. A Jewish lad who eventually managed to be accepted in the wished-for High School was considered very happy and all the other children envied him when they saw him on the street wearing the school's uniform. There were also rich parents who sent their children to study at the Jewish "*Tarbut*"[2] high school at Rowno (many of Dubno's children studied there), something that clearly required significant expense.

The Soviet Government immediately founded several High Schools simply by adding appropriate classes to existing elementary schools and every child that completed the sixth grade continued into a High School seventh. With that, the *Tarbut* School, which taught in Hebrew, was closed and two national schools, teaching in Yiddish, were opened. At first, village children who had completed elementary school in their villages entered the higher grades to continue their studies. For these children, residential schools were created – but that was an innovation that rarely occurred. Also, during the days of the Polish administration, the children of rich families learned piano or violin with private teachers; they were not especially gifted but simply the children of parents who could afford the fees. Talented children went to study at the School for Music only after passing a suitable qualifying test. The "Pioneer's" palace was also founded with playing fields and a school for folk-dancing and ballet but - again – only for the talented.

All of them, each with a liberal dose of publicity, attracted the youth who distanced themselves from the complaints of their parents who had been burnt by the "flames" of the new regime. At the same time, it is necessary to emphasize that the young Zionists were bitterly disappointed when their clubs were closed, and contact was lost with their friends who had immigrated to Palestine. Every letter that arrived from there strengthened and encouraged them and became the topic of the day.

Students who had completed High School received a grant and went to study in Lvov, in the University or Technical College. Even during Polish rule there were few students who studied in Lwow because of the rampant anti-Semitism there made it difficult at the higher institutes of learning, so the wealthy parents sent their children to study abroad: Brussels, Paris, or London.

The German Invasion

On 23rd June 1941 German aircraft began to bomb the town. The office staff, teachers and all the Russians that came and settled in our town during the previous two years hurried to send their families away from the Front; they too began to leave. Jews also had the opportunity to flee but they were mostly the younger people. Among those that fled was a family that had worked for the Russians, fearing the Germans would suspect them of being Communists. In the same way members of the Communist Party fled with their families. Many young men who had been mobilized and sent for training retreated to inside the Soviet Union. In all about 3,000 people fled; the escape lasted for two days, and the town mourned. There were parents who strongly objected to their sons' self-imposed exile stating, "there is no devil like the one you are describing," saying that if they managed to get along with the Bolsheviks they could certainly do so with the more highly cultured Germans. But there were also those who foresaw the coming Holocaust; although they were in the minority, while the majority gave credence neither to a doom-like outlook nor to the rumors of what was being perpetrated in central Poland. A son who separated from his parents and went to the Soviet Union had no idea that he was seeing them for the last time.

There wasn't much time to consider whether to run or to remain because on the third day after the declaration of war it was already impossible to get out of town; the battle was getting closer and people who left that morning either returned or were killed.

That same morning, just four kilometers from town, a battle was raging between a Soviet army unit and the German army. We all sat in our cellars because shells were falling ceaselessly all over hitting some houses and killing a number of people. The Germans defeated the defending army at the approaches to the town having held the Soviet soldiers under siege and killing all of them and on the fourth day of the war they invaded the town.

I sat in the cellar together with all the other residents of the surrounding houses. The atmosphere in the cellar was terrible: one woman was seriously ill with heart problems, and another was paralyzed, and both would break out in moans and groans of terror at the sound of every grenade or shell-burst. We the children laughed at the groans, one of us even mimicking the funny voices of the two sick women with great hilarity while the adults tried to keep us quiet and explain to us the seriousness of the situation, though I was sure they felt a little relieved that we introduced a little life and levity into the otherwise heavy and frightened atmosphere.

Through a small thick glass skylight, we looked outside. Silence reigned and not a living soul could be seen. At about twelve o'clock we heard the rattling sound of tanks and other vehicles driving past and the voices of people coming closer. Because the skylight opened in the direction of the main street it was possible to see the German invasion of the city in its entire "splendor."

As if out of the ground people began to appear from both sides of the street: Ukrainians, Poles and others, who had been waiting long for this moment, all dressed in their finest and carrying bouquets of flowers to welcome the invaders. A shudder passed through me at the sight: these were the same people who, less than two years earlier had greeted the Red Army with fictitious gratitude and shown them esteem and respect for liberating them from the yoke of their Polish masters. Now they stood receiving the Germans with cries of "Heil Hitler", scattering flowers in their path as they went by.

At the front was a large tank with two Nazi flags fluttering followed by a black luxury limousine with – presumably – the Commandant sitting inside. After him two soldiers on motor-bikes and after them an endless convoy of armored vehicles – tanks and various artillery pieces. Within a few minutes the soldiers spread throughout the town. The sound of artillery was silenced. From the vehicles, which travelled in all directions, loud-speakers announced in German, Polish and Ukrainian, that all the residents should return to their homes because the German army controlled the town, and their orders were to be obeyed. There was more: the German army was continuing to advance eastwards and after the capture of Moscow the war would end.

We continued to sit in the cellar for another few hours. We noticed people, including Jews, moving about outside and decided that there was no point in continuing to sit in the cellar and we needed to go home. We felt terrible. We knew that if the Ukrainians were given a free hand their deep hatred towards us would break out and then – it would be the end for the Jews. There were already some, even in those first few hours, who said that we had to go, even by foot, leaving everything behind and flee to the Soviet Union. There were others who said that it was possible to "buy" the Ukrainians with money and presents.

The Ukrainians plundering and beating

We went up to our house. It was already about six o'clock in the evening, but it was still light, and we looked around. The streets were full of German soldiers and Polish girls were trying to befriend them. We went to bed late. We awoke early in the morning to the sound of shutters and windows being broken and the shouts of rowdy people. We went outside and it immediately became clear what was happening: the Germans had given orders to the Ukrainian Police that had been created during the night, to break into all the Russian warehouses and government shops and allow the mobs to take whatever they wanted. It was the first scheme of the invaders to capture the hearts of their new subjects. To further that "program" they sent cars to the suburbs and the local villages to bring the villagers to share in the plunder, given to them by the "good-hearted Germans". And indeed, it was a ploy that hit the target and awoke in the robbers

[Columns 477–478]

support for the new regime. I have no doubts that it was probably the first time in their lives that the villagers had ever ridden in a car and that experience in itself, together with the promise that in a few weeks, with the further movement of the Front, it would be possible to rob and kill the Jews was enough to encourage them in the wholesale robbery. They arrived in town with the cars decorated in the yellow flags of the Bandera[3] faction of the Organization of Ukrainian Nationalists, and Nazi flags. When they arrived at the warehouses, they were already half-crazed and fell upon the booty immediately.

Shock and breath-taking horror gripped me. They grabbed sacks of sugar weighing a hundred kilograms and dragged them to their wagons and the cars, sacks of salt that had been torn mixed with the sugar; soap-powder thrown into flour and large piles of unprocessed skins, bolts of cloth and other materials dragged along the ground; barrels of oil and kerosene were tipped over and spilled and the sidewalks in front of the shops turned into quagmires of trash. Arguments and fights broke out among them over a lady's leather purse that one of them took. The conflicts worsened and eventually blood was spilled.

Suddenly I saw a terrible sight: a young man about sixteen years old, from the Poltorak family, living in our neighborhood apparently decided that if everyone else was stealing then he, too could grab some of the booty but a Polish man fell upon him shouting: "You filthy Yid, your reign is over, now we're in charge and we'll show you…" Hearing the shameful language others gathered round and began beating the Jewish lad and other Jews who by chance happened to be standing around. An older Jewish man who courageously dared to say he would call the police if they didn't stop attacking innocent by-standers was also seriously beaten up while being told that they were the police and the masters now and the Jews had no rights to call the police – no one would come to save them.

The first edicts

It is superfluous to state what an impression all these events and disturbances made on me, all of which occurred in the very first few hours after the invasion. But the coming days would show that they were absolutely nothing compared to what the future held for us.

The tumult continued until late at night and then there was silence. Armed soldiers patrolled the streets and all night long we heard their noisy footsteps. I wondered: what is likely to happen tomorrow if on the first day of the conquest they have already given us such a surprise!? And indeed, the following morning we found large posters in Ukrainian and Polish informing all that Jews must wear a white arm-band with a blue Star of David on their left arm so that the authorities could distinguish between Jews and Aryans. The posters also detailed what size the arm-band must be – its width and length and the size of the Star of David. The poster also warned that any Jew caught not wearing an arm-band will be shot on the spot without warning. The order was signed by the town Commissar and a Municipality that had already been created on the first day of the invasion. The Jews lowered their heads. It was now clear to everyone that this was only the beginning. And who knew what to expect in the coming days?

There was no longer any doubt that those who had advised fleeing from the advancing murdering Nazis had been right.

The devastating incitement was conducted by the Christians against the Jews. The belief that the Jews were the source of all their troubles and woes was deeply embedded within them. Therefore, it was necessary to destroy them and put an end to their own sufferings. Announcements and posters with similar messages signed by the Andeks and other veteran anti-Semites made their appearance in town. It was enough for the common people - and it was a mental preparation for what was to come. Later came announcements from the Municipality and the new military authorities about inspections and with them a new edict every day. Jews were also ordered to surrender any radio in their possession by a certain date, any Jew found with a radio after that date would be shot on the spot - and every edict against the Jews concluded with those words.

On the fourth day of the conquest, bread rationing began: the Jews in certain shops and Christians in others. The Jews' ration was one-hundred grams a day and the Christians two-hundred and fifty grams. The bread allocated to the Jews was black and intentionally moist to increase the apparent weight. Many, many people would get up at midnight to line up and queue in order to be sure of getting their meager ration and then they would finish eating it by the time they got home. Many times, they would return home empty-handed because there was not always sufficient bread available for everyone. The supply of food that we had stored got smaller and smaller and slowly we began to feel hunger. Entry into the market was forbidden to the Jews and in order to obtain anything we were forced to sneak in by way of little-used lanes and alleys that led to the market square, stop the farmer on a corner and buy something from him. The farmers quickly caught on to the situation and immediately began to demand higher and higher prices compared to those in the market. For the time being the Soviet money remained in use, but it was rumored that it would be discontinued and replaced by the German mark. It was clear that those most affected by the exchange would be the Jews who would be forced to buy their necessities from the farmers with the new coinage whose value would certainly be higher than that of the Soviet's.

[Columns 479–480]

Jews, both with and without a profession or trade were ordered to report for work, taken out of their houses by force and beaten by the Ukrainian militia who invaded their homes, and taken to the central square next to the theater and the Greenberg House, where German officers and soldiers were waiting to divide them into groups and dispatch them to dig ditches and clear forests, etc. Old people who were there in the square were abused; they were beaten, their beards were ripped out by force, their legs were kicked, and they were forced to crawl home on all fours because they were not seen as fit for work. Families separated from a man who went to work as if forever and if he did return there was great joy because, indeed, there were many who went out on forced labor and never returned.

The first "*Aktzia*" the "Eighty"

Early in July 1941, two weeks after the invasion, the first "*Aktzia*" took place.

At 11 o'clock in the morning, the Militia suddenly broke into the homes of the Jews, took about eighty men for urgent work supposedly for a couple of hours, loaded them onto trucks and took them straight to the Jewish cemetery. Christians who lived close by later related how they were executed.

A platoon of armed soldiers was waiting for the men in the cemetery. When the trucks arrived, the men were ordered down and told to throw all their documentation to one side. They were then stood alongside an already prepared trench, shot and thrown half-dead into the trench one on top of the other. The trench was then filled in and the papers burned. The local residents were warned not to tell anyone what they had seen.

Apparently, this "*Aktzia*" had been an experiment but two days later the Jews of the town already knew that the eighty young men had been executed. The day after the "*Aktzia*" a Jew died and people who went to the funeral found some of the charred remains of the documents blowing in the wind. They collected them and examined them; grave suspicions arose about the fate of the eighty men. The family members of the victims spoke to the local residents promising money and presents and begged them to tell what happened and the tragedy fell upon them as a ghastly shock difficult to bear. On previous occasions a few men – sometimes two or three, sometimes a few more – had been taken and after they had not returned the relatives went to the authorities and were told that they were found fit and had been sent to work. It was now clear to everyone that if someone didn't return home in the evening from work – he was no longer alive.

A search began, seeking ways to escape work and thus began the trade in release from casual labor and obtaining regular work with an "*Ausweis*"[4] promising exemption to the owner from other work. People paid enormous sums of money for a doctor's certificate of illness, signed by a doctor of the "*arbeitsamt*"[5] exempting the holder from labor; Poles who posed as friends of both the Jews and the Nazis made a good living out of the situation.

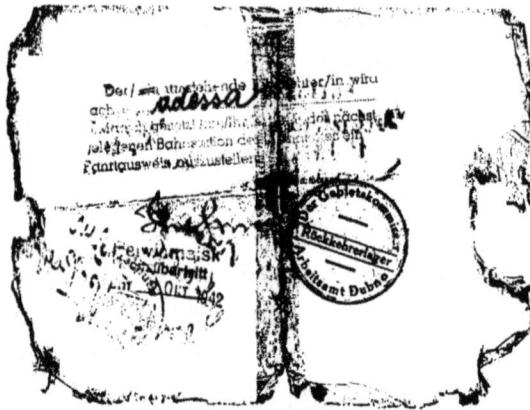

The Jewish people became poorer and poorer by the day. The farmers began to demand higher and higher imaginative prices for the most essential produce – an overcoat or dress for a loaf of bread, a suit of clothes for a sack of potatoes, a carpet for a kilogram of butter. They began to acquire items for themselves that even in their dreams they had never imagined possessing. Their hardness and cruelty reached such proportions that they would likely demand from a Jew that he actually take off the clothes that he was wearing as payment for the food he needed. Babies especially suffered from lack of milk. A neighbor of ours, for example, was forced to give an excellent wardrobe with three doors for two fluid ounces of fresh milk a day for one month.

The victimized families demonstrated at the offices of the *"Judenrat"*[6] established by the authorities a few weeks previously, demanding an explanation from the council members who, fearing the anger of the crowd, disappeared from the building. In fact, their hands were tied but the embittered community saw the council as the intermediary between them and the authorities and put the blame on the council, certain that if they had wanted to they could have prevented the tragedy.

[Columns 481–482]

Wild and organized theft

About a week before the murder of the eighty men two Gendarmes with drawn bayonets appeared at our house. They demanded all the money we had in the house, warning us that if we withheld as much as a cent and they discovered it by a search, we would be killed on the spot. My mother, terrified, gave them everything we had. After they had it they laughed and gave us a note saying the money would be returned at the end of the war. We were ordered not to leave the house for one hour and then they disappeared. We later learned that we had been robbed by a gang of Germans that was operating in the area and demanding money from the Jews using dire threats. The theft hit us hard because it left us with nothing to exist on.

A few days later notices appeared ordering the Jews to surrender all their silverware, gold and any dollars and jewelry to the authorities giving the last date for depositing it under penalty of death, as usual, for anyone found still possessing anything of the above after that date. The operation was organized with impeccable German efficiency and precision: every day according to an alphabetical list, the people stood in line to hand in their valuables. It was easy to guess the mood and feelings of the people regarding the constant flow of daily edicts not knowing what the following day will bring asking each other: "What's new"? – meaning what new misery will fall upon us? And since one got used even to that state of affairs, people began to look for ways of evading every new edict, to obstruct or avoid obeying every order. Thus, it came about that many people came to the decision to hide their valuables with Christian friends – if they agree to pay fifty percent of the value for their assistance.

The *Judenrat* and the Jewish Militia

At the head of the *Judenrat* stood Mr. Toibenfeld, who when Poland still ruled, had been the teacher of Geography and Polish history in the *"Tarbut"* school. Although he was highly educated, the Polish government did not permit him to teach in the gymnasium. He also gave private lessons in German and during the Russian regime taught German in the high school. He was apparently chosen to head the *Judenrat* because of his knowledge of German and being a man of some standing.

The secretary of the *Judenrat*, also a teacher, was Margolis. The rest of the members of the *Judenrat* were Jews from western Poland who had arrived in 1939 fleeing, at that time, from the Germans, and a few from our town, and all together – thirteen men.

Next to the *Judenrat* was the *Arbeitsamt* obliged to put into effect the orders of the Municipal *Arbeitsamt* headed by the German, Hammerstein.

The *Judenrat* was also obliged to replace the functions of the disbanded Jewish Community institutions: control of the Jewish hospital, the orphanage, old people's home and so on. Although in protecting the Jews from the murders and depredations their hands were tied because those atrocities were perpetrated by the authorities themselves with the participation of the Ukrainian Militia and incidental thefts and murders by individual volunteers.

In the meantime, a Jewish Militia had been formed. In order to be accepted into the Militia two things were essential: influence and money. The men of the Militia wore distinctive blue hats with a yellow stripe and a yellow arm-band with a number. They carried a thick stick about half a meter long with a leather loop. Their function was to ensure that the people went to work as scheduled, that they deposit all cash resources and precious metals in their possession and that they didn't leave town, that they didn't sneak into the market to shop and that they didn't leave their homes after six in the evening. From the moment of the creation of the Militia, there was an intense hatred against them from within the Jewish community; they were seen as the lowest of the low, fawning upon, and aiding the murderers. Even the non-Jews themselves mocked them and said, "Only Jews would betray their own in time of stress." But the drive to survive whatever the cost was so strong that for the sake of that "*Ausweis*" that promises the Militia exemption from being taken for "labor" they were prepared to erase the "Image of G-d"⁅ in which they were created and commit acts of cruelty against their brethren and betray their own people.

The Jewish militia was housed in the Karaulnik house, a two storied building from which the residents had been evacuated. It set up a special room for punishment. The Militia showed itself to be eager in fulfilling the Government's wishes and orders. They searched for those attempting to evade orders and were not satisfied with simply ensuring that they were sent to work but instituted punishment sometimes causing a loss of consciousness.

Above the entrances to cinemas, coffee-bars, restaurants and other public places were signs "Entry to Jews forbidden".

The workers would go out in organized groups and as Jews were forbidden to use the sidewalks, walked along the side of the road, arranged in ranks of three and accompanied by men of the Militia. Artisans and others with a trade such as engineers, welders, builders, glaziers and so on, were holders of *Ausweise* and worked for the Germans as wage-earners; but the wage was minimal. But on the other hand, as holders of the *Ausweis* they were able to exit the town and purchase food.

[Columns 483–484]

A knitting factory was established for the Jewish women and for the purpose they too were issued *Ausweise*. Only the younger women, who had some kind of influence with the *Judenrat*, were accepted in the factory. Parents who managed to arrange for their daughter to work there were happy knowing never again would she be in danger of being sent to a German military camp or the Ukrainian Militia where she would likely be a rape victim or the victim of simple physical bullying by the Militia.

There were rumors that the members of the *Judenrat* were enriching themselves at the expense of the Jewish public from the money being collected by them as bribes to the authorities, but no proof was ever found of this.

AUSWEIS

Der _____ Gorbatюk Nikolaus
(Beruf) (Vor- u. Zuname)
beschäftigt bei _____ Sokoliwska (Raumelda)

ist zur einmaligen Benutzung der Eisenb... _____
von _____ Dubno _____ nach _____ Odessa

ohne besonderen Fahrausweis berechtigt.

Der Ausweis verliert nach Beendigung der Reise seine Gültigkeit und ist auf de...

Bestimmungsbahnhof ohne besondere Aufforderung abzugeben.

29.IX.42
Ausgestellt im _____
Transportdienststelle

Siegel
der ausstellen
den Dienststei...

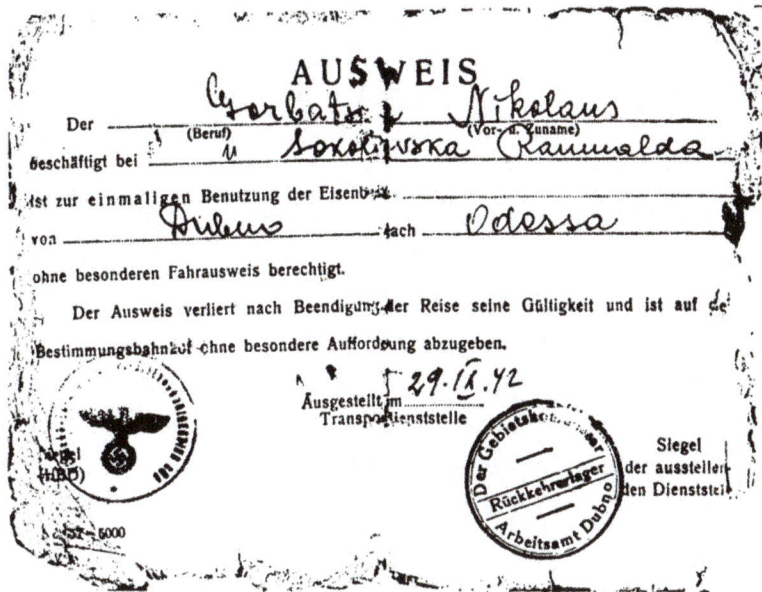

On one occasion the *Judenrat* carried out a collection of blankets and bed-linen for the Ukrainian Militia. They said they wanted to bribe them to prevent them sending people to labor camps. Everyone began hauling blankets and bed-linen to the *Judenrat* storerooms and from there everything was transferred to the authorities. "*Aktzias*" of this nature became a daily occurrence and the Jewish population became more and more impoverished.

Christians who saw what was happening understood it as an opportunity to do it for themselves: in the attics and cellars of their homes they prepared small hiding places for Jews of their acquaintance in which they could hide when the time came to round up people for labor and for this, they received good money and expensive gifts.

At the same time anti-Semitic incitement continued without interference against the Jewish capitalists who had always exploited the farmer and the communists who wanted to force them to organize Kolkhozes.[8]

Abuse and maltreatment

The Jew was like a gateway that everyone could run over and trample on with his heel. He was forbidden to walk on the sidewalk and any German could approach a Jew in the street and order him to bow down to him with his face on the ground, slap his cheek just for the pleasure alone, instruct him to crawl several hundred meters and so on. Later the order went out that every Jew had to bow down and doff his hat to every German passer-by. The Jews began to avoid the Germans, hiding in nearby entrances to houses or escaping down lanes and alleys.

The Ukrainian Militia saw the Germans' actions and followed suit. They would usually copy all the actions of the German behavior in relation to the Jews and sometimes even exceed the cruelty and savagery of their teachers. Thus, they would incite children to throw stones at the Jews on the street while they stood and laughed at the Jews' attempts to flee for their lives.

In September 1941 a school was opened for the Christians but not even one for the Jewish children. Because even under the terrible conditions they were in, the Jewish people could not ignore the study of the Torah they returned to the "*Heder*" system with a "Rabbi" and thus there was no break in the religious education of the young children even in the terrible days when each day was worse than the preceding one.

Eye-witnesses to events relate that a Ukrainian Militia man met an old man whose beard matched his age and who had no Star of David band on his arm. He cursed him. The Jew began to explain his error that he had changed his coat and had forgotten to transfer the band to the second coat and was prepared to return home immediately and put it on. The Ukrainian began to beat the old man with the old man begging for his life. Passers-by attempted to approach and help the old man and awaken some pity in the Ukrainian, but they too were attacked and warned to move away or be shot. The Ukrainian then wrapped the man's long beard round his truncheon and dragged the Jew by his beard along the street. Crying out the "Hear, O, Israel…" affirmation of faith, the old man finally collapsed and fainted. Then the Ukrainian shot him and walked away.

That event carried with it the rumor that a second "*Aktzia*" was to take place. People began to arrange hiding-places in cellars, toilets and in any place where it was possible to build a double wall. The main idea of the adults was to save the young children because, yet they were far from believing that the Germans intended to exterminate everyone. The *Judenrat* was helpless; its members continued without pause to collect money and gifts for the Nazis and the local authorities but without a guarantee from their side that it would help to save the lives of any Jews

[Columns 485–486]

to say nothing of what little personal property they still retained in their possession. They said quite openly that they "…don't do a thing without an order from the higher command" and the complaints about hooliganism from soldiers and the Militia didn't even penetrate their ears.

Oberleutnant Hammerstein, who was the *Arbeitsamt* manager, would appear in the work-places to check that everything was in order and the fear of death fell on everyone. He would call one of the men to him and start beating him with his baton and kicking him about the legs. The injured man was forbidden to cry out in pain and if he was unable to bear his agony and did cry out, he was shot and killed on the spot. Hammerstein was an Austrian, evil and sadistic and he vented all his rage on the Jews.

All the many elements that went into preparing hiding places and obtaining *Ausweise* for fixed employment, etc., were intended only to safeguard the youngsters. No one thought that there was a need to prepare hiding places for the women, children, and old people. When there was a rumor of a "man-hunt" the men hurried to hide while the women remained at home in order to explain to the searchers that the men were working or weren't at home thus preventing searches.

Occasionally it could happen that a soldier would enter one of the homes and announce that he had heard from "reliable sources" that an "*Aktzia*" was about to take place and demand money for the warning and of course he was paid. Within hours the information would spread to the entire Jewish community and great anxiety would fall upon them. Then it would become clear that it was a false alarm that was used only to extort money from the Jews. Although fear was always present in any case. The Sword of Damocles was permanently suspended above their heads, carrying with it a negation of traditional Jewish values resulting in selfishness, ignoring entirely the possibility of assisting the individual even in the threatening circumstances in which they found themselves. The moral degeneration continued to spread.

There was a family in Dubno by the name of Hoffman. The father, a lawyer, was of German extraction and the mother pure Russian. For generations the family had been considered Russian: Russian was spoken in the home. The children studied in the high school and had friends among the Jewish children. At this time the father received a high appointment in the municipality and the senior son, Vania became the assistant and advisor to the town Commissar and the second, who was about twenty, was a commander in the Militia. They became *Volksdeutsche*[2] serving the Germans and wreaking vengeance on the Jews. One cannot imagine how these human beings can execute such horrific and cruel acts against other human beings cast in the same "Image of G-d" in general and the Jews in particular – recently their friends.

The High School teachers, Reibek and Kolomowycz obtained positions in the Municipality and organized endless anti-Semitic incitements.

The second "*Aktzia*"

On Thursday 21st August 1941 at 10:00 am the second "*Aktzia*" began during which nine-hundred people were murdered, among them seven women.

Men from the Militia and some Gendarmes spread throughout the town and began taking Jews. Many Jewish men, who had gone out to work that morning were sent home on the pretext of being given a day-off so that nearly all of them were in their homes. Suddenly, like pouncing wild beasts, they broke into the houses taking the people out to where trucks awaited them. A major panic arose: the people began to run and hide, escape, running hither and thither, the women crying and the children begging the captors for the lives of their dear ones rent the skies. I was witness to the round-up, but I was later given the details of the "*Aktzia*" itself by Pinchas Steinberg, who was also captured but managed to escape. He related: "They took the people by trucks to the prison in the suburban town of Surmicze. There were long lines of Militia and Gendarmes lining both sides of the road leading into the town. When the trucks got to the gates the Jews were ordered to get down and one by one to run or crawl along the rows of guards as far as the courtyard of the prison. Whether running or crawling according to an arbitrary decision, they were beaten by the murderers wielding their clubs; those who succeeded in getting as far as the prison were bruised, injured and covered in blood while those who were beaten so severely that they lost consciousness under the blows were shot to death where they lay and dragged to one side. Within the courtyard the unfortunate people were ordered to sit in a large circle on the ground. The murderers walked among them, counting them and registering their names while continuing to beat them while the men huddled together with the certain feeling that their fate was sealed. Many began praying, many who could not tolerate any more blows begged the murderers to kill them outright without more ado and put an end to their misery. From time to time more trucks appeared until there were about nine-hundred souls there. Apparently, that was the number of people allotted in this operation because the Militia left the town and came to join the "*Aktzia*" in the prison. At two o'clock in the afternoon the town fell completely

[Columns 487–488]

silent." Those who were hiding continued to sit in their hiding place while the families of those taken ran in the direction of the prison although they were not permitted to approach, and full of despair they returned home as they came. They began running to all their Christian friends in their distress, who knew the Germans, asking for their help, all to no avail. The *Judenrat* was closed and sealed-off; people knocked on the doors and windows of the building but were dispersed and sent away.

At one o'clock in the afternoon, about twenty or thirty men from the prison were taken to the Jewish cemetery. There, they were forced to dig a large trench and when they were finished, they were shot by the murderers. Between four and five o'clock all the people from the prison were brought to the cemetery in trucks and there, one by one, they were shot dead and either fell or were flung into the trench. The murderers worked until late at night covering the grave and when they left, Christians living in the vicinity of the cemetery related details on the "*Aktzia*". The people arrived at the cemetery badly injured, covered in blood with their clothing torn. They were weak and exhausted, falling down and helpless. They offered no resistance.

A common grave

Pinchas Steinberg himself was shot at the prison after he had fainted, but the bullet didn't hit a vital organ. The murderers supposed that he was dead and left him where he lay. During the night, he recovered consciousness and crawled home. What had been done that night is indescribable.

In that "*Aktzia*" my mother's brother, Eliezer Horwitz was killed; he left behind his wife and two small children. The woman tried several times during the night to kill herself but after they sedated her with an injection they were able to treat my grandmother, Eliezer being her third sacrifice since the revolution of Petliura[10] after the First World War. It was difficult to watch the old lady's great suffering and anguish; she was the very personification of pain and despair. She became deaf and confused during the night to the point of total unawareness of her surroundings.

Mrs. Deibog, whose husband and only son were killed in that "*Aktzia*" was seen the following day in the streets behaving erratically. She accosted every youngster in the street, biting him and shouting:

"Why are you alive when Lusik is dead?" The Militia ordered her family to keep her in the house, if not they would kill her, but it was impossible to stop her; she would escape from the house running around the streets threatening everyone. After a while she calmed down, but her clarity of mind never returned. All the great, deep Jewish tragedy from hell gazed out of the eyes of that unhappy figure.

Most of the people never left their hiding places that night for fear that the murderers would continue their horrific work. In their despair many busied themselves with digging fresh hiding places, shaking from the slightest sound in the street and speaking among themselves in whispers like thieves in the underworld. But the following day nothing happened; the *Judenrat* announced that everyone must report for work and life returned to what was "normal" for those days. The topic of the "*Aktzia*" and the nine-hundred killed was never mentioned and conversation was diverted away from it…someone spread a rumor that some of the victims were sent to work and

541

only the weak ones killed. Many people from those families rushed to the *Judenrat* demanding from the chairman that he clarify which of them was still alive and who not. The reply was for the Militia to disperse them all saying it wasn't yet known. It was supposed that the rumor was started by the Christians as a ruse to squeeze money from the mourning families with false promises of clarifying where the survivors had been sent.

A slight recovery

Most shocking of all was the sight of the womenfolk whose husbands had been killed. They congregated every morning outside the *Judenrat* building with their children until they were sent away by force. While the families who had not been involved up to this time recovered quickly in spite of the generally tragic situation and the permanent fear of tomorrow, they tried to continue with their daily lives with their most personal worries, pushing from their minds what had happened "yesterday and the day before". Nevertheless, they were far from serene and had no false illusions because every day there were fresh rumors about another "*Aktzia*" that was to take place; but since these rumors proved to be false, people ceased to believe them.

[Columns 489–490]

The winter of 1941/2 passed in relative quiet although new edicts and persecutions were not lacking and the economic situation was also very difficult: shortage of food, shortage of coal and firewood, and robberies with an occasional murder occurred every day but there were no more organized "*Aktzias*", and people began to relax and become accustomed to the depressed situation. The survival instinct was very strong, and everyone was concerned to hang on at all costs until…the anger passed, and better days arrived. The Jewish people dreamed of the return of the Red Army whom they saw as their only hope of salvation. Rumors spread of Red Army victories, but they were only wishful thinking – yearned for heart-felt wishes far removed from reality.

In November 1941 an order was given to change the blue and white arm band with two yellow patches, one of which was to be stitched on to the upper back of the coat and the second on the chest – it was a return to the days of the middle-ages and the sense of insult was overwhelming and hateful, but it was impossible to ignore and anyone daring to do so paid with his life. The Jews in the street provoked both laughter and pity when walking at the edges of the street with the yellow patch on the arm and back. The Christian population became crueler from day to day towards their Jewish neighbors. The milkman, for example, who brought milk to my uncle for years, said to my aunt that she can give him my murdered uncle's clothes since he no longer needed them, for milk and butter for the children…

The Ukrainians become crueler

In one of the suburbs of the town was an immense prisoner of war camp for captured Russians, about ten thousand of them. They were treated horribly. They were under the control of the German army and Ukrainian Militia and the Jewish and non-Jewish population was forbidden contact with them. They were hungry and bare-foot. Many died from the cold, thousands from hunger. Every day they brought their dead through the town for burial at the other edge of the town. Eight of them were harnessed to a trailer full of the dead and others walked alongside bare-foot in the snow, without a coat since most of them had given their great-coats for a crust of bread. The weak among them would lean on the shoulders of their comrades and were helped along and those that were unable to keep up were shot on the spot and half-dead thrown onto the trailer hauled by their comrades. There were events when some Jews tried to throw bread to the prisoners of war and were shot for their "crime". Once, one of the prisoners managed to sneak a beet from a farmer's wagon as he walked past and was shot by a Ukrainian Militia. After he had shot him, he stooped down to take a gold ring from the dead man's finger and recognized his own brother who was serving in the Red Army and been taken prisoner. His parents and friends wanted to beat him to death for killing his own brother, but he ran away to the forests and became a thief and murderer. The incident found an echo in the Ukrainian population of the area and their blind devotion to the Germans was somewhat undermined, seeing the extent to which matters had come, that a brother kills a brother – and for what! The awakening within the Ukrainian population against the Germans didn't bring with it any change in the attitude towards the Jews. Their hatred of the Jews knew no bounds, and it was "permissible" for them to kill all the Jews even before the next "*Aktzias*".

A witness related that a few of the prisoners became cannibals, eating the flesh of their dead comrades. The Germans used the horrible fact for their vile propaganda pointing to the Bolsheviks as wild men and it helped them to increase the hatred of the Ukrainians towards them.

During the winter, the camp itself was liquidated. A few of the remaining prisoners of Ukrainian origin managed to escape to surrounding villages and acquire some civilian clothes and to hide. For others of Asian and Russian extraction the consideration to help them or not was based on their appearance: If they were recognizable nobody wanted to help them (it carried the death penalty) and they either died or were shot.

"*Aktzia*" of robbery

In January 1942, during the days of one of the Orthodox Christian festivals an "*Aktzia*" of organized robbery took place. The farmers received permission to come into town with their wagons and carts, enter the homes of the Jews and take out whatever took their fancy: clothes, furniture, kitchen-ware and bedding – everything. The Jewish people began to hide things in their cellars and other places, but it didn't help because in the light of day the robbers were able to find everything. Most of the looted articles were pieces of furniture. From morning until late evening carts left the town laden down with furniture taken from the Jewish homes. After this "*Aktzia*" the Jews began to give their furniture in barter for food because it was clear that whatever remained of their furniture was not "theirs" – after the first robbery a second will come and everything will go without any return. So, it was better to get some essentials for the articles like food and fuel rather than just let everything go for nothing. Thus, the Jews of Dubno passed the winter of 1942.

The ghetto

At the beginning of March rumors about the creation of a ghetto were already multiplying. The people who had long been accustomed to misfortunes appearing every day received this new information without any special emotion. There were even those who greeted the idea with the thought that from the point of view of security it would be better for them that the ghetto

[Columns 491–492]

would be closed and the thieves would be unable to rob them. The majority tended to think that concentrating the Jews in one place was a way of making it more difficult for the murderers to liquidate them completely. In March notices appeared detailing the parts of the town that would be included in the ghetto: the Jewish neighborhoods alongside the river Ikwa. The Jews lived in all parts of town, even those sections where the majority of the residents were Christians and also in the suburbs. According to the notifications all those whose dwelling-place was outside the designated area were ordered to evacuate apartments and move into the ghetto. Thus, the question of accommodation became desperate, for most of the ghetto area was inhabited mainly by people of little means or were even impoverished and overcrowding was prevalent even before the establishment of the ghetto. The *Judenrat* managed to confiscate some of the properties and distribute them among the neediest but mostly it was necessary to pay extortionate sums of "key-money" to obtain a room. Because we now had no money at all, we dwelt in what had been a shop. The front door of the shop faced the "Aryan" side and was secured with planks of timber and tin, and we used the back door that opened onto the main street of the ghetto. For the first few weeks, until about Passover, the ghetto remained open but afterwards they began to close it in on all sides with a fence of barbed-wire the poles of which were about three or four meters apart. It was built according to the instructions of authorities from *Judenrat* money and erected by Jewish workers – An ironic joke of the Devil! The Jews imprisoned themselves within the walls of the ghetto with their own hands! Movement in and of the ghetto was controlled at the two ends by gates incorporated into the fence. On both sides of the gate were little trenches; in the outside trench two Ukrainian Militia men stood guard and in the inside one two from the Jewish Militia. In addition, guards were stationed along the entire length of the fence surrounding the ghetto.

With the completion of the ghetto the economic situation became even worse. All contact with the farmers was lost and it became impossible to acquire supplies of food. The only opening that helped save the situation was the side of the ghetto backing on to the river Ikwa. Here the Jews and non-Jews smuggled food and other necessities into the ghetto. The smugglers were risking their lives to make money, but it eased the terrible conditions of those enclosed inside the ghetto and helped them to survive. The river was, for all that, well-guarded and the Ukrainian Militia-man were bribed to allow boats to pass to and fro. Indeed, there were not a few cases where the Militia accepted the bribes and then reported the smugglers to the authorities and the smugglers were shot and killed. Only owners with documented permission were allowed to leave the ghetto.

Christian children would gather along the fence and throw stones over the fence at the Jews inside shouting cat-calls and insults and laughing at those inside while adults outside took no notice. Those few who showed - if not support - at least not hate towards the Jews under siege in the ghetto, were the Czechs. There were about ten Czech families in Dubno, and the villages close by were also settled by Czechs. Most of them were wealthy and some even substantially rich and compared to the Ukrainian population, their standard of living was very high and the relationships between them and the Jews had always been very good. But with the coming of the Nazis, they, too, were influenced by the destructive propaganda and some of the younger ones joined the Gendarmes. Nevertheless, many of them continued to maintain excellent relationships with their Jewish friends and acquaintances, supplying them with food and even hiding them in times of danger. A few of the survivors of the Dubno ghetto owe their lives to their friends among those Czechs.

The division of the ghetto

After Passover, an order appeared informing all the Jews working outside the ghetto who were master-craftsmen in one or other of the essential trades, that their work permits must be renewed because the ghetto was going to be divided into two sections: in one section would live all those with the special work-permits and their families and in the other – all the rest of the population. It was not known at this time that the Germans intended to liquidate half the Jewish population in one fell swoop, but it was clear that it was better to remain living in the section reserved for those with the special permits as essential workers, in spite of the already overcrowded situation that would get even worse. Our hearts told us something bad was ahead and everyone began to try and get one of the work-permits. A "black-market" opened up for these documents and even fictitious marriages took place where a man who had one would marry a woman whose husband had been murdered in one of the earlier "*Aktzias*" or had fled to Russia, if the woman could afford to pay a fair price for marrying her. Both bachelors, who had such a permit and the authorities, did a good "business" out of the situation.

Again, the Jewish people began carrying their meager possessions from one dwelling-place to another within the ghetto. We – that is, my family and I, remained in the section of the "unprivileged" and placed the burden of our fate on hope that this was not simply another trick to extort more money from the Jews. The transfer from one section of the ghetto to the other was free and even that fact perhaps was only in order to lull us into a false sense of security. But all these things were merely illusions because the heart didn't want to believe that the worst of all nightmares was about to unfold without any interference. In fact – the entire episode had been carefully planned by the murderers ahead of time.

[Columns 493–494]

I am saved by a miracle

On 27th May 1942 the big "*Aktzia*" began in Dubno in which more than 4,000 Jewish souls of the town were exterminated. During the night our section of the ghetto was surrounded by hundreds of soldiers, Gendarmes and Militia and early in the morning they began their terrible work. We awoke to the sound of loud knocking on the door and insulting cries directed at the Jews, windows being smashed and the terrified cries of children. Then it was the turn of our street. The murderers went from door to door, knocking on the doors with batons and kicking the doors with their feet and if they weren't answered immediately, they smashed the doors open and dragged the people out throwing them into the street where they were formed into groups at the street corner. Within seconds, before we had time to grasp what was happening outside, we already heard them knocking on the door next to ours where there was a family with two children, and we immediately heard the knocking on our door. My mother dragged me at the very last second and hid me under a table standing in the corner, covered me with a blanket and some old newspapers before the door burst open. At that same moment as she replaced the table and opened the trap-door to the cellar in the other corner of the room, the door burst open and three Gendarmes broke in, got hold of my mother and grandmother and dragged them out. I heard my mother begging them not to hit my grandmother. A shower of curses accompanied her words and then she was gone. That was the last I ever saw of my mother. Whenever I am reminded of those moments my throat closes as if a bone is stuck there. The murderers searched the cellar (my mother had opened and shut the door deliberately to mislead them into thinking someone was hiding there), opened and searched cupboards and then left the house.

From the shop next door, we heard shouts and the cries of the six-year old girl who begged of the murderers: "'Uncle' – please don't hurt my mother and sister." They tried to pull the baby from the arms of her mother who resisted with all her strength. One of them got hold of the little girl's legs and with an immense pull dragged the baby out of her arms and swung the baby's head against the wall. I heard the most terrible shriek from the mother, then a shot and then - silence...

When they had finished their "work" in our street, I stayed lying down in my hiding place for hours and when I heard footsteps approaching my heart stopped beating. I kept counting to myself and said if I count to a number, I fix for myself and nobody comes, it's a sign that I am saved. But several times, as I arrived at the number, I heard footsteps and I was sure my fate was sealed – now they will find me but, in my heart, I felt that I would not die. I remembered my grandmother's words and her promise to me that they will not kill me, because I hadn't begun to live, and every person is entitled to live a little. That's why I was born. After some time, I heard footsteps. Two Germans entered – apparently to confirm that no one remained. They searched everywhere. First, they went down to the cellar. Afterwards they lifted the table I was hiding beneath. I was trembling all over lest they discover me. It was the only time in my life that I prayed with all my heart. But they replaced the table without finding me. I heard them go down into the cellar a second time afterwards coming up and saying to each other: "It seems there were Jews living here but they have already been found and taken – the door was open."

I felt a little relieved when they left. My mother had saved my life – for the time being, at least by opening the cellar door at that last critical moment...

For now, I could hear voices from outside the ghetto. I slowly approached the door of the shop opening onto the street outside the ghetto and saw groups of girls – about 200 people, surrounded by Gendarmes, urging them to hurry along in the direction of the cemetery. The people were shouting in pain from the blows that were being rained on their heads and the murderers shouting threats. I couldn't watch any longer and felt dizzy. I got back to my hiding place, covered myself with the newspapers and up-ended the table on myself but at one edge I put my shoes so that I could let a little air in. Apparently, I must have fainted because I heard nothing more.

I awoke when I heard someone calling my mother's name and mine. I looked out of a crack and saw it was already dark. I was very alarmed and decided not to answer; I thought they had come to search once more, and I only imagined that I heard the names. But again, I heard the names being called and this time I recognized the voice of my uncle Moshe Horvitz, my mother's brother. I answered him. He helped me to lift the table and climb out. He didn't ask about my mother and grandmother – there was nothing to ask: According to what had been done to the house and the door, the upturned beds, he could see there had been a thorough search and that I had been spared by a miracle...

I could hardly stand on my feet. He sat me on a chair and gave me some water to drink and he told me that he had lost his wife and son while he and his daughter Bracha, had survived. His wife had closed him up in the special hiding place they had prepared, thinking that the murderers were only looking for the workers while she and the little boy of seven stayed at home. Thus, they took her and the boy while he and his daughter remained undetected. Since he lived close to the border between the two parts of the ghetto, he moved with his daughter to the other, somewhat safer zone after the murderers had left the area where the "*Aktzia*" hadn't been carried out. All that had occurred about three hours previously. He left his daughter in a safe place and went looking to see if he had anyone left.

We decided to crawl to the other side of the ghetto on all-fours from fear that there might still be Gendarmes wandering around who would certainly shoot us if we were spotted. But no one was to be seen and silence reigned. When we went out, we peeked into the shop next door: we saw the body of the little girl, whose skull had been shattered, laying on the floor and next to her the body of her shot mother. Petrified with fear from so many horrifying sights I was no longer shaken by anything but the sight of this little girl, a victim of a "vendetta against a tiny

[Columns 495–496]

little child could only be created by the Devil" and to this very day the vision of that little child with the shattered head has never left me; and when I wake up at night with silence all around me, I get out of bed and go to look at the beds of my children bend over them and listen to their breathing and only then can I return to my bed and sleep...

We crossed all our section of the deserted and silent ghetto (we were living at the farthest end) and arrived at the first street of the still-populated area. We met no one on the way and the streets that yesterday were bustling with life, running around frightened, were empty and as quiet and as silent as a grave-yard. Movement in this area of the ghetto was minimal because the people were still apprehensive that the murderers may start their work again here and they didn't relax until information was received from the *Judenrat* that the decree was over, that is – the murderers had drunk their fill of blood and had no need of further victims…

In all a total of some tens of people managed to evade the destruction and escape from the destroyed half of the ghetto. A platoon of Ukrainian Militia stood guard around the area making sure that there was no looting of the abandoned property by Jews and non-Jews alike. From our family another aunt had been saved – Neora Horvitz and together with her I passed the entire period of the occupation in various hideouts in the nearby villages. Her husband and daughter were the only members of our family who had escaped to the Soviet Union. She remained with her son Naphtali who was my age and studied together with me in school. In that "*Aktzia*" the son was killed and she, like me, was saved by chance. In her great despair and distress, she thought it better to commit suicide after losing her son and knowing nothing of the fate of her husband and daughter whom she was sure had perished at the beginning of the war. But I was so sad and miserable that everyone was moved to have compassion on me, and she gave in to their requests and took me under care in place of her lost son. She was a qualified nurse and found work in the sanitation department of the ghetto. She registered me as her daughter, and I was able to receive meals at lunch and in the evening in the kitchen of the Jewish institutions.

The following day everyone had orders to start work as usual. The *Judenrat* also restarted its operations. It was now clear to everyone that gifts and bribes were of no help because the *Judenrat* and the Jewish Militia's hands were tied and were helpless to assist in anything and everyone had to do everything to save himself in time before the next wave of liquidation took place. Feverish activity took place especially by those who had means, to acquire documentation as Christians or to obtain work in the nearby villages and farms with a work-permit and place to sleep. But only a very few were able to use that method. A few doctors and dentists succeeded in getting permits to live there.

My own situation was difficult: everyone felt sorry for me but pity alone without real help to back it up only angered me and hurt. I cried day and night. I had nothing to wear, and I had no shoes because I had escaped without them and I hadn't been able to get any others.

A thief in the night

One day, I was walking bare-foot and trod on a piece of glass and hurt my foot. That same night I decided to sneak into the deserted part of the ghetto, get to our house and bring back some clothes and shoes. We had seen they had begun removing everything from the houses and taking them to a store-room for sorting before sending everything to Germany. Jews were engaged in the sorting areas, and we were told by them that our street had not yet been reached. I left my room one night without my aunt knowing. I knew she would refuse to let me go because of the great danger for if I were caught, I would be shot on the spot. Indeed, I knew she also suffered a lot because of me, that I didn't have anything to wear and that if I should be successful in bringing some essential articles, she would be happy and relieved. Most of the way I crawled. Complete silence reigned in that part of the ghetto, only the heavy tread of the Gendarmes and the Militia coming and going up and down on their guard route protecting the empty houses from looting, broke the total silence of the night. I crawled through side-streets keeping as far as possible from contacts with the guards close to the walls of the buildings and avoiding moonlit areas...

As I went on farther and farther, my early fear diminished, and I began to feel like a dauntless heroine. The mere thought that tomorrow will find me dressed and shod and that I wouldn't appear crushed, depressed and miserable like today, encouraged me and sped me on. I arrived safely at our house. The door was wide open but inside everything seemed normal and in place. I could see that the houses on the other side of the street were already empty and at the front of the houses piles of rags and papers and so on – trash; everything good had been taken. I went inside. Fortunately for me a lamp-post in front of the shop facing the Aryan side had a powerful light that shed light through the cracks in the shutters ...

I saw that our beds were still in place and complete with the sheets – and I trembled...only two or three days ago we were all here together and now only I was here, alone. Thoughts ran wildly through my head, but I quickly recovered and reminded myself why I had come. From outside I could hear the echo of the guard's footsteps from the Aryan side. I knew I

[Columns 497–498]

must do everything with the utmost care without arousing the suspicions of the guard. I waited until his footsteps got fainter and then began to look for the things I needed. When I heard the guard's footsteps coming nearer, I lay down on the floor and waited. In the end I gathered together a few dresses, shoes, a pillow and a blanket. I placed them all on a blanket and wrapped them up in a sheet. The bundle was big and heavy, but I decided to risk it. Then I decided to take a few mementoes from the house as it was the last opportunity, I had to see them. I took a large photograph album, a few things I had received for my birthday, a head scarf of my grandmother's that she liked to use in the winter and a leather purse of my mother's. All those I tied up in a small bundle in a brown cloth. I swung the large bundle on my shoulder and the small one I carried in my hand and started out. I didn't dare to look behind me and began to hurry on, fearful of the smallest sound of a wind-blown leaf.
I got half-way without a problem or raising suspicions, but it didn't last all the way. The large bundle wrapped in a white sheet made me quite visible; one of the guards noticed something white and began to come towards me. I threw the large bundle on the ground while holding on to the smaller one and began running. I heard a shot, and

the bullet sang past close to me but didn't hit me. I didn't stop but continued running. I heard no more shots, but the big bundle was left behind and all my efforts that were at the risk of my life had been in vain…tired and disappointed I arrived back, went into my room, lay down and went to sleep. I didn't think about the fact that I should be glad that I had again played with my life and yet again saved from certain death. I was just very sorry about the lost bundle…though I was pleased that my aunt knew nothing of my escapade - that I went out and came back in again. I was unable to relax for hours, and I was shaking all over reliving the experience of what I had been through. In the morning I told my aunt everything and showed her the photographs and mementoes. With the passage of time and our many wanderings virtually every item was lost except my grandmother's head scarf that has stayed with me as a reminder of the life and home that was…

From the ghetto to "freedom"

The situation in the ghetto was very tense. In spite of the fact that the authorities had promised there was no "*Aktzia*" in the near future we didn't believe them, and people's thoughts turned to the preparation of good hiding-places for the time of need. They worked at night: digging holes, preparing bunkers and equipping them for a long stay.

My aunt had grievances against the *Judenrat*. As a nurse working in the sanitary department, she needed to obtain a valid work-permit allowing her to live in the workers' ghetto. If they had done so her son would not have been taken and killed. A public enquiry was set up and it was found that her permit had been sold to someone else and he was saved together with his family. To compensate for the injustice caused to her – as if it were possible to compensate her for the loss of her son – to say nothing of the terrible conditions she endured, they promised to send her to work in the village of Studinka about 28 kilometers from Dubno. There were peat-bogs there and they were creating a work-camp for Jewish youth from the surrounding towns and villages but not urban centers. Just one nurse and two Jewish Militia-men were scheduled to be sent there. Many would jump at the chance to work there, and it was with great difficulty that it was my aunt who got the position to travel. Then arose the question…what about me? I was too young to work in the mines and to remain alone in the ghetto – can it be done? It was true I was registered as her foster-child, and she was my provider but to obtain an entry permit to Studinka for me was very difficult. Up until now I had been working in the clothing-stores in the deserted area of the ghetto. These were the clothes that had been left behind in the deserted houses and tens of Jewish women under the control of guards sorted the clothes for quality, size and so on. Physically the work was not hard but mentally it was unbearable. The sorting of clothes, especially those of the children, many of them with the embroidered names, was heart-breaking and depressing and haunted us. Occasionally we found photographs, books and documents of relatives and acquaintances. All these things we arranged for destruction or dispatch.

Every day we met at eight o'clock at a fixed place and accompanied by guards taken to work. Baskets and purses that we had with us were taken from us so that we would be unable to sneak any articles. At four in the afternoon when we were ready to return from work, we were carefully checked by the Militia-men who made us undress to make sure that we had taken nothing. Incidentally, thus they would laugh at us and also touch us. While I was no longer afraid having got used to the situation, the shame, embarrassment and degradation gnawed at my heart... once a guard ordered a young woman to take off her dress and walk home half-naked because he thought she had come in an old dress and changed it for a better newer one...and one woman was punished with forty-eight hours imprisonment because they found a pair of woolen gloves in her pocket. In spite of all, I managed to take home from there quite a few dresses and a

[Columns 499–500]

pair of shoes. I would walk to work with a torn dress that I had taken from someone and return in one I had taken. Terror filled me at the search because it always seemed to me that they remembered the dress I had worn in the morning coming to work. Only when I got through the search did I breathe more easily.

In the meantime, there were again many rumors about another "*Aktzia*" and people would try to get hold of documents as Christians at any price. A few of the members of the *Judenrat* sent their families to other towns with documentation as Aryans but it didn't often work and most of them had to come back again. A few guaranteed themselves a place with Christians in the villages and suburbs for a very high payment, but most remained in the ghetto, close to their hide-out or took their chance at escaping at the last minute...

In August 1942 I received the permit to go to Studinka. The people who worked there all the time were the villagers and from around harvest time they had to go back and tend to their fields so the Germans who were interested in producing large quantities of peat, built a work-camp for the Jewish youth living in the surrounding towns: Mlynow, Ostrow and Demidovka. My aunt, as I said, was installed there as nurse and inspector of sanitary matters while I was sent to work half a day in the peat bogs and half a day to help my aunt in the clinic. Two Jewish Militia men – Moshe and Leib Kagan – with their families were sent to control and regulate the work. They needed a very strong influence to be sent to Studinka.

We were nine people: Moshe Kagan with his wife and two sons, Leib Kagan with his wife and daughter, my aunt and me.

We rented a cart and started our journey. The journey that would normally take a few hours took us a whole day because of searches and examinations made from time to time by German soldiers. But we went through one stop and after having our documents examined, we started up again but then heard "Halt!" and were commanded to raise our hands above our heads and remain like that until we were allowed to move on. The farmer, the owner of the horse and cart was very angry at the many stoppages and now and again threatened to leave us half-way and return home because he felt sorry for his horses (for us, of course, he had no pity). With every threat he made of that type we would thrust a present at him – a watch, a ring, money and he would calm down for a while.

Late in the evening we arrived at the approaches to the village. Because it had rained the previous night the road was very muddy and we were forced to go by foot, to spare the horses from pulling the heavy load through the mud. About two kilometers from the village, we arrived at a place where the road was so very muddy that we had to remove our shoes and go bare-footed. To make matters worse it began to drizzle with a light rain, the horses stopped and wouldn't move. Here the patience of the farmer was gone, and he forgot all the presents and cash we had given him for the journey. He simply threw all our belongings in the mud. The horses felt the lightening of the load and immediately began to move, and the farmer took himself off. Despair hit us: we were unable to carry all the things, and neither could we leave them where they were. Not only were they all that we had left in the world, but we were also carrying on trust articles that parents had entrusted to us for their children who were working in the peat bogs. With no alternative we remained stuck there in the mud and rain until morning, chilled to the bone and shivering and fearful of every sound we heard or of a dog barking in the distance. Thus passed the first night of our exit from the ghetto to "freedom".

The village of Studinka

With the dawn we began to move, dragging our possessions with us. We made slow progress and at about eight o'clock arrived at the village. The yellow patch on our clothes told everyone who we were, and they welcomed us with shouts of "Yids!" At last, we arrived at the work camp.

They were all youths, boys and girls, who welcomed us warm-heartedly. They lived in old unused barns with thatched roofs that dripped water all over the piles of straw that were their beds. Nevertheless, their spirits were relatively good because they were happy to be out of the ghetto. They felt themselves somewhat freer, nobody troubled them about wearing the yellow patch and they had plenty of food from the farmers for helping them in the fields and at home; they chopped wood, picked fruit, and did their laundry and the girls who knew how to sew received butter and meat for their work. All these extra things they did after their day's work in the peat bogs that began at six in the morning and lasted until two in the afternoon because the peat they harvested had to be dried before it could be loaded and moved.

When the youngsters heard that there was a nurse among us who would be looking after their health, their joy was great; many had injuries on the hands and feet that were badly infected from the work in the peat bogs. In the whole village there was neither doctor nor nurse. The villagers took their sick people to a nearby Polish hamlet of Smiga (Smyga) six kilometers away while the Jews had been entirely without medical aid until now. When we told them that we had to report to Khamalniczenchor with a letter from the *Arbeitsamt*, that he must provide us with a place for the clinic and also accommodation for us, they told us that he was the work manager, a rabid anti-Semite and a drunkard and had two sons in the Militia. He would appear unexpectedly where they were working, call a couple of people to come to him, hit them a few times and send them back to work. Those below him in the chain of command would copy him and do the same thing.

It was a pleasant surprise for us when he received us with reasonable courtesy and kindness, went with us to one of the farmers' houses and commandeered one of the rooms for the clinic. In one of the corners of the room we arranged a bed of planks and a mattress of a sack stuffed with straw. The two men of the Militia with their families were quartered in another part of the house that was not yet completed and the doorway and windows were gaping holes.

My aunt started to work immediately while I was busy preparing bandages from the old sheets, we had brought with us from Dubno, from the *Judenrat* store-room. We gave the farmer's wife some of the things we had brought for her (for all sorts of reasons we made sure of preparing suitable "hidden gifts" that open hearts). She was very pleased and in return gave us two good meals that day after months of hunger for simple bread. The following day, early in the morning, I went to work in the peat bogs. The work was hard and performed primitively. There were some mechanical diggers that removed the earth and extracted big piles of peat; the boys cut the peat with special knives into rectangular slabs and the girls arranged the slabs to dry. The exposed holes were very wet and only a few had rubber or leather boots, everyone else worked barefoot. The two Jewish "policemen" and eight Ukrainians oversaw the workers. There was a "brigadier" to each group of three. The Ukrainian police wandered around all the time among the workers urging them on, not sparing the blows whether necessary or not. I could see that not all the girls were treated rudely – on the contrary, some of the girls even received smiles and cigarettes and were allowed to rest and even return home early. I learned afterwards that these girls were enjoying a "relationship" with the Ukrainians who promised to hide them in the event of an "*Aktzia*" …

At ten o'clock they would bring breakfast: bread and milk. Everyone received a mug of milk and a chunk of fresh black bread. It was wonderful. For the first time since the outbreak of war I ate good bread!

My aunt also treated the residents of the village; she performed injections according to the directions of the doctor from Smiga and also treated their emergencies. The farmers knew her well and she made friends with a few of them. These promised her she would be hidden safely in the event of an "*Aktzia*"

In an atmosphere of seething hatred, it was inevitable that not everything would go smoothly and so it was that one day a Jew was murdered by a Ukrainian. The Ukrainian, who worked as a mechanic on one of the diggers, ordered one of the Jews to lubricate the machine. The moment that the Jew bent over the machine the man drew a knife and stabbed him! The Jew died on the spot. Panic ensued, all the workers and the guards came running to the place, but the murderer had fled afraid of revenge. Khamalniczenchor was alerted and immediately restored order: he commanded one of the farmers to hitch up a wagon and with a few Jewish friends of the murdered man, to take the body fifteen kilometers from the village and bury it. After that he ordered the murderer to return to work and instructed everyone to forget the incident. But we couldn't forget it and the camp became a volcano waiting to erupt: It was decided not to go to work. The following day the guards waited until ten o'clock and when they saw no one had appeared they spread out and began to bring the people to work by force. Khamalniczenchor also ordered that if there was ever a similar breakdown in discipline everyone will be sent back to the ghetto and other Jews will be brought in to replace them. A warning such as that was enough to suppress any action from us.

In October 1942 the final "*Aktzia*" took place in Kremenets, where all the Jews remaining in the town were exterminated. The killings took place in Poczajow between Studinka and Kremenets. The distance between Studinka and Poczajow is about six kilometers, and we could hear all that was going on as the "*Aktzia*" took place. A few managed to escape from the killings and hide in holes left from peat mining.

A few days after the "*Aktzia*" in Kremenets, Khamalniczenchor informed us that in a few weeks with the approach of autumn and the rains, the work in the peat bogs will stop and we will be returned to the ghettos or towns we came from. He also warned that no one should consider escaping because anyone found in Studinka or the surroundings will be shot on the spot. The majority chose to return and whatever befell their families would also be their fate too. But a few men decided to escape to the forests and all of them were found and shot during a sweeping search carried out there. Others succeeded in securing for themselves hiding places with the Christians in the village but those too were nearly all killed. I knew of seven people in the camp in Studinka who remained alive.

[Columns 503–504]

The final "*Aktzia*"

On Simchat Torah (the Festival of the Rejoicing of the Law"), 5th October 1942, the final "*Aktzia*" began in the ghetto of Dubno. About a week before we, the group from Dubno, received an order to return there. Moshe Kagan and his family returned there after he had failed to find a secure hiding place for himself and his family. He also thought that no danger awaited him there because for some time now he had been in the Militia. At that time, it was still thought that members of the *Judenrat* and the Militia were relatively safe. After some time, I heard that Moshe Kagan and all his family had committed suicide when their bunker was put under siege. Leib Kagan hid his 4-year-old daughter with farmers and he and his wife returned to the ghetto where they were killed. The daughter was saved and survived and lives with her aunt in Paris.

A hiding-place in the forest

My aunt decided that we would not return to the ghetto because there, everyone would most certainly be killed. We had an acquaintance in Smiga - Stefan Savchuk, a forester. He was Ukrainian and his wife was a Pole. My aunt had treated their daughter who had fallen ill with Scarlet Fever. The mother made a good impression on us and once said, in passing, that if anything was going to happen, they would be ready to help us. There was no explicit promise to hide us in what she said but as we know a drowning man clutches at straws. We decided to try. For two days we were busy with preparations to return, and we told everyone that we were going back to Dubno. We informed Khamalniczenchor officially that we were going and to his wife, who that same day went to Dubno, we gave some of our belongings to deliver to some of our acquaintances and tell them we would be returning the following day. We did all that in order not to raise suspicions that we intended to remain in the area. The following morning, we started on our way with just a few packages in our hands as if to look for a wagon going to Dubno. After we had gone about two kilometers from the village, we entered the forest and stayed there until the evening. When it was dark, we turned towards Smiga. The route was very dangerous because the forest was full of all sorts of people: Ukrainians who had run from the Militia, escaping Soviet prisoners, Jews, gangs of thieves and even deserters from the German army itself. All these were fighting each other, and local residents locked themselves up in their homes as soon as evening came, allowing no one to enter. We arrived safely and knocked on the door. The people were a little scared but when they heard who it was, they opened the door. As soon as we entered, we realized that the promise that had been made was not entirely reliable because they were not able to keep us at home. Savchuk explained that the area was teeming with Militia and Gendarmes making searches day and night and if they learned we were there, they would kill them as well as us. After the "*Aktzia*" in Kremenets – he told us – notices were posted everywhere that for anyone hiding Jews the punishment was death and their property confiscated. Even food he was unable to give us because he barely made a living himself. We asked him to allow us to stay a day or two and if during these two days nothing happened in Dubno, we would return there. In the end he agreed to lead us into the forest and his wife would bring us food there. He also promised to find a place for us far from any path or forest road and to dig a trench for us in case of rain. He demanded from us that we promise – should we by chance be discovered – we would say that we had got here entirely on our own and that no one had helped us or even knew we were here. For the time being he prepared a place for us to sleep in his barn.

Two days later we were informed that an "*Aktzia*" had started in Dubno and there was no point in returning there. In Studinka they had liquidated the work camp and those who had not returned to the ghetto were transported to the nearby village of Werba (Verba) where they were taken out and slaughtered. Savchuk understood that if he sent us away, we would be killed, and he assured us didn't want to be responsible for our death. After we had been there a couple of days, he felt a certain responsibility towards us and his wife also convinced him to keep us another couple of days saying perhaps the immediate German anger will pass and we can go out freely. They didn't know that this was the final "*Aktzia*" and the aim was to liquidate the last remnants of the Jews that remained as refugees from the previous "*Aktzia*". And indeed, we knew our situation very well, but we couldn't force him.

We considered returning to Dubno but we had plenty of time to walk knowingly towards our death so why hurry – there's time! We left for the forest and the spot that Savchuk had chosen for us was dense with bushes so that it was very dim there the whole day and we could see virtually nothing beyond three or four meters around us. We were at the beginning of November, and it was rainy. The ground had no time to dry out before it was raining again. Good clothes and shoes we didn't have and just one blanket; the cold and damp troubled us a lot; all that was in addition to the ever-present fear. Our ears were alert for the least whisper of sound whether from shepherds with their flocks just outside the forest or from people picking mushrooms and we were fearful in case they came close to us and discovered us. Savchuk had warned us that if someone comes very close to us, we should run immediately and that if we didn't there was a real chance that they would kill us. Towards evening his wife brought us some potatoes and bread and sometimes tea or milk. She would cry with pity at our situation, and we used to comfort her.

[Columns 505–506]

After we had been two weeks in the forest the first snow came. The cold at night was intolerable. In addition, no one brought us any food. We understood why: the tracks in the snow would lead anyone and everyone to where we were… and also to those who were helping us. We fed ourselves for two days on a few nuts that we found and drank water from the snow that melted on our hands. On the third day the weather warmed up slightly and the snow melted and towards evening Mrs. Savchuk arrived. She had with her a full basket of food: two loaves of bread, plenty of boiled potatoes in their jackets, and some apples. She cried while telling us that her husband had gotten a little drunk at a wedding party they had attended and told where we were hiding and that we should leave here as soon as possible. But because night was coming on and

557

the farmers were afraid to go out at night because of the gangs roaming around, we should stay here until morning. My aunt, who had suffered heart attacks since her son was killed, now suffered a serious attack. We did everything we could to help her relax and Mrs. Savchuk parted from us and went her way.

In the farm of the Evangelists

We dove deep into our thoughts. Time was pressing and the clock was ticking, and we had to come to some sort of decision. We were almost certain that the wedding story was nothing but a story – they simply wanted to get rid of us and used it as an excuse. But be that as it may, we now needed to get out of there and soon or die of starvation and exposure. We began to sift through the names of all our acquaintances in Studinka and match them with the chances of them helping us to find shelter for ourselves. We could think of no one. On the contrary – it was more than likely that they would give us away to the police. There was only one family that lived in a tiny isolated far distant hamlet, and they were Evangelical Christians. The man was ill with Tuberculosis and my aunt had injected him several times. His condition was beyond hope. They had tried to explain to us the basic tenets of their faith and it was clear beyond doubt that they would not kill us. They were desperately poor but had food. More than that: the farmer needed help and perhaps because of that they were willing to keep us there for a while. The place was well-suited for hiding, the house was far from any settlement and bordered by a forest.

We started on our way keeping all the time on forest paths and away from any highway or a frequented road. We arrived at the hamlet very late. The dog began to bark. Hearing the barking, the woman, Domka, came out. Fearful that perhaps a gang was closing in on the house, she unleashed the dog and went back inside closing the door. The dog rushed at us angrily, ready to tear us to pieces. In addition, our fears grew that patrols patrolling the area would hear the barking and come to investigate what was happening – and that would be the end for us. We gave the dog bread and some sugar, and he became quiet. We stood in the bushes and waited. After about an hour Domka came out again and saw us. Fearfully she asked us what we wanted. "We know that anyone caught helping Jews paid for it with their lives." We told her that we knew but nevertheless she had to help us because we had nowhere to go.

We stayed with them. They prepared a place for us in the loft of the cow-shed. The children represented a serious problem, because they couldn't understand why we had to hide. We explained what the situation was and explained again and after a week they learned to keep quiet about us.

About a kilometer away from where we were, they found a Jewish woman with her child living with a Christian family. They were taken out and executed. The Christian family as well could expect the death penalty but, in the end, they commuted the sentence: the father and one of the daughters were sent to a labor camp in Germany and the livestock – horses and cows, impounded.

We now waited to be told to leave the place, but the farmer did the opposite, filled with anger against the Germans and also the hamlet authority for submitting itself entirely to the orders of the Germans, he promised us that as long as he was alive, he would not desert us. And indeed – he started at once to prepare an additional hiding place for us, safer than the one we had, in the event of a sudden search. It was a small cave under the edge of the house where we could barely sit down even stooped over. The entrance was small and concealed and we could get in only by crawling very carefully because the walls were very thin and fragile and likely to collapse and bury us under a landslide. The children learned to guard us from everyone. They would try to keep visitors – adults and children alike, from approaching the cow-shed so that we wouldn't be discovered. We received enough bread and a hot meal at least once a day. When there were no strangers in the vicinity, at least one of them would come to us and comfort us and when the snow came and there was no fear of anyone coming to the house, they would let us come down to the house to bathe and warm up by the fire and also launder our clothes. When that happened, one of the children would always be outside keeping watch and warn us in case anyone approached the house. Many times, there were false alarms that only caused panic. Out of caution they milled flour on mill-stones in the house in case someone questioned why the family needed so much flour.

When there is no air to breathe

The Germans laid a heavy burden of taxes, especially on farm produce, on the villagers who began to bury their produce in pits they dug at night in their fields.

[Columns 507–508]

In February 1943 the Germans ran a search in the village. In our house there was a double problem: to hide us and to hide the produce which was, in fact, what the Germans were searching for. We had to hide in the little cave under the house. The children closed the entrance and there we sat for a whole day doubled-up and cramped without being able even to straighten our back because the place was less than a meter in height. We also suffered from lack of air to breathe although we opened just a little the hole we used for entry. The searches continued all day and throughout the night into the following day. It was cold and my legs felt like two lumps of ice. The mice scampered all around us and there were moments that I thought it would have been better to remain in the cow-shed even if we got caught, rather than freeze here in this hole. At last, I fell asleep. I awoke in the morning to a slight rustling sound: the children had come to bring us some hot food. They were very careful because the searches were still going on. They told us that the searchers had reached the edge of the village and would probably soon be here. The child closed the entrance with planks and sprinkled a thin layer of earth over them. Indeed, from the point of view of security the hiding place was perfect but our situation inside it was terrible. We had the feeling of complete suffocation.

During the afternoon hours three Germans came accompanied by two local Militia men from Smiga, to search the house of our benefactor. They stood all the family against the wall and told them to raise their arms. The searches were exacting: They dug up random parts of the courtyard and in the buildings – in the barns and stables, the chicken houses and the cow-shed and after they had found nothing, they took for themselves a fat pig weighing about 100 kilograms and went. Domka was very sad about the pig but when we heard what they had taken from others in the village we were pleased we got rid of them so cheaply.

With nightfall Domka came and told us to come to the house to bathe and warm up because after a day like that it was certain that no one would come to visit. My legs were frozen, and I couldn't move from my place. With an effort of desperation, I managed to crawl out, but my aunt was unable to do so. She was weak and frozen and couldn't push herself. After much effort she fainted and lay down with her head outside and the rest of her body still in the cave. We dug a sort of small trench underneath her, but we couldn't drag her out. The children cried and Domka got angry and started shouting towards the house: "After a day like that – troubles like this and because of who? Because of the Jews." And her husband was guilty of it all! Her shouting brought her sick husband from his bed, and he dragged my aunt up with all his strength. We took her into the house, warmed her up with warmed towels and she regained consciousness. That same evening the farmer suffered a hemorrhage from his lungs and bled from the mouth, something that hadn't happened for a long time. He was very ill, and it could easily have happened even without the effort of raising my aunt from the cave but both Domka and the children saw in us the cause of the trouble and their faces showed that they had suffered enough from us. We went up to our loft in the cow-shed but I was so tense after two nights of suffering from cold and fear that I couldn't sleep. The thoughts chased each other through my head and left me restless. According to the mood in the house we needed to go and leave these people in peace but where to go? The following morning no one came to us, only at midday the daughter came up to us and brought some food hidden in her clothes. She said that everyone was angry with us and wished that we would go, only the father wasn't angry, and we should wait until he felt better.

That same day it became known in the village that the searches and the robberies carried out by the Germans, without talking first with the village elders, angered all the farmers intensely. The council decided to cancel its affiliation with the Ukrainian Militia and collect weapons for self-defense in case they should come again to steal. They also decided not to allow their youngsters to go to Germany to work there. They became aware that the Germans simply tricked them although they killed the Jews, but no Ukrainian authority had been founded and they didn't distribute Jewish property among the farmers. When they invited us into the house that same evening, with two of the children outside on the look-out we sensed a different attitude in the atmosphere. Domka asked for forgiveness from my aunt for her behavior of yesterday regarding her attitude towards us, explaining that her outburst was the result of the many months of high tension under which she had been living.

Encouraging rumors

She told us what had been happening in the village. Rumors were beginning to come in of victories by the Soviet army over the Germans. Our farmer, who had been a member of the village council in 1939-1940 was one of the few who didn't object to the Russian regime (we didn't know that until now) and was very happy to hear these rumors. They decided to allow us to remain with them but to be careful not to let our presence be known to the villagers because they were likely to attack us. "Look," they said, "winter is coming to an end, summer will be easier for us and by next winter perhaps our salvation will be here."

But still the days were hard to bear: The Germans carried out searches nearly every week and more than once we had to retreat to the cave under the house. Food was scarce because

[Columns 509–510]

the family sold everything in order to buy medicines for the sick man. The children, who had been ordered to Germany to work, refused to obey the order and escaped to the forests. Chaos reigned and it was impossible to know who to be careful of and who not, who was dangerous and who not. German pressure got stronger but so too did the resistance of the farmers.

One day, we suggested to Domka that she should go to Dubno, to the Czech family where my aunt had hidden many belongings and bring as much as she could. She went and the family was overjoyed to know that we had survived but they warned her to be careful and not to come there again, because their daughter was friendly with the Germans and the son even helped in some searches in the ghetto after the last "*Aktzia*". They were likely to notice that a farmer's wife from a distant village was visiting their house. The family gave Domka many things belonging to us. They also gave her some sugar for the sick man and medicines that they had acquired, with some influence, from the dispensary. They told her to come again but only in June when the children would be away for holidays. Domka returned impressed and full of admiration for these good people, for their generosity, their courteousness and their good-hearted kindness. The happiness at home was great: we took nothing but gave everything to the family and stayed only with our own worn dresses…

The yearning for freedom grew stronger day by day. Sitting in hide-outs became more and more irksome and depressing and our patience shorter and shorter. Thoughts ran ceaselessly through our minds concerning every one of our friends and acquaintances that almost certainly were no longer alive; around every child I had studied with at school, and now – where is he?

Sunny days and spring came. The condition of the sick man gradually worsened. During his last days he said to his wife that she should try to keep us in the house until the liberation, or until she can have us help her with the difficult days that will come after his death. He understood that the Soviets would not forgive the villagers for their service to the Germans and also the Russian prisoners of war who betrayed their country. While she, Domka, will be her own best proof by the fact that she kept us safe in spite of the very real, ever-present threat of death for not obeying their commands and not serving their needs.

In April 1943 the farmer died. For many days before his death and also afterwards, Domka didn't come to us. The children's visits also became rarer, only Nadia didn't forget us and brought us food from time to time. Domka was very attached to the sick man and all the heavy chores about the farm now fell upon the children and they had little time to spare for us. For weeks we were unable to bathe or change our clothes and the lack of cleanliness that troubled us was now so bad that it caused us much suffering. About two weeks after the death of her husband Domka came to us. She said that she would very much like for us to leave the house because her "…nerves are completely shattered". The busy season on the farm was approaching and many strangers would be wandering around making it very difficult to prevent them discovering us. She was more afraid of the villagers than of the Germans. We didn't know what to do. We began to plead with her, persuade her and remind her of her husband's last words before he died and promising much after the liberation which was clearly on its way.

The surroundings burn with hatred

In the meantime, there was open conflict between the village and the Germans. In July, with the beginning of the harvest, the Germans surrounded the village on every side searching for deserters from the Militia and those evading going to labor camps in Germany. They stole fruit, horses and everything they could lay their hands on accompanied by threats of blowing up houses in the village if there was any resistance or argument. Most of the residents of Studinka escaped together with their livestock to the peat bogs that spread over an area of four kilometers. Grouped together in one place they prepared to resist the Germans by force. Domka and her children also fled but we couldn't join them because the villagers themselves would have killed us. We had no alternative but to stay where we were and trust in fate. But we knew we couldn't stay in Domka's house for fear of giving an opening to the Ukrainians and Poles to put her and her children in danger because of everything that they did for us. We left the house crawling and got to the closest field and hid there among the standing wheat that had not yet been harvested.

The Germans began blowing up houses and in some places smoke and flames reached high into the sky. The Germans passed close to where we were, shooting in all directions and bullets flew above our heads, so far without hitting us. After a while we heard them leaving the village. They took a lot of cattle, pigs and horses and a few deserters that they had caught, with them. In the evening the villagers returned to their homes with their hatred of the Germans burning like fire in their hearts. There was no way peace could be made between them.

We sent Domka to Dubno and again she brought a large package of things with her: this time with many precious articles of my aunt: furs, woolen blankets, women's suits and underwear. Domka had never seen such things in her life and thus we had the possibility of again "buying" time from her for a while and she promised to let us remain until the end, providing we weren't discovered.

At the end of the summer of 1943 all the rumors of Russian victories began circulating again and the collapse of the German army. Again, we were raised up and carried on the wings of our imagination that the liberation was coming closer and closer. But the residents of Studinka weren't happy with the Soviet victories: they expected that the Germans and the Russians were bloodthirsty and would exhaust each other with long drawn-out battles and out of it all would arise an independent Ukraine. They joined the national Bandera movement that was striving to rid the country of the Germans, to expel the Poles and if somewhere a single Jew was found – to exterminate him.

[Columns 511–512]

There were a couple of Polish villages in the area and a couple of mixed villages with Ukrainians. The "Bandarists" killed the Poles cruelly, burned their homes and stole their property and belongings. A Pole who managed to escape with his life to town or the forest joined the Jews hiding there. The Germans no longer dared to enter the village in small groups. They came to collect taxes only as a full corps; at night the Ukrainians were in complete control, and they burned Polish property and murdered Poles with all the cruelty they could. It was some small consolation for us in revenge for all that they had done to us.

The approach of the Soviets

Between August and December 1943 there were four searches conducted in the village and we were forced four times to hide in the forest after Domka and the children escaped with the villagers to the bogs. I was full of festering sores, especially my legs.

We had no bandages or medical ointments to treat them. I was also troubled with my eyes from hiding in completely dark places and then coming out into the bright sunlight. I could see nothing and became dizzy. It recurred several times and my aunt was very worried about me. I saw much better at night than I did during the day, and I was frightened that I would go blind. My greatest wish was to survive to see the day that the Soviet army returned and redeemed us and more than the redemption to see the fall of the German army. Then came the winter of 1943-44 and salvation was still not here. Disappointed with the slowness of the Soviet advance we almost stopped believing the many rumors of the German collapse. Although the fact that even the Ukrainians, haters of the Soviets, spoke all the time of the Russian victories, encouraged us and kept our faith up that the end was near for the oppressive regime.

Again, it was time to suffer the snow and cold. Domka and the children were forced to restrict their meals in order to pay a large amount from their seeds to the workers during the harvest season. The yield was not good and part of it was destroyed by fire caused by the Germans and was not harvested. There were doubts if there would be enough bread to last until the next harvest. Nevertheless, the relationship between Domka, the children and us changed for the better: the mutual fears and problems we shared tied us together and we were like one family in suffering and hopes for better days. Anya, the older daughter, was already seventeen years old and received a travel order to work in Germany. Domka decided not to let her go and Anya took our place in the hideout under the house. There was a fear that a search for her would uncover us. We sat for a week in the forest, because every day they came searching for her until, at last, they believed her mother's explanation that she had run away without permission with a boyfriend, and she didn't know where. When they stopped coming for her, we returned to our loft above the cow-shed. Now Anya was together with us in the underground.

The last time we hid in the forest I became ill with a bad attack of bronchitis. The cough was severe and choking; I was afraid that my constant heavy coughing would be heard outside. Everyone in the house tried to help to ease my suffering: they brought me hot milk, hot water-bottles to warm my legs and the son, Wassia, walked twelve kilometers in the snow to bring me aspirin and cough syrup – the only medicines easily available. There was also some concern that I might have pneumonia and the temperature was 20 degrees F. We had no fuel to fire the heater – and even if we had it was too dangerous – everything around us was straw. Eventually I began to improve and overcome that illness as well, but I was so exhausted that I didn't even have the strength to sit. I dedicated myself to knitting; I knitted woolen shirts, gloves and ear-muffs for all the family.

January and February 1944 passed in relative quiet. Then artillery-fire rolled around the heavens and could be heard in the stillness of the night.

Cooperating with the Russians

One morning – it was January or February 1944 – we heard many wagons coming closer and the sounds of people. We listened carefully – they were speaking Russian! We rejoiced with great happiness, quite certain that they were Russian Partisans dressed like Germans who had stolen their uniforms after killing the Nazis. If so, it was certain that the Red Army must be following along close behind. My aunt said to go down to them and ask them to take us with them to Dubno because here we were in danger from the villagers themselves. A few of them came into the courtyard to water their horses and one of them turned to Domka and asked if she knew of any Soviet Partisans in the area, adding that they had been sent by the authorities to liquidate them. It all immediately became clear to us: they were soldiers of the Russian general Vlasov who cooperated with the conquerors. We were lucky not to have rushed down and avoided putting our own heads in a noose…

[Columns 513–514]

Domka worried about us and told us to be more careful and not be in so much of a hurry. In the year and a half that we had been in her house we became attached to each other, and she protected us until the day of the liberation. She couldn't go to Dubno again to bring sugar, salt and kerosene and we had to be satisfied with what we had. In the meantime, farmers had arrived in the village from other areas where battles were raging. Three families of refugees from the area of Rowno were guests in Domka's house. We were forced to be very careful of these people, each of whom was famous for heroism in the killing of Jews. These were the hardest of times for us that same winter of 1943/44. We couldn't move from the place and the children couldn't come up to us and only when they came to milk the cows would they bring us a few slices of bread. During the first two weeks of March the Germans bombarded the village several times. All the people fled to the forest and the bogs; only we remained alone up in our loft above the cow shed. The Germans never appeared again in the village while the Ukrainians were armed and ready to defend themselves against both sides at one and the same time.

The Red Army liberates Studinka

In the middle of March rumors circulated that there were battles in Dubno. A few days later, that Dubno had been liberated. But the Germans were still in control where we were, and they were digging defensive trenches in the peat bogs. The morning following the announcement of the liberation of Dubno, the Soviets laid a heavy bombardment on the area, but the Germans took no part. We were located somewhere in the middle of the Front. The Russian lines were on the approaches to the village on

565

the Smiga side and on the edge of the village on the way to Verba the Germans were arrayed. The bombardment went on for hours and we were frightened that now, right at the end, on the eve of liberation, it was going to be the end for us. Why, then – if it were to be so – did we have to endure, we asked ourselves, these many, many months of suffering?

On the 26th March 1944, as evening approached, silence came. Then there was a loud explosion, and we learned the Germans in their retreat had blown up a bridge. The night passed quietly but the people didn't return to their homes and everywhere silence reigned. Early in the morning of 27th of March the Red Army took the village. We were the first to see them. My hand is not capable of describing our feelings and our excitement at that moment. It was like walking out of great darkness into a great light, something bigger than life itself. To know that your fate was sealed two years previously with no possible chance of reprieve from the clutches of death and yet for all that to struggle against a bitter death every single day and through will-power alone – subdue it; to hope to see and wake up to the day in which the murderers are vanquished – and to see, too, the realization of the hope to breathe the air of freedom, nothing could bring greater happiness than that!

At the same time, we knew: not to get too excited and not to be too rash lest the village discovers who we are and will take vengeance on Domka after the liberation. Indeed, as I later learned, some Jews were killed in Dubno after the liberation – they came out of hiding to greet the liberators and the Ukrainians murdered them.

The soldiers came and started searching for gangs of Germans, asking the head of the family and after they received explanations from us, they left. In the meantime, people began to return to the village and we saw the need for us to hide from them until a more settled time. For a few days the sounds of artillery and explosions were heard and on 29th March there was also a heavy German bombing. Two German bombs fell on the village causing two big fires. No one was killed. The 30th of March was completely quiet, and we decided to return to Dubno.

We return to Dubno

On the 1st April we started out for Dubno. We got up at dawn so that no one would see us leaving the village. Wassia led us through the fields and forests as far as the highway avoiding every village and house out of caution for Domka and her children. We parted from the youth amidst great emotion. He took a small photo of his father from his pocket that he had asked to give us as a memento when we go free. He had signed it two days before he died…

The distance from the village to Dubno was twenty-eight kilometers. According to the season it should already have been springtime in the country, but the weather was still wintry. Damp snow was falling that melted underfoot. There were puddles of water and mud all along the road. Our shoes were completely ragged and tattered,

566

totally wet and freezing our feet, but the feeling of freedom sped us on our way. After we had gone several hundred meters, we saw a military vehicle and waved him down for a ride. The driver stopped but told us it was absolutely forbidden to pick up people on the road. We continued onwards. After seventeen kilometers a car stopped for us, and we were allowed to climb on.

We arrived at Dubno around mid-day. The town looked almost destroyed as a result of the battles that had been fought there. The people who had fled the town had not yet returned and

[Columns 515–516]

half the population of the town – the Jews – was no longer alive. The houses in the ghetto seemed mostly destroyed and those that remained standing had been appropriated by Christians. We wandered around the town for a while among the houses without seeing anyone we knew but, in the evening, we decided to go and visit the Czech family, Shakuda. They received us very warmly and were happy to see us. Their home had been destroyed; three shells had hit it, but they had managed to salvage one room and the kitchen and in those they lived. The parents were living on their own: the daughter had gone to Prague a year before and the son – to Germany against his parents' wishes that he remain with them. We got everything at once – clothes, shoes, comfortable beds and good food aplenty. We heard from them that there were about thirty Jewish survivors in town from Dubno and from other places as well. All the neighbors crowded in to see us and everyone tried to prove that he had done much to help the Jews in the ghetto and for certain he would have hidden Jews in his very house had not the Germans been right next door…
Among our callers I met a friend from school Polina Muller (she is now in the United States) and our happiness was boundless. We both endured a period of terrible years in our short lives and withstood the most terrible of sufferings. In the meantime, we had grown and become young women. There was no difference between us except one: she had survived together with her parents and sister, while I was left alone without my family…

The following morning my aunt began the search for her husband and daughter who had fled to Russia. She found work with a clinic, and I wandered round the town all day long among the rubble, around where our house, near the school where I had learned – and before my eyes passed the ghostly memories of those good days that had gone and would return no more. Food we now had in plenty and also suitable medical treatment; the injuries to my legs formed correct scabs and after a while completely disappeared. Life began slowly to become organized, and even registration for school started – suddenly…

The town is bombed again

The Germans began to bomb the town night and day for weeks. In one of the attacks the military hospital close to our house was hit and all the patients and staff were buried underneath the rubble. We stayed lying on the floor in our room because we had no time to go down to the cellar and the blast shattered all the windows in the house leaving me with a light wound from one of the flying shards of glass. Clearing the debris from the military hospital in order to get at the victims buried under the mountain of rubble took days. Men to do the work were virtually non-existent in town so the women-folk were mobilized for the job. I too worked there for six straight days. The bombing continued throughout the time. They were the last bombings the area suffered from the Germans.

German prisoners

For a short time, there was a German prisoner-of-war camp in Dubno. They worked in clearing up all the debris in town, but their appearance was much different to that of the Russian prisoners of 1941/42. They didn't die of starvation, and they weren't barefoot; all that was required of them was discipline at work. Indeed, the fact that our murderers and oppressors were now prisoners and they had to obey the orders of the Soviet soldiers among who were quite a few Jews, gave me great pleasure. Among the Jewish people in town were those who threw insults at the prisoners releasing some of their hatred of the murderers but to injure them was forbidden. One Jewish man who threw a stone at one of the prisoners was arrested and fined. He said in his defense that he recognized the German who had murdered his father. He was told that he could press charges against the man, but he could not take the law into his own hands.

The return to school and studies

On the 5th July 1944 the school opened and there were special classes for children who had not studied throughout the war. Studies were conducted intensively in small groups and every one of the pupils could receive extra explanations after school hours. The teachers were polite, generous and patient and did everything they could to help the children absorb the material being taught. There was not one single book [to study from] and all the subjects were taught verbally by the teachers and written down by the pupils. I was dedicated to learning; using the opportunity to drive from my mind all that had happened to me and what was happening at the battle fronts that were still actively engaged, with thousands of casualties every day.

At the New Year festival of Rosh Hashanah of 1945 that was to be held in the school, they intended to distribute to war-orphans parcels of clothes from the Red

Cross. I knew about this, and I told my teacher that I didn't want a parcel and I didn't want my name mentioned or included among the orphans receiving aid, in the presence of the teachers and pupils. I was revolted at the feelings of pity that everyone expressed to me, and I tried to hide from my class-mates the fact that I had no home, that my aunt and I lived with a Czech family in only one small, dilapidated room. I suffered from an inferiority complex and strove to overcome it.

In the meantime, I received a letter from a cousin and her husband. I was pleased to know that they were well and would shortly be coming to Dubno. I succeeded at my studies and was encouraged, and it added to my efforts and even awakened within me the ambition to continue my education.

Translator's Comments

1. Probably a reference to the Hebrew idiom "to pass through the seven circles of hell [*shiv'at medurey gehinom*], based on the ancient rabbinic idea that hell (*Gehinom* in Hebrew) concists of seven layers. (Translation editor's comment)
2. A secular–academic Jewish school system founded in 1922 mainly in eastern Europe against the prevailing traditional Jewish religious–based system of education. Some still exist. The word itself means "culture".
3. Stepan Bandera, leader of the Ukrainian nationalistic organization OUN, which murdered Jews and Poles during the war.
4. Official identity card.
5. Works department.
6. Jewish Council
7. See Genesis 1: 26
8. Collective farms
9. A Nazi designation proclaiming people of German extraction and race to be German irrespective of nationality.
10. A supposed rabid anti–Semite and instigator of many post–WWI pogroms until his assassination in Paris in 1925. However, much dispute still lingers today among historians – even Jewish ones – as to his involvement and guilt. See: https://en.wikipedia.org/wiki/Symon_Petliura

Testimony about the Slaughter in Dubno at the Nuremberg Trials

Hermann Graebe

Translation from Hebrew by Jerrold Landau and partly based on text kindly provided by the *Holocaust Education & Archive Research Team* (www.HolocaustResearchProject.org)

The frightful testimony brought here is only one of many that appear in the book[1].

I, the undersigned, Hermann Freidrich Graebe, state the following under oath:

From September 1941 to January 1944, I worked as a director and chief engineer at the Zdolbunow (Zdołbunów) branch of the Jozef Jung construction company. In this capacity I had to visit various workplaces of our firm. Under the terms of a contract with the army construction services, the company was to build, among other things, grain warehouses on the old Dubno airfield in the Ukraine.

On the 5 October 1942, when I visited the building office at Dubno, my foreman Hort[2] Moennikes told me that in the vicinity of the site, Jews from Dubno had been shot in three large pits, each about thirty metres long and three metres deep. Between 1,500 and 5,000 Jews who had lived in Dubno prior to the pogrom and were slated for death were killed daily. As the shootings had taken place in Moennikes' presence, they left a deep impression upon him.

I went to the place accompanied by my work supervisor. I saw great mounds of earth about 30 meters long and 2 meters high. Many trucks were parked nearby. Armed Ukrainian militia were making people get out, under the surveillance of SS soldiers. The same militiamen were responsible for guard duty and driving the trucks back and forth. The people in the trucks wore on their clothing the obligatory yellow pieces of cloth that identified them as Jews.

1000 Pairs of Shoes

The people who had got off the trucks – men, women and children – had to undress upon the order of an SS man, who carried a whip. They had to put their clothes on separate piles of shoes, outer clothing, and underclothing. I saw a heap of shoes that must have contained eight hundred to one thousand pairs, great piles of clothes and undergarments.

Without screaming or weeping these people undressed, stood in family groups, kissed each other, said their farewells, and waited for a sign from another SS man, who was also armed with a whip. During the fifteen minutes that I stood near the pit, I did not hear anyone complain or beg for mercy.

I watched a family of eight: a man and woman about fifty years old, surrounded by their children of about one, eight, and ten, and two grown girls about twenty and twenty-nine. An old woman with snow-white hair was holding the one-year-old child in her arms, singing something to it. The child was crowing with delight. Those around looked on with tears in their eyes. The father was holding the hand of the ten-year-old boy, speaking to him softly. The boy was fighting back his tears. The father pointed to the sky, stroked the boy's head, explained something to him.

The Dead Moved

At that moment the SS man at the pit shouted something to his comrade, who separated off about twenty persons and ordered them to go behind the mound of earth. Among them was the family I mentioned above. I still clearly remember a dark-haired, slim girl who pointed to herself as she passed close to me and said, "Twenty-three!"

Mass grave

I walked to the other side of the mound and found myself standing before an enormous grave. The people lay so closely packed, one on top of the other, that only their heads were visible. Nearly all had blood flowing from their shoulders and heads. Some of them were still moving. Some lifted an arm and turned a head to show us that they were still alive.

The pit was already two-thirds full. I estimated that it already contained about one thousand people.

[Columns 519–520]

I looked at the man who had shot them. He was an SS man who was sitting on the edge of the narrow end of the pit, his legs dangling into it. He had a sub-machine gun across his knees and was smoking a cigarette.

Smoking Between the Acts of Murder

The people, completely naked, went down some steps which had been cut in the clay wall of the pit and climbed over the heads of those already lying there, to the place indicated by the SS man. They laid down in front of the dead or injured people. Some of them caressed those who were still alive and spoke to them softly.

Again, I heard a series of shots. I looked into the pit and saw twitching bodies with the heads not moving. Blood was pouring from their necks.

I was surprised I was not ordered away.

The next batch was already approaching. They climbed into the pit, lined up against the previous victims and were shot.

I returned to the pit the next morning. I saw about thirty naked people lying near the pit, about thirty to fifty metres away from it. Some of them were still alive. They looked straight in front of them with a fixed stare and seemed not to notice neither the chillness of the morning nor the workers of my firm who stood around.

A girl of about twenty spoke to me and asked me to give her clothes and help her escape. At that moment we heard an SS car approach, and I returned to my worksite.

Ten minutes later we heard shots from the vicinity of the pit. Those Jews who were still alive had been ordered to throw the corpses into the pit. Then they themselves had to lie down in the pit, to be shot in the neck.

Signed: M[3]. Graebe

Wiesbaden, November 10, 1945

Original and Translator's Comments

1. From the book of testimony "The Third Reich and the Jews" by Leon Poliakov and Josef Wulf, Jewish authors who compiled their book from documents taken from the Nazi archives. (Yediot Achronot, 16 Cheshvan 5704 [1953], number 8341).
2. Should be Hubert (trans)
3. Probably a typo in the original text since his first name is Hermann Friedrich (trans)

The End of the Partisan, a Member of Betar[1], Aizia Wassermann

By Asher Ben–Oni

Translated from Hebrew by Selwyn Rose

Aizia Wassermann was born in Międzyrzec in 1919. His parents became wealthy while he was still a child and were considered so among those of standing in the area. They acquired the Tackser House which, because of its size and luxuriousness was conspicuous in town and became a small palace. Aizia was educated in the local school and was also an active and dedicated member of the local *Betar* branch. At the age of thirteen, he entered the Polish government Gymnasium in Rowno. It was there that he first encountered anti–Semitism in all its nakedness and from that moment, he became an ardent *Betar* activist and began to influence his father into liquidating his business interests and immigrating to Palestine. With the outbreak of the Second World War, the Russians entered Międzyrzec and began to nationalize all the assets of everyone and it was known that they were destined to be sent to Siberia. His father managed to save a significant part of his capital and through the timely advice of a Soviet officer, he moved the family to Dubno. There, he found work, and no one knew of his past.

The German conquest found the Wassermann family ensconced in Dubno. When the first command of the Germans was to order all the Jews to wear the yellow patch, Aizia rebelled and went to live with his Polish friends, the Yugilevych family.

When the Germans began to mobilize the citizens for forced labor in Germany (before the liquidation of the town's ghetto), he, and two members of the Yugilevych family, …

...escaped to the forest. They acquired arms and lived by the weapons. Slowly they were joined by some other rebellious people and when their number had increased to fifteen men, they stopped accepting any further people.

When the Dubno ghetto was liquidated, the platoon began armed military style operations against the Germans and their collaborators. The Soviets tried to contact them and the underground Home Army[2] also sought to have the group join their force but they remained independent. They were light travelers and wherever they were during the day, it was never where they slept at night. Because of their strong connections with the population, so hostile to the Germans, it was easy for them to follow, and investigate their movement causing the Gestapo many headaches through their activities. From the forests of Dubno, they moved to the forests near the village of Kamienna Gora, fortifying themselves there on a cliff called Duma.

Winter was at its height. After three whole days of non–stop snowing, the universe was covered as if with a white sheet. A freezing cold penetrating wind swept over everything. Not a human soul was seen on the streets of the village and the streets glowed brightly and shone white in the sunlight. The villagers remained closeted in their homes keeping their fires well fuelled.

Thick dark gray smoke belched from the chimneys and from the windows and doors leaked the aromas of cooking and fresh baking....[3]

[Column 521]

The Only Son of the Wassermanns is not with his Parents

That same hour, the Wassermann family sat in the warmth of the cellar of the Polish family Umanski, waiting for the husband to bring them some hot tea, a little food and some news to calm their souls. They remembered their home with its spaciousness and comfort, light and warmth and gave thanks to G–d for providing a roof over their head in these troubled days, a time when the whole area – Rowno, Dubno, Zdolbunow and Ostrow were defined as "*Judenrein*", and all the Jews exterminated without leaving a single trace of their existence. The oil lamp, casting its dim illumination brought up memories of "the good old days" when they spent the winter evenings in their home in the company of friends and acquaintances, seated round a table full of delicacies and thinking that the gold and jewelry they possessed would suffice them for at least ten years. Until then.......

One thing only guided the peace of mind of the Wassermann family – their only son Aizia refused to hide and wait patiently until the anger passed. The moment the Germans invaded, and the Jews were ordered to wear the yellow patch, he obtained a firearm and escaped to the forest. Up until the liquidation of the Dubno ghetto, nothing was heard of him. Only later, when they survived that liquidation, they heard that their son was alive and that he was leading a small, courageous band of partisans. They also met with him and since then he would occasionally visit them.

When he came to visit them, he never spoke to them of his activities with the partisans, of his fight with the Germans or the help he gave to Jews in the forest. It was only from Christians and Jews from Mizoch (Mizocz, Mizotch) and Dubno, who would occasionally meet in the forest, did they hear of the fearless spirit of their Aizia and the reputation he and his group had gained among the German outposts scattered around the region and the punishments they visited upon those in the population suspected of collaborating with the Germans or refusing to assist the hiding Jews.

Three days previously, he was expected to visit them, but he had not arrived. His parents consoled themselves with the thought that it was because of the heavy snow and fierce cold. Nevertheless, the householder told them in the morning, that after rather a bloody battle with the German *Gendarmerie*, in a nearby village, in which all the Germans were killed and their weapons taken, Aizia and his band escaped to the forest near Kremenets.

Aizia's mother, Beyla Wassermann, sensed that something tragic had happened to her beloved son and she asked her son–in–law, Moshe Meizlish, who was married to her daughter Malia, Aizia's sister, to go out at night from his hiding place and find out exactly what had happened to Aizia.

The agreed knocking on the door to the cellar scared the dwellers inside. The father, Yosef Wassermann, opened the door. The house owner entered bearing bread, hot tea, meat fat and even some vodka.

The house holder would supply their needs through a secret panel while the door was used only when it was necessary…

[Column 522]

…to convey something verbally. He told them that the Germans were making extensive house–to–house searches for Aizia and his partisans. They plan to visit this village either tonight or tomorrow morning. There is no doubt that their search will be exact because someone had "whispered" to the Germans about the connections of the family to the Jews. Therefore, it was best for all of them to leave the cellar for a few days until the searches were finished. He had already prepared a suitable hiding place for them in the nearby forest and when it gets dark, he will take them there. Yosef Wassermann gave the villager a suitable present and the plan was agreed between them that when the Germans approach, he will lead them to the hiding place he had prepared for them; immediately after the search the farmer's son will bring them back to the cellar.

The villager left and the Wassermanns sat down to eat. Grief pervaded the cellar and sorrow gnawed at the heart; again, a life of wandering, again a life under the stars at the mercy of the wind and snow with the threat of death hovering over their heads…

Moshe, who was to leave the cellar at night to find out about the fate of Aizia, prepared for himself something to eat on the way, some camouflaged clothing, a little money, matches and candles and waited impatiently until the residents of the village all went to bed.

The Farmer Leads Them to the Forest

Suddenly they were frightened by the shouts of their neighbor, Kraschitzka, whose voice had penetrated the cellar; they could hear clearly that she was saying: "The Germans are already in the village, they are looting and beating and burning. Run and save yourselves!"

Before they even had time to grasp what was happening, they heard the urgent knocking on the door. The farmer entered angrily and told them to follow him quickly because the Germans were only three houses away.

Half dressed, confused and frightened the Wassermanns followed the farmer out towards the forest. The farmer ran, with them following. They were gasping for breath, falling over from the belongings they were carrying and from the effort but rising up and continuing to run.

When they got into the thick of the forest, close to the hiding place, Moshe separated from them and went off in the direction of a nearby village to find out the reason for Aizia's nonappearance on the agreed day. Moshe's watch showed that it was still early – eight in the evening – and it was dangerous to be wandering around at that hour, with the Germans in the vicinity. He slowed his steps, gazed round about him and sat down somewhere comfortably to rest for a while and plan his next move.

He barely had time to take one breath and relax when in the silence of the frozen forest, he heard worrying shouts. It seemed to Moshe that the voice was known to him. He jumped up and stood erect, tense and all ears but the shouting…

[Column 523]

…was not repeated – did he imagine it? Did his excited state of mind mislead him? No, no it can't be! Yes, he heard it – definitely, with his own ears, the frightened voice of his wife? He hurried his steps and hastened in the direction of the shouts. At a distance of twenty meters or so four figures were running towards him. Moshe stopped behind a large tree and looked at the four escaping figures. He identified among them the tall figure of Uzbek, the escaped Russian deserter, who worked for the owner of the cellar in which they stayed. Moshe sprinted down the path and found a place from which he could see but not be seen. He immediately identified all the remaining figures. The man with the club in his hand was the house owner who had led the family to the supposed new hiding place. The older boy, Vladek ran on the left of his father with a hatchet in his hand and the third figure was the son–in–law of the homeowner from the nearby village.

Moshe backtracked towards the hiding place in the forest. A few meters from where he had parted from his loved ones, he found all of them with their skulls smashed in. It was all understood and clear....

The murderers returned home happy and satisfied. The liquidation of the hated Jews went off without a hitch and without resistance. Only one or two screams were let out by the victims. Umanski had not yet washed the blood off his hands and face and had already run to the cellar in which the murdered family had hidden. Like a wild predator leaping on its prey, he fell upon the suitcases hidden under the beds. He up–ended them on the bed and his head swam as he beheld their contents: gold and silver coins in quantities he had never seen in his life, jewelry such as were beyond his imagination and clothes of a quality unbeknown to him and such as he had certainly never worn in his life. He closed the cellar and secured it with a lock and a bolt, went upstairs, washed himself and changed his clothes. Immediately after that, he called to his worker and the rest of his family to come and sit and enjoy a glass of vodka to celebrate the "removal" of the Jews from the house. They were all overjoyed at the riches that had fallen upon them and as an added pleasure that no one else except the neighbor Kraschitzka knew anything about it. Every member of the family, the neighbor Kraschitzka and the servant, Uzbek, received some profit from the property of the Wassermanns and the promise of some of the clothes. Only the old father failed to take part in the celebrations and sat unhappily in the corner. It is true he agreed that because of the danger to them all it was better to get rid of the Jews, but it was enough to get them out of the house and be satisfied with their property. For murder there is no atonement, even the Germans will find no penance from G–d. Thus, he spoke to his son. But the son stood his ground and claimed that if they had just robbed them of their property and left them alive, they would never have a moment's rest, who knew when they could suddenly appear in the future when times had changed and demand their property back. Now he can stay safe and secure and undisturbed.

[Column 524]

Aizia a Leader of the Partisan Platoon

Tired and exhausted but deeply satisfied, Aizia and his men returned to their base on the cliff in the forest. Their operation this time was a resounding success. The German unit in town surrendered to them with almost no fight. They slew the guard before he managed to make a sound. When they entered the building they occupied, they caught the unit completely unprepared, sprawled on their cots and without their arms within reach. After only verbal resistance, their hands were tied, their arms taken together with their money and documents and the rest of their property and taken to the depths of the forest. There, they were put on trial, their participation in the liquidation of the ghetto investigated, their robberies of the civilian population, conquest of a country and condemned to death. They were a pitiful lot as captives, begging for their lives, cursing Hitler, appealing to the mercy of the partisans, swearing they had never harmed the Jews, but their guilt was known, and they were all shot.

From the foodstuffs that the partisans took from the Germans, they prepared for themselves an excellent meal that they finished off with pleasant–scented cigarettes they found in the desk of the garrison's German commander. This time they lay down to sleep without setting up even a nominal guard; they simply closed the door, blocked by three hefty sand–bags and fell into a deep sleep. Only Aizia was somewhat restless and in spite of his fatigue was unable to fall asleep. Strange and bad thoughts troubled him and feelings of homesickness for his family unlike anything he had experienced previously attacked him. The snoring of his colleagues angered him, and he got up, dressed and went outside.

From too much drinking, added exhaustion and lethargy in all his limbs from the hard efforts of the evening, he had a bitter taste in his mouth and felt a slight dizziness in his head. All around was a threatening silence. The thick trees hid not only the partisan's camp but also the heavens and the snow-covered fields.

Aizia strolled among the trees and reached the open fields. The fresh, cold air drove away the fatigue and also the dizzy feeling he had disappeared. He stopped, drew out of his knapsack his pistol, laying the cold metal along his forehead and his cheek, examined its function, fed a round into the breech and strode out along the way. A large grey rabbit sped across his path in the twinkling of an eye and disappeared into the forest. The skies were clear, and a full moon shed its light as it floated between the scattered clouds and shone on his worried, agonized countenance. "The nights of Canaan are beautiful, cool they are and clear,"[4] he suddenly began to hum. What a lovely night! – he said aloud, to himself. On normal nights like this he would harness two horses to an upholstered sleigh, climb aboard with his girlfriend and gallop off in pleasure, while now… "The nights of Canaan are beautiful, cool they are and clear," they are without doubt – he mused to himself in pleasure – when I get to the Land of Israel, I will miss these skies on more than one occasion, the pure white snow and the thick forests. And when, in his visions, he would be there, he no longer recalled his present situation, his status and function and even his homesickness…

…for his parents melted away but their images appeared before him intermixed with events and visions that were brought to mind.

He decided that tomorrow he would go to visit them; he will visit them and demand that they move to a hiding place close to him. Aizia did not know that he will never see them again and will not be able to attend to their interment.

The Vengeance Exacted for his Butchered Parents

"For a bird of the air shall carry the voice and that which hath wings shall tell the matter."[5] And even before Moshe had time to tell anyone of the traitorous murder, the surroundings already knew that the Wassermann family had been murdered by the owner of the very cellar in which they had been given refuge, out of greed for their money and property. The news of the crime was brought to Aizia without delay by two Poles from his group who told him of the despicable deed by two of their own compatriots.

The vengeance and style of the punishment to be meted out was already formed in his heart and he asked for three volunteers from among his men for the execution of his parents' murderer and his helpers. The entire platoon volunteered in spite of the danger and difficulties involved. Aizia chose from among them two early members of the group, his good friends the Yugilevych brothers, Poles from Dubno and his girlfriend, Anda. On separating from the group, the friends swore they would never lay down their arms until Hitler had been defeated and the people and their freedom from bondage realized. He delegated himself as his own replacement expressing his supreme confidence that he and his companions would return safe and sound, parting from them affectionately.

It was six in the evening when the four partisans left their encampment in the forest and made their way to the village where their target lived.

After a march of two and a half hours, they stopped about half a kilometer from their destination. Anda was sent forward to scout out the village and report. She returned and announced that the villagers were mostly asleep and that she could detect no sense of preparedness or special awareness, nor any signs of the presence of the police or *Gendarmerie*. After a brief consultation, they decided to enter the village without delay or hesitation. They advanced carefully with Aizia carrying a machine–gun, the senior Yugilevych a Luger and a grenade, his brother armed with a sub–machinegun and ammunition and Anda a pistol with a lovely silver butt taken from a German officer on one of their raids. The murderer's home stood at the edge of the village, a little isolated but well–built and defended structurally. The younger Yugilevych knocked on the window and shouted in German to open the door. When a voice came back questioning why they were being bothered so late at night, he replied that he had been informed from a reliable source that in this house Jews were being hidden and they were here to search the house. The house–owner replied that there were no Jews in there and while opening the door, that he would have liquidated them himself. When he saw Aizia standing there, he fainted.

The entire household was dragged out of their beds, stood in a row in front of a wall and were made to answer questions. The farmer who had fainted had recovered, denied…

[Column 526]

…everything and began to beg for his life. The investigation was short and cruel. Aizia heard from the murderer a description of the killing and the motive for perpetrating the killings. The worker, the Uzbek, was shot first and after him all the rest. Only the old father of the murderer was left alive. Afterwards, gasoline and other flammable liquids were poured out over and inside the house and the structure burnt to the ground with all its contents.

The Meeting with the Gestapo Commander in Dubno

The following day the entire area was riddled with anxiety and fear. The Jews hiding in the adjoining villages fled to the forest or more distant villages. The fear of Aizia and his platoon fell upon everyone who had blood on their hands or guilty consciences due to suspicion of collaboration or informing. The Germans also woke up and sent a large and powerful Lithuanian unit to the area.

In the meantime, stories and legends spread from mouth to mouth concerning the heroic and wonderful deeds and military successes of the partisans against the Germans. Clearly, this was not pleasant for the Germans, and they determined to catch him at all costs and when they failed to do so, they tried guile, suggesting a meeting between Aizia and the Gestapo commandant of Dubno to discuss the conditions under which Aizia would be willing to disband his unit. According to many stories that spread around Dubno and the surroundings, between the survivors of Mizoch and also among the Germans themselves it can be assumed that Aizia did meet the Gestapo commandant of Dubno and told him that he will not lay down his arms until he has avenged all the blood that had been shed of his people and that he lives to see the destruction of Nazi Hitlerite Germany.

How he managed to go free from such a situation is not known: it is said that the platoon was holding a hostage of great importance. The Germans said that the Commandant didn't approve of the murder of the Jews and was secretly very much against Hitler. I heard from a Ukrainian from Mizoch that a platoon of partisans stood guard over the two of them throughout the conversation and that this prevented the *Gendarmerie* from getting to him…nevertheless, the fact that there was such a meeting between Aizia in the office of the Gestapo in a town the size and importance of Dubno is proven beyond the shadow of a doubt because he was indeed a partisan of exceptional courage and insufferable to the Germans. These stories only reinforced their determination to liquidate him.

The Last Battle in which the Heroes Fell

Determined searches were launched throughout the whole region of Volhynia to find Aizia and his platoon. Large rewards were offered for any information that went towards his discovery and whereabouts. And serious punishments were laid upon villages that allowed them entry. But none of it helped. In fact, the attacks by the group increased and became ever more severe. Once they caught two German policemen and forced them to march along the streets of the village shouting: "Hitler is a farce" …

[Column 527]

…Afterwards they made them dress in tattered clothing with the yellow patch on them and sent the men to the village. In broad daylight, they fell upon a convoy that was carrying stolen property from the citizens and returned everything to the villagers. Later on, they stopped killing the Germans immediately but simply defamed them and belittled them and set them free. The fear of being attacked by Aizia's partisans spread throughout the region and they were determined to be rid of him at any cost.

By chance, or perhaps by informers, the Germans discovered his whereabouts toward the end of summer 1944: a farmer, bringing supplies to his base was caught by the Germans on his return from there and they forced…

[Column 528]

…him to take them to the platoon's hiding place. There are those that say that it was all by chance and a misfortune and others that say it was an act of treachery. Whatever the truth, the hiding place was discovered. A large, strong force of Germans was mobilized and brought to the place where a long hard bloody battle took place. The Germans suffered tens of casualties in that last battle and even so were unable to subdue the partisans entirely until they brought in some artillery pieces and captured the stronghold.

The Partisans fought to the bitter end and the last man. To this day, they are remembered by the villagers and farmers of the area and all the Jewish survivors of the Dubno ghetto, Mizoch and the area with admiration and deep respect and pride for the name of Aizia Wassermann.

May his memory be for a blessing.

The banner in the photograph says: "Brit Trumpeldor Dubno Chapter –1930" [6]

Translator's Comments

1. *Betar* is the name of the Zionist Revisionist movement founded by Ze'ev Jabotinsky in1923. *Betar* was the last Jewish stronghold to fall during the Bar Koḥbar revolt in 136 C.E.
2. The Home Army (Polish: *Armia Krajowa*, AK); was the dominant Polish resistance movement in Poland. see: https://en.wikipedia.org/wiki/Home_Army
3. [Note to the reader: the remainder of this line and some additional – unknown – text is missing in our source material; we have no means of recovering it or of identifying what it might be. Trans.]
4. From a poem by Yitzhak Katzenelson
5. Ecclesiastes 10:20
6. *Brit Yosef Trumpeldor* is the mnemonic of the Covenant of Trumpeldor, an earlier close associate of Jabotinsky and an early modern Zionist hero. Joseph Trumpeldor (1880 –1920) was a Russian soldier and an early Zionist activist who helped to organize the Zion Mule Corps and bring Jewish immigrants to Palestine. Trumpeldor died defending the settlement of Tel Hai in 1920 and subsequently became a Zionist national hero.

Historical Questionnaire [1]

About Jewish Communities Destroyed and People Exterminated

Translated from Hebrew by Selwyn Rose

1. The town Dubno. County: Dubno. Country: Poland

2. For how many years was there a Jewish community?

Nearly three-hundred years.

3. How many Jews lived there up until the war?

Nearly ten thousand.

4. What were their main sources of sustenance?

Artisans, laborers, wholesale and retail trading, manufacturing.

5. What community services, charities and societies existed there and how many were there? What socio-cultural foundations, organizations and unions were there in town and what is their fate today? (Such as: synagogues, *Batei-Midrash*, *Yeshivot*, cemeteries, old people's homes, children's hostels, hospitals, society-organized home-visits for the sick and bed-ridden, educational establishments, libraries, evening classes, theatrical groups, cooperatives, banks, charity groups, professional societies and unions of artisans, political parties, etc., etc.).

Apparently, there were: 2 synagogues, one from the year 1700 after the census and the second from about 1850. 34 *Batei-Midrash* and "*Steible*s" (built in the 19th Century). A cemetery from 1750; an old people's home from 1856; a hospital from 1845; a sick visit society from 1890; a library (culture) established in 1923; a private Hebrew gymnasium (Jewish?) named after Dr. Margalit, 1922. A municipal

585

library (1925), Theatrical group (1915), Artisans' supermarket/storehouse (1923), Traders' Bank (1910).

6. What valuable properties and assets were in the hands of the community and owned privately and what was their fate? (Structures, buildings, quarries, registries, holy ritual articles, curtains, perfumes, books, pictures, etc.).

The Community owned: synagogues and *Batei-Midrash*, a hospital, an Old People's Home, an "Ort" educational center for orphans, and a complete row of houses of community owned properties. A *Beit Ha-Midrash*, and about fifteen prayer-rooms and all the *Torah* scrolls were destroyed by fire.

7. The important and significant disturbances since the beginning of the war (1/9/1939)?

[Column 530]

a) Until the Nazi invasion:

The Ukrainians started bullying and robbing the Jewish people and their homes before the Nazi invasion.

b) During the days of the Nazi authority: (The date of the invasion, the first anti-Jewish edicts and laws. The taking of hostages, confiscations and other seizures. Ghettoes (open and closed), tortures, the forced shearing of beards, stigmatization, forced labor, transfer of Jews to other locations and the opposite, pogroms, executions, plunder. How was the final destruction implemented? [the date]).

The Germans entered Dubno 25th June 1941.

On the 28th June 1941, the order was published to wear a white arm-band with a blue Star of David.

On the 30th June 1941, 23 Jews were snatched from the street among them Hershel Rosenfeld, the Rabbi and Father of the Rabbinic Court of Dubno, age about 70, Avraham Eisenberg aged about 45, Doctor Shimon Kagan, aged about 43 (both active Zionists), Meir Geker aged about 30, Khotiner aged about 30 (two Communist supporters), Doctor David Kagan, a Zionist and others. They released Doctor Kagan through the intervention of the Polish priest; the rest suffered torture and terrible beatings. They were shot on the 3rd of August 1941. The remaining Jews were detailed for the hardest and dirtiest of work.

Starting on 10th December 1941, The *Judenrat* was required to supply 1000 men each day for forced labor.

On 29th July 1941, 83 Jews were snatched from the streets among them was Michael Ing, aged about 42, Moshe Gilburt aged about 45, Feldman aged about 40, Milman aged about 35 – all of them important merchants. They were shot to death.

On 19th August 1941, an order was issued to wear a yellow patch.

On 21st August 1941, nearly 1075 Jews were dragged in among them just 3 women and that same day they were all executed by shooting.

On 22nd November 1941, an "*Aktzia*" took place, collecting property: all valuables and food. The "*Aktzia*" affected only the Jewish population according to the registered location of their homes.

On 1st December 1941, fur- and other warm winter-coats confiscated.

On 20th and 21st December 1941, the "*Aktzia*" of collecting valuables from the rest of the refugees who had not until then been plundered, was completed.

On 1st April 1942, a closed ghetto was created for the Jews of Dubno.

[Column 531]

On 27th April 1942, an unruly, wild Nazi "*Aktzia*" took place during which 4000 Jews were liquidated (3800 in pits and 200 in the ghetto).

At the end of May 1942, the Nazis brought into the ghetto about 200 professionals from the villages of Varkovychi (Warkowicze, Varkovitchi) and Ozeryany (Oziran).

On 5th October 1942, the Nazis performed another "*Aktzia*" in which about 4,000 Jews were murdered (about 3500 at a distance of about 3-4 kilometers from Dubno alongside some hay-stacks. Hundreds were killed inside the ghetto. After the "*Aktzia*", 373 souls remained alive (of them 10 excellent professionals and a few counselors).

On 24th October 1942, the last Jewish settlement was liquidated.

8. The relationship of the non-Jewish population toward the Jews and its activities:

The relationship of the non-Jewish Polish and Ukrainian population towards the Jews was decisively hostile and full of hatred.

9. Did the local Jewish population organize any sort of resistance?

There was no organized form of resistance in town.[2]

10. How many Jewish residents of the town remained alive?

About 400.
>   a. About 280 returned from the Soviet Union
>   b. About 60 partisans returned from the forests.

11. Known personages (Liquidated) (name, age, profession, field of activity, date of murder).

1. Rabbi Hershel Bar Mendel Auerbach-Rosenfeld, the esteemed member of the dynastic family of Dubno for many generations, aged about 70, shot on 3/7/41.
2. Dr. Shimon Kagan, aged about 43, a doctor respected by all and a public activist, shot and killed on 3/7/1941.
3. Shmuel Horovitz, a past-chairman of the Community, shot 21/8/1941.
4. Dr. David Kagan, a doctor respected by all.
5. Doctor Toivenfeld, a teacher in the "*Tarbut*" school, head of the *Judenrat*, elected to that post by the Jewish community, he made conspicuous efforts to help the Jewish population of Dubno and was shot to death on 21/7/1942.

Registered in the city of Eggenfelden
Protocol written by: Siritco
4/11/1947
Signed by: Yehuda Schneider
Translated from the Yiddish in Latin characters Yn"Ay

Identified in Yad Va-Shem under the tag 1219/65 Jerusalem
The Central Historical Committee of the liberated Jews of America.

Original Editorial Notes

1. The numbers are not accurate. There are differences – but not big ones – in the dates of the different "*Aktzia*" given here and those provided in the lists of Weisberg and others. We have cited the dates as they were provided to us by different eye-witnesses; it is impossible to determine which dates are the most accurate.
2. Nevertheless, Jews of Dubno did join the partisans in the forests.

Historical Questionnaire [2]

About Jewish Settlements Destroyed and Jewish People Exterminated

Translated from Hebrew by Selwyn Rose

1. The town Dubno, County of Dubno. Country: Poland.

2. How old was the Jewish settlement?

Hundreds of years.

3. How many Jews were there up until the war?

12,000

4. What were the main sources of their sustenance?

Trade and artisans.

5. What public institutions existed there? How many? What is their fate today?
    (Such as: Cultural institutions and activities, synagogues, *Bate-Midrash, Yeshivot,*
    cemeteries; old people's homes, day-care centers, hospitals, charitable
    organizations, sick visits for the bed-ridden and otherwise confined to home;
    educational institutions, libraries, evening-classes, drama groups; cooperatives,
    banks, loan foundations, professional and trade-unions, political parties, etc.,
    etc.).

A Jewish gymnasium. Synagogues and *Batei-Midrash*. Old People' home. Day-care
center. Hospital. Cemetery. All political parties and organizations. Labor and
professional unions.

6. What articles of value were owned by the community, and privately and what was
    their fate?

7. The major disturbances since the beginning of the war (1939).

a)   Up until the Nazi invasion

A revival of Jewish culture under the Soviet regime. The destruction of Jewish entrepreneurship, Jewish high schools were opened.

b)   During the Nazi occupation

[Column 533]

The date of the Nazi invasion. The first anti-Jewish laws. The taking of hostages. Enforced contributions. Confiscations, the ghetto (open or closed), tortures, cutting of beards, distinguishing markings. Forced labor. The transfer of Jews to other places and vice versa. Pogroms. Liquidations. Plundering. How was the community finally destroyed? (Date).

On 25th June 1941 the Nazis entered the town. They took hostages. 100 thousand rubles ransom. The plundering of gold and silver and other valuables. The wearing of a yellow patch from 17.10.41. The initiation of a closed ghetto, the forced labor of men from the age of 13-15 until the age of 65.

  i. There was an "*Aktzia*" on 21.7.41 when 20 Jews were shot to death.
 ii. The second "*Aktzia*" was on 21.8.41 when 1000 Jews were shot to death.
iii. There were two economic "*Aktzia*" on 5.3.42 and 23.3.42
 iv. The creation of the ghetto 2.4.1942. The largest "*Aktzia*" took place on 27.5.1947[1]. Nearly 8000 Jews were executed. They were buried in an air-strip close to town and the Jewish cemetery.
  v. The last economic "*Aktzia*" in the ghetto (the theft of all foodstuffs), took place on 16.7.1942.
 vi. The liquidation of the Jewish ghetto took place on 5.10.1942 (more than 3000 Jews were murdered) and buried in the air-strip and the cemetery.
vii. On 23.10.1942, the last 150 Jews, hiding in bunkers, were executed.

8.   The attitude of the non-Jewish population and its activities.

The Ukrainians behaved towards the Jews worse than the Nazis and were responsible for actively perpetrating virtually all the "*Aktzias*". The Poles and the Russians were no better.

9.   Did the local Jewish population organize any resistance?

- No.

10. How many Dubno Jews remained alive?

- No more than 250 souls.
a.   By unknown means
b.   By various strategies, some in Russia.
- Some were hidden by the Czechs, some in the forests.

11. Known personalities: (Name, age, profession, fields of activity, date of demise).

No persons of prominence or specific public activity are known.

The Historical Society of Landsburg.
Text: M. Weisberg,
Date: 20.5.1947
Witness's signature: M. Weisberg
Translated from the Yiddish.

Original Editorial Note

1.   Clearly an error – it should be 1942

Passover after the Shoah

by Yakov Netaneli–Roitman

Translated from Hebrew by Selwyn Rose

Passover came in '46: in Dubno, the *shul* stayed closed the eve that made holy the day.
Though the snow was melting and the cherry–tree bloomed – each house was bent and ruined, and each roof was in decay.

The streets were bare and empty, not a soul was passing by, the doors gaped wide, as did the gates, yet no one came that way.
Of all the things we dearly loved, the flames devoured them wholly
And only the night's chill wind lamented "This is the bread of our sorrow."

Abandoned seemed each household, a brick from the walls cried out,
An unseen hand strikes out and a buried voice bemoans.
A grateful Christian voice cries out while a flickering alien flame
Eats at the bricks, like a silver candlestick stolen by the Haidamaks.

From "Ha–Boker" [1] 14th Nisan 1946

Translator's Comments

1. *"Ha–Boker"* "This morning" or "The Morning" was a Hebrew–language daily newspaper in Mandate Palestine and later Israel associated with the General Zionists, founded in 1935 by the right–wing of the General Zionists, with the first edition published on 11 October that year.

2. Advising the adoption of my collaborator, Ms. Shirley Ginzburg's erudite analysis of the Hebrew poem's esoteric and literary language; "The author mingles references to traditional parts of the Haggadah, the guide for Passover rituals, celebrated on the Hebrew date 14 Nisan. The family Seder meal would be observed in Dubno, if there were any Jews left to do so. The houses are destroyed and vacant, the synagogue abandoned. The 'doors gaped wide, as did the gates;': During the Seder, a child opens the front door of the home, and all sing to welcome the metaphoric arrival of Elijah the Prophet. Here, they are open—for no one at all! 'This is the bread of our sorrow' recalls the opening line of the Haggadah: *"Ha–lahma Aniyah"* 'A brick cried out...' The Egyptian slaves made bricks for the pyramids. 'An unseen hand strikes out;' alludes to the final plague, killing of the first born, recounted in the Seder. The Haidamaks were Ukrainian Cossacks, who infamously fomented a massacre of Jews in Uman in 1768. Periodically, Cossacks and rioters stole wantonly during pogroms, especially the prized candlesticks used weekly to inaugurate holy times. Without them, there were no flames kindled to usher in the Passover holiday. Profane flames had destroyed Dubno's Jews, their homes and Temple."

From the Bitter Spring

by Netanel Bahiri (Bilizki)

Translated from Hebrew by Jerrold Landau

My pen and paper tremble – with convulsions

What strength do I have to describe everything to you...

I only know this –

To my city, it was as if the ruler prepared against it,

And he, his wife, and children came down, and it fell.

I knew you, my city, as a person knows the palm of his hand

Not one corner was hidden from my eyes

And I did not know only this –

Where the lad was hiding, strong in build

And where he was spilled like blood at the frightening time...

I knew that they destroyed my city from the face of the earth –

The poretz, uncircumcised Stas, and Ivan;

And now, woe to life,

Did they destroy the image of the honor of G-d within you,

Or did you fall full of indignation, as a partisan falls?

You stand before my eyes alive, young, bustling

Even though I have already lost your picture, for some time,

The nobility of your splendor, which was so spellbinding and enchanting,

It storms upon me heavily, and with bitter sadness.

And with you everything is emptied out, and they live: Father, Mother, and the like

Your small room, which filled me with great happiness, so great,

Even your enchanting aunt, Aunt Breina,

Stands before me with a kerchief wrapped around her elderly head.

I will remember what you said: Father and Mother, I will not abandon you…

(I knew, you were one with them, pampered and alone)

And I indeed left them, and the wind erased my footsteps,

In the remote station, snowy, stormy, and isolated.

I will ask – and who does not know my mouth – where are you, where are you both together?

Alas, what happened to you there, oh proper daughter of Israel?

During the time of destruction and fear, did the dark, evil hands of the murderers

Also hone over your head the cutting knife?...

From Yiddish: Y. Netaneli

Translator's Comments

1.   A poretz is a term for a landowner.
2.   I reversed some of the stiches of the last two lines for clarity.

The Krypister family who poisoned themselves in their home on the day of the "Aktzia"

The Empty Heavens

By Rabbi Leibish Vinokur[1]

Translated from Hebrew by Selwyn Rose

The event occurred three days after the *Shavuot* festival in the year TRZ"G[2] (1942) 14th. At that time, I was in the home of Rabbi Eliyahu Guttmann (May G–d avenge his blood), when they came and took Rabbi Yisrael Yudl Diamond, a known businessman and the son–in–law of Perl, for execution. "Rabbi!" I screamed – "Rabbi, can you see who they are taking?"

Rabbi Eliyahu, who was standing next to the window, raised his eyes skyward and cried "Hear, O Israel! The Lord our God is One!" and he fell silent.

After a few moments, he lowered his gaze and murmured: "Escape for your lives...the heavens are empty..."

Original and Translator's Comments

1. As recalled by Rabbi Leibish Vinokur of Dubno, in Israel in TSH"T (1949)
2. The author has defined the year in both everyday Arabic numerals and also the Hebrew system. There is a definite conflict between the two: the Hebrew year TRZ"G is quite definitely 1933 and NOT 1942. (trans)

The Days of Suffering and Pain

by Shoshana Somberg-Gon

Translated from Yiddish by Pamela Russ

From the first moment that the German captors entered Dubno, they cast terror over everyone. They immediately began snatching up people for work. Whoever went out into the street – risked his own life. A German, or a Ukrainian assistant, was able to capture him. And capturing meant – not necessarily for work, but also for torturing, which ended in death.

This happened at the time we lived in the ghetto. One of the members of the Judenrat was moving to a more comfortable room and in order to move his things, he mobilized some workers from the Jewish workers' office. There were no means of transport and the people worked hard bringing over his things quite a distance away. After putting his things inside, it appeared that a washing tub was missing, which they found by one of the laborers – Berko Meidit, who had a paralyzed hand, and whom the Germans themselves freed from work. The Jewish police decided to pass an "open judgement" on him, and that was no more than cruelty, because they beat him so severely that he ended up needing a doctor.

Participating in this act was the commandant Fritz Siss, whose name will be cursed eternally, along with others, among whom was – Groisblat.

This act of the Jewish police stirred up the ghetto residents, and in protest, some of Meidit's neighbors carried him home in front of everybody's eyes. My husband and I tried to turn in one of the

policemen whom we met en route. But he informed on us to the commandant Siss and they told us to present ourselves to the police. What was waiting for us was very clear. We escaped through a window and hid in a bunker which was a place the police did not know about. We remained there for more than twenty-four hours, went through great fear hearing how the police were in the same room and were emptying out everything. Afterwards, we found out that they had even taken the pillows. That's how we escaped our punishment.

However, the other Jews who supported Meidit, were punished by the Jewish police receiving twenty lashes each.

This was the regime of terror of the Jewish police in the ghetto, with Commandant Siss at the head. They were convinced that "Nothing will happen to us". And their end was no different than that of the other ghetto residents, with the difference only being time…

*

When it became clear that they were going to enclose the Jews into a ghetto, I went to Meisliches' mill to buy some flour for these difficult times. It was I who went because the men were afraid to be seen in the streets.

As soon as I went into the street, I noticed an unusual group of Ukrainian police who were chasing the Jews. I was not afraid and continued on my way. Two policemen stopped me and without a word, they began to beat me and drag me off to "work."

We came to the prison building. Groups of Jews appeared on all sides. Among these groups were – a number of Jewish women. They chased us into the prison yard and told us to lie down on the ground, face down. Whoever spoke even one word or made even the slightest movement was beaten murderously by the policemen. After such tortures for several hours, the "*selektzia*"[selection] began. The young and healthy were ordered to go to a table around which there were Gestapo men, and they sorted: right, left. Those who had "work permits" were freed, but in the process, they were given many beatings.

One Ukrainian mercilessly made fun of the respected elder Sh. Hurwich. He tore out his beard. After that, he tied up the elderly man with a wire, and showed off his achievement to his fellow murderers.

My brother Pesakh was shot on the spot. Someone else had his ear cut off in one motion, and he was left lying in a puddle of blood.

In every corner and place there were terrible screams. New groups kept on coming. They were given shovels and ordered to go dig ditches.

It was my row's turn to appear before the murderers. I begged them to release me because I had left a small child behind. Because this "*Aktzia*" was mainly for men, they let me go. As I left the prison, I had to pass in front of rows of Ukrainians who beat me until I fell over, all bloodied and with torn clothes. How I was lucky enough to reach the first Jewish house – I don't know, but there I received help for the first time, they washed me up and changed my clothing. Later I went home. I still heard shooting on the way. They were shooting the captured Jews whom I had seen in the prison yard. 1,400 men died on that dark day. Fathers and sons, among them – 13 women. There were 14 women, and I remained the only one alive…

This is a photograph taken in Germany of Dubno survivors.
They are holding a Memorial to the Martyrs of Dubno.

A Necklace of Sadness for Senele
and the Eight Hundred Children who Perished in One
Day[1]

by Yacov Netaneli-Roitman

Translated from Hebrew by Selwyn Rose

As I stood gazing mournfully at the devastated town of Dubno, all that met my eye was a solitary cherry-tree standing in the garden of what had been our home, beladen with the ripe, blood-red fruit. All that could be seen in the deathly silence was the glow of a red-hot bar of iron from the burning rubble rending asunder the bricks enclosing it as its heat caused the bricks to split. Only the cherry-tree was afire, its glowing-red fruit calling out in the silence for rebellion.

As market day came to a close in Dubno on the banks of the River Ikwa, Jewish homes were set ablaze and a thick pall of smoke covering the town lay like a carpet over everything.

The unspeakably evil Asmodeus, who knew only to create horror among Man, became personified by the rioting Germans, shooting at everyone with their machine guns or force-marching young children along, among whom was Senele, with volleys of shots; it was not far to walk…

An evil one grasped the young artist with the soul of a poet who, clutching a stick of charcoal created a living breathing image of Marshal Pilsudski with his magnificent mustache on the pavement. Then uncle and grandfather quickly appeared chatting with the neighbor Malka-Etta, gazing wonderingly at the innocent child's creation on the ground.

The fresh ripening fruit on the cherry-tree attracted the attention of passersby and from the *Heder* came the sounds of *"Akdamot Milin"*[2] carried on the air as a warming refrain arising from the razed fields after the pain and suffering of the destruction.

The diminutive Nethaniel now appeared alone at the doorway of the Rabbi's house and study and entered the pit of hell. He bore in his hand a brush well-dipped in color and he carried it into the heavens like a magician wafted on high from the thick branches of the tree. And there in the skies appeared a castle, a river, the hillsides of Dubno her meadows, forests and suburbs, her markets and fairs, the hustle, bustle and confusion of her streets, the synagogue with its magnificent Holy Ark, all in contrast to the ringing of the church bells pealing out their glee at the suffering of the Jews.

And among them stood the cherry-tree beneath which stood two others and over all yet two more, bearing between them the first fruits on their way to *Yerushalyim*…And again, a puzzling grandfather and father will come, unable to understand how the senses of such a small child could create such complex images?...

And today behold: there is no Senele…while a toad and a frog in a springtime chorus are heard incessantly…So come and see as the street awakens, weep with mourners in the street. The hand of a Haidamak has strewn arrows around leaving only brush and thorn-bushes. On the ground beneath the cherry-tree, *Tikun Shavuot*[3] is taking place and we weep together with them and strike our heads against the wall…

Come and see – there is no Senele – his glowing eye has weakened, and the colorful sky has become grey and dull like a leaden bullet.

Today, in the Baratz *Beit-Midrash* I saw a dancing competition taking place. It was not night-time and there was no dawn and torches were lighted at dusk. From every side, from every grave night-clothes flew in the air and there was a pile of bodiless heads of children heaped against the walls. They came out to read the *"Akdamot"* together, but their mouths brought forth only dry canes and reeds for the event.

It was as if on a blooming colorful flowerbed of azure, yellow and red, silence poured all over a disappointed orchestra of what had gone before; mouths whispering from decapitated heads the story of the robbery and pillage and the helpless dancing without bodies, without blood and without limbs.

Oh, cherry-tree, oh, cherry-tree, for whom do you bloom? If it is for the devouring German then deprive him of it…cherry-tree oh, cherry-tree for whom are your berries? If for the Haidamaks may you cause your blossoms to rot…

Land, oh, land. Oh, grazing meadows of Satan, let no peace come upon you, may eternal silence be your fate; may the fruit bring forth nothing but a curse upon you and may your soul be placed upon the pyre.

Tel-Aviv, the Festival of Shavuot 1946.

Translator's Comments

1. The Hebrew original to this piece appears as a poem. However, the poem contains many local and highly esoteric allegories, metaphors and imagery that made it advisable to render it into everyday prose.
2. *Akdamot*: A highly esoteric and *Talmudic*, encoded Aramaic prayer written around 1095 and recited on the Festival of Shavuot, mainly - but not exclusively - in Ashkenazi communities. For a full commentary see: https://en.wikipedia.org/wiki/Akdamut
3. *Tikun Shavuot* A religious debate special to the Festival of Weeks – Pentecost, *Shavuot*

Dubno after the Liberation

by Sioma
(From a private letter)

Translated from Yiddish by Pamela Russ

Many friends have already received letters from their acquaintances, and everyone is asking the same thing: "Who is left alive?" Because of a population of 12,000 souls, only 40–50 are left, and in conditions that are unimaginable – in forests, ditches, and the like. I will try to describe what we experienced in that terrible period. Even if I would write an entire book, it would still be doubtful whether I could recount that of our hellish lives. But I will try, in general strokes, to describe that period.

Standing at the edge of a mass grave

In the years of 1939–41, I occupied a head office in a willow tree sawmill. Our physical lives were good, we lived peacefully, and even went to Lvov frequently. But this ended very quickly. The sudden assault on June 22 put an end to everything. Oh, how the tragic Yona wanted to go deep into Russia, but we did not allow him. And now I blame myself for his death because I allowed myself to be convinced by my wife Priva not to let him go. The end was that both were killed.

With the first moment that the Germans entered, the horrors began. The first sign was – the yellow patch. Every German could spit at a Jew, denigrate, and insult him, for which there was no

[Column 727–728]

Survivors standing at the edge of a mass grave

punishment. Every Jew had to bow down or even stretch out on the ground in front of every passing German. Woe to that Jew who did not heed these orders stringently. Capturing Jews and beating them was a daily activity.

Two months after the German occupation of the city, all the Jews were transported to the ghetto. Everything was quickly "organized" in an administrative manner, because you could not take anything or any food with you. That's how some families were taken there to live in unimaginable crowdedness, without any sanitation conditions, always being harassed, young and old, from morning to night, and taken to hard labor.

Every day we thought that it could not be worse. But that which never even came into our minds, was not even difficult for the thugs. They were not satisfied with starving, terrorizing, and humiliating us – because they knew that Jews lived with the faith that the rage would pass. One fine Thursday, they assembled the best of the Jewish youth, the handsome and healthy ones, took them off to prison, and from there – to the cemetery, and told them to dig out graves, and there they met their death. But the murderers were not happy with this and two days later they murdered another 200 victims in the same manner.

From that time on, each Jew considered himself a living dead. Death was always with us. The people were already very skilled at interpreting the events, and various horrific rumors were our daily servings. Fear consumed every spark of hope that remained in our hearts. At dawn, on February 27, the Germans sorted all the ghetto residents into skilled workers and non-workers. Those "so-called" without a skill,

[Column 729–730]

were evacuated to Surmicze where mass graves had been prepared in order to kill them there. Rivers of blood and tears flowed. Many lost their minds, and their cries reached the heavens. But all was for nothing. German precision demanded that the people position themselves four in a row, in an organized manner – and "disciplined" and "organized" like that, 3,500 pure and holy souls were murdered only because they were born as Jews.

Among the victims – were my dear mother and father and other relatives. Those who survived were Yankel, Zelda, Loybe, Priva, Yona, and I. In October, on *Shemini Atzeres* and *Simkhas Torah* [the last two days of the Sukos holiday], the ghetto was once again encircled. From the remaining population, they selected 350 skilled workers and 3,800 others, and transported them all to their death, all the while beating, punishing, and shooting young children on the way. Among those who died were my relatives. I, Priva, and Yona escaped into the forest. After this *Aktzia*, we returned to the ghetto thinking that with this final act it was over. But one tragic Sabbath, a gang of Ukrainians under German command arrived, and as in the previous manner, they murdered the last survivors.

The city had become a cemetery. The peasants took to looting and wherever they discovered a Jew, they handed him over to the Germans for a reward.

In a camouflaged hiding place, we were able to save ourselves from a slaughter. It is impossible to imagine the risks we took as we escaped into the forest and hid there by Gurbik. We were there for three weeks with only the shirts on our backs – and this right in the winter. We went into the city, and they saw us, recognized us, and captured us. They killed Priva, and I escaped, wandering around like a shadow. Yona was not around, and Priva was also dead. They murdered the dearest people. And in my heart, there was the thought that I was left alive in order to be able to take revenge. This feeling of revenge gave me the strength to live. I fled into the forest, suffered hunger and cold, and begged for death to relieve me from the ghosts by day and by night – but I lived despite it all.

The Red Army began to come closer and the Germans – to recede. As a Polish forced laborer (I had Aryan papers under the name of

[Column 731–732]

Butnar Kowycz), they sent me over to Krakow. And from there, 5,000 forced laborers were sent to dig the defense line on the San River. I felt that victory was near and I had to remain alive in order to be able to retell what we had experienced and to take revenge. I began to work well, energetically. A German colonel arrived, and they summoned me to him, and the Nazi officer presented me as an example of a Pole that loyally serves the Germans, and blessed be the Polish nation that they have such a son...

The Russians continued to attack. I and another eighteen people were lucky to escape from the camp and hide in the forest until the Russians came and freed us. I went 500 kilometers on foot and finally arrived in Lutsk. I was arrested by the NKVD [Soviet Secret Police] and sat in prison for 14 days. When I proved that I was a Jew, they let me go free.

I am alive. Is this a life? I am wandering among the destruction, lonely and alone, without a living soul with whom I can exchange one word, without anyone recognizing me. I work as a bookkeeper, but after work, life is not really life. I am looking for a way to take revenge: for Priva's death – 100 Germans; Yona's death – 1,000 Germans!

Yes, I found Batya with her two daughters. That's it. As I am writing, blood is dripping out of my heart, tears are running from my eyes. For how much longer will I be able to go on? Greetings to all.

Your Sioma[1]

I would so much like to be together with you, see someone from the family, from our nation, tell of the German horrors of death, tell and tell, so that the future generations will know.

No resting! Let no Jew in this world be silent! We all have to take revenge! Revenge!

The survivors of Dubno Jews in Germany

Dubner [those from Dubno] after planting trees in the "Martyrs' Forest"

The banner in the photo says:
"19 years after the Shoah of the community of Dubno – 5722 [1962]

Original Comments

1. The author of these lines later died in a car accident.
2. The text has been translated from Russian.

Necrology

List of the holy victims of the Dubno community

[Please note that the numbers in "Column No." refer to the column numbers of the original book.]

Last Name	Maiden Name	First Name	Gender	Spouse's First Name	Column no.
ADLER		Pesakh	Male		733
ADLER		Rakhel	Female		733
ADLER		Yekhezkel	Male		733
ADLER		Yitzkhak	Male		733
AKSMAN		Boris	Male		733
AKSMAN		Sara	Female		733
ALEKSANDER		Beniamin	Male		733
ALEKSANDER		Max	Male		733
ALEKSANDER		Moshe	Male		733
ALEKSANDER		Tzila	Female		733
ALTERMAN		Avraham	Male		733
ALTERMAN		Feiga	Female		733
ALTERMAN		Khava	Female		733
BALABAN		Ben Ami	Male		734
BALABAN		Hinda	Female		734
BALABAN		Shlomo	Male		734
BARDIGA		Feiga	Female		735
BARDIGA		Khana	Female		735
BARDIGA		Mirl	Female		735
BARDIGA		Rakhel	Female		735
BARDIGA		Reizl	Female		735
BARDIGA		Yehuda	Male		735
BARU		Masha			735
BARU		Menukha	Female		735
BARU		Pinkhas	Male		735
BARU		Tzvi	Male		735
BAT					751
BELFER		Bela	Female		734
BELFER		Beril	Male		734
BELFER		David	Male		734

BELFER		Khana	Female		734
BELFER		Meir	Male		734
BELFER		Miriam	Female		734
BELFER		Motil	Male		734
BELFER		Roza	Female		735
BELFER		Sara	Female		735
BELFER		Sheike	Male		735
BELFER		Shlomo	Male		735
BELFER		Yehudi	Male		734
BELFER		Yehudit	Female		734
BERGER		Barukh	Male		735
BERGER		Barukh	Male		735
BERGER		Batia	Female		735
BERGER		Batia	Female		735
BERGER		Bila	Female		735
BERGER		Chila			735
BERGER		Dina	Female		751
BERGER		Efraim	Male		735
BERGER		Efraim	Male		735
BERGER		Elka	Female		735
BERGER		Ester	Female		735
BERGER		Gitel	Female		735
BERGER		Hertzel	Male		751
BERGER		Hirsh	Male		735
BERGER		Junda			735
BERGER		Lea	Female		735
BERGER		Liba			735
BERGER		Lova	Female		735
BERGER		Melia	Female		735
BERGER		Melia			735
BERGER		Mordekhai	Male		735
BERGER		Moshe	Male		735

BERGER		Moshe	Male		735
BERGER		Motel	Male		735
BERGER		Natan	Male		735
BERGER		Nisan	Male		735
BERGER		Pesia	Female		735
BERGER		Pinkhas	Male		735
BERGER		Pinkhas	Male		735
BERGER		Risia	Female		735
BERGER		Rivka	Female		735
BERGER		Rivka	Female		735
BERGER		Ruzia	Female		735
BERGER		Shprintza	Female		735
BERGER		Shprintza	Female		735
BERGER		Tova	Female		735
BERGER		Tzvi	Male		735
BERGER		Yekhiel	Male		735
BERGER		Yekhiel	Male		735
BERGER		Yona			735
BERGER		Zlata	Female		735
BERKOVSKI					735
BIBERMAN		Efraim	Male		734
BIBERMAN		Khaia	Female		734
BIKHMAN		Anshel	Male		734
BIKHMAN		Ester	Female		734
BIKHMAN		Golda	Female		734
BIKHMAN		Khaia	Female		734
BIKHMAN		Mania	Female		734
BIKHMAN		Reuven	Male		734
BINSHTOK		Batia	Female		736
BINSHTOK		Malka	Female		734
BINSHTOK		Motil			736
BINSHTOK		Perel	Female		736

BINSHTOK		Pnina	Female		734
BINSHTOK		Sara	Female		736
BINSHTOK		Yisrael	Male		734
BITELMAN		Bila	Female		734
BITELMAN		David	Male		734
BLAT		Berish	Male		751
BLUMAN		Aharon	Male		734
BLUMAN		Malka	Female		734
BLUMAN		Mordekhai	Male		734
BLUMAN		Pesia	Female		734
BLUMAN		Shmuel	Male		734
BLUMAN		Yosef	Male		734
BLUMAN		Zlata	Female		734
BOBER		Arie Leib	Male		734
BOBER		Dvora	Female		734
BOBER		Ester	Female		734
BOBER		Golda	Female		733
BOBER		Golda	Female		734
BOBER		Hersh	Male		733
BOBER		Khava	Female		734
BOBER		Moshe	Male		734
BOBER		Tzvi	Male		734
BOIDER		Yitzkhak	Male		751
BOKSER		Bluma	Female		734
BOKSER		Hersh	Male		734
BRANSHTEIN		Asher	Male		751
BRANSHTEIN		Malka	Female		735
BRANSHTEIN		Mikhael	Male		735
BRED		Tema			735
BRED		Yitzkhak	Male		735
BRIDER		Shmuel	Male		735
BRILIANT		Rivka	Female		735

619

BRILIANT		Ester	Female		735
BRILIANT		Meir	Male		735
BRILIANT		Tibel			735
BRONSHTEIN		Asher	Male		735
BRONSHTEIN		Fridl			735
BRONSHTEIN		Gitel			735
BRONSHTEIN	KAGAN	Khaia	Female		735
BRONSHTEIN		Lea	Female		735
BRONSHTEIN		Mania	Female		735
BRONSHTEIN		Nesi			735
BRONSHTEIN		Nusia			735
BRONSHTEIN		Rivka	Female		735
BRONSHTEIN		Yaakov	Male		735
BRONSHTEIN		Yitzkhak	Male		735
BRONSHTEIN		Yosef	Male		735
BUDOKER		Rakhel	Female		734
BUDOKER		Rivka	Female		734
BUDOKER		Yosef	Male		734
BUKHBINDER		Alter	Male		734
BUKHBINDER		Bluma	Female		734
BUKHBINDER		Feiga	Female		734
BUKHBINDER		Henia	Female		734
BUKHBINDER	DRATUR	Ita	Female		734
BUKHBINDER		Roza	Female		734
BUNDUR		Yitzkhak	Male		734
BURSHTEIN		Avraham	Male		734
BURSHTEIN		Avraham	Male		735
BURSHTEIN		Bila	Female		734
BURSHTEIN		Bluma	Female		734
BURSHTEIN		Hersh	Male		734
BURSHTEIN		Mania			735
BURSHTEIN		Yenta	Female		734

BURSHTEIN		Yosef	Male		734
BURSHTEIN		Zeev	Male		735
BUSKIS		Bila	Female		734
BUSKIS		Feiga	Female		734
BUSKIS		Felik	Male		734
BUSKIS		Genya	Female		734
BUSKIS		Khana	Female		734
BUSKIS		Lea	Female		734
BUSKIS		Libka	Male		734
BUSKIS		Moshe	Male		734
BUSKIS		Yenta	Female		734
BUSKIS		Zunia	Female		734
BUSKIS		Eliezer	Male		734
BUSKIS		Reuven	Male		734
BUSKIS		Zelda	Female		734
CHERNIAVSKI		Batia	Female		747
CHERNIAVSKI		Brakha	Female		747
CHERNIAVSKI		Kopel	Male		747
CHERNIAVSKI		Mendel	Male		747
CHERNIAVSKI		Moshe	Male		747
CHERNIAVSKI		Rizel	Female		747
CHERNIAVSKI		Yosef	Male		747
DAJCZMAN		Aharon	Male		737
DAJCZMAN		Barukh	Male		737
DAJCZMAN		Reuven	Male		737
DAJCZMAN		Sara	Female		737
DAJCZMAN		Yosef	Male		737
DANZIGER		David	Male		738
DANZIGER		Khaia	Female		738
DANZIGER		Tova	Female		738
DANZIGER		Yehoshua	Male		738
DEIBOG		Anushka			737

DEIBOG		Lusik			737
DEIBOG		Moti	Male		737
DEMB		Khava	Female		738
DEMB		Lea	Female		738
DEMB		Moshe	Male		738
DEMB		Nekhemia	Male		738
DEMB		Rakhel	Female		738
DEMB		Rakhel	Female		738
DEMB		Rivka	Female		738
DEMB		Sara	Female		738
DEMB		Sara	Female		738
DEMB		Tzvi	Male		738
DIAMANT		Malka	Female		737
DIAMANT		Yisrael Yehuda	Male		737
DRATVER		Bluma	Female		738
DRATVER		Ester	Female		738
DRATVER		Hinda	Female		738
DRATVER		Ita	Female		738
DRATVER		Khaim	Male		738
DRATVER		Shlomo	Male		738
DRATVER		Tehila	Female		738
DRATVER		Tolik			738
DRATVER		Yitzkhak	Male		738
EIZEN		David	Male		751
EIZEN		Giser			751
EIZENBERG		Brakha	Female		733
EIZENBERG		Gdaliahu	Male		733
EIZENBERG		Kalman	Male		733
EIZENBERG	GUTMAN	Khaia	Female		733
EIZENBERG		Libish	Male		733
EIZENBERG		Rakhel	Female		733
EIZENBERG		Sheindl	Female		733

EIZENBERG		Yosef	Male		733
EIZENBERG		Zlata			733
EIZENSHTAT		Asik	Male		751
EIZENSHTAT		David	Male		751
EIZENSHTAT		Ester	Female		751
EIZENSHTAT		Greisha	Male		751
EIZENSHTAT		Reuven	Male		751
EIZENSHTAT		Yitzkhak	Male		751
EIZENSHTAT		Zelik	Male		751
ELBERT		David	Male		751
ENGELMAN		Frida	Female		733
ENGELMAN		Yehuda	Male		733
EPSHTEIN		Moshe	Male		733
ERDMAN		Ada	Female		733
ERDMAN		Moshe	Male		733
ERDMAN		Roza	Female		733
ERDMAN		Yaakov	Male		733
FEFER		Hinda	Female		746
FEFER		Shimon David	Male		746
FEFER		Sonia	Female		746
FELDMAN		Avraham	Male		752
FELDMAN		Charna	Female		745
FELDMAN		Doba	Male		745
FELDMAN		Eli Moshe	Male		745
FELDMAN		Hinda	Female		745
FELDMAN		Khana	Female		745
FELDMAN		Lea	Female		745
FELDMAN		Malka	Female		745
FELDMAN		Motel	Male		745
FELDMAN		Nakhum	Male		745
FELDMAN		Vitia	Male		745
FELISHER		Batia	Female		745

FELISHER		David	Male		745
FELISHER		Ester	Female		745
FELISHER		Rivka	Female		745
FELISHER		Sosia			745
FELISHER		Yehoshua	Male		745
FELISHER		Yukel			745
FELISHER		Zusia	Male		745
FIERMAN		David	Male		745
FIERMAN		Dina	Female		745
FIERMAN		Dov Berl	Male		745
FIERMAN		Eti	Female		745
FIERMAN		Khana	Female		745
FIERMAN		Liba	Female		745
FIERMAN		Riba	Female		745
FIERMAN		Sheindl	Female		745
FIERMAN		Shmariahu	Male		745
FIERMAN		Zlata	Female		745
FIGORILIDER		Bluma	Female		752
FIGORILIDER		Charni	Female		752
FIGORILIDER		Fani	Female		752
FIKS		Moshe	Male		745
FIKS		Munia	Female		745
FIKS	EFRAT	Pulia	Female		745
FIKS		Shlomo	Male		745
FIKS		Yokheved	Female		745
FINKELSHTEIN		Batsheva	Female		745
FINKELSHTEIN		Shlomo	Male		744
FIRER		Velvil	Male		745
FIRER		Yosef	Male		745
FISHBIN		Aharon	Male		745
FISHBIN		Aharon	Male		745
FISHBIN		Avraham	Male		745

FISHBIN		Dina	Female		745
FISHBIN		Ita	Female		745
FISHBIN		Khaia	Female		745
FISHBIN		Khaia	Female		745
FISHBIN		Mordekhai	Male		745
FISHBIN		Moshe	Male		745
FISHBIN		Munia			745
FISHBIN		Rivka	Female		745
FISHBIN		Sara	Female		745
FISHBIN		Shimon	Male		745
FISHBIN		Tzila	Female		745
FISHBIN		Tzvi	Male		745
FISHBIN		Yisrael	Male		745
FISHBIN		Yosef	Male		745
FISHER		Brakha	Female		745
FISHER		David	Male		745
FISHER		David	Male		745
FISHER		Ester	Female		745
FISHER		Frida	Female		745
FISHER		Gitel	Female		745
FISHER		Khana	Female		745
FISHER		Lea	Female		745
FISHER		Libka			745
FISHER		Mikhael	Male		745
FISHER		Shlomo	Male		745
FISHMAN		Itamar	Male		745
FISHMAN		Khaikel	Male		745
FISHMAN		Mikhael	Male		745
FISHMAN		Perel	Female		745
FISHMAN		Pinkhas	Male		745
FISHMAN		Sara	Female		745
FISHMAN		Sara	Female		745

FISHMAN		Shula	Female		745
FLEISHER		Shmariahu	Male		752
FLEISHMAN		Avraham	Male		752
FLEISHMAN		Yehuda	Male		752
FREKHTER		Henia	Female		746
FREKHTER		Peril	Female		746
FREKHTER		Rizel	Female		746
FREKHTER		Yitzkhak	Male		746
FRENKEL		Bila	Female		746
FRENKEL		Eliahu	Male		746
FRENKEL		Khaia	Female		746
FRENKEL		Khaim	Male		746
FRENKEL		Malka	Female		746
FRENKEL		Meita			746
FRENKEL		Menukha	Female		746
FRENKEL		Sara	Female		746
FRENKEL		Tova	Female		746
FRIDMAN		Khana	Female		746
FRIDMAN		Yosef	Male		746
FRIMAN		Avraham	Male		746
FRIMAN		Barukh	Male		746
FRIMAN		Bila	Female		746
FRIMAN		Brakha	Female		746
FRIMAN		Kila			746
FRIMAN		Rakhel	Female		746
FRIMAN		Sara	Female		746
FRIMAN		Yisrael	Male		746
FRIMAN		Yosef	Male		746
FRIMERMAN		Rivka	Female		746
FRIMERMAN		Sheindl	Female		746
FRIMERMAN		Tova	Female		746
FRIMERMAN		Yaakov	Male		746

FRIMERMAN		Yitzkhak	Male		746
FUKS		Avraham	Male		751
FUKS		Mordekhai	Male		752
FUKS		Shmuel	Male		752
FUKS			Male	Avraham	751
GALPERSON		Avraham	Male		737
GALPERSON		Hershel	Male		737
GALPERSON		Shmuel	Male		737
GALPERSON		Yaakov	Male		737
GALURIN		Luzia	Female		735
GALURIN		Sonia	Female		735
GAMBURG		Feiga	Female		737
GAMBURG		Moshe	Male		737
GAMBURG		Reizl	Female		737
GAMBURG		Simkha			737
GAMBURG		Yaakov	Male		737
GARELNIK		Avraham	Male		737
GEIERMAN		Fania	Female		737
GEIERMAN		Yekhezkel	Male		737
GEIFLER		Barukh Leib	Male		737
GEIFLER		Bela	Female		737
GEIFLER		Etil			737
GEIFLER		Feiga	Female		737
GEIFLER		Peretz	Male		737
GEIFLER		Rivka	Female		737
GEIFLER		Yaakov	Male		737
GEKER		Hersh	Male		751
GEKER		Sheindl	Female		751
GELFENBOIM					737
GERSHTEIN		Moshe	Male		737
GERSHTEIN		Rafael	Male		737
GERSHTEIN		Tehila	Female		737

GERSHTEIN		Tzvi	Male		737
GERTZ		Khana	Female		737
GERTZ		Roza	Female		737
GERTZ		Sara	Female		737
GERTZ		Yeshayahu	Male		737
GERTZ		Yitzkhak	Male		737
GIL		Eli	Male		736
GIL		Feiga	Female		736
GIL		Hertzel	Male		736
GIL		Khaim	Male		736
GIL		Lea	Female		736
GIL		Mikhael	Male		736
GILBURG		Ester	Female		736
GILBURG		Ezra	Male		736
GILBURG		Ita	Female		736
GILBURG		Sara	Female		736
GILBURG		Shoshana	Female		736
GILRANT		Lusia	Female		737
GILRANT		Sheindl	Female		737
GILRANT		Yosef	Male		737
GIMAN		Aharon	Male		737
GIMAN		Eliezer	Male		737
GIMAN		Moshe	Male		737
GIMAN		Roza	Female		737
GITELMAN		Eliezer	Male		736
GITELMAN		Gershon	Male		736
GITELMAN		Lea	Female		736
GITELMAN	KOLISH	Mina	Female		736
GITELMAN		Soni			736
GOBERMAN		Avraham	Male		751
GOBERMAN		Gitel	Female		751
GOHEN		Meir	Male		736

GOHEN		Sima	Female		736
GOHEN		Yitzkhak	Male		736
GOKHBERG		Eliezer	Male		736
GOKHBERG		Ester	Female		736
GOKHBERG		Izik	Male		736
GOKHBERG		Khaia	Female		736
GOKHBERG		Khaia	Female		736
GOKHBERG		Khaim	Male		736
GOKHBERG		Malka	Female		736
GOKHBERG		Moshe	Male		736
GOKHBERG		Motil			736
GOKHBERG		Risel	Female		736
GOKHBERG		Sosia	Female		736
GOKHBERG		Susil			736
GOKHBERG		Yaakov	Male		736
GOLCEKER		Bela	Female		736
GOLCEKER		Beniamin	Male		736
GOLCEKER		Ita	Female		736
GOLCEKER		Khaia	Female		736
GOLCEKER		Khinka	Female		736
GOLCEKER		Mania	Female		736
GOLCEKER		Moshe	Male		736
GOLCEKER		Yeshayahu	Male		736
GOLCEKER		Yosef	Male		736
GOLDARBEITER		Bluma	Female		736
GOLDARBEITER		Eliezer Tzvi	Male		736
GOLDARBEITER		Feiga	Female		736
GOLDARBEITER		Golda	Female		736
GOLDARBEITER		Khava	Female		736
GOLDARBEITER		Lea	Female		736
GOLDARBEITER		Leib	Male		736
GOLDARBEITER		Nekhama	Female		736

GOLDARBEITER		Paltiel	Male		736
GOLDARBEITER		Rivka	Female		736
GOLDARBEITER		Yosef	Male		736
GOLDBLAT			Male		751
GOLDENBERG		Frida	Female		736
GOLDENBERG		Zelig	Male		736
GOLDMAN		Gitel	Female		736
GOLDMAN		Rakhel	Female		736
GOLDMAN		Sonia	Female		736
GOLDSHTEIN		Khana	Female		751
GOLDSHTEIN		Moti	Male		751
GOLDSHTEIN		Shefi	Male		751
GOLDSHTEIN		Shlomo	Male		751
GOLMETZER		Fania	Female		737
GOLMETZER		Malka	Female		737
GOLMETZER		Melia	Female		737
GOLMETZER		Yael	Female		737
GOSHKIS		Eliahu	Male		736
GOSHKIS		Fruma	Female		736
GOSHKIS		Klara	Female		736
GOSHKIS		Sara	Female		736
GOSHKIS	MENKES	Yafa	Female		736
GOTLIB		Frida	Female		736
GOTLIB		Rika	Female		736
GRINSHPUN		Bebi			737
GRINSHPUN		Khaia	Female		737
GRINSHPUN		Rozshka	Female		737
GRINZWEIG		Azriel	Male		737
GRINZWEIG		Berta	Female		737
GRINZWEIG		Brunia	Female		737
GRINZWEIG		Fishel	Male		737
GRINZWEIG		Hinda	Female		737

GRINZWEIG		Malka	Female		737
GRINZWEIG		Memtzi			737
GRINZWEIG		Mordekhai	Male		737
GRINZWEIG		Nakhum	Male		737
GRINZWEIG		Niusa			737
GRINZWEIG		Osna	Female		737
GRINZWEIG		Sara	Female		737
GRINZWEIG		Sonia	Female		737
GRINZWEIG		Tzvi	Male		737
GRINZWEIG		Yitzkhak	Male		737
GROINEM		Yitzkhak	Male		737
GROIPEN		Aharon	Male		751
GROISBLAT		Bentzion	Male		737
GROISBLAT		David	Male		737
GROISBLAT		Mikhael	Male		737
GROISBLAT		Shlomo	Male		737
GROISBLAT		Tzipora	Female		737
GROIZAN		Izik	Male		737
GRUBER		Irka			737
GRUBER		Khaim	Male		737
GRUBER		Manis			737
GRUBER		Mathel			737
GRUBER		Nakhum	Male		737
GRUBER		Riba	Female		737
GRUBER		Shprintza	Female		737
GURNTZOIT			Male		751
GURTENBERG		Aharon	Male		736
GURTENBERG		Bluma	Female		736
GURTENBERG		Henia	Female		736
GURTENBERG		Khaia	Female		736
GURTENBERG		Khasia	Female		736
GURTENBERG		Miriam	Female		736

GURTENBERG		Moshe	Male		736
GURTENBERG		Sonia	Female		736
GURTENBERG		Tzipora	Female		736
GURTENBERG		Yaakov	Male		736
GURTENBERG		Yoel	Male		736
GURTENBERG		Zeev	Male		736
GUZ		Avraham	Male		736
GUZ	POVCHER	Gitel			736

Last Name	Maiden Name	First Name	Gender	Spouse's First Name	Column no.
HAMBURG			Male		738
HAMBURG		Lea	Female		738
HAMBURG		Meir	Male		738
HAMBURG		Meir Aharon	Male		738
HAMBURG		Pesil	Female		738
HAMBURG		Rakhel	Female		738
HAMBURG		Rivka	Female		738
HAMBURG		Sara	Female		738
HAMBURG		Shmuel	Male		738
HAMBURG		Tema	Female		738
HAMBURG		Tzvi	Male		738
HECHT		Aharon	Male		738
HECHT		Beniamin	Male		738
HECHT		Efraim	Male		738
HECHT		Khaim	Male		738
HECHT		Mikhla	Female		738
HECHT		Miriam	Female		738
HECHT		Myshka	Male		738
HECHT		Siuma	Male		738
HECHT		Sumekh			738
HECHT		Yaakov	Male		738
HOKHBERG		Khaikel	Male		738
HOKHBERG		Mania	Female		738
HOKHBERG		Mikhael	Male		738
HOKHBERG		Sonia	Female		738
HOLPER		Moshe	Male		751
HOLPER		Udia	Female		751
HOROVITZ		Avraham	Male		738
HOROVITZ		Bila	Female		738
HOROVITZ		David	Male		738
HOROVITZ		Dreizia			738
HOROVITZ	SITERMAN	Dvora	Female		738
HOROVITZ		Eliezer	Male		738

HOROVITZ		Moshe	Male		738
HOROVITZ		Naftali	Male		738
HOROVITZ		Rakhel	Female		738
HOROVITZ		Shifra	Female		738
HOROVITZ		Shmuel	Male		738
HOROVITZ		Yaakov	Male		738
HOROVITZ		Zelda	Female		738
HUNGER		Eli Moshe			738
IADLIN		Mania	Female		751
IADLIN		Volf	Male		751
IADLIN		Zysl	Male		751
IAKIRA		Ber	Male		740
IAKIRA		Batia	Female		740
IAKIRA		Dov	Male		740
IAKIRA		Dov	Male		740
IAKIRA	VAKSMAN	Fania	Female		740
IAKIRA		Golda	Female		740
IAKIRA		Khana	Female		740
IAKIRA		Libish	Male		740
IAKIRA		Matatiahu	Male		740
IAKIRA		Moshe	Male		740
IAKIRA		Pinkhas	Male		740
IAKIRA		Sara	Female		740
IAKIRA		Shifra	Female		740
IAKIRA		Yekhiel	Male		740
IDELMAN		Matatiahu	Male		733
IDELMAN		Pesia	Female		733
INGBER		Brakha	Female		733
INGBER		Fridl	Female		733
INGBER		Henia	Female		733
INGBER		Khaia	Female		733
INGBER		Rakhel	Female		733

INGBER		Roza	Female		733
INGBER		Shlomo	Male		733
INGBER		Tzvia	Female		733
INSPEKTOR		Avraham	Male		733
INSPEKTOR		Avraham	Male		733
INSPEKTOR	KOITEL	Pepa	Female		733
INSPEKTOR	KORN	Rusia	Female		733
INSPEKTOR		Shifra	Female		733
INSPEKTOR		Shlomo	Male		733
INSPEKTOR		Zeev	Male		733
INSPEKTOR		Zeev	Male		733
KACHKA		Avraham	Male		748
KACHKA		Khasia	Female		748
KACHKA		Mendil	Male		748
KACHKA		Miriam Lea	Female		748
KAGAN		Aharon	Male		740
KAGAN		Avraham	Male		740
KAGAN		Avraham	Male		740
KAGAN		Brakha	Female		740
KAGAN		Charna	Female		740
KAGAN		David	Male		740
KAGAN		Dov	Male		740
KAGAN		Khana	Female		740
KAGAN		Mordekhai	Male		740
KAGAN		Moshe	Male		751
KAGAN		Nitza	Female		740
KAGAN		Rizel	Female		740
KAGAN		Roza	Female		740
KAGAN		Sara	Female		740
KAGAN		Shlomo	Male		740
KAGAN		Tibel			740
KAGAN		Yaakov	Male		740

635

KAGAN		Yenta	Female		740
KAGAN		Yona	Male		751
KAGAN		Yosef	Male		740
KAGAN		Zysl			740
KAHANA		Avraham	Male		740
KAHANA		Dina	Female		740
KAHANA		Dov Berish	Male		740
KAHANA		Gur Arie	Male		740
KAHANA		Khaim	Male		740
KAHANA		Tonia	Female		740
KAMTZAN		Avraham	Male		748
KAMTZAN		Mendel	Male		748
KAMTZAN	SHTIBEL	Sara	Female		748
KANDINER		Eti	Female		748
KANDINER		Henia	Female		748
KANDINER		Ozer	Male		748
KANDINER		Volf	Male		748
KANTERMAN		Batia	Female		748
KANTERMAN		Feiga	Female		748
KANTERMAN		Moshe	Male		748
KANTERMAN		Tzvi	Male		748
KANTERMAN		Yosef	Male		748
KANTOR		Genya	Female		748
KANTOR		Gershon	Male		748
KANTOR		Khinka	Female		748
KANTOR		Lova	Female		748
KANTOR		Moshe	Male		748
KANTOR		Rivka	Female		748
KAPLAN		Friba			752
KAPLAN		Siuma	Female		752
KAPLAN		Zalman	Male		752
KARAULNIK		Tosia	Female		748

KARAULNIK		Zysl	Male		748
KATZ		Batia	Female		740
KATZ		Rivka	Female		740
KELNER		Khaia	Female		748
KELNER		Moshe	Male		748
KELNER		Yoel	Male		748
KERSHENBLIT		Shlomo	Male		749
KHAIAT		Bila	Female		740
KHAIAT		David	Male		740
KHAIAT		David Leib	Male		740
KHAIAT		Muni	Male		740
KHAIAT		Roza	Female		740
KHAIAT		Shmariahu	Male		739
KHAIAT		Yekhiel	Male		740
KHOTINER		Batia	Female		739
KHOTINER		Dina	Female		739
KHOTINER		Feiga	Female		739
KHOTINER		Khaia	Female		739
KHOTINER		Mordekhai	Male		739
KHOTINER		Perel	Female		739
KHOTINER		Tzvia	Female		739
KHOTINER		Yaakov	Male		739
KLEINER		Sosel			752
KLEIZER		Rakhel	Female		752
KLEIZER		Anshel	Male		752
KLEIZER		Ester	Female		748
KLEIZER		Ester Rakhel	Female		748
KLEIZER		Feiga	Female		752
KLEIZER		Hersh	Male		748
KLEIZER		Khana	Female		748
KLEIZER		Lea	Female		748
KLEIZER		Mania	Female		748

KLEIZER		Sara	Female		748
KLEIZER		Sonia	Female		748
KLEIZER		Velvel	Male		752
KLEIZER		Volf	Male		748
KLEIZER		Yisrael	Male		748
KLEMPNER		Aliza	Female		748
KLEMPNER		Avraham	Male		748
KLEMPNER		Bluma	Female		748
KLEMPNER		Bluma	Female		748
KLEMPNER		David	Male		748
KLEMPNER		Dov	Male		748
KLEMPNER		Ester	Female		748
KLEMPNER		Ester	Female		748
KLEMPNER		Gitel	Female		748
KLEMPNER		Itamar	Male		748
KLEMPNER		Miriam	Female		748
KLEMPNER		Nakhum	Male		748
KLEMPNER		Sara	Female		748
KLEMPNER		Sara	Female		748
KLEMPNER		Yaakov	Male		748
KLEMPNER		Yitzkhak	Male		748
KLEPKER		Azriel Khaim	Male		748
KLEPKER		Shmuel	Male		748
KLEPKER		Shoshana	Female		748
KLIMACHER		Batia	Female		748
KLIMACHER		Khaim Shmuel	Male		748
KLIMACHER		Menukha	Female		748
KLIMACHER		Yosef	Male		748
KOBERNIK		Avraham	Male		747
KOBERNIK		Ester	Female		747
KOBERNIK		Feiga	Female		747
KOBERNIK		Meir	Male		747

KOBERNIK		Rakhel	Female		747
KOBERNIK		Shifra	Female		747
KOBERNIK		Tula	Male		747
KOBERNIK		Yehuda	Male		747
KOBERNIK		Yosef	Male		747
KOBERNIK		Zeev	Male		747
KOFAIKA		Bluma	Female		752
KOFAIKA		Moshe	Male		752
KOFAIKA		Natan	Male		752
KOFAIKA		Pinkhas	Male		752
KOIFMAN		Aharon	Male		747
KOIFMAN		Beba	Female		747
KOIFMAN		David	Male		747
KOIFMAN		Doba	Female		747
KOIFMAN		Golda	Female		747
KOIFMAN		Grina			747
KOIFMAN		Khaia	Female		747
KOIFMAN		Shmuel	Male		747
KOLTUN		Avraham Moshe	Male		747
KOLTUN		Batia	Female		747
KOLTUN		Batia	Female		747
KOLTUN		Edi			747
KOLTUN		Ester	Female		747
KOLTUN	LAKHMANCHIK	Khava	Female		747
KOLTUN		Meir Maier	Male		747
KOLTUN		Moshe	Male		747
KOLTUN		Pesia	Female		747
KOLTUN		Sheike	Male		747
KOLTUN		Tzila	Female		747
KOLTUN		Yisrael	Male		747
KOLTUN		Zlata	Female		747
KOLTUN		Khava	Female		752

KONSHTEIN		Beril	Male		752
KORCHAK		Barukh	Male		748
KORCHAK		David	Male		748
KORCHAK		David	Male		748
KORCHAK		Eliahu	Male		748
KORCHAK		Elka	Female		748
KORCHAK		Feiga	Female		748
KORCHAK		Frida	Female		748
KORCHAK		Gitel	Female		748
KORCHAK		Izik	Male		748
KORCHAK		Khaim	Male		748
KORCHAK		Leib	Male		748
KORCHAK		Menukha	Female		748
KORCHAK		Pesakh	Male		748
KORCHAK		Udel			748
KORCHAK		Yaakov Moshe	Male		748
KORCHAK		Yitzkhak	Male		748
KORIN		Moshe	Male		752
KORIN		Shmuel	Male		752
KORIN		Velka			752
KORIN		Yisaskhar	Male		752
KORNFELD	LASHCHEVER	Rakhel	Female		748
KORNFELD		Shimon	Male		748
KOZHAK		Brakha	Female		747
KOZHAK		Getzil			747
KOZHAK		Moshe	Male		747
KOZHAK		Rizel	Female		747
KOZHAK		Yenta	Female		747
KOZHAK		Yosef	Male		747
KRAKOVIAK		Hershel	Male		752
KRAKOVIAK		Mordekhai	Male		752
KRAKOVIAK		Shepsel	Male		752

KRANTZOV		Batia	Female		752
KRANTZOV		Dina	Female		752
KRANTZOV		Yosef	Male		752
KREMIN		Ester	Female		749
KREMIN		Frida	Female		749
KREMIN		Yoel	Male		749
KREMIN		Zysl	Female		749
KRUCHNIK		Betzalel	Male		748
KRUCHNIK		Khaia	Female		749
KRUCHNIK		Rizel	Female		748
KRUCHNIK		Tonne	Female		748
KRUCHNIK		Yisrael	Male		748
KRUM		Yisrael	Male		748
KURENITZ		Dvora	Female		747
KURENITZ		Ester	Female		747
KURENITZ		Gershon	Male		747
KURENITZ		Hinda	Female		747
KURENITZ		Yekutiel	Male		747
KURENITZ		Yeshayahu	Male		747
KUZIS		Dora	Female		747
KUZIS		Katia	Female		747
KUZIS		Khava	Female		747
KUZIS		Mania	Female		747
KUZIS		Mania	Female		747
KUZIS		Moshe	Male		747
KUZIS		Pulia	Female		747
KUZIS		Ritza	Female		747
KUZIS		Tania	Female		747
KUZIS		Yehoshua	Male		747
KUZIS		Yisrael	Male		747
KUZIS		Zysl	Male		747
LAKHMANCHIK		David	Male		741

LAKHMANCHIK		Khaia	Female		741
LAKHMANCHIK		Mordekhai	Male		741
LAKHMANCHIK		Risa	Female		741
LAKHMANCHIK		Sonia	Female		741
LAKHMANCHIK		Yehoshua	Male		741
LANDIS		Mordekhai	Male		742
LANDIS		Roza	Female		742
LASHCHEVER		Avrasha	Male		742
LASHCHEVER		Efraim	Male		742
LASHCHEVER		Khana	Female		742
LASHCHEVER		Musia	Female		742
LASHCHEVER		Shalom	Male		742
LASHCHEVER		Shura	Female		742
LASHCHEVER		Sonia	Female		742
LASHCHEVER		Tova Rakhel	Female		742
LASHCHEVER		Yisrael Moshe	Male		742
LASTOV		Nakhum	Male		751
LASTOV		Shmuel	Male		751
LEHMAN		Aharon	Male		741
LEHMAN		Khaia	Female		741
LEIBEL		Aniuta	Female		741
LEIBEL		Bentzion	Male		741
LEIBEL		Mina	Female		741
LEIBEL		Yona	Male		741
LEIBEL		Yosef	Male		741
LERNER		Aharon	Male		742
LERNER		Avraham	Male		742
LERNER		Brindil	Female		742
LERNER		Dvora	Female		742
LERNER		Ester	Female		742
LERNER		Genya	Female		742
LERNER		Khana	Female		742

LERNER		Lea	Female		742
LERNER		Mendel	Male		742
LERNER		Miriam	Female		742
LERNER		Munik	Male		742
LERNER		Rakhel	Female		742
LERNER		Sara	Female		742
LERNER		Shimon	Male		742
LERNER		Shimshon	Male		742
LERNER		Vladimir Zeev	Male		742
LERNER		Yaakov	Male		742
LERNER		Yosef	Male		742
LERNER		#REF!	Male		742
LEVIATIN		Akiva	Male		740
LEVIATIN		Bela	Female		740
LEVIATIN		Ester	Female		740
LEVIATIN		Hirsh	Male		740
LEVIATIN		Mikhael	Male		740
LEVIATIN		Monka	Female		740
LEVIATIN		Motel	Male		740
LEVIATIN		Perel	Female		740
LEVIATIN		Pesia	Female		740
LEVIATIN		Sara	Female		740
LEVIATIN		Sheindl	Female		740
LEVIATIN		Sonia	Female		740
LEVIATIN		Yeli	Female		740
LEVIATIN		Yosef	Male		740
LEVIATIN		Yosef	Male		740
LIDERMAN		Shlomo	Male		741
LIKHT		Avraham	Male		741
LIKHTENSHTEIN		Dov	Male		741
LIKHTENSHTEIN		Susil	Female		741
LIKHTER		Beniamin	Male		741

LIKHTER		David	Male		741
LIKHTER		Henia	Female		741
LIKHTER		Rizel	Female		741
LIKHTER		Sara	Female		741
LIKHTER		Shmuel	Male		741
LIKHTMAKHER		Fruma	Female		741
LIKHTMAKHER		Meir	Male		741
LIKHTMAKHER		Rakhel	Female		741
LIKHTMAKHER		Tzipora	Female		741
LIKHTMAKHER		Yaakov	Male		741
LIPIN		Rizel	Female		741
LIS		Avraham	Male		741
LIS		Pesakh	Male		741
LIS		Rakhel	Female		741
LIS		Shlomo	Male		741
LISI		Bluma	Female		741
LISI		Doba	Male		741
LISI		Shlomo	Male		741
LISTUK		Lemel	Male		741
LISTUK		Mekhla	Female		741
LISTUK		Rivka	Female		741
LISTUK		Sara	Female		741
LISTUK		Sonia	Female		741
LISTUK		Tzila	Female		741
LITVAK		Barukh	Male		741
LITVAK		Friba	Female		741
LITVAK		Moshe	Male		741
LITVAK		Rizel	Female		741
LITVAK		Zelda	Female		741
LITZMAN		Asher	Male		742
LITZMAN		Avraham	Male		741
LITZMAN		Batia	Female		741

LITZMAN		Berish	Male		742
LITZMAN		David	Male		741
LITZMAN		Ester	Female		741
LITZMAN		Itelna	Female		741
LITZMAN		Khaia	Female		742
LITZMAN		Kioptzi			742
LITZMAN		Motel	Male		742
LITZMAN		Rakhel	Female		741
LITZMAN		Rakhel	Female		742
LITZMAN		Shlomo	Male		742
LITZMAN		Tova	Female		742
LITZMAN		Tzvi	Male		741
LITZMAN		Tzvi	Male		742
LITZMAN		Yenta	Female		742
LIVGORIN		Bentzion	Male		741
LIVGORIN		Khaia	Female		741
LIVGORION		Bela	Female		741
LIVGORION		Nakhman	Male		741
LOSHAK		Avraham	Male		741
LOSHAK		Barukh	Male		741
LOSHAK		Beniamin	Male		741
LOSHAK		Brakha	Female		741
LOSHAK		Kila	Female		741
LOSHAK		Rakhel	Female		741
LOSHAK		Rivka	Female		741
LOSHAK		Rizel	Female		741
LOSHAK		Shlomo	Male		741
LOSHAK		Shmuel	Male		741
LUCHNIK		Ester	Female		741
LUCHNIK		Mordekhai Leib	Male		741
LUKHMAN		Dina	Female		741
LUKHMAN		Shalom	Male		741

LUVSHIS		David	Male		741
LUVSHIS		Elik	Male		741
LUVSHIS		Khaim	Male		741
LUVSHIS		Khana	Female		741
LUVSHIS		Mindl			741
LUVSHIS		Mordekhai	Male		741
LUVSHIS		Rivka	Female		741
LUVSHIS		Shlomo	Male		741
LUVSHIS		Shoshana	Female		741
LUVSHIS		Yosef	Male		741
MAKHROK		David	Male		742
MAKHROK		Ester	Female		742
MAKHROK		Yehudit	Female		742
MALER		David	Male		742
MALER		Liuba	Female		742
MALER		Miriam	Female		742
MALER		Moshe Khaim	Male		742
MALER		Yekhezkel	Male		742
MANDELKER		Bunia	Female		743
MANDELKER		Roza	Female		742
MANDELKER		Sharlota	Female		743
MANDELKER		Volf	Male		742
MANDELKER		Yisrael	Male		742
MANDELKER		Zitna	Female		743
MANUSOVITZ		Ester	Female		743
MANUSOVITZ		Khana	Female		743
MANUSOVITZ		Mordekhai	Male		743
MANUSOVITZ		Moshe	Male		743
MANUSOVITZ		Shalom	Male		743
MANUSOVITZ		Yehoshua Zeev	Male		743
MANUSOVITZ		Yitzkhak Dov	Male		743
MARGALIT		Avraham	Male		743

MARGALIT		Bila	Female		743
MARGALIT		Dov	Male		743
MARGALIT		Fridl	Female		743
MARGALIT		Izidor	Male		743
MARGALIT		Khaia	Female		743
MARGALIT		Niuna	Female		743
MARGALIT		Rakhel	Female		743
MARGALIT		Shabtai	Male		743
MARGALIT		Yaakov	Male		743
MARGALIT		Zeev	Male		743
MATZIS		Khana	Female		743
MAZUREK		Lipa	Male		742
MAZUREK		Simkha	Male		742
MEIERZON		Batia	Female		742
MEIERZON		Dov	Male		742
MEIERZON		Feiga	Female		742
MEIERZON		Khava	Female		742
MEIERZON		Lea	Female		742
MEIERZON		Mordekhai	Male		742
MEIERZON		Rema	Female		742
MEIERZON		Shimon	Male		742
MEIERZON		Sima	Female		742
MEIERZON		Yisrael	Male		742
MEIERZON		Yona	Male		742
MEISTER		Dora	Female		742
MEISTER		Nekha	Female		742
MEIZLER		Eliahu	Male		742
MEIZLER		Mania	Female		742
MEIZLER		Rakhel	Female		742
MEIZLER		Tzvi Hersh	Male		742
MENIS		Gershon	Male		743
MENIS		Rivka	Female		743

MENIS		Yisrael	Male		743
MERDER		Khaia	Female		743
MERDER		Moshe	Male		743
MERDER		Yaakov	Male		743
MERDER		Yosef	Male		743
MINIUK		Bila	Female		742
MINIUK		Khaia	Female		742
MINIUK		Shalom	Male		742
MINIUK		Tzvia	Female		742
MISPANIS		Pesakh	Male		751
MISPANIS		Pinkhas	Male		751
MTZIS		Avraham	Male		743
MUZ		Khaia	Female		742
MUZ		Mertzi			742
MUZ		Motel	Male		742
MUZ		Pesia	Female		742
MUZ		Sara	Female		742
MUZ		Yehoshua	Male		742
MUZ		Yehudit	Female		742
MUZ		Yeshayahu	Male		742

Last Name	Maiden Name	First Name	Gender	Spouse's First Name	Column no.
NAKHTMAN		Dina	Female		751
NAKHTMAN		Nekhama	Female		751
NAKHTMAN		Yaakov	Male		751
NELIK		Ami	Female		743
NELIK	KACHKA	Feiga	Female		743
NELIK		Meir	Male		743
NUDLER		Buzin			743
NUDLER		Motel	Male		751
NUDLER		Yaakov	Male		751
OBSHTEIN		Ester	Female		733

OBSHTEIN		Genya	Female		733
OBSHTEIN		Lea	Female		733
OBSHTEIN		Nekhama	Female		733
OBSHTEIN		Pesakh	Male		733
OBSHTEIN		Sara	Female		733
OBSHTEIN		Simkha			733
ORZEK	GURTENBERG	Khaia	Female		733
ORZEK		Tzvi	Male		733
OSTROVSKI		Levi			733
OSTROVSKI		Lea	Female		733
OSTROVSKI		Mordekhai	Male		733
PAK		Ester	Female		746
PAK		Seril	Female		746
PAK		Yehuda	Male		746
PAVSHEVSKI		Krinitzi			744
PAVSHEVSKI		Mikhael	Male		744
PELTENSOHN		Rakhel	Female		745
PELTENSOHN		Yaakov	Male		745
PERL		Avraham Tzvi	Male		746
PERL		David	Male		746
PERLIUK		Batia	Female		746
PERLIUK		David	Male		746
PERLIUK		Ita	Female		746
PERLIUK		Khana	Female		746
PERLIUK		Mordekhai	Male		746
PERLIUK		Zhenia			746
PERLMUTER		Aharon	Male		746
PERLMUTER		Betzalel	Male		746
PERLMUTER		Dov Beril	Male		746
PERLMUTER		Liba	Female		746
PERLMUTER		Miriam	Female		746
PESIS		Alter	Male		746

PESIS		Bila	Female		746
PESIS		Khaia	Female		746
PESIS		Shmuel	Male		746
PESIS		Zanvil	Male		745
PIATIGORSK		Liba			744
PIATIGORSK		Yenta	Female		744
PICHNIUK		Moshe	Male		744
PINCHUK		Brakha	Female		744
PINCHUK		Feibel	Male		744
PINCHUK	MINUK	Khana	Female		744
PINKHASUVITZ		Beril	Male		745
PINKHASUVITZ		Gitel	Female		745
PINKHASUVITZ		Rivka	Female		745
PINKHASUVITZ		Sara	Female		745
PINKHASUVITZ		Sheindl	Female		745
PINKHASUVITZ		Shmuel	Male		745
PINKHASUVITZ		Zalman	Male		745
PINSBERG					744
PODISOK		Grina			744
PODISOK		Khaim	Male		744
PODISOK		Khinka	Female		744
PODISOK		Motel	Male		744
PODISOK		Pinkhas	Male		744
PODISOK		Sara	Female		744
PODISOK		Shalom	Male		744
PODISOK		Yisrael	Male		744
PODLOTZKI		Avraham	Male		744
PODLOTZKI		Batia	Female		744
PODLOTZKI		Shoshana	Female		744
PODLOTZKI		Yosef	Male		744
POGORILTZER		Avraham	Male		744
POGORILTZER		Brindil	Female		744

POGORILTZER	INGBERG	Pesia	Female		744
POGORILTZER		Rivka	Female		744
POGORILTZER		Rivka	Female		744
POGORILTZER		Yehuda	Male		744
POGORILTZER		Yehudit	Female		744
POGORILTZER		Yisrael	Male		751
POLISHUK		Alte	Female		744
POLISHUK		Avraham	Male		744
POLISHUK		Batsheva	Female		744
POLISHUK		Bentzion	Male		744
POLISHUK		David	Male		744
POLISHUK		Volf	Male		744
POLTURAK		Berko	Male		744
POLTURAK		David	Male		744
POLTURAK		Frida	Female		744
POLTURAK		Khanokh	Male		744
POLTURAK		Mania	Female		744
POLTURAK		Munia			744
POLTURAK		Rakhel	Female		744
POLTURAK		Sara	Female		744
POLTURAK		Shlomo	Male		744
POLTURAK		Simkha	Male		744
POLTURAK		Yenta	Female		744
POPLAR		Yosef	Male		751
POTIKHA		Akiva	Male		744
POTIKHA		Peretz	Male		744
POVCHER		Moshe	Male		744
PRAKER		Bila	Female		746
PRAKER		Brakha	Female		746
PRAKER		Idel	Female		746
PRAKER		Khaia	Female		746
PRAKER		Libish	Male		746

PRAKER		Nekha	Female		746
PRAKER		Shalom	Male		746
PRAKER		Yaakov	Male		746
PRAKER		Yisrael	Male		747
PRESMAN		Rakhel	Female		746
PRESMAN		Asher	Male		746
PRESMAN		David	Male		746
PRESMAN		Eli	Male		746
PRESMAN		Ester	Female		746
PRESMAN		Ester	Female		746
PRESMAN		Gutman	Male		746
PRESMAN		Hershel	Male		746
PRESMAN		Khaia	Female		746
PRESMAN		Khaia	Female		746
PRESMAN		Lipa	Male		746
PRESMAN		Nekhama	Female		746
PRESMAN		Rakhel	Female		746
PRESMAN		Ratzia			746
PRESMAN		Sara	Female		746
PRESMAN		Tova	Female		746
PRESMAN		Vili	Male		746
PRESMAN		Wanda	Female		746
PRESMAN		Yisrael	Male		746
PRESMAN		Yitzkhak	Male		746
PRESMAN		Yitzkhak	Male		746
PRESMAN		Zelda	Female		746
RABINSHTEIN		Bila	Female		749
RABINSHTEIN		Dov	Male		749
RABINSHTEIN		Rakhel	Female		749
RADIKHOVSKI		Brindil	Female		749
RADIKHOVSKI		Moshe	Male		749
RADIKHOVSKI		Rakhel	Female		749

RADIKHOVSKI		Rivka	Female		749
RADIKHOVSKI		Udi	Male		749
RADIKHOVSKI		Zeev	Male		749
REIF		Hinda	Female		749
RIKHMAN	DREISHPUN	Khaia	Female		749
RIKHMAN		Sara	Female		749
RIKHMAN		Shlomo	Male		749
RINSBERG		Ester	Female		749
RINSBERG		Lea	Female		749
RINSBERG		Yaakov	Male		749
ROIS		Aba	Male		752
ROIS			Male	Aba	752
ROITMAN		Avraham	Male		749
ROITMAN		Efraim Elkhanan	Male		749
ROITMAN		Feiga	Female		749
ROITMAN		Manis			749
ROITMAN		Natanel	Male		749
ROITMAN		Rafael	Male		749
ROITMAN		Sarka			749
ROITMAN		Tzipora	Female		749
ROITMAN		Yisrael	Male		749
ROTSHTEIN		Klara	Female		749
ROTSHTEIN		Lusia	Female		749
ROTSHTEIN		Mordekhai	Male		749
ROTSHTEIN		Yosef	Male		749
ROZENBERG		Eva	Female		749
ROZENBERG		Hertzel	Male		749
ROZENBERG		Leib	Male		749
ROZENBERG		Mendel	Male		749
ROZENBERG		Rakhel	Female		749
ROZENBERG		Rizel	Female		749
ROZENBERG		Shlomo	Male		749

ROZENBOIM		Aharon	Male		749
ROZENBOIM		Avraham	Male		749
ROZENBOIM		Elka	Female		749
ROZENBOIM		Ita	Female		749
ROZENBOIM		Khana	Female		749
ROZENBOIM		Malka	Female		749
ROZENBOIM		Nekhama	Female		749
ROZENBOIM		Sheindl	Female		749
ROZENBOIM		Yisrael	Male		749
ROZENFELD	MEIERZON	Batia	Female		749
ROZENFELD		Feibel	Male		749
ROZENFELD		Khaim Moshe	Male		749
SADOVNIK		Berl	Male		743
SADOVNIK		Berl	Male		743
SADOVNIK		David	Male		743
SADOVNIK		Elka	Female		743
SADOVNIK		Helena	Female		743
SADOVNIK		Izik	Male		743
SADOVNIK		Malvina	Female		743
SADOVNIK		Sara	Female		743
SADOVNIK		Sheina	Female		743
SADOVNIK		Shlomo	Male		743
SAFIAN		Dvora	Female		744
SAFIAN		Ester	Female		744
SAFIAN	LASHCHEVER	Miriam	Female		744
SAFIAN		Munia			744
SAFIR		Etil	Female		744
SAFIR		Sara	Female		744
SAFIR		Tzvi	Male		744
SANDES		Ester	Female		744
SANDES		Khana	Female		744
SANDES		Mania	Female		744

SANDES		Vikhni			744
SANDES		Yehoshua	Male		744
SEGAL		Avraham	Male		743
SEGAL		Elik	Male		743
SEGAL		Hinda	Female		743
SEGAL		Khaia	Female		743
SEGAL		Khana	Female		743
SEGAL		Meir	Male		743
SEGAL		Moshe	Male		743
SEGAL		Reiza	Female		743
SEGAL		Yosef	Male		743
SEGAL		Zlata	Female		743
SHAPIRA		Asher	Male		751
SHAPIRA		Buzia	Female		750
SHAPIRA		Doba	Female		751
SHAPIRA		Gitel	Female		750
SHAPIRA		Nusia	Female		750
SHAPIRA		Rivka	Female		751
SHAPIRA		Tzirel	Female		750
SHAPIRA		Yaakov	Male		750
SHAPOVNIK		Beniamin	Male		750
SHAPOVNIK		Khana	Female		750
SHAPOVNIK		Khanan	Male		750
SHAPOVNIK		Melekh	Male		750
SHAPOVNIK		Miriam	Female		750
SHARGEL		Avraham	Male		752
SHARGEL		Bluma	Female		751
SHARGEL		Brindil	Female		751
SHARGEL		David	Male		752
SHARGEL		Ester	Female		751
SHARGEL		Hersh	Male		751
SHARGEL		Khaim	Male		751

SHARGEL		Krintza	Female		752
SHARGEL		Malka	Female		752
SHARGEL		Mikhla	Female		751
SHARGEL		Moshe	Male		752
SHARGEL		Rizel	Female		751
SHARGEL		Sara	Female		751
SHARGEL		Shlomo	Male		751
SHARGEL		Tzvi	Male		751
SHARGEL		Volf	Male		751
SHARGEL		Zlata	Female		752
SHEBINSKI		Mikhael	Male		749
SHEBINSKI	MEIZLER	Mina	Female		749
SHEINAK		Meir	Male		750
SHEINAK		Mina	Female		750
SHEINAK		Rizel	Female		750
SHEINAK		Sara	Female		750
SHEINDELZON		Asia	Female		750
SHEINDELZON		Avi	Male		750
SHEINDELZON		Avraham	Male		750
SHEINDELZON		Elkhanan	Male		750
SHEINDELZON		Mindl			750
SHIKH	KLEIZER	Feiga	Female		750
SHIKH		Leib	Male		750
SHIKH		Mania	Female		750
SHIKH		Yisrael	Male		750
SHIKHMAN		Aharon	Male		750
SHIKHMAN		Asher	Male		750
SHIKHMAN		Dvora	Female		750
SHIKHMAN		Efraim	Male		750
SHIKHMAN		Etil	Female		750
SHIKHMAN		Gitel	Female		750
SHIKHMAN		Miriam	Female		750

SHIKHMAN		Moshe	Male		750
SHIKHMAN		Rizel	Female		750
SHINDELMAN		Bitzia	Female		750
SHINDELMAN		Khaim	Male		750
SHINDELMAN		Khuma	Female		750
SHINDELMAN		Masha	Female		750
SHITERMAN		Asher	Male		750
SHITERMAN		Avraham	Male		750
SHKOLNIK		Avraham	Male		751
SHKOLNIK		Azriel	Male		751
SHKOLNIK		Henia	Female		751
SHKOLNIK		Khaia	Female		751
SHKOLNIK		Tova	Female		751
SHKOLNIK		Yenta	Female		751
SHNITER		Ida	Female		750
SHNITER		Pinkhas	Male		750
SHNITER		Risia	Female		750
SHNITER		Rizel	Female		750
SHNITER		Shmuel	Male		750
SHNITER		Volf	Male		750
SHOKHET		Shlomo	Male		749
SHPRINGER		Bila	Female		751
SHPRINGER		Eliahu	Male		751
SHPRINGER		Ester	Female		751
SHPRINGER		Gitel	Female		751
SHPRINGER		Malka	Female		751
SHPRINGER		Rivka	Female		751
SHREIBMAN		David	Male		752
SHREIBMAN		Feiga	Female		752
SHREIBMAN		Munik	Male		752
SHREIBMAN		Rakhel	Female		752
SHREIBMAN		Velvil	Male		752

SHREIBMAN		Yisrael	Male		752
SHREIER		Avraham	Male		752
SHREIER		Ester	Female		752
SHRENTZEL		Bunia			752
SHRENTZEL		Feiga	Female		752
SHRENTZEL		Nisa	Female		752
SHRENTZEL		Sheindl	Female		752
SHRENTZEL		Shlomo	Male		752
SHRITNIK		Avraham	Male		752
SHRITNIK		Batia	Female		752
SHRITNIK		David	Male		752
SHRITNIK		Hinda Rakhel	Female		752
SHRITNIK		Moshe	Male		752
SHRITNIK		Tzirel	Female		752
SHTAKHER		Khaia	Female		749
SHTAKHER		Khana	Female		749
SHTAKHER		Libish	Male		749
SHTAKHER		Nesia	Female		749
SHTAKHER		Sara	Female		749
SHTAKHER		Sara	Female		749
SHTAKHER		Sheindl	Female		749
SHTEIN		Batia	Female		750
SHTEIN		Dov	Male		750
SHTEIN		Feiga	Female		750
SHTEIN		Leib	Male		749
SHTEIN		Meir	Male		750
SHTEIN		Moshe	Male		750
SHTEIN		Nakhman	Male		750
SHTEIN		Niuma			750
SHTEIN		Pia	Female		750
SHTEIN		Rakhel	Female		750
SHTEIN		Reuven	Male		750

SHTEIN		Shaul	Male		749
SHTEINSHNID		Aharon	Male		750
SHTEINSHNID		Avraham	Male		750
SHTEINSHNID		Barukh	Male		750
SHTEINSHNID		Eli	Male		750
SHTEINSHNID		Hinda	Female		750
SHTEINSHNID		Khaia Sara	Female		750
SHTEINSHNID		Lea	Female		750
SHTEINSHNID		Mordekhai	Male		752
SHTEINSHNID		Naftali	Male		750
SHTEINSHNID		Peril	Female		750
SHTEINSHNID		Riba	Female		750
SHTEINSHNID		Tzvi	Male		750
SHTEINSHNID		Yehuda Leib	Male		750
SHTEINSHNID		Zeev	Male		750
SHTEINVORTZEL		Asher	Male		750
SHTEINVORTZEL		Avraham	Male		750
SHTEINVORTZEL		Betzalel	Male		750
SHTEINVORTZEL		Etil	Female		750
SHTEINVORTZEL		Feibel	Male		750
SHTEINVORTZEL		Khaia	Female		750
SHTEINVORTZEL		Malka	Female		750
SHTEINVORTZEL		Mendel	Male		750
SHTERN		Bela	Female		750
SHTERN		Khaim	Male		750
SHTERN		Leib	Male		750
SHTERN		Moshe	Male		750
SHTERN		Moshe	Male		750
SHTERN		Yaakov	Male		750
SHTERN		Zlata	Female		750
SHTIBEL		Avraham	Male		749
SHTIBEL		Berl	Male		749

SHTIBEL		Fania	Female		749
SHTIBEL		Khaim	Male		749
SHTIBEL		Moshe	Male		749
SHTIBEL		Rivka	Female		749
SHTIBEL		Yaakov	Male		749
SHTIMER		Golda	Female		749
SHTIMER		Idel	Female		749
SHTIMER		Mania	Female		749
SHTIMER		Nekhama	Female		749
SHTIMER		Rizel	Female		749
SHTIMER		Shamai	Male		749
SHTIMER		Shaul	Male		749
SHTINGARTEN		Hertzel	Male		752
SHTINGARTEN		Pura			752
SHTINGARTEN			Male	Hertzel	752
SHTOF		Bentzion	Male		752
SHUKHMAN		David	Male		752
SHVAKHIM		Khaim	Male		752
SHVAKHIM		Sender	Male		752
SIKOLNIK		Riba	Female		744
SIRKIS		Adela	Female		744
SIRKIS		Bluma	Female		744
SIRKIS		Etel	Female		744
SIRKIS		Golda	Female		744
SIRKIS		Hersh	Male		744
SIRKIS		Khaim	Male		744
SIRKIS		Khava	Female		744
SIRKIS		Manis			744
SIRKIS		Meir	Male		744
SIRKIS		Moshe	Male		744
SIRKIS		Sheindl	Female		744
SIRKIS		Sheva	Female		744

SIRKIS		Sonia	Female		744
SIRKIS		Yekhezkel	Male		744
SIRKIS		Yelna	Female		744
SITERMAN		Asia	Female		744
SITERMAN		Fania	Female		744
SITERMAN		Rakhel	Female		744
SITERMAN		Sara	Female		743
SITERMAN		Vitia	Male		744
SITERMAN		Yoel	Male		744
SITERMAN		Zisia	Female		743
SITMAN		Arie	Male		743
SITMAN		Brakha	Female		743
SITMAN		Eliahu	Male		743
SITMAN		Ester	Female		743
SITMAN		Ester	Female		743
SITMAN		Lova	Female		743
SITMAN		Meir	Male		743
SITMAN	KOBERNIK	Mirl	Female		743
SITMAN		Rakhel	Female		743
SITMAN	LIKHTER	Rakhel	Female		743
SITMAN		Rivka	Female		743
SITMAN		Velvel	Male		743
SITMAN		Yehudit	Female		743
SITMAN		Yitzkhak	Male		743
SITMAN		Yosef	Male		743
SITNIK		Aharon	Male		743
SITNIK		Fridl	Female		743
SITNIK		Khava	Female		743
SITNIK		Vova	Male		743
SITNIK		Yitzkhak	Male		743
SOBOL		Menukha	Female		743
SOBOL		Sheindl	Female		743

SOBOL		Yaakov	Male		743
SOBOL		Yisrael	Male		743
STRINER		Shlomo	Male		743
TAKS		Aharon	Male		740
TAKS		Khaia	Female		740
TAKS		Rakhel	Female		740
TAKS		Zahava	Female		740
TAKS KOFMAN		Brindil	Female		740
TAKS KOFMAN		David	Male		740
TAKS KOFMAN		Malka	Female		740
TAKS KOFMAN		Sara	Female		740
TAKS KOFMAN		Shendel	Female		740
TESLER		Yaakov	Male		740
TESLER		Yisrael	Male		740
TOISTER		David	Male		740
TOISTER		Rakhel	Female		740
TOISTER		Yosef	Male		740
TUKER		Birish	Male		740
TUKER		Khana Pesia	Female		740
TUKER		Miriam	Female		740
TUKER		Sara	Female		740
TUKER		Shprintza	Female		740
TUKER		Yosef	Male		740
TZENTNER		Avrasha	Male		747
TZENTNER		Dvora	Female		747
TZENTNER		Eliahu	Male		747
TZENTNER		Peretz	Male		747
TZIMERMAN		David	Male		747
TZIMERMAN		Genya	Female		747
TZIMERMAN		Khaim	Male		747
TZIMERMAN		Max	Male		747
TZIMERMAN		Naftali	Male		747

TZIMERMAN		Perla	Female		747
TZIMERMAN		Siuma	Male		747
TZIMRING		Batia	Female		747
TZIMRING		Moshe	Male		747
TZIMRING		Roza	Female		747
TZIMRING		Yeshayahu	Male		747
TZUKER		Rafael	Male		752
TZUKERMAN		Fishel	Male		752
TZUKERMAN		Frida	Female		747
TZVANGER		Efraim	Male		747
TZVANGER		Henia	Female		747
TZVANGER		Rakhel	Female		747
UNG		Bumek	Male		733
UNG		Mikhael	Male		733
UNG		Sheike	Male		733
UNG		Shimon	Male		733
UNG		Tzvia	Female		733
UNG		Zlata	Female		733
USTATSHER		David	Male		733
USTATSHER		David	Male		733
USTATSHER		Hinda	Female		733
USTATSHER		Khaia	Female		733
VALDER		Brunia	Female		739
VALDER		Lea	Female		739
VALDER		Liuba			739
VALDER		Mania	Female		739
VALDER		Mikhael	Male		739
VALDER		Pesakh	Male		739
VALDER		Sonia	Female		739
VALDER		Volf	Male		739
VAR		David	Male		739
VAR		Levi	Male		739

VAR		Moshe	Male		739
VAR		Rakhel	Female		739
VEINTROIB		Bela	Female		739
VEINTROIB		Bluma	Female		738
VEINTROIB		Elka	Female		739
VEINTROIB		Ita	Female		738
VEINTROIB		Ita	Female		739
VEINTROIB		Rivka	Female		739
VEINTROIB		Shmuel	Male		738
VEINTROIB		Yisrael	Male		739
VEINTROIB			Male	Yisrael	739
VEITZMAN		Ester	Female		739
VEITZMAN		Khaia	Female		739
VEITZMAN		Yoel	Male		739
VERKH		Avraham	Male		739
VERKH		Bila	Female		739
VERKH		David	Male		739
VERKH		Shmuel	Male		739
VERKOVSKI		Miriam	Female		739
VERKOVSKI		Moshe	Male		739
VIDERMAN		Akiva	Male		738
VINER		Yaakov	Male		739
VINOKUR		Aharon	Male		738
VINOKUR		Dvora	Female		738
VINOKUR	LASHCHEVER	Roza	Female		738
VINOKUR		Yehoshua	Male		738
VISMAN		Avraham	Male		739
VISMAN		Batia	Female		739
VISMAN		Gusia	Female		739
VISMAN		Izik	Male		739
VISMAN		Matil	Female		739
VISMAN		Moshe	Male		739

VISMAN		Pulia	Female		739
VISMAN		Rakhel	Female		739
VOLMAN		Aniuta	Female		739
VOLMAN		Yosef	Male		739
VOLOVELSKI		Sara	Female		739
VOLOVELSKI		Tzipora	Female		739
VOLOVELSKI		Yeshayahu	Male		739
VOSKOBOINIK		Shmuel	Male		739
VOVK		Golda	Male		738
VOVK		Beniamin	Male		738
VOVK		Elka	Female		738
VOVK		Khaia Feiga	Female		738
VOVK		Kula	Male		738
VOVK		Mania	Female		738
VOVK		Mordekhai	Male		738
VOVK		Rakhel	Female		738
VOVK		Rivka	Female		738
VOVK		Sonia	Female		738
VOVK		Tova	Female		738
VOVK		Zysl			738
VUSITZER		Sara	Female		739
VUSITZER		Yehoshua	Male		739
VUSITZER		Yitzkhak	Male		739
VUSITZER		Zalman	Male		739
ZAMBERG		Khaia	Female		739
ZAMBERG		Khana	Female		739
ZAMBERG		Meir	Male		739
ZAMBERG		Mendel	Male		739
ZAMBERG		Sara	Female		739
ZAMBERG		Shimon	Male		739
ZAMOROCHENSKI	IAKIRA	Ester	Female		739
ZAMOROCHENSKI		Rivka	Female		739

ZAMOROCHENSKI		Yehoshua	Male		739
ZAMOROCHENSKI		Yitzkhak	Male		739
ZEIGER		Aharon	Male		739
ZEIGER		Aleksander	Male		739
ZEIGER		Brindil	Female		739
ZEIGER		Feiga	Female		739
ZEIGER		Mikhael	Male		739
ZEIGER		Rakhel	Female		739
ZEIGER		Sara	Female		739
ZEIGER		Shlomo	Male		739
ZEIGER		Tzirel	Female		739
ZEIGER		Yitzkhak	Male		739
ZILBERMAN		David	Male		739
ZILBERMAN		Khana	Female		739
ZILBERMAN		Yosef	Male		739
ZILBERMAN			Male	Yosef	739
ZORNE		Adela	Female		739
ZORNE		Moshe	Male		739
ZORNE		Selia	Female		739
ZORNE		Shlomo Sonia	Male		739
	Khaim Dov		Male		733

Name Index

Not part of the original book.

Vinokur, 599
Vinokur, 664
Visman, 664, 665
Vize, 504
Volman, 665
Volovelski, 665
Von Werdum, 30, 32
Voskoboinik, 665
Vovk, 665
Vusitzer, 665

W

Wajnberg, 185
Waldman, 184
Wallitzer, 447
Warech, 353
Wassermann, 575, 576, 577, 581, 583
Weiderman, 316
Weinberg, 67
Weinryb, 66
Weisberg, 62, 90, 91, 501, 509, 588, 591
Weisboim, 509, 518
Wejsberg, 502
Wertheim, 406
Wessel, 37
Wieliczka, 39
Wiener, 52
Wiesel, 69
Wilner, 351, 353, 355
Witecka, 201
Wiza, 513
Woczkowa, 35
Wojciechówna, 34, 35
Wolitzer, 385
Wovek, 503
Wyzotsky, 107

Y

Yaari, 266
Yakira, 368
Yannai, 459, 460
Yavetz, 72
Yohannis, 299, 300, 301
Yoski, 325
Yozefob, 395
Yozpov, 58
Yugilevych, 575, 581
Yuspowicz, 35

Z

Zaiger, 111
Zaks, 61, 62, 369, 399, 408, 434
Zalizniak, 38
Zamberg, 665
Zamorochenski, 665, 666
Zederbaum, 71, 97
Zeidel, 305, 306
Zeiger, 666
Zekzer, 264
Zgatavtchk, 385
Zharne, 451
Zigelbaum, 408
Zilberman, 97, 298
Zilberman, 666
Zimerman, 289
Zimmerman, 111, 206, 316
Ziskind, 309
Zisman, 125
Zohar, 5, 113, 329, 453
Zorne, 316, 322
Zorne, 666
Zuckerman, 72, 437
Zukerman, 104, 110
Zuradky, 347
Zygmunt Ii August, 24

www.ingramcontent.com/pod-product-compliance
Lightning Source LLC
Chambersburg PA
CBHW062020090426

42811CB00005B/912